CONCORDIA COLLEGE LIBRARY
BRONXVILLE, NY 10708

Teacher Guide

Grade 6

CONCORDIA PUBLISHING HOUSE · SAINT LOUIS

Copyright © 2012 Concordia Publishing House
3558 S. Jefferson Avenue, St. Louis, MO 63118-3968
1-800-325-3040 • www.cph.org

All rights reserved. Unless specifically noted, no part of this publication may be reproduced, stored in a retrieval system, or transmitted, in any form or by any means, electronic, mechanical, photocopying, recording, or otherwise, without the prior written permission of Concordia Publishing House.

The purchaser of this publication is allowed to reproduce the marked portions contained herein for use with this curriculum. These resources may not be transferred or copied to another user.

Written by Jane Fryar, Carol Geisler, Joan Gerber, Diane Grebing, Judy Lillquist, Mark Lucas, Eileen Ritter, Karla Roeglin

Edited by Carolyn Bergt

Series editors: Rodney L. Rathmann, Carolyn Bergt, Brenda Trunkhill

Editorial assistant: Amanda G. Lansche

Unless otherwise indicated, Scripture quotations from the ESV Bible® (The Holy Bible, English Standard Version®), copyright © 2001 by Crossway Bibles, a publishing ministry of Good News Publishers. Used by permission. All rights reserved.

Scripture quotations marked NIV are taken from the Holy Bible, New International Version®. NIV®. Copyright © 1973, 1978, 1984 by Biblica, Inc.™ Used by permission of Zondervan. All rights reserved.

Quotations marked KJV are from the King James or Authorized Version of the Bible.

Quotations marked *TLSB* are taken from the notes, introductory material, or original articles from *The Lutheran Study Bible* © 2009 by Concordia Publishing House. All rights reserved.

Quotations marked *LSB* are from *Lutheran Service Book*, copyright © 2006 Concordia Publishing House. All rights reserved.

Quotations from Luther's Small Catechism are from *Luther's Small Catechism with Explanation*, copyright © 1986, 1991 Concordia Publishing House. All rights reserved.

A Select Library of Nicene and Post-Nicene Fathers of the Christian Church, eds. Philip Schaff and Henry Wace [New York: The Christian Literature Series, 1890–99. Reprint, Grand Rapids, MI: Eerdmans, 1952, 1961], vol. 12, p. 15. Used by permission.

Cover photo: © Liza McCorkle/iStockphoto.com

Manufactured in the United States of America

Contents

Unit 1—Beginnings and Patriarchs
1. Creation and Fall 11
2. Cain and Abel 15
3. The Great Flood 19
4. The Tower of Babel 23
5. God's Promises to Abraham 27
6. The Offering of Isaac 31
7. Isaac and Rebekah 35
8. Isaac Blesses His Sons 39
9. Jacob and Laban 43
10. Joseph 47
11. Job 51

Unit 2—To the Promised Land
12. The Call of Moses 57
13. Plagues and Passover 61
14. Holding Up the Prophet's Hands ... 65
15. Moses and Jethro 69
16. The Tent Church 73
17. Korah's Rebellion 77
18. Water at Meribah 81
19. Balaam 85
20. God's People Build a Monument ... 89
21. The Fall of Jericho 93
22. Deborah and Barak 97
23. Samson 101

Unit 3—Prophets and Kings
24. God Calls Samuel 107
25. Israel's First King 111
26. Samuel Anoints David 115
27. David and Goliath 119
28. David and Saul 123
29. Saul's Downfall 127
30. David and Bathsheba 131
31. Solomon Builds a Temple 135
32. Rehoboam and Jeroboam 139
33. The Prophet Elijah 143
34. Naboth's Vineyard 147

Unit 4—Collapse and Captivity
35. The Prophet Elisha 153
36. Joash 157
37. Hezekiah Prays 161
38. Josiah 165
39. Jonah 169
40. Jeremiah 173
41. Daniel and His Friends 177
42. Three Men in the Fiery Furnace ... 181
43. Daniel and the King's Dreams ... 185
44. The Writing on the Wall 189
45. Queen Esther Saves Her People .. 193

Unit 5—The Promised One Is Here!
46. God's People Return Home 199
47. Jesus Is Born 203
48. The Boy Jesus in the Temple 207
49. John Prepares the Way 211
50. The Baptism of Jesus 215
51. The Temptation of Jesus 219
52. Jesus' First Disciples 223
53. Nicodemus Visits Jesus 227
54. Jesus and the Woman at the Well ... 231
55. Jesus and the Children 235
56. Sermon on the Mount 239

Unit 6—The Ministry of Jesus
57. The Faith of the Roman Centurion . 245
58. Friends Bring a Man to Jesus 249
59. Ten Men with Leprosy 253
60. The Parable of the Sower 257
61. Jesus Is Transfigured 261
62. Jesus Feeds a Crowd 265
63. A Woman Is Judged 269
64. Peter's Confession 273
65. Stormy Seas 277
66. The Parable of a Foolish Rich Man 281
67. Jesus Raises Lazarus from the Dead 285

Unit 7—Jesus Completes Our Salvation
68. Banquet Parables 291
69. Zacchaeus 295
70. The Pharisee and the Publican ... 299
71. A Woman Anoints Jesus 303
72. Jesus Rides Into Jerusalem 307
73. Jesus in the Temple 311
74. The Last Supper 315
75. Peter Denies Jesus 319

76. Jesus on Trial...................... 323
77. Jesus Dies and Is Buried........... 327
78. Jesus Rises from the Dead......... 331

Unit 8—The Spread of the Gospel
79. The Emmaus Disciples............. 337
80. Doubting Thomas.................. 341
81. Jesus at the Sea of Tiberias........ 345
82. The Ascension..................... 349
83. Pentecost......................... 353
84. Peter, John, and the Lame Man.... 357
85. Peter and John in Prison.......... 361
86. Ananias and Sapphira............. 365
87. Stephen........................... 369
88. Philip and the Ethiopian.......... 373
89. Saul Becomes a Christian......... 377

Unit 9—The Christian Church Grows
90. Cornelius......................... 383
91. Rhoda............................ 387
92. Tabitha........................... 391
93. A Mission Trip.................... 395
94. Lydia............................. 399
95. The Jailer at Philippi.............. 403
96. Paul at Mars Hill.................. 407
97. Paul's Nephew to the Rescue....... 411
98. Paul on Trial...................... 415
99. Shipwrecked...................... 419
100. Paul and Timothy................. 423

Appendix

Preface

A Look at Your Role

You Are a Teacher of the Faith!

God has gifted you with a tremendous privilege. As a teacher of the faith, you have the opportunity to teach the most important truths anyone can ever learn. You can tell the Good News of Jesus, our Savior, who lived, died, and now lives again. He offers us forgiveness of our sins, the opportunity to begin over again with the slate wiped clean, and a happy home with Him in heaven. As a teacher of the faith, you can show what Jesus means to you in your actions as well as in your words. You can show that you care about each student, genuinely and individually, just as Jesus loves and cares for you. You can handle disappointments and frustrations in ways that show the power of God's Spirit in your life. You can demonstrate what Jesus' forgiveness means to you in your willingness to forgive others.

The challenges of the classroom are many; at times, they may seem overwhelming. We live and teach in a world damaged by sin and its contaminating effects in the lives of our students as well as in our own lives. But the good news is that no one who follows Jesus need ever feel he or she is doing it alone. We serve a God "who daily bears us up; God is our salvation" (Psalm 68:19). In His Word, He promises to strengthen and encourage us for the challenges we face. He promises to give our work meaning, our efforts effective outcomes, and our lives joy.

You Are Part of Something Big!

Before Jesus ascended into heaven, He told His disciples, "Go therefore and make disciples of all nations, baptizing them in the name of the Father and of the Son and of the Holy Spirit, teaching them to observe all that I have commanded you" (Matthew 28:19–20). Christian schools focus on disciple making. They are "workshops in Christian living," where discipleship is practiced as lessons are taught, relationships are established, and the issues of everyday life are experienced. This curriculum has been designed to assist those teaching the faith so that through the Word and Spirit of God, people of all ages may

- know the one true God—Father, Son, and Holy Spirit—and the forgiveness and salvation offered through Jesus' death and resurrection;
- come to faith and grow into Christian maturity;
- identify ourselves as members of the Body of Christ, the Church;
- live in joy, contentment, and harmony with God, ourselves, and all others;
- express faith in the worship of God and in the service of God and others;
- value all of God's creation and care for it wisely and well;
- witness faith in Jesus, our personal Savior and the Savior of all people; and
- live in the Christian hope of a new and eternal life in Christ Jesus.

With an emphasis on these goals, the One in Christ curriculum focuses on Christ. It seeks to assist teachers in providing students with optimal opportunities for growing in their faith and Christian lives. By God's grace, those teaching in Lutheran schools join in one voice with the writers, editors, marketers, and others who helped prepare this curriculum in the sentiment of 1 John 1:3: "That which we have seen and heard we proclaim also to you, so that you too may have fellowship with us; and indeed our fellowship is with the Father and with His Son Jesus Christ."

A Look at Your Students

You Are a Teacher of Sixth Graders!

What are sixth graders like? Consider the common physical, social, psychological, intellectual, and faith-development characteristics of children between the ages of 11 and 12. A list of these characteristics is given on the One in Christ Portal, but no child will display all the characteristics listed. Your students are growing in different areas at different rates. A person who is exceptionally gifted in social skills may have difficulty with intellectual skills. Others may seem intellectually gifted but may lack spiritual maturity. On certain days, you may observe behaviors that make you question whether any of the attention you have given to your students' spiritual nurturing is making any difference. On these days especially, remember that growing faith and producing the words, actions, and attitudes that evidence the presence of faith are the work of the Holy Spirit. Trust in God's mighty power to work faith and spiritual maturity in the lives of all for whom Jesus died. Hold up your students in prayer, encourage them in the faith, and trust in God to work the results.

A note about Baptism: Typically, you will have a number of students in your class who have not been baptized. Perhaps some of your students' parents have questions and concerns about what your church body teaches about Baptism and when, how, and under what circumstances this blessing from God is to be received. In your approach, take care not to leave unbaptized children with feelings of inadequacy or guilt. As Scripture tells, we are saved through faith, and we are brought to faith through God's Word; do not imply that unbaptized children are excluded from the community of faith. However, do not react by simply avoiding Baptism, especially when the topic flows naturally from lesson discussions. Instead, stress the clear teachings of God's Word that Baptism welcomes sinners into the family of God, where they receive Jesus' gifts of forgiveness, life, and salvation; that God desires Baptism for all people; and that Baptism applies the words and promises of God together with water, which connects with the recipient by faith. Also, prayerfully look for opportunities to talk with parents of unbaptized children about Baptism. Many children and their families receive the blessings of Holy Baptism each year through the ministry of Lutheran teachers. Speak readily of the joy of being a baptized Christian and of the joy that those in faith have as they look forward to being baptized someday.

A Look at the Sixth-Grade Curriculum

You Are Teaching with One in Christ Materials!

God's Word reminds us that our faith unites us with Christ just as it unites us with other Christians. Our faith in Jesus makes the Christian classroom a unique and wonderful place, different from any other classroom. Jesus Himself has promised, "For where two or three are gathered in My name, there am I among them" (Matthew 18:20). Classrooms dedicated to Jesus look, feel, and sound unlike all other classrooms. One in Christ materials do more than guide and equip the teacher for helping students learn God's Word. They also provide practical, engaging ideas and suggestions for connecting the lesson to all that takes place in and extends from the classroom, reaching into the other areas of the curriculum as well as into the playground, the playing field, the home and neighborhood, and ultimately, around the world.

With a special emphasis on Bible literacy and discipleship, materials for grades 1, 2, 4, 6, and 8 consist of a chronological Bible survey, while those for grades 3, 5, and 7 are organized around a theme-based Bible story approach. Popular features of previous curricula remain, with increased attention given to helping students make real-life connections. In addition, Teacher Guides direct teachers to the One in Christ Portal, which includes updated features for each lesson, such as PowerPoint and interactive whiteboard activities, video clips, and other lesson extensions that involve and engage the family.

Sixth-grade One in Christ materials consist of a Bible survey of one hundred Bible stories. Each lesson has been planned and developed so that it may be taught in approximately thirty-five to forty-five minutes per session. In order to plan and teach One in Christ, you will need the English Standard Version (ESV) Bible, a Teacher Guide, Student Books, and other resources available on the One in Christ Portal. If you do not have access to the portal, specific resources are repeated in the *Teacher Resource Book* (which has reproducible activities, unit tests, parent letters, and memory work lists, all of which are also included on the One in Christ Portal). You will also want to have *Luther's Small Catechism with Explanation* (from Concordia Publishing House) available for quick and easy reference.

Designed to continue the focus on the Bible literacy characteristic of One in Christ, the sixth-grade materials have been developed to give a sequential survey of the Bible—Old and New Testaments. There is an emphasis on the Bible as one big and continuing story of God's love for all people and His plan of salvation for them through the death and resurrection of Jesus Christ. Each lesson, even in the Old Testament, will focus on how the Bible narrative relates to God's plan of redeeming mercy and grace. There will be references along the way to the Six Chief Parts of doctrine because these are all based on Scripture. These Six Chief Parts consist of the Ten Commandments, the Apostles' Creed, the Lord's Prayer, Baptism, Confession, and Holy Communion. They are referenced wherever they apply specifically to the sequence of Bible stories. The goal of the materials for sixth grade is to help students grow in discipleship as they explore Scripture and apply it to their lives. Bulletin boards, available for purchase from Concordia Publishing House (CPH), are designed for visual reinforcement to help students apply unit themes and concepts.

A Look at the Teacher Guide

Unit Organization

One in Christ materials at most grade levels are organized into nine units. Though varying somewhat in length, these units coincide roughly with the time of year in which they will be taught. Look for supplemental ideas and activities to enhance your observance of seasonal events, such as Reformation, Thanksgiving, Advent, Christmas, Lent, and Easter, in the lessons taught during these times in the Church Year.

Music suggestions in the curriculum refer to the *Lutheran Service Book* (*LSB*) and particularly to those hymns recorded on the CD sets called *Hymns of the Month* (*HOM*) and *Hymns of the Season* (*HOS*). These suggestions provide an organized and progressing hymnody curriculum. As you learn the hymns of the month or season, always review hymns learned at previous grade levels so that students retain their familiarity with those hymns too. Suggestions are also made for *All God's People Sing!* (*AGPS*), particularly from the list of fifty songs recorded on the accompanying CD set, *Jesus' People Sing!* (*JPS*). Of course, be sure to include other hymns and songs that appropriately fit the lesson theme and give glory to God alone!

By God's grace, each lesson follows a threefold objective. First, it confronts learners with the Law, showing human sin and our need for a Savior. Second, it leads learners to see God's grace in sending Jesus to redeem us from sin, death, and the power of the devil. Third, it encourages learners as they daily live in Christ, empowered by the Holy Spirit. You will want to use the Teacher Guide together with the *Teacher Resource Book* or the One in Christ Portal. These resources provide reproducible activity sheets together with a host of ideas and other resources to assist you in teaching the faith.

Unit Introduction Pages

The nine units correspond fairly closely to the nine months of the school year. You will want to pace yourself accordingly, extending some lessons as needed, especially so you can use some of the enrichment ideas in the "Lesson Support" sections of the guide. (Note: Teachers continually say they can never cover all the material in the guide, so we have purposely cut back on the number of lessons while increasing the number of options so that you can work at a pace that suits the needs of your individual situation.) The following Teacher Guide features, provided in each two-page unit overview, will assist you in your planning.

Unit Theme: This summarizes the main theme of the unit while also providing helpful suggestions for emphasizing, applying, and extending unit concepts.

Unit Worship: This section provides suggestions for relating your opening devotions to the unit theme.

Unit Resources: These are suggestions or reminders about the curriculum Web resources that can enlighten and enrich your students' learning. Suggestions may also be made about other related CPH products.

Unit Contents: This list of the lesson titles in the unit provides the teacher with at-a-glance information about the scope and content of the unit. At the close of the unit, you may want to use some of these titles to assess student learning, asking students to write three or four sentences to summarize their choice of three or four stories. (Summarizing in their own words will tell you how well they really have grasped the key elements of a Bible narrative.)

Unit Bulletin Board: A unique bulletin board has been designed specifically for each of the nine units at this level. These are available for purchase from CPH. This section explains how to construct and display the bulletin board. Information in this section will also tell you how to use the bulletin board to involve students and extend lesson applications.

Bible Book Overviews: This section of the Unit Introduction refers you and the students to the Appendix in the back of the Student Book (and in the Teacher Guide). This Appendix is not just an add-on. It is more like a Bible handbook, with a Bible dictionary, concordance, timelines, maps, and more. It is suggested that in each unit, you particularly take time to look at the Bible Book Overview, looking at just a few of these Bible summaries each month to help students become familiar with where to find particular content. The overviews also will show how all of Scripture connects to our Savior and salvation.

A Look at Teaching the Lesson

Lesson Overview

The first page of every lesson in the Teacher Guide begins with the lesson's "Background" section. This provides additional information for the teacher's own growth and development while also giving high-interest facts that may be helpful in presenting and discussing the lesson.

A special feature is the "Devotion," which can be read to the class. These life-application stories always relate directly to the day's theme and can be used as introductions to the lesson itself.

An accompanying sidebar always lists key information for your preparations for the lesson, including the "Central Truth," which is a statement that provides the main theme of the lesson. Each lesson also has three "Objectives." As you review these statements, keep in mind the importance of including Law (God's expectations of us, which remind us of our sinfulness), Gospel (what God has done for us in Christ Jesus to restore us to Himself), and our response (how we respond to the Gospel in the new life God empowers us to live). You may choose to read these statements to students at the beginning of the lesson or refer to them at the lesson's conclusion. Research suggests that students are more likely to achieve lesson objectives if the objectives are clearly identified for them.

A "Materials" list notes items needed to teach the lesson. "The Basics" (used in every lesson) include the Student Books, ESV Bibles, and pencils.

The "Bible Prep" list is very important. It includes the Bible references students will need throughout the lesson. Post them on the board in advance so students can bookmark these verses before class begins. This will make the lesson flow more efficiently as well as level the playing field so as not to single out students unfamiliar with finding references in the Bible.

The Lesson Plan

One in Christ lessons make use of various technologies to achieve lesson objectives. Be sure to check out the Web resources accompanying the lessons to access interactive whiteboard activities, slide presentations, video segments, and so forth. These resources are only available on the One in Christ Portal, organized by grade level and lesson number.

Inserted on the second and third pages of each Teacher Guide lesson are reductions of the two Student Pages and the Reproducible with answers written in. You will find many of the questions and directions given in the Teacher Guide rather than in the Student Book, because this series places an emphasis on group discussion and group work. Please note the Gospel highlighted in red in the Teacher Guide as a reminder to give a clear presentation of the Gospel in the teaching of the lesson. The Student Book is not meant to be a workbook in which you assign pages; instead, students will use these pages to respond to the lesson and to record group interactions.

All lessons follow an easy-to-teach format of three distinct parts: "Into the Lesson," "Into the Word," and "Into Our Lives." The "Into the Lesson" section is designed to capture students' interest and to delve into the lesson concepts. The "Into the Word" section provides the Bible story or Bible study that supports the theme of the lesson. Finally, the "Into Our Lives" section encourages students to react, or respond to and apply, the concepts they have learned. The Reproducible, one designed for each lesson, can be reproduced from the *Teacher Resource Book*, or, if you prefer, it can be downloaded from the One in Christ Portal.

Each lesson concludes with the "Lesson Support" section, which provides a variety of articles, teaching tips, lesson extensions, and enrichment ideas.

Student Book

This level of One in Christ consists of one hundred lessons. Two facing pages have been dedicated to each lesson of the Student Book. These pages are also reproduced in the Teacher Guide with answers provided for easy teacher reference. The One in Christ emphasis on God's Word and discipleship is readily apparent upon a quick review of these pages. All studies of God's Word, life-related activities, and memory verses have been chosen and included with the overall goal of helping students learn more about God's love for them in Jesus Christ.

One in Christ materials have been prepared with the goal of replacing academic activities with more of a focus on reflection, discussion, and application. By God's grace and through the working of His Spirit, your students will experience the oneness in Christ that occurs when God's people gather around His Word in times of study, reflection, and prayer. The goal of those who have prepared these lessons is to help make the portion of the day devoted to the study of God's Word unique and distinctive—the students' favorite time of the school day.

A Special Resource

One of the special features designed to be used at the sixth-grade level is a series of books (biographies) on heroes of the faith. Middle-school classrooms commonly feature high-interest paperbacks in class quantities for students to read and discuss together. Young people often learn from, find inspiration in, and guide their lives according to the heroes they choose. Biographies show us how those we admire met and dealt with the challenges and struggles they faced. Regardless of the time and circumstances in which we live as God's people, we have much in common. The same God gives us life and provides us with all we are and possess; the same Spirit equips, guides, and encourages us through God's Word. The same Savior promises always to be with us. The following persons of faith are featured in the paperbacks designed for use at the sixth-grade level. (Note the variety in the selection of subjects: both men and women; persons from different centuries and different callings, serving during times of reformation or revolution, or serving by teaching or healing.) You may want to read the books aloud to your class and discuss the relevance of each character as a group, but it will be even more effective if you have class quantities so each student can read a section and then discuss it with partners, groups, or the class as a whole.

The biographies are *Martin Luther* (by Edward C. Grube), *Heinrich Melchior Muhlenberg* (by Stephenie Hovland), *Dorothea Craemer* (by Julie Stiegemeyer), and *Dr. Bessie Rehwinkel* (by A. Trevor Sutton).

Unit 1—Beginnings and Patriarchs

Theme

This first unit of the sixth-grade level of One in Christ focuses on beginnings, starting with God creating all things. This glorious beginning, however, was damaged by the beginning of sin. But then, by God's grace, came the beginning of the promise of a Messiah, who would come to save His people from their sins. We see another beginning after the great flood as Noah's family remained faithful, though also tarnished by sin. We then move on to the beginning of a special family chosen by God to carry the promise of the Savior who would be a blessing to the whole world. The patriarchs of this family were Abraham, Isaac, and Jacob, who passed the promise on to succeeding generations until the fullness of time had come and God sent, to be born of this family, His own Son, Jesus. These Bible stories also provide an opportunity to look at a subtheme—the Ten Commandments, which God gives to us to show us the Law (we are sinners who need a Savior). But we will also see the Gospel in these Old Testament stories because all of Scripture points to Jesus, our Savior; each lesson has a "Covenant Connection" that relates the Bible narrative to the promise of the Messiah. This curriculum has nine units to roughly correspond to the nine months of a school year. Unit 1 is suggested for use in August and September. You will find that there is not one lesson for every day of the week because some of these lessons will take more than one day to cover the material (depending on your students, their interest, and their abilities).

Unit 1

1. Creation and Fall
2. Cain and Abel
3. The Great Flood
4. The Tower of Babel
5. God's Promises to Abraham
6. The Offering of Isaac
7. Isaac and Rebekah
8. Isaac Blesses His Sons
9. Jacob and Laban
10. Joseph
11. Job

Worship

Each lesson in this curriculum has a classroom devotion that you may read to your students at the opening of your day together. (The devotions always have a direct connection to the day's Bible lesson. If you already have an established plan for opening devotions, you can still use the one suggested in the Teacher Guide as an introduction to the lesson.) It is suggested that your devotions this month include the reading of Psalm 100. Each month, a different Psalm of the Month will be suggested. You will probably notice that, through frequent use, most students will know the psalm by memory by the end of the month. (Putting the psalm to use is a much more effective means for memorization than as an assignment.) By the end of the school year, your students will have a basic understanding of nine key psalms. Though you can feel free to choose a variety of hymns and songs, suggestions will be made mostly from the *LSB* hymnal and the *AGPS* songbook. It will always be noted if the hymns are on the recorded set of *Hymns of the Month* or *Hymns of the Season*, available from CPH, which will give students a good background in Christian hymnody and will also help them to more readily participate in church worship services. Note that the CPH recording *Jesus' People Sing! (JPS)* consists of fifty songs, all from *AGPS*.

Resources

A key resource for this curriculum can be found on the One in Christ Web Portal. Individual lessons will be listed on this site, providing downloadable reproducibles, links to other Web sites, interactive whiteboard applications, slide presentations, and other resources for the lesson of the day. The Portal will also have a listing of available materials related to the unit as a whole, such as a list of the Bible memory verses for the unit, a letter to make available to parents, and a unit test. These last three items and the reproducibles are also available in print in the *Teacher Resource Book*. (A parents letter in Spanish is available only online.) The unit tests are mostly multiple-choice tests that provide immediate feedback to the student and are self-correcting for the teacher. You can give the test to the whole class at once or to smaller groups in your computer lab, if available. If you have only one computer available, you can have students sign up to take the quiz during study periods, or they can be printed out. Unit 1 test answers are (1) c; (2) b; (3) a; (4) c; (5) a; (6) b; (7) c; (8) b; (9) b; (10) a. Note that the titles of this unit's lessons are listed in the column above to give you an overview of the material covered in this unit. On the next page, you will find an illustration of a Bulletin Board for this unit, available from CPH, and an explanation of how to use it. There is also a section for ideas on exploring the content of the books of the Bible over the course of the year.

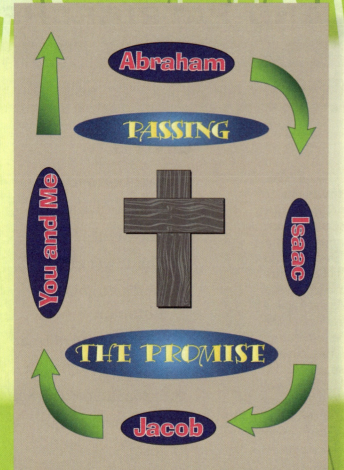

Bulletin Board

This bulletin board is available, ready to cut out and pin up, from Concordia Publishing House. There will be a bulletin board available for each unit/month that focuses on the unit's theme. This one presents a basic message that is essential to this unit. In the beginning, humankind had the image of God's holiness and righteousness; but that was lost by sinful disobedience. The consequences affected all creation. However, it could never affect God's love for His people. Right from the beginning, God was ready with a plan of salvation. He spoke of it in Genesis 3:15 and continued to reveal more and more of His plan as the years passed. God chose one family to "Pass the Promise." This was the family of Abraham, through whom all the world (including you and me) would be blessed. Abraham passed the promise of the Savior to his son Isaac, and he passed the promise to his son Jacob, and the promise continued until Jesus fulfilled it by dying on the cross and rising at Easter to save the world. We have this promise of salvation, and we, too, are commissioned by the Lord to pass this promise to people all over the world—and to future generations!

Bible Book Overview

The Student Book Appendix has a valuable feature that gives a summary of each book of the Bible. Looking at the summaries of sixty-six books can be overwhelming, so it is suggested that each month/unit, your class look at the summaries of just a few of these books. Start this month by looking at the first five books of the Bible. Point out that these are often called "the Books of Moses" (because Moses wrote down what had been passed down orally). These are also called "the Books of the Law," because the Ten Commandments are recorded twice in this section of books, along with laws of ceremonies and sacrifices. The five books are *Genesis, Exodus, Leviticus, Numbers,* and *Deuteronomy*. Ten of the stories in Unit 1 are from the Book of Genesis. (The final story of the unit takes place in this time period, but it is a book of poetry.) Most of the Bible narratives in Unit 2 are covered in the remaining Books of the Law (which are also called "the Pentateuch" because they include five books). Read together and discuss the five summaries in the Appendix when you have time.

UNIT 1—BEGINNINGS AND PATRIARCHS

LESSON 1

Creation and Fall
GENESIS 1–3

Background

Oliver Wendell Holmes once penned this limerick:

God's plan made a hopeful beginning.
But man spoiled his chances by sinning.
We trust that the story
Will end in God's glory.
But, at present, the other side's winning.

That's how it feels sometimes, doesn't it? Adam and Eve introduced sin into God's perfect creation, and human beings have suffered ever since. Tsunamis and cyberbullying. Parkinson's and poverty. Cataracts, cancer, and crises of every kind. Adam blamed Eve, and she blamed the serpent. We blame our circumstances, our neighbors, our personal history. But the responsibility for the mess we're in rests squarely on our own shoulders. We cause plenty of hurt. We contribute to the hurt initiated by others. We get hurt by the sinful, selfish decisions others make. Hurting people hurt people, and round and round it goes.

But that's not the end of the story. The story of salvation will indeed end in God's glory. It will end in our good—and all because the woman's offspring, our Lord Jesus, took the guilt of our sin off our shoulders and put it on His own. He carried it to the cross and suffered for it in our place.

The story of how that happened can't be told in ten minutes. In fact, the story of our salvation took centuries to unfold. It takes sixty-six books of the Bible to tell that story. From Genesis to Malachi, from Matthew to Revelation, the Holy Spirit describes inerrantly and infallibly the twists and turns that story took down through human history. That's the story you will share with your students this year—and a wonderful, intriguing story it is! Knowing Christ, you get to make Christ known—in your classroom, your school, your family, your community, your church, and your world. Welcome to the great adventure of the greatest story ever told!

Central Truth

God created all things, but humankind's rebellion broke the image of holiness and perfection God created in them; God immediately acted—moving from creation to restoration.

Objectives

- Realize that the sin of Adam and Eve, and all sinners, is placing personal will above God's will (breaking the First Commandment).
- Praise God that His response to humankind's broken image was to establish a plan and a promise to restore it through Christ Jesus.
- Dedicate ourselves to the Lord, who has created and re-created us.

Materials

- Hymnals and music CDs
- Web Resource 1a
- Web Resource 1b
- Web Resource 1c
- Reproducible 1

Bible Prep

Post in advance so students can bookmark references before class time.
- Genesis 1–3

Devotions

As we begin to look at God's great story, let's first consider a little story that is something of a parable. Little Jackie came running into the house, proud of the little clay bowl she had made in first grade. She was going to give it to her big brother, who was in high school, so he would have a special place to keep his car keys. But as Jackie ran into the house, she slipped and fell, and her clay bowl broke into many pieces. Her brother, Jonathan, reading his homework in the other room, heard her say, "Everything is broken!" And then he heard her quietly hurrying around the house. Finally, she sadly walked over to him. She handed him a very lumpy clay bowl. Jackie sniffed and said, "I tried to glue the pieces together myself, but I just couldn't do it right." Jonathan quickly said, "I think you need help from someone who has the right tools." Jackie watched as Jonathan added a new layer to the bowl to make it smooth, then added mosaic glass squares to make it beautiful. It was a new creation.

This parable can remind us of God's creation, which was broken by humankind's sin. We try to repair things we do wrong to make things better—but we can't do it ourselves. We need the help of God's Son, our Brother, who has the right tools (His righteousness, death, and resurrection) to cover our mistakes (sins) and smooth things over (in our relationship to God). Because of Jesus, each of us is now a beautiful new creation! We read in 2 Corinthians 5:17: "Therefore, if anyone is in Christ, he is a new creation. The old has passed away; behold, the new has come." Read together the words of praise in Psalm 100 and then sing "What a Friend We Have in Jesus" (*LSB* 770; recorded as *Hymn of the Month* for grade 6, September).

INTO the lesson

One Big Story—One in Christ

The opening section of the Student Book has a somewhat poetic review of the days of creation. (You may choose to read related verses from Genesis 1.) Discuss what the special creation was on Day 6 and what made it so special. (Adam and Eve were the special creation; each was created in a unique way [see Genesis 2]; they were unique because, unlike all other living things, they were created in God's image—not in looks, but in character, which was holy.) Questions (a) and (b) explore what creation tells us about God: His greatness and also His infinite, caring love.

Emphasize that the story of creation is not just a nice story—it is God's truth. Point out that there are people today who dismiss the story as fiction because they have placed their faith in evolution. These people are committing the same sin as Adam and Eve—placing their own thoughts and ideas ahead of God's will, breaking the First Commandment. Faith-filled believers will not pick and choose what they want to believe from the Bible, thinking that their "knowledge" is above God's. The creation story is the foundation for learning about God's greatness and His love—factors that are also basic to the story of God's salvation in Christ Jesus.

(Look again at the earlier phrase about people who have "placed their faith in evolution." Evolution is not a science. It is a belief system based on hypotheses rather than facts. DNA studies today contradict facets of evolution. Mathematicians look at evolution through the laws of probability and recognize that human evolution is impossible. Scientific laws of entropy [note these are *laws*, not hypotheses] say that matter in time deteriorates rather than improves [as evolution would suggest]. There is no evidence of evolution from one species to another; mutations of a species tend to be of a lesser form and are usually unable to reproduce, rather than improve the species. Evolution is a philosophical view of the world rather than a scientific fact.)

Review

Point out that this review section will always note how the lesson connects to the overall picture of the story of God's saving love. Genesis 1 is not just a story of how the world was made. Its focus is on God's love for His people as He prepares a home for them. God knows all things, and right from the start, He knew people would sin—but that did not stop Him from expressing His love. We could compare this to a married couple who decide they want to have a baby. They want to have someone to love and care for. They know it won't be easy. They know there will be dirty diapers and spit-up milk, but those things do not stop them from expressing their love to a new creation! Parents know what to expect from a baby; God knows what to expect of His people, and that's why, from the very beginning, He was ready to save His people through Christ Jesus.

INTO the Word

Second Half of the First Narrative

Point out: **Usually the story of creation and the story of the fall into sin are taught as two separate stories. Actually, the two belong together to set the stage for all the rest of the events in the Bible. Creation is about a home created for God's people, who, because of their brokenness after their fall into sin, needed God to restore them through the promise of a Savior.**

Discuss the picture at the top of the page. Point out that sin did not just affect Adam and Eve. Sin broke everything! It even broke the image of God

Second Half of the First Narrative

Sin broke everything in creation; but God would not break His covenant relationship with His people. Sin brought horrific consequences; but God brought mercy, grace, and a promise to restore that relationship.

> God created a garden home for His people—
> but sin intervened.
> God planned a heavenly home for His people—
> as the Savior intervened.

Here's the Plan

 God made a wonderful world, which sin ruined.

 Because God is loving, He made a plan to save us.

 He sent His Son to set us free from sin and death.

 He grows faith in our hearts so we can live in faith.

○ He promises us life forever in heaven, through Jesus.

Do those five little pictures look familiar? Put them together as one symbol, drawing and then coloring them in the box above.

Remember

"If, because of one man's __trespass__ , __death__ reigned through that one man [__Adam__], much more will those who receive the abundance of __grace__ and the free gift of righteousness reign in __life__ through the one man __Jesus Christ__ ." (Romans 5:17)

---

created in people. That is why we are all born as sinners; this is part of the human condition. Our condition, our human nature, is to need oxygen, water, and food, and another part of our human nature is sin.

Read Genesis 3:1–15. Ask students, **What was the first sin? Why is eating fruit such a big deal?** The significant factor was not the fruit; it was the disobedience to God's will as Adam and Eve chose to do what *they* wanted rather than what *God* wanted. It was their desire to become gods themselves, setting their own rules and doing as they pleased. Such behavior continues to be the main cause of sin in the world today.

Discuss further the promise of the Savior in Genesis 3:15. It may seem obscure, so use Web Resource 1a to help their understanding. Emphasize that Satan won that battle—Adam and Eve sinned. Satan continues to win battles in our world and in our lives today. But the final, ultimate victory belongs to Jesus. There may be battles, but He has already won the war, conquering sin, death, and Satan. And amazingly, Jesus takes His victory and gives it to us so that we have forgiveness, life, and salvation.

Discuss the word *intervened* as it is used in the Student Book. When Satan intervened, he brought destruction. When Christ intervened, He brought restoration.

INTO our lives

Here's the Plan

Genesis 3:15 may be somewhat difficult to understand, but God continued to reveal more and more about His plan over the centuries through His prophets. We will see this plan unfolding in the course of this year.

Have students read through the steps of God's plan as listed in the Student Book. Ask if they recognize the little symbols pictured. These are the elements in the seal or symbol that Martin Luther designed to tell the whole story of salvation. Have students draw and color the symbol in the blank box. Web Resource 1b displays a version of the symbol.

As you wrap up today, have students sit back, close their eyes, and listen as you read aloud the story from 1 Corinthians 15:51–58. As you finish reading, move directly into this prayer:

Lord Jesus, because of You, the story of salvation will end in God's glory and in our eternal joy. As we hear more about that story of salvation this year, give us open hearts to love and serve You more and more. Amen.

Remember

This Bible verse summarizes today's lesson, where we see brokenness resulting from Adam and restoration through Christ Jesus. Look again at the symbol in the review box, and also show Web Resource 1c. This is a Chi-Rho symbol, which consists of the first two letters (*P* and *X*) in the Greek word for Christ. The symbol, topped by a circle, reminds us that Christ came to save the world. We see how Christ saved us as we look at the yellow *X* (which represents the manger) and the yellow cross, reminding us that from the cradle to the cross, Christ Jesus did all things for our restoration; and by faith in Him, we are a new creation. This symbol reminds us that everything in the Bible connects to and focuses on Jesus. He is the fulfillment of God's covenant promises.

Lesson Support

Technology

Using the Internet to do basic research and to collect appropriate illustrations, put together a PowerPoint presentation that celebrates specific aspects of the creation. Choose beautiful, complex, and/or powerful features on display in God's universe. Caption each slide using eight to ten words. Add appropriate spoken narration and perhaps a musical accompaniment. Present it as part of an upcoming chapel worship service.

Faith in Action

Because we believe that our planet is the home created uniquely for us by our heavenly Father, Christians have a deep concern for the environment. Work together with your class and other classes in your school to develop a specific project that will make a positive impact in your community.

- Find a way to recycle the paper used in your school.
- Consider ways to cut down on lunchroom trash.
- Enlist a group of adults to help weatherize the homes of elderly residents in your community.
- Collect burned-out CFL light bulbs and take them to an agency that offers safe disposal.
- Collect and recycle used athletic shoes.

Bringing it home

Use Reproducible 1 to share the message of creation with others. Students can use the activity to tell the story to family members and friends. (Family is usually the first witness target for students. Witnessing to those who already are believers encourages them in the faith, plus it provides opportunities for students to practice the vocabulary of sharing the faith.) Encourage students to use this tool as a witness tool that helps them to speak of the greatness of God, praising and thanking Him for all He has done.

Critical thinking

Everyone has a worldview, whether we realize it or not. We're not always consistent in our worldview. Furthermore, the ideas and beliefs of some worldviews overlap. Worldviews are important because they influence our thinking about right and wrong. They also affect our behavior. In general, human beings make decisions about what to do based on what they believe. As you look around at your world, what do you see? How do you make sense of all those inputs, all those messages? The story of salvation is one story—or "frame of reference"—for making sense of it all. Here are some other frames of reference. Each of them is popular. Read the descriptions, asking yourself how they differ from the Christian frame of reference.

The Story of Stuff—People who tell themselves this story (materialism) believe that money will keep them secure and material things will make them happy. They live for the latest electronics, the most stylish home, the biggest swimming pool in the backyard, and the best vacations. Life is about collecting more and more things and experiences.

The Story of Me, Me, Me—People who tell themselves this story (self-centeredness) put themselves in the center of the universe. They don't think much about how their decisions and actions affect their family, friends, or community. What they want matters much more to them than what others need. They decide what's right and wrong, making it up by looking at what will benefit them the most. Life is about getting what makes them feel satisfied and happiest.

The Story of Only Matter Matters—According to this story (experiential knowledge), only what we can see, taste, touch, hear, or smell matters. In fact, if you can't measure it, you can't scientifically study it, and you can't trust it. Everything that happens follows the "laws of nature." Life is about exploring the things that are really real, and then you die. Your consciousness stops forever. The story is over.

The Story of Superficial Spirituality—This story (New Age philosophy) is almost the opposite of "Only Matter Matters." It teaches people that they are divine—little gods, really. Their life quest is about finding and releasing the power within them. They explore all kinds of spiritual practices as they try to free their higher self, often using horoscopes, tarot cards, channeling the spirits of the dead, and the like.

How does the story of salvation through Jesus differ from all of these worldviews?

Curriculum Connection

Check the sixth-grade Visual Arts volume of the Concordia Curriculum Guide series for a connection to this lesson; look at section 6.2.2.3, "Using Observation, Life Experience, and Imagination as Sources for Visual Symbols and Images." In a sense, God has created "recycled art" out of us, re-creating us in the image of Christ after sin spoiled God's image in us the first time. As a class, make recycled art together—projects that are not only beautiful but also good for God's creation.

UNIT 1—BEGINNINGS AND PATRIARCHS

LESSON 2

Cain and Abel

GENESIS 4:1–16

Background

People often act in arbitrary ways. God never does. Yet, as we read the opening verses of Genesis 4, we may wonder: What really was wrong with Cain's sacrifice? Why did God accept Abel's offering, but not his brother's? Hebrews 11:4–5 tells us. Faith—Abel's God-given faith—made this younger son's sacrifice acceptable. Cain's sacrifice was not "mixed with faith"—faith in the Savior who would one day, as God promised, offer the one final, perfect sacrifice for human sin—Himself.

Genesis 3:21 set the pattern for sin's proper sacrifice. The Lord slaughtered animals and covered Adam and Eve's nakedness with the animals' skins. What must our first parents have thought as they experienced the deaths that made this covering of their shame possible? Shock at the horrors their longing to "be like God" (v. 5) had unleashed into God's once-good creation? Whatever their reaction, the consequences of their sin were enormous. As the days went on, this enormity slowly but certainly must have weighed more and more heavily on their hearts. The death of their younger son at the hands of the older must have crushed them. And yet, in an ironic twist, God would one day send a Savior who would die to destroy death. Consider: "Indeed, under the law almost everything is purified with blood, and without the shedding of blood there is no forgiveness of sins" (Hebrews 9:22). "Through death He [Christ] might destroy the one who has the power of death, that is, the devil, and deliver all those who through fear of death were subject to lifelong slavery" (Hebrews 2:14–15).

Abel's blood cried out for vengeance. Jesus' blood cried for mercy. God heard. He still hears today. And He forgives those who come to Him in faith for pardon.

Central Truth

Sin has consequences that are far-reaching; we are blessed that one consequence of God's love was the cross of Christ.

Objectives

- Recognize that an individual's sin has consequences that include punishment for the sinner and distress for those around him or her, including innocent people and the environment around them.
- Give thanks that God is not only just, demanding punishment, but He is also merciful, placing that punishment on Jesus on the cross.
- Respond to others in love and mercy as God has done to us.

Materials

- Hymnals and music CDs
- Reproducible 2

Bible Prep

Post in advance so students can bookmark references before class time.

- Genesis 4:1–16
- 1 Samuel 16:7
- Hebrews 11:4
- Matthew 25:31–46

Devotions

Can you think of a time when one sin led to another? For example, Dad said, "Do your homework," but you texted your friends for the next two hours instead. Mom asked, "Is your homework done?" You lied: "Yes, it's done." The next morning, when you got to school, you asked if you could copy your best friend's answers. He said yes, but the teacher caught you. She wrote a note to your parents—and to your friend's parents too. Consequences loomed large on the horizon! What other examples can you give of one sin leading to another and, finally, to sad consequences? The Bible says that sin is "deceitful." Listen: "But exhort one another every day, as long as it is called 'today,' that none of you may be hardened by the deceitfulness of sin" (Hebrews 3:13). *Deceitful* means "tricky." Sin fools us. We think we can get away with it. We think it's harmless—and maybe even fun! But sin is serious business. When we give in to it, our hearts get a little bit harder. In fact, that's one of sin's worst consequences! We might fool the people around us, but we can't fool God. Sin hurts us. It hurts the people around us. Sometimes, it even hurts the society we live in—and the creation itself! We can't control those consequences, hard as we may try. In today's Bible study, we'll see a sad example of that. We can't fool God. Sin's consequences are very bad news. The Good News, the Gospel, is that we don't have to suffer! Our heavenly Father loves us despite our sin. The consequence of God's love is that He sent His very own Son to endure the punishment we had earned! He took away our punishment; He took away our sins. Praise God by speaking together Psalm 100 and then singing "O Blessed, Holy Trinity" (*LSB* 876; recorded as *Hymn of the Season for grade 6, Christian Education Month*).

INTO the lesson

The Big Picture: More Than the Fifth Commandment

Discuss the title of this section. Usually the focus of a lesson on Cain and Abel is on the Fifth Commandment. (Review this commandment, referring students to the portion of Luther's Small Catechism included in the Appendix of their Student Book.) The title says that this story is about hatred, harming, and murder, but it is also about much more. The bigger picture is of our human condition as sinners. Do a quick survey of your class. Ask, **How many of you inherited brown hair from your parents when you were born? blond? black? red? How many of you inherited blue eyes from your parents when you were born? green? brown? How many of you inherited original sin from your parents when you were born? These are all conditions we are born with. It's not a matter of choice; it's who we are by human nature.** This is not an excuse. We cannot blame someone else for our condition. Being born into this sin-damaged world means we are born in original sin.

Point out that the other type of sin is called "actual sin," in which we think, say, or do specific things that disobey God's will. Ask, **What can we do about all of this? Nothing—there is nothing we can do! That is why we look to our Savior, Jesus, for forgiveness and new life to live as His people.**

INTO the Word

A Sinner (Genesis 4:1–16)

Work together as a class on this Bible study. Allow students to change answers if they have learned something from another student. (This is not meant to be a graded assignment; it is meant to be a learning experience through group discussion.) Challenge students to consider times when they have acted like Cain—not as a murderer, but as someone who was angry at the accuser when he or she should have felt sorry that he or she did wrong; as someone who looked for excuses or blamed others rather than admitting errors; as someone who did not repent or change his or her ways. Cain was only interested in protecting himself; he did not recognize that our greatest protection is in the forgiveness Jesus offers to the faithful who repent. **Cain was worried about the punishment of his sin; we do not worry, because Jesus died on the cross to take away the punishment, which is received by all who truly believe in Him.**

Review

Point out that Adam and Eve probably hoped that their first son was the promised Savior. He definitely was not! A sinner born of sinners could not save sinners. God's plan would gradually unfold as He worked in His people through His Word. The Savior would come in the "fullness of time," at the time God knew was best for the fulfillment of His plan of salvation.

A Savior

We cannot look at the story of Cain without also looking at the story of Christ. The comparisons you develop as a group to list on the chart in the Student Book show contrasts. Cain and Christ are opposites—but this is more than just a matter of being different. These opposites were *in opposition*, *opposing* one another. Since Satan ruled Cain's heart, Cain was an enemy of God. That is why we see such hostility in him and such antagonistic behavior. Cain and Christ's purposes in life were antithetical.

In your discussion, emphasize that we are not just looking at the history of a bad guy because we, too, were born in sin. When we continue in sin unrepentantly, we are in opposition to Christ, and we are enemies of God. (See the words to remember from Romans 5:10.) Below the chart, we see two aspects of our condition,

16

A Savior

Sinners have been described as "curved in on themselves." Like dead stars—black holes, so massive that no light can escape from them—we live for ourselves; we indulge in self-centeredness. But instead of curving in on Himself, Jesus focused outward. His love moved Him to leave heaven and to suffer and die for us. Fill in the chart below with as many differences between Jesus and Cain as you can name.

Cain	Christ
He was born sinful, and he focused on himself.	Born sinless; focused on saving us!
Cain killed his brother.	Christ, our brother, died so we could live.
Cain complained about the consequences of his sins.	Christ willingly bore the consequences—not of His own sins, but of ours.
God let Cain live, giving him the opportunity for faith and repentance.	Christ had to die so we could have the opportunity for faith and repentance.

We are born in sin. *We are reborn in Baptism.*

So What about Me?

1. What is your human-nature reaction when someone confronts you because you've done something wrong? **So often it is self-protective, resentful; anger at the accuser for identifying your mistakes; blaming someone else.**

   What is God's will? **God wants you to admit you've done wrong, be sorry about it, repent, ask forgiveness, and change your ways.**

2. What is your human-nature reaction when you are told to be "your brother's keeper"? **So often it is a lack of concern, unwillingness to help unless there is a benefit to you.**

   What is God's will? **That we eagerly want to help others, even if they don't know us or don't even like us, and that we do so without expecting anything in return, such as a thank you**

Remember

"For if while we were enemies we were reconciled to God by the death of His Son, much more, now that we are reconciled, shall we be saved by His life." (Romans 5:10)

INTO our lives

So What about Me?

Use the next section to again look at this dichotomy of the old self and the new self. Encourage students to give honest answers to these questions.

1. Our human nature, when someone tells us we are wrong, is to get angry at that person for confronting us. We excuse ourselves: "Not me"; "It was an accident"; "I have a right to do this"; "Everyone does this"; "I'll say I'm sorry (if it gets you off my back and avoids punishment)"; "I'll say I'm sorry (but I won't stop doing it)." It is God's will that we acknowledge our sin, confess it, have sorrow over sin, receive forgiveness in faith, and change behavior through the working of the Holy Spirit in us.

2. Our human nature is interested in helping ourselves and not in helping others. We sometimes react by saying, "It's *their* problem, not mine; they deserve those troubles." God's will looks at things in the opposite way. He reaches out in kindness, and He calls on us to do the same as His people. (See Matthew 25:31–46.)

Lead students to see that by regularly confessing our sins and receiving Christ's forgiveness, we use the escape route He opened on Calvary's cross. That is why each worship service begins with words of confession of our sins and words of absolution through Christ Jesus. (Read these words together in *LSB* on p. 151, 167, or 184.) *Option:* Reproducible 2 extends some of the lesson concepts further.

and we see how we are related to this Bible story. Emphasize that we are born in sin and are enemies of God. Cain's symbol is also our symbol when we turn in on ourselves, doing only what we want and what we think is good for us. Our only hope is in Christ, who offers forgiveness, life, and salvation. This change happens as we are reborn in Baptism and by faith in God's Word. By faith, Christ has put His mark on us—the sign of the cross—and He leads us to reach out to others in Christian love.

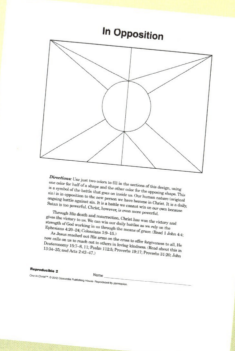

Lesson Support

Searching Further

Sin's consequences extend far beyond our individual lives, damaging the creation itself. Find and study Isaiah 24:4–12 or Jeremiah 10–11. List the specific consequences of sin in nature named by the prophets. Then consider an environmental problem that has been in the news recently. What elements of the problem seem similar to those described in the Scripture verses you read? Evaluate what happened to cause the damage. Where has human sin played a part (e.g., a worker is too lazy to check a valve; shoddy safety equipment is made cheaply because of greed; those responsible show a lack of concern for the consequences of a company's actions)? Whom might God use to help fix or clean up the damage? In what different careers do people make a difference in preventing or repairing damage? Which students might be interested in and gifted for those careers? Why should Christians care about the environment? Have students work individually or in groups to write a letter to other Christians, posing this question and answering it based on what they've learned in today's session and the previous one. Consider publishing the best letters in your school or church newsletter. Ask students to use professional word-processing software and submit a work product of high quality.

Digging Deeper

Have students read Genesis 4:25–26. The birth of Seth must have comforted a grieving Adam and Eve. Through the line of Seth, God's promise to send a Savior would continue. Martin Luther understood the phrase "people began to call upon the name of the Lord" as referring to the beginning of true worship. God's people knew and believed His Messianic promise. By faith, their worship was acceptable to and accepted by Him. Have students explore one or more of the orders of service your congregation uses on a regular basis. When in the service do the assembled believers "call upon the name of the Lord"?

Curriculum Connection

For many of your students, their biggest encounter with Fifth Commandment sins will come in the area of cyberbullying (using computers or other electronic means to harm someone through words and pictures). Let this become an ongoing discussion this year about using new means of communication in a Christian way; how to deal with being a victim; how to defend other people who are being harmed in these ways and not become an accessory to the wrongdoing by inaction. In connection with this, consider using section 6.1.2.4, "Dealing with Frustration, Anger, and Anxiety," found in the sixth grade Physical Education volume of the Concordia Curriculum Guide series. Discuss with students how they can work through negative emotions with God's help and without causing damage to themselves or others.

Reaching Every Child

Even though you've probably completed only the first few days of a new school year, you've likely already begun to note individual differences among your students. Perhaps you've also noticed challenges these differences have introduced. What to do? First, examine realistically your expectations for yourself and the ideal classroom decorum. Of course, learning requires order. But it may take a few days or weeks before every student adjusts to the expectations you customarily set for the classroom environment. Pray for patience, and partner with your principal and possibly the teacher who worked with your students last year too. Don't forget that parents can be helpful allies as well. Enlist them before you feel you must. Second, approach the situation as a learning challenge—with yourself as the key learner! Get curious. Experiment and record results. What kinds of activities and approaches seem to produce the results you're looking for? How can you incorporate more of them? An attitude of curiosity will not only lead to better outcomes; it also will be less likely to create discouragement in you and probably in your students too. Third, work to build trust between you, the students, the parents, and your administration. Do what you say you will do. Keep your emotions under control. Act rather than reacting. Evaluate your behaviors in terms of whether they will build or deflate your relationships with your class and individual members in it. Send notes home when you "catch kids being good." Eat lunch with your class, even if you're not required to do so. Spend time with them on the playground too. Show genuine interest and concern. Note the positive—even if it's minor at first. In general, behavior that is noticed and rewarded will be repeated. Fourth, work to discover and highlight the positive skills and abilities of every student.

18

UNIT 1—BEGINNINGS AND PATRIARCHS

LESSON 3

The Great Flood
GENESIS 6:1–9:17

Background

"I the LORD do not change," God tells us (Malachi 3:6a). That changelessness is a good thing. Because of it, "You, O children of Jacob, are not consumed" (v. 6b). The Lord is changeless in justice, changeless in mercy. Justice and mercy. Law and Gospel. Accusation and salvation. These themes repeat again and again throughout both testaments in Holy Scripture. The account of the great flood is but one example:

- Violence and wickedness filled the earth, grieving God's heart. In justice, He made plans to act (Genesis 6:5–7).
- In merciful concern that Noah and his family not be drawn into the morass, God created a way to preserve them (vv. 13–22).
- Judgment did not fall right away. In mercy, God commissioned Noah to preach about the righteousness He offers freely to all repentant sinners (2 Peter 2:5).
- The "world of the ungodly" (Hebrews 11:7) refused repentance, even though God in mercy "waited patiently" (1 Peter 3:20 NIV). Finally, in justice, the Lord acted. A cataclysmic flood occurred.
- Throughout the time of judgment, the Lord preserved Noah and his family—both physically and in faith. When Noah left the ark, he built an altar and sacrificed animals as a reminder of the one final, perfect sacrifice to come—the promised Messiah.

God mercifully preserved Noah in righteousness. The promised Messiah came in the fullness of time. Today, every baptized child of God can claim the righteousness He won on the cross for Noah and for us! God's mercy toward Noah was in a very real sense mercy toward you and me!

Central Truth
Throughout this one long story, we continually see the pattern of Law and Gospel (sin and grace; accusation and salvation; judgment and mercy).

Objectives
- Acknowledge that God is holy and cannot accept or ignore the sins of humankind.
- Affirm that God is also gracious, providing deliverance for all who believe in His salvation.
- Trust in the Lord to give us new life, set us free from the guilt of sin, and enable us by the Holy Spirit to grow in faith.

Materials
- Hymnals and music CDs
- Beach balls (as many as you can gather)
- Reproducible 3
- Web Resource 3a

Bible Prep
Post in advance so students can bookmark references before class time.
- Genesis 5–9
- Job 22:15–17
- Hebrews 11:7
- 1 Peter 3:18–22
- 2 Peter 2:5

Devotions

Does someone in your family keep track of your family tree? What is a family tree, anyway? (Let a volunteer or two answer.) It's fun to learn about our relatives from past generations. Who knows? Maybe someone has a great-great-uncle who lived in a sod house on the prairie in Nebraska or a great-great-great-grandmother who served as a nurse in the Civil War.

Today, though, I'd like you to think about a different family tree—our "faith family tree." All of us who believe in Jesus are part of this faith family tree. It started with Adam and Eve, who had many children. Each of those children was born with an overwhelming defect: the problem of original sin. Adam and Eve passed the condition of sin on to each of their sons and daughters. Still, the family tree of faith did not die out. Many of Adam and Eve's children, grandchildren, and great-grandchildren believed in the Savior whom God had promised to send. By grace, God counted these believers as righteous.

But most did not believe. They lived rebellious, ungodly lives. In patience, God waited for them to repent. He waited for centuries, from the time of Cain onward! But one day, God said, "Enough!" The fountains of the deep exploded. Water poured from the sky in torrents. Only Noah and his family were safe in the ark God had told Noah to build. Everyone else drowned. The great flood was a sad time, but it was also a happy time because God spared His believing children, even as He punished the rebellious unbelievers. Law and Gospel. Sin and grace. Judgment and mercy. That's our family story. It's the story of your life too. And mine. The Law tells us we deserve punishment. But in Jesus, the Gospel tells of salvation. Let's praise the Lord for it now. Say together Psalm 100, and sing "Father Welcomes" (*LSB* 605; recorded as *Hymn of the Month* for grade 3, April).

19

INTO the lesson

Drowning a Beach Ball?

Begin by tossing one, two, three, or more beach balls to students and challenging them to keep all the balls from touching the ground. After a minute or two, collect the balls and read the opening paragraph from the Student Book to the class. Then talk about the questions listed beneath it.

Focus special attention on this fact: **Even with the best technique, no one can keep a beach ball under water for very long. It's like the sin in our lives. We can get help from others. We can try with all our might to hide it, pass it on to someone else, or try to ignore it. But sooner or later, disrespectful attitudes, curse words, loveless actions, neglect of prayer, failure to be thankful—some sin or another—will inevitably pop to the surface.**

It's no better when people band together in organizations or governments to keep the sin in society under control. Sometimes people or societies give up, and that makes things even worse! God gave human beings His Law to keep sin under control in society, to minimize the ways we hurt one another so we can live together in relative peace. Societies that ignore God's Law and make rules of their own based on human opinions do even worse than those who try (even while failing) to keep God's Law. Ask for examples.

Say, **Today's lesson focuses on a time when society did this, leaving only one small family that still lived in fear, love, and trust of God. This family is on the faith family tree. They are some of our faith ancestors.**

Review

Review the meaning of the word *righteous*. Point out that *righteous* does not mean "never sinning." Instead, it is the verdict our Judge has already passed on our lives because of what Jesus did for us. His perfect life, sacrificial death, and victorious resurrection—all accomplished in our place—make us right with God, who now sees us as innocent and blameless because of Jesus.

LESSON 3

The Great Flood

Drowning a Beach Ball?

Think about your last trip to the swimming pool, lake, or ocean. Did you take a beach ball along? Have you ever tried to "drown" a beach ball by forcing it completely under the water? What techniques have you tried? What happens?

- How is trying to drown a beach ball a little like trying to get rid of the sin in our lives? What happens?
- How is trying to drown a beach ball a little like trying to stop the sin in the world?
- What techniques do people try in order to deal with sin?
- Do people ever just give up and let the sin surface and float along?
- What happens to the person (and the society) that ignores sin?

Review

Covenant Connection

The Bible says Noah was "righteous" (Genesis 6:9). He was a sinner, but he had faith in God's promise of a Savior, so he "became an heir of the righteousness that comes by faith" (Hebrews 11:7). That same Savior has made us righteous, taking our sins to the cross "so that in Him we might become the righteousness of God" (2 Corinthians 5:21).

INTO the Word

Drowning Sin— in Judgment

Though the story of Noah and the flood brings up images of animals, that is not what the story is about. **As is true of every portion of Scripture, the event is about Law and Gospel. In other words, it is about judgment and mercy, sin and grace, justice and forgiveness. Law and Gospel is the constant theme of Scripture.** The biblical account of this narrative is quite long. Rather than reading it verbatim, distribute Reproducible 3 and ask students to follow the directions there, using the page to review the biblical account, and reading specific key verses. Have the class work on one section at a time so you can discuss each section before moving on to the next.

The sum of the correct answers for Section A is 4; all the statements are false. Use the Bible verses referenced on the sheet if students disagree or ask for further explanation. Stress item 3—Noah stood out *because of the righteousness God gave him*. Noah's *faith*, not what he did, made Noah righteous. In the same way today, God gives us faith in Jesus and then declares us righteous because of it.

The sum of the correct answers for Section B is 12; all the statements are true. Again, refer to the Bible verses

Drowning Sin—in Judgment

Because God is just and holy, He cannot just ignore sin. He's not some old man up above whom we can fool by lying, pretending, blaming, or hiding from the wrong we do and the hurt we cause when we sin. God must punish sin. But He loves sinners—that's us! In love, He promised to send a Savior for the sins of Adam, Eve, Cain, Abel, Noah, and every other sinful person born on earth.

At one point in earth's history, though, Satan nearly succeeded in wiping out that promise. Only one little family remained that still trusted God to keep His promise. Just think—eight godly people surrounded by thousands of unbelievers! Can you imagine the ridicule, the bullying, the jokes, the pressure on Noah and his family to give in to ungodliness? In mercy toward Noah and justice toward everyone else, God acted. Genesis 6–9 shows us that sin is serious; God is angry at sin, and He is determined to destroy it.

Drowning Sin—in Mercy

We have two big problems with sin:

- First, God can't just ignore our sin. He is holy and just, so He must punish it—just as He had to punish the sin of Noah's day.
- Second, we can't stop committing sins. It's impossible for us to drown them, even when we try our hardest—and we don't always try!

Jesus conquered both problems for us. And because He did, we're free!

- First, instead of punishing *us* for sin, God punished Jesus. By faith in Him, we are made righteous—all right with God. In Baptism, God daily drowns our sin.
- Second, when we struggle with sin, Jesus is near to remind us that in Baptism, He drowned sin's power in us. He invites us to confess our sins and to receive His forgiveness. Just as the Great Flood washed sin off the earth, your Baptism in Christ washes away sin's power in us.

1 Peter 3:18–22

Remember

"Baptism, which corresponds to this, now saves you, not as a removal of dirt from the body but as an appeal to God for a good conscience, through the resurrection of Jesus Christ." (1 Peter 3:21)

INTO our lives

Drowning Sin—in Mercy

In the great flood, the waters drowned the wickedness that was rampant and brought judgment. In our lives, the waters of Baptism drown sin and our sinful nature through the promise of forgiveness in Christ Jesus as He brings us mercy. Ask students to turn to the Small Catechism in the Appendix in the back of their Student Book and read what Martin Luther said about Baptism (see the Fourth Part, "What does such baptizing with water indicate?"). Have students bookmark the catechism in their Student Books so that it is always ready for quick reference. The Small Catechism is also printed in *LSB* (p. 321), in *AGPS* (p. 35), and in the *Faith Alive Bible*.

Ask students to find the beach balls on the pages of this lesson and write types of sins on them. Then ask a volunteer to read the rest of the text in this section (or do so yourself) as meaningfully as possible. Comment on the comfort and reassurance you personally derive from your Baptism, and invite students to do so too. Then close with a prayer like this one:

Lord Jesus, thank You so much for acting in both justice and mercy. You let Yourself be punished in our place, and now You are patient and merciful with us in our sins. Keep assuring us of Your forgiveness, Lord, and stand with us as we rely on the power of Baptism to drown the sins that hurt us and others. Thank You for Your cross and empty tomb! Amen.

Remember

Point out that the verse compares what happened to Noah during the great flood with what happened in our lives when we were baptized.

---

referenced in each item for further clarification. Because Noah took seven pairs of ceremonially "clean" animals onto the ark, he could offer sacrifices in thanksgiving to God when the judgment had passed, the floodwaters had receded, and he and his family were safe.

The sum of the correct answers for Section C is 8; statements 9 and 10 are false, while 11 and 12 are true. Explain that it did rain very hard, but that wasn't all that happened; Scripture speaks of the waters deep in the earth bursting forth. Both the Hebrew of the Old Testament and the Greek of the New Testament refer to the great flood by using a word other than the ordinary word in those languages for "flood." The rain lasted forty days and nights, but that was not the end of the flood, because it took months for the waters to dry up. This was a unique and terrible judgment—a cataclysm! Justice was served as God destroyed the wickedness. He was also merciful in sparing Noah. This justice and mercy are the Law and Gospel themes, followed by a response of worship and thanks.

Abel offered a sacrifice. Now, Noah offers a sacrifice. Why? What did these sacrifices mean? Allow the students time to think, if necessary. The sacrifices pointed ahead to the one final, perfect sacrifice the Savior would make for all people on His cross. Use Web Resource 3a to "dig deeper" into the events of the Bible story.

Lesson Support

Working in Groups

Consider asking students to work on Reproducible 3 with partners, two or three students per group. It may speed up the activity, and it's likely students will read and understand more of the Bible passages referenced as they collaborate on the task.

Technology

Research shows that a decline in face-to-face contact may contribute to a lessening of social skills and to more bullying and mean behaviors in children and adolescents, both in the classroom and outside it. Talk about this with your class, and relate it to their personal use of technology. Is more screen time leading to more problems in their relationships at home and in school? Does it make the "beach balls" in their lives more difficult to drown? How can we use God's good gift of technology more wisely so that He is honored by it?

Reaching Every Child

Use one of the beach balls you brought to class to organize spontaneous ("popcorn") prayers for one another as today's session ends. Tell students the object is twofold: (1) to keep the ball from touching the ground; and (2) to pray for ourselves and others as we catch the ball and pass it from one person to another.

As a student catches the ball, he or she should say a quick prayer; for example, "Jesus, teach me to be more patient," or "Lord, help Michael to know what a good friend he is."

Encourage students to have one or two petitions in mind before each new set begins. The activity should be fun, but discourage silliness or irreverence.

Searching Further

One of the main reasons God gave for His wrath before the flood was the violence that filled the world. See Genesis 6:11 and 13. Use a concordance or an online Bible study tool to explore other Scripture passages that refer specifically to violence. What do these verses say about God's attitude toward it? What conclusions can you draw about what He might think about "entertainment" in our culture? What changes might you want to make in your life as a result of this study?

Teacher Tips

This narrative opens many possibilities for students gifted in art. Encourage them to illustrate Genesis 7:10–12, either musically or by creating a drawing or painting. Or help your class divide the account of Genesis 6–9 into about a dozen distinct scenes. Assign each scene to a different student or to pairs of students, and ask each to create a PowerPoint illustration for their assigned scene. If you have students gifted in music, perhaps they could find or even create a background score. Have those who like to write create and record a suitable narration. Find a way to use the presentation as part of your school chapel service sometime during the year. Don't just tell the story, though. Find a way to tie it to the blessings of Baptism. Another option is the musical *Noah's RemARKable Voyage*, available from Concordia Publishing House (item no. 976108).

Critical thinking

Few incidents from the Old Testament are mentioned as often by New Testament writers as the great flood. Explore these references and ask, "Why might the Holy Spirit have chosen to include New Testament comments about the great flood so frequently? See Matthew 24:37–39; Luke 17:26–27; Hebrews 11:7; 1 Peter 3:20–21; and 2 Peter 2:5.

Curriculum Connection

Consider the character of Noah and the effect it had on his actions while using section 6.2.2.2, "Character Qualities, Effect on Plot and Resolution," in the sixth grade Language Arts volume of the Concordia Curriculum Guide series. What kind of person was Noah? What kind of "person" did he understand God to be? How did this shape Noah's actions? Working together, list as many adjectives as you can, both for Noah's character and for God's character as displayed in this story. Genesis 7:1 speaks of Noah as *righteous*. Use a concordance to find other Scripture verses that teach us more about righteousness.

UNIT **1**—BEGINNINGS AND PATRIARCHS

LESSON **4**

The Tower of Babel
GENESIS 11:1–9

Background

The great flood destroyed the sinful world in which Noah and his family lived. God preserved Noah and his family, blessed them, and commanded them to "be fruitful and multiply and fill the earth" (Genesis 9:1). But the sinful nature inherited from Adam remained in Noah and his family. In their sinfulness, Noah's descendants willfully thwarted God's command to "fill the earth." The tower they planned would give them a focal point to keep their civilization powerful and in one place. In their planning and their building, Noah's descendants put themselves in the place of God, a sin against the First Commandment. God knew that this self-centered idolatry would lead to continual sinning. He confused their language, effectively ending the tower building and dispersing the builders.

But God does not leave His people in brokenness. In His mercy, He sent His Son to redeem our sinful world. At Pentecost, the Holy Spirit descended on Jesus' disciples with "a sound like a mighty rushing wind. . . . And they were all filled with the Holy Spirit and began to speak in other tongues as the Spirit gave them utterance" (Acts 2:2–4). Peter stood with the other disciples and proclaimed the Good News of Jesus, the Savior, to the international crowds gathered on Pentecost, and each person heard in his own language the mighty works of God (v. 11). By the power of the Holy Spirit, "those who received his word were baptized, and there were added that day about three thousand souls" (v. 41). The people heard in all their languages the powerful and essential message of salvation by faith in Christ Jesus. They were united not by pride, but by faith.

Central Truth
We are called to glorify God's name in all things; giving glory to ourselves instead is rebellion against God. (See the Second Commandment.)

Objectives
- Recognize that as sinners, we, too, often want to make a name for ourselves, putting ourselves first, failing to appreciate and give credit due to the name of the Lord.
- Realize that God calls us to repentance, humility, and service to others in the name of Jesus.
- Proclaim the true honor God gives to us as He names us as His own children by grace through faith.

Materials
- Hymnals and music CDs
- Web Resource 4a
- Reproducible 4

Bible Prep
Post in advance so students can bookmark references before class time.
- Genesis 9:1
- Genesis 11:1–9
- Philippians 2:9–11

Devotions

Jake and Ed loved football. They started playing together in a kids' league back in their hometown, and they starred together on their high school team. Jake established a new record for yards gained rushing; Ed led the team to a perfect season as quarterback. Together they helped the team win the state championship. When Ed and Jake were recruited by the same university, they were glad they would be able to play together again. During football season of their third year, sportscasters took notice, and they began to see their names in newspaper sports reports. In the first game of their senior year, Jake set a new record for yards rushing. The next week, Ed completed passes for two touchdowns. Their team was ranked number one in the nation. Soon the two friends were mentioned as rivals for the Heisman Trophy. Professional football teams planned to draft both players at the end of the season.

After an important game, Jake was interviewed by a television broadcaster who asked, "To what do you credit your great performance on the field today?" Jake answered, "Some of it is natural talent, but I have always worked out and practiced harder than anyone else. I can't wait to sign a great contract with the pros and make all the money I want. My goal is to be the greatest running back that ever played football." The same broadcaster asked Ed the same question. Ed answered, "I thank God for giving me a strong body and the ability to play football. For many years, I practiced hard to make the most of the gifts He has given me. He protected me from serious injuries and healed me when I was hurt. Through Jesus, my Savior, I have peace with God. I plan to use my abilities to serve God and other people in whatever way He chooses." Ask, *Whose name did each of the players glorify? How can you glorify God's name in your own life?* Glorify God's name together by singing "Jesus, Name above All Names" (*AGPS* 145; recorded on *JPS*, CD2) and/or "How Sweet the Name of Jesus Sounds" (*LSB* 524; recorded as *Hymn of the Season* for grade 4, Epiphany).

23

INTO the lesson

What's in a Name?

An important word in this Bible story and in the Second Commandment is the word *name*, so begin by studying the importance of a name. The illustration in the Student Book shows the word *rose* in Italian, Indonesian, Finnish, Romanian, Croatian, Dutch, Vietnamese, and Welsh. As Shakespeare notes, it doesn't matter what you call the rose; it is still a fragrant rose. However, we also know that the significance of a name goes far beyond the word itself. (The word *rose* brings to mind not only the fragrance, but also the color and texture of the blossom and the leaves and thorns along the stem.)

Various dictionaries define the word *name* in several ways, such as (a) "what somebody or something is called"; (b) "an uncomplimentary, descriptive word spoken about somebody"; (c) "reputation—how you are perceived or valued"; and (d) "a famous person." Discuss these definitions with your students. Although sixth graders most often use the word *name* in the sense of its first definition, they will be familiar with name-calling (second definition) and with celebrities who are "big names" in show business or sports (fourth definition). Challenge them to give a sentence using each definition of the word.

God's name stands for God "as He has revealed Himself to us, His essence and His attributes" (*Luther's Small Catechism with Explanation,* Question 25). When Moses asked for His name, God replied, "I AM WHO I AM" (Exodus 3:14). God exists and always has and always will. God's name includes all He does for us as Creator, Provider, and Preserver; as Savior, Redeemer, and Lord; and as Sanctifier and Source of faith. In the Second Commandment, God forbids misuse of His name. Review the Second Commandment and its meaning with your students. If students have not yet memorized this commandment and its meaning, have them do so now. Discuss the misuses of God's name listed in the explanation. Note, however, that it focuses more on the positive use of God's name: Luther says we rightly use God's name when we "call upon it in every trouble, pray, praise, and give thanks" (Small Catechism, explanation of the Second Commandment). When we depend only on ourselves in times of trouble, when we praise and honor ourselves for our accomplishments, or when we neglect to thank God for all He does, we deprive God of the glory He deserves, and we improperly use His name. As you explore the significance of God's name, praise His name by singing "All Hail the Power of Jesus' Name" (*LSB* 549; recorded as *Hymn of the Month for grade 5, May*) or "How Majestic Is Your Name" (*AGPS* 122; recorded on *JPS,* CD1).

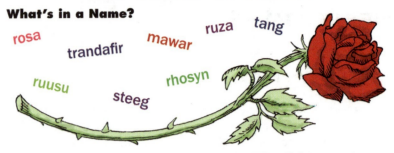

LESSON 4
The Tower of Babel
What's in a Name?

Why are names so important to us? In *Romeo and Juliet,* William Shakespeare wrote, "What's in a name? That which we call a rose By any other name would smell as sweet" (Act 2, Scene 2).

A person's name stands for that person—who he or she is, and what he or she has done. Athletes practice endlessly to become a big name in their sport. Business owners work hard to establish a good name, or reputation, for their services. A person accused of doing something wrong wants to "clear" his name. A politician running for office makes sure his name appears everywhere.

God's name stands for God Himself. He has created the world and still preserves it. He has redeemed us through Jesus' death on the cross in our place. Through the Holy Spirit, He has brought us to faith, and He helps us to serve Him and one another. God's name is holy and worthy of praise.

In the Second Commandment, God tells us, "You shall not misuse the name of the Lord your God." Martin Luther explained the Second Commandment in this way: "We should fear and love God so that we do not curse, swear, use satanic arts, lie, or deceive by His name, but call upon it in every trouble, pray, praise, and give thanks" (Small Catechism).

When we receive honor for that which God deserves the glory, we are honoring our own names instead of His name. According to Exodus 20:7, "The LORD will not hold him guiltless who takes His name in vain." God promises punishment to those who break His Commandments. But He sent Jesus to lead us to repentance, forgiveness, and new life lived according to His will.

Review

Covenant Connection

Names for God such as "heavenly Father" and "Good Shepherd" tell us about who God is and what He does. Many of God's names point to His plan of salvation; such names include "promised Messiah"; "Anointed (or Chosen) One"; "Redeemer" (which refers to "one who buys back"); "Jesus" (which means "saves His people from their sins"); and "Immanuel" ("God with us"). When we honor and praise God's name, we also show respect for who He is and gratitude for what He has done for us.

INTO the Word

The Boastful Builders of Babel

All people on earth after the flood were descendants of Noah and lived in the region where they had emerged from the ark. According to Genesis 9:1, God commanded Noah's family to "be fruitful and multiply and fill the earth." Subsequent generations of Noah's descendants would need to move far away from their relatives to fulfill God's directive. Many generations passed, and again, the rebellious willfulness of the sinful people was evident. Read together Genesis 11:1–9. The descendants of Noah wanted to join together as one powerful nation. In rebellion against God's command, they began building a tower to serve as a focal point of their greatness. This tower was probably a ziggurat similar to those found in archaeological excavations in Mesopotamia. A ziggurat was a pyramid built with several receding stories erected upon a rectangular, round, or square base. (Use the keyword *ziggurat* to find examples of this style of building on the Internet.)

Making a tall building is not a sin, but the peoples' purpose for doing so was wrong. They had made gods of themselves instead of honoring the true God. They trusted in their own power and might. Their glorification of self misplaced the glory that was

The Boastful Builders of Babel

After the Great Flood, the family of Noah grew quickly. God had commanded them to (1) **be fruitful and multiply and fill the earth** (Genesis 9:1). But Noah's descendants wanted to stay together as a powerful group. They planned to build a (2) **city** and a great (3) **tower** with its top in the (4) **heavens** (Genesis 11:4a). They hoped to (5) **make a name** for themselves (Genesis 11:4b).

When God saw what Noah's descendants were building and their purpose in doing so, He was not pleased. The Lord said, "Behold, they are one people, and they have all one (6) **language**" (Genesis 11:6). God knew that in their pride, they believed they could do anything. They would continue to disobey Him.

God said, "Come, let Us go down and there (7) **confuse their language**, so they may not understand one another's (8) **speech**" (Genesis 11:7). So the Lord dispersed them from there over the face of all the earth, and they stopped building the city. Therefore the city's name was called (9) **Babel** (Genesis 11:9), because there the Lord confused the language of all the earth. And from there the Lord dispersed the descendants of Noah over the face of all the earth. What was God's reaction to their building project? Why would the language problem cause the people to stop building and move to other places?

Raise Praise

The men of Babel wanted to make a great name for themselves. But God wants us to glorify His name above all other names. We glorify God's name when we give Him credit for all that we have, all that we do, and all that He has done. We praise Him most of all for redeeming us through His Son, Jesus.

The people of Babel built up a tower for their glory. We lift up our prayers for the glory of God. On each line list a blessing for which you praise the Lord.

Remember

"Therefore God has highly **exalted** Him and bestowed on Him the **name** that is above every **name**, so that at the name of **Jesus** every knee should bow, in heaven and on earth and under the earth." (Philippians 2:9–10)

---

due God's holy name. Discuss how breaking the First Commandment leads to breaking other commandments—in this case, the Second Commandment. *Option:* To see the effect of the confusion of languages on that building project, let students use the Internet to search for the key phrase "language tools." At a Web site that makes translations, key in the phrase "Where is my hammer?" Look at some of the many possibilities as the phrase is translated into other languages. Even a simple task would become very difficult with the confusion of languages.

Notice God's reference to Himself in the first-person plural in Genesis 11:7: "Come, let *Us* go down" (emphasis added). This reference to the Holy Trinity echoes Genesis 1:26: "Let *Us* make man in *Our* own image, after *Our* likeness" (emphasis added). From the beginning, God presents Himself as Father, Son, and Holy Spirit.

Confusion in Babel Clarity in Christ

Across
4. Call something superior; praise
6. The one that comes after the first
8. Use in the wrong way
9. Reputation
10. Mesopotamian tower

Down
1. Telling someone he is great
2. Earthen material used to make bricks
3. One of the rules God gave for living
5. Location of tower in Genesis 11
7. Tall building

Reproducible 4

INTO our lives

Raise Praise

Because of original sin, it is natural for human beings to give glory to themselves instead of to God and to honor their own names when they should honor His name. Divide your students into small groups. Ask each group to list three ways in which people honor their own names instead of God's name. Possible examples would include sports figures who boast of their success; entertainment celebrities who do anything—even break the law—to get their names in the news; politicians who take credit for successes while blaming their opponents for failures; and parents who brag about their successful children. As groups report their lists to the class, ask how each example deprives God of honor that is rightly due His name. Call attention to instances where celebrities and athletes have first given praise to God for their accomplishments.

Help students to understand that we have all been guilty of seeking honor and glory for ourselves instead of glorifying God's name and giving Him the credit for all that He has done. Reassure students that God has promised to forgive this and all other sins for the sake of Jesus, who took sin's punishment in our place. "If we confess our sins, He is faithful and just to forgive us our sins and to cleanse us from all unrighteousness" (1 John 1:9).

Direct students' attention to the line drawing of a Mesopotamian ziggurat in the Student Book. This may have been the style of the ancient tower of Babel. Then emphasize that our focus of praise is on the Lord. Help students brainstorm ways in which we can glorify the name of the true God. Possible answers might include the following:

He gave me a strong, healthy body.
He gave me a family to care for me.
He gives me all that I need.
He gave me special talents or abilities.
He gives me friends.
He helps me to serve others.
He protects me from danger.
He makes me better when I am sick.
He gives me faith in Jesus as my Savior.

Remind students that we praise God's name because of the redeeming work of Jesus, who gives us forgiveness of sins and eternal life. To review aspects of the lesson, use Reproducible 4 at this time. Sing "Jesus! Name of Wondrous Love" (*LSB* 900; recorded as *Hymn of the Season* for grade 5, Epiphany).

Lesson Support

Technology

At the tower of Babel, God "confused the language" of Noah's descendants. Today, 6,909 languages are spoken by the 7 billion people in the world. All or a portion of the Bible has been translated into 2,479 of those languages. But 4,430 languages have no Scripture at all. In 1964, Lutheran Bible Translators was incorporated to translate the Word of God into languages in which it was not available. As of this writing, Lutheran Bible Translators has forty-one missionaries and thirty-one associate missionaries, plus a Service Center with nineteen full-time and two part-time staff members. Twenty-two translation programs are in progress in fifteen countries. The thirty-two New Testament translations that have been completed give 7 million people access to God's Word for the first time. Learn more about the work of Lutheran Bible Translators through the Internet (www.lbt.org) or from their promotional materials. Present what you have learned to your congregation, and encourage a special offering for the work of Lutheran Bible Translators.

Help your students to access a Web site offering different translations of the Bible, such as www.biblegateway.com. Type in the chapter-verse reference for one of your favorite Bible passages (you may want to use Philippians 2:9–11, this lesson's "Remember" verse). Print this verse in several different languages. Make a poster showing the verse in various languages, and accompany each translation with a picture from the corresponding country.

If you know a person who speaks a foreign language, invite that person to visit your class. Ask him or her to share several words from that language and their pronunciations with your students. Practice saying the words together. After the visit, send a letter of appreciation from your class. If possible, include one or more of the new words you learned.

Searching Further

When the builders of the tower of Babel set out to make a name for themselves, they refused to recognize that their building abilities and their very lives were gifts from God to be used for His purposes. Jesus' parable of the talents tells us more about how He expects us to use His gifts. Read the parable in Matthew 25:14–30. A silver talent in Jesus' day was a unit of currency equal to about 7,300 denarii (a denarius equaled one day's wage for a laborer), and a gold talent could be thirty times more valuable. But the parable applies equally well to our definition of *talents*—natural abilities God has given to each of us. God expects us to use our talents for His glory and to serve others, and not only to bring glory to ourselves. Think about the talents God has given you. Do you take credit for those special abilities? Do you use them only to advance your own reputation? How can you serve others and glorify God's name through the use of your talents?

Hands to Serve

God has given each of His children talents to be used for His glory and in service to others. Think of the variety of talents represented in the children in your classroom. You may have writers, artists, musicians, group leaders, and mathematicians. Other children may have talents for caring for or encouraging others. As a group, decide on a service project in your community. Possibilities appropriate for this age group might include a collection of nonperishable foods, a coat and winter clothing drive, or a project to make cards or crafts to be delivered to a nursing home or other care facility. Encourage each child to use his or her God-given talents to participate in the project. Upon completion of the project, write an article detailing the project for the school or church newsletter. Be sure to give God the glory and credit instead of glorifying personal efforts.

Art Connection

God's temple—His Church—is not built of bricks or stones, like the tower of Babel. In this temple, all of the glory goes to God and not to sinful people. Read 1 Peter 2:5 and Ephesians 2:19–22 and see that God's Church is built of "living stones"—people who are alive in Christ! On a large sheet of poster paper, draw an outline of your church building. Have students sign their own names inside this outline, and add the names of other people who are living stones in the Church of God. Include your pastors, teachers, family members, and others.

UNIT 1—BEGINNINGS AND PATRIARCHS LESSON 5

God's Promises to Abraham
GENESIS 12:1–4; 15:1–6; 17:1–8, 15–17; 18:1–15; 21:1–6

Background

The apostle Paul explores the case of Abraham in Romans 4, asking, "What then shall we say was gained by Abraham . . . ? For if Abraham was justified by works, he has something to boast about, but not before God" (vv. 1–2). Paul quotes Genesis 15:6: "[Abraham] believed the Lord, and He counted it to him as righteousness." The money we receive on payday isn't counted as a gift; it is money we have earned. But the righteousness we receive through faith in Jesus is a gift of God's grace.

God's promises to Abraham didn't come through the Law, but through faith. Because these promises rest on God's grace, they are guaranteed to all who believe in Him, regardless of their sinful condition. Abraham believed God's promises in spite of the evidence, the fact that he was one hundred years old and had no children. When sin caused his faith to weaken, even his weak faith was made righteous—justified—because of Christ's work on his behalf. Paul concluded that this faith "will be counted to us who believe in Him who raised from the dead Jesus our Lord, who was delivered up for our trespasses and raised for our justification" (Romans 4:24–25).

Central Truth

God's word of promise came to His people through the prophets, focusing on the Messiah (Jesus) who is the Word in the flesh. (This lesson also relates to the Third Commandment.)

Objectives

- Acknowledge that God comes to us in His Word, confronting us with the Law and comforting us with the Gospel.
- Appreciate that God chose one family to whom He spoke the messianic promises that are a blessing for all the world, received by faith.
- Worship God as we hear His Holy Word and rejoice in the Word made flesh (in Jesus).

Materials

- Hymnals and music CDs
- Reproducible 5
- Bible atlas or other resource books
- Art materials for a mural

Bible Prep

Post in advance so students can bookmark references before class time.
- Genesis 12, 15, 17, 18, 21
- Jeremiah 29:11
- Hebrews 1:1–2, 8–16
- 1 John 1:9
- 2 Timothy 3:14–17
- Romans 4:20–25
- 2 Corinthians 5:21

Devotions

A young Russian student named Sergei walked across the campus of an American university. He smiled and waved as he approached a young woman who was in his math class. "Hi, Sergei," called the woman. "What's the good word?" "Good word?" thought Sergei. "I have learned many new words in English, but I don't know which one is the good word." He did not yet understand that this phrase is a cliché that is just a greeting. It means "What's happening?" or "What's new with you?"

Sergei walked on. As he entered the chemistry lab, the professor greeted him. "Good morning, Sergei. What's the good word?" "Good word? Why are they asking me? They have been speaking this language much longer than I have," mumbled Sergei.

"Hey, Sergei, what's the good word?" called another young man as he zoomed past on his bicycle. "Good word, good word," Sergei puzzled. "How am I supposed to know this 'good word'?"

When Sergei returned to his dorm room, his roommate Tom looked up from the book he was studying. "What's the good word, Sergei?" Tom asked. "Good word, good word! Everyone wants to know. Could someone tell me, please? What *is* this 'good word' that I am supposed to know?" Sergei pleaded.

"'What's the good word?' is just an expression, Sergei," Tom explained, "like 'How are you doing?' or 'How's it going?'" Tom thought quietly for a minute. Then he said, "But I do know a *really* good word. It's the good word about Jesus," Tom explained. "God sent His Son, Jesus, to earth to live as a human being and die on the cross to pay for our sins. Jesus is God's Word in the flesh." Sergei smiled and said, "*Jesus* is a *really* good word, Tom. Now I know which good word to give to everyone."

Let's pray: Dear Lord, we thank You for the Good News about Jesus that we read in Your Word. Help us to share this good word with others. Amen. Sing "O Blessed, Holy Trinity" (*LSB* 876; recorded as *Hymn of the Season* for grade 6, Christian Education Month).

27

INTO the Word

Have You Heard the Good Word?

"Long ago, at many times and in many ways, God spoke to our fathers by the prophets" (Hebrews 1:1). The Old Testament is filled with accounts of God speaking to His people in a variety of ways. Share with your students the story of God walking in the Garden of Eden and speaking to Adam and Eve (Genesis 3:8–22), questioning Cain after Abel's murder (4:9–15), instructing Noah to build the ark (6:13–22), and blessing Noah and his family at the end of the great flood (9:1–17). God called Abram to go to a country He would show him, and He promised to make a great nation of Abram's descendants (12:1–3). As "the angel of the Lord," He appeared to Abraham (chs. 17–18). He tested Abraham with His command to sacrifice his son, Isaac (22:1–2, 11–12, 15–18). God spoke from a burning bush to Moses (Exodus 3–4) and continued to speak to him throughout the delivery from Egypt and the exodus. He spoke to all of the Israelites from the top of Mount Sinai, and they heard His voice as thunder, saw lightning and a thick cloud, and heard a loud trumpet blast as they all trembled in fear (19:16). After Moses' death, God spoke to Joshua, reassuring him and giving instructions for the conquest of the Promised Land (Joshua 1:2–9). Throughout the centuries preceding the birth of the Messiah, God spoke through prophets to remind His people of His promise to send a Savior. He repeatedly confronted them concerning the practice of idolatry and reassured them of His faithful love for them.

"But when the fullness of time had come, God sent forth His Son, born of a woman . . . so that we might receive adoption as sons" (Galatians 4:4–5). God revealed Himself to us in His Son. In Jesus, God's "Word became flesh and dwelt among us, and we have seen His glory, glory as of the only Son from the Father, full of grace and truth" (John 1:14). When His disciple Philip asked to see the Father, Jesus replied, "Whoever has seen Me has seen the Father" (14:9). Jesus is God's "good Word" to us in the flesh.

Sing or read the hymn that is related to this lesson: "God Has Spoken By His Prophets" (*LSB* 583).

If your students have not already memorized the Third Commandment and its explanation, this would be an excellent time to have them do so. Discuss the opportunities we have to learn more about God through His Word: personal and group Bible studies, worship attendance, Sunday School, and Lutheran Day School.

Lesson 5

God's Promises to Abraham

Have You Heard the Good Word?

Wouldn't it be great if God would speak to us directly the way He spoke to people in Bible times? You know, say things like "Don't worry about your future—I've got it covered for you," or "I can see you're sorry you did that; I forgive you, and I still love you." We think life would be so much easier if we knew exactly what God wanted and how He really felt about us. Actually, we do know what He wants and says—from His Holy Word.

The writer of the Epistle to the Hebrews wrote, "Long ago, at many times and in many ways, God spoke to our fathers by the prophets, but in these last days He has spoken to us by His Son" (Hebrews 1:1–2). In Jesus, God's Word became a human being. John wrote, "The Word became flesh and dwelt among us" (John 1:14). Jesus fed the hungry, healed the sick, and gave sight to the blind and hearing to the deaf. Jesus cast out demons and held little children in His arms. Jesus made the lame walk and raised the dead to life. Then Jesus took all of our sins upon Himself and died on the cross in our place. When we see Jesus, we see God's Word with skin on! This is even better than the messages of the prophets—Jesus is the fulfillment of the prophecies (Acts 10:43).

In the Third Commandment, God tells us to "Remember the Sabbath day by keeping it holy." Martin Luther explains the commandment this way: "We should fear and love God so that we do not despise preaching and His Word, but hold it sacred and gladly hear and learn it" (Small Catechism). We hear God speak to us when we read and study the accounts of His faithfulness to His people of promise in the Old Testament. We hear Him speak in the life of Jesus as recorded in the Gospels and in the history and letters of the Early Church in the New Testament. We hear Him speak as we gather in worship with God's people. Can you hear God speaking about your future? What does God say to you in Jeremiah 29:11? Do you want to hear God's words of forgiveness? What God says to you in 1 John 1:9?

Review

Covenant Connection

Read Romans 4:20–25 to see the connection between Abraham, Jesus, you, and me. Abraham was a sinner, like you and me. He received righteousness from God by faith in the promised Savior. We, too, are made righteous by faith in Jesus (in the "Great Exchange"; see 2 Corinthians 5:21). Jesus is the "Chosen One" (Luke 9:35); Abraham's family was chosen to carry the promise of the Savior (Genesis 12:3); and we have been chosen to live as members of God's family of faith (1 Peter 2:9).

16

INTO the lesson

God's Good Word to Abraham

The story of "God's Promises to Abraham" is the account of God's grace to Abraham and to all people through Abraham's descendant Jesus. God chose one family to carry this promise; and by faith, we are part of that family, according to Galatians 3:7–8. Study Reproducible 5, which gives a summary of some of the early events in Abraham's life. Then use the information here and in the Student Book to learn more about his journey of faith.

God called Abram, the son of Terah, out of idolatry. According to Joshua 24:2, "Long ago, your fathers lived beyond the Euphrates, Terah, the father of Abraham and of Nahor; and they served other gods." God commanded Abram to move away from his country and his kindred to a land that God would show him. He promised to make of Abram a great nation, to bless him, and to make his name great. God would bless those who blessed Abram and curse those who cursed him. Through Abram, all of the families of the earth would be blessed. Abram obeyed God and, with his wife, Sarai, and nephew Lot, moved to the land of Canaan. Abram "believed the Lord, and He counted it to him as righteousness" (Genesis 15:6).

It would be easy to view Abram as the hero of this story. But God called

28

God's Good Word to Abraham

★ "Abram, Abram," God called. "Go from your own country and your relatives and your father's house to a land that I will show you. I will make of you a great nation, and I will bless you and make your name great, so that you will be a blessing. I will bless those who bless you and curse anyone who dishonors you. In you, all the families of the earth will be blessed" (Genesis 12:1–3). Abram followed the Lord's command (Hebrews 11:8–10).

★ Abram wondered how God could make a great nation of his descendants when he and Sarai had no children. God spoke to him in a vision and said, "Look toward heaven, and number the stars, if you are able to number them. So shall your offspring be" (Genesis 15:5). Abram believed God's words, and God "counted it to him as righteousness" (Genesis 15:6).

★ God appeared to Abram again. "This is My promise to you. You shall be the father of many nations, and kings will come from your descendants. I will keep My promise to you forever, to be your God and the God of your descendants. I will give the land of Canaan to you and your descendants, and I will be their God." God changed Abram's name to "Abraham," meaning "father of many nations" (Genesis 17:1–8, 15–17).

★ The next time God spoke to Abraham, He appeared in human form along with two angels. He repeated His promise. Abraham and Sarah laughed with joy and surprise (Genesis 18:9–14; also 17:17). God kept His promises. The next year, they had a baby boy named "Isaac," meaning "laughter" (Genesis 21:1–7). Centuries later, Abraham's descendant Jesus was born. Through Jesus' death and resurrection, all the families of the earth are blessed.

God's Good Word to Me

For hundreds of years, God's Word came to His people through prophets. Then God revealed His Word through His Son, Jesus, the "Word made flesh." The very heart of God is revealed in His Son, Jesus, who said, "Whoever has seen Me has seen the Father" (John 14:9). Today we hear God speak to us when we read and study His Holy Word.

Not only do we have God's Word, but we also have the example of Jesus as He fulfilled God's Word, and we have the gift of the Holy Spirit, who works through the Means of Grace. God asks us in the Third Commandment to honor, use, and apply these great gifts in our lives. Read 2 Timothy 3:14–17 and write one or two sentences telling why God's Word is so important. <u>It brings salvation through faith in Jesus; it gives correction and training in righteousness; and it equips us through the power of God for every good work.</u>

Remember

"Long ago, at many times and in many ways, God spoke to our fathers by the prophets, but in these last days He has spoken to us by His Son." (Hebrews 1:1–2)

Abram the idol worshiper to follow Him by grace, without any merit on Abram's part. God chooses the weak and unexpected and grows faith in them so that we can see that their strength or success is a gift from God, not of their own doing. Abram believed God, but his faith—like ours—had its moments of weakness. When Abram and Sarai traveled to Egypt during a time of famine, Abram passed Sarai off to Pharaoh as his sister so the Egyptians would not kill him (12:10–20). He later tried the same trick with Abimelech, king of Gerar (chapter 20). When he grew weary of waiting for God to keep His promise of an heir, he suggested adopting his servant Eliezer as his son. He fathered a child by Sarai's servant Hagar, hoping that this would be the son God had promised. Although Abram was not always faithful to God, God was always faithful to Abram.

INTO our lives

God's Good Word to Me

God's promises to Abraham were words of grace, blessing him with land and material possessions during his lifetime and the lifetimes of his descendants. Through Abraham and his descendants, God blessed all people with a Savior.

We do not deserve God's promised blessings any more than Abraham did. **Although we have been unfaithful to God, He has been faithful to His promises to us. In Abraham's descendant Jesus, God's very Word became flesh to live and die in our place. Through Jesus' death and resurrection, God counts us righteous by faith.**

Encourage students to explore these four situations: **How could you respond to each?**

1. **Your friend says, "The company my father works for is closing, and he won't have a job. I'm worried about what will happen to my family. If only God still spoke to people like He did in Bible times."** (You might tell your friend that God *does* still speak to us today, through His Word, the Bible. Suggest reading Joshua 1:5; Jeremiah 29:11; Matthew 6:25–34; 28:20; and Hebrews 13:5.)

2. **Your brother is frightened by the reports of terrorists he sees on the news. "Where is God when we need Him?" he asks. "I'd feel so much better if He'd speak to us about this."** (Assure him that God knows how he feels and is always with him. Read together Psalm 3:6; 46; 91:7; and Matthew 28:20.)

3. **Your sister took some makeup from a store when she thought no one was watching. But the manager saw her on the security camera and called the police. Because she was a juvenile, she was released, but she feels terrible about what she did.** (Remind your sister that God tells us in His Word that He welcomes and forgives sinners who repent. Read together Psalm 51; Luke 15:11–32; and 1 John 1:9.)

4. **Your friend tells you, "I'm not going to church anymore. It's old-fashioned and doesn't really speak to me."** (Remind your friend that God commands us to hold His Word sacred and gladly hear and learn it. In our worship services, we hear the timeless, unchanging Word of God with other believers. Read together John 8:47; Colossians 3:16; Psalm 26:8; and Hebrews 13:8.)

29

Lesson Support

Technology

Cell phones, Twitter, Facebook, e-mails, instant messaging—students today are accustomed to instant feedback. Contrast instant feedback with God's communication with us in Holy Scripture. God's Old Testament promises are still relevant to us today, thousands of years later. As we study the life, death, and resurrection of Jesus, we hear God tell us how much He loves us. Today's instant messages come quickly and are forgotten almost as fast. God's Word, however, is eternal: "The grass withers, the flower fades, but the word of our God will stand forever" (Isaiah 40:8).

Ideas for the Gifted

Genesis 18 records the visit of three men to Abraham's camp. Two of the men were angels, and one was the Lord Himself in human form. Abraham bowed before the men and brought water to wash their feet. He offered to bring them "a morsel of bread" (v. 5), and he arranged for Sarah and his servants to prepare a feast of bread and freshly slaughtered meat. This type of hospitality was typical of people in the Middle East and is still common today. Using the Internet or a resource book about life in Old Testament times, plan and prepare some of the foods Abraham would have served his guests.

Celebrating GROWTH

Make a timeline of Abraham's life. We know that Abraham lived 175 years (Genesis 25:7). On a whiteboard or a length of roll paper, draw a straight line 175 cm long (69 inches). On your timeline, 1 cm will equal one year. Measuring from the left end of the line, mark off as many centimeters as you are old and write your name at that point. Then, again measuring from the left end of the line, mark your father or mother's age in centimeters and write his or her name. Add another line to show the age of one of your grandparents. The writer of Genesis picks up the life story of Abram when Abram obeys God's command and moves to Canaan (Genesis 12:4). Draw a line on your timeline to show Abram's age at that time. How old was Abram when God visited him and promised him a son (17:1)? Show his age on the timeline, and label it "God promises Abram and Sarah a son." God kept His promise and gave Abraham and Sarah a son. Draw a line to show how old Abraham was when Isaac was born (v. 17), and label it "Isaac's birth." How old was Sarah when she died (23:1)? Go back to Genesis 17:17 to find out how much older Abraham was than Sarah; then you do the math. Label this line "Sarah's death." Label the right endpoint of the line "Abraham's death." *Bonus question for math geeks:* How old was Isaac when Sarah died?

Searching Further

Use the Bible atlas in the Appendix of the Student Book or the maps in your Bible to trace the journeys of Abraham. According to Genesis 11:27–28, Abram and his family lived in Ur of the Chaldeans. This ancient city was located near the Euphrates River, not far from the Persian Gulf, in present-day Iraq. Abram's father, Terah, left Ur to move to Canaan, but when they came to Haran, the family settled there (vv. 31–32). Haran is near the headwaters of the Euphrates River, in the area of the border between Syria and Turkey. In Haran, God called Abram to move to the land He would show him—the land of Canaan (12:1–8). Abram, Sarai, and Lot went to Egypt during a famine, then returned to Canaan. Lot moved to Sodom (ch. 13), which is located on the Dead Sea. The sacrifice of the ram in place of Isaac (ch. 22) occurred on Mount Moriah, possibly the later temple site in Jerusalem, where Melchizedek reigned in Abraham's time (14:17–24). Abraham and Sarah were buried near Mamre (25:9–10), close to Kiriath-arba (between Jerusalem and Beersheba).

Although God had promised all of the land of Canaan to Abraham and his descendants, Abraham owned no land in Canaan until he bought the Cave of Machpelah to bury Sarah. "These all died in faith, not having received the things promised, but having seen them and greeted them from afar, and having acknowledged that they were strangers and exiles on the earth. . . . But as it is, they desire a better country, that is, a heavenly one. Therefore God is not ashamed to be called their God, for He has prepared for them a city" (Hebrews 11:13, 16).

Working in Groups

Abraham, Sarah, and Lot lived as tribal herdsmen, wandering from place to place and living in tents, much as the Bedouin live in the same region today. Use the Internet or a resource book about people in Old Testament times to learn more about Abraham's way of life. Draw and paint a mural showing Abraham's way of life. *Bonus:* Use the Internet to learn more about the Bedouin living in the Middle East today.

UNIT 1—BEGINNINGS AND PATRIARCHS

LESSON 6

The Offering of Isaac
GENESIS 22:1–18

Background

The Old Testament system of offerings and sacrifices for sin seems outmoded and irrelevant today. But God's demand for holiness didn't end with the old covenant. In the New Testament, God demands, "Present your bodies as a living sacrifice, holy and acceptable to God" (Romans 12:1), and, "We should be holy and blameless before Him" (Ephesians 1:4). But since unholiness awaits God's people at every corner of life, they (like Israel) must be *accounted* holy: "For in Him all the fullness of God was pleased to dwell, and through Him to reconcile to Himself all things, . . . making peace by the blood of His cross. . . . He has now reconciled [you] in His body of flesh by His death, in order to present you holy and blameless and above reproach before Him" (Colossians 1:19–23). This reconciliation is once and for all. . . . People can do nothing to make themselves acceptable to God. Their forfeited lives can be redeemed only by an atonement, a substitution, that God has "given on the altar." People daily need to seek the forgiving mercy of God. Total redemption calls forth a total response and commitment to God. Holy living is living wholly to God.

Walter R. Roehrs, *Survey of Covenant History: A Historical Overview of the Old Testament* (St. Louis: Concordia, 1989), 64; Scripture quotations changed to ESV.

Central Truth
God is demanding, but He demands no more than He Himself was willing to do for us. (This lesson is also related to the First Commandment.)

Objectives
- Acknowledge that God requires a complete commitment in faith and obedience toward Him—an impossible task for any and all people.
- Observe that God sent Jesus—true God and true man—to do the impossible for us, serving as our substitute and sacrifice.
- Live for the Lord who died for us so that we may live eternally.

Materials
- Hymnals and music CDs
- Reproducible 6
- Web Resource 6a
- Art materials, including large paper for banner

Bible Prep
Post in advance so students can bookmark references before class time.
- Genesis 22:1–18
- Psalm 50:14
- Psalm 51:17
- Proverbs 21:3
- Hosea 6:6

Devotions

Open your devotions by singing "Go to Dark Gethsemane" (*LSB* 436; recorded as *Hymn of the Season* for grade 3, Lent).

Read again stanza 3 of the hymn. The writer speaks of "God's own sacrifice complete." What is a sacrifice? What would motivate someone to make a sacrifice? What was God's sacrifice that was completed on "Calv'ry's mournful mountain"?

The author O. Henry wrote a short story in 1906 titled "The Gift of the Magi." The story is about a young couple, Jim Young and his wife, Della, who loved each other very much. Jim and Della had very little money and could hardly afford the rent on their one-bedroom apartment. As Christmas approached, they knew they had no extra money to buy Christmas presents. But because they loved each other so much, each wanted to give the other a special gift. Della decided to buy Jim an expensive chain for his prized pocket watch, which his grandfather had given him. To get the money for the chain, she had her beautiful long hair cut off and sold to a wigmaker. In the meantime, Jim decided to buy Della a set of combs made of tortoiseshell and jewels to wear in her lovely, brown hair. To get the money, he sold his grandfather's pocket watch. What sacrifice did Della make for Jim? What sacrifice did Jim make for Della? Why were they willing to make these sacrifices? The Bible tells us that God made the greatest sacrifice of all time. Like Della and Jim, God's sacrifice was motivated by love. But unlike Della and Jim, the people for whom God made His sacrifice didn't love Him in return. God gave His sacrifice for His enemies, that they might become His redeemed children. God sacrificed much more than a gold watch or knee-length hair. "God so loved the world, that He gave His only Son" (John 3:16). Let's pray: Dear God, You have sacrificed so much to make me Your forgiven child. Help me to live for You in everything I do. Amen. Thank God by saying together the words of Psalm 100; then close by singing "What a Friend We Have in Jesus" (*LSB* 770; recorded as *Hymn of the Month* for grade 6, September).

31

INTO the lesson

What Is a Sacrifice?

Use the Student Book story to clarify that a sacrifice involves giving up something that is very important to the giver, although it does not always cost the giver his or her life. While all sacrifices are offerings, not all offerings are sacrifices. In the account in Luke 21:1–4, the rich people gave an *offering*; the widow made a *sacrifice* because she gave all that she had. Jesus praised her giving, which showed her priorities. By giving all she had to God, she obeyed the First Commandment: "You shall have no other gods." Luther explained this commandment by saying, "We should fear, love, and trust in God above all things."

The sacrifices demanded by God in the Old Testament laws reminded the Israelites that God was to be their first priority. For a table listing the kinds of offerings God commanded, the focus of enactment, and the purpose of each, see *The Lutheran Study Bible* (St. Louis: Concordia, 2009), page 171. Notice that forgiveness of sins always involved the shedding of blood and sacrifice of an animal: a young bull, sheep, goat, turtledoves, or pigeons. The writer of Hebrews explained, "Indeed, under the law almost everything is purified with blood, and without the shedding of blood there is no forgiveness of sins" (Hebrews 9:22). During the ordination of the Old Testament priests, the blood of sacrificial animals was sprinkled on them to cover their sin and set them apart for service before the Lord (Exodus 29:21). The priests collected the blood from sacrificed animals and applied it daily to the tabernacle altar. In this daily blood rite, the life of the animal was a substitute for the life of the people. Once a year, on the Day of Atonement, the high priest entered the Most Holy Place and approached the ark of the covenant. He applied some of the sacrificial animal's blood to the Mercy Seat.

All of the Old Testament sacrifices pointed to the one all-sufficient sacrifice of Jesus, the Lamb of God. Shedding His own blood on the cross, He offered His life in exchange for the life of the world. His blood is the required blood covering for the world's sins. Just as the high priest took the animal's blood into God's presence in the Most Holy Place and brought the blood out to cleanse the altar, so Jesus offered His own blood, rose from the dead, ascended to heaven, and entered into the heavenly sanctuary with His blood and flesh to be with His Father. These sacrifices *foreshadowed* the sacrifice of Jesus on the cross. Look at Web Resource 6a for examples in the Old Testament foreshadowing the Savior, shedding His blood on the cross and arising at Easter.

LESSON 6
The Offering of Isaac
What Is a Sacrifice?

Emily's class had been learning about worship in Old Testament times. Emily was fascinated by the sacrifices the Israelites placed on the altars. She compared these sacrifices with the offerings she and her parents brought when they attended church. "Dad," Emily asked one evening, "what is the difference between an offering and a sacrifice?" Emily's dad thought for a moment. "Well," he answered, "I guess it's like the difference between eggs and bacon. When a hen gives an egg, that's an offering; but when a pig gives bacon, *that's* a sacrifice because he gives all that he has."

God commanded the Israelites to offer sacrifices to pay for their sins. The sacrifice of an animal such as a lamb was required to atone for sins. Sacrifices had to be made again and again as people continued to sin. These sacrifices gave the Israelites a picture of the ultimate sacrifice—the Messiah, whom God promised to send to take away the sins of all people. According to the writer of the Epistle to the Hebrews, "When Christ had offered for all time a single sacrifice for sins, He sat down at the right hand of God. . . . For by a single offering He has perfected for all time those who are being sanctified" (Hebrews 10:12, 14).

Martin Luther explained the sacrificial work of Jesus in his explanation of the Second Article of the Apostles' Creed. Read about it in the Small Catechism in the Appendix of this book.

Jesus is the full and complete sacrifice for our sins; no other blood sacrifices are needed. Now that we have been made blameless in God's sight and have received His righteousness, what kind of sacrifice does God desire? (Read Psalm 50:14; Psalm 51:17; Proverbs 21:3; Hosea 6:6.) _____
God desires that we offer thanksgiving and repentance, act righteously and justly, and show steadfast love.

Review

Covenant Connection

The story of the sacrifice of Isaac foreshadows the crucifixion of Christ Jesus. "Foreshadowing" is giving a preview of events to come. Throughout the Old Testament, God gave the people and the prophets more information about the coming of the Messiah. What God did not demand of Abraham (sacrificing his son), God was willing to do Himself for us (sacrificing His Son). We see God's grace and mercy to Abraham and Isaac, and we also recognize God's greater grace and mercy to the whole world in Christ Jesus.

18

INTO the Word

A Mountain and an Offering

Read the story of Abraham and Isaac from the Student Book. Then read the account from Genesis 22:1–18. To help students understand the emotional impact of the events in this story, encourage students to tell the story from the point of view of Abraham, Isaac, and one of the servants who accompanied them on the first and last portions of this journey.

Direct students to verse 1 and the words "God tested Abraham." Discuss the difference between "testing" and "tempting." God uses testing as a way of strengthening faith through trial and hardship. Satan, the world, and our sinful flesh tempt us to sin and fall away from God. In his explanation of the Sixth Petition of the Lord's Prayer, Luther writes, "God tempts no one. We pray in this petition that God would guard and keep us so that the devil, the world, and our sinful nature may not deceive us or mislead us into false belief, despair, and other great shame and vice" (Small Catechism).

Ask students: **How did Abraham's obedience to God's command show that he put God first in his life?** Read God's answer in verse 12. **How is this related to the First Commandment?** (The explanation of the First Commandment tells us to

A Mountain and an Offering

Step by step, Isaac struggled up the slope of Mount Moriah with his father. The two of them pressed on to the place of sacrifice. Isaac carried the firewood, while Abraham brought the pot of fire and the knife.

"Father," asked Isaac, "we have brought the fire and the wood. But where is the lamb for the sacrifice?"

Abraham answered, "God will provide a lamb for the burnt offering." As he walked, Abraham thought about God's shocking words to him: "Take your son, your only son Isaac, whom you love, and go to the land of Moriah, and offer him there as a burnt offering."

Abraham could not understand how God, who had promised him many descendants, could demand the life of his only son. Abraham's heart ached. But Abraham obeyed God and believed His promises.

When they came to the place God had commanded, Abraham built an altar. Then he tied up Isaac and laid him on the altar. Just as Abraham raised the knife to kill his only son, God called to him from heaven. "Abraham, Abraham!" God called. "Do not lay your hand on the boy or do anything to him. Now I know that you fear God, seeing you have not withheld your only son from Me."

Abraham looked up and saw a ram caught in a thicket by its horns. Abraham killed the ram, placed it on the altar, and offered it as a burnt offering in place of Isaac. Abraham called the name of that place "The Lord will provide." God repeated His promises to bless Abraham and to bless all people through Abraham's greatest descendant, Jesus.

A Mountain and a Sacrifice

Step by step, Jesus struggled up the slope of Mount Calvary. He pressed on to the place of sacrifice, carrying the wooden cross. The Father's heart ached at the suffering and death of His only Son, whom He loved. God had provided the Lamb—Jesus, the Lamb of God—to atone for the sins of all people. Because of Jesus, God looks at us and calls us righteous. Write a prayer offering thanksgiving to God for providing His own Son as the perfect sacrifice for our sins.

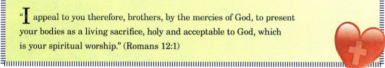

"I appeal to you therefore, brothers, by the mercies of God, to present your bodies as a living sacrifice, holy and acceptable to God, which is your spiritual worship." (Romans 12:1)

INTO our lives

A Mountain and a Sacrifice

Through the account of Abraham and Isaac, God gave His people a picture of what He would do in the future through His own Son, Jesus Christ. Help your students find the parallels in the two stories. As Abraham and Isaac struggled up Mount Moriah to make their sacrifice, so Jesus struggled up Mount Calvary. Abraham loved his only son, Isaac; God the Father loved His only Son, Jesus. Both sacrifices were the result of love—Abraham's by his love for God, and God's by His love for sinners. Abraham believed that God could raise Isaac from the dead; God did raise His Son, Jesus, on the third day. Isaac carried the firewood on his shoulders; Jesus carried the wooden cross. On Mount Moriah, Abraham said, "God will provide a lamb for the sacrifice," and God caused a ram to be caught in a thicket; on Mount Calvary, God did provide the perfect Lamb to be sacrificed for the sins of the world. On Mount Moriah, God blessed Abraham and his descendants; on Mount Calvary, all people were blessed.

Here, however, the similarities end. If Abraham had sacrificed Isaac, Abraham's sins would not have been forgiven. Because Isaac was a sinner, he would have only been receiving the punishment for his own sins. But Jesus lived a perfect life without sin. He took the sins of the whole world to the cross and died to atone for them. Through Jesus' life, death, and resurrection, we have forgiveness of sins and eternal life.

Remember

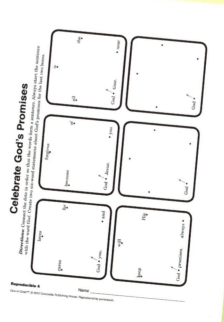

In conjunction with the Bible verse, read what Samuel said to King Saul when the king disobeyed God's command; see 1 Samuel 15:22–23. Also look at Psalm 116:12–14 and 17–19, in which we again see that the sacrifice God wants is an obedient and faithful heart.

---

fear, love, and trust in God above all things.)

Direct students' attention to verse 5, where Abraham tells the servants, "I and the boy will go over there and worship and come again to you." Abraham planned to sacrifice Isaac as God had commanded, but he knew that the God of life and death had the power to raise Isaac from the dead. Compare this verse to Hebrews 11:19: "He considered that God was able even to raise him from the dead."

The Angel of the Lord, the messenger referred to in verse 11, is the Son of God Himself. In verse 12, He declares that Abraham has passed the test successfully: "Now I know that you fear God, seeing you have not withheld your son, your only son, from Me."

God the provider provides a substitute for Isaac. Abraham finds a ram caught by his horns in a thicket and offers it to God as a burnt offering on the altar he had built for Isaac.

Then, "because you [Abraham] have done this and have not withheld your son" (v. 16), God repeats the promises He had made to Abraham and his descendants: God would bless Abraham and multiply his offspring; his offspring would possess the gates of their enemies; and through Abraham's offspring, all the nations of the earth would be blessed. God blessed Abraham out of His free mercy through faith. Explore some of the promises of God by using Reproducible 6.

Lesson Support

Bringing it home

Encourage students to interview their parents about sacrifices they have made for their families. What sacrifices were necessary when the children were babies? What did parents sacrifice as the children started school? What sacrifices do parents see in the future as their children are ready for college? Then instruct the students to ask their parents to tell them about sacrifices *their* parents made for *them* as they were growing up. What motivated these sacrifices? Were the results worth the sacrifices?

Invite students and parents to look for stories of sacrifice in the newspaper and on television. Keep a record of these stories, collecting newspaper clippings in a scrapbook. Then discuss the following: How are all of these sacrifices like God's sacrifice when He gave His only Son to die for sinners? How are they different? Remind students that while almost all sacrifices are motivated by love, God loved people who had rebelled against Him and disobeyed Him. The results of sacrifices on the part of parents affect a few family members; God's sacrifice affected all people who ever lived. While the sacrifices of parents and other people may be forgotten, God's sacrifice was good for all time and affects eternity.

Searching Further

The laws concerning sacrifices and offerings were given by God through Moses during Israel's forty-year journey through the wilderness of Sinai. But God's people had been giving Him offerings and sacrifices beginning in Adam and Eve's own family. According to Genesis 4:3–7, Cain offered "the fruit of the ground," and Abel brought "the firstborn of his flock and of their fat portions." When Noah and his family emerged from the ark, Noah built an altar to the Lord and sacrificed "some of every clean animal and some of every clean bird" (8:20). Abram "built an altar to the Lord, who had appeared to him" at Shechem and again at Bethel when he first arrived in Canaan, the land God had promised to give him (12:7–9). Use the Internet or a resource book to learn more about Old Testament altars. Then draw a picture showing an Old Testament sacrifice.

Critical thinking

Make a large First Commandment banner to display in your church or school. Under the title "The First Commandment," write Question 22 and its answer from *Luther's Small Catechism with Explanation*: "What does God require of us in the First Commandment? God requires that we fear, love, and trust in Him above all things. . . . We love God above all things when we cling to Him alone as our God and gladly devote our lives to His service." Ask each student to draw a picture showing things that a person might do to show his or her love for God. Have students write prayers asking God to help them keep Him foremost in their lives. Place several of the students' prayers on the banner.

Celebrating GROWTH

Isaac was possibly about twelve years old when Abraham was commanded to sacrifice him on Mount Moriah (about the same age as students in your class). In Genesis 22:5, Abraham refers to him as "the boy," but he must have been old enough to carry the firewood on his shoulders (v. 6). The Bible is full of stories about children who acted in faith. A little girl from the land of Israel told Naaman about Elisha the prophet, through whom God cured his leprosy (2 Kings 5:1–14). David the shepherd boy was chosen by God and anointed by Samuel to be the next king of Israel (1 Samuel 16:1–13). A boy gave Jesus his lunch—five barley loaves and two fish—and Jesus fed five thousand men, plus women and children (John 6:1–15). Assure your students that God can and will use them for His purposes, even at their young age. "Let no one despise you for your youth, but set the believers an example in speech, in conduct, in love, in faith, in purity" (1 Timothy 4:12).

Ideas for the Gifted

Abraham's offering of Isaac gave Old Testament believers a foreshadowing, or picture, of something God would do in the future—in this case, sacrifice His own beloved Son, Jesus. Challenge gifted students to find other such previews in the Old Testament. The forty-year wandering of the Israelites in the wilderness of Sinai served as a picture of Jesus' forty days of temptation in the wilderness of Judea. Or compare Numbers 21:8–9 with John 3:14–15). Help students make a chart showing these and the other examples of foreshadowing they find.

UNIT 1—BEGINNINGS AND PATRIARCHS

LESSON 7

Isaac and Rebekah
GENESIS 24

Background

This Bible story offers a very appropriate opportunity to emphasize that marriage is a commitment between one man and one woman to remain faithful to each other for the rest of their lives! Marriage should not be based on physical appearances and worldly status, but on the will of God, our heavenly Father, who knows what is best for our lives! Since approximately 50 percent of marriages end in divorce, it is likely that there will be students in your classroom whose parents are divorced. For the sake of these students, we must acknowledge that divorce does happen and that God forgives those who are repentant. Acknowledge that problems in relationships can hurt everyone involved. Above all, emphasize that divorce is never a child's fault! The amount of time needed for this topic will depend on the needs and emotions of those in your class; you will need to monitor your students very carefully and act accordingly. The goal of this lesson is to focus on the dos rather than the don'ts of the Sixth Commandment. Teaching young men and young women to love and respect each other will be a blessing for students who are on the brink of going through many physical, emotional, social, and spiritual changes.

Central Truth

From the very beginning, God established a pattern in creation of male and female and of families, desiring that people respect, love, and serve one another. (Relate this lesson to the Sixth Commandment.)

Objectives

- Recognize that relationships in the world too often focus on physical appearances and personal gratification rather than on Christ-centered relationships.
- Affirm that with Jesus at the center of our lives, families and relationships will center on the forgiveness, peace, and joy found only in the Lord.
- Pray that God will bless our families with His guiding and gracious hand.

Materials

- Yellow highlighter
- Hymnals and music CDs
- Web Resource 7a
- Reproducible 7

Bible Prep

Post in advance so students can bookmark references before class time.
- Ephesians 4:1–3
- Matthew 19:5–6
- Genesis 24
- Philippians 4:8
- Matthew 19:9
- Psalm 103:12

Devotions

Consider this little story and the relationships involved: "What's Abby crying about?" Megan asked. "I don't know, but she looks really weird!" whispered Ramon. "You're right! When she cries, her face gets really red!" Jack exclaimed. "What's wrong, Abby?" asked Daniel. "My grandma died this morning," Abby sniffled. "I'm so sorry," Daniel said. Abby continued: "And the sad thing is that now my grandparents won't get to celebrate their fiftieth anniversary this Friday!" Abby started to cry again, but she was interrupted by Mrs. Cunningham. "Really? Fifty years? Time sure flies!" she exclaimed. "Your grandma was my teacher when I went to elementary school. Knowing how strong their marriage was, they didn't *need* an anniversary to remind them how blessed they were. Nowadays, you don't often see people stay together for that many years, but when you do, you can see the blessings flow in their lives!"

"You're right!" Abby agreed. "I'm going to miss Grandma a lot, but they were really blessed!" "Yes, and one of those blessings was being able to see you growing up into such a nice young lady!" Mrs. Cunningham winked. "Thanks!" grinned Abby. "Oh, and Daniel," continued Mrs. Cunningham, "I'm happy to see you being so respectful of your friend's feelings." "Yeah, thanks, Daniel," Abby said. "It's nice to know I have some people who are looking out for me!" "Yes, but don't forget the most important person looking out for you," reminded Daniel, pointing upward. "You're right! How could I forget God? Thanks, Daniel, for being an understanding friend," Abby said as the kids got on the school bus.

Let's pray: Dear Jesus, help us to love and respect other people in our lives, and keep us mindful of the blessings You give us through Christ-centered relationships. In Your name we pray! Amen.

Then sing together "What a Friend We Have in Jesus" (*LSB* 770; recorded as *Hymn of the Month for grade 6, September*). Close by saying together Psalm 100.

INTO the lesson

Teacher Note: The Student Book pages are not meant to be self-directing or used just as an assignment. They are meant to guide class discussions along with additional material from the Teacher Guide.

God Speaks!

Review briefly the story of Abraham and Isaac from Lesson 6, and recall Abraham's trust in the Lord. Then have students read the opening paragraph in the section entitled "God Speaks!" Have students highlight "they would live a life filled with respect, love, and service to each other." Then ask, **How can we show respect, love, and service to our families, to our friends and neighbors, and in our classroom?** Allow students to contribute several ideas and write these on the board. (For example, by doing classroom, home, or community jobs; by not laughing at other classmates', siblings', or friends' ideas; by standing up for what is right; by cleaning up trash outside; by talking to a person about a problem rather than gossiping; by helping and showing respect to the elderly and handicapped.)

Discuss the Sixth Commandment and its meaning from Luther's Small Catechism, found in the Appendix of the Student Book. Say, **Leading a "sexually pure and decent life" means that husbands and wives remain faithful to each other.** Then ask, **What does it mean to love and honor each other?** One important aspect of this is to put the other person's needs above your own. Read aloud Philippians 2:4.

Emphasize that the Sixth Commandment covers three broad areas: marriage, family, and gender. This commandment encompasses God's will for us in all of these areas. Marriage, family, and gender (maleness and femaleness) are part of God's good creation. Problems occur only when they are abused or misused by sinful intentions. **There are many controversial issues in our society today regarding marriage, family, and gender. Too often, these issues are responded to with the phrase "I have a right to do this," or "It's my right, and you can't tell me what to do," or "I have a legal right to do this." These types of "rights" do not make an action right in God's eyes. These types of "rights" do not count for us as righteousness. In dealing with these issues, we need to ask, "Who sets the standards? Whose will do I follow? Who decides what is right?" If your answer to these questions is not God, then you have set yourself up as your own god and have also broken the First Commandment.**

LESSON 7
Isaac and Rebekah

God Speaks!

Abraham was committed to trusting and obeying God to the point that he was willing to offer his son, Isaac, as a sacrifice to the Lord. What faith that must have taken! Years later, another "faith challenge" happened. Abraham trusted God's will as he sent his servant to find a wife for Isaac. God played the part of the ultimate matchmaker in order to carry out His plan for Isaac's life! God desired that Isaac would marry one woman, Rebekah, and that they would live a life filled with respect, love, and service to each other. Rebekah was chosen not for her good looks, but for her qualities of kindness and especially her love of the true God. The Sixth Commandment in Luther's Small Catechism tells us God's divine plan for marriage. Read this commandment and Luther's explanation of it (see the Appendix in the back of this book) and fill in the blanks below.

The Sixth Commandment: You shall not commit adultery.

What does this mean? We **should** fear and love God so that we lead a **sexually pure** and **decent** life in what we say and do, and **husband** and **wife love** and honor each other.

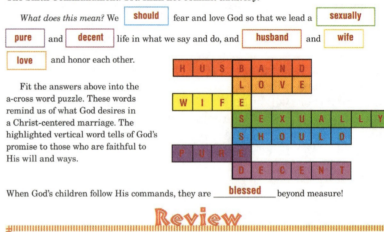

Fit the answers above into the a-cross word puzzle. These words remind us of what God desires in a Christ-centered marriage. The highlighted vertical word tells of God's promise to those who are faithful to His will and ways.

When God's children follow His commands, they are ___**blessed**___ beyond measure!

Review

Covenant Connection

God promised that the Messiah would come from Abraham's family line. This family line would continue through Abraham's son, Isaac, and Isaac's son Jacob. These three were known as "forefathers," or "patriarchs," of this family line. When it was the right time ("in the fullness of time"), Jesus was born—a descendant of Abraham, Isaac, and Jacob. Through faith in Jesus, we have become members of the family of God!

So what is God's will? What has God determined is right in regard to marriage, family, and gender? In Scripture, God has said that **marriage is a commitment of faithfulness between one man and one woman. It excludes physical, sexual relationships outside of marriage. The marriage commitment of faithfulness is a commitment to honor and respect everyone in the whole family.**

What about the issue of gender? This is an immediate concern to your students now and in the future. This means that, male or female, we are to treat one another with respect in our thoughts, words, and actions. Obedience to the Commandments is not "giving up your rights"; it is a matter of following God's plan for us. We can be certain that God's plans are always best. Read about them in Jeremiah 29:11 and Romans 8:28.

Extend the discussion by looking at Jesus as the perfect example of unselfish love. Read aloud John 15:13: "Greater love has no one than this, that someone lay down his life for his friends." Also read and discuss Ephesians 5:25: "Husbands, love your wives, as Christ loved the church and gave Himself up for her." Then read and discuss John 3:16: "For God so loved the world, that He gave His only Son, that whoever believes in Him should not perish but have eternal life." Say, **Jesus is the greatest example of love. He gave His life for us when He died on the cross to forgive us of our sins!**

Then have students work alone or

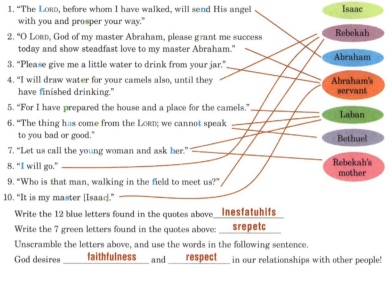

We Listen!

In the story of Isaac and Rebekah, God gives many people lots of opportunities to trust in God's plan and in His work through other people. Read Genesis 24, the true story of how Isaac and Rebekah were led to be together even though neither one had a choice in the matter. Then read each quote below and draw a line to the name of the person who said those words. Some names may be used more than once.

1. "The Lord, before whom I have walked, will send His angel with you and prosper your way."
2. "O Lord, God of my master Abraham, please grant me success today and show steadfast love to my master Abraham."
3. "Please give me a little water to drink from your jar."
4. "I will draw water for your camels also, until they have finished drinking."
5. "For I have prepared the house and a place for the camels."
6. "The thing has come from the Lord; we cannot speak to you bad or good."
7. "Let us call the young woman and ask her."
8. "I will go."
9. "Who is that man, walking in the field to meet us?"
10. "It is my master [Isaac]."

Write the 12 blue letters found in the quotes above: **lnesfatuhifs**
Write the 7 green letters found in the quotes above: **srepetc**
Unscramble the letters above, and use the words in the following sentence.
God desires **faithfulness** and **respect** in our relationships with other people!

We Pray!

Just as Abraham's servant prayed that God would lead him to find a faith-filled wife for Isaac, God invites us to pray about the relationships in our lives as well. Take time now to pray, asking God to bless all marriages and all families around the world. Additionally, ask God to forgive you for times when you do not show proper respect to people at home, at school, and in your community! Pray this in the name of Jesus, our Savior.

Remember

"'For this reason a man will leave his father and mother and be united to his wife, and the two will become one flesh.' So they are no longer two, but one. Therefore what God has joined together, let man not separate." (Matthew 19:5–6 NIV)

INTO the Word

We Listen!

Emphasize this continuing connection: All of the Old Testament points to our Savior, Jesus. God was faithful to His promises to the patriarchs. And by faith in Jesus, we are their descendants too. Galatians 3:7, 9 says, "Know then that it is those of faith who are the sons [and daughters] of Abraham. . . . So then, those who are of faith are blessed along with Abraham, the man of faith." Use Web Resource 7a to help unscramble the two main words of this section.

in pairs to fit the boxed words into the a-cross puzzle. Read the sentence below it together: **When God's children follow His commands, they are blessed beyond measure!** You may also wish to clarify that these blessings aren't "awards or prizes" given by God for good behavior; they are often natural good results that are given to us by God when we, with the help of the Holy Spirit, follow God's plan. Say, **When we follow God's commands, we are blessed with forgiveness, peace, and joy in our lives!**

INTO our lives

We Pray!

Isaac and Rebekah never even saw each other before their marriage was arranged, and yet they remained faithful to their marriage vows. Their marriage was based on God's plan, not on the world's ideas about marriage. Too often, people focus on physical appearances and wealth in their choices; God's choice for us is that we respect one another and remain loyal to the promises and commitments we have made. Seek God's will for the relationships in your lives. God desires that men, women, boys, and girls keep Christ as the center of their lives.

Discuss respect. Ask, **In what ways do people show disrespect at home, at school, or in the community? If you repent of your sins, what will happen?** (God forgives those who repent and believe in Jesus.) **Who can help you become more respectful?** (The Holy Spirit has power to transform us.) **What are ways you can show respect to other people?** *Option:* Use Reproducible 7 to study how respect is the basis for obedience to all the Commandments, as we are led by the Holy Spirit to live as children of God.

Read the narrative under the heading in the corresponding section of the Student Book. Say, **Just as Abraham's servant prayed to God for His will to be done, take some time now to write your own prayer. Consider giving praise for good relationships and asking for God's guidance where there are problems.**

37

Lesson Support

Bringing it home

Give students the opportunity to explore how God has blessed their family. Send students home with a long piece of paper (9 × 36 inches or so). Ask each child to work together with his or her parent(s) to create "a timeline of blessings" that have taken place in his or her family. The timeline may begin at the child's birth, or it may extend back into the life of a parent or grandparent. Exact dates are not important, but years or general decades would be helpful. Possible ideas could include birth and Baptism dates; God helping someone through a serious illness, surgery, or accident; engagement or marriage anniversaries; important family events and celebrations.

Be sure that students give their outlines a title (perhaps "A Timeline of Blessings"), and have students illustrate, add photos, or create symbols of the various blessings as well. Encourage neatness, and explain that their timelines may be displayed in the hallway!

Older adults have lived long enough to value the basic concepts of respect and service to one another. Many of them also know what it means to honor their marriage vows. Give students the chance to spend time showing respect and service to some of these older adults by allowing them to serve as volunteers at a nursing home, group home, or an assisted-living facility.

Be sure to visit the same place at least two or three times, and try to make sure that students are matched up with the same person/people each visit so that they can really get to know someone older than they are. Perhaps you as the teacher can encourage the older adults who feel comfortable doing so to share some of their life experiences and examples of how they have learned to respect people, marriage vows, authority figures, and so forth. At the end of the final visit with their "older friend," have students each give their person/people a small gift that was made for them as a token of appreciation for their time and for their ideas.

Working in Groups

Thinking of ways to show respect and love to people is not always easy. However, there is strength in numbers! Divide students into groups of four and have then work together to brainstorm ways that they can show love and respect to all people at school, at home, and in their community. Then have students make a large poster showing their ideas for showing respect in these different settings. (Some groups may want to make three different posters.)

After ideas are brainstormed and recorded and posters are completed, guide each group to choose one idea from their poster(s) and have them write a narrative or script that can be presented to the class. Teachers should walk around the room as students are deciding which idea to dramatize so that they can monitor students as they decide which scene to act out. This way, the same scenarios are not repeated several times. Discuss each scenario and say a prayer with the children, asking that God would help the class (students and teacher) show respect throughout their days!

Ideas for the Gifted

Abraham sent his servant to Nahor with ten of his camels! Camels were a sign of wealth, and he wanted the family of the one chosen as Isaac's wife to know that Isaac came from a wealthy family. Since camels are such fascinating animals, encourage students who would appreciate and could handle extra work to do some research on camels and present their information to the class. Perhaps knowing more about camels and their capabilities will help students realize their value back in Bible times!

Direct students to use the Internet, library books, magazines, and other sources as they search for information on the camel's habitat, food and water sources, traveling capabilities, and other interesting facts. After they have gathered all necessary information, encourage students to present their findings to the class through a speech, a PowerPoint presentation, or any other creative means.

If these students are still looking for more camel activities, encourage them to name one of the servant's camels and have them write a story from that camel's perspective as it journeyed with Abraham's servant to go and find a wife for Isaac.

UNIT 1—BEGINNINGS AND PATRIARCHS

LESSON 8

Isaac Blesses His Sons
GENESIS 27–28

Background

Today's lesson encompasses two stories in one. First, Jacob steals the blessing of the firstborn from his brother, Esau; then Jacob must flee from his brother's wrath, and along the way, he receives God's assurance and promise. While they are two separate events, they are related: Jacob sins, and then Jacob flees, but the Lord remains constant. The fact that sin does have consequences is a very important concept to teach. Sometimes children think sin always involves direct punishment given by someone in authority, such as having a privilege taken away. However, God often uses the natural consequences of sin to teach us how we ought to live (for example, not doing well at a competition because you stayed up too late the night before). As you teach this lesson, emphasize that God wants us to obey parents and other authority figures (Fourth Commandment) because He loves us and He cares for us through them. Another interesting concept to explore is Jacob's reputation for scheming. His name even means "he cheats"! Even though Esau was the older twin, Jacob fought to be the oldest by holding on to Esau's heel at birth—almost as if to say he "tied" with Esau at being the firstborn. (See Proverbs 20:11.) Always emphasize that God forgives sinners and sends the Holy Spirit to help us in our weaknesses.

Central Truth

Even though people and families are weak and sinful, God works through them to carry out His purposes. (Relate this lesson to the Fourth Commandment.)

Objectives

- Admit that all of us in families are sinners—moms, dads, kids, and other relatives.
- As Christ has forgiven us, share that forgiveness with all our family members and with members of the family of God.
- Celebrate that God can work His purposes even through weak and sinful people like us, because His strength is far greater than our weakness.

Materials

- Hymnals and music CDs
- Web Resource 8a
- Reproducible 8

Bible Prep

Post in advance so students can bookmark references before class time.
- Genesis 27:1–45
- Acts 5:29
- Ephesians 6:2–3
- Genesis 28:10–22

Devotions

Marcus was sitting at the kitchen table, doing his homework. His father came in and said, "Hey, Marcus, it looks like you are really wrapped up in your work." Marcus looked up and said, "It's funny you would say that, because I am studying spiderwebs. Did you know that spiders build their webs for hunting? Webs ensnare and entrap a spider's food source. Did you know that spiders create at least three different kinds of silk threads from spinnerets on their bodies? One type of silk makes a safety-line trail; a sticky kind of silk traps prey; and a fine silk wraps up the victims. Did you know that sometimes spiders eat their own webs for nourishment? They are recycling the silk proteins!"

"Wow!" said Dad. "You really know a lot about spiderwebs. See if you can answer a few questions for me: What is the difference between a spiderweb and a cobweb?" "That's an easy one," Marcus replied. "A cobweb is a spiderweb that has been abandoned, probably because it is no longer sticky enough to be functional." "Very good," said Dad. "Can you tell me how the World Wide Web is like a spiderweb?" "Interesting," said Marcus. "I'll take a guess at that one. Is it because the World Wide Web is many files, documents, and sites that are all interconnected and linked together like the strands on a spiderweb?"

"Quite right," said Dad. "Now try this one. How are temptations and sin like a spiderweb?" Marcus answered, "I don't have to guess on this one. Just like a spiderweb, temptations ensnare and entrap us. Once you are caught in sin, things just keep getting worse and worse, no matter how hard you try to get away. That's just like an insect caught in a web. It might try to fight to be free, but eventually it gives up and is doomed. The main difference, though, is that we have the way to be set free from sin—Jesus sets us free from sin!" Dad replied, "I couldn't have said it better myself. We can be very thankful for Jesus, who rescues us." Praise God for His goodness by reading together Psalm 100 and singing "O Blessed, Holy Trinity" (*LSB* 876; recorded as *Hymn of the Season for grade 6, Christian Education Month*).

INTO the lesson

Web of Lies!

Display Web Resource 8a, which illustrates today's Bible story. Leave it up throughout the lesson. Introduce the key players in the Bible narrative, and then establish some background: In ancient times, it was often the custom that the oldest son received special favors, with a birthright that offered at least double the privileges and promises offered to other sons in the family. This birthright became an issue in Isaac's family. When his twin sons were born, Esau was born first, but Jacob was born holding on to his brother's foot as if to signify that they were "tied" in being firstborn and having the birthright. Years later, Esau showed that he didn't care about the privileges and promises because he was willing to trade it all for a hot meal. This showed disdain and disrespect for the promises of God. However, what is most significant is that God intended right from the start that Jacob would be the heir apparent. The father, Isaac, never should have considered giving the birthright to Esau, contrary to God's plan. Jacob, rather than scheming to get the birthright, should have trusted God to work out all things according to His plan. And Esau continued to show his disrespect for God and the messianic promises by marrying an idol-worshiping Canaanite woman. After your introduction to the lesson, say, **Let's read the first paragraph in our lesson today! Let's learn more about this tangled web of sin.** Look at the opening section of the Student Book, and read aloud the narrative from Genesis 27:1–45. Then work on the activity that describes the many lies in which Jacob was involved. The concluding statement of this section leads into the next portion of the lesson.

Spinning the Web

This section relates the Bible narrative to the Fourth Commandment. Have students read it and the explanation from Luther's Small Catechism that is printed in the Appendix of the Student Book.

Emphasize that this commandment is not just about kids obeying parents. It refers to anyone who is in authority. Who would that be in the classroom? on a baseball team? in a car on the highway? while working in a factory? when a patient in the hospital? as a citizen of a city, state, and nation? Discuss the extended implications of the Fourth Commandment, using the questions in the Student Book. Note again that this commandment was broken in many ways in the Bible story. We see how Jacob disrespected and lied to his father. Rebekah broke the commandment by encouraging her son to sin against his father. Esau's whole life showed self-centeredness and disregard for others. And Isaac broke this commandment by disobeying his heavenly Father, thereby also breaking the First Commandment. Yet God chose to work His will through these weak and sinful people. Thus this story also can encourage us, reminding us that God's love for us is unconditional, based on the saving grace we have in Christ Jesus.

Review

Discuss this review section after completing the other portions of the Student Book. Point out that God's amazing grace is seen in His willingness to use even the weakest of sinners to effect His purpose. We need never feel too guilty or too useless to receive the unconditional love of God. There are many things we can learn from the Bible narrative, but the most significant point is that God continued to carry out His plan; He continued to use sinners to "pass the promise." **Emphasize that this promise is the covenant agreement that God would send the Messiah—the Savior—to rescue us from sin so that we can live as people of God.** This would be a good time to either present or review the bulletin board (available from CPH) titled "Passing the Promise." Emphasize the three patriarchs—Abraham, Isaac, Jacob—through whose family line all the world would be blessed in Christ Jesus. Throughout the Old Testament, we will see this messianic prophecy explained by prophets, passed on by families, and clarified by God's messages to His people. Today we know that this promise

Tangled Web!

This was truly a dysfunctional family! None of the four people acted righteously. They all were sinners needing to repent and receive God's forgiveness. They were all caught up in deceitfulness, disobedience, and unkindness. In this tangled web, write what each person did that was contrary to God's will and God's plans.

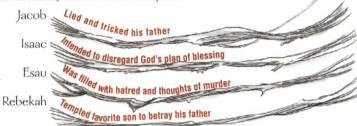

Jacob — *Lied and tricked his father*
Isaac — *Intended to disregard God's plan of blessing*
Esau — *Was filled with hatred and thoughts of murder*
Rebekah — *Tempted favorite son to betray his father*

Set Free!

God's grace is greater than our sinfulness. Jacob recognized God's unconditional love. Even though he had to flee for his life, Jacob was still surrounded by the love of God. Read about God's special message that came while Jacob was homeless. See Genesis 28:10–22. God's forgiveness set Jacob free. The last part of verse 14 and the first part of verse 15 speak of two of God's great promises. Write each one beside the stairway pictured below.

In you and your offspring shall all the families of the earth be blessed.

I am with you and will keep you wherever you go.

We, too, sin daily and need forgiveness. We are thankful that God sent His Son, Jesus, to die on the cross and forgive our sins. Young and old, we all need God's forgiveness! On the cross, write the names of people in your family and other relatives and friends who are forgiven through Christ Jesus!

Remember

"I will never leave you nor forsake you." (Hebrews 13:5b)

INTO the Word

Tangled Web!

None of the people in this Bible narrative was righteous. Have partners work together on this section of the Student Book. Then discuss together where our righteousness comes from. Read aloud Romans 5:17–18; 1 Corinthians 1:30; 2 Corinthians 5:21; and Philippians 3:9.

Then read together the readers theater on Reproducible 8. As you look at the box at the bottom of the page, ask who the hero of the story is—is it Jacob, Isaac, Esau, or Rebekah, as the letters and lines would indicate? No, *God* is the hero of every story in the Bible. Ask students to select words to write in the blanks (like an acronym) that would say this. One possibility that fits well with today's theme is "**J**esus **I**s **E**ternal **R**ighteousness."

INTO our lives

Set Free!

Emphasize that God never leaves His people without hope and redemption. As sinful as Jacob was, God came to him with the promise of the Savior and the promise to always be with him. **What did Jacob say in Genesis 28:16–17 that showed that he recognized God's presence and blessings?** ("Surely the Lord is in this place" and "This is none other than the house of God, and this is the gate of heaven.") As a class, turn to the concordance in the Appendix of the Student Book and read aloud Scripture verses that speak of the freedom we have in Christ Jesus. We are set free from sin, death, and the devil, and we are set free to live as God's people with the free gifts of forgiveness, life, and salvation.

has been fulfilled in the death and resurrection of Jesus. Now it is our turn to "pass the promise" to others. Discuss to whom we can pass the promise, how we can do that, and when and where we can pass it on. *Option:* Sing "Pass It On" (*AGPS* 196; recorded on *JPS*, CD 2, track 11).

Lesson Support

Technology

Encourage students to work in groups of three; one person should be Jacob, one should be a news reporter, and one should be a producer/videographer. Have them pretend to be a crew from Mesopotamia Live News Network. Because the reporter accidentally stumbles on Jacob as he is sleeping with his head on a rock, he or she gives a feature report on Jacob and his life. Be sure that the students write a script for their reporting debut, and make sure that all involved know what their responsibilities are. Each report should include the who, what, when, where, why, and how of Jacob's situation, and students should be encouraged to use props to make their reports as authentic as possible.

When the videos are completed, pop some popcorn and enjoy watching them as a fun classroom activity! If possible, have students critique at least two of the videos as they watch them. A rubric could be made to evaluate the following categories: assignment completed on time (10 points), organization (10 points), delivery (10 points), message content (who, what, when, where, why, and how, 10 points each for 60 points total), and cooperation of team (10 points), for a total possible score of 100 points.

Bringing it home

God wants children to obey their parents and others in authority. Children need to know what parents expect of them so that they know what to do to obey their parents. Assign a project for parents and their children to discuss which jobs need to be done around the house, who should do them, and how they should be completed so that children are clear about their responsibilities. After students are sure of what their parents want, parents should decide on any rewards that children will be given for obeying their parents' rules and any consequences that will be imposed upon children for disobeying those rules.

If children earn an allowance for the work they do, now is a great time to teach children (or reteach them, if necessary) to tithe (note the last verse of Genesis 28). Encourage them to set aside a specified portion of their earnings (Scripture recommends 10 percent, but that is only a guideline) and give it to the Lord by supporting the mission and ministry of the Church.

Ideas for the Gifted

Have students work in pairs to create a poster that shows ways students can obey their parents and others in authority. Allow students to be creative and use several different types of media (such as colored pencils, markers, crayons, pastels, watercolor paints, poster paints, charcoal, magazine pictures). Lessons on how to use the different media could be covered in art class in the weeks preceding this activity. Each poster should have a title that has something to do with the Fourth Commandment and should contain at least six different examples of children honoring parents and others in authority. Posters should also have a balance of images (not all images on one side with lots of blank spaces and the like), and images should clearly show that the main subject(s) is following the Fourth Commandment.

Posters should be judged in terms of neatness (20 points), creativity (20 points), content of items on the poster (30 points), placement of items on the poster (10 points), and use of media (variety, effectiveness, and the like; 20 points) for a total possible score of 100 points. If possible, have other teachers judge the posters for a more objective assessment. When all is said and done, display the posters in the hallway for parents and others to see and enjoy.

Working in Groups

Most children love to work in groups with others their own age. In order to encourage children to honor their parents and others in authority, help students in the class form service groups of four or five students each. Then have each service group do volunteer work at least once at each group member's house (coordination with parents will, of course, be necessary). This not only teaches each child to serve his or her own parents, but it also allows students to see service modeled by their peers!

Ideas for service might include raking leaves, shoveling snow, trimming bushes, cleaning up yard and neighborhood litter, dusting the house, cleaning bathrooms, sweeping or mopping floors, organizing a basement or closet, washing or folding laundry, and so forth. Anything that gets the kids moving and serving is a great idea for group work!

After each servant event, have students fill out a learning inventory survey that asks them what they did, what they learned, how they learned it, what challenges or problems they had, and how they could fix or minimize their problems next time.

Unit 1—Beginnings and Patriarchs Lesson 9

Jacob and Laban
Genesis 29–32, summarized

Background

"Cheaters never prosper" goes the saying—except in today's Bible lesson. Jacob, his Uncle Laban, Laban's daughters, and their maidservants are involved in a twisted plot of theft, jealousy, and cheating. This is not a story about obedience to the Commandments. In this story, Jacob, whose name means "deceiver and cheater," prospers. "The man increased greatly," the text tells us (Genesis 30:43), and by the end of the story, Jacob has gained for himself wives, sons, servants, flocks, and herds. Is that the lesson to be learned—that cheaters do, in fact, prosper? Jacob cheated his brother out of the blessing that was Esau's by right of birth. Laban was dishonest as he gave his daughters to Jacob in marriage. Rachel and Leah were jealous of each other's children, each desperate to keep Jacob's love and favor for herself. Each wife gave her maid to Jacob to bear sons for him on her behalf. Laban kept the best of his flocks from Jacob, yet through the grace of God and clever breeding practices, Jacob's flocks prospered. Cheaters may prosper, as Jacob did, but in so doing, they violate the will and commands of God, and they suffer considerable grief as they deal with the consequences of their sin. In the story of Jacob and Laban, we learn once again that people are sinners and that our almighty God works through sinners and their sinful, selfish behavior to accomplish His purposes and fulfill His promises. Through Jacob, God worked to fulfill His promise to bless Abraham with land and with descendants as countless as the stars. The Messiah was born into the family line of Judah, Jacob's fourth son. Jesus Christ, the promised Messiah and "Lion of the tribe of Judah" (Revelation 5:5), conquered sin and death for us all.

Central Truth

God's will is always for the good of His people. (Relate this lesson to the Ninth and Seventh Commandments.)

Objectives

- Recognize that coveting thoughts often lead to stealing actions; both are sinful.
- Rely on God to forgive and transform us, trusting His power over any evil in or around us.
- Depend on the grace of God to do what is best for His people at the time He knows is best for His purposes.

Materials

- Yellow highlighters
- Art supplies: poster paper, pencils, markers, paint
- Reproducible 9

Bible Prep

Post in advance so students can bookmark references before class time.
- Genesis 29–32; 33:4, 9
- 1 Timothy 3:12
- Psalm 121:8

Devotions

Carrie Anne was in her room, sitting at her desk, writing her thoughts in a journal. She wrote, "In the Bible we are reading about a bunch of people who seem to do nothing but wrong things—people like Jacob and Esau and Laban. You would think the Bible would just tell us good things. Another thing I can't understand is how God could be so patient with these people. Why didn't He just get rid of them, kick them out, or walk away?" Just then, she heard her mother calling to her from downstairs. She sounded annoyed as she said, "Carrie Anne, you still have not taken care of the dirty dishes from dinner. I did my part by fixing a good meal. Now you are responsible for the cleanup. We will not go shopping until you have done your jobs." Immediately, Carrie Anne leaned over with her head on her desk as she prayed in her heart: "Dear Lord, I get it now! You loved Jacob just like my mom loves me. Sometimes I disappoint her, but she never gives up on me, just like You didn't give up on Jacob. Even after I've messed up, Mom forgives me and keeps trying to teach me how to live as a child of God. You did the same with Jacob after he messed up; You forgave him and kept on teaching him how to live as Your child." Just then, Carrie  Anne's mother walked past her room and saw her sitting there with her head down. She came in and put her hand on Carrie Anne's shoulder and asked if she was all right. Carrie Anne continued her prayer, but this time she spoke it out loud: "And, dear Lord, thank You for giving me a mom who is so patient and loving and kind. I know I continue to make mistakes and I don't always obey. Please make me strong to live as Your child. Amen." Carrie Anne sat up, gave her mom a hug, and then ran downstairs to take care of the dishes. She didn't see the tears in her mother's eyes, and she didn't hear her mother's simple prayer: "Dear Jesus, thank You, thank You." Sing "Let Us Ever Walk with Jesus" (*LSB* 685; recorded as *Hymn of the Month* for grade 6, September).

INTO the lesson

A Lesson in Disobedience

Point out: **Today's lesson does not give us good examples of Bible heroes. In fact, the people in the lesson are all sinners who cheat, trick, covet, envy, and are seriously unkind to their own families. Right from the start, we need to ask ourselves, how did this whole mess begin? In each case, the problem begins with their thoughts as they see something someone else has, become envious, and then scheme and plan to make it their own. This starting point breaks the Ninth Commandment.** Take time to look at this commandment and its explanation in the Small Catechism in the Student Book Appendix. Have students highlight the words "get it in a way which only appears right." We will see this method used by Laban, who tried to make excuses for what was outright cheating and stealing. Making something "appear right" does not make it right in God's eyes. Ask if students can give modern-day examples of this (for example, seeing a clerk give you too much change and keeping it because "he gave it to me"; or copying music from a friend's MP3 player, reasoning that "she paid for it"—even though you did not). The attitudes of coveting and scheming lead to open and outright stealing, which is breaking the Seventh Commandment. The sinful thinking that breaks the Ninth Commandment leads to the actions that break the Seventh Commandment. Look at the explanation of this commandment, and have students highlight the words "get them in any dishonest way." **Some people think taking things is okay as long as you don't get caught. That just isn't true. God knows, God sees, and God judges those actions as sinful. You are accountable to Him. You might ask, "Doesn't Jesus forgive all sins?"** Read more about this in 1 John 1:8–9. **We receive the gift of forgiveness by faith—which involves recognizing our sin (confession) and trusting our Savior (in repentance).** Let's explore this further in God's Word.

Lesson 9

Jacob and Laban

Family Troubles

Jacob had deceived his father, Isaac, and tricked his brother, Esau. To escape the trouble he was in, he rushed to another country to stay with his Uncle Laban. It was there that the cheater got cheated.

Problem 1

Jacob worked for his uncle for a month. His uncle asked what he wanted for wages. Jacob knew what he wanted. He said he would work seven years if he could then marry Laban's beautiful daughter, Rachel. Jacob was in love, so the years seemed to go by quickly (Genesis 29:20). After the wedding, he realized that he had been tricked into marrying the older (not-so-pretty) sister, Leah. His uncle tried to make it look like it was the right thing to do and was not a trick. Laban said it was their custom that the older sister had to get married before the younger one. However, greedy Laban said Jacob could also marry Rachel *if* he worked for another seven years! This was just the beginning of more troubles. (What does 1 Timothy 3:12 say about marriage? **A husband should have one wife.**)

Problem 2

There was a lot of jealousy between Jacob's two wives. Jacob obviously loved Rachel, and Leah was despised. But God felt sorry for Leah and gave her many children: Reuben, Simeon, Levi, Judah, Issachar, and Zebulun. Rachel had no children and was envious of Leah's family. So she gave Jacob her servant Bilhah, who had two sons for Rachel: Dan and Naphtali. This made Leah jealous because she had stopped having children, so she gave Jacob her servant Zilpah, who had two sons for Leah: Gad and Asher. Finally, Rachel had two sons of her own: Joseph and Benjamin. This was just the beginning of *more* troubles! Not only were the mothers jealous of each other, but the brothers were jealous and unkind too. Who do you think were Jacob's two favorites? **Joseph and Benjamin**

The brothers were each unique, so it could be expected that they would each be treated differently. However, what was wrong with having favorites in a family? **All should receive love and kindness; favoritism causes troubles for everyone.**

Review

Covenant Connection

The continuing story of Jacob and his family is interesting, but more than that, it is connected to God's plan for sending the Messiah. Jacob eventually passed the promise to his son Judah that the Savior, the King of kings, would come from Judah's family (Genesis 49:10). We will see in Bible stories to come how Jacob's family grew into a large nation of twelve tribes, or family groups—the twelve tribes of Israel.

24

INTO the Word

Family Troubles

Isaac sent his son Jacob to his relatives to find a wife, a daughter of Jacob's uncle Laban. On the way, God appeared to Jacob in a dream and promised to bless him with land and children. The God of Abraham and Isaac was Jacob's God too.

God was faithful, but the deceit and lies of Jacob and his whole family caused serious troubles. Read in the Student Book about the three major problems faced by Jacob and the family he married into. His father-in-law tricked him into doing fourteen years of labor. His two wives were sisters, but were jealous of each other; this rivalry continued among their sons.

Jacob's father-in-law, Laban, changed their working agreement ten times. But none of this could affect God's plan for His people. Jacob continued to be blessed because that was the will of God.

When Jacob left with his wives, servants, and flocks, Laban pursued him. But in a dream, God told Laban not to harm Jacob. Read Genesis 31:36–42. What did Jacob tell Laban about his work? (He had worked hard for Laban, but if God had not been on his side, he would have received nothing for his work.) Finally, Jacob and his uncle made peace. They set up a pile of stones as a monument. Read Genesis 31:46–50. What did the

PROBLEM 3

Jacob knew it was time to take his large family to his homeland, but Laban didn't want this to happen. Laban knew that his son-in-law was a good worker. Laban knew that God had blessed him through Jacob's hard work and had made him rich (Genesis 30:27). So Laban made a deal with Jacob—a deal he manipulated over and over again. At first he said Jacob could have all the spotted lambs; but when the flocks suddenly had *many* spotted lambs, Laban changed the terms of the deal. However, no matter how he changed the arrangement, God always saw to it that Jacob was blessed. Jacob said to his wives, "Your father has cheated me and changed my wages ten times. But God did not permit him to harm me" (Genesis 31:7). It had taken a long time, but Jacob was finally learning that bad behavior had bad consequences, but the faithfulness of God could always be trusted. How does this change of heart show in Jacob's prayer in Genesis 32:9–10? _____
Jacob was humble and admitted that he did not deserve God's goodness.

Family Blessings

In all of this mess, God did not give up on His people. Jacob's sins, Laban's sins, Leah's sins, and Rachel's sins would not divert God from His plans. God remained faithful. As He says in Malachi 3:6, "I the LORD do not change." Jacob was again running away from danger; his father-in-law, Laban, had chased after him, and now it looked like his brother, Esau, was ready to attack. So God came to Jacob one night in the shape of a man to reassure Jacob that God was always with him. Jacob would not let Him go without a blessing, so they wrestled all night. Finally God said to him, "Your name shall no longer be called Jacob, but Israel, for you have striven with God and with men, and have prevailed" (Genesis 32:28). (*Note:* God also worked on the hearts of Laban and Esau. They did not attack Jacob, but blessed him. See Genesis 31:48–53 and 33:4, 9.) After this, Jacob's family, which grew into a large nation of people, was always called "the children of Israel." Abraham, Isaac, and Israel (Jacob) were ancestors of the Messiah, the Savior, Jesus—a blessing to all people!

Label the children of Israel pictured above.

Remember

"The LORD will keep your ___**going out**___ and your ___**coming in**___ from this time forth and ___**forevermore**___." (Psalm 121:8)

stones mean? (The stones were called "Mizpah," which means "watchpost." The Lord would watch over Jacob and Laban to be sure that neither man cheated or harmed the other.) Use Reproducible 9 to learn more.

Through all of Jacob's schemes, Laban's deception, and the jealousy of Rachel and Leah, God was at work, carrying out His plans. Jacob's sons and their families formed the twelve tribes of Israel (Genesis 35:23-26). **Jacob and his fourth son, Judah, were ancestors of Jesus Christ, who came to give His life as a sacrifice for the sins of Jacob and his family—and for our sins.**

INTO our lives

Family Blessings

Say, **Praise and thank God that His actions toward us are not dependent on our actions toward Him. He remains faithful, trustworthy, powerful, and kind at all times. This does not change, in spite of our frequent failures and sins. Hebrews 13:8 says, "Jesus Christ is the same yesterday and today and forever." As we look at Jacob's story, we also see our story—the story of sinners. Thankfully, Jacob's story is blessed by the grace and mercy of God. Our life stories are similarly blessed. God is faithful, even when we aren't.**

Jacob and his wives did not always obey God's commands about coveting and stealing. They wanted what they did not have, and they tricked others into getting what they wanted. Obeying the Commandments is not just about "not coveting" or "not stealing." We can also actively obey the commands of God. Discuss these questions with your class: **How can we be satisfied with what we have? How can we help others keep what is theirs?**

Work together in groups to plan skits showing ways in which the Seventh and Ninth Commandments might be obeyed or disobeyed. Write a description of each scenario given below, or think of your own stories to role-play.

- A student takes markers from another student's desk during a recess.
- A girl shows off a new jacket while other girls watch.
- Students pick up trash and rake leaves.
- One student looks at another student's test answers.

Remember that Jesus, "the Lion of the tribe of Judah," came to obey the Commandments perfectly in our place and to die for our sins. Remind the students that in our disobedience and obedience, God is at work in our lives, calling us to repentance and guiding us in following His will.

Lesson Support

Bringing it home

Jacob, Laban, Rachel, and Leah struggled with one another in their family relationships. They were often jealous and dishonest with one another. Sometimes your students will also have difficult relationships and troubled times with parents, brothers, and sisters. Discuss with your students the ways in which jealousy, dishonesty, coveting, or stealing might be expressed within their families. Are they ever jealous of what a brother or sister has? Have they ever been dishonest in what they have said to their parents? Have they taken something that belonged to another family member? How can we follow God's will as we live within our families? Pray together and ask God to bless and protect our families. Ask the Spirit to help us show the love of Christ in the way we treat one another. Using the Commandments as themes, have students write prayers that they can use in family devotions.

Critical thinking

Suppose Laban and Jacob had gone before a judge to settle their disagreements. Who was really in the wrong? Did Laban treat Jacob unfairly, or was Jacob dishonest with his uncle? How should their differences have been settled? Discuss the evidence with your students. Remind your students that God chose to bless Jacob because He is a gracious God, not because Jacob was a good person. God chose Abraham and his descendants, including Jacob and his sons, to carry forward His plan of salvation.

Faith in Action

In his explanation of the Seventh Commandment, Martin Luther says that we should help our neighbor "improve and protect his possessions and income." Help your class decide on some possible service projects that will help your church and school "improve and protect" its property. Is there cleaning or painting that needs to be done? Can your students pick up trash, clean lunch tables, or help to clean and dust the church for Sunday services? Are there elderly church members or neighbors who need help caring for their property, sweeping, raking, or pulling weeds? Think about ways you and your students can help others improve and protect their possessions.

Searching Further

Have students work in groups to read all of Genesis 29–31. Thinking about the Ninth and Seventh Commandments, find all of the incidents of dishonesty and cheating that happen in the story of Jacob and Laban. How do the people in the story go against God's will? How does God help and protect Jacob and the others? Remember that some Bible stories are a *description* of what happens in the lives of sinners and not a *prescription* for the way we should behave! We can learn what *not* to do. We can see that people in the Bible were like us—sinners. Thankfully we also know God forgives us for the sake of Jesus.

Check it Out

There are many cultural aspects involved in this Old Testament story. It was the custom for the groom to pay a "bride-price" to the family of the bride. This price was compensation to the family for the loss of a working member of their household. When Jacob chose Rachel as his wife, he agreed to work for Laban for seven years; his work would be the bride-price. Laban tricked Jacob, giving him instead his older, apparently less attractive daughter, Leah, whose identity would have been concealed behind the customary veils that brides wore on their wedding day. Laban eventually agreed to give Rachel to Jacob as a wife, but Jacob had to work another seven years to pay the bride-price for her.

Although from the beginning God willed that marriage was to be between one man and one woman (Matthew 19:4–8), the Old Testament patriarchs and kings often took more than one wife. It was not unusual for a childless woman to give her maid to her husband so that the servant would have children on her behalf. The female servant's infant would be received at birth "on the knees" of the wife, showing that the baby was to be considered as the wife's own child (Genesis 16:1–4; Job 3:12).

In an incident in Genesis 30:14–18, Rachel bargains with Leah for some mandrake plants that Reuben found in the field. The berries and roots of the mandrake were believed to encourage fertility. Rachel had not yet had any children, and no doubt she believed the mandrakes would help her become pregnant. It was God, however, who helped her, blessing her with the gift of her son Joseph (v. 22).

When Laban withheld the spotted sheep and goats from his nephew, Jacob had the stronger sheep and goats breed in front of peeled, striped branches (vv. 37–42) so that the young animals would be born with spots. This was only a superstition on Jacob's part; it was God who blessed Jacob's flock (31:7–9).

UNIT 1—BEGINNINGS AND PATRIARCHS

LESSON 10

Joseph
GENESIS 37–50, SUMMARIZED

Background

The jealous competition among Jacob's wives and maidservants continues into the lives of his sons. Joseph, Rachel's firstborn, is Jacob's favorite son. Joseph's brothers are jealous of the favor he finds in his father's eyes—and Joseph's dreams of ruling over his family don't sit well with them either. The story of Joseph and his brothers repeatedly presents us with examples of disobedience against the Tenth Commandment (which prohibits coveting relationships) and against the Eighth Commandment (which prohibits lies and betrayal). For example, Joseph's brothers covet Joseph's favored status, so they conspire to sell their brother and lie to their father; also, in Egypt, Potiphar's wife falsely accuses Joseph, and he is sent to prison as a result. Through these sinners, God is at work to bring about His holy will. By the power of God, Joseph is raised up from prison to rule Egypt, second only to Pharaoh. God's people, the children of Israel, arrive in Egypt. There, Israel will become a great nation, although they will endure years of enslavement. At the right time, God will call His people out of Egypt, just as one day far in the future, He would call His own Son, with Mary and Joseph, out of exile in Egypt. That Son, Jesus, like Joseph, would be betrayed and sold. He would be arrested and imprisoned by death itself. As Joseph ruled Egypt, saving the people from starvation and forgiving his brothers, Jesus would be raised up in triumph from death to rule, forgive, and save His people, including you and me!

Central Truth

God is with us in good times and also during bad times, blessing us. (Relate to the Tenth and Eighth Commandments.)

Objectives

- Acknowledge that covetous and envious attitudes can lead to words and actions that belie and betray others.
- Depend on God to give us hearts that look at others and respond to them in Christian love and kindness, through the redemptive work of Christ in us.
- Dedicate what we say and do to others for the glory of God (all through a Christian perspective).

Materials

- Hymnals and music CDs
- Web Resource 10a
- Reproducible 10
- Art supplies: poster paper, pencils, markers, paint

Bible Prep

Post in advance so students can bookmark the reference before class time.
- Genesis 37; 39–50

Devotions

On her way to the playground, Ann walked past the open door of Mrs. Bryan's sixth-grade classroom. She almost continued on by, but then she stopped to look in again. The sixth graders were at recess, and the room was empty—except for one person. Jenny, the new fifth-grade girl, was alone in the room. Ann watched her reach into a student's desk and pull out a cell phone. Jenny came outside, looked around, and walked quickly away. Ann hurried over to a group of seventh-grade girls gathered on the playground. As they gathered around her, Ann whispered, "You won't believe what I saw! That new fifth-grade girl stole a cell phone from a sixth grader!" "I don't believe it," said Sandy. "Maybe someone told her to find it." "No," said Ann, "I'm sure she was stealing it, because she looked scared. She didn't want anyone to see her." "I can't believe it!" said Sandy, and she hurried off to whisper the secret to other students. Before long, students all through the middle school were pointing at Jenny and whispering to one another. Jenny saw people looking at her and wondered about it.

It wasn't until the end of the day that Ann found out the truth. Waiting for her ride, she heard Mrs. Bryan say to Jenny, "Thank you for going back to my classroom and getting Lynn's cell phone from her desk. She needed to call her mom since she wasn't feeling well." Ann felt awful. Jenny hadn't been stealing; she had been helping one of the sixth graders! "I need to tell Sandy and everyone else," Ann thought. "And I guess I should apologize to Jenny." Before they left school, Ann found Jenny and apologized. Ann explained to the other girls what had happened and said, "I think we have all learned that it is important to make sure you get all the facts first, because what you say could hurt someone."

We pray: Lord Jesus, help us to speak well about others and explain their actions with kindness. Amen. Sing "What a Friend We Have in Jesus" (*LSB* 770; recorded as *Hymn of the Month* for grade 6, September). Together say Psalm 100.

INTO the lesson

Refer to today's devotion, asking, **What lesson did Ann learn about words?** (Ann learned that words do have the power to hurt someone.) By her hurtful words and lies about Jenny, Ann hurt the new girl's reputation. In today's story of Joseph and his brothers, hurtful words are only the beginning. The story of Laban, Jacob, and Jacob's wives is a story filled with jealousy and cheating. Now Jacob's sons add more lies and jealousy to their family history. The Eighth Commandment, like the Seventh, is about stealing, but it is about stealing someone's good reputation by telling lies. The Tenth Commandment, like the Ninth, warns against wanting what belongs to others, but this command is about people and relationships too.

Read the Eighth and Tenth Commandments aloud from the Small Catechism in the Student Book Appendix and discuss their meanings. Point out that the Eighth Commandment is especially relevant to the lives of your students as they use social-media networking. Discuss the incredible harm that is caused by unkind texting, blogs, downloadable photos, and more. Discuss why these unkind communications hurt so much and why they are more than "anonymous words."

After discussing how we break the Eighth Commandment, spend time talking about ways to keep it. The explanation in the catechism gives three key possibilities for the way we talk about other people:

1. Defend them.
2. Speak well of them.
3. Explain everything in the kindest way.

Have students give you positive examples of how this could be done. Set up a classroom project for the next week where students may post ideas, comments, and even fictional narratives about positive, Christian behavior in these contexts. These can be posted on three separate charts having the titles of the three key possibilities. It may encourage even more interest and participation if this is set up as a classroom blog.

Good and Bad Times

Say, **The story of Joseph and his brothers is filled with jealousy, lies, and coveting, beginning with Joseph's brothers, who covet the good favor from their father that only Joseph enjoys. Joseph's brothers betray him and sell him into slavery. But just as God was at work to carry out His purposes in the story of Jacob, God is at work in the life of Joseph too.**

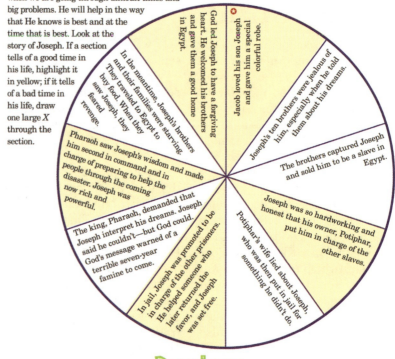

He works through the lives of sinners, and in the story of Joseph, He gives us a picture, a preview, of the life of our Savior, Jesus. As we read and study the story of Joseph, look for ways in which his story is like the story of Jesus.

Joseph's story is very long and complex. It reads like a novel, with many chapters. To review the essence of his story, use Web Resource 10a in connection with the diagram in the Student Book. The ten sections of the diagram correspond with the ten sections of Web Resource 10a. Then examine again the diagram in the Student Book, following the directions to indicate the good and bad times in Joseph's life. Relate this to the Bible words to remember from Jeremiah 29:11. Discuss the common question that some people ask: why do bad things happen to good people? Emphasize that God never promises that Christians will not have troubles. We are sinners living in a sin-filled world; bad things, unfair things, will happen. However, God does promise to be with us at all times—He never abandons us. Look for ways that He blesses you, even as the troubles of this world surround you. Read aloud Genesis 50:20, where Joseph speaks to his brothers, realizing how God worked through all these good and bad times in order to save the lives of many people.

A Big Story—in Five Acts

Act 1: Joseph's Family
(Genesis 37:1–11)

Act 2: The Brothers Capture Joseph
(Genesis 37:12–36)

Act 3: Joseph—a Slave and a Prisoner
(Genesis 39)

Act 4: Pharaoh's Dreams
(Genesis 41)

Act 5: Joseph Forgives His Brothers
(Genesis 42:1–11; 45:1–20)

(*Option:* Read Genesis 42–45 to get the whole story.)

A "Comparative Type"

In literature, a "comparative type" is someone who shares some similar characteristics with another person. In biblical literature, a "type" is something or someone in the Old Testament that prefigures something or someone in the New Testament. In the first chart, read the statements about Joseph. Whom does he prefigure? Discuss similar New Testament events.

Joseph and Jesus	Only Jesus
He came to help but was attacked in anger.	Jesus is true God and never sinned.
He was betrayed for silver coins.	Jesus died to save us from eternal disaster.
He was treated unfairly and like a criminal.	Jesus arose and offers us eternal life.
He forgave his enemies.	Jesus saves the whole world (John 3:16).

Remember

"For I know the plans I have for you, declares the Lord, plans for welfare and not for evil, to give you a future and a hope." (Jeremiah 29:11)

INTO the Word

A Big Story—in Five Acts

Take a closer look at Joseph's story. Keep in mind that you may have students in your class who have heard this story since they were in preschool, and some who may be hearing it for the very first time. Therefore, approach the story in a new way, working in five groups, encouraging students to find ways *they* can communicate the story, challenging them to look for concepts they have not thought of before.

Assign one of the acts of the story as listed in the Student Book to each student group. They are to read the text from the Bible and then write a summary narration or script that tells that portion of Joseph's story. (Another option would be to read this portion of the story from a Bible story book.) When finished, each group will present their summary narrative or script to the whole class. See the Lesson Support Page for additional ideas to support these presentations.

INTO our lives

A "Comparative Type"

This is probably the most important part of the lesson, as we see how Joseph's story connects to Jesus and to all of our lives. Ask students to look at the first chart and give examples in each category from the lives of both Joseph and Jesus. Then point out that while Joseph prefigures Christ Jesus, the comparison is only partial. Have students suggest ways that Jesus was different from Joseph. Note that the suggested answers all pertain to Jesus' role as the Savior/Messiah.

The story of Joseph is in many ways a picture of the life of Jesus. Like Joseph, Jesus was betrayed and sold. Even though He was innocent, He was arrested and condemned. While Joseph was only imprisoned, Jesus was crucified. As Joseph was raised up from prison to rule Egypt, Jesus was raised up and ascended to the place of authority at God's right hand. He rules in grace so that many people, including you and me, can be saved through faith in His name.

Joseph had the power and authority to harm his brothers. Instead, he forgave them. He was merciful to them just as God had been merciful to him. He "comforted them and spoke kindly to them" (Genesis 50:21). **God has forgiven our sins. Now we can share that forgiveness with others.** Help your students learn to build people up instead of giving "false testimony" or speaking in a harmful way. Building people up is not just a matter of complimenting someone on their clothes or athletic ability. Your students can also show appreciation for someone with simple words such as "I know you're always there for me" or "Thanks for explaining that question in math; now I understand it." They can invite a new or less popular student to join them at recess or lunch. Discuss specific ways in which your students can speak kindly to others at school and at home. Just as God loves and forgives us, we can love and forgive others.

Working in Groups

After students present their summaries or skits on Joseph's life, the class may respond in song, as presented on Reproducible 10. Note that these are very simple tunes; students may have other suggestions for tunes that can piggyback with the words. Stress, though, that a match in rhythm and word count must apply. *Option:* Listen to the portion of a recording of *Joseph and the Amazing Technicolor Dreamcoat* (by Andrew Lloyd Webber and Tim Rice) that relates to each of the acts. *Option:* Students can create drawings of the story's events in ways that imitate the Egyptian style of artwork after exploring books and the Internet to see how Egyptians illustrated their history in painted artwork and stone carvings. Take note of the ways in which the Egyptian artists drew the human body and how they filled their paintings with decorative designs of trees, flowers, and animals. *Option:* Egyptians sometimes wrote the names of their rulers in an upright, narrow oval called a "cartouche" (pronounced kar-TOOSH), filled with symbols to illustrate the name's meaning. Students can research the way different Egyptian names, such as "Tutankhamen," were written in a cartouche. Scholars are unsure of the meaning of Joseph's Egyptian name, "Zaphenath-paneah," but some have suggested that it may mean "The God speaks; he lives." Such a meaning could indicate Pharaoh's acknowledgement of Joseph's powerful, living God, who warned of the future in Pharaoh's dreams. Have students design symbols and a cartouche for Joseph's Egyptian name.

Searching Further

In Genesis 49, as Jacob (also called "Israel") neared death, he gathered his sons around him and gave his blessing to each one. His prophetic words tell something about the future of each son and of the Israelite tribe that will be descended from that son. Even though Reuben, Simeon, and Levi are the first three sons according to birth, they do not receive the blessing of promise. All three had grievously sinned against the Lord. Reuben slept with his father's concubine Bilhah (Genesis 35:22), and Simeon and Levi brought trouble to the family by murdering the citizens of Shechem in revenge for the rape of their sister, Dinah (34:30). The promise first given to Abraham, that the Messiah would be born into his family, is passed on through Judah, the fourth son. Read Judah's blessing in Genesis 49:8–12. Judah is described as a lion, ruling his family. "The scepter shall not depart from Judah" (v. 10) until the One is born to whom it rightfully belongs. In Revelation 5:5, Jesus is called "the Lion of the tribe of Judah." He conquered sin and death and reigns as King! The scepter promised to Judah belongs to Him.

Critical thinking

Obedience to the Eighth Commandment calls us to speak well of others instead of telling lies about them or speaking in hurtful ways. Bullying is a serious problem among students of all ages, especially those in their preteen and teenage years. Difficulties at home or school, low self-esteem, and teasing are among the issues that cause some students to belittle and bully others in a futile effort to build themselves up. Discuss the problem of bullying with your students. What can they do if they see someone else being teased or hurt by a bully? What can they say to stop the situation? To whom should they report the incident? Is there some way they can reach out in kindness to the bully, helping him or her to learn better ways of relating to others? Obeying God's Commandments is not only about avoiding what is wrong, but also about doing what is right. As Christians, we can express the love of Jesus by showing love and kindness to others.

Bringing it home

Sibling relationships often provide the circumstances for jealousy and hurtful words, just as such relationships did in the story of Joseph. A young sister is hurt because her idolized older sister ignores her. The older sister is annoyed by her younger sibling's constant attempts to follow and imitate her. A son becomes jealous of the attention that parents give to his brother. Discuss relationships like these with your students. Even those students with no brothers and sisters have very likely experienced similar problems within their friendships. The Eighth and Tenth Commandments apply to our relationships with family and friends. Help your students to see that they can extend the love and forgiveness we have received from Jesus, our Savior, to the members of their family and to their friends!

UNIT 1—BEGINNINGS AND PATRIARCHS

LESSON 11

Job
THE BOOK OF JOB

Background

When we experience trouble, it is not unusual to ask, "Why me? What did I do to deserve this?" The Book of Job addresses those common questions, but it begins with a very different question, as Satan challenges God concerning the faithful and wealthy Job: "Does Job fear God for no reason?" (1:9). Satan suggests that Job is faithful only because God has blessed him. Take away those blessings, Satan challenges, and Job will curse God. God permits Satan to afflict Job with disaster and illness, but not to take his life. Job's friends come to comfort him in his distress, each offering an explanation for the trouble that has come upon him. Throughout the testing, Job remains faithful, looking with hope for his Redeemer. Job does maintain his innocence, protesting that he does not deserve what has happened to him. Finally, God Himself enters the discussion, silencing every argument with question after question, revealing a divine majesty that is beyond human understanding. Even faithful Job falls silent, realizing that his claims of innocence cannot stand before the power of his Creator. Evil, trouble, illness, and disaster are the result of sin in the world; yet, behind it all, God remains in control of His creation. He does not cause evil; yet, for reasons beyond our human understanding, He permits it, as He permitted Satan to afflict Job. Yet even that evil—as seen in the testing of Job—can be bent to His purpose. At one point, Job asks God, "Do You see as man sees?" Yes, God has seen as man sees. God took on human flesh in the person of Jesus Christ and suffered the penalty for our sins. It is for Jesus' sake, and not because of our imagined innocence, that God blesses us with life and forgiveness.

Central Truth

Evil is the result of sin in this world (don't blame God); God blesses us out of His own goodness for Christ's sake (don't take credit for yourself).

Objectives
- Differentiate the consequences of sin and evil in this world from the actions of God, which are always just and holy.
- Believe, even during times of trouble, that God is near and able to bless us.
- Live in obedience to the Lord—not to *obtain* salvation, but rather because we *have* salvation, through Christ alone.

Materials
- Hymnals and music CDs
- Reproducible 11

Bible Prep
Post in advance so students can bookmark the reference before class time.
- The Book of Job

Devotions

Lucas was really mad at God. Barker was Lucas's best friend. Sure, Barker had been old for a dog, but not *that* old. Why did his dog have to die? Barker used to sleep beside Lucas's bed. He was always waiting at the door when Lucas came home from school. He would lie down behind Lucas's chair at dinner. On the weekends, Lucas and Barker would hike in the woods and run around the park. Why did God have to take Barker away? That's what Lucas asked his dad one night. Dad answered, "There is sin in this world. Because the whole world and everything God created is hurt by sin, people—and animals too—grow old, get sick, and die. Barker didn't do anything wrong, but because he is part of the sinful world, he suffered along with it." "Why doesn't God stop that?" asked Lucas. "Why doesn't He *do* something about it?" Dad said, "He *has* done something about it. God Himself came into the world, and He suffered the same pain and trouble that we experience." "You mean Jesus," said Lucas. "That's right," said his dad. "Jesus died on the cross. He never did anything wrong, but He was punished for our sins so that we can be forgiven. We still experience sin and trouble now, and we are still tempted and disobey God. But when Jesus rose from the dead, He defeated death and sin. Those things can't hurt us or keep us away from God." "But why did Barker have to die *now*?" asked Lucas. His dad replied, "We don't know why God allowed Barker to die right now. But we can trust God and know that His reasons are best, even when we don't understand why things happen. Jesus loves you, and He knows how much you loved Barker. You can be sure of that."

Let's pray: Jesus, help us to trust You, even when things happen that we do not understand. Help us to focus on Your greatness and goodness to us. Amen. Sing "O Blessed, Holy Trinity" (*LSB* 876; recorded as *Hymn of the Season for grade 6, Christian Education Month*). Praise God with the words of Psalm 100.

INTO the lesson

Establish the setting of the Book of Job. Say, **We don't know the exact "where" and "when" of today's Bible narrative. It most likely took place around the time of Abraham, during the time of the patriarchs. It is also most likely that this took place in the area of the Mideast where most people lived at that time. This would be the area of modern-day Israel, Iraq, or Iran, an area often called the "cradle of civilization."**

The story begins with a conversation between God and Satan, who challenges God with some questions. God has pointed out that Job is an example of a godly man who honors the Lord and turns away from evil. Satan replies, "Does Job fear God for no reason?" In other words, Satan is saying that *of course* Job loves God, because God has been so good to him and blessed him so much. Satan issues the challenge, saying that if God took away all those blessings, Job would curse God. Then God, in effect, says, "Let's see who is right," and He allows Satan to turn against Job. This is important to remember: God allowed Satan to cause disaster in Job's life; the Lord Himself *never* causes evil. Continue by exploring the activities in the Student Book.

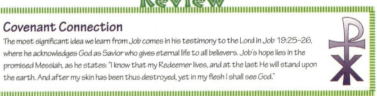

INTO the Word

Disaster

Discuss not only the totality of Job's tragedies, but also the timing—one right after the other. Point out: **Most people would say, "Why is this happening to me? Why did God do this to me? It's so unfair—I'm a good person." Instead, Job responds, "The L**ORD** gave, and the L**ORD** has taken away; blessed be the name of the L**ORD**" (Job 1:21). Job recognized that all the blessings he had were gifts from God and that Job did not deserve any of them; no one does, because we are all sinners. Job focused on the greatness of God rather than on his own despair. His trust remained firm.**

As we see how Job struggles with what is happening in his life, we can learn about the trouble that comes into our lives. We can learn, with Job, to trust God, even when we don't understand why things happen. We live in a sinful world filled with trouble and pain, and we experience things that we don't understand. Sometimes we think we don't deserve things that happen to us. But God loves us and sent His Son to save us, and that was something we certainly did not deserve. God watches over us and cares for us, and, as Job will learn, we can trust God in everything that happens.

Conversations

The organizational pattern for the Book of Job is *Prologue, Dialogue,* and *Epilogue*. Most of the book is dialogue—conversations. The first two chapters are prologue—setting up the events of the story. The last chapter is the epilogue—telling what happened after the conversations.

As you work together on the Student Book activity, point out how these statements are representative of the flow of the conversations in the story. Job's wife and his three friends (Eliphaz, Bildad, and Zophar) blame Job for his troubles, saying that this is a punishment for his sins. Job says they are no comfort—and they are no better than he is. Then we have a turning point. Elihu speaks up. He had hesitated to speak earlier because he is younger than the others and thought they would be wiser (32:6); but he is angry at Job for trying to justify himself rather than focusing on God as a just God, and he is angry at the three friends because blaming Job is not the answer (vv. 2–3). After this, God speaks of His own greatness and goodness as the Creator of all things, and He asks why the created ones would question their Creator. Job falls silent; he has nothing to say when faced with

Deliverance

Describe how God delivered Job. (See Job 42:10, 12–13, 16.) <u>God blessed Job with 10 more children, and God made him twice as rich as before. He lived 140 more years.</u>

God is with us today too. Here are some of the ways God delivers us today.

1. God can give His help directly to us, even in a miraculous way.
2. God can bless us with other people and methods to help us in our need.
3. God can help us cope and live with a problem that doesn't seem to go away.
4. God will remove all pain and problems when He takes all believers to heaven, through the salvation we have by faith in the death and resurrection of Jesus, which He offers in grace and mercy.

Conclusions

God Creates — Remember: Don't blame God for evil in this world; He does not cause it.

Satan Destroys — Remember: Don't take credit yourself for good; recognize good as a blessing from God.

We Sin

Jesus Saves — Focus on God's greatness: "The Lord gave, and the Lord has taken away; blessed be the name of the Lord" (Job 1:21).

Remember

"For My thoughts are not your thoughts, neither are your ways My ways, declares the LORD." (Isaiah 55:8)

God's overwhelming power. Then Job replies in humility and repentance, realizing that which is also true for us: we are blessed *for Christ's sake*, not because of our own goodness.

Review

We deserve to be punished for our sins. The Good News is that God does not give us what we deserve. He sent Jesus, our Redeemer, to suffer the punishment that we deserve. Because Jesus died on the cross, our sins are forgiven. Even death cannot defeat us, because Jesus rose from the dead to defeat death. When Jesus returns on the Last Day, we will be raised from death, and like Job, we will see our Redeemer!

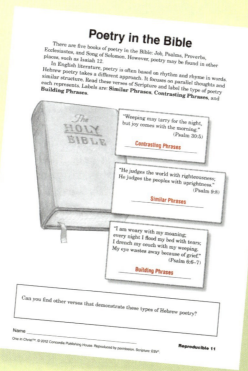

INTO our lives

Deliverance

Discuss with the entire class some of the ways God continues to deliver us today. (1) Sometimes we don't even recognize God's direct hand in our lives, attributing it to "good luck" when it really is God's grace. (2) Doctors, firefighters, parents, and the tools they use are blessings from God through which He works to rescue us. Pray for God's guidance of these people and methods, recognizing that these are gifts from God. (3) We don't understand why, but sometimes, God does not choose to remove a problem. We must trust that He knows all things and does what is best, and at the right time. He may have a purpose that we never recognize, but we trust that He will help us live with or adjust to the difficulty as we rely on Him. (4) We can be certain that eventually all troubles will be gone, because we are assured of life in heaven through the promise of our Savior. (See Revelation 21:4.)

For further study on this subject, look at 1 Corinthians 10:13 (where Scripture says we will not be troubled more than we can stand); 2 Corinthians 1:3–4 (God comforts us in our afflictions so we can understand and do the same for other people); and 2 Corinthians 12:7–10 (we can ask, but we will not always get what we want because God's grace is sufficient—it is enough for what we need).

Conclusions

This last lesson in Unit 1 brings us full circle back to the first lesson in the unit. The story of creation and the fall and the story of Job relate particularly to the First Commandment. Point out that the larger box in the Student Book could serve as an outline for both stories. In Lesson 1, we learned that God created all things by His mighty power; in the story of Job, God proclaims His goodness and power in all that He created, and therefore we should not question Him. Satan is a key figure in both lessons as he causes evil; the weakest element in both stories is humankind; people are lowly sinners, undeserving of God's grace and mercy. Yet, in both lessons—and throughout our lives—we see that God continues to bless us, particularly through the promise of the Messiah and its fulfillment in Christ Jesus.

Briefly discuss the other concluding statements that review key points of the lesson. *Option:* You may want to explore the fact that the Book of Job is a book of Hebrew poetry by studying Reproducible 11. This explains that Hebrew poetry (as in Psalms and Proverbs) is not like English poetry. It does not have parallel sounds (rhymes); instead, it has parallel ideas (similar or contrasting).

Lesson Support

Bringing it home

In the Book of Job, God speaks to Job from a whirlwind, asking question after question concerning His divine power and majesty. We are humbled along with Job as we consider God's creative power reflected in earth, sea, and sky. Students can involve their classmates and families in projects to study and preserve the gift of God's creation. List the names of the animals mentioned in Job 38–41, where God shares His delight in the wonderful things He has created. Use the Internet and other sources to find pictures and information on each of these. (*Note:* The "Behemoth" mentioned in 40:15 is thought to be a hippopotamus, and the "Leviathan" in 41:1 is thought to be a crocodile.) Perhaps students can work together to make PowerPoint presentations of the information and illustrations they have found. Use Psalm 104 to praise God for the many magnificent features of His creation.

A helpful resource is the 2010 book *Together with All Creatures: Caring for God's Living Earth*, produced by the Commission on Theology and Church Relations of the Lutheran Church—Missouri Synod. The book in both its longer and shorter formats is available from the Synod's Web site (www.lcms.org/514). The book offers many suggestions for study and conservation projects, including the identification of local plants and animals, learning about endangered species and their habitats, and creating community gardens. Ideas are suggested for individuals, families, churches, and schools.

Check it Out

Satan challenged God with the question "Does Job fear God for no reason?" Satan believed that Job only trusted God because God had blessed him. Satan thought Job was faithful because there was something to be gained by it. Satan's challenge is really a very old question and one common to sin in all its forms: "What's in it for me?" Satan used that temptation in the garden of Eden, showing Eve what could be gained by eating the forbidden fruit, and Eve then saw "that the tree was to be desired to make one wise" (Genesis 3:6). Satan tempts us to think that sin will lead to gain for ourselves, when in reality, sin results in the loss of human relationships and our relationship with God. It was our Redeemer, Jesus Christ, who, although He had everything to gain for Himself, gave up everything, even His life, for us. The apostle Paul writes that Jesus "made Himself nothing, taking the form of a servant" and "humbled Himself by becoming obedient to the point of death, even death on a cross" (Philippians 2:7–8). Jesus' loss is our eternal gain!

Curriculum Connection

Confronted with Job's terrible suffering, Job's friends constructed theories about why God allowed it to happen. Since they were familiar with the idea of punishment following sin, they supposed that this dynamic was at work in Job's case. But they were wrong, because in mathematical terms, Job was what is called an "outlier"—a piece of data that is very different from the majority of cases. Help your students learn about central tendency and outliers using section 6.5.3, "Data Affecting Measures of Central Tendency." You can find this in the sixth grade Math volume of the Concordia Curriculum Guide series.

HANDS TO SERVE

Have your students create cards for residents of nursing homes, for people in the hospital, or for shut-ins from your own congregation. Students can write messages of comfort and hope in their cards, telling people about the love of Jesus and leaving room for the residents to write their own greetings. Provide envelopes so the cards can be mailed. Parents may be willing to donate stamps as part of the gift. (Note that it is good to send cards to those in nursing homes; but it is also important to provide cards that they can send to others, especially since they may no longer be able to shop for such purchases.) Talk to your pastor or a local nursing home or hospital to arrange a visit from your students. Your class can deliver their handmade notes, sing songs, and greet the residents. Share the love of Jesus, the Redeemer, with those who are lonely!

Faith in Action

Job suffered pain and loss. Many people around us today suffer from hunger, from illness, or from the loss of their homes. If space and weather permit, students could start a garden, donating the vegetables and herbs raised to a food bank or similar charity. Find ways to help your students offer comfort and hope in the name of Christ.

Unit 2—To the Promised Land

Theme

This unit follows the people of Israel from slavery in Egypt, through the desert wilderness, and into the Promised Land of Canaan. We will see the weakness and sinfulness of the people who continually complain, fail to trust God, and fall away from Him. In these people we also see ourselves, for we, too, are sinners. However, we rejoice in God's unconditional love, a love that is not based on what we do, but on what the Lord Himself does for us through Jesus, our Savior. Though these are Old Testament stories, they always direct us to our need for the Savior and God's great promises fulfilled in Him. We will also see the Gospel in these stories because all of Scripture points to Jesus; each lesson has a "Covenant Connection" that relates the Bible narrative to the promise of the Messiah. In this unit, you will also find a subtheme: as you study the Old Testament Church on the move, you will also study the Church of the Reformation, as we lead up to the celebration of Reformation Day on October 31. The Reformation occurred in the sixteenth century, and it reminds us that, though the Church continues to have problems because it consists of sinful people, God's Word endures. God continues to raise up leaders to speak the truth of the Gospel. The one constant throughout history is the grace of God in Christ Jesus!

Worship

Each lesson in this curriculum has a classroom devotion that you may read to students during the opening of your day. (The devotions always have a direct connection to the day's Bible lesson. If you already have an established plan for opening devotions, you can still use the one suggested in the Teacher Guide as an introduction to the lesson.) It is suggested that your devotions this month include the reading of Psalm 46, a psalm of reliance on God, and also the psalm on which Luther's hymn of the Reformation, "A Mighty Fortress Is Our God," was based. Each month, a different Psalm of the Month will be suggested. You will probably notice that, through frequent use, most students will know the psalm by memory by the end of the month. (Putting the psalm to use is a much more effective means for memorization than as an assignment.) By the end of the school year, your students will have a basic understanding of many key psalms. Though you can feel free to choose a variety of hymns and songs, suggestions will be made mostly from the *LSB* hymnal and the *AGPS* songbook. It will always be noted if the hymns are on the recorded set of *Hymns of the Month* or *Hymns of the Season* CDs, available from CPH, which will give students a good background in Christian hymnody and will also help them to more readily participate in church worship services. Note that the CPH recording *Jesus' People Sing! (JPS)* consists of fifty songs, all from *AGPS*.

Resources

A key resource for this curriculum can be found on the One in Christ Portal. Individual lessons will be listed there, providing downloadable reproducibles, links to other Web sites, interactive whiteboard applications, slides, and other resources for the lesson of the day. Each unit will also have a listing of available materials related to the unit as a whole, such as a list of the Bible memory verses for the unit, a letter to make available to parents (by print or online), and a unit test. These last three items and the reproducibles are also available in print in the *Teacher Resource Book*. The unit tests are mostly multiple-choice tests that provide immediate feedback to the student and are self-correcting for the teacher. You can give the test to the whole class at once or to smaller groups in your computer lab, if available. If you have only one computer available, you can have students sign up to take the test during study periods, or they can be printed out. Unit 2 on-print test answers are (1) c; (2) b; (3) b; (4) a; (5) c; (6) a; (7) b; (8) d; (9) b; (10) c. Note that the titles of this unit's lessons are listed in the column above to give you an overview of the material covered in this unit. On the next page, you will find an illustration of a bulletin board for this unit, available from CPH, and an explanation of how to use it. There is also a section for ideas on exploring the content of the books of the Bible over the course of the year.

Unit 2

12. The Call of Moses
13. Plagues and Passover
14. Holding Up the Prophet's Hands
15. Moses and Jethro
16. The Tent Church
17. Korah's Rebellion
18. Water at Meribah
19. Balaam
20. God's People Build a Monument
21. The Fall of Jericho
22. Deborah and Barak
23. Samson

Bulletin Board

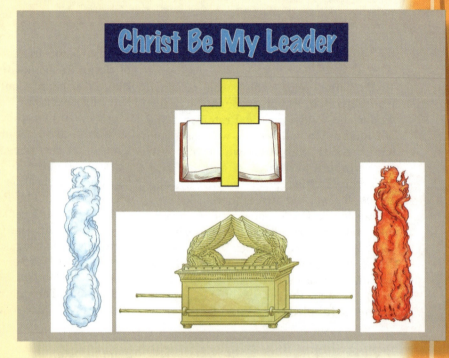

This bulletin board is available, ready to cut out and pin up, from CPH. There will be a bulletin board available for each unit/month, which focuses on the unit's theme. This one presents a basic message that is essential to this unit. Jesus leads us (takes us) to the promised land (heaven) through His death on the cross and resurrection. He sends the Holy Spirit, working through the Word of God, to bring us to faith and to enable us to live in faith as followers of Jesus. So why do we also have the Old Testament symbols on this bulletin board that is about Christ Jesus? While it is true that God was leading the people of Israel to the Promised Land of Canaan by day in the cloud and by night in the pillar of fire, consider that God was acting on His covenant promises—therefore the name "ark of the covenant," pictured here as a golden box. A covenant is an agreement and a promise. The Lord said, "I will be your God, and you will be My people." That was the agreement. The covenant promise was the promise of the Messiah. It is Jesus—the Messiah—who takes away our sins and makes us people of God. He completed our part of the agreement. So the Old Testament and New Testament are totally connected by the covenant, and that covenant is fulfilled in Christ Jesus. All of Scripture directs sinners to the Savior!

Bible Book Overview

The Student Book Appendix has a valuable feature that gives a summary of each book of the Bible. Looking at the summaries of sixty-six books can be overwhelming, so it is suggested that each month/unit, your class look at the summaries of just a few of these books. Remind students that you have been looking at the first five books of the Bible, which are often called "the Books of Moses," because God inspired Moses to write down what had been passed down orally. Unit 2 will continue with stories from this portion of the Old Testament, but will also venture into the next section of historical books. This section covers the period of the judges who led the people of Israel as God directed them in their new homeland. The books are Joshua, Judges, Ruth, and 1 and 2 Samuel. Samuel was the last of the judges; he was also a prophet and a priest. Samuel was the judge who anointed the first two kings, Saul and David. Read together and discuss the summaries of these five books in the Student Book Appendix when you have available time. (Note that a copy of the Student Book Appendix is included in the back of this Teacher Guide.)

Unit 2—To the Promised Land

Lesson 12

The Call of Moses
Exodus 1–4

Background

Moses' encounter with God is significant in many ways. This is the first time God tells His personal name, "YHWH," to a human being. The name is related to the Hebrew verb "to be" and can be translated "I am" (the phrase used by Jesus so often!) or "I will be what I will be."

The encounter is also notable for God's gentleness and patience with Moses. Instead of a spectacular, frightening display, God allows a bush that is burning in an odd way to attract the shepherd Moses' attention. When Moses comes over to see, God speaks to him and immediately identifies Himself as "the God of your father" (Exodus 3:6), the same familiar God Moses had always worshiped. When Moses tries to back out of God's plan, God promises to be with him and help him speak, gives him miraculous credentials to present to anyone who doubts him, and finally offers him a helper and encourager, Moses' own brother, Aaron.

It is interesting to see that Moses does not *want* to become God's chosen rescuer for His people. Forty years earlier, Moses had tried to protect the Israelites by force; this resulted in him having to flee from Pharaoh as a murderer. Now, at age 80, all Moses wants is to be left alone to live as a shepherd. It is at this time in his life, not earlier, that God judges him ready to serve as rescuer and shepherd of Israel. God has prepared Moses so that now he can challenge the Pharaoh—but not with human weapons. He will indeed be a shepherd in the wilderness—not of sheep, but of God's chosen people.

Central Truth
God has a plan for our lives and prepares us for His good purposes.

Objectives
- Moses tried to say no to God, but God was determined, having prepared Moses as a child in faith in a godly home, in the ways of Egypt as a young man, and as an adult to lead his people through the desert.
- Recognize that God calls us too—to hear His Word, to repent, and to live in service to others.
- Respect God and His Word as we worship Him, our almighty and only true God.

Materials
- Hymnals and music CDs
- Web Resource 12a
- Reproducible 12

Bible Prep
Post in advance so students can bookmark references before class time.
- Exodus 3:1–4:17
- Acts 2:38
- John 13:34–35
- Matthew 28:20
- Isaiah 41:13

Devotions

Anthony sat down at the lunch table with a bunch of other sixth graders. Marcy said, "What's up, Anthony? You look kind of grumpy." Anthony replied, "Oh, it's just that my great-aunt Martha is coming to visit us this weekend. I know the first question she'll ask me: 'What do you want to be when you grow up?' I hear that all the time." "What's wrong with that?" asked Rachel. "I get that from people all the time too. They are just showing an interest in you." Anthony shrugged and said, "I just never have a good answer for her. Sometimes I want to be a lawyer, and other times, I want to build rides for amusement parks, and then I think it would be great to be a cowboy and ride horses or jeeps all over." Marcy interrupted, "You know, you don't have to decide now. My dad was a TV reporter. He studied that at college. But after a few years, he changed his mind, went back to school, and now, you know, he's a pastor. People can change their careers and occupations." Jason joined the conversation, saying, "Marcy's right. In the Bible, Moses was eighty years old when *he* changed from being a shepherd to a leader of a nation! All of those years, God had a plan for Moses and was preparing him for that purpose." Anthony asked, "Do you think God has a plan for me?" "I know He does," said Rachel. "And part of that plan is that God wants you to be a servant." "Not me!" exclaimed Anthony. "That sounds like a lot of hard work with very little pay." Jason broke in, "I think Rachel is talking about your *purpose*, not your job. Whatever jobs we may have, now or someday in the future, God wants us to do them in a way that serves other people and also gives glory to God." "How can a lawyer be a servant of God?" asked Anthony. "That's easy," replied Marcy. "He or she can be honest and fair." "And," Jason added, "a person who builds amusement parks can serve others by ensuring that people are safe on all the rides." Anthony chimed in, "I get it now. Whatever we do, we can do it for the Lord, showing loving kindness to others." That's a very important part of God's plan and purpose for each one of us! Give glory to God now by saying together the words of Psalm 46. Sing "Make Me a Servant" (*AGPS* 174; recorded on *JPS*).

57

INTO the lesson

Say, **Before we can study today's Bible story about the call of Moses, we need to find out how we got to this point in time. How did we get from Genesis to Exodus? In Genesis, we learned that God chose the family of Abraham, Isaac, and Jacob to be His special people. Jacob's son Joseph rescued the family during a famine by bringing them to Egypt, where the Pharaoh—the king—gave them the best land for raising sheep** (Genesis 47:5–6).

Over the years, this family of seventy people grew to be a large nation of hundreds of thousands of people. In time, Joseph was forgotten, new kings came and went, and a new Pharaoh came to power who was afraid that this large nation of Israel would join forces with Egypt's enemies. So in order to control them, the Egyptians made the Hebrew people their slaves. God heard the prayers of the oppressed people and created a plan to rescue them.

Before we can study the Bible story, we also need to find out how Moses got to this point. Throughout Moses' life, God was preparing him for one main purpose: to rescue the people of Israel. God protected Moses as a baby so that from his earliest childhood years, his family could teach him about the true Lord God. (See Exodus 1:22–2:9.) **When Moses was no longer a little child, he was raised in an Egyptian palace, instructed there in the Egyptian language and customs and the procedures of the royal palace. There was still more for Moses to learn, though, and God worked through events in Moses' life to teach him how to survive and live in the desert. Even though Moses was unaware of this plan and purpose, God knew that the time had come for His plan to be set in motion.**

Use Web Resource 12a to review these concepts. Then continue with the Bible story, using the Student Book and the Bible (Exodus 3:1–4:17).

LESSON 12

The Call of Moses

God Gives Moses a Purpose in Life

God had an excellent plan for Moses. He prepared Moses, saving him when he was a baby so he could be raised in a God-fearing Hebrew home. Then God prepared Moses to know the ways, language, and customs of Egypt as he grew up in the house of Pharaoh's daughter. Later, it was time for more training, as God led Moses to learn how to survive in the desert while tending sheep in Midian. Finally, when the time was right, God revealed Himself to Moses on Mount Sinai through a bush that seemed to be burning but was not being consumed by the fire. God gave Moses a calling, a purpose: to lead the people of Israel out of Egypt to the Promised Land. (See Exodus 3:1–10.) But at first, Moses did not want this task.

Moses Says No!

Look up the four times Moses said no to God and tell what excuses Moses gave.

a. Exodus 3:11 — I'm not a leader; I'm unimportant (no confidence).

b. Exodus 4:1 — The people will not listen to me or believe me.

c. Exodus 4:10 — I am not good at speaking.

d. Exodus 4:13 — Please send someone else.

Review

Covenant Connection

God made an unexpected choice for a leader—an eighty-year-old shepherd named Moses—to lead His people to the Promised Land in Canaan. This foreshadows the coming of the Messiah: Jesus was not what most people expected. Even though God continually revealed more and more about the Messiah through the prophets, the people were not expecting a Savior who would die on a cross. But that was exactly God's plan for leading us to the promised land in heaven!

INTO the Word

God Gives Moses a Purpose in Life

Refer again to the title of this lesson, "The Call of Moses." **This obviously is not talking about a phone call, because Moses lived thousands of years ago.** *Call* **can also mean "to speak loudly or directly"; God did speak to Moses, but we are searching for a different definition of the word** *call.* **A** *call* **or** *calling* **can be a person's occupation or career, but it is usually more than that. A calling is your specialty, the purpose that motivates what you do, or your mission in life. One man described it this way: "My** *career* is flying jet planes; my *calling* is to share the love of God with others." **God calls on us to be His people; He calls us to repentance and faith and to new life in Jesus.**

God caught Moses' attention with a bush that was on fire, yet was not burning up. Explore how God presented Himself to Moses and called him to lead the Israelites out of slavery. The activity in this section may be completed individually, although it would be more effective if students worked in small groups.

Point out that Moses is overwhelmed; he has poor self-esteem, and just seems too afraid. He starts making excuses for not "taking on the proj-

God Says Yes!

How did God reply to each refusal?

a. Exodus 3:12, 15 God would be with Moses as He had been with Abraham, Isaac, and Jacob.
b. Exodus 4:2–9 God equipped Moses with miraculous signs.
c. Exodus 4:11–12 God would tell Moses what to say.
d. Exodus 4:14–17 God would send a helper—Moses' brother, Aaron.

God Gives You a Purpose in Life

Some people think their purpose in life is to get rich and do whatever they want. That is not how God sees it—He has a purpose for you that will bring true joy. "For I know the plans I have for you, declares the LORD, plans for welfare and not for evil, to give you a future and a hope" (Jeremiah 29:11). God calls you to this purpose—to believe and to serve.

God's Will for My Life

Acts 2:38 Repent and be baptized in the name of Jesus Christ.
John 13:34–35 Love one another, serving in kindness.

God's Promises for My Life

Matthew 28:20 He is always with us.
Isaiah 41:13 He holds our hand, ready to help us.

Remember

[God has] "saved us and called us to a holy calling, not because of our works but because of His own purpose and grace, which He gave us in Christ Jesus." (2 Timothy 1:9)

31

---

ect." Emphasize God's patient answers to every excuse Moses gives. (See the top of the Student Book page.) God enables and empowers Moses by offering His presence, miraculous signs, and help from others to aid Moses with his task. Finally, in Exodus 4:14, not only the bush is on fire, for the Lord's anger is kindled against Moses after all his excuses. Yet God still offers another excellent solution. Now Moses has run out of excuses, but he also feels more capable at this juncture. Ask the class if this sounds familiar to anyone. We also often make excuses and reach a point where there just aren't any more reasons to deny God's plan for our lives. At this point, begin the next section of the lesson, in which students will discuss their callings from the Lord.

INTO our lives

God Gives You a Purpose in Life

Before starting this section of the Student Book, look at the illustration and ask, **Why is there a fire on this page? I can understand the fire on the burning bush that Moses saw. What does a flame symbolize for you and me? What does this have to do with you and me?** Guide the discussion to consider another important time when a nonconsuming fire appeared in Scripture. This would be on the day of Pentecost in Acts 2. Point out that a flame gets your attention—it got Moses's attention and it also got the attention of the disciples gathered on Pentecost Day. One of the most significant things about fire is that it changes things (e.g., fire on a grill changes a slab of raw meat into a delicious steak). Discuss why a flame is a good symbol for the Holy Spirit: **What change does the Holy Spirit make in us? (He brings us to faith in Christ Jesus as our Savior and empowers us to live as people of God.) The disciples on Pentecost Day were "fired up" to speak the Gospel, glorify God, and serve others. God calls on us to be His disciples today; He blesses us with the Holy Spirit, who transforms our lives so that we can be "fired up" to serve God and to serve other people!** Continue by examining God's plan for us as guided by the text in the Student Book. Reproducible 12 may also be used at this time.

Be sure to look at the Lesson Support page, which gives important ideas for examining the life of Martin Luther and how God worked His will and purpose through him. Since you will most likely be teaching this unit during October, use the suggested ideas throughout the month to focus on the celebration of the Reformation on October 31. Also keep in mind that the year 2017 is the five hundredth anniversary of the Reformation, and celebrations will be held worldwide at that time.

59

Lesson Support

Technology

As you begin a study of Martin Luther, it is important to see the times in context. God works through history to bless His people and spread His message. Many converging factors led to the Reformation at that time in history. This was a time of change that supported the growth and spread of the Reformation. Have student groups explore these topics: (1) The changing from a feudal system with serfs, knights, and castles to the development of cities, trades, and a business (or middle) class. (2) The secular power of the Roman Catholic Church and of the Holy Roman Empire. (3) The height of the Renaissance (which encouraged new ideas and new explorations in many fields, leading people to also be more receptive to new thinking about the Church). (4) The impact of widening travel, new horizons, new inventions (particularly the printing press, useful in spreading the ideas of the Reformation). (5) The monastic life that Luther lived and left. (6) Luther's predecessors (he was not the first person to challenge the leadership of the Church; people who came before him, such as Savanarola, laid the groundwork, so that when the time was right, and according to God's plan, the Reformation would grow and have a profound effect). The Reformation was not an accident or random occurrence—God was working throughout history, preparing people to learn, speak, and share the truths of God's Word.

Searching Further

Relate today's Bible story to a study of Martin Luther. The main similarity between Moses and Luther is that God had a momentous purpose in the life of each man that would be a blessing to God's people. There are other parallels and contrasts that are interesting to note. Moses lived about fifteen hundred years *before* Christ Jesus; Martin Luther lived about fifteen hundred years *after* Jesus. Moses wrote some of the books of the Bible (the first five—the Pentateuch, or "Books of the Law"). Martin Luther wrote *about* the Bible and its interpretation. Emphasize that Martin Luther is not in the Bible, but he helped us to understand the truths that are in God's Word. Moses was called to serve God in a dramatic manner, as God spoke through the burning bush. Some people may consider the dramatic story of Luther promising to become a monk during a terrible lightning storm to be his moment of calling, but his cries to St. Anne would have gone unheard. God worked through all the events of Luther's life, but his moment of being called to his life's purpose came not through a burning bush or a lightning strike, but through the Word of God. While studying Scripture, Luther read the words "the righteous shall live by faith" (Habakkuk 2:4; Romans 1:17; Galatians 3:11) and came to realize that there is nothing we can do to be saved; all depends on the grace of God, which we have by faith, not by works. We are saved by God's actions alone. This turning point gave Luther his purpose for his life, focusing on the three pillars of Christianity (and the Reformation), which are *sola gratia*, *sola Scriptura*, and *sola fide*—we are saved by grace alone, through God's Word alone, by faith alone. It is all God's doing in Christ Jesus. As Moses' life purpose was epic in clarifying the Law of God for the people, Luther's life purpose was epic in clarifying the Gospel. (*Note:* this does not mean Law and Gospel were exclusive to each other's teachings, as both taught about our sin and God's grace; this is merely a comparison of emphasis.)

Check it Out

The year 2017 will be (or was, depending on when you read this) the worldwide celebration of the five hundredth anniversary of the Reformation. The Reformation, beginning on October 31, 1517, had an enormous effect on world history. However, as Christians and as Lutherans, we have particular reason to rejoice at how God worked through Luther and these events to bring a clearer understanding of God's Word. Be aware of special publications that will be developed at this time. Even the leader of the Roman Catholic Church, Pope Benedict XVI, has stated that Luther was correct in his emphasis on Scripture and that we have salvation through the grace of God. The pope recognizes that the Reformation had an impact on the Roman Catholic Church too (which was Luther's original intent), and the pope would, therefore, encourage Catholics to be part of this celebration. It is important to recognize that this is not an "us against them" kind of celebration. The focus should be on God and the truth of His Word; Luther was just God's tool. While we still do not agree with some of the doctrinal practices of the Roman Catholic Church, we do want to have friendly, positive, and open communication, praying that God will use this observance to further enlighten His people and His Church about the saving truth of Christ Jesus.

(As you study these events, you will see sinful things happening in the Church, such as the corruption among some members of the Church hierarchy preceding the Reformation and the excesses of violent change by extremist reformers afterward. Emphasize that the evil comes from sinful mankind and not from God and His Church. Because people are sinful, there have been and continue to be human errors in the interpretation and application of God's Word. Pray that God will guide us to understand and live His Word in its truth and purity.)

Unit 2—To the Promised Land

Lesson 13

Plagues and Passover
Exodus 7–12

Central Truth

There is one true God—one Ruler over all—who delivers His people from evil, especially the great evil of sin.

Objectives

- Recognize that when we love, trust, or depend on anything more than God, we are sinning.
- Rejoice that God delivers us from the greatest evil (sin) through the death and resurrection of Jesus.
- Worship the Lord as we are blessed by the Means of Grace.

Materials

- Hymnals and music CDs
- Reproducible 13a and 13b
- Yellow highlighters
- Web Resource 13a

Bible Prep

Post in advance so students can bookmark references before class time.

- Exodus 7–12
- Galatians 5
- Jeremiah 31:31–34
- Matthew 26:26–28

Background

After 430 years in Egypt, the Israelite slaves had almost forgotten God. But God showed that He had not forgotten His people. Throughout the ten plagues, God took aim at the oppressors of His people, and in particular, at their gods. The Egyptians worshiped many gods, including the sun god Ra; cow-headed Hathor; the goddess Heket, who was depicted with the head of a frog; and Seth, the god of storms. The true God brought upon them plagues that made it clear that these "gods" were no gods at all—darkness for three days, sickness and death for their cattle, millions of frogs, a hailstorm so dangerous that anyone outside in it died. And yet, the Lord protected His own people, Israel. And the final plague, the death of the firstborn, made it clear that none of Egypt's gods or powers could stand against the Lord: "For I will pass through the land of Egypt that night, and I will strike all the firstborn in the land of Egypt, both man and beast; and on all the gods of Egypt I will execute judgments: I am the Lord" (Exodus 12:12). To ensure that Israel would never forget God's deliverance, the Lord instituted the Passover meal. At the center of this celebration was a sacrificed lamb, whose blood was instrumental in saving the Israelite families that first Passover night. Many years later, God sent the true Lamb of God, His own Son, Jesus, who poured out His blood to save not only Israel but also everyone who believes in Him. And it was at Passover that Jesus instituted the new meal that we eat in remembrance of Him, the Lord's Supper.

Devotions

In the school cafeteria one day, Shania said, "Can you believe what the pastor did, coming into our classroom to ask for volunteers to help with the cleanup of the church property after the storm? What was he *thinking*? On a Saturday! Listen, when I'm away from school, my time is for *me*. And this is *not* about me!" Jermond replied, "The only way I'll volunteer is if I'm paid to do it. Money talks to me. What does it say? It says, 'More, more, more!'" The kids laughed, and then Roland added, "Seriously, I can't help on a Saturday. For me, Saturday means football practice. My coach owns me during football season." "I know what you mean," said Jacob. "Games are my life—but I'm talking electronic games. Nothing is as important to me. I'm a tech guy, and my goal is to master any new game that comes on the market. I've got a reputation to maintain!" A couple more kids joined their table and brought up a new subject to talk about, saying, "I looked at the next Bible story we will study. It's about Moses and the Egyptians. Did you know that those people worshiped a river and called the sun a god? They even thought animals like frogs and beetles were sacred! What were they thinking? How could they think such ordinary things were that important?" Roland laughed, "Who was in charge there—Pharaoh or frogs? Oh, wait a minute. Pharaoh thought he was a sacred god too." Let's stop a minute and examine these conversations. These kids were ridiculing the Egyptians and their gods, but look closely at what was most important in their own lives. Who was in charge of the lives of these kids? What was sacred to them? (In most cases, they considered themselves most important; their own wants and desires were in charge of their choices. They placed highest importance on things like money, sports, electronics, and texting. These are the things they were devoted to.) **Let's pray that the Lord Jesus will rule in the choices we make, and that He will lead our time and our priorities. That means giving up some personal choices and making Him of first importance—but that is what He did for us on the cross.** Sing together "Let Me Be Thine Forever" (*LSB* 689; recorded as *Hymn of the Season for grade 5, Pentecost*). Praise the greatness of God, who rules over all nations and all creation, by saying together Psalm 46.

Into the Lesson

God Preps Egypt for the Exodus

God freeing His people Israel from slavery in Egypt reminds the Israelites, sends a message to the Egyptians, and witnesses to the world that He is the "one and only" God. In Luther's Small Catechism, three words are used as wonderful descriptions of who God is. Share these words and their meanings with your class.

Omnipotent: all powerful, almighty. Matthew 19:26 says, "With God all things are possible." God demonstrated His power with the plagues; they occurred at His timing, and nothing could stop them except His word.

Omniscient: all knowing. John 21:17 says, "Lord, You know everything." God knew that Pharaoh would harden his heart after each plague and not set the Israelites free. He also knew Pharaoh would pursue the people, even after the tenth plague.

Omnipresent: present everywhere. Jeremiah 23:24 says, "Can a man hide himself in secret places so that I cannot see him? declares the Lord. Do I not fill heaven and earth? declares the Lord." God was present with the people during the plagues, striking the Egyptians while protecting the Israelites.

As you work together on this section in the Student Book and Reproducible 13a, point out, **These were not just random calamities. They occurred and ceased at God's command. They gradually increased in intensity. They attacked the Egyptians' sense of power and autonomy as the plagues devastated the economy, the agriculture, and even the concept of the religious deities. All of the plagues were testifying to the almighty power of the one true God. As the prophet stated, "The Lord is the true God; He is the living God and the everlasting King. At His wrath the earth quakes, and the nations cannot endure His indignation"** (Jeremiah 10:10). (You might point out that the blue, red, and purple colors in this section relate to the colors used by Egyptian royalty in décor and jewelry.)

Lesson 13

Plagues and Passover

God Preps Egypt for the Exodus

God had prepared Moses well for the task. Empowered by God, Moses bravely went before Pharaoh and demanded the release of the Hebrew people. Knowing Pharaoh would be resistant, God had a plan to send plagues and pestilence that went beyond annoyance and pain to attack the very gods the Egyptian people believed in and to attack their pride in their own power and wealth. God demonstrated His greatness and might as He exposed the weakness of the Egyptian economy, government, and deities. Once again, God showed that He is Lord over all.

God sent plagues that increased in intensity and destruction. These diagrams, along with information on Reproducible 13a, detail the first nine plagues, leading up to the tenth and most devastative disaster, which led to the Egyptians begging the Israelites to leave.

Covenant Connection

The lifesaving blessings of the first Passover foreshadow the lifesaving blessings we have through Jesus' death on the cross. Compare these events of the old covenant (testament) and the new covenant (testament).

Into the Word

God Preps Israel for Freedom

What preparation did the people of Israel need? They prepared by packing and by fixing the Passover meal, but the most significant preparation was in their hearts, as God called on them to trust His commands and have faith in His promises. Read the paragraph in the Student Book and also the account of the tenth plague in Exodus 11:1–12:42. Draw parallels between the Old Testament Passover and the New Testament plan of salvation through Jesus as you work on the "Comparisons" section of Reproducible 13b. It is so amazing and faith building to compare the Passover with what Jesus did on the cross and to refer to Jesus as "the Lamb of God." God sent His only Son to be the sacrifice for all mankind; and Jesus shed His blood to set man free from slavery—the slavery of sin, death, and the devil.

Compare the Hebrews' Passover celebration with the Christians' Lord's Supper. After completing the Passover meal with His disciples, Jesus instituted this new Supper for the new covenant. It was to be a memorial of His sacrifice for the sins of the world, offering forgiveness through Christ's body and blood, which are in, with, and under the bread and wine. It is a meal of remembrance and more

God Preps Israel for Freedom

Special preparations were made for the last plague as God prepared His people to leave the land and escape from slavery. God gave instructions that might have seemed unusual, but He wanted the people to show their faith in the actions and requests of God. He told them to pack up and be ready to leave in a hurry with their belongings. They should be dressed, with sandals on and walking sticks ready, as they ate a meal of roasted lamb. There would be no time to wait for bread dough to rise high and fluffy, so the unleavened bread would be baked without yeast and would be flat and crunchy. They also prepared a salad of bitter herbs and spices to remind them of the bitter tears they had shed as slaves. Blood from the lamb was to be painted on the doorframes of the houses as a sign of their faith in the promises of God. That night at midnight, the Lord passed over the homes in Egypt; in any home without the sign of faith (blood on the doorframe), the firstborn son died. After this tenth plague, the Egyptian people and their king urged the Hebrews to leave, even giving them gold and silver gifts to send them on their way. In remembrance of this special night, the people of Israel were to celebrate the Passover meal every year in thanks to God for their deliverance and freedom.

Jesus Sets Us Free

The Israelites were freed from slavery and death by the blood of a lamb spread on their doorframes; we are saved from slavery to sin and death by Jesus shedding His blood on a cross for us. In Jesus, we are part of a new covenant. A covenant is an agreement between two parties/people. God has kept His part of the covenant through the forgiveness we have in Jesus. We cannot now just say, "Thanks Jesus; now I'll do whatever I want," because that leads us right back to the slavery of sin and breaks the covenant. Read Galatians 5:1, 13, 22–25. Summarize what this tells about our new freedom:

Jesus sets us free to live as His people, serving others, following the ways of the Spirit—the way of righteousness.

THE NEW COVENANT

Jeremiah 31:31–34
Matthew 26:26–28

Remember

Explore the new covenant relationship we have in Christ Jesus by studying Martin Luther's Explanation of the Second Article of the Apostles' Creed in the Appendix.

because it actively bestows God's blessings on believers. It is at times called "the breaking of bread," while the Passover is referred to as "the Feast of Unleavened Bread." The Hebrew word *pasah* means "to pass over." We refer to Jesus as "the Paschal Lamb," the word *paschal* being derived from that Hebrew word. For us, the Lord's Supper replaces the Feast of the Passover. Mention to your students that Christ's giving of His body and blood as sacrifice for our sins fulfilled God's promise to Adam and Eve. Jesus is the new covenant between us and God through His shed blood.

INTO our lives

Jesus Sets Us Free

Start this section of the Student Book by stating the inarguable fact that mankind is in slavery to sin. Quote Ecclesiastes 7:20: "Surely there is not a righteous man on earth who does good and never sins." We fall into trusting ourselves. (Proverbs 3:5 says, "Trust in the Lord with all your heart, and do not lean on your own understanding.") Or we put our faith in money. (Mark 10:23 says, "And Jesus looked around and said to His disciples, 'How difficult it will be for those who have wealth to enter the kingdom of God!'") Explain to the students that having wealth is not evil; it only becomes so when wealth replaces God in our lives. At other times, we put our possessions first. (Philippians 3:19 says, "Their end is destruction, their god is their belly, and they glory in their shame, with minds set on earthly things.") We are all slaves to sin and the devil, headed for eternal death, if we believe that we can remain in a right relationship with God of our own doing.

Share the wonderful news that Jesus broke the chains of sin around us through His death on the cross. We are no longer slaves to sin. Sin and the devil do not rule our hearts when we have faith in Jesus as our Lord and Savior, our Paschal Lamb. He took upon Himself the punishment we deserved; He became the sacrifice for us. He restored a right relationship between us and God—our new covenant!

Also explore Romans 6:15–23. Look up the Bible verses below the illustration, and read the related paragraph in the Student Book. Look also at Luther's explanation of Jesus' redemptive action for us in the bottom box on Reproducible 13b. Have students highlight the words that indicate that we now belong to Jesus. (He purchased us, so that we might be His own.) Also highlight the words that indicate what our new life in the new covenant is like—a life dedicated to the One who dedicated Himself to us.

In this unit, we see Moses as a heroic Bible character. Concurrently, the Lesson Support page encourages that you also study Martin Luther, a hero of faith. However, in all of Scripture and all of life, we know that the true and ultimate hero in all matters is Jesus. Use Web Resource 13a to sing about this. (Have students listen to the stanza and join in on the refrain until they are comfortable singing the whole song. Comment on the last phrase of the refrain, and have students use a concordance to discover where these words can be found in Scripture.) Conclude by reading John 1:29 and singing "The Lamb" (*LSB* 547; recorded as *Hymn of the Season for grade 5, Lent*).

Curriculum Connection

Encourage students to explore the life of Luther using several key printed resources. CPH offers a minicourse on his life, *Martin Luther Mini-curriculum: Grades 5 and 6* (item no. 223119). Also consider the book *Luther—Biography of a Reformer* by Frederick Nohl (copyright © 2003 CPH; item no. 124226). This gives an extensive look at Luther's life in a format appropriate for this grade level. Consider having class copies of the book and using it during the portion of the daily schedule designated for studying literature. Another book that takes a different approach to the study of Luther is Edward Grube's biography of Luther from the CPH Heroes of Faith collection, which is a companion to this One in Christ curriculum. This book takes the perspective of Luther's "Table Talks," in which he asked and answered questions of his students as they sat informally around a table; however, in this book, the students are modern-day sixth graders! Again, this book is most effective in class quantities, with assigned sections followed by group discussions.

Music Connection

Point out that Martin Luther wrote many hymns. Especially noteworthy is "A Mighty Fortress Is Our God" (*LSB* 656 and 657). Explain that the words are based on Psalm 46, the psalm being used in devotions this month. Compare the psalm and song lyrics. Relate the word *fortress* to the time in Luther's life when he went into hiding in a fortress, or castle. Learn more about that adventure, finding pictures of the castle as it appears today, discovering the new "identity" Luther assumed at that time, and finding out how he occupied his time while in hiding. After a year in hiding, Luther was able to return home, where he was no longer in danger because he was now famous, enjoyed political protection from friends, and—most of all—remained secure in the grace of God.

Study the two versions of "A Mighty Fortress Is Our God" in *LSB*. Ask, **Which do you think is the original version?** (Neither; it was originally written in German; both are translations.) Compare the differences in wording, but note the similarity in meaning of each stanza. Listen to the two versions as recorded for *Hymn of the Season for grade 3, Reformation*, and *Hymn of the Month for grade 3, October*. Discuss which version students prefer and ask why that is their preference. Note, too, that one version is very stately and rhythmic; the other is more lyrical and isorhythmic. Sing both versions.

CPH offers *Martin Luther: Hymns, Ballads, Chants, Truth*, a CD set of Martin Luther's music (item no. 991726). This might be good background/listening music during study time. Ask students how they would describe Luther's musical style.

Searching Further

It took a lot of courage for Moses to stand up before Pharaoh, who at that time was probably the most powerful leader of the most powerful nation on earth. Discuss the source of Moses' courage, especially after he was so weak and shy when God first approached him about the task. (The courage came from God; Moses realized God was with him and that God equipped him with miraculous signs and significant words.) Make a parallel to your study of the life of Martin Luther. He also showed great courage when he stood trial before the emperor of the Holy Roman Empire and refused to do as he was told. (When asked to take back the things he had written, he said he could not and would not recant unless they proved by Scripture that he was wrong.) It took courage for Luther to continue his work when he was declared an outlaw, "wanted: dead or alive." Again, the courage came from God and the conviction that God was with him and would guide him for God's own purposes. The courage to stand up for what is right in God's sight is not easy, and it must be based on the strength of God and not our own personal strength. As we have been reading in Psalm 46, "God is our refuge and strength, a very present help in trouble" (v. 1). Continue to study about Martin Luther this month in preparation for the celebration of Reformation Day, October 31.

Technology

Have students explore the ten plagues further, using resources on the Internet and video clips based on this Bible narrative. There are many illustrated books on the exodus; bookmark the plagues in a collection or display of such books. Assign one plague to each of ten pairs or groups and have them create a sculpture or mural representing it.

Unit 2—To the Promised Land

Lesson 14

Holding Up the Prophet's Hands
Exodus 17:8–16

Background

On the face of it, this is an odd story: the success of the Israelite army depends on whether Moses' hands are up or down. It sounds almost like magic. But there are many places in Scripture where God teaches us through acted-out messages (especially through the prophets Jeremiah and Ezekiel). In this case, the meaning seems clear: no Christian leader can carry out his duties without the help and support of God's people around him. Aaron and Hur were absolutely necessary that day for God's people to triumph. And because this took place on a mountain, all Israel would have seen it and known that this was true.

It is true for us as well. No pastor, no teacher, no missionary can serve well without the prayers, help, and support of God's people. The scriptural truths explored in this lesson remind us of the importance of showing support and giving encouragement to the pastor and the other spiritual leaders God graciously gives us. The general disregard for authority in our culture today has also infiltrated the Church. But as we read and study the Bible, we find this phenomenon to be nothing new.

As the Israelites traveled in the wilderness, they doubted Moses' leadership. Because Moses was God's representative, by dishonoring Moses, the people also dishonored God's guidance and care for them. When we unfairly criticize our pastor, speak ill of him, doubt his leadership skills despite his faithful obedience to the Word, fail to worship regularly, fail to support our pastor, we, like the Israelites, dishonor God by not honoring His representatives. As you teach this lesson, help your students see that the Church does not belong to us, nor to the pastor, but to God. Pastors lead and guide us as God's representatives.

Central Truth

God gives us spiritual leaders, and He desires that we respect and support them.

Objectives

- Recognize that the Church does not belong to the pastor or to us—it belongs to God. He shares that gift with us, and He blesses us with pastors to help carry out His ministry.
- In humility, affirm the blessing that the pastor and other leaders are as they serve the kingdom of God.
- Support and encourage the leaders God gives us.

Materials

- Hymnals and music CDs
- Reproducible 14

Bible Prep

Post in advance so students can bookmark references before class time.
- Exodus 13–18
- Psalm 40

Devotions

"Abby, please put the salad on the table for lunch," Grandma said. As Abby took the salad out of her grandma's refrigerator, she saw a note taped to the freezer door that said, "Pray for Pastor Steen." Abby walked over to the sink and stood beside her grandma and asked, "Why is Pastor Steen on your list? Is he sick or something?" "No," said Grandma. "Pastor Steen's not sick. I pray for God's wisdom, guidance, protection and care for him." "I don't get it," said Abby. "Pastor Steen knows more about God than anyone I know. Why would *he* need our prayers?" "Well," said Grandma, "Pastor Steen spends many hours every week reading and studying the Bible so he makes sure that the message in his Sunday sermon is true to God's Word. He leads Bible studies. He visits with people who are sick or injured and those having surgery. He spends time with homebound people. He talks with people about their problems and worries and shares God's comfort with them. He makes a point to share Jesus' love with everyone. He teaches confirmation class and leads chapel for all of you students at school. He prays for us. He also has a wife and two children to care for and love." "Wow!" said Abby. "Pastor Steen has so much to do! We *do* need to pray for him." Grandma replied, "Let's ask God to give Pastor strength and good health so he can continue to serve the Lord."

Continue: God blesses us with pastors who carry out His ministry. Pastors are representatives of God. They proclaim God's Word and share the Good News of Jesus' saving love through their words and actions. They serve God. Let's pray for our pastor, that God may be with him in all that he does, and that we may support and encourage our pastor as our leader and friend. Lead students in prayer, and then sing "Thy Strong Word" (*LSB* 578; recorded as *Hymn of the Month for grade 6, October*) to celebrate the power of God's Word. As you learn the hymn, sing just one stanza, adding another one each day while listening to the remaining stanzas in order to focus on the meaning of the words.

INTO the lesson

The Exit

This section provides the context for today's Bible narrative. We can't skip from the Passover directly to an incident in the desert. The narratives flow together as a river of God's grace to His people. Reread or retell the story from Exodus 14. Marvel at the magnitude of this miracle. Emphasize that the power and direction did not come from Moses or his staff, which was such a visual reminder of power; no, the power always came from God as He worked through His tool, Moses. After reading the response of Moses and the people in Exodus 15, join Moses and his sister, Miriam, and sing to the Lord. Sing "O Sing to the Lord" (*LSB* 808), using the accompaniment track (track 7) on Disc 10 of *Hymns of the Month (Hymns with Spanish Lyrics)*. Then listen to the same song on the vocal track (track 1) as it is sung in Spanish. Encourage students to join in singing it in Spanish after they have had a chance to study the printed words in the hymnal. Ask, **Do you know what language the Israelites would have used when they sang?** (Hebrew)

Note: There is a lot to explore in this lesson. This might be as far as you get on the first day of study.

INTO the Word

Handy Support

Look at the map of the Israelites' travels in the wilderness. Point out that it would have been a much shorter route if they had traveled along the coast. There were two reasons for not doing so: (1) according to Exodus 13:17, God did not lead them that way because He wanted them to avoid the powerful and warlike Philistines, whom the Hebrews were not yet ready or strong enough to deal with; and (2) when God had spoken to Moses from the burning bush at Mount Sinai, God had said that Moses would return to that place with the Israelites to worship Him at that mountain (3:12).

Emphasize that Moses was an unlikely leader, particularly because he was over eighty years old. God, however, likes to work through the unexpected so that we will recognize that the results come from God alone. Encourage students to trust in God to work in unexpected ways in their lives too.

Then ask, **What do Aaron and Hur's actions in this Bible narrative show about their relationship with Moses and their feelings toward him?** (By helping Moses in battle, they honored Moses and supported him, both physically and emotionally. Aaron and Hur recognized Moses as their God-given leader.) Also have students look at Exodus 17:13 and ask, **Whom was God already preparing to be the next leader?** (Joshua would become the leader forty years later.)

Review

This prayer gesture or posture is a sign of asking and longing for God's help. Early Christians also regarded this prayer posture as a symbol of Jesus' crucifixion. (See "Postures and Gestures" in *TLSB*, p. 1,276.)

Give God a "Hand"

The title of this section refers to "giving a hand" of appreciation, applause, or congratulations. In other words, "Take time to praise the Lord!" Point out that a banner was often carried to identify a group of people. Each of the twelve tribes of Israel had an identifying banner; at sporting events, a banner is often waved whenever points are scored; the banners we see in church identify who God is and what He has done for us. **God's identifying feature is** *love*; 1 John 4:16 says, "God is love." Song of Solomon 2:4 says, "He brought me to the banqueting house, and His banner over me was love." Sing together "His Banner over Me Is Love" (*AGPS* 118; also recorded on *JPS*). Read together Psalm 40, on which the song is based. Though this psalm was written by David, it relates well to the difficulties and the deliverance that the Israelites experienced—and which we, too, must face.

LESSON 14
Holding Up the Prophet's Hands
The Exit (Exodus 14)

Moses was the political head and spiritual leader of the people of Israel when they left slavery in Egypt. This was an unwieldy group of two million people, plus all their livestock. Actually, Moses was just a representative of the true leader, God Himself. In what way did God continually remind the people of that fact? (Exodus 13:21–22) **A pillar of cloud led them by day, and a pillar of fire stayed with them by night**.

When Pharaoh changed his mind and came after the people with a full army and over six hundred chariots, the Hebrew people's first reaction was panic, not prayer (Exodus 14:11–12). What instructions did Moses give the people? (See Exodus 14:13–14.) **Fear not; stand firm; see the salvation of the Lord; be silent**

Modern skeptics try to explain away the next event, which was truly a miracle, saying that the Red Sea crossing was just a tsunami. While waters do recede before a tsunami, they do not (Exodus 14:22) **stand like a wall on both sides as two million people pass by**.

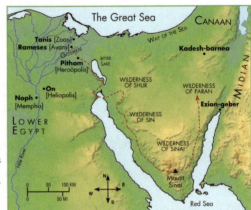

Other skeptics try to say that there was a spelling mistake and that this happened not at the great Red Sea, but at the Reed Sea, which is only knee deep. This, too, doesn't make sense, because why would knee-deep water (Exodus 14:27–28) **destroy a whole army**? This can't be explained away as good luck or accidental timing. The Israelites knew that it was the hand of God. Read their response in Exodus 15:1–21.

Review

Covenant Connection

When Moses held up his hands on his own, or when Aaron and Hur held them up for him, the Israelites were victorious in battle. This same prayer posture with arms extended foreshadows Jesus on the cross. What victory did Jesus gain for us as His hands were uplifted?
Through His crucifixion and resurrection, Jesus gained victory for us over sin, death, and Satan.

34

Handy Support

This was just the first of many encounters with enemies. As Moses led the Israelites through the wilderness to the Promised Land of Canaan, they often encountered nomadic tribes and other groups of people who regarded them as enemies and intruders. Early in their journey, God's people met resistance from the Amalekites at Rephidim in the wilderness. Read Exodus 17:8–13.

What battle plan did the Israelites follow? **Moses stood on a hill above them, holding up his hands in prayer, asking God for help and victory.**

What happened whenever Moses held up his hands in prayer, according to Exodus 17:11? **The Israelites prevailed in battle.**

Whenever Moses' hands would lower, what happened? **The Amalekites prevailed.**

Why did Moses' hands lower, according to verse 12? **Moses grew physically tired. He needed help.**

Who helped Moses, and how did they do so? **While Moses sat on a stone, Aaron and Hur held up his hands. This kept Moses' hands steady in prayer to God throughout the rest of the day. By depending on God's strength in battle instead of their own, Joshua and the Israelite soldiers defeated Amalek.**

Give God a "Hand"

God doesn't need our help, but He does desire our thanks and praise. Read Moses' response to God's care (Exodus 17:15). Then design a banner that gives thanks and praise to God for His blessings in your life.

Remember

"Encourage one another and build one another up." (1 Thessalonians 5:11)

INTO our lives

Supportive Hands

After reading the paragraphs on Reproducible 14, point out that many people today have a wrong attitude toward their pastor, considering him more as "hired help" than as God's representative. A pastor is not hired to do whatever we want him to do or to do the work we don't want to do. The pastor is responsible to God, and so are we; so we should be working together, supporting one another spiritually and encouraging one another. Read stanzas 3 and 4 from "Hark, the Voice of Jesus Calling" (*LSB* 826). The words relate well to the Bible story and also to our role as people of God.

Give this oral true/false quiz, and discuss with students why they agree or disagree with each statement.

1. **The pastor of a church is its head.** (False. Based on Colossians 1:18, Christ is the Head of the Church.)

2. **All people who believe in Jesus Christ as their Lord and Savior are a part of God's Church.** (True. All who believe in Jesus are joined together in Him as a "holy temple in the Lord" [Ephesians 2:21]. "You yourselves like living stones are being built up as a spiritual house" [1 Peter 2:5].)

3. **It is okay to have disagreements about the truth of the Bible within God's Church.** (False. In 1 Corinthians 1:10, we read that in the name of Jesus, we are to agree with one another and be unified in faith. Church members within a specific congregation may disagree about what color of carpet to place in the church sanctuary or about what time to start the service every Sunday, but there is to be no disagreement about the truth of Holy Scripture.)

4. **Members of the Church don't need to know the truths of the Bible very completely, as they can trust in everything the pastor says.** (False. All Christians need to be continually reading and studying God's Word so they can recognize if the truth is being taught [Matthew 7:15–16]. Each individual Christian needs to "[be] prepared to make a defense to anyone who asks you for a reason for the hope that is in you" [1 Peter 3:15]. While we have the blessing of seminaries where our pastors are very well trained in the Scriptures and in their accurate meaning, we cannot rely on anyone else's knowledge or beliefs for our own faith.)

5. **If you don't like a pastor's personality or style of preaching, it's okay not to come to worship.** (False. We come to worship God. God's Word tells that if a pastor is preaching the true Word of God, we are to respect him [1 Thessalonians 5:12–13].)

6. **It is important that church members pray for their pastors and spiritual leaders and that they monetarily support them.** (True. Acts 4:23–37 tells that prayer was offered and monetary gifts were given to the apostles by members of the Early Church. This gives an example for us as to how we are to support our pastors today.) The Church belongs to God. It is not owned by a pastor or by a congregation. **Every aspect of every activity that takes place within the Church should find its purpose as a way of glorifying and proclaiming Jesus Christ as Lord and Savior, who gives forgiveness and eternal life** (1 Peter 4:10–11; 1 Corinthians 10:31).

Lesson Support

Curriculum Connection

Cooperation is a gift God has given us to use not only in the Church, but in our families and schools as well. Take a look at section 6.7.4, Cooperation to Achieve Goals, found in the grade 6 Health volume of the Concordia Curriculum Guide series. What cooperative projects might your class take on in order to serve others in your school, church, or community?

Check it Out

Relate this lesson to Martin Luther, noting that he was the pastor/priest of the Castle Church in Wittenberg, Germany. He knew that his first responsibility was to God and God's truth. When John Tetzel came to town, selling indulgences to buy forgiveness of sins, Luther knew he had to speak up for the truth. Though the sale of indulgences was sanctioned by church leaders in order to raise money to build a large cathedral in Rome, Luther knew that forgiveness is a free gift from God—not something that can be purchased with money or good works. His responsibility to the Lord led Luther to place the Ninety-five Theses, or statements, on the church door on October 31, 1517. He wanted to open a debate/discussion to search out the truth as found in Scripture.

Searching Further

Invite the pastor who serves the congregation of your school to your classroom to speak about the schooling that he received at the seminary. If he can't attend your class, arrange an interview by Skype or e-mail. Provide in advance a possible list of topics such as the following:

- Describe your path to the seminary, including where you did your undergraduate work. Tell how God led you into the ministry.
- Describe the kinds of classes pastoral candidates take at the seminary. Explain how each class helped prepare you for the work you do as a pastor. What was your favorite class? What was your most challenging class?
- What does it mean to "go on vicarage"? How did your vicarage during your third year of preparation differ from your other three years of instruction?
- Do you have any specialized ministry training (e.g., missions, inner city ministry, foreign language skills, chaplain training)? How do you use these special skills?
- Why is the kind of preparation the LCMS offers at its seminaries so important in the training of pastors?

Hands to Serve

Many congregations observe Pastor Appreciation Day during October. Encourage students to show love and support to the pastor(s) of your congregation by participating in one or more of the following activities:

- Write thank-you cards to the pastor that express appreciation for something specific he does (such as leading devotions or chapel, being a good listener, preaching God's true Word, praying for your school, visiting the sick and homebound, having a kind smile).
- Plant a tree or shrub on your school or church property in honor of your pastor serving God as an "[oak] of righteousness" (Isaiah 61:3).
- Illustrate a poster with a meaningful Bible verse that the pastor can display in his office.
- If your pastor enjoys sports, invite him to play a game of softball or kickball with your class at recess.
- Find out your pastor's favorite snack. Make or buy it for him. Decorate a container in which to place the snack. Place it on his desk in his office as a Friday afternoon surprise.
- At chapel, offer a special student-led prayer specifically for your pastor. Use the ideas developed on Reproducible 14.

Working in Groups

Plan to create a video entitled "A Day in the Life of Pastor [your pastor's name]." Help the students form groups and give each a specific job to do in the planning, filming, and presentation of the video. Groups might include script writers, one or two videographers, video editors, set construction workers, publicists who will advertise the showing of the video, and a snack crew who will provide refreshments during the filming as well as at the showing of the video. Show the students' completed production at a school open house or perhaps during a Sunday morning fellowship time during Pastor Appreciation Month. Present a copy of the video to your pastor and his family.

UNIT 2—TO THE PROMISED LAND   LESSON 15

Moses and Jethro
Exodus 18

Central Truth
The work of the Church is not just the pastor's job—we all have opportunities and responsibilities to serve God in His kingdom.

Objectives
- Confess that we sometimes fail to take an active and supportive role in the Church.
- Pray for God's forgiveness and strength to not only support pastors, but to also use our God-given talents for the good of God's kingdom.
- Serve joyfully, knowing that we are never giving up time or money, because God's return in blessings is always more than abundant.

Materials
- Reproducible 15
- Hymnals and music CDs
- Web Resource 15a
- Web Resource 15b
- Yellow highlighters

Bible Prep
Post in advance so students can bookmark references before class time.
- Exodus 18–19
- Exodus 32:15–16; 33:11
- Numbers 2
- Acts 6:1–7
- 1 Peter 2:9

Background

Scripture says that the number of Israelites God brought out of Egypt was "about six hundred thousand men on foot, besides women and children" (Exodus 12:37). A conservative estimate would make that over 2 million people—who were constantly clamoring for Moses' attention and guidance.

Jethro was a wise man. When he saw the heavy burden Moses was attempting to carry by himself, he suggested a workable alternative: appoint others to help! "Look for able men from all the people, men who fear God, who are trustworthy and hate a bribe, and place such men over the people," Jethro suggested (18:21).

This is still great advice for God's people today. No pastor, no leader can do everything alone. God has given gifts to all His people to enable them to serve in many different ways. "Now there are varieties of gifts, but the same Spirit; and there are varieties of service, but the same Lord; and there are varieties of activities, but it is the same God who empowers them all in everyone. To each is given the manifestation of the Spirit for the common good" (1 Corinthians 12:4–7). God blesses people with pastors. God also blesses pastors with people.

As you teach this lesson, let your attitude reflect the joy you experience as you serve the Lord. Seize this opportunity to lead your students to recognize the talents with which God has blessed them. Help them see the importance of sharing these talents to glorify God as they serve Him, their pastor, and one another, now and in the future.

Devotions

Consider these four incidents: (1) As Rashon and Darrell walked through the church parking lot on their way to Sunday School, they noticed Mrs. Williams struggling with several heavy sacks of groceries for the food pantry. "Hey, Mrs. Williams," Darrell called out. "Let us give you a hand with those sacks." (2) Shanna and Amy stopped by Mrs. Henry's preschool room at the end of Sunday School. The room was littered with toys and supplies. "Hi, Mrs. Henry," said Shanna. "Let us give you a hand to clean up." (3) As Trevor and Katie rode their bikes past their church, they noticed the church custodian raking the thick layer of leaves that covered the lawn. "Mr. Jacobs," called Katie as she and Trevor parked their bikes, "let us give you a hand and help you rake up these leaves." (4) As Drew walked past the pastor's office, he saw Pastor Greene surrounded by stacks of Bibles and several large cardboard boxes. "Good morning, Pastor Greene," said Drew. "Let me give you a hand packing up these Bibles." What happens when more than just one pair of hands work together? (Many important tasks are completed.) **In our previous** lesson, we saw how Aaron and Hur helped Moses. In today's Bible story, we will see how another individual helps Moses carry out another important task. As always, when we listen to these Old Testament Bible stories, let's consider what they are telling about our lives today.

Listen to the recording of the song "El Shaddai" (recorded on *JPS*). Point out that this song contains many of the names for God that the Israelites in the Old Testament would have known. Sing this song as a class (*AGPS* 92), and consider the connection you have through faith in God with people who lived thousands of years ago.

69

INTO the lesson

Orderly Arrangement

This section sets up context for the narrative in today's lesson. Once again we can see that God prefers orderliness, efficiency, and logical systems.

As you look at the populations of the various tribes, point out again that just the men were counted, so the census was really about the number of families.

The Israelites most likely camped for a longer period of time at an oasis or at a wadi. (Explore the Internet to find examples of these.) An oasis was a fertile area within the desert wilderness. An oasis usually had a well or a spring that could support vegetation, which would also be good for the people and their livestock. A wadi is a small valley that carries away water after one of the few brief rains in the wilderness. (A wadi would more likely be called an "arroyo," "gulch," or "gully" if it were in the western part of the Unites States.) A wadi had a dry riverbed for most of the year, but brief rains could fill it with rushing or even flooding waters. The water that soaked into the ground often fed wells and vegetation.

You may want to point out that the tribal pattern for camping was also the pattern for marching when the Israelites traveled. They marched in four rows of three tribes each. The first row included Judah, Issachar, and Zebulun; the second row, Reuben, Simeon, and Gad; the third row, Ephraim, Manasseh, and Benjamin; and the fourth row, Dan, Asher, and Naphtali. With such a plan, everyone knew what was expected, no one rushed or pushed to be first in line, and the process could move smoothly and efficiently with little or no further direction. (This is true in classroom management too—more can be accomplished when things are done in an orderly way, rather than with each person doing whatever he or she wants.)

INTO the Word

Wise Advice

Work together on Reproducible 15. Jethro gave good advice to Moses about his work overload; but there is another, even more significant reason for this advice. The people had a tendency to go to Moses first for help rather than to the Lord; they too often saw Moses as their leader, rather than God, who worked through Moses as His representative. (Note that Jethro's plan for a judicial system continues to work even today. In our country, we have a system of lower courts, state courts, and federal courts that make decisions unless a matter must go all the way to the Supreme Court.)

Jethro's plan was a legal system based on the laws of God. This same solution was suggested to the disciples in the early days of the Christian Church. Jesus' twelve disciples tried to take care of all the concerns of the Church, but it was too big—and growing more each day. The plan was a division of labor. Read about it in Acts 6:1–7. The same problem can occur in the Church today. Emphasize that the Church does not belong to the pastor, and he should not be required to do all the work. At the same time, the Church does not belong to the people, and they are not to give orders to the pastor to do the work so they don't have to. The Church belongs to God, and Christ Jesus is the Head of the Church. So what is our part? We are the members, or parts, of the Body of Christ. We all need to function and work together. We have different talents and abilities that are needed. Read aloud 1 Corinthians 12:27. (Consider expanding on this topic using Web Resource 15a, reading all of 1 Corinthians 12, and using the "Searching Further" section on the Lesson Support page.)

Also consider how division of labor is a blessing in churches today. A pastor's work load can be shared by other professional church workers such as music directors, deaconesses, and Directors of Christian Education (DCEs). Do you have any of these workers or other professional church workers in your congregation? Perhaps you could

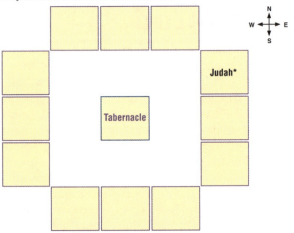

Lesson 15
Moses and Jethro

Orderly Arrangement

God prefers order to chaos. To ensure order among such a multitude of people, God established a plan for setting up the Israelite camp in the desert wilderness. Use Numbers 2 to complete this map of the twelve tribes. The first tribe mentioned in each group of three was the leading tribe of that group. (Place an asterisk beside the group leaders.) As we will see in the next lesson, the tabernacle was at the center, reminding everyone that God is central to all that we do.

As you work on the map, notice the populations of these tribes, which are often comparable in size to large cities today. Setting up camp was a major effort, so the people often stayed weeks or even months in an area that had good water and vegetation for their livestock.

The twelve tribes of Israel were named after and carried banners of the names of the twelve sons of Israel (Jacob). However, the families of Levi were not granted a division of land because they were dedicated to worship duties (eventually in the tabernacle and then the temple) and were distributed among and supported by the other tribes. Instead, the two sons of Joseph, Ephraim and Manasseh, were given tribal designations. (See Genesis 48:5.)

Review

Covenant Connection

God continually repeated His covenant promises to His people. In Exodus 19:5–6, God asked Moses to give a message to the people that if they obeyed Him and kept their part of the covenant, "you shall be My treasured possession among all peoples, for all the earth is Mine; and you shall be to Me a kingdom of priests and a holy nation." Through Christ Jesus, that covenant promise carried through to the New Testament and to all believers today. Turn to 1 Peter 2:9 and highlight all the words that compare to the promise in Exodus 19.

By God's Hand

Moses was a good leader, but his authority came from the Lord; so Moses gave the Law to the people as it was given to him by God. What was especially unique and important about this Law, according to Exodus 32:15–16? **It was not only the words but also the writing of God engraved on the stone tablets.**

What was unique about God's relationship with Moses (Exodus 33:11)? **God spoke to Moses face-to-face, as a man speaks to his friend.**

The Law of God speaks to us today too. It works to stop our sinful behavior (like a curb), and it shows us what we have done wrong (like a mirror). However, Jesus Christ has fulfilled the Law for us and has taken our punishment to the cross. Now, as redeemed children of God, we look at the Law in a new way—showing us how to live a godly life (as a guide)—as we are enabled by the power of the Holy Spirit.

My Family Tribe

1. There are many aspects of God's plan for the families/tribes of Israel that are also true for your own family (tribe). Who is the head of the family, who sets the standards of how you are to live? **God**

2. Who are God's representatives who established your particular tribe and to whom God has given authority as His representatives? **Your parents**

3. "Rights" are not automatic. Moses gave special rights to people who were capable, honest, and God-fearing. What rights have your parents given you? **Answers will vary.**

4. "Rights" are not automatic; they involve responsibilities. Moses established a division of labor, expecting cooperation as he divided up the work for the good of the whole community. In your home, what is the division of labor? What are your responsibilities? **Answers will vary.**

5. What is the result when people want to have their own way and do whatever they want? **Sin, chaos, unhappiness**

6. As with the tribes of Israel, what does God want to see guiding the life of your tribe? (See the verses in the "Remember" section for clues.) L**ove**, F**orgiveness**, and P**eace**.

Remember

"The LORD is slow to anger and abounding in steadfast love, forgiving iniquity." (Numbers 14:18)

"The LORD bless you and keep you; the LORD make His face to shine upon you and be gracious to you; the LORD lift up His countenance upon you and give you peace." (Numbers 6:24–26)

Skype or make a video of a conversation with one of them. Remember that professional church workers assist the Church but are not supposed to do all the work of the congregation; all people in the Church have responsibilities to keep it functioning well. Discuss some types of volunteer work done in your own congregation as people use their God-given talents to support the ministry of the Church.

Review

The words to highlight in 1 Peter 2:9 are "a royal priesthood, a holy nation, a people for His own possession."

By God's Hand

As you explore this section in the Student Book, take time to review God's Law as it is written in the Ten Commandments. Use Web Resource 15b to count off each commandment as you study it in Luther's Small Catechism as found in the Appendix of the Student Book.

In addition to the Ten Commandments, God gave other moral, ceremonial, and civil laws. Point out that the ceremonial laws foreshadowed the coming of the Messiah, so these laws are no longer in effect since the coming of the Savior. Jesus gave us a new covenant—we worship Him, but not in the Old Testament ways. (This was signified when the temple curtain tore at the time of Jesus' death on the cross.) The civil laws determined justice when civil infractions took place. The moral laws of the Ten Commandments, however, apply to all people and are true for all times.

Discuss the diagram in the Student Book. Explain that the Law shows our sin and the need for a savior. However, **since we have been justified through Christ Jesus, we look at the Law differently. Knowing that Jesus has fulfilled the Law for us by His perfect obedience, and knowing that He has taken the punishment of the Law for all people on the cross, we can now look at the Law not in a fearsome way, but as a guide for the Christian life.** For further study, explore "The Purposes of the Law" in *Luther's Small Catechism with Explanation*. Question 77 examines the three purposes of the Law—to serve as a curb, a mirror, and a guide. Emphasize that we can live a Christian life through the power of God as He justifies us (in Christ) and sanctifies us (through the Holy Spirit).

INTO our lives

My Family Tribe

It is very interesting to make a direct comparison between the organizational plans for the Israelites and the organization of families today. God is to be the center of both, in all matters.

One of the problems in society and in families today is an overemphasis on rights for everything. While we do have certain rights, we do not have a right to do whatever we want or to possess whatever we want. Those types of "rights" are beyond the boundaries of God's Law and are motivated by sin and selfishness. True order and peace will be evident when God's love and forgiveness abound and when that same love and forgiveness are shared by all.

Curriculum Connection

Consider using section 6.2.4, Mathematical Problems, as a curriculum connection to the Bible story about Jethro's advice to Moses. You'll find the section in the Math volume of the Concordia Curriculum Guide series for sixth grade. Use math to visualize the new judicial system in this story. Assume that there were 603,550 adult men in the official census (which did not include women, children, or Levites, according to Numbers 1:45–46), and that these were divided into groups of tens, fifties, hundreds, and thousands, as Jethro suggested. How many officials would be needed to handle each level? To how many levels would a person need to appeal his case before reaching Moses himself? Assuming that nine out of ten cases were solved at each level, and only one passed upward, to what extent would this cut down on Moses' work load? If you like, figure this as a class using fractions or percentages.

DIGGING DEEPER

Relate one of the key concepts in this lesson to your study of Martin Luther. It was important that God's Word and Law be written down so that all Israelite people could read and learn about God's will for their lives rather than be completely dependent on their leader, Moses. In Luther's time, the Bible and religious writings were usually written in Latin, leaving the common people dependent on their church leaders as the people sought to learn about God. Luther realized the importance of writing God's Word in the language the people could read, so he translated Scripture into German. He also wrote many books in German that explained what Scripture means. One of these was the Small Catechism, a book of questions and answers explaining the main teachings (concepts, doctrines) of the Bible. Luther's Small Catechism is included in the Appendix of the One in Christ Student Book; in *LSB* on pages 321–30, immediately preceding the first hymn; and in *AGPS* beginning on page 35. Using questions and answers was one of Luther's favorite ways to teach. His students at the university where he was a professor often came to his home to study with Luther in what became known as his "Table Talks." This concept is put in a modern setting in which contemporary sixth graders ask Luther questions in Edward A. Grube's biography of Luther, which is part of the CPH Heroes of Faith series that is a companion to this level of One in Christ. Consider ordering class quantities of this book to learn more about the Reformation.

Reaching Every Child

This stage of your students' physical and emotional development can be challenging for the students themselves as well as for those who care about them. Leading students to see their value as redeemed children of God to whom He has given important skills and talents gives them the kind of self-worth we want them to develop as Christians. Helping your students see their roles as children of God is an important way for you to reach out to the quiet student, the academically challenged student, the behaviorally challenged student, and the lonely student to help each one see that God values him or her as His child, a member of His family, a part of Christ's Body. Talk with students individually, and encourage them by sharing with them achievements you've seen them accomplish and talents you've seen them use. Be as specific as possible, and help the students see that even the very small acts of kindness they show are extremely important and are used by Jesus to build up His Body in love.

UNIT 2—TO THE PROMISED LAND

LESSON 16

The Tent Church
Exodus 25–26; 36; 39–40

Background

One of the first tasks God gave to the new nation of Israel was to establish a place of worship, a place where God would dwell among them. This tabernacle, a portable tent church, remained the center of the Lord's worship for more than four hundred years, until the temple was built. God gave Moses a very detailed design to follow; He also ordered that the tabernacle was to be built using the offerings of the people (Exodus 35:4–29) and under the supervision of Bezalel and Oholiab, two Israelite men who had received gifts from the Holy Spirit to carry out this work (vv. 30–35). The tabernacle was about half the size of a football field, and in today's economy, the materials used to build the tabernacle would cost more than $1 million. The word used for "ark" (25:10) when speaking of the ark of the covenant is the same Hebrew word used for Noah's boat (Genesis 6:14) and Moses' basket (Exodus 2:3). Though these all varied in size and design, each was mobile and under God's protection. Like any good teacher, the Lord used all five senses to teach the people of Israel about Himself. Much of the tabernacle was overlaid with gold, formed of silver, or made of multi-colored fabric, appealing to the sense of sight. Taste and smell were involved in the sacrifices of the altar, as well as the use of holy incense and anointing oil. Hearing was involved through the bells added to the hem of the high priest's robe (28:33–35), as well as through prayer and teaching. And the whole action of sacrifice, as well as the many washing rituals, taught Israel about the holiness of God using the sense of touch. Above all, the tabernacle was to be a place where the Lord dwelt among His people as their God. Today we meet for worship in buildings of many types, or even outside; but we always meet together in the presence of Jesus (Matthew 18:20).

Central Truth
God desires that we gather together with other believers in worship.

Objectives
- Admit that we often allow our wants to take over our hearts rather than doing what God desires—hearing His Word and worshiping with other believers.
- Thank God that He comes to us with grace and mercy, choosing to dwell with us in His sanctuary and in our hearts and lives.
- Live for the Lord as one dedicated, or set aside, for His good purposes.

Materials
- Hymnals and music CDs
- Web Resource 16a
- Web Resource 16b
- Web Resource 16c
- Web Resource 16d
- Reproducible 16

Bible Prep
Post in advance so students can bookmark references before class time.
- Exodus 25–26; 36; 39–40
- 1 John 2:2
- John 8:12
- John 6:51
- Hebrews 7:26–27
- Romans 8:34

Devotions

Keeshon was busy helping his mother get ready for a presentation at the family reunion. He was scanning old photographs so the pictures could be projected on a screen for everyone to see. His mother squealed with delight as she showed him a picture of her family when she was just a little girl. "Look, there's your Aunt Rhoda when she wore her hair in braids! And look, it's Uncle Leon when he still had hair on his head!" Keeshon and his mom laughed at how much everyone had changed. Keeshon noticed, "Grandpa sure looks duded up in that suit and hat! And wow! Grandma sure looks pretty! What was going on here? You all look like you are dressed for some kind of special occasion." "Yes, we were," Mom replied. "We were dressed to go to church. On Sunday mornings, your grandma always dressed me in what she called my 'Sunday best.' Grandma said it was one way we could show our respect to Jesus, who always does the very best for us." Continue, **It's not necessary to wear fancy clothing to church. But how can wearing something clean, neat, and special—not what we wear every day—help us to prepare for spending time at worship?** (Let students respond. It is indeed true that our outward appearance does not matter to God. But when we wear clothing that is set aside for church, we remember that going to church is a special blessing that God gives us. We go to God's house not for our own personal comfort and entertainment, but to focus on Him. The focus of worship is God's true Word; that is also the focus of the Reformation, celebrated later this month. Turn to the hymn "Thy Strong Word" (*LSB* 578; recorded as *Hymn of the Month for grade 6, October*). Have students listen to each stanza as it is sung while they read the words silently, and have them join together to sing the repeated refrain at the end of each stanza.

INTO the Word

Before talking about building the tabernacle, establish the context of this narrative. Remind students that in the previous lesson, the giving of the Law to Moses was discussed. Explain that Moses was on Mount Sinai, talking with God for a long time. The people of Israel began to fear that their leader had died. This again showed a lack of understanding that God Himself was their leader. After all that God had done to rescue and provide for the people, their fear grew as their faith dwindled. They reverted back to the ways of the Egyptians, asking Aaron to make a golden calf to worship, similar to the gods of Egypt. Aaron was weak and fearful; instead of standing up as a true priest and leader, he did what the people wanted. When Moses returned, he was angry, and it is safe to say that God was even angrier—and there were consequences. Moses interceded for the people, asking God to forgive these stiff-necked, stubborn people, saying, "Consider too that this nation is Your people" (Exodus 33:13). And God replied, "My presence will go with you, and I will give you rest" (v. 14). (For more details, see Exodus 32–34.) Say, **Despite the people's sins, God forgave them mercifully and renewed His covenant with them. Knowing that the people needed a constant reminder of God's presence with them, the Lord told Moses to build a sanctuary. This would be a tent church so they could take it with them as they traveled.** God gave directions to Moses that are recorded in Scripture, giving exact details and precise measurements. The people were to provide the materials from the gifts the Egyptians had given them when they left Egypt after the Passover. These gifts of gold and silver, precious gems, and cloth of royal colors would be used to honor the Lord and to emphasize that God dwelled right there among them.

INTO the lesson

God Dwells with His People

Work together as a group on the crossword puzzle in the Student Book. Divide the Scripture readings among the students to read aloud as they learn important facts about the tabernacle. (If you prefer, you could divide the class into four groups, with group 1 reading any references from Exodus 25, group 2 reading verses found in chapters 26 and 36, group 3 reading from chapter 39, and group 4 from chapter 40.) Also use Web Resource 16a, which duplicates this puzzle, to help students locate the correct positions of answers in their Student Book. This type of resource is especially helpful for children who have difficulty moving from one task to another.

Follow this activity with Web Resources 16b, 16c, and 16d, which give more images, details, and explanations of the tabernacle. Always emphasize that God Himself has directed that we have a place of worship where we regularly gather together. Either at this point in the lesson or on another day, take time to discuss present-day houses of worship. Encourage students to explore the Internet to find pictures of various styles of churches, from great cathedrals to simple, steepled, white-frame buildings. Point out that God desires us to gather together to worship; in fact, He commands it in the Third Commandment. Our motivation to worship, however, is to respond to God for all that He has done for us. List some of the blessings we receive when we gather together in worship (such as hearing the truth of God's Word proclaimed and explained; fellowship with other believers; encouragement and comfort through the Word and Sacraments; encouragement and comfort from fellow believers; joyful hearts; peace in knowing that we are forgiven for Jesus' sake). As you continue this lesson, think about this question: is worship something that we just stop and do once a week, or is it a constant part of our lives?

The Tabernacle Foreshadows

The structure and elements of the Old Testament tabernacle are foreshadowings, or previews, of what Jesus would do for us as our Savior. Read the listed Bible passages to discover how the tabernacle and its features related to Jesus and how they apply to our Christian identity today.

The Tabernacle	New Testament Worship
	1. Read 1 John 2:2. How do the sacrifices made by the priests on the bronze altar relate to Jesus? <u>Jesus was sacrificed on the cross for the sins of all people.</u>
	2. Read John 8:12. How does the lampstand relate to Jesus? <u>Jesus is the light of the world, showing the way through the darkness of sin.</u>
	3. Read John 6:51. How does the bread apply to Jesus? <u>Jesus is the bread of life. He provides what is needed for life eternal in heaven.</u>
	4. Read Hebrews 7:26–27. How does Jesus compare to the high priest of the Old Testament? <u>Jesus is our great High Priest. We are redeemed through His sacrifice.</u>
	5. Read Romans 8:34. The pleasing aroma of incense was smelled by God when it was burned on this altar. What action of Jesus does this signify? <u>Jesus prays for us and pleads on our behalf to God the Father.</u>

God Dwells with Us and in Us

God directed Moses and the Israelites to build the tabernacle so that He could dwell (live) among His people, have fellowship with them, and communicate with them (Exodus 25:22). Today, God dwells with us in His church sanctuary and also in our hearts and lives. Tell what each Bible verse says about how God dwells in us.

- "Do you not know that your body is a temple of the Holy Spirit within you, whom you have from God?" (1 Corinthians 6:19a) <u>We are God's dwelling place; He lives in our hearts.</u>
- "I appeal to you therefore, brothers, by the mercies of God, to present your bodies as a living sacrifice, holy and acceptable to God, which is your spiritual worship." (Romans 12:1) <u>Redeemed by Jesus and made holy by Him, we live for the Lord in all that we do and say, wherever we are.</u>

Remember

"Whoever confesses that Jesus is the Son of God, God abides in him, and he in God. . . . God is love, and whoever abides in love abides in God, and God abides in him." (1 John 4:15–16)

39

Review

Also refer to John 1:14, where "the Word [Jesus] became flesh [was born] and dwelt among us [lived with us]" as the fulfillment of the prophecies, promises, and previews of the Old Testament.

The Tabernacle Foreshadows

The Scripture passages and questions in this activity show Jesus to be the fulfillment of the sacrificial and other actions first performed by the Levite priests, and which continued until the Christian Church began after Pentecost. Emphasize the point that **Jesus, our great High Priest, did everything necessary to gain salvation for us.** Because of Jesus' actions as our Savior, who died and rose for our sins, the rituals and sacrifices carried out by the priests in the tabernacle—and later, in the Jerusalem temple and the synagogues—are no longer necessary. As you discuss the questions of this activity, share how the tabernacle events and the way that the tabernacle was built point to Jesus, the future Savior, and how He would rescue His people from sin. Our worship today focuses on what Jesus did for us and what He continues to do in our lives and to eternity.

INTO our lives

God Dwells with Us and in Us

Say, **God's desire is to be with us always. The tabernacle that Moses and the Israelites built was a place where God could dwell with His people. He moved with them and led them as they traveled to Canaan. Later, God sent His Son, Jesus, to live among people in the flesh as He fulfilled all the Old Testament prophecies and kept God's covenant with His people. Through Jesus' death and resurrection, a new covenant was established. Jesus alone earned salvation and a new eternal life for us. When we trust and depend on Him as our Lord and Savior, these gifts are ours. No other sacrifices are ever again needed.**

We have been "set aside" for God's good purposes and as His people. Worship is not just something that we do once a week; it is to be a constant part of our lives. Help students realize that since we are God's temples, He is constantly with us, in us, and leading us. Say, **As God's New Testament people, through Baptism, the Holy Spirit dwells in us and empowers us to live for God and to serve Him. By the power of the Holy Spirit, we live and show the truths of His Word as we live for Him, both inside and outside His sanctuary.**

The Israelites were incredibly giving when Moses asked for materials to build the tabernacle. As a matter of fact, they gave so much that they were asked (Exodus 36:6–7) to stop! What a wonderful attitude they had! By the power of the Holy Spirit, what can *you* offer to God that maybe you haven't thought about giving before? Consider not just monetary or material items, but also actions that you can perform.

75

Lesson Support

Searching Further

In your studies this month about the Reformation and Martin Luther, investigate Andreas Karlstadt, an associate briefly of Luther. Luther continually had to calm Karlstadt down, counter some of his actions, and discuss their disagreements. Karlstadt may be described as overzealous, impetuous, and argumentative. In his zeal to make changes in the Church, he often tried to get rid of everything that was Roman Catholic. Today he would be considered a radical. When he started destroying statues and pictures in churches, he went too far. Luther said that not everything needed to be changed. Only that which was not in agreement with Scripture needed to be removed, and then only in a peaceful, nonviolent manner. Luther said that there was much in the Church that was good and always had been. Explore books and Web sites to learn more about the differences in thought between these two men.

Hands to Serve

Is there a special need or a special project that you, your students, and their families could undertake to enhance the atmosphere of your church sanctuary or to advertise the importance of worship in the life of a Christian? Here are a few ideas: make a banner; clean pew cushions and hymnal racks; make Scripture bookmarks for use in the sanctuary hymnals and Bibles; fill "busy bags" for preschool-age children with books and activities that tell about Jesus and about what goes on during worship; plan a skit or short presentation that encourages people to come and spend time with God at His house, then film it and place it on your church's Web site; design a new Web page or additions to current Web pages on your church's Web site that creatively share the importance of spending time in God's house.

Curriculum Connection

The tabernacle was created to meet the challenges of providing a worship space for a nation on the move. Everything in it was portable, and the materials from which it was made were readily available and easily packed and transported. Take a look at section 6.2.1.6, Using Appropriate Materials and Tools to Solve an Artistic Problem, which appears in the Visual Arts volume of the Concordia Curriculum Guide series for grade 6. Together, identify some of the challenges the architect of the tabernacle (God!) faced, and how He overcame them. For example, consider the altar—it had to be fireproof, yet light enough to be carried. For an extra activity, imagine how you might meet the challenges of constructing a modern church that had to be portable—one for a migrant community, for example, or one that is used in a location (such as a public school) where everything must be removed by Sunday night.

Working in Groups

Work as a class to design a living history exhibit of the tabernacle. Secure an area of the gymnasium or multipurpose room for your exhibit. Assign different groups to work on building the tabernacle and its elements, to make the curtains, and to assemble costumes for the high priest, for Moses, and for other Israelites. You will also need several students to serve as tabernacle guides, or "experts," who will share information about the construction of the tabernacle and the elements inside it based on accurate biblical information. PVC pipe could be put together to construct the "fenced" area that surrounded the tabernacle. The pipe could also be used as frames from which to hang fabric to form the curtains in the tabernacle. Cardboard boxes spray painted gold or bronze could be used to make the ark of the covenant, the bronze altar, and the incense altar. Thick dowel rods could be used for the poles that carried the ark. Card tables covered with fabric could be used to symbolize the tents of the twelve tribes that surrounded the tabernacle area. Raid your school's costume box for robes and other items for the Israelites. Then invite younger classes in your school to tour the tabernacle. Guides from your class can take them through the tabernacle and explain what it is all about. Reproducible 16 can be distributed to the children who visit the display, either as an activity to do at home, or to complete at a table set up for that purpose in the display area.

Unit 2—To the Promised Land

Lesson 17

Korah's Rebellion
Numbers 16

Central Truth
The visible Church on earth is not untouched by sin and sinners; God calls us to His Word to discern the truth.

Objectives
- Be alert, knowing that there are some false leaders in the Church today (as at the time of Moses and Luther).
- Rejoice that Christ has made atonement for us, so we can look to Him for deliverance.
- Rely on God's Word alone for the truth.

Materials
- Hymnals and music CDs
- Reproducible 17a and 17b
- Web Resource 17a

Bible Prep
Post in advance so students can bookmark references before class time.
- Numbers 13–16
- Psalm 79:9

Background

The story of Korah's rebellion is one of the scariest stories in the Bible. Korah was highly favored by the Lord, being one of the Levites who was charged with looking after the holiest things of the tabernacle. Yet this was not enough for him. He and his followers became proud and presumptuous, and they attempted to grab positions God had not given to them. Therefore, as Moses pointed out, they were not rebelling against Aaron and Moses, but against God Himself (Numbers 16:11). And like the devil, the "arch-rebel" against God, they were doomed to a horrible end. The frightening reality is that false teachers like Korah still exist in some churches today. Though they have been entrusted with holy things, they rebel against the Lord out of pride and presumption. And like Korah, they lead many people astray, to their great loss and destruction. The whole Bible warns us against such people, whom Paul called "fierce wolves" and "men speaking twisted things, to draw away the disciples after them" (Acts 20:29–30). But how can we tell if their teaching is true or false? Isaiah gives us the answer: "To the teaching and to the testimony! If they will not speak according to this word, it is because they have no dawn" (8:20). The Holy Scripture is our protection and our measure of truth. If anyone teaches in contradiction to God's Word, he is a liar (Proverbs 30:5–6). Rejoice with your students in the glorious gift God has given us in His Word, Jesus, and in His ever-true and holy Scriptures. Proclaim that God's Word alone tells the amazing truth of Jesus, which saves us and gives us eternal life.

Devotions

Where do you go for the source of truth? There are plenty of outrageous and untruthful Web sites on the Internet mixed in with the good. Television and movie producers usually have high financial standards to determine which shows are 'successful,' but they often don't enforce high standards where truth is concerned. Your source of information needs to be honest, knowledgeable, and accurate. Ask, **Who would be your best source for finding an answer to the following questions?**

1. How many fins does a whale shark have?
    (a) A veterinarian (b) A marine biologist (c) An oceanographer
2. What is the current population of Thailand?
    (a) The U.S. Census Bureau (b) Expedia.com (c) The Government Bureau of Population in Thailand
3. What is the Queen of England's favorite food?
    (a) The Queen herself (b) The World Book Encyclopedia (c) A current London gossip magazine
4. What are the symptoms of the latest flu virus?
    (a) *The New York Times* (b) The World Health Organization (c) Your school nurse
5. Where can you find out more about Jesus and His miracles?
    (a) Your soccer coach (b) Wikipedia (c) God's Word

Especially when it comes to questions about our eternal salvation, it's vital to go to the source of the truth: the Bible. Martin Luther realized this too. When he was asked to disavow the things he had written because his writings spoke against the church leaders, Luther refused, even though he risked his life by doing so. Luther proclaimed that the only measure and standard for judging truth was the Word of God. He said that he must stand solely on the Word of God. God gave Luther the knowledge, the courage, and the conviction to confront the false teachers of his time. Luther tested the truth of a teaching by measuring it against the truth found in God's Word. May God help us remember that His Word is the only truth we will ever need for salvation. Our Church and our faith are built on the solid rock of God's Word in the Gospel message of salvation through Jesus. Let's sing about that rock now. Sing "Built on the Rock" (*LSB* 645; recorded as *Hymn of the Season* for grade 6, *Reformation*).

INTO the lesson

The Grumbling Escalates

As you discuss this section of the lesson, emphasize the point that whenever we rebel against authorities that God has placed before us, we break the Fourth Commandment. Remind students of the truths discussed in previous lessons concerning the importance of respecting and supporting our pastors and other church leaders because they are God's representatives. When we dishonor them, we dishonor God. However, it is also important to be discerning, because false leaders do arise—even in the Church, and even today. The source of truth must always be the Word of God.

To set the story of the rebellion into context, we need to step back and look at events that preceded it. So begin the lesson by looking at a pivotal point—the point of turning around, when the people failed to trust God's guidance and were thus punished with forty years of wandering in the wilderness (one year for each day that the spies had explored Canaan before they returned with a bad report). After God had rescued them from the greatest earthly power of that time—Egypt—they still failed to trust that He could help them again. Use the first section of the Student Book lesson to explore this part of the narrative.

Following this is the story of rebellion, which could be called a tipping point. This was almost the last straw, as false leaders spoke against Moses and Aaron (but were really speaking against God). The consequences were very destructive, but it would have been still worse if not for the interceding of Moses and Aaron as they relied on God's grace and mercy. **As sinners, we too need an intercessor, and we have that in Christ Jesus, who through His death and resurrection has reconciled us to God, so that we now live in His perfect grace and mercy.**

LESSON 17

Korah's Rebellion

The Grumbling Escalates

After traveling for one year in the wilderness, the people of Israel reached Canaan—the land God had promised to them (and to Abraham, Isaac, and Jacob). Twelve spies were sent ahead to check it out. See Numbers 13–14 to find out about their report.

Good News (13:23, 27): The land is fruitful, flowing with milk and honey

Bad News (13:28): The people are strong with fortified cities

Majority Report *(ten other spies)* (13:31, 33): We cannot fight them; we are like grasshoppers to them

Minority Report *(Caleb and Joshua)* (13:30; 14:9): We can overcome them; God is on our side

People's Response *(once again)* (14:1–4): They cried loudly, "Why did you bring us out of Egypt to die here?"

Moses Intercedes *(once again)* (14:17–19): Moses prayed to God, asking Him to show His steadfast love and forgiveness

The Consequence (14:22–24, 30–34): Except for faithful Caleb and Joshua, none of the people who left Egypt would enter the Promised Land; but after forty years of wandering, their children would get to go in

Review

Covenant Connection

In Numbers 16:42–48, Moses and Aaron atoned for the sinful people. This was another preview of the Messiah. Atone means "to go between to fix a relationship, to intercede, to be in the middle, to make amends for what was wrong, and to bring unity." This is what Jesus did for us when He died on the cross. Read Psalm 79:9.

INTO the Word

"You Have Gone Too Far!"

This story is quite complex. You can read it in Numbers 16, but first share the simplified version on Reproducibles 17a and 17b. To gain more insight, use Web Resource 17a. Then ask, **What do the events of this Bible story tell you about God?** (God is just and punishes sin. He is greatly angered when people disobey His representatives because this also is rebellion against Him. But God also listens to prayers on behalf of His people and is merciful.)

Point out the interesting thing about the title of this section. Korah spoke these words in Numbers 16:3, and then, in verse 7, Moses turned around and used the same words *against* Korah.

"You Have Gone Too Far!"

Did the people learn to stop sinning? (Do we learn to stop sinning?) Read Numbers 16 to find out about a large rebellion led by a man named Korah. He was a Levite who wanted to be a priest.

Korah complained about the power Moses and Aaron had, but actually: (eh ntawde het owrep) **he wanted the power**

Korah complained that Moses and Aaron had exalted themselves, but actually: (odG dha eonsch htme) **God had chosen them**

Jesus, Our Great High Priest

The actions of Aaron, the high priest, on behalf of God's rebellious people brought about atonement, or reconciliation, between God and the Israelites. As Aaron made an incense offering, God's anger was appeased, and the punishing plague stopped. Aaron's actions foreshadow what Jesus would do for all people as our great High Priest: He offered Himself as the sacrifice that appeased God's anger at our sin, ending eternal punishment for all believers. These New Testament Bible verses point to Jesus as the fulfillment of the Old Testament prophecies.

"[Jesus] had to be made like His brothers in every respect, so that He might become a merciful and faithful high priest in the service of God, to make propitiation [atonement] for the sins of the people." (Hebrews 2:17)

"For it was indeed fitting that we should have such a high priest, holy, innocent, unstained, separated from sinners, and exalted above the heavens. He has no need, like those high priests, to offer sacrifices daily, first for His own sins and then for those of the people, since He did this once for all when offered up Himself." (Hebrews 7:26–27)

"[Jesus] is the propitiation [atoning sacrifice] for our sins, and not for ours only but also for the sins of the whole world." (1 John 2:2)

"In this is love, not that we have loved God but that He loved us and sent His Son to be the propitiation [atoning reconciliation] for our sins." (1 John 4:10)

Search a dictionary or Bible glossary and write a definition for these words:

- Atonement — **Bringing together those who had been separated**
- Propitiation — **The substitute who atones**
- Reconciliation — **Establishing a right and peaceful relationship, bringing unity**

Remember

"Sanctify them in the truth; Your word is truth." (John 17:17)

INTO our lives

The Source of Truth

Read together the closing section of Reproducible 17b. Then say, **We know by the abundance of false teachings and false teachers in the world that false teachers can be very persuasive and engaging. Fortunately, God gives us His Holy Scripture so that we can test every teaching to see whether it agrees with God's truth. Why is it important that we test all teachings that speak about God and the way to salvation?** (We want to make sure that we are not trusting in a false teaching or sharing false teachings with others.) Read about the Bereans, who searched Scripture for truth, in Acts 17:10–12.

Jesus, Our Great High Priest

After discussing together the activity in this portion of the Student Book, say, **One of the most amazing aspects of the Bible is how the story of Jesus is shown throughout the thousands of years of history that are covered in its writings. This is yet another proof that the Bible is God's true Word, for there is no other book written by so many different authors over so many years of history that keeps at its heart the same consistent point: we are saved through faith in Christ Jesus. Only God could write such a book!**

Take a moment in the lesson to look carefully at the lyrics of the hymn "Thy Strong Word" (*LSB* 578). Ask, **What phrases in the hymn show the power of God's Word?** (Such phrases include [1] "did cleave the darkness," reminding us that all creation—except for people—was called into existence simply at the spoken word of God; [2] God's Word "bespeaks us righteous"; and [3] "From the cross forever beameth" all redemption and hope for mankind.) Say, **Holy Scripture also speaks of the power of the Word in Isaiah 55:11: "So shall My word be that goes out from My mouth; it shall not return to Me empty, but it shall accomplish that which I purpose, and shall succeed in the thing for which I sent it." We may not understand God's ways, but we can always trust that His Word is true and will do what it says.**

Technology

Martin Luther faced death threats due to his defense of God's Word. Many Christians throughout the world today face separation from family, prison, physical and mental abuse, and even death because they believe and defend God's true Word. The Voice of the Martyrs is an organization that seeks to make known the stories of these Christians and that works to support Christians who are living in areas where Christians are hated and oppressed. We all can support persecuted Christians through prayer, interceding for them as we ask for God's grace and mercy.

Curriculum Connection

A possible connection for this lesson is section 6.3.2.9, Cultural Relativism, in the sixth-grade Social Studies volume of the Concordia Curriculum Guide series. Korah's rebellion against God's ordained system was based partly on his belief that he could create his own truth, disregarding what God had already said. Discuss with students: **What happens when people follow their own cherished ideas without taking hard realities into account? Is this kind of mind-set a wise one when driving, taking medicine, or doing math? In spiritual matters also, there are hard realities, which God has made known to us in the Bible. With this in mind, is it a good idea to adopt or create religious beliefs based solely on how appealing they are to you?**

Searching Further

Have students study other individuals who embraced and proclaimed the truth of God's Word despite threats against them. Some people to consider include Daniel; Shadrach, Meshach, and Abednego; Stephen; Peter; and Paul. Emphasize that the only true hero is Jesus Christ. But each of these individuals trusted in the truth of God's Word and was not afraid to share it.

Teacher Tips

Chapter 2 of 1 John discusses many other truths and topics of discussion related to this lesson. In your own personal devotions, take time to read and study it. This chapter, particularly verses 21–25, is a "pep talk" for all Christians concerning the importance of clinging to the main Bible teachings that Martin Luther so dearly loved: faith alone, grace alone, Christ alone, Scripture alone.

Critical Thinking

To understand world events, it is important to understand other religions and their teachings. Compare the true teachings of the Bible with those of other religions practiced in the world today, including Islam, Hinduism, Mormonism, and Judaism. Rose Publishing (www.rose-publishing.com) offers several excellent charts that compare the teachings of other religions with Christianity and clearly show their false teachings. This might also be a topic that your pastor could present to your class.

Faith in Action

Celebrate the gift of the Holy Scriptures by hosting a Bible collection for a local prison ministry or for missionary distribution. Or make bookmarks that illustrate a Bible passage proclaiming the truth of God's Word (e.g., John 17:17; John 3:16; Ephesians 2:8–9). Distribute these bookmarks at a community event, at a church-sponsored dinner for the community, or with canned foods in a food drive ("Food for the Body and Soul").

Unit 2—To the Promised Land
Lesson 18

Water at Meribah
Numbers 20:1–13

Central Truth
Our sinful human nature leads us to blame others and blame God when things go wrong; God's grace leads us to forgiveness and to forgive.

Objectives
- Recognize that quarrels and personal inadequacies exist in the Church as in other places; even "good leaders" make mistakes and sin.
- Look to God and His Word for the decisive guidance we need, knowing that He alone is perfect, patient, and constant.
- Rely on God's forgiveness to take away our sins and to guide us to be forgiving of others.

Materials
- Hymnals and music CDs
- Web Resource 18a
- Web Resource 18b
- Reproducible 18

Bible Prep
Post in advance so students can bookmark references before class time.
- Numbers 20
- Exodus 15:22–25
- Exodus 17:1–7
- Ephesians 4:29–32
- Luke 18:9–14
- Psalm 103

Background
This is a significant event because it explains why Moses was not allowed to enter the Promised Land. Why was Moses' sin so serious? God's displeasure with Moses was for taking joint credit with God for producing the water (see Numbers 20:12). Moses was supposed to point to God; instead, he implied a share in that focus. It was the public claim of power and righteousness, a claim undeserved, by God's own chosen leader that was a matter of serious consequence, both in Moses' day and in God's Church today.

There is something else going on that is of even greater significance in foreshadowing the Messiah. The apostle writes, "For I want you to know, brothers, that our fathers . . . all ate the same spiritual food, and all drank the same spiritual drink. For they drank from the spiritual Rock that followed them, and the Rock was Christ" (1 Corinthians 10:1–4). Much of the Old Testament foretells the coming of Jesus, sometimes in straightforward prophecy (His birth in Bethlehem foretold in Micah 5:2), and sometimes through an acted-out symbolic prophecy called "typology." For example, Moses has always symbolized God's Law since it was to him that God gave the Commandments. And it was the just and holy Law of God that "struck" Jesus Christ, our Rock, on the day He carried our sins to the cross. Because He took that blow for us, we have living water to drink—everlasting life.

Devotions
Erin hopped onto the city bus as usual, hoping the ride to school would go quickly. The only seat left was next to a girl named Sofia who was wearing a uniform that identified her as a student at the Catholic school. Erin had spoken with her a few times, and she wondered how Sofia's school day compared with her own schedule at Christ Lutheran School. They began to talk, and soon the discussion led to the subject of their faith. They both agreed that Jesus lived, died, and rose again to save them from their sins. They both talked about how important prayer was in their life. Then it happened. They each began to tell why their school was better. "Our buildings are newer," said Erin." "Important people in town go to my church," Sofia retorted. "Our school has a new gym," added Erin. "We have more students at my school," countered Sofia. Erin shouted, "Well, we don't pray to saints!" Sofia shot back, "Well, you treat Luther like he is God!" Erin told her that it wasn't true, but it was too late. Sofia wouldn't listen. After that day, both girls avoided each other on the bus. Erin talked to her pastor about this argument and why someone would think Lutherans pray to Luther. Her pastor reminded her that words said in the heat of an argument are often distorted. Arguments end up as personal battles over who is right and who is wrong. Instead, we should give a simple and loving witness to God's action in our lives. God's truth will do the convincing, not the loudness of our voices or the heated replies we give. That day, on the way home from school, as she stared out of the bus window, Erin asked God for forgiveness. From that time on, Erin shared her faith carefully, with kindness. She knew that her thoughts, words, and actions had consequences that affected her relationship with others. She learned to trust God's Holy Spirit to change the hearts of people, and she saw her role as sharing God's love and grace. As 1 Peter 3:15 states, "Always [be] prepared to make a defense to anyone who asks you for a reason for the hope that is in you; yet do it with gentleness and respect." Together say Psalm 46, and sing "Thy Strong Word" (*LSB* 578; recorded as *Hymn of the Month* for grade 6, October).

INTO the lesson

Fussing and Fighting

Like the girls on the bus in today's devotion, the Israelites were unable to see beyond their own fears when challenged. The girls were afraid they would lose something they had (the importance of their beliefs). The Israelites were afraid they wouldn't get what they wanted (enough water to survive the rigors of the desert). In both cases, the resulting anger closed the hearts of those involved to God's will for the situation, and relationships were damaged. *Option:* Share an occasion from your youth when your words or deeds negatively impacted someone else. Tell why you remember this even now, and how you know God has forgiven you. Your witness will help students understand the process of confession and absolution. Remind them that the Bible encourages us to "confess your sins to one another and pray for one another, that you may be healed" (James 5:16).

INTO the Word

The Blame Game

The wilderness of Zin, where the Israelites were camped in this thirty-ninth year of wandering, afforded few creature comforts. There were few trees for shade and precious little grass for the animals to eat. Their need for water was real. Imagine several million people (counting women and children) waking up each day and not finding enough water to drink, wash, cook, or bathe. How long would you last before you began to wonder whether you would survive? Their goal of reaching the Promised Land seemed unimportant when they couldn't find enough water. We can understand how fearful thoughts created discontent. Complaints began as they agreed that someone must be at fault. The blaming started, and trust in the Lord vanished. Words changed into actions as a leader arose to challenge Moses. The people could not see God's provision—or the consequences that would result from their lack of faith. Yes, when our "flesh" rises up, we sin in thought, word, and deed.

Imagine the frustration Moses felt as he heard the complaints. After all the signs and wonders God had performed for the Israelites over nearly forty years in the wilderness, they *still* didn't trust God! Even after God's glory was revealed to him, Moses' angry thoughts became angry words: "Hear now, you rebels: shall we bring water for you out of this rock?" (Numbers 20:10). During his angry outburst, Moses took credit for giving them the water! *That* was why he was punished by not being allowed to go into the Promised Land. It wasn't because he struck the rock; it was because he did not point to *God* as the sole provider. He undeservedly took some of the credit for this miracle. View Web Resource 18a to learn more about this.

Psalm 103 was written by King David, a man who understood sin and its consequences. His sins of murder and adultery resulted in a difficult family life. How could this flawed person write such a beautiful poem? He saw beyond this world and its difficulties. His spirit soared, knowing that God's love and forgiveness gave him a relationship with God for eternity. David knew that his glass was not half empty or half full as some people today describe their life. It was overflowing!

82

Why do you think the consequences for Moses and Aaron were so severe (Numbers 20:12)? <u>God needed leaders who would follow instructions exactly and not proudly take credit for God's actions. God knew that Moses and Aaron had served Him well, but a new leader was needed as they marched into the Promised Land</u>. All leaders and followers make mistakes. Those who look to God for mercy discover His perfect will for their lives. Read Psalm 103 aloud and underline in your Bibles the phrases that tell what God does for those who trust Him.

Fall on Your Face

The first thing Moses and Aaron did after arguing with the Israelites was to fall facedown at the entrance to the tabernacle. They knew they needed forgiveness for their part in the argument and courage to replace their fear. God acknowledged their humble approach and showed them His glory (Numbers 20:6–8). Today, when we humbly approach God in times of trouble, we fall on our faces before Him when we pray in repentance and in need. When we read His Word, He is speaking to us as His Holy Spirit gives us eyes to see. Why do we need the Holy Spirit to help us? <u>Our physical eyes cannot discern (clearly see) spiritual matters, so God puts His Spirit into our hearts so that we may understand His will for our lives.</u> No matter what problems we have, God promises to forgive our sins, calm our fears, and provide direction for our lives. He will give us courage to overcome challenges that would otherwise confound and confuse us. What does Jesus teach about humility and forgiveness in the parable of the tax collector and the Pharisee in Luke 18:9–14? <u>It is not what we do, nor any "goodness" we may claim, that brings us blessings; we are forgiven and blessed because of God's goodness and love in Jesus. We recognize that we are to come to Him in humility.</u>

The Face of Forgiveness

The Hebrew word for *anger* comes from two words meaning "face" and "nostrils." If you have seen someone who is full of rage, you know why! Moses struggled with anger all his life. (He killed an Egyptian in a fury; he broke the tablets of stone with the Commandments written in God's hand; he struck the rock without giving God full credit for the miracle of water.) Each time, Moses and the people around him suffered. Imagine what it looked like to see him angry! How do you think Moses' face changed when God forgave him and restored His relationship with him?

Paul explained anger further in Ephesians 4:29–31. Give examples of other negative behaviors listed that can be seen in today's world. <u>Corrupting talk, grieving the Holy Spirit, bitterness, wrath, anger, clamor, slander, malice.</u> In your own heart, consider which of these are problems for you, and then read Ephesians 4:32 together. What advice does Paul give to you and all believers to help avoid the difficulties anger causes? <u>"Be kind to one another, tenderhearted, forgiving one another, as God in Christ forgave you."</u>

Remember

"Bless the LORD, O my soul, and forget not all His benefits,
who forgives all your iniquity, who heals all your diseases,
who redeems your life from the pit, who crowns you with steadfast love and mercy." (Psalm 103:2–4)

---

overcome. Encourage them to pray for wisdom and understanding.

"I want what I want when I want it." That sums up our lives before we learn to trust God. In Ephesians 4, Paul shows believers how to live as followers of Christ. He emphasizes unity, one body, one Spirit, the gift of grace, leaders who equip the saints, and people who speak the truth in love. Ask students to think of one person they have difficulty forgiving (but do not speak the name). Brainstorm specific kind actions that would help them mend the strained or broken relationship. Remind them that God will give them courage to work through any fear of rejection.

It is important to point out that the water at Meribah is not the end of the story. In the very next chapter, Numbers 21, we see the people again complaining about food and water. We see that Moses has learned his lesson, for he follows God's commands humbly. We also see the great patience of God as His people continue to fall into sin. This is a great comfort to us, because we, too, keep making the same mistakes over and over. This time, however, **we see one of the most beautiful images in the Old Testament that points so strongly to the Messiah, who would hang on a cross to deliver us from death and the devil.** Use Reproducible 18 to discover together the parallels between the bronze serpent and the crucifixion—both offering God's redeeming grace and mercy. Review the story using Web Resource 18b, if you wish.

INTO our lives

Fall on Your Face

Say, **Moses, Aaron, and the tax collector show how God grants mercy to those who come to Him, confess their need, and humbly seek His face. When Moses and the Israelites argued, they could not see how their behavior damaged their relationship with God and one another. God calls us to repentance, to come to Him in humility, and He will not turn us away.** Write the words "Communion of Saints" on the board. Emphasize: **All Christians are saints because our sins have been forgiven through Christ Jesus and our relationship with the Father has been restored.**

The Face of Forgiveness

Moses didn't know how he appeared to others until he had time to calm down and reflect on the consequences of his behavior. We all have weaknesses of character that can cause us to sin when our "flesh rises up." The sooner we get honest about them, the sooner God can make a difference in our lives. Brainstorm a list of "character defects," and place them on the board. Answers include selfishness, prejudice, conceit, greed, lust, indifference, phoniness, fear, self-pity, self-righteousness, laziness, gluttony, perfectionism, impatience. Give students quiet time to reflect on which ones they need God's help to

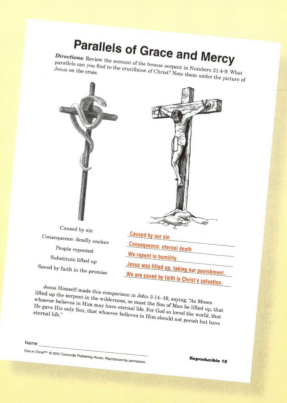

Lesson Support

Curriculum Connection

Water is a basic natural resource that every human community needs. Learn about the water cycle with your class. You'll find ideas and activities in section 6.3.2.12, Water Cycle, in the sixth grade Science volume of the Concordia Curriculum Guide series.

Searching Further

Discover Jesus' instructions for dealing with someone who has hurt you. Read Matthew 18:15–20, and note the following steps: (1) Speak privately with him; if he listens, you have gained a brother. (2) If he won't listen, take one or two others along as witnesses (not accusers) and try again. (3) If he still won't listen, tell the church (fellow believers in a position of authority, like parents, pastors, or teachers). (4) If he *still* won't listen, confront him with the facts again and give him an opportunity to repent and receive God's forgiveness. Jesus knew just how to relieve anger and resentment!

Critical thinking

Video games, movies, and rap song lyrics often exploit anger and physical violence. Discuss how our "flesh" (human nature) gravitates to the messages they show. Why is that? Satan wants us to think we are better than others and that they don't matter. Tell about the frog that jumps into a pot of cool water just placed on a hot flame. The frog doesn't realize how hot it is getting until it is too late. How does this relate to exposure to violent or sexually explicit media? We become accustomed to seeing "pretend" violence, and when something truly fearful happens, we become insensitive and it doesn't seem as bad to us as it really is.

Technology

Write this old saying on the board: "What I hear, I forget; what I see, I remember; what I write, I understand." Ask students to close their eyes and visualize Psalm 103:1–8 while you read it aloud. List on the board what they "saw" in each verse. Assign one phrase to each pair or group of students, and instruct them to locate an appropriate illustration for it from the Internet. Create a class PowerPoint presentation of each verse to share in chapel.

Art Connection

In regard to the performing arts, as a special project, students could create puppets and a script for telling Luther's life story. "The Adventures of Martin Luther" Big Book (copyright © 1999 CPH; item no. 222808) is large enough to be used as the backdrop scenery for such a production.

View two very respected video productions of Luther's life—the 2003 movie *Luther,* starring Joseph Fiennes (in color) and the older (1953), black-and-white version titled *Martin Luther*, starring Niall MacGinnis. After viewing both, compare styles, actors, scripts, and so forth. Point out that even though we are used to seeing films in color, the black-and-white version depicts a somber atmosphere, reflecting the seriousness of these events.

Unit 2—To the Promised Land

Lesson 19

Balaam
Numbers 22–24

Background

The story of Balaam is a strange one. He is a prophet torn between obedience and disobedience to the Lord. He says all the right things: "Though Balak were to give me his house full of silver and gold, I could not go beyond the command of the LORD my God to do less or more" (Numbers 22:18). But his actions contradict his words: he invites the messengers to stay in case the Lord changes His mind; he agrees to visit the king, even though he already knows God has refused the king's request; and ultimately, he gives the king advice that causes Israel to fall into sin and lose God's protection for a time (Numbers 31:16; Revelation 2:14). The Bible tells us that Balaam turned traitor for money (2 Peter 2:15). And yet, the Lord used even this traitor for His own good purposes. He caused Balaam to bless, not curse, the people of Israel, much against Balaam's will (Numbers 24). He even spoke a prophecy of the coming Messiah, Jesus, through Balaam. (See Numbers 24:17.) This may be the very prophecy that led the Wise Men to the baby Jesus! The story of Balaam is ultimately a comfort to us, because it shows us that God can use even His enemies to bless His beloved people.

Central Truth

Unbelievers try to disparage and work against God, but God's great power can use even them to accomplish His will.

Objectives

- Trust in the Lord because we are too weak on our own to stand up for the truth.
- Believe that God forgives us and empowers us to do His will, even in difficult times.
- Rejoice that God's plans and ways are always for the good of His people.

Materials

- Hymnals and music CDs
- Web Resource 19a
- Reproducible 19

Bible Prep

Post in advance so students can bookmark references before class time.
- Numbers 22–24
- Malachi 3:6
- John 14:6
- John 17:17
- Hebrews 13:8
- 1 Peter 1:25

Devotions

Today we will hear a Bible story about an ungodly prophet, and we will see that God's will was carried out nevertheless. Because of sinful human nature, we will find dishonest and unscrupulous people even in the Church. It is important to always remember that this is not God's fault, and it is not the fault of the Church—the guilty parties are sinful people. For this reason, it is important to pray for the Church and that the truth of God's Word will be supreme. It is also important to be discerning; that means to be cautious about what we hear, always checking what people say with the source of truth—God's Word. Imagine what it must have been like in Martin Luther's day. Most people did not know how to read or write! They had to rely on what others told them about God. A priest named John Tetzel convinced many people that buying pieces of paper called "indulgences" would guarantee forgiveness of sins. He even said that they could buy indulgences to get dead relatives into heaven. People didn't know that the real purpose of selling indulgences was to get money to build a cathedral in Rome. When Martin Luther heard about this, he was angry because he knew that faith in Jesus' sacrifice on the cross is all the assurance of forgiveness we need. It was silly to think you could buy your way into heaven! He included this problem in ninety-five statements he posted on the church door, where other monks might see them and take time to discuss them with him. Since there were no forms of public communication like radio, television, newspapers, or computers, the church door was used for all public notices. The printing press had recently been invented, however, and God was about to use both of these things to change His Church and free His people. Someone grabbed the paper from the door and had copies printed and distributed all over Germany. How happy people were to know that God loved them! Then Luther wrote a book of questions and answers about God for parents to discuss with their children. It is called the Small Catechism. Within a few years, the whole Bible was being printed in the German language, and people began to read it for themselves. No longer would dishonest preachers be able to trick them. This shows us that God sometimes uses worldly things like printing presses and even dishonest priests to give believers courage to stand up for their faith. As Scripture promises, the Word of God will prevail—it endures forever! Sing together "Built on the Rock" (*LSB* 645; recorded as *Hymn of the Season* for grade 6, *Reformation*). Also speak together Psalm 46.

INTO the Word

What Was He Thinking?

Today's narrative is unusual and even humorous in places, but it does direct us to simple and solid truths. The main lesson is that it is foolish to work against the will and ways of God, because He will prevail. This was the problem Adam and Eve had in the Garden of Eden. They knew God's will, yet they thought they knew better. The end result was that God did prevail. Sin was punished; but a Savior was also proclaimed. That is another thing we can learn from today's narrative—the Savior was proclaimed! Balaam may have been the mouthpiece, but the words of Numbers 24:17 are the words of the Lord, reaffirming the messianic promise that the Savior, who would reign over all, would come from the family of Jacob.

We learn from the narrative that going against God is futile. Balaam is mentioned in the Book of Revelation (2:14) as eventually working with Balak to undermine the people by tempting them to sin. He couldn't go up against God on his own, so he sided with Satan and idolatry.

What Are You Saying?

Balaam was a false prophet. Luther encountered falsehood in the priests and Church of his day; and today, there are news reports of religious cults and evangelists who have deceived their churches and led people astray. While condemning those practices, we must never doubt or tarnish the true Church of God and His Word. Satan works especially hard to try to capture the souls of the faithful. Pray to God and trust Him to guide us to the truth.

Say, **We will have questions and even doubts, but we can be reassured through the truth of God's Word, which will never fail us. Consider some of the following questions that people may ask.** Read the passages as noted to help your students consider and answer each question.

(1 John 1:1–5) **How can people who claim to be walking in the light of Christ do bad things?** (Our sinful nature is still present in our earthly bodies.)

(1 Peter 1:3–9) **Since our salvation is assured by faith in Christ, why do we still have temptations?** (Sanctification is a lifelong process. We are justified, but our minds must be renewed through the Holy Spirit working through the Means of Grace.)

(Romans 8:28) **How can something good come from a bad experiences?** (God continues to work in all things to accomplish His good will.)

(Psalm 32:1–5) **When can guilt be a good thing?** (It serves its purpose if it draws us to the Lord for forgiveness.)

It is the Holy Spirit who gives us understanding of the Word. Martin Luther gave sound advice on what to do when we read a passage of Scripture we don't understand: "Praise the Lord and go on." God reveals understanding as we need it.

LESSON 19

Balaam

What Was He Thinking?

As the Israelites neared the land of Moab, King Balak was afraid Israel would "chew them up" (Numbers 22:4). So he sent for Balaam, a prophet who was greedy, deceitful, and not a good person. Balak offered Balaam money to put a curse on the people of Israel. But Balaam was smart enough to know he could not oppose the true Word of the true God. The Lord knew He could work His will even through an unfaithful person like Balaam. God said, "Don't go." The king offered more money, so Balaam talked to God again. This time, the Lord said, "Go with them; but only do what I tell you" (Numbers 22:20). God now was very angry and certainly did not trust Balaam, so God sent a dramatic warning to Balaam as he rode on a donkey—just as stubborn as Balaam. What happened to the donkey (Numbers 22:23)? __The donkey saw the angel of the Lord with a fiery sword, so she left the road and ran into a field—as Balaam hit her.__ What happened the second time (vv. 24–25)? __When she again saw the angel, the donkey pressed up against a wall, catching Balaam's foot between her body and the wall, as Balaam again struck her.__ What happened the third time (vv. 26–27)? __The donkey had nowhere to go to get away from the angel, so she just lay down, as Balaam struck her again.__

Balaam wasn't getting the message, so God did two miraculous things. What happened in verses 28 and 31? __God opened the mouth of the donkey so she could speak to Balaam; then, God opened Balaam's eyes so he could see the angel__. Balaam was warned again to only speak what God would tell him. This event seems humorous, but more than anything, it shows the foolishness of Balaam and of King Balak to think they could oppose the will of God.

Review

Covenant Connection

Balaam was a foolish man. But he did speak words of wisdom when he said what God told him to say. In Numbers 24:17, God had him speak these words of prophecy about the Messiah: "I see Him, but not now; I behold Him, but not near: a star shall come out of Jacob, and a scepter shall rise out of Israel." These words echo Genesis 49:10, where Jacob gave the promise of the Messiah to Judah, saying, "The scepter shall not depart from Judah, nor the ruler's staff from between his feet." Jesus was born from this royal family, but as a heavenly King, the King of kings.

44

What Are You Saying?

King Balak of Moab was happy to see Balaam when he arrived. At last, they had their weapon against the people of Israel. They went to a high point where they could see some of the Israelites. God spoke to Balaam, who then said (Numbers 23:8) that _he could not curse someone whom God had not cursed._ The king was shocked, and he said, "What have you done to me? I took you to curse my enemies, and behold, you have done nothing but bless them" (v. 11).

The king took Balaam to another place to try again. What did Balaam say this time (vv. 19–20)? _God is not like a man who changes his mind; God said to bless Israel; I can't revoke it._

King Balak was exasperated. He said, "If you won't curse them, at least don't *bless* them!"

The king was not quite ready to give up. He took Balaam to a third location to try again. What did Balaam say this time about Israel (Numbers 24:9b)? _"Blessed are those who bless you, and cursed are those who curse you."_ Read aloud the special words of blessing in Numbers 24:5–7. After hearing this, King Balak was done. He told Balaam that he had better flee. So they parted ways. And the people of God moved on.

What Does This Mean for Me Today?

The Bible narrative is interesting and has a lot of unusual things happening. But does it have anything to say to kids in the twenty-first century? The people were wishy-washy-wacky, but the lesson from Scripture is solid: God's Word is true. God's will *will* be done. We pray for that very thing in the Lord's Prayer—"Thy will be done." Rewrite the words of these Bible verses in the correct order to learn more about what Scripture tells us.

John 17:17: is truth in the truth Your word them Sanctify _"Sanctify them in the truth; Your word is truth."_

1 Peter 1:25: remains the word forever The of Lord _"The word of the Lord remains forever."_

Malachi 3:6: I For change not do Lord the _"For I the Lord do not change."_

John 14:6: the the the am life way truth and and I _"I am the way, and the truth, and the life."_

Hebrews 13:8: Christ today and and is same Jesus the forever yesterday _"Jesus Christ is the same yesterday and today and forever."_

Remember

"Bless the Lord, O my soul, and all that is within me, bless His holy name! Bless the Lord, O my soul, and forget not all His benefits, who forgives all your iniquity, who heals all your diseases, who redeems your life from the pit, who crowns you with steadfast love and mercy." (Psalm 103:1–4)

INTO our lives

What Does This Mean for Me Today?

The Holy Spirit works in our lives to give us the desire to put God's will before our own. He enables us to begin to live according to God's purposes for us. But this is not always easy. When we follow God, we may have to say or do things that seem unpopular with those around us (like standing up for the truth or refusing to give in to a temptation).

Sometimes we fail to let God's power work in us. Yet, even at those times, God still loves us. He leads us to repent of our failures, and He forgives us for Jesus' sake. Through His Word and Sacraments, God offers us new strength to do His will.

Jesus knows our struggle. In Gethsemane, Jesus asked His Father to take away His suffering; but He ended His prayer with the words "nevertheless, not as I will, but as You will" (Matthew 26:39).

Jesus Himself taught us how to pray for strength to do God's will in the Lord's Prayer. Read aloud Luther's explanation of the prayer's Third Petition (direct students to the Small Catechism in the Appendix in the Student Book).

Thy will be done on earth as it is in heaven. **What does this mean? The good and gracious will of God is done even without our prayer, but we pray in this petition that it may be done among us also.**

How is God's will done? **God's will is done when He breaks and hinders every evil plan and purpose of the devil, the world, and our sinful nature... and when He strengthens and keeps us firm in His Word and faith until we die. This is His good and gracious will.**

Remember these important words from Philippians 2:13: "It is God who works in you, both to will and to work for His good pleasure." Use Web Resource 19a to learn more about exactly what the will of God is.

Curriculum Connection

The story of Balaam and his donkey provides plenty of material for reflection and drawing conclusions! Look at section 6.1.3.3, Post-reading Strategies—Reflecting, Analyzing, and Drawing Conclusions, which is found in the sixth-grade Language Arts volume of the Concordia Curriculum Guide series. What can students learn from this story? Consider questions like these: Why did God choose a donkey to speak to Balaam, instead of having the angel announce himself directly? Why did Balaam argue with the donkey, seeming not to notice the absurdity (and miracle!) of arguing with an animal? We know from Revelation 2:14 that in spite of this warning, Balaam went on to betray God and God's people by giving Balak advice on how to draw Israel into sin. What does that tell us about human nature?

Searching Further

Use Reproducible 19 to explore the term "a land of milk and honey." On one level, it means a land where there would be plenty to eat and drink. Taking it further, the milk and honey can have a spiritual implication. Discuss with your class that we are on a journey too—a spiritual journey to the promised land of heaven. Along the way, we need nourishment (milk and honey), and we face things that can sidetrack or even destroy us (junk food). Discuss why the listed items can harm us or help us grow; add others to the list. Then emphasize that our faith growth is nourished by Jesus Himself in His Holy Word and Sacraments.

Technology

The texts regarding Balaam are often misunderstood or interpreted in different ways. Ask your pastor to explain any difficult passages, including cultural practices of the time. Then invite him to visit the class or answer student questions via e-mail or Skype.

Working in Groups

Tell students that the books attributed to Moses are called the "Pentateuch," from a Greek word that means "five books." Jews call them the "Torah," which means "instruction." These books include Genesis, Exodus, Leviticus, Numbers, and Deuteronomy. Divide the class into five groups, and assign each a different book of the Pentateuch to review. Have them scan the book and write Bible *Jeopardy!* questions about events and people they remember. Use one card for each question. Write the question on one side and the answer on the other side. Use this as a review before going on to the Book of Joshua.

Ideas for the Gifted

Have students make a board game based on the exodus route. Draw and color a map of the area on a large piece of poster board. Add steps between locales. Call it "Journey to the Promised Land." Make cards labeled "Blessings" and "Consequences" that reference details of their journey. Players take turns drawing cards. If they draw a "Blessings" card, they move forward a set number of spaces; if it is a "Consequences" card, they lose a turn. Give each participant a marker to move around the board to reach the Promised Land.

Unit 2—To the Promised Land

Lesson 20

God's People Build a Monument
Joshua 3–4

Background

Stone monuments were a common way of commemorating important events or agreements in the Old Testament. Jacob, Moses, Saul, and the Transjordan tribes of Israel all set up stone monuments on different occasions (Genesis 28:18–22; 31:45–54; Exodus 17:15–16; 1 Samuel 15:12; Joshua 22:10–34). Moses commanded Israel to create a stone monument with the words of the Law on it when they had entered the Promised Land (Deuteronomy 27:2–8). The hope was that a stone monument would last long and remind the people of Israel to be faithful to the Lord and to live as His people.

Joshua's monument was built with stones taken from the very riverbed that God had made safe for the Israelites to cross over. The stones themselves were a witness to the miracle God had performed, for it would be difficult—if not impossible—for ordinary human strength to obtain large stones from that location, particularly when the Jordan was in flood. As long as the stones remained in place and the Israelites remembered the story, they would tell their children of the miracle God had done for them.

Devotions

We've seen how the Lord prepared Moses for his leadership role later in life. His early years in a God-fearing home, his middle years in an Egyptian palace, and later years as a shepherd in Midian were not random events. God was training Moses in skills he would need to lead the people of Israel out of slavery. Today we will see how God prepared Joshua—also over many years—to be the next leader of the people.

God's plans and actions in the lives of His people are not seen only in Bible stories. They continue throughout history. The twists and turns in Martin Luther's life in the sixteenth century were part of God's plan to train Luther and to place him in the right environments to become a great reformer.

Consider also the famous artist Henri Matisse, who lived at the turn of the nineteenth century and into the twentieth century. In his early years, Matisse was well-known for his paintings, which were filled with colors and patterns. But as he became older, his health was poor. Eventually he was confined to a wheelchair, and he was afflicted so badly with arthritis in his hands that he could no longer hold a brush to paint without suffering severe pain. However, he still wanted to express his creative ideas; so he "painted with scissors." In other words, he cut large shapes from colored paper, then arranged them and pasted them in place to make glorious creations. Some critics say that his paper cutouts far surpass the beauty of his earlier works.

Now think about your own life. Consider that God has plans for each of us. Sometimes those plans take turns that we don't expect. But we can trust that God's will for us is always for our good. Whether you are going through good times or bad times, remember the words of Jeremiah 29:11: "For I know the plans I have for you, declares the LORD, plans for welfare and not for evil, to give you a future and a hope." Sing together "Thy Strong Word" (*LSB* 578; recorded as *Hymn of the Month* for grade 6, October). As an alternative anytime this month, sing "A Mighty Fortress Is Our God" (*LSB* 656, 657; recorded as *Hymn of the Month* for grade 3, October [656], and as *Hymn of the Season* for grade 3, Reformation [657]). After singing this "Hymn of the Reformation," read together Psalm 46, on which the words of the hymn are based.

Central Truth

God prepares His people through various ways, and He always keeps His promises to them.

Objectives

- Acknowledge that it is not our own strength, wealth, intellect, or even goodness that leads us to the ultimate victory.
- Rely on the grace of God to go before us and deliver us.
- Celebrate that through the waters of Baptism, God works in us, making us His people through faith and forgiveness as He leads us to the promised land of heaven.

Materials

- Hymnals and music CDs
- Web Resource 20a
- Web Resource 20b
- Web Resource 20c
- Reproducible 20

Bible Prep

Post in advance so students can bookmark references before class time.

- Joshua 1:16
- Joshua 3–4
- Numbers 27:18–23
- Psalm 18:2; 19:14; 31:3; 62:2; 71:3; 78:35; 89:26; 94:22; and 95:1

INTO the lesson

Prepared to Lead

As you study this section in the Student Book together, emphasize how God was molding the life of Joshua so that one day he would be a good leader. One important concept we can learn from this is that the Church is not dependent on a person or a personality. When a leader in the Church passes on, the Church does not come to a standstill. The Church goes on because its true leader is the ever-living Savior, Jesus Christ. Say, **God is active throughout history in the lives of His people. In fact, *history* is really "His story." All the events of humankind have a purpose in God's great design. There is no history apart from God.** The Heroes of Faith biography series that accompanies the One in Christ curriculum reminds us of Christian leaders throughout the ages—leaders who were guided and supported by the Lord.

Read aloud Joshua 24:14–15 and then point out that he was "taking a stand." He was letting everyone know that he and his family would continue to follow the Lord. Compare this with the words of Martin Luther when he was placed on trial and responded, "Here I stand; I cannot do otherwise. God help me. Amen." He, too, followed the Lord and used Scripture as his guide. Take time to explore and sing two songs that share this theme. "Thine Forever, God of Love" (*LSB* 687; recorded as *Hymn of the Month for grade 6, May*) is a poem asking God to keep us faithful to Him throughout our entire lives. The song "Here I Stand" (Web Resource 20a) relates well to the stand of faithfulness that both Joshua and Martin Luther made. In this hymn, we are relating this to our own lives, relying on God's power to keep us firm in faith.

Lesson 20

God's People Build a Monument

Prepared to Lead

After forty years in the desert wilderness, the people of Israel looked to a new leader. Moses had died at the age of 120. God chose Joshua to lead the people into Canaan, the land promised long ago to Abraham, Isaac, and Jacob. Since the early years of Joshua's life in Egypt, God had been preparing him to be the next leader. Here are some of the events that occurred and the characteristics Joshua developed as a result.

Life Experiences	Characteristics
Slavery in Egypt	Self-control and discipline
Crossing the Red Sea	Trust in God alone
Standing with Moses at Mount Sinai	Awe and respect for God
Guarding the temple of meeting	Sense of duty
Leading troops against the Amalekites	Military strategy
Representing his tribe as a spy	Bravery and confidence in God
Following Moses' orders	Obedience to superiors

Read Numbers 27:18–23 and write the most important quality of leadership that Joshua possessed. **God's Spirit**

Now the people of Israel were beside the Jordan River with the Promised Land of Canaan on the other side. The nation had been at the same spot forty years earlier, but at that time, they had cried out in fear, failing to trust in the Lord. In the meantime, the rebellious people had passed away, and their children formed this new nation with a new response. Read Joshua 1:16 and write the response of the people to their new leader, Joshua. **"They answered Joshua, 'All that you have commanded us we will do, and wherever you send us we will go.'"**

Read Joshua 3:5. What words of encouragement did Joshua give the people? **"Tomorrow the Lord will do wonders among you."**

Read Joshua 3:7. What words of encouragement did God give Joshua? **"As I was with Moses, so I will be with you."**

Covenant Connection

The name *Joshua* is a form of the name *Jesus*. Joshua was a preview of the Savior Messiah to come. Both would lead their people into the Promised Land. At this point, however, we see major differences. Joshua fought heathen nations, but he never completely won the victory. Jesus fought sin and death—and His victory is complete. On the cross, He said, "It is finished." And He gives the victory to us (1 Corinthians 15:57).

46

INTO the Word

Powerful Parallels

Once again, we see God's wisdom and planning. These were not random events. These parallels would be an obvious reminder of God's action in both events. God is present throughout history and in our own lives today.

Ready to Follow

Use the Student Book and Web Resource 20b to tell the story of the crossing of the Jordan River. Once again, we see the beautiful symmetry in God's plan. These were not random events. They occurred at God's command. The "Review" section shows again the connections between the Old and New Testaments. As pointed out, one of the major differences is that Israel, led by Joshua, never completed the task of removing the unbelievers from the Promised Land; this is something that would plague them for the remainder of their years as a nation. On the other hand, we **look at Jesus, who has obtained complete victory over sin, death, and the devil.**

The Jordan River is also a prominent feature in the New Testament narrative of Jesus' Baptism. In Baptism, as we receive faith and forgiveness, we are crossing over from our old sinful self to a new creation in Christ Jesus. We are encouraged to daily remember our baptismal covenant, mak-

The Jordan River was overflowing with floodwaters. What two-part plan did God carry out? (1) Joshua 3:6, 13: **The priests carried the ark of the covenant into the middle of the river and the water stopped.** (2) Joshua 4:11, 18: **The people crossed over, the priests walked out of the dry riverbed, and the water started overflowing again.**

Powerful Parallels

Parallels are events or ideas that follow a similar path. The beginning and ending of the journey of the children of Israel have very interesting parallels. Read the following paragraph. When you come to a box, read just the purple word. Then read the paragraph again, but when you come to the box, read just the green word. This will help you to see the similarities between the two events.

God's chosen people [exited entered] [Egypt Canaan], a land of [slavery promise]. God's miracle held back the waters of the [Red Jordan Sea River]. The people joined their leader, [Moses Joshua], in praising God with a [song memorial].

Ready to Follow

Why did God tell them to use *twelve* stones to build the memorial (Joshua 4:1–4)? **Each stone represented one of the twelve tribes of Israel.** Eventually, the land would be divided into sections, one for each of the twelve tribes. But there was still much work to be done; the heathen, idol-worshiping people needed to be removed from the land so that it could be dedicated to the Lord.

Remember

"The LORD will keep your going out and your coming in from this time forth and forevermore." (Psalm 121:8)

47

INTO our lives

Rocks of Remembrance

Even today, memorials are constructed to call attention to and encourage people to remember something significant. Use Web Resource 20c as you consider several American memorials. Ask students to identify other memorials they are aware of. The Student Book in the "Remember" section pictures the memorial; however, the addition of the Bible verse, for memory work, reminds us that memorials can be words in our hearts rather than stones plastered together. Say, **That is why learning these Bible verses is so important—it is taking God's Word, as a memorial in our hearts, wherever we go!**

This lesson started by connecting to the past—to Israel's time in Egypt and in the wilderness. At this point, connect the lesson to the future of Israel. Crossing the Jordan River was a starting point for the twelve tribes. In the years to come, they would face challenges to establish themselves in this new land. Distribute Reproducible 20 and study the map, which shows the eventual division of the land and where the various tribes settled. (Point out that the tribe of Levi was dispersed throughout all parts of the nation so that they could be worship leaders wherever the people settled.)

As you examine the Bible verses pointing to God as our Rock, also examine the hymn "My Hope Is Built on Nothing Less" (*LSB* 575; recorded as *Hymn of the Month for grade 5, October*). The refrain is especially appropriate, as it states, "on Christ, the solid rock, I stand." Sing again "Here I Stand" (Web Resource 20a), noting that here, too, we sing of our "Rock," who is Jesus!

ing us members of God's family as our sins are washed away through the blood of Jesus.

Note: Some people who read the Book of Joshua see the violent battles and wonder how we can say that God is love. Remember that the Canaanites violated the most important command of God through the worship of idols. They sought to please their gods through practices that included the sacrifice of children and sexual orgies. The culture of the Canaanites was said to be the most barbaric of its time. The humane laws given to the Israelites stood in sharp contrast to the practices they observed in the cultures around them. God instructed the Israelites to kill those people to remove their influence. The pockets of idol worshipers that remained were like a cancer that infected the people of Israel time and again, in spite of God's warning of the danger that association with those people would cause.

91

Lesson Support

Create a classroom memorial. Have each student write a personal "letter to God"; assure students that no one else will look at these letters, not even the teacher. In the letter, they are to mention (1) something they are particularly thankful for that day, (2) a question they would like to ask God about the Bible, (3) a question they would like to ask God about life in this world today, and (4) something they would like to improve or change about themselves. Give each student an envelope in which to place the letter, seal it, and write his or her name on it. Place these letters (which are much like prayers because they are talking to God) in a box that can be locked and placed in a secure place. We are now at Lesson 20. Tell students that when the class discusses Lesson 80, you will open the box, pass back the letters, and let students consider how much they have changed or grown during the intervening months. Remind the students that God has been with them during that whole time.

Curriculum Connection

Cultures around the world create monuments to mark important events. Take a look at section 6.3.2.1, Contrasting and Comparing the Representative Images or Designs and Stylistic Characteristics from at Least Two Cultures. This is found in the sixth-grade Visual Arts volume of the Concordia Curriculum Guide series. Then compare Joshua's monument with several others from various countries—perhaps the Vietnam Veterans Memorial, the Taj Mahal, the Great Pyramid of Giza, and the statue of Christ the Redeemer in Rio de Janeiro, Brazil. What purposes do these monuments serve? What meanings do they carry? Look at their artistic style and material. How are they different? How are they similar?

Searching Further

At the end of Joshua's time of leadership, he made the famous statement "as for me and my house, we will serve the LORD" (Joshua 24:15). These words are often found on plaques and other Christian artwork that people display in their homes. (Point out that when Joshua said "house," he was referring to his family, not to a building.) Ask students to simply be aware of this and notice if there is a piece of art in their home, a grandparent's home, or somewhere else on which the Bible verse is displayed. If possible, encourage students to bring such a piece of art into the classroom; you might then arrange the students' items in a display, showing the various ways in which this verse is presented.

Bringing it home

Paint "Rocks of Remembrance" to share with family members. Collect smooth stones 3 to 6 inches long, and use permanent markers to write a word or draw a Christian symbol on each rock.

Unit 2—To the Promised Land

Lesson 21

The Fall of Jericho
Joshua 1; 2; 6–8

Central Truth
God desires to lead His people in all things—He leads, we follow.

Objectives
- Admit our physical and spiritual weakness.
- Turn all things over to God and follow Him—He faithfully does the hard part, and we get the victory through the cross of Christ.
- Share the Good News of salvation with others.

Materials
- Hymnals and music CDs
- Web Resource 21a
- Reproducible 21

Bible Prep
Post in advance so students can bookmark the reference before class time.
- Joshua 1–8

Background

What odd instructions for overcoming a city: walk around it, blow trumpets, and be silent until it is time to shout. Surely some of the Israelites felt foolish as they obeyed God's instructions. But then, maybe not. They had seen His miracles in the desert. They had seen Him part the Jordan River to let them walk through on dry land. God's instructions are never foolish, no matter how strange they may appear.

Even the Canaanites knew that by the time of this story. As Rahab says, "I know that the Lord has given you the land. . . . For we have heard how the Lord dried up the water of the Red Sea before you when you came out of Egypt, and what you did to the two kings of the Amorites. . . . And as soon as we heard it, our hearts melted, and there was no spirit left in any man because of you, for the Lord your God, He is God in the heavens above and on the earth beneath" (Joshua 2:9–11). And so, in wisdom, Rahab hid the spies and followed their instructions, even at the risk of her own life.

The Lord has given us odd instructions also. "Repent and be baptized every one of you in the name of Jesus Christ for the forgiveness of your sins" (Acts 2:38). "Take, eat. . . . Drink of it, all of you" (Matthew 26:26–27). "Go therefore and make disciples of all nations" (Matthew 28:19). We follow Him because we know that His words lead to life eternal.

Devotions

In today's Bible lesson, we will see that two of the things God desires of His people are trust and obedience. Consider how these traits are or are not shown in this story: Adam admired his older brother Josh because he made good decisions. So when Josh finally received his driver's license, their parents agreed that the two of them could go to a movie together without parental supervision. It would be the first time Adam rode in the family car with only Josh behind the wheel. It felt like true freedom for both of the boys. They turned up the radio and laughed most of the way there. While standing in line, Adam begged Josh to take him to the newest, scariest R-rated movie in the theater. Josh stood his ground, refusing to allow it. "Mom and Dad trust me, and I'm not going to blow it on some dumb movie," Josh stated. "Besides, it might give you nightmares, and then they would find out for sure and blame it on me." Adam continued to beg, insisting he wouldn't be bothered by the bad movie. But it was pointless. Josh paid for their tickets to see the comedy flick that their parents had agreed upon. They headed in just as the lights dimmed. About halfway through, Adam said he needed to use the restroom. He slipped out of the dark theater and made his way down to the R-rated movie. He could only stand it for about ten minutes. When he returned to his seat beside Josh, he felt extremely guilty. It only made him feel worse when he lied to his brother about why it had taken him so long. "There was a really long line, and I saw a friend from school," he stammered. He couldn't enjoy the rest of the movie, and he remained quiet on the ride home. The next morning, Josh was allowed to drive Adam to school. Adam confessed to Josh what he had done and apologized for being dishonest. "You have to talk to Mom and Dad, you know," Josh said. "I know. Can you help me out and stick around while I 'fess up?" Adam asked, trying not to sound too frightened. "Sure, but only if you tell the truth. And tell them that I said no way about fifty times!" Josh sounded more annoyed than angry. "It's a deal," Adam lamented. He was starting to feel better, but he said a prayer on the way to school, asking for forgiveness and the courage to face his parents. He would need all the help he could get. His parents would ground him for sure. He knew he had it coming.

We are blessed to know that while God demands obedience and justice, He also shows grace and mercy. Jesus led an obedient life for us, and His death on the cross obtained justice for all who believe in Him. *Praise God, our refuge and strength, by reading Psalm 46 and singing "Thy Strong Word" (LSB 578; recorded as Hymn of the Month for grade 6, October).*

INTO the Word

Ask, **Does God get fed up when people disobey Him? Does He grow impatient with the disobedience of His people?** We find many examples of the continued disobedience of God's people in the Old Testament. Yet God continued to forgive them, and He desired a relationship with them. He provided leadership, guidance, and redemption, and yet demanded obedience. This still holds true today.

Before starting the Bible story for today, we will look at the ending! Much happens in the Bible narrative in Joshua 1–8, but when all is said and done, Joshua built an altar and offered sacrifices to the Lord. The interesting thing about this altar is that Joshua carved on the stones the words of the Law that God gave to Moses (Joshua 8:32). Joshua, with all of the people, was renewing the covenant that the Lord would be their God, and they would be His people.

Lesson 21

The Fall of Jericho

Unexpected Help

Read Joshua 2. Forty years had passed since Joshua had been a spy, scouting the land of Canaan. Now he was the leader of the Israelites, sending out spies himself, particularly to Jericho—a key city to their entrance into the Promised Land. The spies were helped by Rahab, a woman who had led a wicked life, but who now recognized the true God, saying, "The Lord your God, He is God in the heavens above and on the earth beneath" (Joshua 2:11).

Name three dangerous things Rahab did to help the Israelite spies. **Answers may include: hid the spies on her roof; lied to the king's messengers and sent them on a useless pursuit; used a rope to lower the spies to safety outside the city walls; sent the spies on a safe route.**

What was the plan to protect Rahab because of her kindness? **She was to place a scarlet (red) cord in her window—a sign that she and all in there would be safe when Jericho fell.**

God's long-range plan for Rahab was even more amazing. Matthew 1:5 tells us that Rahab was the mother of Boaz, the great-great-grandmother of King David, and an ancestor of Jesus Christ. Why is this so amazing? **It shows God's grace and forgiveness; He is not unwilling to associate with very sinful people, but offers faith and a new life for them. We are not saved by what we do, but by what God has done for us in Christ Jesus.**

Unexpected Report

The report of ten of the spies forty years earlier had been filled with fear, saying that the people of Israel would be crushed like grasshoppers by the powerful people of Canaan. What was the report this time (Joshua 2:24)? **"Truly the Lord has given all the land into our hands. And also, all the inhabitants of the land melt away because of us."**

Covenant Connection

So many things related to Jericho's fall were unexpected, showing us aspects of the character of God. He works in unexpected ways, as Isaiah 55:8 says: "My thoughts are not your thoughts, neither are your ways My ways, declares the Lord." When the Messiah, Christ Jesus, came, He was not what the people expected. They thought He would be a powerful king. Instead, He was born in a stable and became a humble teacher, serving people. Even though Jesus said it would happen, people never expected the Messiah to die on a cross and, three days later, arise from death and the tomb! In Acts 17:6, the message of salvation in Jesus was said to "[turn] the world upside down." Praise God for His unexpected grace and blessings.

48

INTO the lesson

Unexpected Help

God so often chooses to work through the unexpected person to carry out His will. Rahab was a prostitute, Gideon was a coward, many of the disciples were fishermen, Zacchaeus was a tax collector, and Paul persecuted Christians. God wants us to know that *He* is working in our lives—it has nothing to do with our power, intelligence, or goodness. This is something that Martin Luther also came to recognize. As a monk, he tried all sorts of techniques to gain God's pity or favor, but it was never enough. He felt peace only when he relied totally on the righteousness of Jesus.

Unexpected Report

As you work together on this section of the Student Book, the "Covenant Connection," and the remainder of the lesson, emphasize that God works in mysterious ways! He works in ways that we can't expect or comprehend. That's why He's God, and we're not! If our simple minds could understand God, if God's ways could fit into our small brains, He would be a very small God. Praise Him that He is so much more than we can ever understand, and therefore trust Him completely. Use Web Resource 21a to sing about the greatness of God, "Our Hero"!

Unexpected Strategy

Read Joshua 6:1–20. What was God's battle plan for the first six days? _Once each day, the people would parade around the city without making a sound. They would be led by the priests carrying the ark of the covenant and by seven priests who would be blowing rams' horns._

What was the strategy for the seventh day? _It was the same plan except that it was done seven times, and the last time, as the priests blew their horns, the people shouted._

What reason could God have for such an unusual strategy? _God wanted the people to trust Him completely; He wanted them to know that they did not win by their power, but by His._

What special order did God give the people in Joshua 6:19? _All silver, gold, bronze, and iron from Jericho was to be given to the treasury of the Lord._

Some people try to explain away the destruction of Jericho, saying it was just an earthquake. Because God is the Creator and Ruler of all creation, He very well could have used an earthquake to do this—it is within His power to control all of nature. However, this was not "just an earthquake," because no one has ever been able to call an earthquake into happening at an exact instant of time. Again, we must say that it is in God's power to control all of nature! He rules heaven and earth!

Unexpected Defeat

The next battle was against a small, unimportant town named Ai (which means "ruined"). What was the report from the spies who returned from Ai (Joshua 7:3)? _The spies said to not bother taking all the people into battle; they said two or three thousand soldiers would be enough to win a victory._

What was the unexpected result in verses 4–5? _The little army of Ai chased away the army of Israel and killed some of the Israelites. Now it was the hearts of Israel that melted with fear._

Why had God allowed this defeat (see vv. 10–13)? _Someone had disobeyed God's orders by stealing for himself some of the metals from Jericho that where supposed to be given to the Lord's treasury._

Once the guilty person (Achan) confessed (7:20) and was punished, God sent Joshua and the army back to Ai with an ambush plan (8:3–7). Most of the army stayed hidden while Joshua approached the city with a small group. The people of Ai came out of the city and chased them away, thinking it was just like before. However, as they chased Joshua, the main portion of the Israelite army stormed into the city of Ai and destroyed it. What can we learn from these Bible narratives?

We can see two things that God expects of His people:

TRUST and OBEDIENCE

We can see two things that we can expect from God:

MIGHTY POWER and GRACIOUS FORGIVENESS

Remember

"Commit to the Lord whatever you do, and your plans will succeed." (Proverbs 16:3 NIV)

INTO our lives

Unexpected Strategy

After discussing the unusual strategy God presented to the people, ask your students if they have considered any unusual strategies with God's people today. Ask them to consider Baptism—what an unusual strategy! In his Small Catechism, Martin Luther even asks, "How can water do such great things?" Then Luther gives this answer: "Certainly not just water, but the word of God in and with the water does these things, along with the faith which trusts this word of God." (Direct students to the Small Catechism in the Appendix of their Student Book.) Our sins are indeed washed away in Baptism, not by the water, but by the Word of God in Christ Jesus.

Or consider another unusual strategy—the Lord's Supper. Some church bodies believe the bread and wine are just symbols that help us remember Jesus. However, in the Small Catechism, Luther focuses on the true Word of God spoken by Jesus Himself. Luther says, "These words, 'Given and shed for you for the forgiveness of sins,' show us that in the Sacrament forgiveness of sins, life, and salvation are given us through these words. For where there is forgiveness of sins, there is also life and salvation." He also assures us, "Whoever believes these words has exactly what they say: 'forgiveness of sins.'"

Unexpected Defeat

Though the title of this section speaks of defeat, it does end in victory. **We see again that God takes sin seriously; He does want our obedience. But we also see His great grace and forgiveness as He calls us to repentance. This lesson ends in victory, but the greater lesson is found in the victory Christ has won for all of us through His death and resurrection.** As stated in 1 Corinthians 15:57, "Thanks be to God, who gives us the victory through our Lord Jesus Christ." Rejoice in this, using Web Resource 21b to sing "Hope's Celebration." Explore words and phrases that are especially related to today's Bible lesson.

Lesson Support

Curriculum Connection

While the fall of Jericho involved some dramatic moments at the end, it was preceded by hours and hours of endless walking. Get your students involved in walking, running, and other forms of healthy activity. You'll find help and ideas in section 6.1.3.2, Locomotor Skills Demonstrated in Dynamic Fitness, Sport, and Rhythmic Activities. This is in the sixth-grade Physical Education volume of the Concordia Curriculum Guide series.

Technology

Use an interactive whiteboard to display Bible verses through biblegateway.com. Students may choral-read or alternately read the verses.

Visit a Web site related to the city of Jericho. Keyword suggestions to aid you in your search include "city of Jericho," "map of Jericho," and "battle of Jericho." Emphasize that Jericho is a real place that has been examined by archaeologists.

Searching Further

Consider using Reproducible 21 as an optional discussion starter on the many battles in Joshua, Judges, and other books of the Bible.

Working in Groups

Divide the class into groups of three or four. Give each group a stack of index cards. Instruct the students to build a house of cards as tall as they can, but to remain silent during the construction. Encourage them to use nonverbal communication and to work quickly and cooperatively. Give them exactly two minutes to complete the challenge. The winners of the challenge will then elect someone from each group to silently bring down their tower in a nonthreatening way; for example, a student might gently blow the tower down or apply a light flick of the finger. Remind the students that while the Israelites were marching, their faith grew. While they were silent, they were not able to express doubt or disobedience. On the seventh day, they were able to let loose a victory shout and express their joy. Faith can break down barriers. Use Hebrews 11:30 to reinforce this.

Faith in Action

Have the students imagine that they are news anchors; have them create an on-the-scene news report as if they were interviewing eyewitnesses to the fall of Jericho. Give them five to ten minutes of preparation time in groups of two or three to plan their "action news" reports. Suggest they use a "who, what, when, where, why, how" approach. Then have students present their news reports to the class.

Ideas for the Gifted

Have students research the Berlin Wall. Have them look for details about its size, construction, location, years of existence, reasons for existence, and its eventual fall. Ask them to make correlations to the city of Jericho, posing questions about God's role in the fall of the Berlin Wall and the fall of the city of Jericho. Have them decide if there are any connections.

Unit 2—To the Promised Land

Lesson 22

Deborah and Barak
Judges 4–5

Central Truth
Throughout all of history, the cycle continues: people sin, suffer consequences, and cry for help; then God sends deliverance, and joy is restored.

Objectives
- Realize that the cycle of sin continues while we live in this sin-filled world.
- Acknowledge that the only thing that stops the cycle is Jesus.
- Rejoice that God calls us to repentance and faith by His grace and mercy.

Materials
- Reproducible 22
- Web Resource 22a
- Hymnals and music CDs

Bible Prep
Post in advance so students can bookmark references before class time.
- Judges 4–5
- 2 Corinthians 5:21
- Romans 12:2
- 1 Thessalonians 5:17
- 2 Thessalonians 1:3
- 1 Peter 2:2
- 2 Peter 3:18
- Ephesians 6:10–18
- Galatians 5:22–23

Background

The Book of Judges shows a grim cycle, which is described in Judges 2:11–19. The careful reader can count at least seven of these sin/judgment/rescue cycles in the book, and possibly more. This was the case at the time of Deborah. The previous judges, Ehud and Shamgar, had died, and Israel promptly returned to evil. This time, God raised up Deborah, who called on Barak to assemble an army. God saved Israel once again, "and the land had rest for forty years" (5:31)—after which, of course, Israel fell into sin again! It is easy to be impatient with Israel. But we know that our own lives are not as faithful as they should be either. In fact, it is only through Jesus Christ that we are able to stay as close to the Lord as we do! He has given us forgiveness and salvation through His death and resurrection. Now God the Holy Spirit dwells in our hearts and pulls us back whenever we stray from the Lord. Even when we insist on going our own way and fall into major sin and trouble, He still calls us back to repentance, faith, and forgiveness through Jesus. None of this is our doing. It is all God's gracious, patient love.

Devotions

Today's Bible story has a familiar cycle of sin, consequences, repentant prayer, and rescue. We often find this same cycle in our lives. Here is a story of a family in the middle of such a painful cycle. The only comfort that lasts is in the forgiveness, strengthening, and deliverance we have in Jesus.

Samantha looked across the breakfast table at her mom. Both of them were tired from the long night before. Samantha began to wonder what things would be like when her parents got the divorce. She knew it was only a few short weeks away before things were finalized, and she could feel the tears well up in her eyes. She wanted to talk to her mom about last night, but she was too tired. She decided to pray instead.

"Dear Lord," Samantha silently began, "please help my dad stop drinking. He wants to do what is right, but he is helpless on his own. He knows what he needs to do to follow You, and to be Your servant, but he continues to mess up. Help him to realize that he needs to go to his meetings to get support for his fight against alcoholism. Help him find another job so that he can feel good about himself again. Please give him the strength to break this terrible cycle. He stops drinking, finds a job, starts drinking again, and then loses his job again. The fighting starts up, and my mom yells at him when he comes home drunk. Please help us."

Samantha looked up just as her little brother came in the room from a restless night's sleep. Samantha smiled as she watched him make his way over to their mom, who folded him into her arms when he reached for her. Samantha continued the prayer in her heart. "Lord, be with my little brother, Jack. He is so young and scared. He doesn't really understand what is going on. He is so much like Dad that I worry about him already. Please, Lord, don't let him grow up to be an alcoholic! I pray with all my heart that he doesn't mess up his own family too, like Dad has messed up ours!"

Lastly, she wanted to pray for her parents' relationship, but she didn't know how. She began, "Lord, I don't even know what to pray for now . . ." God was with her in spite of her uncertainty, and He would continue to be with her and her broken family in this cycle of heartache. She knew this was most certainly true. She would just keep praying, waiting for God's plans and God's timing.

Sing together "O God, Our Help in Ages Past" (*LSB* 733; recorded on *Hymns of the Month, grade 3, November*).

INTO the lesson

Readers Theater

This is a comfortable way to introduce what might be a complicated Bible narrative with complex concepts. After reading the script in the Student Book, read the psalm of praise in Judges 5 aloud together, assigning verses or alternating sections, because this is another way to summarize the Bible story.

INTO the Word

Use Reproducible 22 to discuss how this Bible story is actually a *type* of what happens over and over again in the Bible (at least seven times in the Book of Judges alone). A *type*, or *archetype*, is an example that is not unique, but represents something that occurs often. This type of story is true not only for the actions of the people of Israel, but it can be seen throughout history because all people are sinful.

Discuss a contemporary example of this *type*. Europe at one time represented the height of Christianity, with huge cathedrals in most large cities. There were difficulties, such as those that caused the need for the Reformation, but in general, Europe was Christian. In recent years, many of those giant cathedrals are largely empty except for tourists who come to look at the artwork. In many European countries, the percentage of people who attend church regularly is under 20 percent. On the other hand, the rising Muslim population in Europe seems to be foreshadowing a time when Christianity might be replaced by Islam. Some people say, "That could never happen there" or "That could never happen here." But it *has* happened elsewhere. It happened in what today is modern Turkey. Two thousand years ago, that area was called "Asia Minor," and it was home to many Christian communities, including many that were nurtured by missionaries such as the apostle Paul, Titus, Timothy, Silas, and Barnabas. A thousand years ago, that area was the location of the Byzantine Empire, which carried on orthodox Christianity after the collapse of Rome. One of the most magnificent cathedrals in the world, St. Sophia's in Istanbul, was turned into a mosque, with minarets instead of crosses, and many of its golden mosaics dedicated to Christ have been taken down or covered over. Today it is a museum where public prayer is strictly prohibited. It happened there.

Lesson 22

Deborah and Barak

Readers Theater

KEY PLAYERS:

Narrator (explains details)
Israelites (unfaithful to God; repentantly seek His help)
The Good Guys: Deborah (the prophetess who gives messages from the Lord)
Barak (leader of Israel's army who relies on Deborah's wisdom)
Jael (a brave woman, Sisera's assassin, wife of Heber)
The Bad Guys: King Jabin (king of Canaan, oppressor of the Israelites)
Sisera (commander of Jabin's army)
Heber (Jael's husband and a traitor who informs Sisera's army of Barak's military plans)

Narrator: Long after the death of Moses and Joshua, the Israelites strayed far from God and did evil in His sight, worshiping Canaanite gods. So God allowed the Canaanites to overpower the Israelites. For twenty years, King Jabin ruled cruelly over them.

King Jabin: I, King Jabin, ruler of Canaan, do decree the tribes of Israel to be under my control.

Israelites: Deborah, you are wise. Give us a message from the Lord. Has He forgotten us? For so many years, we have been ruled by these thieves and thugs. What should we do?

Deborah: You are constantly coming to my court for advice, and yet you continue to disobey the Lord. No wonder you have a life of trouble! You suffer the consequences of your sin.

Israelites: But we have been praying to God for twenty years, and He is bound to hear our prayers and deliver us! We can't take the oppression of Jabin's army any longer! But we are hopeless against his army commander Sisera, who has nine hundred iron chariots. No one can defeat him!

Deborah: God listens to the prayers of the faithful. Why should He listen to you when you don't listen to Him? I have a message from God, but it is important for you to listen this time. God gave me the role of judge to help lead you to peace in this Promised Land, but first I must ask you to go and get Barak. God is summoning him to be His flashing sword, His thunderbolt, in battle.

Narrator: The Israelites did as she asked, and Barak came to Deborah to hear her plan.

Deborah: Barak, the Lord God of Israel commands you to take with you ten thousand men of the tribes of Naphtali and Zebulun and lead the way to Mount Tabor. God will lure Sisera, the commander of Jabin's army, into a

Review

Covenant Connection

This story seems to have a happy ending, but it really doesn't. Notice the last statement: "The people praised God and rested in peace for forty years." What do you think happened at the end of the forty years? Once again, the people forgot about God's grace. They turned away from the Lord and ended up in trouble. We might feel tempted to criticize the people of Israel, but we, too, continually sin, even though we know God's grace and goodness. Where is there hope? Only in Jesus! He forgives us, and He transforms us. Pray that God will keep us faithful to His Word, forgive us when we fail, and lift us up when we fall.

50

INTO our lives

So what does the Old Testament teach us, and what does European history teach us today as we sit in a sixth-grade classroom? Ask, **How can we keep this cycle from happening again? There is one answer—the victory is in Jesus. God calls us to be watchful and vigilant and to be armed and ready with the Word of God. Turn to Ephesians 6:10–18 and read about the defense and weapon we have in our constant fight against sin, death, and the devil. It is a battle that continues every day. But we know we have the ultimate victory in Christ.**

As the memory verses say, it is necessary that we be faithful to God. But we are not strong enough to do this on our own. That is why it is so important to stay connected to the Means of Grace—God's Word and the Sacraments—because the Holy Spirit works through these means to strengthen our faith and to build us up in faithfulness and godliness. That faithfulness is one of the fruit of the Spirit, which God grows in us. See Galatians 5:22–23.

Discuss the role of Barak in this Bible story. Some say that he was a cow-

98

vulnerable spot near the Kishon River. God will be with you. Even though your army is smaller and not as powerful, God will give the victory to the Israelites.

Barak: I will, but only if you come with me.

Deborah: I'll go with you, but understand that there will be no glory in it for you. God will win the battle, and God will use a woman's hand to destroy Sisera.

Narrator: So Barak called together the tribes of Naphtali and Zebulun, and, with Deborah, they went to Mount Tabor to prepare for battle. Meanwhile, Heber, a traitor to his own people of Israel, told Sisera about Deborah and Barak's plans.

Heber: Sisera, word on the street says that the army of Israel is headed for Mount Tabor. They think they can defeat you in battle.

Sisera: Really! Looks like I'll take my nine hundred chariots for a little scenic drive. We'll be waiting for them in the valley as they come down the mountain. Troops, let's get ready to win an easy one!

Deborah: *(To Barak and his army)* This is the day the Lord has given Sisera into your hands! God is marching before you! Charge!

Narrator: God did indeed go before the army of His people. He went ahead of them with a cloudburst of rain. It was the dry season—no one expected rain—but God opened up the heavens. The water roared in a flood down the mountain in front of the army of Barak. The waters roared into the valley below into what had been the dry bed of the Kishon River. Sisera had positioned his chariots there—in the worst possible place.

Israelites: Praise the Lord! He is sweeping the army away before us! Look at the chariots being washed away by the powerful floodwaters! Look at the chariots that remain—they are stuck in the mud! Look at the army of Sisera, running away in fear! This day belongs to the Lord!

Sisera: Yikes! I better get out of here. I've been so cruel to these people—they will surely want to get revenge on me! I must find my friend Heber. He will hide me and protect me.

Narrator: Sisera was a coward, abandoning his army. He rushed to Heber's home. There, Sisera was greeted by Heber's wife, Jael, who invited him to come inside to safety.

Jael: Come in, sir. Stay here. Don't be afraid. We will protect you. Rest under this blanket while the danger passes by.

Sisera: Wow, thanks! Do me a favor and stand in the doorway of the tent. If anyone comes by and asks you if you have company, just say no.

Jael: Okay, whatever you say.

Narrator: Sisera fell sound asleep because he was so exhausted and because he thought Jael was a traitor like her husband. But he was wrong. Jael knew the wickedness of Sisera, Jabin, and Canaan. She trusted that God had put the enemy into her people's hands. While Sisera was asleep, Jael killed the powerful commander. Jael used the weapons she had nearby—a tent peg and a hammer—to kill him. Then she called out to Barak, who was outside, chasing the Canaanite army.

Jael: Barak, I will show you the man you are looking for. I will show you what I have done.

Narrator: Deborah and Barak joined together in a song of praise to God. They had served as partners who were tools, or instruments, for God. They knew that it was God who had won the victory for them. The people praised God and rested in peace for forty years.

Remember

"Be faithful unto death, and I will give you the crown of life." (Revelation 2:10) "The Lord is faithful. He will establish you and guard you against the evil one. . . . May the Lord direct your hearts to the love of God and to the steadfastness of Christ." (2 Thessalonians 3:3, 5)

---

ard because he would go into battle only if Deborah went with him. It isn't fair to judge others because we don't know what is in their hearts. (Scripture speaks of the faith of Barak in Hebrews 11:32.) Only God can judge, and He does so based on His Holy Word. Perhaps Barak recognized the value of a partnership with someone who was so close to the Lord and was blessed by God. Perhaps Barak trusted that God could use a woman like Deborah just as well as God could use a man like Barak to accomplish His purposes. We see this cooperative attitude between Deborah and Barak in Judges 5, as together they create a psalm of praise to God.

Option: Try a game of *Jeopardy!* to review the Bible narrative. Divide the class into teams. Students can refer to Judges 4 and 5 to respond to the following answers given by the teacher. Participants should phrase their responses in the form of questions.

I defeated the enemy commander, as was prophesied. (Who was Jael?)

I led the charge of an army of ten thousand. (Who was Deborah?)

I was commander of the Canaanite army, and I fled on foot from the battle. (Who was Sisera?)

I was a prophet and a judge over Israel. (Who was Deborah?)

I was uncertain about leading the battle. (Who was Barak?)

I said I "owned" the people of Israel. (Who was King Jabin?)

I acted like a spy and revealed battle plans to the enemy. (Who was Heber?)

This was crushed in the tent of Jael. (What was Sisera's head?)

These were the showpieces of a mighty and oppressive army. (What are the nine hundred iron chariots?)

We were victorious at the battle at Mount Tabor. (Who were the Israelites?)

I am the Ruler and mighty King of all nations. (Who is our God?)

Faith in Action

Use Ephesians 6:10–18 to draw connections to our daily battle with sin, our need for protection, and God's powerful army of believers. Have students take turns reading the Bible verses. Have them form groups, and assign each group one of the following words from the Scripture references: *truth, righteousness, readiness, peace, faith, salvation,* and *prayer.* Have the groups write a real-life scenario in which someone must battle a problem by applying one of these seven concepts. The scenarios might include an encounter with a bully, a family problem, a situation with an unbeliever, a test of faith, or a personal inner struggle. Groups should be prepared to share their work, and they may create a PowerPoint presentation of the concepts. Review our battle against sin and the ultimate victory we have in Christ by singing "I'm in the Lord's Army" (Web Resource 22a) or "Stand Up, Stand Up for Jesus" (*LSB* 660; recorded as *Hymn of the Month* for grade 7, April).

Celebrating GROWTH

Be a tent pole! In advance, the teacher should bring in a large sheet or, if possible, use a parachute from your school's physical education department for this activity. Explain to the students that several of them will become tent poles for the rest of the class by holding up four ends of the sheet. The rest of the class will be allowed inside the tent to sit and listen to the Bible connection.

Ask the students if they have ever been in a tent in which the poles collapsed. Ask them to think about how important it is to have strong tent poles to support the shelter. Tell them that we can all be strong supporters of other Christians, and we can offer our services to God so that He may use us for His purposes. Much like tent poles, we can provide the support needed to help others. Let students know that God used Jael for His own purpose and that God wants us to trust Him. Ask them to think of ways in which God shelters us from the sins of the world. Remind them that there may be times they will be asked to be strong leaders for Christ and provide help for others in order to further God's kingdom.

Read 2 Corinthians 5:1: **"We know that if the tent that is our earthly home is destroyed, we have a building from God, a house not made with hands, eternal in the heavens."** Ask the students to draw a parallel between the temporary body we possess here on earth and that tent in the Bible passage. Look for responses that include our vulnerability as humans and our need for God's strength and help. (While here on earth, we may be weak, but God provides us with all we need to be strong, even if it is merely becoming like a tent pole.)

Check it Out

What's in a name? Say, **The name *Deborah* means "bee." Why is this an appropriate name for her?** (She was a leader and a prophetess, so perhaps she seemed like a queen bee. She certainly was busy as a bee, solving disputes. She took charge of the battle and led the people to victory.)

The name *Barak* means "thunderbolt." What does this name suggest? (He was a military leader. He stormed the enemy at the charge of Deborah. But the *real* thunderbolt came from God, as He sent the rains, causing a flood, and thereby defeating the enemy.)

The name *Heber* means "ally." How is this name fitting? (Heber allied himself with the Canaanite king and was likely the informer of Barak's military plans.)

The name *Jael* means "mountain goat." What is the connection to her and her actions? (Sisera asked for water, and Jael was wise enough to give him milk—most likely, goat's milk—which helped put him to sleep so that she could put an end to his treacherous life.)

Have students research the meaning of their own name, asking their parents to explain why their name was selected just for them. Students may share their findings with the rest of the class.

Bringing it home

Research the Bible and find other examples in which the Israelites continued the cycle of sin. Tell the students to be prepared to share specific stories in which the people sinned and God showed His grace. Emphasize how Law and Gospel are evident throughout the Old and New Testaments. Have students draw a parallel to people today. Remind them that though His people become wayward and weak, God never changes.

Unit 2—To the Promised Land

Lesson 23

Samson

Judges 13–16

Background

Samson was a lifelong Nazirite. Nazirites were Israelites, men and women, who vowed to dedicate themselves to the Lord for a specific period of time. During that time, the Nazirite could not cut his or her hair, drink wine or eat anything made from grapes, or go near a dead body, even that of a relative. They were to live as people who were dedicated—separated—to the Lord (Numbers 6:1–21). This vow demonstrated more than just self-discipline; it meant complete and total devotion to the Lord.

It's clear that Samson was not faithful in his obedience to the Lord. He tried to intermarry with foreign idol worshipers; he visited prostitutes; and he ate ritually defiled food, even offering it to his unsuspecting parents (Judges 14:8–9). And it's not clear how much of his over-the-top violence can be excused by his role as God's appointed judge.

Yet, in spite of all this, it is clear that God cared for him, forgave him, and used him to protect and help God's people. This gives us hope that God will forgive our sins as well in Jesus Christ and use us in His service.

Central Truth

Relying on our own strength or on the will of ungodly people leads to failure; trust in God lifts us up, according to His will.

Objectives

- Admit that often when we think we are great, we are destined to fail; God does not leave us in our defeat, but continually strives to deliver us.
- Rejoice in the constant love of God that is always working to pull us back to faith in Him.
- Discern the effects of our acquaintances, seeking friendships with those who share God's love in the family of faith.

Materials

- Hymnals and music CDs
- Reproducible 23
- Web Resource 23a

Bible Prep

Post in advance so students can bookmark the reference before class time.
- Judges 13–16

Devotions

Sophie shouted, "Mom, I'm going over to Miranda's house!" "Wait a minute and sit down here with me," replied her mother. "Sophie, you sounded like you were *telling* me rather than *asking* me. We've talked before about Miranda. Ever since you and she became friends, you have picked up some bad habits. You know I don't approve of the language you've added to your conversations, and I don't like the way you slam the door when you don't get your way. That may be what happens at Miranda's house, but that is not the way of our family." "Aw, Mom, Miranda's *cool*," said Sophie. Mom replied, "I would rather that she was Christian." Sophie snapped back, "Miranda *is* a Christian!" Mom asked, "Is that just a label, or does she *live* as a Christian?" "Well," said Sophie, "Miranda needs a good friend, just like everyone else." "But Sophie," said Mom, "that's the point—there is no goodness in the friendship. Miranda influences you to do the wrong things. And you are not influencing her for good." Sophie ran off and slammed her bedroom door. Her mom silently prayed that God would give her the right words to say.

A few days later, Sophie came home from school and announced that she had indeed been a good friend to Miranda. "I was a loyal friend and defended her when Elaine said Miranda cheated in the game we were playing." Quietly, her mom asked, *"Did* Miranda cheat?" Reluctantly, Sophie said, "Yes, but I protected her—and that's a good thing." "Oh, Sophie, I wish you could see that this is *not* a good thing," her mom said. "You followed Miranda's will, not God's will!" Sophie slumped into the chair. "Oh, Mom, this friendship is so *difficult*!" Her mother held Sophie's hand as she said, "It doesn't have to be if you put Jesus first. Live as Jesus wants you to live." "And if I mess up?" asked Sophie. "Oh, you will," said Mom. "We all do. But you can ask Him for forgiveness and ask Him to make you stronger." "But Mom, what if Miranda hates me for not doing things her way?" "Then," said Mom, "it's time to find a new friend. Friendships are much easier when both friends are walking the same way—with Jesus!" Point out that this was probably just the first of many conversations that Sophie and her mom had about friendships. Today's Bible lesson will demonstrate someone who not only followed the ways of his friends, but mostly followed his own way of doing things. But he was only truly successful when he relied on the Lord. Sing together about the Friend who leads us—and who, we hope, is also the way and path for our friends. Sing "What a Friend We Have in Jesus" (*LSB* 770; recorded as *Hymn of the Month* for grade 6, September).

INTO the Word

Superhero or Antihero?

Focus on Samson as the antihero, the one whose example we are not to follow. His bad example points us in the opposite direction—to the mercy we have in Christ Jesus, who came in humility to serve and to give Himself on the cross to obtain forgiveness, life, and salvation to all who believe.

Have students work in groups to list the events of the three disastrous chapters of Samson's life. Have each group work on a different chapter and then share their results with the whole class. Here are some of the possibilities. (Accept reasonable answers; do not expect a list as complete as the ones that follow.)

A Disastrous Marriage

- Samson saw a Philistine woman whom he wanted to marry, but his parents did not approve.
- While they were traveling together to meet the wife for Samson, a young lion came roaring toward them, and God gave Samson the power to tear the lion apart with his bare hands.
- Some time later, when Samson went back to her, he turned aside to look at the lion's carcass, which was swarming with bees and now contained honey. Samson scooped the honey out of the lion's carcass and ate some.
- At the wedding feast, Samson told his guests a riddle, betting them thirty linen garments that they couldn't solve it within the seven days of the feast.
- The guests threatened Samson's wife unless she convinced him to explain the riddle to her. Samson's wife cried for the entire seven days of the feast until he finally explained it to her.
- When the guests solved the riddle, Samson knew he had been tricked. He killed thirty Philistines and used their clothes to pay off his wager. Because Samson left in such a rage, his wife's father had her marry another man.
- Later, Samson went to visit his wife to give her a young goat as a gift. The woman's father wouldn't let Samson see her because he thought Samson hated her.
- Samson became angry and wanted to get even with the Philistines, so he went out and caught three hundred foxes. Tying them tail to tail in pairs, he then fastened a torch to every pair of tails, lit the torches on fire, and let the foxes loose in the fields of ripe grain, where everything burned up.
- When the Philistines found out, they burned the house of Samson's wife, killing her and her father.
- Samson was so angry about the murder of his wife, he attacked and slaughtered many of the Philistines. Using the jawbone of a donkey, he struck down a thousand men.

A Disastrous Girlfriend

- Samson went to spend the night with a Philistine prostitute. The people of Gaza plotted to lock him up and kill him at dawn. But Samson got up in the middle of the night, tore off the doors and posts to the city gates, and carried them to the top of a hill.
- Some time later, he fell in love with a woman named Delilah. The rulers of the Philistines, who wanted to overpower him, told her they would pay her to find out the secret of Samson's strength.
- When Delilah asked Samson the secret of his strength, he said that he would become weak if he were tied up with seven fresh bowstrings. Delilah did this while the Philistines were hiding nearby; but when she called out, "Samson, the Philistines are upon you!" Samson easily snapped the bowstrings and was not captured.
- Delilah complained that Samson had made her look foolish, and she again pressed him for the secret of his strength. This time, he said

---

Lesson 23

Samson

Superhero or Antihero?

When you hear of Samson, you probably think of a muscle man with unusual strength. He could hardly be called a "superhero," however, because he was very weak in other areas: he had weak values; he was weak in giving in to suspicious people; he was weak in giving in to his temper; and he was weak in making decisions. Work in groups to make outlines or lists of the things that happened to Samson in the following "chapters" of his life. Record each chapter on a separate sheet of paper.

Chapter 1: A Disastrous Marriage. Samson was selfish and self-willed. He married a Philistine—one of the enemy. He ignored God's will and followed his own judgment: "She is right in my eyes" (Judges 14:3). This resulted in nothing but trouble. On a sheet of paper, list the events recounted in Judges 14–15, as Samson used his power to show off, acting out in violence, anger, and revenge.

Chapter 2: A Disastrous Girlfriend. Samson should have been suspicious when, time after time, his girlfriend, Delilah, tried to trick him. He was just too sure of himself to be cautious. Read Judges 16:1–22 and make a list of the things that happened in this chapter. Then consider: what does long hair have to do with it? His hair was a sign of dedication and faithfulness to God. Even more significant than losing his hair was the fact that Samson had lost his dedication to God, and because of that, he also lost the power God had given him.

Chapter 3: A Glorious Disaster. Read Judges 16:23–30 and describe what happened. It is ironic (a turn or reversal of events) that Samson, who once had killed people with the bone of a donkey, was now doing a donkey's work; he had torn off a city's gates and was now held prisoner within the gates of a city; he had destroyed Philistine wheat fields and now had to grind their wheat into flour. Samson was brought low. But at this low point, he looked to God for help and humbly prayed. God's will for Samson's life was to use him to save Israel from the Philistines; now, in this final disaster, Samson brought about the death of more enemies than at any other time in his life. The antihero finally became a hero as he finally placed his trust in the Lord God.

Covenant Connection

In Samson, the antihero, we can see a contrast with Jesus. Samson was proud; Jesus was humble. Samson was violent; Jesus was peaceful. Samson was selfish, doing only what he wanted to do; Jesus was selfless, doing the will of God the Father, saying, "Thy will be done." One similarity between the two is that there was victory in death. Even this, however, has striking differences. The death of Jesus on the cross was for the saving of all people. And the death of Jesus was followed by His victory over that death when He arose on Easter, claiming the ultimate victory of life in heaven for all who believe!

Pillars of Parallels

Look for parallels, or similarities, between Samson and the whole nation of Israel. Record your findings in the space provided on the pillar.

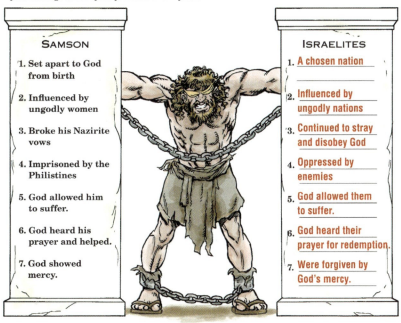

SAMSON
1. Set apart to God from birth
2. Influenced by ungodly women
3. Broke his Nazirite vows
4. Imprisoned by the Philistines
5. God allowed him to suffer.
6. God heard his prayer and helped.
7. God showed mercy.

ISRAELITES
1. A chosen nation
2. Influenced by ungodly nations
3. Continued to stray and disobey God
4. Oppressed by enemies
5. God allowed them to suffer.
6. God heard their prayer for redemption.
7. Were forgiven by God's mercy.

It is God's desire to bring all sinners to repentance and faith. God wants to restore the unfaithful, like Samson and like the thief on the cross. God is patient and compassionate. You need never think that you have done something that God will not forgive. Samson's greatest victories came at the end of his life, and both were totally the work of God. While it is true that destroying the Philistines was a great victory, the even greater victory is God's gifts to Samson—hearing his prayer and having mercy on him.

Remember

"Therefore I will boast all the more gladly of my weaknesses, so that the power of Christ may rest upon me." (2 Corinthians 12:9)
What does the apostle Paul mean? Is it a contrast? Is it a paradox? Look for clues to the meaning in 1 Corinthians 1:26–31 and in the song "Jesus Loves Me" (LSB 588; AGPS 144), especially in the last line of stanza 1.

---

that new ropes would bind him and make him weak. This didn't work either.

- Delilah continued to pester Samson. So Samson told her to weave the seven braids of his hair into the fabric on her loom and tighten it with a pin. Delilah did this while he slept. Then, for the third time, she called out, "Samson, the Philistines are upon you!" Samson woke up and pulled up the pin and loom with the fabric. (He was, however, getting closer to the truth by involving his hair.)
- Finally Delilah said, "How can you say you love me when you won't confide in me?" She nagged him day after day until he finally told her everything. Samson revealed the secret that because God had set him apart as a Nazirite, his strength would leave him if his hair were cut.
- When Delilah heard this, she sent word to the Philistines, who returned with the money. Delilah put Samson to sleep in her lap and cut his hair. The Lord left Samson because he had been unfaithful, so he became weak. Now when she called, "Samson, the Philistines are upon you!" Samson couldn't defend himself.

A Glorious Disaster

- The Philistines seized Samson, gouged out his eyes, and put him in prison. But the hair on his head began to grow back.
- The Philistines held a celebration to their false god, Dagon, and brought Samson out to entertain them. It was a huge gathering, with three thousand people on the roof of the building and even more inside.
- When Samson stood among the many rulers, men, and women, he prayed to God for strength. He reached toward the two central pillars and pushed with all his might, collapsing the temple, and killing himself and all the people in it.

INTO our lives

Pillars of Parallels

After working on this section of the Student Book, ask the class to consider how we today are like Samson and like the Israelites. Tell the students that even though Samson broke every vow set before him by God, the Lord still used him and loved him. Remind the students that God will use us however He sees fit, and we should rejoice in His continual deliverance. Consider these discussion questions: **Have you ever relied on your own strength while failing to see God's greater plan? How might others try to influence you in a negative way? How important is it to have other Christian friends? What could you say to a friend who needs God's help? You were created for the purpose of upholding God's truth, sharing the Lord's loving kindness, and spreading the Gospel message of salvation in Jesus. Ask God to give you strength in times of trouble and forgiveness in times of disobedience.** Use Reproducible 23 in connection with this discussion.

Both Sinner and Saint

Like Samson, each of us is both a saint and a sinner. Because we were born into this sin-filled world with a sinful human nature, and because we suffer the consequences of sin around us, we cannot escape sin, no matter how hard we try. Like Samson, we often sin by misusing the good gifts God gives to us. But by faith in Jesus Christ, we are also saints. We stand perfect and forgiven before almighty God, clothed in the innocence Christ earned for us by His life, death, and resurrection.

Consider each of the following gifts from God. For each, give one example of how, as sinners, we may be tempted to use this gift in a sinful way. Also, give an example of how the Holy Spirit can enable God's saints to use this same gift to serve and give glory to God.

A sense of humor
Sinner: *Answers will vary.*
Saint:

Leadership qualities
Sinner: *Answers will vary.*
Saint:

Musical talent
Sinner: *Answers will vary.*
Saint:

Physical strength
Sinner: *Answers will vary.*
Saint:

Intelligence
Sinner: *Answers will vary.*
Saint:

Reproducible 23

Searching Further

Refer to those mentioned in the "Hall of Faith" in Hebrews 11:31–40. Have students list the people referenced in this passage, and discuss how these people are commended for their faith as stated in verses 39–40. Ask the students to match the names listed in verse 32 with the actions listed in verses 33–38. Samson's actions are seen in verses 33–34, 36, and 38. Students may also recall heroes of Lessons 21 and 22 as mentioned again in Hebrews. Remind students that the stories in the Old Testament were used to teach people in the New Testament as well as us today. Stress that Hebrews doesn't focus on these heroes' failures, but rather on God's goodness to them as He forgave them, gave them faith, and guided them to live in faith. It's not what *we* do, but what *God* has done for us.

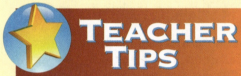

You may want to note the similarities in the birth announcements of Samson (Judges 13) and Jesus (Luke 1). Both were announced by an angel and both said his purpose would be to save the people. After this, it is the differences that are most notable. What made Jesus so different from Samson? Jesus was born as true man, but He was also born as true God. He was without sin; even from the early age of twelve, He knew that He was born to serve the purpose of the heavenly Father; in Gethsemane, He prayed to the Father, saying, "Not as I will, but as You will." We learn something from Samson too: the lesson of Samson is God's great mercy.

Ideas for the Gifted

What may seem like random acts actually were part of God's plan. Have students draw on what they know about the nature of God and how He teaches us a lesson today with the events of Samson's life. Ask the students to think about what certain parts of Samson's story might symbolize.

The lion—This could represent the way in which God gives us strength to overcome the power of sin. A lion may seem like a fierce adversary, but we can tear sin apart with the help of the Holy Spirit.

The honey in the lion's carcass—God can take something bad or scary and bring blessings to us.

Samson's great thirst following his victory—Samson, much like us, was never fully satisfied with the work God was doing in his life. He wanted more, and he often behaved like a spoiled, demanding child. But God still answered his prayer, quenched his thirst, and allowed him to lead the Israelites. We continue to thirst for more, and yet, God can work with very little to accomplish great things.

Delilah and her betrayal—We should resist temptation and not fall for the tricks of those who wish to deceive us time and time again.

The blinding of Samson—We, too, are blinded by sin and imprisoned by our bad decisions.

Samson's hair growing back—God's deliverance is there for us, and sometimes we need to be patient and allow it to grow again within us in order to carry out God's plan.

Students may create a newspaper account of the great feats of strength demonstrated by Samson. The story of Samson contains fantastic accounts of his exploits, which would prove newsworthy. Students should give their newspaper a name, headings, and a byline for each reporter. Illustrations or graphics should be included in the paper, and the layout should resemble a newspaper of today. Students might enjoy sharing their newspaper with other classes or grade levels.

Faith in Action

Generate the following discussion. Ask, **What might it be like to face a lion? Are there times when your troubles seem as though you are staring into the jaws of a lion? What are those troubles? How can you feel strong enough to tear that lion apart with your bare hands? Is your faith being tested?** Remind the students that God wants to tackle our troubles with us, and we need to trust in Him to give us this strength. Have the students write a prayer expressing their need for God to deliver them from temptation, asking Him to bring strong Christian friendships into their lives, and thanking Him for bringing them back to Him each day.

UNIT 3—PROPHETS AND KINGS

Theme

This unit focuses on the historical biblical period of the united and the divided kingdoms. During this time, God spoke to His people through many prophets. Each king that we look at will be associated with one or more prophets. We will see the Gospel in these Old Testament stories because all of Scripture points to Jesus, our Savior. A subtheme for most of the unit is a connection to the Lord's Prayer, seeing how the Old Testament stories relate to our ever-present and unchanging Lord. As Hebrews 13:8 says, "Jesus Christ is the same yesterday and today and forever." As you know, the curriculum has nine units to roughly correspond to the nine months of a school year, so Unit 3 is suggested for use in November, bringing in another related subtheme of thanksgiving and giving glory to God.

Worship

Each lesson in this curriculum has a classroom devotion. If you already have an established plan for your opening worship, you can use the devotion suggested in the Teacher Guide as an introduction to the lesson instead. Each month, a different psalm is suggested for use as part of your opening devotions. Using one psalm per month leads to familiarity and better understanding. In fact, most students will have learned these psalms by memory by the end of the month, just through frequent use. It is suggested that your devotions this month include the reading of Psalm 23, as this month, we think of thanksgiving for all the care God provides for us. One web resource introduces the possibility of chanting the psalm after students have become familiar with speaking it. This procedure is beneficial in leading students to grow in their use of various worship formats. The hymn of the month (November) is "God of Grace and God of Glory" (*LSB* 850), and the hymn of the season (Thanksgiving) is "Sing to the Lord of Harvest" (*LSB* 893). Always feel free to make additional hymn choices, including songs from *All God's People Sing!* (with fifty of these songs recorded on *Jesus' People Sing!*). Consider frequently reviewing hymns learned in previous years also.

Resources

A key resource for this curriculum can be found on the One in Christ Portal. Individual lesson materials will be listed there, providing downloadable reproducibles, links to other Web sites, interactive whiteboard applications, slide presentations, and other resources for the lesson of the day. Each unit will also have a listing of available materials related to the unit as a whole, such as a list of the Bible memory verses for the unit, a letter to make available to parents (by print or online), and a unit test. These last three items and the reproducible pages are also available in print in the *Teacher Resource Book*. The unit tests are multiple-choice tests that provide immediate feedback to the student and are self-correcting for the teacher. You can give the test to the whole class at once or to smaller groups in your computer lab, if available. If you have only one computer available, you can have students sign up to take the test during study periods, or it can be printed out. (Unit 3 test answers are: 1-d; 2-c; 3-b; 4-c; 5-b; 6-d; 7-a; 8-c; 9-e; 10-a.) Note that the titles of this unit's lessons are listed in the column at the right to give you an overview of the material to be covered.

Unit 3

24. God Calls Samuel
25. Israel's First King
26. Samuel Anoints David
27. David and Goliath
28. David and Saul
29. Saul's Downfall
30. David and Bathsheba
31. Solomon Builds a Temple
32. Rehoboam and Jeroboam
33. The Prophet Elijah
34. Naboth's Vineyard

Bulletin Board

This bulletin board is available, ready to cut out and pin up, from CPH. There will be a bulletin board available for each unit/month that focuses on the unit's theme. This bulletin board combines several themes from this unit. First, display the stones to make an Old Testament type of altar. Place in the order of the petitions of the Lord's Prayer as listed at the bottom of each stone. Explain that a priest would place wood and an animal sacrifice on the altar. Smoke from the burning sacrifice would rise as incense to God in heaven for the atonement of the sins of the people. Place the cross above the altar, noting that Jesus is the complete sacrifice—no others are needed. He has made complete atonement for our sins. Now we can go directly to God in prayer, for we are His children, made holy and blameless through forgiveness. Read Psalm 141:2, then note that the words on the stones are summary statements of the Lord's Prayer, each relating to lessons in Unit 3. (*Note:* The Introduction and First Petition are related to Lesson 24; then the petitions proceed in order until Lessons 29 and 30, which switch the Sixth and Seventh Petitions. This will also be noted in the lesson guide.) As each part of the prayer is studied, place a red heart on the stone as a reminder that the sacrifice God now desires from us is a contrite heart (see Psalm 51:17). When your class has completed Lesson 31, the hearts can be rearranged to form a title above or below the altar shape.

Bible Book Overview

The Student Book Appendix has a valuable feature that gives a summary of each book of the Bible. Looking at the summaries of sixty-six books can be overwhelming, so it is suggested that each month/unit, your class look at the summaries of just a few of these books. During Unit 3, introduce the remainder of the Old Testament historical books: 1 and 2 Kings, 1 and 2 Chronicles, Ezra, Nehemiah, and Esther. These books cover the history of the kings of the united and divided kingdoms, and also the time of captivity and return from captivity. Read together and discuss the summaries of these seven books in the Student Book Appendix when you have available time. (Note that a copy of the Student Book Appendix is included in the back of this Teacher Guide.)

UNIT 3—PROPHETS AND KINGS

LESSON **24**

God Calls Samuel
1 SAMUEL 3

Background

"Long ago, at many times and in many ways, God spoke to our fathers by the prophets, but in these last days He has spoken to us by His Son" (Hebrews 1:1–2).

What exactly is a prophet? And how did God use prophets like Samuel to speak to His people? The books of the Old Testament show that a prophet was not simply a preacher who explained and applied an existing text of the Scriptures. God delivered messages directly to the prophets. Another important name for a prophet is "seer," from the same Hebrew root as *seeing* and *perceiving*. The most common indicators that the prophet was conveying God's message are the words "Thus says the Lord" and "declares the Lord."

Moses was called by God to speak God's words to Pharaoh and the Israelites and to perform miracles on God's behalf. Like later prophets, these words often brought him into conflict with the people God had called him to lead. Samuel was a prophet who served as a judge and then later as an advisor to the king.

After the division of the kingdom into Israel and Judah, God used the prophets to call His people to repentance. Elijah's showdown with the prophets of Baal demonstrates the existence of both true and false prophets in ancient Israel. The activities of the prophets grew along with the rising threat of Assyria and Babylon. After the Judeans returned from captivity in Babylon, they compiled the writings of the prophets along with the Books of Moses.

But then the prophets grew silent, because God had grown silent. He was about to reveal His Word in the person of His Son.

Central Truth

God spoke His messages of warning, repentance, and redemption directly to the Old Testament prophets; He speaks the same messages to us in Holy Scripture; we speak to Him in prayer.

Objectives

- Realize that God calls us to obedience and service, but we often fail and sin.
- Understand that God also calls us to repentance, calling to us through the Means of Grace to receive redemption in Christ Jesus.
- Dedicate our lives to obedience to God and service to others, giving all glory to God.

Materials

- Hymnals and music CDs
- Reproducible 24
- Web Resource 24a

Bible Prep

Post in advance so students can bookmark references before class time.

- 1 Samuel 1–3
- Luke 1–2
- Matthew 25:40
- Matthew 28:19–20
- John 13:34
- Romans 12:4–8
- Ephesians 4:32
- The Book of Psalms

Devotions

"Call me," Mom reminded Jake as he tucked his cell phone into his pocket. "When baseball practice is over, give me a call. I'll come get you and bring you home."

"Call me," Mom said to Dad as he picked up his briefcase. "I'll be thinking about you in that meeting today and wondering how it's going. I'll be waiting to hear from you."

"Call me," Mom told Sarah as she dropped her off at Julie's house. "I know sleepovers are a lot of fun, and you'll have a great time with the other girls. I trust you to know what is right and what is wrong. If anything at the party makes you uncomfortable, please call me. I'll be glad to come and take you home."

Cell phones provide a great way to keep in contact with our families. We can call our parents when we need a ride or forget our lunch or homework assignment. We can talk to our parents about events at school or what we're doing with our friends. We can call to ask for help when faced with a difficult or dangerous situation.

Christians have a means of communication with God that is more wonderful than any cell phone. Through prayer, we can talk to God any time, any place, in any situation. Sometimes we ask God for things we need and thank Him for all He has done for us. Sometimes we just want to talk to Him as a friend. Sometimes we ask Him to deliver us from a difficult or dangerous situation. When we have done something wrong, we tell God about our sins and ask Him to forgive us for Jesus' sake.

God invites us to come to Him in prayer. "Call upon Me in the day of trouble; I will deliver you, and you shall glorify Me" (Psalm 50:15). Jesus said, "Ask, and it will be given to you" (Matthew 7:7). He answers our prayers in His own way and His own time, according to His will. Let's call on God in word and in song. Pray together the Lord's Prayer. Sing together "Children of the Heavenly Father" (*LSB* 725; recorded as *Hymn of the Month* for grade 5, November).

INTO the lesson

Samuel's Journal

Help students understand who Samuel was and what he was doing in the temple by summarizing the events of 1 Samuel 1–2. (Note that the temple mentioned was the tabernacle tent church; Solomon's temple was not built until some years later.) Read the account of God's call in the Student Book and also from the Bible in 1 Samuel 3. (Samuel may have been about twelve years old at this time.)

Who's Calling?

Samuel's communication with God was very direct. We still communicate with God today, but in a different way: we speak to God in prayer; God speaks to us in His Word. Look at the Student Book diagram and use this as a graphic organizer to guide your classroom discussion as you label this two-way communication.

Say, **God asks us to call upon Him in prayer. He invites us to pray regularly and frequently, especially in times of trouble. We can pray everywhere—when we are alone, with our families, or in church. We pray in the name of Jesus, that is, with faith in Him as our Savior. We pray with confidence, believing that for Jesus' sake, God hears the prayers of all believers and answers in the way and at the time that is best.**

Looking at the same diagram, relate it to the words of Jesus in the prayer He gave to us. Jesus' told His disciples to call God "Our Father who art in heaven." The disciples must have been shocked to hear this. (People in Jesus' time were forbidden to say God's name out loud.) The word *Father* tells us that God loves us and wants us to pray to Him confidently and without fear. Because of Jesus, we can come directly to God in prayer. Hebrews 4:16 says, "Let us then with confidence draw near to the throne of grace, that we may receive mercy and find grace to help in time of need." In Jesus, all believers are children of one Father and should pray with and for one another.

The words "hallowed be Thy name" relate directly to the Word of God as we listen to it and keep it in our hearts and lives. "How is God's name kept holy? God's name is kept holy when the Word of God is taught in its truth and purity, and we, as the children of God, also lead holy lives according to it" (Small Catechism, The Lord's Prayer, explanation of the First Petition). This is all part of that two-way communication.

Option: At this point in the lesson, or at a later time, use Reproducible 24, which is explained in the article "Faith in Action" on the "Lesson Support" page. This activity extends the focus on prayer.

INTO the Word

Called to . . .

Emphasize: **God spoke to His people in the Old Testament through prophets. God gave His message to the prophets, and they gave that message to the people. We have the words of the prophets in Scripture, in the Old Testament, mostly in the books starting with Isaiah and continuing through Malachi.** From a Bible's table of contents, read aloud together the names of the prophets from Isaiah through Malachi. Briefly scan the Book of Jeremiah, noting that very often, a chapter will begin with words like "thus spoke the Lord" or "the word of the Lord came." Turn to the hymn "God Has Spoken by His Prophets" (*LSB* 583). Either read together or sing stanza 1.

Continue: **When God sent Jesus into this world, He no longer needed to send any more prophets. In Jesus, we have the embodiment of God and His Word. John 1:14 says, "And the Word became flesh and dwelt among us, and we have seen His glory, glory as of the only Son from the Father, full of grace and truth." Jesus is the complete and perfect Prophet, Priest, and King. Jesus is the fulfillment of all the messianic prophecies. We no longer need prophets to tell us God's message because Jesus Himself *is* God, and He speaks His message**

Called to . . .

Have you heard any prophets lately? While cartoons sometimes show bearded men in long robes carrying signs declaring that "The End Is Near," the truth is that God speaks today through His Word. God sent His Son, Jesus, to be His Word in human form. In Jesus, we see all that we need to know about God. We learn about Jesus in the Bible; it is God's Word that speaks to us today.

Through the Bible, God calls us to serve Him in many ways. Read the following Bible passages. What is God calling you to do?

a. Matthew 25:40 — **To serve less fortunate people as we would serve Christ Himself**
b. Matthew 28:19–20 — **To carry the Gospel into all the world**
c. John 13:34 — **To love one another as He has loved us**
d. Romans 12:4–8 — **To use our gifts to serve the Church, the Body of Christ**
e. Ephesians 4:32 — **To be kind and forgive one another as God in Christ forgives us**

Dedicated

Even before he was born, Samuel's whole life was dedicated to the Lord (see 1 Samuel 1:11, 27–28). What can you dedicate to honor and worship God? The Lord has made you a unique individual and has given you particular abilities, characteristics, and interests. Perhaps you like to paint or play a musical instrument. Maybe you are good at math or science. Do you like to write or speak in front of groups of people? Do you have an interest in helping people who are sick or hurting? All of these may be part of what God is calling you to do. How could you dedicate these blessings from God to give Him glory and to serve others?

HOW COULD YOU DEDICATE THESE TO THE LORD?

Talent or Ability	
Personal Characteristic	
Special Interest	

Remember

"Long ago, at many times and in many ways, God spoke to our fathers by the prophets, but in these last days He has spoken to us by His Son." (Hebrews 1:1–2)

INTO our lives

Dedicated

Point out that Samuel was dedicated to the Lord even before he was born. It was a lifetime commitment. Your pastor and teacher have made a commitment to professional church work. The truth is, being a true Christian is a lifetime commitment for everyone! Whatever your profession may be, you can dedicate what you do to the Lord. And furthermore, this does not just involve professions, and it is not only an adult concern. Just like Samuel, as a child, teenager, grown-up, and on into old age, being a Christian is a lifetime commitment. Say, **Being "dedicated" means, first of all, that we are set apart. We are to be set apart, different from the rest of the world. Being "dedicated" also means that we have a special purpose. Our special purpose is discipleship—living in faith, serving others, and giving glory to God. This lifetime commitment is also a full-time commitment. Discipleship is not a part-time thing. If you are baking a cake, doing homework, playing basketball, watching TV, texting a friend—*whatever* you do—do it living in faith, serving others, and giving glory to God.**

Display Web Resource 24a, which emphasizes this theme. (Refer to this frequently throughout the year. Perhaps have students make a poster to keep this as a constant reminder.) Carry on this theme by working on the Student Book activity.

An important song of dedication is "Take My Life and Let It Be" (*LSB* 783; recorded as *Hymn of the Month* for grade 6, January). Have students scan through the text and identify the different aspects of our identity (who we are) that we are setting aside and consecrating for God's purposes. Sing the hymn together.

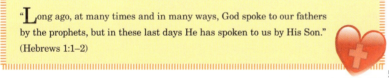

---

to us in the Gospel. In Jesus, we have God's words directly! Read or sing together stanza 2 of "God Has Spoken by His Prophets."

Continue: **Today, God communicates directly to us through Scripture. When we hear or read those words, we are hearing God Himself. God the Holy Spirit works through the Word of God as a Means of Grace. We say that the Word of God is *efficacious*, which means that it is active, working, and powerful. As the Holy Spirit works through those words of God, He is active in us, growing our faith, giving us comfort and peace, building us up, and strengthening us in faith.** Read or sing together stanza 3 of the hymn.

Say, **In our Bible story, God called Samuel for a special purpose: to give a message to Eli. God calls us today too. For what purpose has God called us? Find out in His Word.** Continue with the Student Book activity.

Summarize: **God revealed Himself fully to us when His plan of salvation was fulfilled in the birth, life, death, and resurrection of Jesus. In Jesus we see God's justice carried out and sin punished. In Jesus we see God's grace and mercy to sinners. In Jesus we see God's plan to justify us and take us to heaven eternally. We know Jesus and the salvation He accomplished for us as we study His Word.**

109

Lesson Support

Curriculum Connection

Samuel ran to Eli's bedside because of a mistake in reasoning. He assumed that the only other human being present was the source of the voice he heard calling him. Samuel failed to take into account the presence of the Lord! We, too, make mistakes in reasoning. Explore this topic with your students using 6.1.5.8, Unsupported Inferences, Fallacious Reasoning, Persuasion, and Propaganda. You will find it in the sixth-grade Language Arts volume of the Concordia Curriculum Guide series.

Faith in Action

As we continue to explore communication with God through prayer, it is good to analyze the types of prayer. The type we tend to use most often is *asking* God for what we need or want. (Distinguish between needs and wants.) One way prayer is often analyzed is through the acronym *ACTS* (for **A**doration, **C**onfession, **T**hanksgiving, **S**upplication). Sometimes the letters are reorganized to spell *CAST*, standing for the same key words. *CAST* refers to 1 Peter 5:7, which speaks of "casting" our cares, worries, and anxieties on the Lord in prayer. However, let's use a different acronym that seems less formal and may be less intimidating to children. Let's use the acronym *CHAT*. Children can understand that *chat* means "to talk." (They know about chat rooms on the Internet and chatting as they text.) In this case, *CHAT* refers to talking to God in prayer. Use Reproducible 24 and the following information to discuss this.

C: The letter *C* in the acronym stands for "**C**onfession." God promises, "If we confess our sins, He is faithful and just to forgive us our sins and to cleanse us from all unrighteousness" (1 John 1:9). Ask volunteers to read these passages of confession: Psalm 41:4; 51:1–12; 130:1–6. (All verses in this activity come from the Book of Psalms.) Then have students write a brief confession statement/prayer on their reproducible.

H: The letter *H* stands for "**H**onor." We honor and praise God, telling Him how great He is and acknowledging all He has done for us. Examples to read from the Psalms are Psalm 8; 18:1–3; 90:1–2; 145:1–3. Then challenge students to write their own short prayer honoring the Lord.

A: Finally we get to the type we use most often—the letter *A* stands for "**A**sk." This type includes a multitude of prayers: asking for something for yourself or someone else, asking for physical or spiritual needs, and so on. Have volunteers read these verses where the psalmists ask for God's help: Psalm 86; 88; 102:1–15; 109:1–5. Then ask students to write their own short prayer in which they ask something of God.

T: The letter *T* in the acronym stands for "**T**hank." Read examples of thanksgiving prayers in Psalm 105:1–3; 107:1–3; 136; 138:1–3. Then practice writing short prayers of thanksgiving.

Combine prayers of students to use as prayers for classroom devotions.

Teacher Tips

Each child in your classroom has been created by God and given unique gifts. Along with different gifts come different learning styles. Some of your students learn best by listening; others excel with written materials. Many students learn through music, art, or physical activity. When we use a "one size fits all" approach in our teaching methods, we ignore the variety of gifts God has given our students. But varying our methods will help us meet each student's needs and help all students learn to the best of their abilities.

Bringing it home

Samuel was a child when God called him to serve as His prophet. God was with Samuel, and soon, all of the Israelites recognized him as God's prophet. Does God still call children to serve Him today? Explore the service opportunities available for children of your students' age in your congregation. They may be able to serve as an acolyte, lighting the candles before worship, or a crucifer, carrying the processional cross at the beginning of special services. If your congregation or school has a children's choir or school band, students may be able to provide special worship music at a church service. As they grow older, students may assume the responsibility of ushering or reading Scripture lessons at church services. Remind your class that Paul wrote to young Timothy, "Let no one despise you for your youth, but set the believers an example in speech, in conduct, in love, in faith, in purity" (1 Timothy 4:12).

UNIT 3—PROPHETS AND KINGS   LESSON 25

Israel's First King
1 SAMUEL 8–15

Background

From the time of Adam and Eve, believers had acknowledged God as the ultimate authority in the world. God told Noah of the coming flood and spoke to the patriarchs such as Abraham directly or through visions. He spoke to Moses from a burning bush. Through Moses, He gave the Law and led the Israelites through their wilderness wanderings, appearing as a cloud by day and a pillar of fire by night. When the Israelites came to the Promised Land, God appointed judges through whom He ruled the people. But God was the ultimate ruler. A form of government in which God is recognized as the civil ruler is known as a *theocracy*. Samuel served as judge as well as prophet. Although the roles of judge and prophet were not hereditary, Samuel was grooming his sons to follow him. The sons, however, "did not walk in his ways but turned aside after gain" (1 Samuel 8:3). This approaching vacuum of power coupled with the growing menace of the Philistines caused the Israelites' trust in God to be shaken. Their desire was to be like the nations around them, rather than to exist as a people set apart by God. They went to Samuel to demand a king. God told Samuel, "They have not rejected you, but they have rejected Me from being king over them" (v. 7). With the proclamation of Saul as king of Israel, the theocracy ended and the monarchy began. When Saul disobeyed God, God chose David, "a man after His own heart" (13:14), to succeed Saul as king. David the shepherd-king was a preview, foreshadowing Jesus, the Good Shepherd and King of kings.

Central Truth
Though some governments and their leaders may think otherwise, God is King of kings and rules supreme.

Objectives
- Confess that we sometimes try to separate our faith life from our daily life, though they should be unified.
- Praise God that He graciously chooses to influence and affect all aspects of our lives.
- Proclaim that our citizenship is in God's kingdom, now and eternally.

Materials
- Hymnals and music CDs
- Reproducible 25

Bible Prep
Post in advance so students can bookmark references before class time.
- 1 Samuel 8–15

Devotions

Dad was watching the news on television when Eric came into the family room. Eric flopped down on the sofa and watched for a few minutes without saying anything. The reporter was talking about terrorist threats in several European capital cities. He said those same threats could affect major cities in the United States too. "What will happen if the terrorists decide to strike here, Dad? Do you think our government is strong enough to protect us?"

"Well, son, there is always the possibility of a terrorist attack," Dad said as he folded his newspaper. "You know it has happened before. The government has done everything it can to protect us, but sometimes bad things happen anyway."

Eric responded, "Can't they try harder? Can't we get more missiles and bombs and airplanes? Can't we send spies all over the world to catch them before they hurt us?"

"Even the most advanced weapons and the smartest spies can't always protect us, Eric. If we could screen every traveler and every piece of baggage coming in or going out of our country, we would still face the possibility of attack."

"So is it hopeless, Dad?"

"Well," replied his father, "depending entirely on human beings or human governments is hopeless. But we have a Ruler who is stronger than any government on earth."

Eric's mouth dropped open. "Do you mean . . ."

Eric paused and Dad finished his sentence for him: "I mean the Ruler the Bible calls the King of kings and Lord of lords—God Himself. He alone is really in charge of everything that happens. He is the one certain hope that we have, a certainty and hope that lasts to eternity."

"So the terrorists will never attack again?" Eric asked.

"I didn't say that," Dad answered. "But whether they attack or not, God has promised to do what is best for us, now and eternally. He will protect and preserve our souls. When you're afraid, remember His promise: 'I am with you always, to the end of the age'" (Matthew 28:20).

Let's pray together: Dear Lord, we confess that we sometimes let our fears overcome our faith in You. Forgive us, and help us to acknowledge Your lordship in all areas of our lives. In Jesus' name we pray. Amen. Sing together "God of Grace and God of Glory" (*LSB* 850; recorded as *Hymn of the Month* for grade 6, November), pointing out that today, we will learn more about God's kingdoms of grace and glory!

111

INTO the lesson

A Story Map of 1 Samuel 8–15

Remind students that God had called Samuel to serve God and Israel as prophet, priest, and judge for many years. When the people demanded a king, they had three reasons for doing this: (1) Samuel's two sons were raised to be priests, but they had openly rejected the ways of the Lord, leaving no one to succeed Samuel. (2) The Philistines, Israel's pagan neighbors, were growing more powerful and were challenging Israel militarily. (3) The Israelites saw that their neighbors all had kings, and they hoped a king would help to unify the loosely joined tribes of Israel. Their sin was not that they wanted to have a king, but that they placed their trust in human government when they should have trusted in God alone. Direct your students through the Bible readings in the top two boxes of the story map.

Note the change in the story (indicated by the jagged line) where Saul changed. Saul had seemed like the perfect choice to be Israel's first king. Physically tall and attractive, he seemed shy and humble when Samuel revealed God's decision to make him king. But as Saul grew into his royal role, his pride and will grew also. Soon Saul was obsessed with his own importance, though before coming to power, he had been truly humble. Gregory the Great wrote, "When he was little with himself, he was great with God; but, when he appeared great with himself, he was little with God" (*Fathers of the Christian Church*, p. 15).

In the next row of boxes, we see two significant events of Saul's disobedience. Saul was in a legitimate pickle—Samuel had kept him waiting for seven days. His troops were deserting, and the Philistines were ready to attack. But only the priest was allowed to offer the burnt offering. Saul took matters into his own hands and offered the sacrifice. Samuel, speaking for the Lord, told Saul that his dynasty would be cut short. Jonathan, Saul's son, would never become king. David, the man after God's own heart, would succeed Saul.

In the battle against the Amalekites, Saul again followed his own desires and will instead of God's command. Because Saul had not obeyed Him, God rebuked Saul and rejected him as king, tearing the kingdom away from his family. This is a strong reminder to us that whenever we turn from God and place our trust in something or someone else, we are guilty of a form of idolatry.

Lesson 25

Israel's First King

A Story Map of 1 Samuel 8–15

Main Characters: Samuel, Saul, people of Israel

- People's request (8:4–5)
- God's response (8:7)
- Samuel's warning (8:10–18)
- People's response (8:19–20)

- Saul—anointed (9:15–16; 10:1)
- Saul—blessed (10:6–9)
- Saul—humble (10:20–24)
- Saul—forgiving (10:27; 11:12–13)

KING SAUL CHANGED

- Philistines caused fear (13:5–7)
- Saul's disobedience (13:8–13)
- Saul's punishment (13:14)
- Jonathan's victory (14:1–23)

- God's command (15:1–3)
- Saul disobeys (15:9)
- Saul lies (15:10–15)
- Saul punished (15:22–28)

Outcomes and Conclusions:
Possibilities: Power and greed changed Saul; Saul turned away from God and was not faithful; Saul followed his own will instead of God's; God took the kingdom from Saul and his family and gave it to someone whose heart was faithful.

Review

Covenant Connection

There is an interesting contrast between this Old Testament story and the New Testament story of Jesus on trial before the Roman governor Pontius Pilate. In today's story, the people of Israel wanted an earthly king so "that we also may be like all the nations" (1 Samuel 8:20). By contrast, when Pilate asked Jesus if He was the king of the Jews, Jesus answered, "My kingdom is not of this world" (John 18:36). Though many people were expecting an earthly messianic king, Jesus said, "For this purpose I was born and for this purpose I have come into the world—to bear witness to the truth" (John 18:37). Praise God that Jesus came to save us so that someday, He can take us to His heavenly kingdom.

INTO the Word

The Greatest Kingdom of All

Discuss the idea of kingdoms and what makes them powerful. Some of your students may connect this idea with video games they have played. Others may relate it to literature about kingdoms, such as the "Narnia" series by C. S. Lewis. Read the first paragraph in the Student Book. Ask students to name countries in the world today that fit each description. For example, the United States and Russia have large armies with nuclear submarines and intercontinental missiles. China and India have large land areas with enormous populations. Most of the European nations, Canada, and the United States have well-educated citizens with skilled elected officials. Many countries in Europe and Asia can trace their history back more than a thousand years. Point out that the kingdom of God is much greater than any of these kingdoms.

What is the role of a king in an earthly kingdom? In most countries with a monarchy, the king is responsible for administrative duties and foreign affairs as a figurehead or with real authority. God, the King of kings, is unlike any earthly king. (See "Covenant Connection.")

What about the king's subjects? In earthly kingdoms, subjects owe their kings their loyalty, their service, and a portion of their worldly goods as taxes.

The Greatest Kingdom of All

What makes a kingdom great? A large army with nuclear submarines and intercontinental ballistic missiles? A large land area with an enormous population? Well-educated citizens with skilled, elected officials? A national history that has lasted hundreds or even thousands of years?

While all of these may be important to earthly kingdoms, the greatest kingdom of all doesn't depend on any of them. The greatest is the kingdom of God, which is really three kingdoms. The kingdom of God is God's reign as king over the whole universe, the Church on earth, and the Church and angels in heaven.

God rules the whole universe as His kingdom of power. We know that God created all things—from the tiniest microorganisms to the tallest mountains, from algae and atoms to stars and space. He moves the planets in their orbits and causes the seasons to change. He preserves all that He has created, providing food for animals and rain for crops. He created man in His own image and gave him dominion over the created world. No earthly king has ever matched the power of God.

God rules the Church on earth as His kingdom of grace. In this kingdom, God richly forgives the sins of all believers for Jesus' sake. In the kingdom of grace, Christ rules and protects His Church on earth. No earthly king has ever matched the grace of God.

God rules the Church in heaven and the angels as His kingdom of glory. The heavenly members of this kingdom know the joy of living face-to-face with Jesus. When our earthly time as members of the kingdom of grace is over, we will live with Jesus in the kingdom of glory. This kingdom of glory will never end. No earthly king has ever matched the glory of God.

Who Is My King?

God chose Saul to be king of Israel. When Saul was chosen, he was shy and humble—small in his own eyes. But as his years as king passed, Saul grew larger in his own eyes. He trusted in himself and in his army. He forgot that God is King of kings and rules supreme over all.

Have you ever made the same mistake? Have you relied on your own solution to a problem instead of trusting the message in God's Word? Have you worried about wars or natural calamities, forgetting God's promise to be with you in times of trouble?

When we confess these sins to God, our heavenly King forgives us for the sake of His Son, who died in our place. He gives us life now in His kingdom of grace and eternally in His kingdom of glory.

Remember

God "has delivered us from the domain of darkness and transferred us to the kingdom of His beloved Son, in whom we have redemption, the forgiveness of sins." (Colossians 1:13–14)

INTO our lives

Who Is My King?

We acknowledge the Lord as the King of kings. But when we are faced with problems in our lives, we start thinking that everything depends on us. Our reliance on ourselves or on earthly powers results in actions that are sometimes not pleasing to God.

Present the following role-playing situations to your class.

1. You have always been very good at math, but this week you just didn't have time to study for the math test. The boy sitting beside you has left his paper on the edge of his desk, right where you can see it. Your parents will be so proud if you bring home another good grade. What do you do?

2. You heard that your friend Lydia has been telling everyone the secrets that you shared with her. Now another girl has offered to tell you some juicy news about Lydia. Lydia has really hurt your feelings. What do you say?

3. Your friend Jake offered you a cigarette, and you tried it. When you get home, your mother notices the smell of smoke on your hair and coat and asks you about it. You know Mom has warned you about the dangers of smoking. What do you say?

Assure your students that all of us sometimes make the mistake of relying on ourselves or other people instead of putting our trust in God and obeying Him. **God has invited us to confess our sins to Him. He promises to forgive us for the sake of His Son, Jesus.** Use Reproducible 25 to extend this concept.

What do we owe the King of kings? According to *Luther's Small Catechism with Explanation*, Second Article, Christ redeemed us so "that [we] may be His own and live under Him in His kingdom and serve Him in everlasting righteousness, innocence, and blessedness, just as He is risen from the dead, lives and reigns to all eternity."

Read the remainder of the Student Book text in this section, filling in the diagram with the related labels. Connect this to the Lord's Prayer, in which we pray, "Thy kingdom come." But isn't God's kingdom already here? Why are we still praying for His kingdom to come? First, we know that God's kingdom of power is already present everywhere, because we see the wonders of creation and experience the force of nature in earthquakes, hurricanes, and tornadoes; we know that God continues to preserve and bless His creation—His kingdom of power, in which we live our daily lives. Second, we also ask God to give us His Holy Spirit so that we believe His Word and live godly lives as members of His kingdom of grace. This kingdom is God's Church on earth, a spiritual kingdom in the hearts of believers, that comes to us through the Means of Grace. We pray that He would bring others into His kingdom of grace and, through the power of the Holy Spirit, use us to extend His kingdom. And third, we pray that God will hasten the coming of His kingdom of glory so that we may live with Him, in His presence, forever in heaven.

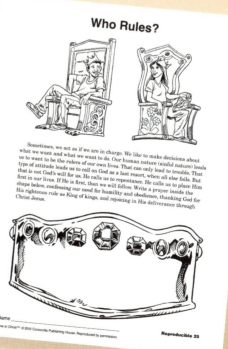

Lesson Support

Curriculum Connection

God warned Israel about the results of choosing a human king. Most would abuse their position, exploiting the people under them. Sadly, this is still the case with many people of high social status today. Consider using section 6.3.3.6, Social Status, which is found in the sixth-grade Social Studies volume of the Concordia Curriculum Guide series. Discuss with students: **Is it even possible to get rid of social status altogether? Can it be used for good? What can you do to use your own status to help others and not harm them?**

Technology

Today a nation that effectively uses technology has an advantage over a nation that does not. The same was true at the time of King Saul. Read 1 Samuel 13:19–23. The Philistines were skilled at metallurgy, probably ironwork and smelting they had learned from the Hittites. The earliest discoveries of iron in Canaan were found in Philistine regions. These artifacts included a sword, knives, and jewelry. The Philistines carefully guarded this skill, keeping it away from their neighbors, the Israelites, "lest [they] make themselves swords or spears" (v. 19), and there were no blacksmiths in all of Israel. This not only kept the Israelites weak militarily, but also provided a profitable business for the Philistines in making and sharpening axes, mattocks, sickles, and plowshares, the tools the Israelites needed for agriculture and building. The result of this strategy was that in battle, the Philistines, wielding swords and spears, faced Israelites armed only with arrows and slingshots. The only Israelites who carried swords and spears were Saul and his son, Jonathan.

Searching Further

Have you heard the expression "It's Greek to me"? Many of the words we use when we speak of forms of government come from the Greek language. For example, the word *democracy* comes from two Greek roots and means "rule of the people." Until the time of King Saul, Israel was a *theocracy*. Students may recognize the Greek root *theo* as being the same as the root of the word *theology*, "the study of God." Theocracy is the system of government in which God is recognized as the civil ruler. In the centuries between the conquest of Canaan and the reign of Saul, Israel was administered by judges who were established by God. As judges were raised up, God conferred the gifts of the Holy Spirit on them. Look up the following Bible references; who were the judges who received the gifts of the Holy Spirit? See Judges 6:34; 11:29; 14:6, 19; 15:14.

Critical thinking

As Christians, we acknowledge Jesus as our King. But what kind of king is He? The people who followed Jesus during His earthly ministry wanted Him to be a king who would free them from the Romans. They had seen Him feed thousands of people with a little bread and a couple of fish. With a king like this, they would always have plenty to eat. Today, people would like to see Jesus as a Superman who uses His powers to get them out of every possible kind of trouble. They would like to bypass the cross, Christ's saving work of redemption. Without the cross, they would never have to acknowledge their sins and repent of them. But the cross is the throne from which Jesus rules His kingdom of grace. Because of the forgiveness He won for us on the cross, we will spend eternity with Him in His kingdom of glory.

DIGGING DEEPER

Jesus used parables to teach His disciples what the kingdom of God or kingdom of heaven is like. Assign groups a parable from the following list. Ask them to tell what the parable tells about the kingdom of God or kingdom of heaven.

Matthew 13:24–30, 37–43 (The parable of the weeds)

Matthew 13:31–32 (The mustard seed)

Matthew 13:33 (The leaven)

Matthew 13:44 (The hidden treasure)

Matthew 13:45–46 (The pearl of great value)

Matthew 13:47–50 (The parable of the net)

Matthew 13:52 (The old and new treasures)

Matthew 20:1–16 (Laborers in the vineyard)

Matthew 25:1–13 (The parable of the ten virgins)

Optional: Make a poster related to each parable and discuss in what way each picture brings to mind something about the kingdom of God. Groups may choose to write a skit to retell the parable and its meaning.

UNIT 3—PROPHETS AND KINGS

LESSON 26

Samuel Anoints David
1 Samuel 16

Background

Today's Bible story is of the anointing of David. "It is doubtful that young David understood the full significance of this simple act. The prophet [Samuel] avoided using the title 'king' and left without offering any explicit instructions to the young man.

"By this simple act, God put a 'reserved' sign on David's life. The Holy Spirit came upon the young shepherd in renewed measure that day. Under the Holy Spirit's guidance, David would grow in faith and love toward God. And in time David would come to appreciate what the Lord had done for him this day—how he had placed him in the line of His Anointed One, the great Good Shepherd and King of all kings.

"Do we always appreciate what God has done for us? He chose us in Christ. In Baptism God put His own 'reserved' sign on our lives. He made us members of His family" (John R. Mittelstaedt, People's Bible Commentary series: *1 and 2 Samuel* [St. Louis: Concordia Publishing House, © 2005], p. 90. Used by permission. All rights reserved.).

Devotions

Camryn thumbed through the pages of her celebrity magazine. "If only I could be as beautiful as Cindy Spinner," she sighed. "I wish I had her hair. I wish I had her eyes. I wish I had . . ."

"But Camryn," her mother interrupted, "you have very nice eyes."

"But Mom," Camryn countered, "hers are bluer and bigger, and she has the longest eyelashes. And the outfits she wears, Mom! If only I had her great clothes."

Just then, Dad looked up from his newspaper. "Is that Cindy Spinner the actress you're talking about?" he asked.

"Yeah, Dad," said Camryn. "Have you heard of her?"

"Well," said Dad, "I was just reading about her in the paper. It seems she was reported driving erratically in her sports car. The police picked her up after she hit a pedestrian. She was under the influence of alcohol at the time, and the police reported finding drugs in her car."

Camryn looked over Dad's shoulder at the picture in the paper. "That's the same Cindy Spinner," she agreed. "I don't understand how she could do something like that. She's just so beautiful!"

"I guess nobody looks very beautiful in a police mug shot," said Dad.

As many people do, Camryn had looked only at her favorite star's outward beauty. But God looks past hair and eyes and clothing. God looks at the heart. When God looks at our hearts, He sees that we are sinners. Jesus said, "Out of the heart come evil thoughts, murder, adultery, sexual immorality, theft, false witness, slander. These are what defile a person" (Matthew 15:19–20). When we confess the sins in our hearts, God forgives us for the sake of His Son, Jesus. Through the

Central Truth

The timing and the will of God are always best, as He works for the good of His people.

Objectives

- Admit that we don't always place God's will first in our lives.
- Explore what it is that God wills for us.
- Pray that God will bless us with the enabling power of the Holy Spirit to follow His will and ways.

Materials

- Hymnals and music CDs
- Reproducible 26
- Web Resource 26a

Bible Prep

Post in advance so students can bookmark references before class time.
- 1 Samuel 16
- Matthew 1
- Luke 3

Holy Spirit, He helps us to live a life that is pleasing to Him.

Point out that in the next few lessons, we will be learning about David, who was chosen by God not for his personal appearance but because of his faithful heart. We see this heart in the psalms that David wrote. For the remainder of this unit, speak together David's Psalm 23, which is especially relevant to this time of the year, as we approach Thanksgiving Day. Also, sing "Sing to the Lord of Harvest" (*LSB* 893; recorded as *Hymn of the Season* for grade 6, Thanksgiving).

INTO the Word

The Boy Who Would Be King

God, through the prophet Samuel, twice told Saul that his kingdom would be torn away from his family. In 1 Samuel 16:1–3, God instructed Samuel to fill his horn with anointing oil and go to the home of Jesse in Bethlehem. A ram's horn was usually used for this purpose, and the recipe for anointing oil had been given to Moses by God (Exodus 30:22–25). God told Samuel He had chosen for Himself a king from among Jesse's sons. Samuel objected to this mission, fearing that Saul would kill him when he found out what Samuel was about to do. But God told Samuel to take along a heifer to sacrifice as a peace offering and to invite Jesse to the sacrifice. God promised to show Samuel what to do and whom to anoint.

Direct students to 1 Samuel 16:4–5. Why did the elders of Bethlehem tremble when they saw Samuel? They knew Samuel represented God's awesome majesty. He often came to rebuke the citizens of a town for their sin. The elders must have been very relieved to hear that Samuel had come peaceably to offer a sacrifice. The elders, Jesse, and his sons consecrated themselves in preparation for the sacrifice.

Choose students to read the skit from the Student Book. At the conclusion, ask students why God didn't choose one of the older sons of Jesse. Remind them that "man looks on the outward appearance, but the LORD looks on the heart" (v. 7). Earlier, Samuel had told Saul that "The LORD has sought out a man after His own heart, and the LORD has commanded him to be prince over His people" (13:14). That man was the boy David, son of Jesse. God had taken what appeared to be a small and insignificant person, and exalted him. David did not look like a future king, but this was in God's hands. "The Spirit of the LORD rushed upon David from that day forward" (16:13). This was God's will, God's way, working through God's power.

Continue with the "Royal Checklist" in the Student Book. Say, **This list indicates characteristics that people might look for when choosing an earthly leader. Draw a line through any characteristics that you think would not be on God's list when making a choice.** (All characteristics will need to be crossed off.) Continue with the questions, noting that even David's father, Jesse, did not consider David as material for becoming a king because he was only a shepherd. God, however, looks at things differently. Read aloud Isaiah 55:8 and 1 Corinthians 1:18–25. Use Reproducible 26 to review the story of the anointing of David.

LESSON 26

Samuel Anoints David

The Boy Who Would Be King

Narrator: God had rejected Saul because of his unfaithfulness and disobedience.
The Lord: Samuel, go to Bethlehem to the home of a man named Jesse. I have chosen one of his sons to become the next king. Go there to offer a sacrifice and to anoint the one who will be king.
Narrator: Samuel traveled to Bethlehem to the home of Jesse.
Jesse: Welcome, Samuel. It is an honor to welcome you to my simple home.
Samuel: Thank you, Jesse. I have come to Bethlehem to make a sacrifice to the Lord. (*Aside:*) I won't tell Jesse yet that God has sent me here to anoint the person He has chosen to be Israel's next king.
Narrator: Jesse had many sons. He brought seven of them forward to meet the prophet.
Jesse: This is my oldest son, Eliab.
Samuel: What a handsome young man! So tall and royal looking! (*Aside:*) He must be the Lord's anointed one.
The Lord: (*Offstage voice*) Do not look on his appearance or height, because I have rejected him. For the Lord sees not as man sees: man looks on the outward appearance, but the Lord looks on the heart.
Jesse: And this is his brother, Abinadab . . .
The Lord: Not this one either, Samuel.
Jesse: And then there is Shammah . . .
The Lord: Not Shammah . . .
Jesse: And their four younger brothers.
The Lord: No, Samuel. None of them.
Samuel: Jesse, are all of your sons here?
Jesse: There's one more—the youngest, but he's out tending the sheep.
The Lord: Arise, anoint him, for this is he.
Narrator: David knelt as Samuel anointed him with oil as the sign that he was chosen by the Lord.

ROYAL CHECKLIST
☐ Good-looking
☐ Intelligent
☐ Wealthy
☐ Brave, strong
☐ Cool dude
☐ Hardworking
☐ Charming, polite

Why didn't Jesse consider David to become the next king? _____
David was young and just a shepherd.

Why did the Lord consider David to become the next king? _____
David had a faithful heart.

Review

Covenant Connection
Messianic promises often called the coming Savior "the Son of David." Jesus was born from this royal family. Centuries would pass, but the direct connection is shown in Matthew 1. David was Jesus' ancestor. Jesus was a descendant of David. Another promise was fulfilled.

Covenant Connection

To help your students put the story of David into its historical context, look at David's family tree on Web Resource 26a. David belonged to the tribe of Judah, and his home was in Bethlehem, in the territory of Judah. David's father was Jesse. Jesse's father was Obed, the son of Boaz and Ruth. This portion of the genealogy is recorded in Ruth 4:21–22. These were all ancestors of Jesus, the Messiah. Ask students to find the genealogy of Jesus in Matthew 1:1–17. Challenge them to find Boaz and Ruth, Obed, Jesse, and David in this genealogy. Then refer to Luke 3:23–38 and find similar information.

Ask students why the writers of the gospels thought it was important to include the genealogy of Jesus. Explain that the birth of Jesus fulfilled prophecies that had been made over many centuries. These prophecies foretold the tribe from which the Savior would come, the name of one of His ancestors, and even the town in which He would be born. The genealogies also show us that God loves all people. In addition to all those fathers, the list in Matthew includes four mothers, none of whom was a typical Jewish woman. Jesus' ancestors included prostitutes, adulterers, violent men, and other sinners of all descriptions—a reminder that there were no people other than sinners to make up His family tree. Jesus' ancestors needed a Savior as much as we do. On this family tree, only Jesus was sinless, because He is true God as well as true man.

God's Way; God's Will

It was God's way to make the unexpected choice of a shepherd for a king. It was God's will that David, son of Jesse, be that king. To learn more about God's will, imagine what it would be like to sit in on an interview with Martin Luther for a sixteenth-century newspaper.

Freida: I am honored to have you as my guest today, Dr. Luther. Let's get right to the issue. People have been praying the Lord's Prayer for years, including that part about "Thy will be done." We've all heard pastors add "if it is Your will" at the end of their prayers. Last week, I interviewed a choir director who said he was going to take his singers on tour next year, "God willing." Why all this interest in God's will? Do people know what they're asking when they pray "Thy will be done"?

Luther: First of all, let me say that God's good and gracious will is done even *without* our prayer, but we pray that it may be done among us also.

Freida: But what exactly *is* God's good and gracious will?

Luther: Good question. It is God's will that His name be kept holy and that His kingdom come, or to say it another way, it is His will that His Word be taught correctly and that sinners be brought to faith in Christ and lead godly lives.

Freida: That sounds harmless enough. Who could be against that?

Luther: The devil, the world, and our own sinful nature oppose the good and gracious will of God.

Freida: How is God's will done in our lives?

Luther: God's will is done when He breaks and hinders the plans of the devil, the world, and our sinful nature, which try to destroy our faith in Christ Jesus. His will is also done when He strengthens and keeps us firm in His Word and faith and helps us lead God-pleasing lives. His will is done when He supports us in all our troubles until He one day takes us to heaven.

Freida: But look around you, Dr. Luther. People die in wars. Millions of children suffer from hunger and the diseases associated with poverty. Others are oppressed because of their race or beliefs. God's will doesn't seem to be working there. Wouldn't it be better to pray "my will be done"?

Luther: Suffering isn't God's will for His people—it's the result of sin in this world. The Bible says God "desires all people to be saved and to come to the knowledge of the truth" (1 Timothy 2:4). That's why God sent His own Son, Jesus, into the world. When He died on the cross, Jesus took the punishment for the sins of everyone who has ever lived. Because of Jesus, we will live with God in heaven forever.

Freida: Thank you, Dr. Luther, for your enlightening words.

Remember

"This is the will of My Father, that everyone who looks on the Son and believes in Him should have eternal life." (John 6:40)

59

INTO the lesson

God's Way; God's Will

We live in a world in which we are bombarded by advertising that tells us we can have everything our own way. Most of this advertising is aimed at self-gratification: look the best, own the best, you deserve it. All of it serves to reinforce the belief that our own will is the only will that counts.

Remind your students of the account of Adam and Eve in the Garden of Eden as recorded in Genesis 3. Adam and Eve's sin came about because they wanted to be their own gods. They wanted to say to God, "My will be done" instead of "Thy will be done." When they chose their own will over God's will, Paradise was lost. When we act like we are our own gods, the world runs according to our will, and its problems multiply.

We pray in the Lord's Prayer, "Thy will be done on earth as it is in heaven." Read together the skit in the Student Book to learn more about God's will.

INTO our lives

How Do We Choose?

What is our standard for making choices? Do we determine decisions according to what we want, or do we base our decisions on God's will? It's not easy to pray "Thy will be done." Our sinfulness makes us strong-willed and tempts us to pray "Not Thy will, but mine be done." But **God's good and gracious will is always best. God's will is that all people be saved and spend eternity with Him. When we pray "Thy will be done," we ask God to open our hearts to accept His will and live according to it. We ask Him to make us a part of His good and gracious will so that, by the power of the Holy Spirit, we may witness to the Good News about Jesus and bring others into His kingdom.**

Direct students to look again at the "Royal Checklist" in their Student Book. Point out, **Very often these are the same characteristics we examine when making choices for ourselves or about our friends. We want to be cool. We like friends who are good-looking and popular. We want to own things that are the latest, most modern, and, often, the most expensive. So many of our decisions are based on what we want—on our own will, rather than looking through a Christian perspective and living according to God's will.**

Living according to God's will isn't easy. That's why we continue to pray that His will be done among us. Ask students, **Have you ever failed to do what you knew was the right thing—God's will—because it made you uncomfortable or it was socially unacceptable? God knows we will face many challenges in living as Christians. He sends His Holy Spirit to help us meet those challenges, and He has promised a reward in heaven, a crown of life, for all who remain faithful, trusting in the salvation we have in Christ Jesus.**

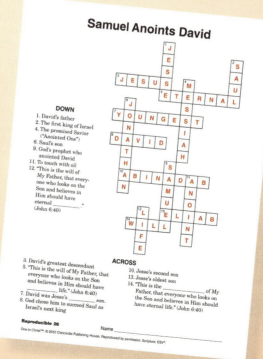

117

Teacher Tips

How do you see the children in your class? Do you assume the attractive, well-groomed child will be well behaved and intelligent? Do you expect trouble from the disheveled kid from the wrong side of town? While most of us would deny this kind of stereotyping, studies have shown that even parents instinctively react more favorably to an attractive child than to an unattractive child. The Bible tells us, "The LORD sees not as man sees: man looks on the outward appearance, but the LORD looks on the heart" (1 Samuel 16:7). An experienced teacher prayed the following prayer each day before school: Lord, help me today to see each child in my class as a precious child of God. Amen.

Searching Further

David was skilled at playing the lyre. A lyre is a stringed instrument of the harp family; it has two curved arms connected at the upper end by a crossbar. It was usually used to accompany singing or the recitation of poetry. The earliest representation of a lyre was found in a Minoan settlement in Crete from the period of the Mycenaean occupation (1400 BC). This lyre had seven strings. The strings of a lyre are usually strummed like a guitar or zither.

DIGGING DEEPER

Consider looking at the remainder of 1 Samuel 16, which serves as an epilogue to this lesson's Bible story. Compare verses 13 and 14. As God's Spirit was increasing in David, the same Spirit left Saul because of his unfaithfulness. Because Saul had followed his own will instead of God's will, God's Spirit had departed from him. The harmful or evil spirit that tormented Saul was under God's control and could only act within divinely determined boundaries. According to Martin Chemnitz, "God permits, allows, suffers sin in the sense of deserting or leaving someone to it" (Loci Theologici, ed. J. A. O. Preus [St. Louis: Concordia Publishing House, 1989], vol. 1, p. 218. Used by permission.). It is evidence of God's mercy that He allowed David's music to temporarily relieve Saul's torment.

Consider how ironic it was that David, the future king, was invited to the palace by the present king. Saul would have been unaware of the anointing by Samuel; at the same time, this would prove a useful training time for David as he had opportunities to observe royal matters close at hand. David's musical talent was a blessing to Saul at that time, but it is also a blessing to the Church throughout the ages, as we continue to read the words of the psalms.

Music Connection

The Jesse Tree is an artistic depiction of the ancestry of Jesus. It is based on the prophecy recorded in Isaiah 11:1, "There shall come forth a shoot from the stump of Jesse, and a branch from his roots shall bear fruit." This theme was popular during the medieval period, and the earliest known example dates from the eleventh century AD. Today, the Jesse Tree often serves as an Advent calendar, with symbols of Christ's ancestors added to the tree each day during the Advent season. Several of the Advent and Christmas hymns in *LSB* refer to the line of Jesse and his family tree, which eventually included Jesus. Sing stanza 2 of "What a Hope! An Eden Prophesied" (*LSB* 342) using the accompaniment track of "The King Shall Come" (*LSB* 348; recorded as *Hymn of the Season for grade 6, Advent*). Read stanza 4 of "O Come, O Come, Emmanuel" (*LSB* 357; recorded as *Hymn of the Season for grade 3, Advent*). Also see stanza 1 of "Lo, How a Rose E'er Blooming" (*LSB* 359; recorded as *Hymn of the Season for grade 6, Christmas*).

Curriculum Connection

God's rejection of Saul and appointment of David to be king set up a competitive situation between them. Competition exists in the natural world as well, among animals and even plants. Using section 6.2.2.6, Competition, encourage students to research examples of competition in nature. For example, they might explore the question of why gardeners and farmers must constantly battle weeds. (This is because most weed species are capable of outcompeting our garden and food plants, which must therefore be protected if they are to survive.) You'll find this section and other useful material in the sixth-grade Science volume of the Concordia Curriculum Guide series.

UNIT 3—PROPHETS AND KINGS

LESSON 27

David and Goliath
1 SAMUEL 17

Central Truth
God provides for our physical needs, which include food and clothing, health and safety.

Objectives
- Acknowledge that we sometimes worry about and fear the obstacles and challenges in life.
- Realize that God forgives our weakness and strengthens our faith to trust His care for us.
- Rejoice that God takes care of what we truly need, at the right time, and in the way that is best.

Materials
- Hymnals and music CDs
- Web Resource 27a
- Reproducible 27

Bible Prep
Post in advance so students can bookmark references before class time.
- 1 Samuel 17
- Psalm 124
- John 18:1–6
- 1 Corinthians 15:55–57
- Ephesians 6:13–18

Background

Today's Bible story is fascinating for students of all ages! A young boy killing a nine-foot giant with only one stone seems almost unreal! Emphasize to the students, however, that this is not just a legend. It really happened! Also take time to explore the Fourth Petition of the Lord's Prayer, and lead your students to discover who it is that really provides for their needs. Students at this age level are very "stuff" oriented, and it is important for them to realize that everything is a gift from God. Also be sensitive to students who do not have as many material things; assure them that God gives everyone their needs (and some wants) according to His good will and timing, and that His will is always what is best for our lives. It may also be intriguing to teach some of the battle strategy used back in Old Testament times. To conserve manpower, each side would often choose one champion to fight each other so that many men would not be lost in a huge battle. Apparently the Israelites also would have been familiar with this tactic, but due to Goliath's extreme size, they became fearful and lost faith in the covenant promise of the Lord. Just as the Lord showed mercy in spite of their sinfulness, so we also receive mercy from our Lord and Savior even when we do not trust in Him to provide for all of our needs! Jesus died once and for all for sinners like you and me! His mercy and grace continue as He continues to strengthen us and build us up in faith through Word and Sacrament.

Devotions

"Are you okay, Jake?" asked Dad. "Yeah," trembled Jake, "and I'm pretty sure Kaylee's okay too. She's still in her car seat, just looking at me."

"Good! We're going to be all right. The ambulance and rescue workers should be here really soon to help us get out of here. I didn't even see anything coming, did you?" Dad asked.

"Well, I did see a blue car turn pretty quickly in front of us, and that's when our car flipped." Jake tried to remember more of the details of the accident, but his mind was becoming cluttered.

"Mama!" cried Kaylee. "I want Mama!" "I know you do, Sweetie. Mama will be here soon too. Help is coming soon," assured Dad.

"How many are in the car?" a voice shouted from outside the car.

"Three of us. One baby, one boy, and me!" shouted Dad, relieved that help had arrived. Within a matter of minutes, Dad, Jake, and Kaylee were all safely out of the vehicle. Everyone involved was basically unharmed.

"Thank God you're all okay!" cried Mom as she held Kaylee and hugged Jake and Dad. "That accident could have had terrible results! Your guardian angels were all working overtime today."

"Another example of God providing for all of our needs in His good timing!" Dad exclaimed.

Let's pray together: Dear Lord our Savior, You are our Redeemer and our Protector. We thank You for providing all that is needed to support our bodies in this life. Forgive us for the times when we take for granted all of the good gifts You give us and for the times when we let discontent creep into our hearts. Help us to be bold as we trust in You above all things. "Grant us wisdom, grant us courage for the facing of this hour." Bless us with energy to share the Good News with those we meet along life's way. In Your holy and precious name we pray, Amen.

Sing "God of Grace and God of Glory" (*LSB* 850; recorded as *Hymn of the Month for grade 6, November*). Say together Psalm 23, pointing out that in today's Bible lesson, we will hear about an incident where David truly was walking "through the valley of the shadow of death" and God was with him! Also use Web Resource 27a. Listen to this chanted version of Psalm 23. In future days, lead the class to join in with chanting the psalm, using the notations to indicate movement in the melody tone.

INTO the Word

Meeting Giants

Have students work either silently or in small groups to read the Bible narrative from 1 Samuel 17. Then gather the class together to answer the questions in the Student Book. Emphasize, **God turns things upside down. His ways are different from the ways of the world around us. He can use simple stones or what seem to be "a bunch of losers" or even people like you and me to accomplish His purposes. We are just tools; the power comes from God.** David was confident—not in his own ability, but in God's faithfulness. Learn about the confidence we have in the Lord by listening to the hymn "Jesus Lives! The Victory's Won" (*LSB* 490; recorded as *Hymn of the Season, grade 7, Easter*). Say, **Because David knew his own strengths and weaknesses, his enemy's strengths and weaknesses, and, most importantly, the strength of God who was with him, he could have confidence in his ability to defeat his giant!**

You may want to discuss the fact that the Old Testament seems to have a lot of violence in it. The fact is, our world today is no different. Look at the news, look at a television program, or look at a video game—they are all filled with violence. Say, **What is significant about the Bible narratives we are studying is that God is always there with His faithful people, helping them to survive and even thrive in spite of the chaos of the world. Instead of focusing on the violence, do as David did and focus on the honor, the faithfulness, and the mighty power of God.**

LESSON 27

David and Goliath

Meeting Giants

Read about David and Goliath in 1 Samuel 17. Then answer these questions.

1. How would you describe Goliath? _He was more than nine feet tall; the point of his spear alone weighed more than six pounds; taunting; uncouth; rough; heavily armored; frightening._

2. This was not the first giant problem David faced. What troubles had he met before? (See verses 34–37.) _He had killed lions and bears with God's help (v. 37)._

3. This was not the last giant problem David faced. See 1 Samuel 22:1–2. Describe his army when he was later being chased by an enemy. _They were a bunch of losers—people in distress, in debt, bitter in soul._

4. Why was David so upset at Goliath? (See 1 Samuel 17:26.) _Goliath's words were a disgrace to Israel and they dishonored God._

5. Why was David so certain he could defeat Goliath? (See vv. 45–47.) _He knew God was on his side; the battle was the Lord's._

Armed and Ready to Go!

David's unfaltering faith in God is what made him stand head and shoulders above the rest of the men—in fact, tall enough to face even the tallest of giants. David tried on Saul's armor—a bronze helmet, a coat of mail (clothing made of strips of metal or leather), and a sword. David tried walking around while wearing it, but he couldn't get used to it. He realized he didn't need it anyway because his help came from the Lord. Centuries later, the apostle Paul wrote about the armor and weapons God gives to us to fight our battles against sin and evil, and once again, these are not made of earthly materials. (See Ephesians 6:13–18.) God's protection consists of things such as truth, the Gospel, peace, faith, God's Word, and prayer.

Jesus taught us to pray for God's support for our earthly needs when He taught us to say, "Give us this day our daily bread." In the Appendix of this book, look in Luther's Small Catechism at the Lord's Prayer, Fourth Petition. Write the list of things we are asking for when we pray for "daily bread": _Food, drink, clothing, shoes, house, home, land, animals, money, goods, a devout husband or wife, devout children, devout workers, devout and faithful rulers, good government, good weather, peace, health, self-control, good reputation, good friends, faithful neighbors, and the like_

Covenant Connection

Compare David and his weapons against his enemy with Jesus in the Garden of Gethsemane. (See John 18:1–6.) When confronted by an armed band of soldiers, Jesus only said a few words and the men fell over. Jesus' word has power. However, Jesus chose not to use that power and gave Himself up willingly to suffer and die for our salvation! Praise the name of Jesus!

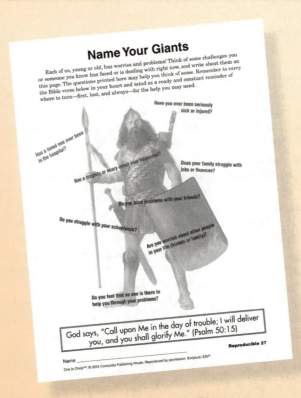

Defeating Giants

In today's Bible narrative, the people of Israel relied on their armies, their armor, and their weapons; when these failed them, they ran away. We are often like those people, trusting in our ideas and plans, things we have, and people we know for the things we want and need rather than trusting first and totally on the power of our gracious God. What does God do when we are sorry for not coming first to Him and relying on Him for all our needs? **He forgives us because of Jesus, our Savior; He sends the Holy Spirit, working through Word and Sacrament, to strengthen us in faith; and He continues to generously bless us and guide us.**

The Victory Is Won!

Even though David chose five stones to bring into battle against Goliath, it only took one stone to do the job. God's power was behind David from the very beginning, and His power is with us too! God's power rescues us from the giant troubles in our lives according to His good will and with His good timing.

Once and for all time, Jesus has crushed the great giants—the power of sin, death, and the devil. And a stone was involved in this battle too. When the stone was rolled from the grave on Easter morning, everyone could see that the victory was complete. Through His death and resurrection, Jesus has won the victory, and He gives His victory to us! (See 1 Corinthians 15:57.)

Remember

"I have said these things to you, that in Me you may have peace. In the world you will have tribulation. But take heart; I have overcome the world." (John 16:33)

INTO our lives

Armed and Ready to Go

Read aloud the first paragraph in the Student Book. Ask, **What is the difference between the armor used in a worldly situation and the armor and protection from God?** (The first trusts the strength of metal and men; the second trusts the power of God to protect us.)

The second paragraph in this section of the Student Book explores praying for God's help, support, and protection. After students write down the list from the explanation of the Fourth Petition of the Lord's Prayer, discuss how each of those factors can be part of a giant problem in someone's life (e.g., weather can be a problem when there are floods or tornadoes). Then talk about specific ways God blesses us in each item on the list (e.g., the blessing of good friends who are faithful and kind). *Option:* Have students read together and highlight key phrases in Luke 12:22–34, which encourages us to not worry, but trust in God.

At this point in the lesson, discuss Reproducible 27. We may not have giant Goliaths in our lives, but we all have giant troubles from time to time. This page looks at some of the possible problems that arise in a person's life. Students don't have to state their own personal problems; encourage them to speak in general terms about people in general. Focus on praying for God's care in all these situations.

Defeating Giants

Do we always trust that God will give us everything we need? (No.) **Why not?** (We doubt because we are weak and sinful; the devil places doubts in our minds.) **Knowing that doubting God is sinful, what should we do?** (We should repent; say we're sorry.) **What happens when we repent?** (God forgives us for the sake of Jesus.) The Student Book explores these concepts. Do allow for slight variation in answers, as long as the same concept is brought out.

After completing this section, have the class turn to Psalm 124 and read it aloud. This is a psalm David wrote. It would be very fitting with this lesson and with many other events in David's life. Have students underline phrases that are particularly related to today's lesson.

The Victory Is Won!

This is an interesting comparison of the significance of two stones—both directed by God. David's single stone from a slingshot eradicated the threat of a Philistine enemy. Jesus' resurrection from the grave with the stone rolled away eradicated the threat of sin, death, and the devil eternally. Have students look up and highlight 1 Corinthians 15:55–57. Say, **Jesus not only crushed death, but it was swallowed up! Jesus' victory over death reminds us that we never need to worry about our battles because they are already won through Jesus Christ.** **Jesus' resurrection means that Jesus was victorious over sin, death, and the devil. Satan and his powers were defeated once and for all, and we now have the promise of eternal life because of Christ's victory over the grave.** Say, **We can place our giants at the foot of the cross and trust that God crushes our giants! Even though it is human nature for us to have fearful emotions, we, like David, can face our giants—our problems—with confidence because we know that God is in us and that His power is greater than any other power in this world!** Celebrate now by singing several Easter songs recored on *Hymns of the Season for Easter (all grade levels).*

Lesson Support

Teacher Tips

Because this lesson asks students to consider some personal concerns, be sure that you, as a teacher, are ready to handle the needs of your students that may arise. Be ready to talk, show care, and refer them to a pastor, counselor, or psychologist whenever necessary. Do not attempt to handle problems that are beyond your expertise. Know that the Lord is with you!

Working in Groups

Divide the class into groups of four or more students and let them have fun designing their own nine-foot giant. Each group will need a ten-foot-long piece of bulletin board paper, some pencils, markers, and other crafty items such as foil, cardboard, buttons, rope strands, yarn, and so forth to outfit their giants. Before they get started, have students study what "six cubits and a span" really means (just over nine feet), and teach them about the different types of Goliath's armor mentioned in the Bible—a bronze helmet, a coat of mail, bronze armor on his legs, a javelin of bronze, a spear of iron, and a shield. Then allow the students to put their creative minds to work and design their own Goliaths with the appropriate armor! Be sure students use pencils to draw their giants first and then go over the outline with markers so as not to waste large amounts of paper.

Art Connection

Have students write and illustrate a comic-strip-style illustration that shows the entire Bible story or a scene from the story. Be sure that students use their rulers for straight, neat lines, and have them measure the boxes and make them proportional to one another. Some suggestions for individual scenes that students may choose to write about and illustrate are David talking with his father, Jesse; David speaking with his brothers and the Israelite men; Saul and David's conversation before David is sent into battle; and David and Goliath in battle. You may choose to assign some segments of the story to certain groups so that the whole story is gradually depicted, or you may just let the students choose their own angles. When the illustrations are finished, display them in the hallway for others to read and view. If applicable, save each student's illustration and place it in his or her portfolio showing progress in art, creative thinking, writing, arithmetic, geometry, and logic.

Curriculum Connection

The story of David and Goliath has been portrayed countless times in painting and sculpture. Compare and contrast several different treatments of this story using section 6.1.1.3, Theme, Genre, Style, Idea, and Media Differences in Selected Works of Art. You'll find it in the sixth-grade Visual Arts volume of the Concordia Curriculum Guide series. Look particularly at the ways the artists highlight the differences between David and Goliath. How do they use angle, perspective, and color to emphasize the danger and God's great deliverance?

Technology

Take two! Divide children into groups of four to six students, and have each group make a video as they reenact today's story. You could have students reenact the entire story, the conversation between Saul and David before David is sent into battle, or the fight between David and Goliath. All of the groups could cover the same scene, or each group could be assigned a scene to eventually show the "big" picture. English and writing connections can be made as each group could also be assigned to write a script complete with dialogue and stage directions. Be sure to share the completed productions with the entire class! Perhaps a fun, healthy popcorn snack during "movie time" could reinforce a job well done!

Unit 3—Prophets and Kings　　　　　　　　　　　　　　　　　　　　　　　　　　Lesson 28

David and Saul
1 Samuel 18; 24; 26

Background

During the years that Saul hunted David in the wilderness, David had opportunities to kill the king and take the kingdom if he so chose. On two occasions, Saul was helpless, undefended, and unaware of David's presence. Moreover, David knew that he himself had been chosen to be the next king of Israel, and that the Lord was withdrawing the kingship from Saul. So why didn't David kill him and assume the throne? The clue lies in David's words to his companion: "Do not destroy him, for who can put out his hand against the LORD's anointed and be guiltless?" (1 Samuel 26:9). When David looked at Saul, he did not see an enemy. He saw someone who had been chosen for this office from the Lord. However evil Saul might be, David could not bring himself to strike back and so dishonor both Saul and God. Today we daily face troubles with people who are also, in a sense, "God's anointed," people whom God has placed in our lives, such as family members, co-workers, pastors, teachers, and neighbors. When there is conflict, we are tempted to take revenge—particularly when justice is on our side. But the Lord's true Anointed, Jesus Christ, tells us to forgive our neighbors. Doing so even against all human reason, honors the God who placed them in our lives.

Central Truth

God's forgiveness is great, and He leads His people to forgive others.

Objectives

- Repent, asking God to forgive our sins, including the sin of being unforgiving.
- Respond to the forgiveness Jesus offers us by forgiving others.
- Recognize that God's way—in love and peace—is always the best way to solve relationship problems.

Materials

- Hymnals and music CDs
- Web Resource 28a
- Yellow highlighter
- Web Resource 28b
- Reproducible 28

Bible Prep

Post in advance so students can bookmark references before class time.
- 1 Samuel 18; 24; 26
- Romans 12
- Isaiah 40; 41; 43

Devotions

Robert and Robin were sitting at the kitchen table, having a snack, when their father came in from work and joined them. He set his hard hat on the table and kicked off his work boots. He seemed a little frustrated, so the twins' mother brought a cup of coffee over for Mr. Larson and joined the group. "Is something bothering you?" she asked. "Yes, there is," he replied. "I think I'm going to talk to my supervisor about it tomorrow. You know that I've been placed on the team that demolishes the old buildings on this new housing project. I am so tired of tearing things down. I want to build something up, not destroy things. I know I will be a lot happier at work if I can create something that improves things and brings happiness to others." "I know exactly how you feel," his wife said. "The problem I see at *my* job is people tearing down other people. At lunchtime, Martha and Liz do nothing but gossip and criticize the new supervisor. When I asked them to not say things that weren't facts, just opinions, they got mad at me. They said it's a free country and they can say what they want. I think I'll have to eat at a new lunch table after this." Robert gasped and said, "If you do that, they'll probably say mean things about you too." "Well," said Mom, "I guess I will just forgive them for that; but I will not sit quietly by while they harm other people." Robin sat there with tears in her eyes and then quickly ran from the room. "Uh-oh," said Mom. "I'd better see what that is all about." Robin was busy texting a message on her phone. "Is something wrong?" asked Mom. "Something is very wrong," said Robin. "Karla texted me earlier about the new girl at school to say she wears dorky clothes and that she thinks the girl's father is in jail. I just laughed when I read that; but now I understand that I was joining in with Karla's mean attitude. Even if I say nothing, I will be wrong. So I'm going to join the conversation, but with kind words. I know Karla is twisting the truth. The new girl's father is in the jail, but that's because he *works* there as a guard. I also know that the new girl is quite a good artist and has even designed some of her own clothes. She's not dorky—she just has a unique personal style. Karla's just trying to build herself up by tearing someone else down." "I am so proud of you," said Dad, who had walked into the room. "I do hope you realize this might affect your friendship with Karla." Robert joined in, saying, "Right, but you'll still have a friend." "Do you mean the new girl?" asked Robin. "No." "Robert, are talking about you and Mom and Dad still being my friends?" "That's true," replied Robert, "but actually, I was thinking of Jesus. He is our never-failing friend." Sing together "What a Friend We Have In Jesus" (*LSB* 770; recorded as *Hymn of the Month for grade 6, September*).

123

INTO the lesson

As the Lord Has Forgiven You

This introductory section explores the idea that the actions of Saul and David resulted from different perspectives. (You may want to demonstrate the two words in the box—*ricochet* and *reflection*.) Saul's hurtful ways ricocheted back on himself, making his own life miserable. On the other hand, David's ways were not influenced by Saul's actions or a desire for revenge; his actions were based on God's love for him in the first place. David's actions were a reflection of God's ways. This is an Old Testament story, but it has very significant relationships to the New Testament. We see this in the forgiving actions of Jesus and in His words in the Lord's Prayer (Fifth Petition). Students are directed to Romans 12; but also look at Ephesians 5:1–2, where we are told to imitate Jesus—which is the same idea as reflecting the love and forgiveness He gives to us in the first place.

INTO the Word

Act 1: Why Won't You Believe Me?

Discuss the idea that the way of people in the world is to get revenge, get back at someone who has harmed you, get the upper hand by putting them down, and so on. Discuss examples of television programs where this kind of thinking is the main part of the plot. Emphasize that God's way is not the way of the world. We should not be learning behaviors and determining our actions based on what we see on TV or video games. Being a Christian is not easy because it is not the way of most people in the world. Being a Christian means we need to live counter to popular culture. We need to be different—and different can be very difficult. That is why we need to rely on the strength and guidance of the Lord. Look at Web Resource 28a. See if students can guess the message. (A jealous heart leads to a joyless life.) Say, **This describes King Saul, but it also describes people in our world today—and if we are honest, we will see evidence of this in our own lives too. Jealousy starts from sinful pride that wants to build itself up while tearing others down. Jealousy is wanting what someone else has or a fear that someone else will exceed what you have. If you are content, you will not be concerned about other people; you will be satisfied with the blessings God has given you. True happiness is found only in this type of contentment, knowing that God gives you all you need for this life and everything you need for eternal life in Christ.**

Act 2: History Repeats Itself

After reading through Act 2, have students go back over the section, comparing it with the events in Act 1. Have them use a yellow highlighter to mark anything that occurs in both stories. There are some differences, but there are also many similarities. Unfortunately, Saul was basically unchanged. Thanks to the Lord, David remained forgiving. Use Web Resource 28b to discuss dealing with jealousy. Saul was caught in expanding bad behaviors. The Bible tells us that he had a jealous eye, a hateful tongue, and hurtful hands. A symbol of this would be that he was inside of an ever-expanding balloon that was ready to pop. Ask, **How do you take the wind out of a jealous or vengeful situation? You do it by joining the celebration!** Use Reproducible 28 to consider modern situations where this would apply. Emphasize that responding positively, even when someone has hurt you, is the way to stop the downward spiral of anger and revenge. It may or may not affect the other person's behavior, but **you can rest assured in the forgiveness and guidance of Jesus Christ, the only source of true peace.**

LESSON 28
David and Saul
As the Lord Has Forgiven You

1. **ricochet:** when something that is tossed or projected out returns, bounces back, is projected back
2. **reflection:** imitation, mirror image, or faithful representation of something else

1. King Saul's troubles started with his pride. When something injured his pride, he became jealous, and that jealousy led to aggression. But these bad attitudes *ricocheted* on him because jealousy is self-destructive. Saul wanted to harm David (twice, Saul threw a spear at him), but he ended up harming himself (becoming paranoid and depressed). Read 1 Samuel 18:6–9, 28–30.
2. David could have taken revenge on Saul, but that only would have caused more harmful ricocheting of bad behaviors. Instead, David was a *reflection* of the Lord. David passed on to King Saul the kindness and forgiveness God gave to him.
3. Read Romans 12:17–21. Summarize this message from Scripture. _Don't let someone's bad actions cause you to act badly; don't repay evil with evil. Let God avenge. Do what is honorable. Overcome evil with good._
4. What words of the Lord's Prayer apply well to this lesson? _Forgive us our trespasses as we forgive those who trespass against us._

Act 1: Why Won't You Believe Me?
1 Samuel 24

Narrator: Saul and his soldiers were in pursuit of David.
Saul: I've heard that David is in the wilderness of Engedi. Let's go after him and put an end to him.
Narrator: David hid with his men in the innermost part of a cave. Amazingly, Saul entered the same cave to take a rest.
David: (*whispering to his men*) I thought this would be a good place to hide. But look who just came in! It's King Saul.
One of David's Men: Now we know what the Lord meant when He said, "I will give your enemy into your hand, and you shall do to him as it shall seem good to you."
Narrator: David was tired of being on the run from his enemy. He could have killed Saul right then and there. But David knew

Review

Covenant Connection

The covenant that Jesus came to fulfill was all about forgiveness and making us His very own people. David knew the forgiveness and salvation of the Lord and looked forward to the promised Messiah. In Psalm 13:5, David said these words of praise to the Lord: "I have trusted in Your steadfast love; my heart shall rejoice in Your salvation."

62

he should not hurt the king God had given to Israel. Instead, David sneaked over and cut off the corner of Saul's robe.

David: Men, listen! Saul is the Lord's anointed. We will not harm him in any way.

Narrator: David followed Saul out of the cave and bowed down before him.

David: My king, why do you listen when men tell you that I am trying to harm you? Believe me, I do not want to hurt you. Today I could have killed you, but I didn't. Here is the proof—I was close enough to take this piece of your robe. May God judge between us and deliver me from your hand.

Saul: David, is that you? You are a better person than I am. You have treated me well even though I treated you badly. May God reward you. Go in peace.

Narrator: Saul then returned home. But David and his men went to a fortified area, knowing that Saul's word could not be trusted. They knew Saul might soon change his mind. (And he did!)

Act 2: History Repeats Itself
1 Samuel 26

Narrator: Time passed, and Saul's jealousy and paranoia returned. He took three thousand men on a search for David. With a volunteer, Abishai, David went down to Saul's camp at night. King Saul and the commander of his army, Abner, lay inside the camp, with soldiers all around them for protection.

Abishai: Look! They're all sleeping. God has delivered your enemy into your hand. Let me take my spear to kill Saul.

David: Don't destroy him. He is God's anointed. God will decide his end. Just take his spear and water jug that are near his head and then let's go.

Narrator: So the two men took the spear and water jug and left. No one in Saul's army saw them. Nor did anyone wake up. God had put them all into a deep sleep. David stood on the top of a hill some distance away and called out to Saul's army.

David: Abner, you didn't do a very good job of guarding your king! Someone sneaked into your camp and could have destroyed the king. Here is Saul's spear and water jug that were near his head. That is how close we came to him!

Saul: Is that your voice, David, my son?

David: Yes it is, my lord. What have I done wrong that you hunt after me? Why are you so angry at me? I have done nothing to harm you.

Saul: I have sinned. Come back, David. Because you did not kill me today, I will not try to harm you again. I've acted foolishly and have made a great mistake.

David: Send one of your young men to get your spear. I will not hurt you. I pray that God will value my life and deliver me from trouble.

Saul: David, may you be blessed. You will do great things and will surely triumph.

Narrator: So David went on his way, and Saul returned home. There is no mention of any other encounter between them after this event.

Remember

"Be kind to one another, tenderhearted, forgiving one another, as God in Christ forgave you." (Ephesians 4:32)

63

Demolition Tools

This is probably the most important section of the lesson because it applies so directly to twenty-first-century kids. Expand on this conversation with your class, bringing in the Law (Eighth Commandment), the Gospel (repentant hearts are forgiven), and sanctification (forgive as the Lord has forgiven you). One difficulty with this scenario is that too many people are reluctant to confess their sins against the Eighth Commandment. Too often, they choose to justify their behavior, saying that a negative statement is not wrong if it is true, or saying that it's not wrong to ask an incriminating question as long as you aren't making an accusation, or it's not wrong as long as you don't name the person (even though there are enough clues to figure it out). People who think this way are only fooling themselves, and they remain unrepentant in their sin.

Refer back to the story in the devotions and what the Larson family learned about tearing down and building up. Read together what Scripture says about this in Ephesians 4:25; Luke 6:37; James 4:11; and 1 Thessalonians 5:11. Emphasize that going against worldly ways takes a lot of courage; it is not the easy path. Read about the blessing of courage we have in the Lord: Deuteronomy 31:6; Joshua 1:7, 9; and Psalm 27:14.

How might someone tear down or build up the people in these situations?

1. Kara is the only girl in her class who is not invited to Marissa's party. Marissa is the most popular girl in the class, and she has never liked Kara. What might Kara's first reaction be? How might Kara respond as she is led by the love of Jesus?

2. Tomas practices basketball after school every day with his older brother. He thinks he is ready to try out for the team. After tryouts, the coach tells Tomas that he is fast but he is too small. Tomas's friend Alex, who is a head taller, makes the team, even though he isn't nearly as good a player as Tomas. What might Tomas's first reaction be? How might Tomas respond as he is led by the love of Jesus?

3. Johanna is well liked by her teachers. She does her best, works hard, and gets A's in every subject. She never fails a test; she participates in after-school activities, takes piano lessons, and helps out in the school library. Darnell says Johanna is just showing off. What might the reaction be of the other students? How might other students respond as they are led by the love of Jesus?

4. Jack is upset and worried. His mother and father seem unhappy all the time. They are always talking together privately and quietly with worried looks on their faces. Jack knows his dad is having trouble at work. A younger man at the office where he works was promoted to supervisor, even though Jack's father has been with the company longer. Today they found out that the younger man will now be his father's boss. What might Jack's father's first reaction be to the situation at work? How might his father respond as he is led by the love of Jesus?

125

Lesson Support

Ideas for the Gifted

It was not uncommon throughout history that a new ruler would seek out and kill every member of the former king's family—including the women and children! Have some students who are especially interested in ancient civilizations (and are able to handle the extra workload) study as much as possible about ancient royal families and rulers. Then allow them to make a PowerPoint presentation and share their newfound information with the class. Be sure to give appropriate extra credit for a job well done.

Bringing it home

"Mirror, mirror, on the wall!" Send home an assignment asking students to take a look at themselves and track their "David and Saul behaviors." Have each student keep a personal journal that logs his or her behavior for two days. If a behavior is seen as not being beneficial to someone, the student should list it under "Saul." If the behavior involves forgiving someone or showing mercy toward someone, the student should list the behavior under "David."

Be sure to send home a note informing parents of the assignment so that they will understand their child's need for extra writing time and so that parents can help students "catch" their "Saul and David behaviors." If time permits, discuss the journaling process with the students.

Curriculum Connection

David's respect, patience, and forgiveness for King Saul set an example of how people of good character behave. Consider using section 6.4.3.2, Good Character (Identifying). This is found in the sixth-grade Social Studies volume of the Concordia Curriculum Guide series. Discuss the ideas found in the section and challenge students: What other historical figures of good character can they name? What examples can they give from their lives to illustrate their virtues? Point out that we should not be discouraged when we see the sins and weaknesses of our "heroes" because we are all sinners. The only perfect hero is Jesus Himself. Look at the Heroes of Faith series for grade 6, learning about people who were followers of Jesus, enabled by the power of the Holy Spirit. Their goodness and righteousness came from Jesus, not from within themselves. They are heroes to us because like them, we can follow the same path of faith as we are justified by Christ Jesus and sanctified by the Holy Spirit.

HANDS TO SERVE

It was not easy for David to be nice to Saul because Saul was not very thankful for David's kind actions. Yet, David continued to be kind to Saul out of respect for his Lord and Savior. Likewise, it's easy to help people when they smile and say thank you, but it's not always easy to want to help if you never see or hear from those you are helping.

Knowing that helping without receiving appreciation is an important skill to build, have your class coordinate a Thanksgiving or Christmas family adoption program. Find out about a family or two that are in need, and have your class arrange to collect food, clothing, and other gifts that are age and size appropriate. After the supplies are collected, have your pastor deliver them to the families, and enjoy the idea that you and your class have just helped people you will never meet!

Reaching Every Child

Today's lesson involves quite a bit of reading (three whole chapters) and writing (several answers and phrases). Some students will consider this a challenge; to others, it will be pure torture. Keep in mind that those students who have difficulty reading and writing usually have a processing disorder that keeps them from doing things as smoothly and as fast as the rest of the students. When pairing up children for reading the Scripture passages and recording answers in the Student Book, be sure to pair challenged students with students who *want* to be challenged, and avoid pairing students whose personalities would clash—those relationships can heal in a different setting at a different time. Set up the challenged students for success by giving them willing partners, extra time to process information, and, if necessary, modified reading and writing requirements.

UNIT 3—PROPHETS AND KINGS

LESSON 29

Saul's Downfall
1 Samuel 28–2 Samuel 5

Background

The story of Saul and the witch of Endor is a tragic one; the man who would not value or obey the Word of the Lord is now so desperate for it that he will even break God's commandment in the hopes of forcing an answer out of God's prophet. Of course, nothing good comes of this, and Saul goes away in despair. Commentators are divided on the question of whether what spoke to Saul was truly the spirit of the prophet Samuel, allowed by God to return for this brief meeting, or simply an evil spirit impersonating Samuel. The spirit speaks the truth, but it does it in a disheartening way that leads Saul to despair instead of faith; and it never encourages Saul to repent or ask forgiveness. Luther may well have been right when he decided this was an evil spirit because God has forbidden necromancy [mediums, witches, satanic arts]. Whatever it was, Saul's downfall is a solemn warning to Christians tempted to use the occult in order to find out things God has not chosen to reveal to them. Saul pursued evil in his selfish desires and in his willful disobedience to the Lord. Sometimes we are like Saul. We become accustomed to the demands, desires, language, and behaviors of the world around us, and we ignore or adopt its evils. In the Lord's Prayer, we ask God to deliver us from evil, from all evils of body and soul. We pray that God would turn our hearts and minds away from our own selfish desires and turn us instead toward our Savior, Jesus Christ.

Central Truth
We are surrounded by evils in this world, and our ultimate deliverance relies on the power and faithfulness of God.

Objectives
- Confess that we become desensitized to many of the evils in the world around us and sometimes do not even recognize the connection to sin.
- Rely on God to protect us from evil and to guide us to follow His good and gracious will.
- Give all glory to God, who has conquered evil and offers salvation in Jesus.

Materials
- Hymnals and music CDs
- Web Resource 29a
- Reproducible 29

Bible Prep
Post in advance so students can bookmark references before class time.
- 1 Samuel 15; 22; 28–31
- 2 Samuel 1–5
- Psalms 10; 22; 23; 27; 46; 91; 109

Devotions

Jack liked scary movies, ghost stories, and "action" video games. And he *really* liked scaring his little sister. He knew it upset her and even made her cry, but he thought, "I'm just having fun!" One day, after his sister ran into the house, Jack's mother came outside and called him over to sit with her on the front steps. She talked about the scary things that he liked and about the way he played tricks on his sister. "Do you remember the Lord's Prayer, Jack?" she asked. "What comes after the words 'And lead us not into temptation'?" "'But deliver us from evil,'" Jack answered. His mother said, "We want God to keep us safe from many things. But we also want Him to deliver us from the bad things we want to see and do." "But all my friends like creepy movies too," said Jack. "And they think it's funny when I scare Sandy!" Then Jack thought for a moment. "Well, I guess Sandy doesn't think it's funny," he said. Jack's Mom reminded him, "Remember that evil can come from inside of us, from things we think, say, and do. We pray that God will deliver us from all kinds of evil, from the bad things in the world around us, and from the bad things that we want to do." "It's not easy to change," said Jack, "especially when other people are doing it too. But I'll pray for God's help." This time when his sister came outside, Jack didn't jump out and scare her. Instead, he said, "Let's play catch!"

When Jack was watching shows and playing games about ghosts and vampires, and when he was teasing his sister, he just thought about the fun he was having. He did not think that he might be doing anything wrong or hurting someone. Many things that we think, see, or experience may lead to sin, although we do not always realize it at the time. It is easy to see that some things are sinful—robbing a bank or killing someone—but other sins are not so easy to recognize. Those sins become "hidden" from us because we see them so often. We get used to the evil things in the world around us. We come to accept the bad language and violent behaviors we see on television or in movies. We see and hear some kinds of evil so often that we no longer think of it as evil. God wants to take us from the darkness of sin and bring us into the light of salvation. Sing the hymn "I Want to Walk as a Child of the Light" (*LSB* 411; recorded as *Hymn of the Season for grade 7, Epiphany*). Then say, **We walk in the light as we follow the Good Shepherd. Let's say the Good Shepherd psalm together, Psalm 23.**

127

INTO the lesson

Deliver Us from Evil

Say, **The story of Saul and the witch of Endor involves frightening things—a witch who can summon spirits, and the spirit of a dead man rising from the grave. It's the scary stuff of Halloween and spooky movies. When we pray in the Lord's Prayer "Deliver us from evil," we may think of such scary things. We also pray for deliverance from evil that makes the evening news—terror threats, traffic accidents, robberies, murders.**

The devil—and note the word *evil* **in his name—is very real and very powerful. The devil wants to do all he can to thwart and destroy the will of God. The devil, however, is not the only cause of evil. The world around us is broken and corrupted by sin. It is a dangerous place for us, physically and spiritually. But we, too, are a source of evil because of our sinful human nature—we, too, must take the blame.**

What's the answer to this grim situation? The answer has already come to our rescue—the answer is Jesus! Through His death on the cross and resurrection at Easter, we have forgiveness of our sin, and we have the promise of eternal life in heaven, where evil can never touch us again. Read aloud Revelation 21:3–4.

In the meantime, we live *in* **this world. But with Christ in us, we are not** *of* **this world. We can avoid some of the evils in this world. Some evils we cannot avoid, but we can be assured that God is with us as we endure the troubles of this world. Some evils are caused by our own sin and weakness; some evils are not directly our fault, but are a consequence of living in a world tarnished by sin.** Discuss these Psalm verses, having students identify the evil from which the psalmist asks to be delivered: Psalm 10:15 (people who are wicked evildoers); 22:21 (wild animals); 23:4 (dangers and death); 27:12 (people who lie and are violent); 46:2 (storms and earthquakes); 91:5 (fear of darkness and the unseen); and 109:3 (hateful attackers). Together read the words that tell about our rescue in Psalm 124:8: **"Our help is in the name of the Lord, who made heaven and earth."**

LESSON 29
Saul's Downfall
"How the Mighty Have Fallen"

1. King Saul had wasted so much time and energy chasing after David, who was not a real enemy, that he was unprepared when a real enemy, the Philistines, waged war. What was Saul's reaction when he saw their large armies (1 Samuel 28:5)? __He was afraid.__
Saul prayed to God, but he got no answer. Why not (1 Samuel 15:23)? __God had rejected Saul because he was unfaithful and disobedient.__

2. Saul got no help from prophets or priests. The prophet Samuel had died. What had happened to many of the priests (1 Samuel 22:18)? __Saul had ordered the deaths of eighty-five priests.__

3. Could things get any worse for King Saul? Yes, indeed! Saul now turned to Satan—he went to a witch at Endor. Saul asked this woman—a medium who called on the devil's powers to supposedly speak to the dead or predict the future—to call Samuel from the grave to find out what would happen. What appeared was most likely a false spirit, but God allowed this to happen so that once more, Saul could be confronted with his sin and his punishment. What was the message for Saul (1 Samuel 28:16–19)? __The next day, the Philistines would conquer Israel, and Saul and his sons, including Jonathan, would be killed.__

4. This is exactly what happened. Who killed Saul the next day (1 Samuel 31:2–4)? __Saul killed himself so he wouldn't be captured.__

5. Despite all that Saul had done, David mourned the death of the king and his sons. He wrote a lament to tell of his sorrow. Write the phrase that he repeated to express his grief over this tragedy. (See 2 Samuel 1:19, 25, 27.) __"How the mighty have fallen."__

Review

Covenant Connection

Saul succumbed to his encounters with sin and Satan. David battled sin and Satan throughout his life, repeatedly coming to God in repentance. The only complete victor against sin and Satan is Jesus Christ Himself. In the Apostles' Creed, we say together that Jesus "descended into hell." Luther's Small Catechism with Explanation explains that statement: "The Scriptures teach that Christ, after He was made alive in His grave, descended into hell, not to suffer punishment, but to proclaim His victory over His enemies in hell" (Apostles' Creed, question 143). Jesus proclaimed His victory over sin and Satan, and He gives the victory to us!

INTO the Word

"How the Mighty Have Fallen"

Use this Bible study in the Student Book to search out the details of this tragic story. *Option:* You may want to also refer to the information in the Background section of this lesson. Emphasize that David saw the tragedy in Saul's story. He did not rejoice in the death of his enemy. As before, he trusted in God's power and might to carry out His will.

David Uplifted

Saul's complete downfall as king was followed by David's rise as king. It was not immediate. People still remained who intended to circumvent or ignore God's will. Eventually, though, in His own time, God's will was accomplished. The reign of David was the high point historically for the Old Testament people of Israel. As always, we must see God working through David. It is God who made him a great ruler. And it is God who forgave him when he stumbled and fell into sin. Praise God that He is there for us too, lifting us up, empowering us to live as His people!

David Uplifted

It was God's will that David, the Lord's anointed, be the next king. But people don't always follow God's will. Abner, the commander of Saul's army, made Ish-bosheth, Saul's son, the king of Israel. But the tribe of Judah (the largest tribe) remained loyal to David and crowned him king of Judah, with Hebron as his capital city (2 Samuel 2:3–4). Eventually, the kingdom was united, with David ruling over both Judah and Israel. The capital of the united kingdom was Jerusalem. How long did David serve in each capital city (2 Samuel 5:4–5)? **Seven years in Hebron and thirty-three in Jerusalem, for a total of forty years**

How is David's rule as king described in 2 Samuel 5:10? **He became greater and greater because God was with him.**

Trust in the Lord

The great tragedy of Saul's life is that he did not show a lifetime commitment of faithfulness to the Lord. When first crowned king, Saul knew the Lord, but soon his trust relied on other things, such as his own strength, his own power, the might of his armies, and even the power of Satan. David, however, remained faithful throughout his life. He was a sinner, like you and me, but he relied on the grace and mercy of God to forgive his sins and restore him to a right relationship with God. He was confident of the forgiveness and salvation he was offered through the promised Messiah, who has been revealed as Jesus Christ. We have that assurance too. Write what these Scripture passages teach us about avoiding evil and about trusting in God.

1 Peter 5:8 **The devil is our enemy, who is sneaking around to harm us; we need to be on our guard.**

1 John 5:19 **The evil one (the devil) has a lot of power in the world, but we are God's.**

1 John 3:8b **Jesus came to destroy the works of the devil.**

2 Thessalonians 3:3 **God faithfully guards us from the evil one.**

Psalm 121:7–8 **Coming and going, God will protect us from evil.**

Colossians 1:13–14 **God delivers us from the kingdom of darkness to His kingdom of light.**

James 4:7–8 **God will help us resist Satan.**

Ephesians 6:10–12 **God makes us strong to stand up to the schemes of the devil.**

2 Timothy 4:18 **The Lord will rescue us from evil and take us to heaven.**

Remember

"Little children, you are from God and have overcome [the false spirits], for He who is in you is greater than he who is in the world." (1 John 4:4)

INTO our lives

Trust in the Lord

Work through the activity in the Student Book together. There are a lot of Bible passages to read aloud. Do not have all students look up all the verses. (That disrupts the flow of the discussion, takes too much time, and is frustrating to students who are just beginning to develop skills with the use of Scripture.) Web Resource 29a projects these verses on a screen. Let volunteers come forward and read aloud a verse, and then share together a possible written response. (If not using Web Resource 29a, have volunteers look up and read the individual passages to the class.)

Evil surrounds us today too. It is not just the evil of witches and spirits. It is not just the evil of terror attacks, robbery, or murder. Those things are frightening, and we pray that God will deliver us from those things. But we are also surrounded by the evil of false beliefs about God, disobedience, sexual relationships apart from marriage, bad language, and much more. These things are all around us, in people we know, in books, movies, and television shows. We become so used to seeing and hearing these evil things that we begin to accept them as a normal part of life, no longer thinking of these things as sin. Sometimes we are so used to them that we start to think or act in the same ways. What are some examples of these kinds of evils around us? Discuss with the students the examples of evil and disobedience to the Lord's commands that can be seen in the surrounding culture. What do they see on television or read in books that does not follow God's will? How are they tempted to act and speak like others who may not know the Lord? Say, **When we pray "Deliver us from evil," we are asking God to deliver us from all kinds of evil—from terror, robbery, murder, and evil spirits. But we are also praying that God would deliver us from the evil of our own sinful desires and from the evils of false beliefs and disobedience that surround us every day. We are asking God to open our eyes and help us recognize the evil around us. We want God to keep us from following our own desires and joining in evil that has become acceptable.** Expand the conversation using Reproducible 29.

Critical thinking

Jack, the boy in the devotion story, did not really think he was doing anything wrong when he teased and scared his little sister. He was just having fun. Often we think of sins as being only "big things" like stealing or telling lies. But Satan can easily trap us into thinking that what we are doing is not really wrong. "I'm just having fun," we may think; or we excuse ourselves by saying, "Everyone else is doing the same thing!" Because we want something or want to have fun, our desires may lead us into sin. Discuss such "small sins" with your students. What temptations do they face at home in their relationships with parents, brothers, and sisters? What temptations do they face at school or at other times with their friends? We pray that God will "deliver us from evil" at all times and in all circumstances.

Working in Groups

Jesus died on the cross to deliver us from the great evils of sin, death, and the devil. Have your students create posters or a mural showing Jesus' death, His resurrection, and His victory over evil. Use the words "But deliver us from evil" on the posters. Students might also wish to illustrate other petitions of the Lord's Prayer by using scenes from the life of Christ. The words "Our Father who art in heaven" could be illustrated with scenes from the birth of Jesus. The caption for the angels rejoicing at His birth could be "Hallowed be Thy name." "Thy kingdom come" could be illustrated with the preaching of John the Baptist and the Baptism of Jesus. Each group of students could be assigned a different petition. Discuss possible events in the life of Jesus to illustrate the other words of the Lord's Prayer.

Searching Further

The Bible does not tell us if the spirit of Samuel summoned up from death by the witch of Endor really was the prophet himself or if it was an evil spirit pretending to be Samuel. Did God permit the prophet's spirit to bring His message to Saul, or did He allow a demon to speak? We do not know if it was Samuel or a demon in disguise, but God used the spirit to speak His truth to Saul. Since the Bible does not tell us, we cannot know which kind of spirit it was. However, we do know that God forbids us to become involved in the satanic arts; Scripture is not silent about such practices (Deuteronomy 18:9–14; Acts 16:16–18; 19:18–20). Martin Luther spoke about such practices in his explanation of the Second Commandment: "We should fear and love God so that we do not curse, swear, use satanic arts, lie, or deceive by His name, but call upon it in every trouble, pray, praise, and give thanks" (Small Catechism). The knowledge of God's will and of His plans and purposes can be found only in His Word.

Faith in Action

We may often pray "Deliver us from evil" when we consider frightening or threatening circumstances in our own lives. The Lord's Prayer begins, however, with the words "*Our* Father," not just "*My* Father." We pray the prayer together in church, in chapel, and in the classroom. Talk to your students about praying for others. There are many people who need the help of God and who need to be delivered from all kinds of evil and trouble. They may be worried, sick, or in need. Help the students to think of people for whom they can pray, and then pray with them. Students might also wish to collect prayer requests from other classrooms or talk to the pastor about people in the congregation for whom they could pray.

Unit 3—Prophets and Kings

Lesson 30

David and Bathsheba
2 Samuel 11:1–12:23

Central Truth
By human nature, there is sin and evil in each of us from which our only rescue is the forgiveness we have in Christ Jesus.

Objectives
- Recognize our responsibility when temptation comes to resist and not give in; making excuses and switching blame are not acceptable ways to deal with it.
- Acknowledge that the strength to resist temptation comes solely from God and through His Word.
- Determine to rely on Jesus to forgive our weakness and to make us strong in faith and in living in faith.

Materials
- Hymnals and music CDs
- Web Resource 30a
- Reproducible 30

Bible Prep
Post in advance so students can bookmark references before class time.
- 2 Samuel 11–12
- Psalm 51
- Romans 4:7
- John 1:29
- 1 John 1:7

Background
The story of David and Bathsheba is cautionary to Christians who love their Lord, because it shows that even someone as strong in faith as David could fall into great sin. It is hard to believe that the same man who wrote so many of the psalms could have spent almost a year so very far from the Lord, and apparently untroubled by it. We say, therefore, in the Sixth Petition of the Lord's Prayer, "Lead us not into temptation." We pray that our own sinful nature may not deceive us or mislead us into sin. When tempted, we begin to think that the tempting offer is a good thing, a desirable thing—just as Eve saw that the forbidden fruit was "a delight to the eyes" and "to be desired to make one wise" (Genesis 3:6). Sin is quite often appealing, leading us to ignore the consequences and forget what God has forbidden. The devil, the world, and our sinful desires are all at work to tempt us and lead us to disobedience. In this petition, we pray that God will help us to resist evil that is disguised as a good choice and open our eyes to see clearly His will for our lives. In our struggle against sin, we can trust Jesus our Savior "who in every respect has been tempted as we are, yet without sin" (Hebrews 4:15). Jesus took our disobedience to the cross and suffered the punishment we deserve for our sin. In exchange, He gives us His own perfect obedience. Through faith in His name, our sins are forgiven. Forgiven and free, we seek to live according to God's will.

Devotions
Jeff and Eric talked about the party as they walked home from school. Almost all of the eighth graders would be at Rob's house, and some of Rob's high school friends would be there too. Eric really wanted to go to the party, but he knew his parents didn't want him to spend time with Rob. They thought Rob and his older friends were a bad influence. Eric came up with a scheme. He would get to go the party, and his parents would never find out. Eric made up a story to tell his parents; he said he was working on a school project with Jeff and had been invited to stay overnight. Eric went to the party, but he didn't have a very good time. He felt guilty about lying to his parents and he was afraid they would find out. After thinking about things for several days, Eric finally told his parents what he had done. They talked for a long time about temptation and the problems that sin brings into our lives. Eric admitted that he could not blame his friends; he was the one who had decided to lie and disobey his parents to get what he wanted. He prayed with his parents about telling the truth and about trust. His parents thanked him for admitting he was wrong; but there would be consequences. They grounded him and said that he had to earn their trust again. Eric promised himself that he would think more carefully about what was truly important.

Discuss why people try to cover up their sins, make excuses, or blame others. Ask, **What things are more important than the fleeting fun Eric had at the party?** (A clear conscience, faithfulness to God, his own integrity, the trust of his parents—these are long-term effects.) **The hardest temptations to resist are often the ones that involve another person. Why is it so difficult to say no to someone when you are tempted?** (You might be concerned about what they think, don't want them to laugh at you, don't want them to hurt you; or you may want to be cool and have cool friends; and so forth.) **As always, our help is in the name of the Lord. Pray for Him to lead us away from temptation, because our natural inclination—our sinful human nature—is to go into it, full speed ahead.** Sing "God of Grace and God of Glory" (*LSB* 850; recorded as *Hymn of the Month* for grade 6, November).

INTO the lesson

Piled Up

The subtitles in this lesson give a brief summary of the story of David and Bathsheba. This was not a matter of one sin—the sins *piled up*. One sin led to another. David tried to *cover up* his sins, but they still remained. God moved David to repentance through the message of the prophet Nathan, so David *'fessed up* (confessed). Until he was ready to acknowledge his sin and feel sorrow over it, he was not ready to hear the Gospel. He heard the Law, repented, and then immediately heard the Gospel. David was assured of God's forgiveness, which we know comes to us, too, because Jesus was *lifted up* on the cross to suffer the penalty for us!

In the previous lesson, we talked about the evils around us in this world that are caused by sin or are a consequence of sin in this world. Today's focus is on the evil within us. David's sin began with impure thoughts, and after that, the sins piled up, and the pile of sins kept getting bigger and bigger.

In the Student Book, look at David's list of sins and read the related Bible verses. Point out that we, too, have our own lists of sins that keep piling up. Again, our help is in the name of the Lord. That is why we pray in the Lord's Prayer, "Lead us not into temptation." In this prayer, we are asking God to lead us away from temptation and make us strong to resist it. Read the explanation of the Sixth Petition of the Lord's Prayer in the Small Catechism in the Appendix of the Student Book. (*Note:* A copy of the Student Book Appendix is in the back of this Teacher Guide.)

Covered Up

Read through the list of various attempts David made to cover up his sins. However, as the illustration suggests, the sins remained. His cover-up became part of the pile of guilt. Examine some of his tactics. **(a)** David's purpose in getting Uriah drunk was to send him home to Bathsheba so everyone would think it was her husband, not the king, who got her pregnant. But Uriah was such a faithful soldier that he refused to enjoy the comforts of home while his fellow soldiers were still in the battlefield. **(b)** Since David's first scheme didn't work, he tried another plan: placing Uriah at the front of the battle line and then pulling the line back so he would be exposed and killed. In effect, David used the Ammonites as his murder weapon. **(c)** When Uriah died, David simply responded that death happens in war, making the death seem insignificant. **(d)** After her time of mourning, Bathsheba married David. This may have appeared to some people as a noble thing—the king marrying the poor widow. But appearances were a lie. **(e)** David's reaction to the parable of Nathan was hypocritical, as he showed outrage about something *he* had done to an even greater degree. **(f)** The worst part of all of this is that David was unfaithful to the Lord. For almost a year, David ignored God's Law and avoided seeking God's forgiveness. Instead, David dealt with his sins by trying to cover them up. He hoped others would not see his guilt, but he could not hide from the Lord. God in His grace and mercy confronted David in order to bring him to repentance.

LESSON 30

David and Bathsheba

Piled Up

David was a great king, but he was not a perfect king. In this Bible narrative, we see how David got caught up in temptation and how the sins kept piling up and piling up. Here is a list of some of his sins mentioned in 2 Samuel 11.

a. He had impure thoughts.
b. He acted on his thoughts by asking questions.
c. He committed adultery.
d. He schemed to get Uriah drunk.
e. He plotted, placing Uriah in the front lines.
f. He murdered, using the Ammonites as a weapon.

F. 11:16–17
D. 11:13   E. 11:14–15
A. 11:2   B. 11:3   C. 11:4–5

Covered Up

David added to his sins by trying to cover them up and trying to make himself look innocent. His cover-up attempts are listed here. The sins were hidden, but they were not gone, and they were not out of God's sight. Consider these cover-ups mentioned in 2 Samuel 11 and 12.

a. He schemed to make it look like Bathsheba's baby was her husband's child.
b. He used the enemy to kill Uriah.
c. He minimized the death as a natural part of war.
d. He married Bathsheba after mourning.
e. He was self-righteous about Nathan's parable.
f. He ignored the Lord.

F. 12:9
D. 11:26–27   E. 12:5–6
A. 11:6–9   B. 11:23–24   C. 11:25

Review

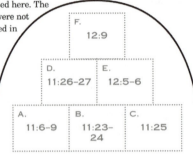

Covenant Connection

David was an imperfect king—a sinner like all other people. But he was also a repentant king who turned faithfully to the Lord for forgiveness. God promised that the Messiah-Savior would come from David's royal family. When the angel Gabriel announced to Mary that she would be the mother of the Messiah, he said of Jesus, "He will be great and will be called the Son of the Most High. And the Lord God will give to Him the throne of His father David, and He will reign over the house of Jacob forever, and of His kingdom there will be no end. . . . The child to be born will be called holy—the Son of God" (Luke 1:32–33, 35). Christ's kingdom was different from David's because Christ's kingdom is holy, spiritual, heavenly, and eternal.

66

Have Mercy on Me

Confession of Sins

Most merciful God, we confess that we are by nature sinful and unclean. We have sinned against You in thought, word, and deed, by what we have done and by what we have left undone. We have not loved You with our whole heart; we have not loved our neighbors as ourselves. We justly deserve Your present and eternal punishment. For the sake of Your Son, Jesus Christ, have mercy on us. Forgive us, renew us, and lead us, so that we may delight in Your will and walk in Your ways to the glory of Your holy name. Amen.

Absolution of Sins

In the mercy of almighty God, Jesus Christ was given to die for us, and for His sake God forgives us all our sins. To those who believe in Jesus Christ He gives the power to become the children of God and bestows on them the Holy Spirit. May the Lord, who has begun this good work in us, bring it to completion in the day of our Lord Jesus Christ. Amen.

Reproducible 30   Name _____

One in Christ™, © 2012 Concordia Publishing House. Confession and Absolution text: LSB © 2006 CPH. All rights reserved. Reproduced by permission.

132

'Fessed Up

David tried to cover up his sins, but they still remained. Because of His gracious love, God had a plan to bring David back to repentance. David needed to see his own sin and confess it—'fess up. God sent the prophet Nathan to confront David. Nathan told the king a parable (an earthly story with a heavenly meaning). Read aloud 2 Samuel 12:1–4.

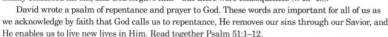

David's response was anger at the man who killed the sheep (v. 5–6). Nathan immediately turned this anger right back at David, saying, "You are the man!" (v. 7–9). David finally confessed his sin, and God forgave him—but there were consequences (v. 13–15).

David wrote a psalm of repentance and prayer to God. These words are important for all of us as we acknowledge by faith that God calls us to repentance, He removes our sins through our Savior, and He enables us to live new lives in Him. Read together Psalm 51:1–12.

In this psalm, what words does David use as synonyms for *sin*? **transgressions, iniquity, evil** What phrases does he use to speak of God's forgiveness? **mercy, blot out, wash me, cleanse, purge me, hide Your face** What words does David use to speak of our new, changed lives in the Lord? **create in me a clean heart, renew a right spirit within me, restore to me the joy of Your salvation, uphold me with a willing spirit**

Lifted Up

David tried to cover up his sins with lies and deceit, but it didn't work. The only thing that covers up, washes away, and removes our sins is the blood of Jesus shed on the cross for us. *God's Son* took our sins on Himself and gives us His righteousness. *God's Son* was lifted up on the cross so that we may be declared sinless in God's sight. (Print the words *God's Son* on the squares on the cross.) How is forgiveness through Christ Jesus described in these New Testament verses?

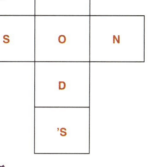

Cross: G / S O N / D / 'S

a. Romans 4:7 — **Our "sins are covered."**
b. John 1:29 — **Jesus "takes away the sin of the world!"**
c. 1 John 1:7 — **Jesus' blood "cleanses us from all sin."**

Remember

"If we say we have no sin, we deceive ourselves, and the truth is not in us. But if we confess our sins, God, who is faithful and just, will forgive our sins and cleanse us from all unrighteousness." (*LSB*, p. 151, adapted from 1 John 1:8–9)

67

INTO the Word

'Fessed Up

(Pardon the colloquial phrase, but it fits the organizational pattern of the lesson.) Follow the discussion of David's confession and repentance in the Student Book. As you look at his words in Psalm 51, also listen to them as they are chanted on Web Resource 30a. (*Note:* This psalm will be used regularly with the devotions in Lent. This method of demonstrating chanting allows the teacher to focus all the children's attention on the same location, particularly providing an opportunity to emphasize when the tones change.)

Lifted Up

David had wanted to cover up his sins with lies and excuses. He learned that sin can only be taken away by the forgiveness we have in the Lord. David did not know about the cross of Jesus, but he did trust the promise of salvation through the coming of the Messiah. We are at a point in history where **God's promise has been revealed in the death and resurrection of Jesus, the Messiah. By faith, we share the same forgiveness from the Lord, knowing that our sins are indeed covered—by the blood of Jesus.**

After working through this section of the Student Book, distribute copies of Reproducible 30. The first section of the activity is private and personal. Ask students to fold their hands on the circle on the page (some may even want to rest their heads on their folded hands, as a sign of humility). Ask students to take some time to think about things they have done wrong and quietly confess this in prayer; also have them think about their weaknesses and quietly pray that God will help them change; finally, have them think about the blessings of faith in Jesus and pray that the Lord will make them stronger in faith.

After allowing a few minutes for this, lead the students in saying together the words of confession printed on this page. Ask, **What are some of the descriptions of sin in this prayer?** ("Sinful," "unclean"; "in thought, word, and deed"; "what we have done and . . . left undone"; half-hearted toward God and unloving toward other people) **This prayer is called a "general confession" because it covers a multitude of sins without listing them specifically. What do we ask God to do for us?** ("Have mercy on us, forgive us, renew us, and lead us.") **What commitment do we make in response to the Lord?** ("That we may delight in Your will and walk in Your ways to the glory of Your holy name.") **Where have you heard these words before?** (In the liturgy in the *Lutheran Service Book,* pages 151, 167, and 213). **These words of confession are always followed by words of absolution, in which we hear about the forgiveness of sins. God does not leave us to wait and wonder about our sins; He is ready and eager to forgive. The Absolution is like an "aah!" moment, a sigh of relief.** Read the words of the Absolution together.

Note: The memory verse for this lesson was not taken from the usual English Standard Version of the Bible. It was taken from the liturgy in *LSB* (pp. 151, 167, and 213) as translated there so that students, having learned this wording, can readily join in saying these words during the Divine Service.

Lesson Support

Searching Further

Explore the idea that saying "I'm sorry" is not a magical phrase that means you get off "scot-free." God wants us to confess our sins; He does forgive our sins; but that does not mean there will be no consequences. Read about one of the consequences of David's sin in 2 Samuel 12:13–23. This needs to be considered a consequence—a result of David's actions—rather than as a punishment, involving retribution. Some of the consequences we suffer in this world are direct results of our actions. For example, if your dad says to not touch that live wire and you do it anyway, the consequence of your disobedience will be an electric shock. Some of the consequences we suffer, such as tornadoes and earthquakes, are the result of living in a world damaged by sin and are not the result of a specific sin. Suffering consequences of sin will end when we are received into God's kingdom of glory in heaven.

Bringing it home

Create discussion questions that can be part of a family letter. Connect this to your discussion of the Lord's Prayer and the Sixth Petition. Encourage families to discuss temptations that surround them—when they are with their peers, with their family members, using Internet and social networking sites, or watching television and movies. Ask parents to discuss with their children the temptations that both they and their children face each day. How does the study of God's Word help them in the face of temptation? Ask families to regularly pray the Lord's Prayer together.

Celebrating GROWTH

When he was confronted with his sin, King David repented and received the Lord's forgiveness through the words of the prophet Nathan. Invite your pastor to talk to your class about the liturgy of Confession and Absolution used during worship (for example, in Divine Service, Setting 1, *LSB,* p. 151). If possible, use Skype to make this easier to fit into your pastor's busy schedule. Ask him to explain any unfamiliar words or phrases used in the confession or in the words of absolution. Are Confession and Absolution part of every service? You might ask your students to read through the service ahead of time and write down questions to ask the pastor when he comes to speak with them. The pastor might also wish to talk about the different orders for corporate and individual confession and absolution (*LSB,* pp. 290 and 292 respectively). How are the two services different? How are they alike? Why might someone want to talk to the pastor in individual, or private, confession? What does it mean to confess our sins together in church and to hear the words of forgiveness?

Critical thinking

Some assume that Bathsheba was a temptress, but that is not necessarily so. It is likely that she was a very young woman, recently married since she had no children yet. For a young woman to refuse to obey an older, powerful king was a dangerous thing. Note also that the prophet Nathan uses the innocent figure of a lamb to represent Bathsheba in the story, suggesting that David has sinned against her as he has sinned against Uriah. (It's not our role to judge.)

Faith in Action

Talk to your students about temptations they may face at school and at home, when they are with friends or with family. Temptations do not lead only to comparatively large and visible sins like robbery or murder. Every day we may be tempted to fall into hidden, inward sins such as hate, coveting, or jealousy, sins that may go no farther than our own thoughts. Yet some of those very thoughts may lead to more outward sins that have an impact on the lives of others. The temptations of the devil, the world, and our sinful flesh may also lead us into sins of gossip, hateful speech, or a lack of respect toward parents, teachers, or others in authority. Both now and in the coming years, students may be tempted by alcohol, drugs, or sexual activity. The petitions of the Lord's Prayer in which we ask God to "deliver us from evil" and "lead us not into temptation" are important as we seek to live according to God's will in thoughts, words, and actions. Pray with and for your students that they may continue to grow strong in faith and in their knowledge of God's Word and will.

UNIT 3—PROPHETS AND KINGS

LESSON 31

Solomon Builds a Temple
1 Kings 5–8

Background

"What's in it for me?" That is a common question in our culture and a question that is found, unfortunately, all too often within our own selfish natures. The right question is "How can I give God the glory?" The Lord's Prayer states the matter correctly. To God alone belong "the kingdom and the power and the glory." God has given us the gift of His Son and forgiveness and life in His name. In thanks and praise, we give God our best, a life of worship that belongs to Him alone. We offer our prayers to Him and He has promised to hear us. When God told Solomon to ask for a gift, the young king asked for wisdom to rule his people wisely. Pleased with Solomon's request, the Lord granted Solomon not only great wisdom but wealth and honor as well, beyond the gifts of other earthly kings. Solomon gave wealth and honor back to the Lord, building a temple to His glory. When the temple was dedicated, Solomon asked the Lord to open His eyes toward the temple "night and day" and "listen to the plea of Your servant and of Your people Israel, when they pray toward this place. And listen in heaven, Your dwelling place, and when You hear, forgive" (1 Kings 8:29–30). What God has given to us we daily give back to Him in a life of worship, love, and service. We pray the prayer that our Lord taught us, knowing without doubt that God, to whom belong "the kingdom and the power and the glory," is turned toward us "night and day" and will hear and answer our prayers.

Central Truth

We worship God and give Him our best, not for our personal interest, but because God deserves praise and glory.

Objectives

- Admit that instead of a life of worship, we often focus on self-interest, what's in it for us, and on personal glory.
- Recognizing the great gifts of forgiveness, life, and salvation, we give God our best because He is the best and deserves the best.
- Honor God in all that we do, giving Him the glory.

Materials

- Hymnals and music CDs
- Web Resource 31a
- Web Resource 31b
- Reproducible 31

Bible Prep

Post in advance so students can bookmark references before class time.

- 1 Kings 5–8
- Genesis 22:1–2
- John 20:31
- Acts 2:38
- 1 Corinthians 11:23–26

Devotions

The students in Mrs. Tracy's sixth-grade class were divided into groups. Each group was planning a different service project in honor of the 40th anniversary of the church and school. Becca, Vicki, Jay, and Trevor were trying to decide on an idea for a project. They suggested ideas and argued with one another about them. "I know!" said Vicki. "The preschool always needs toys and books. We can collect donations of toys and money. We could fill up the preschool rooms with toys, and the little kids would love us!" "Well, I'm not sure we would get enough money to do *that*," said Trevor. "But we could collect food for the church pantry," he said. "I heard that poor people come to the church office to ask for help. We need to have food for them. We could fill the kitchen, and everyone would think we had the best project!" Becca said, "I think the church members would be more impressed if we earned a lot of money for the church painting project. We could have a bake sale and put up a sign to show how much money we raised so far!" "Wait a minute," said Jay. "This is supposed to be a *service project*, not a contest where we are trying to be better than the other groups. We're not trying to impress people. We're trying to find a way to *help* people." "You're right," answered Vicki. "We shouldn't be trying to get attention for ourselves. We're supposed to think of ways to help other people. *They* should get the attention." "There's something even more important than that," said Jay. "If there is *anyone* who should get attention in this, it's God. Serving other people is a way to serve Him. He should get the glory in whatever we decide to do." "You're right. It's not about us." said Becca. "Trevor, what are you doing?" "I'm making a sign for our project," said Trevor. "Whatever we decide, it will be called 'Give God Glory!'" Sing together "Glory Be to God the Father" (*LSB* 506; recorded as *Hymn of the Season* for grade 5, Christian Education month). Say or chant Psalm 23.

135

INTO the Word

Deserving the Best

Use the discussion questions in the Student Book and also Web Resource 31b to learn more about the building of the temple. This gives us just a glimpse of the temple's magnificence. In your discussion, ask questions such as: **Why do you think God wanted a man of peace to build the temple?** (Because God loves and gives peace)

Discuss 1 Kings 5:13, noting that 150,000 workers must have been paid or were volunteers, but 30,000 were forced labor (slaves). These are thought to be some of the Canaanites who were still living in the land of Israel.

Ask, **What's the significance of not having the sound of hammers and tools at the building site?** (A sign of respect; this was not an ordinary building) Ask, **Do you think it was odd that they gave names to the two front pillars of the temple?** (Maybe the people back then would think it's strange that today we give names to bridges. Customs vary.)

Lesson 31
Solomon Builds a Temple

Deserving the Best

These details of the temple were designed for the glory of God:

1. It was in King David's __heart__ to build a sanctuary for the Lord (1 Kings 8:17). But God chose Solomon, a man of peace, not of war, to do so (vv. 15–21). This temple measured 90 feet × 30 feet and it was 45 feet tall; it was not meant for crowds, but for ceremonial worship led by the priests.
2. The "holy hill" on which the temple was built was called "Mount Zion." In earlier times, it had been known as "Mount Moriah." What famous incident had occurred at that very location (Genesis 22:1–2)? __This is where Abraham had been sent to sacrifice Isaac. Now it would be a place of sacrifice for all the people.__
3. It took more than 180,000 men and __seven years__ to build the temple (1 Kings 6:38).
4. The exterior (outside) of the temple building was made of stone. What was unusual about these stones (1 Kings 6:7)? __The stones were prepared at the quarry so that no hammer was heard at the site of the temple building.__ The walls on the interior of the building were covered with sweet-smelling __cedar boards__ (v. 15), overlaid with __gold__ (vv. 15, 21).
5. The temple, as with the tabernacle, had two main rooms. First was the Holy Place, which was separated by a curtain from the smaller __Most Holy Place__, which was where the __ark of the covenant__ was kept (1 Kings 6:16, 19).
6. The porch entrance to the temple was known as a "portico," or __vestibule__. Standing at that entrance were two large pillars, which were named __Jachin and Boaz__ (1 Kings 7:21).
7. The Holy Place had ten __basins__ for water; these "seas" were used for ritualistic washings. Instead of two lampstands, there were __ten__. All of these, as well as the __altar__ of incense, were covered with gold carvings (1 Kings 7:38, 48–50).

Review

Covenant Connection

This temple, God's dwelling place among His people, was destroyed many years later at the time of the Babylonian captivity. It was rebuilt when the exiles returned, but not with the same grandeur. Jesus was in the temple renovated by Herod, speaking to the people in the courtyard area, when He said to them, "Destroy this temple, and in three days I will raise it up" (John 2:19). The people thought Jesus was talking about the building, but He was talking about His own body, for as true God Himself, Immanuel, "God with us," He was the dwelling place of God among us. Jesus was predicting His own death and His resurrection three days later—accomplished for our salvation! In Jesus, God revealed Himself among us.

INTO our lives

God's Presence among Us

Note that the "Covenant Connection" has a very direct connection to this section. Some people think that "religion" is very abstract, ethereal, and just spiritual. But God has chosen to touch our lives in very real and physical ways. The cloud and the ark of the covenant that filled the temple were very physical signs of God's presence with His people. Today we have the power of God that comes to us through His Holy Word, which is also in the Sacraments of Baptism and the Lord's Supper, which offer forgiveness and salvation to us from Christ Jesus. And above all, we have the real presence of God Himself in the person of Christ Jesus, who is Immanuel ("God with us"), and He is the Word made flesh. God is revealed in Jesus. Want to know what God is like? Look at Jesus!

Glorify the Lord

This lesson has quite a few Bible references to look up, so to move the lesson along, use Web Resource 31a, which projects these six verses on the screen. Let volunteers come up to read the verses, and then discuss the responses together. Continue with this discussion of the Conclusion of the Lord's Prayer, which glorifies God.

The ending words of the Lord's Prayer as we know it, "For Thine is the kingdom and the power and the glory forever and ever," are not found in the prayer as Jesus taught it to His disciples, nor as it is written in the Bible. The ending words of praise were added by Christians in the earliest centuries of the Church. The words may have been a response during a worship service. The leader may have said the prayer out loud, and the people may have responded with the ending words of praise. There are many words of praise in the Bible that are very similar to the closing words of the Lord's Prayer. Read **Jude 25**, today's verse to remember. **How are these verses like the ending of the prayer?** Discuss similarities and differences between the verse and the prayer.

We end the Lord's Prayer and our other prayers with the word *amen*. Read Martin Luther's explanation to the Conclusion of the Lord's Prayer in the Small Catechism in your Student Book Appendix. **What does *amen* mean?**

God's Presence among Us

God is always everywhere and at all times present with us. We say He is "omnipresent." For the faith and assurance of His people at the time of the temple's dedication, He chose to reveal His presence with them in what two ways (1 Kings 8:6, 10–11)? **In the ark of the covenant (the Mercy Seat of God) and in a cloud that filled the temple (representing the glory of the Lord filling the house)**

For the faith and assurance of His people today, God chooses to reveal Himself through the Means of Grace—the Word and Sacraments. Identify each Means of Grace spoken of in these Bible passages:

John 20:31 **The Word of God**

Acts 2:38 **Holy Baptism**

1 Corinthians 11:23–26 **The Lord's Supper**

Glorify the Lord

Solomon had the temple built to give glory to God. In the Lord's Prayer, we give glory to God, saying, "For Thine is the kingdom and the power and the glory forever and ever. Amen." God desires that we give Him glory in all that we do. Read the following passages, and in your own words, tell what each says about giving glory to God.

a. Luke 2:13–14 **The angels glorified God when Jesus was born.**

b. Matthew 5:16 **People will glorify God the Father when they see our good works.**

c. Revelation 4:11 **God is glorified because He created all things.**

d. Isaiah 42:8 **God does not share His glory with idols or false gods.**

e. 1 Chronicles 29:11 **Glory is due to God because everything in heaven and earth belongs to Him.**

f. Ephesians 3:20–21 **God is able to do more than we can ask or think.**

Remember

"To the only God, our Savior, through Jesus Christ our Lord, be glory, majesty, dominion, and authority, before all time and now and forever. Amen." (Jude 25)

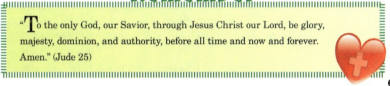

("Yes, it shall be so.") **Amen is the English form of a Hebrew word that means "agreement." It is a way to say "This is true" or "This will happen." What does it mean to say this word at the end of our prayers?** Discuss the use of *amen* as an ending for prayers. **When we say amen, we are saying that we agree with the prayer and we are sure that God will hear and answer us. We know that He loves us. The kingdom, power, and glory are His, and He sent His Son to be our Savior. Our sins are forgiven, and our lives and our worship, our very best, belong to God.**

What's Your Temple Like?

Say, **Solomon's temple had a very high price for all that gold and cedar and stone. What temple was purchased with the blood of Jesus?** (Our bodies were bought with the price of Jesus' blood. Our bodies are temples of the Holy Spirit, and we use our bodies to glorify God.)

Distribute Reproducible 31. To help your students start on their acrostics, consider creating one with your own name, indicating ways of discipleship in which we can glorify God. Here is an example of one for the name *Jack*.

Just praise God whenever you can.

Always do your best, giving God the glory for your success.

Cooperate with friends and family, showing the love of Jesus.

Know that God is always with you.

Option: Extend your discussion with the Lesson Support section. Ask, **How should we use our bodies to bring glory to God?** Read Romans 12:1–2. Say, **Solomon offered animals in sacrifice to dedicate the temple. Jesus was the perfect sacrifice for our sin, so animals do not need to be offered anymore. What sacrifices do we now offer to God?** (Our bodies are living sacrifices. We learn and follow the will of God in our lives.)

Close the lesson by reading together Solomon's words of benediction in 1 Kings 8:54–61. You may also want to sing "God of Grace and God of Glory" (*LSB* 850; recorded as *Hymn of the Month* for grade 6, November).

Searching Further

Solomon's temple was built in Jerusalem, on the site of a threshing floor purchased by King David (2 Samuel 24:18–25); today the temple mount in Jerusalem is the site of a Muslim mosque called "the Dome of the Rock." The skilled workers who built the temple, called "Sidonians" in 1 Kings 5:6, were Phoenician workers. The style and decoration of the temple may have been done in a style similar to Phoenician art and buildings common at that time. Artists today often illustrate the cherubim in the temple in the style of half-bull, half-human Phoenician carvings. The walls were decorated with carvings, and much of the wood was overlaid with gold. A great metal "sea" was made, measuring more than seventeen feet across and holding about ten thousand gallons. The sea rested on the backs of twelve bronze oxen and held water for temple use (1 Kings 7:23–26). Two tall, decorated bronze pillars at the entrance to the temple were named Jachin and Boaz (vv. 15–22). Chapters 2–4 of 2 Chronicles also describe the building of Solomon's temple. The building of the temple was started in the fourth year of Solomon's reign and was finished in the eleventh year of his reign (1 Kings 6:37–38), or about 959 BC. The destruction of the temple by the Babylonians in 586 BC is described in 2 Kings 25:8–17. The temple was burned and the gold and silver carried away. The bronze pillars and bronze sea were broken into pieces and taken to Babylon.

Bringing it home

As you have the opportunity, talk to parents about the importance of attending worship together as a family. As parents, they certainly want to help their children develop all kinds of good habits—brushing their teeth, cleaning their rooms, doing homework on time. Going to church is also a good habit—a habit with many blessings. Our Lord Jesus was in the habit of going to worship each week, as we read in Luke 4:16: "And [Jesus] came to Nazareth, where He had been brought up. And as was His custom, He went to the synagogue on the Sabbath day." It was Jesus' "custom" to go to the synagogue each Sabbath, and we hope that our students will develop a similar custom of going to church each week. You might want to send a letter home with the students, discussing the lesson about Solomon's temple, about our lives as "living sacrifices," and about the importance and joy of worship.

Faith in Action

Our bodies are temples of the Holy Spirit, bought with the blood of Jesus Christ. We are living sacrifices offered to God. As living sacrifices, we want to put our faith into action as we live in love and service toward others. Discuss with your students ways in which they can be "living sacrifices." They can pray for family members, for fellow students, and for church members. Students can gather prayer requests from others or make greeting cards for church members who are hospitalized or "shut in." Discuss with students ways in which they can "discern what is the will of God, what is good and acceptable and perfect" (Romans 12:2) at home and at school.

We want to give God our best, because God has given us the gift of His Son, Jesus, our Savior. In Romans 12:1–2, St. Paul tells us to be "living sacrifices" for God. In Romans 12:9–21, Paul tells us some of the things we can do to be living sacrifices, offering ourselves to God by the way we live each day. Read each verse and consider ways in which we can glorify God in our lives. Verse 9: Show real love to others. Hate evil and do what is good. Verse 11: Don't be lazy about serving the Lord. Verse 12: Rejoice in hope. Be patient in times of trouble. Pray. Verse 14: Bless people who persecute you. Verse 17: Don't pay back evil. Do what is good. Verse 20: Help others, even those who don't like you. Verse 21: Overcome evil by doing what is good.

Ideas for the Gifted

The temple was not just a single building, but involved a series of courtyards and buildings that surrounded the main temple building with its innermost sanctuary. Students might enjoy building a model of the temple, the Most Holy Place, or the ark of the covenant based on artists' illustrations they have found through research. Section 6.1.8, Ratios Used to Make Predictions, introduces the concept of scale models. You can find it in the sixth-grade Math volume of the Concordia Curriculum Guide series. Plan a math and architectural project to build a simplified scale model of the temple as a class. *The Lutheran Study Bible* includes two helpful illustrations with scales on pages 541 and 672. Figure out with students: **How big do you want the finished model to be? What proportion would you have to use in order to represent the real temple correctly in that size of a space?**

UNIT 3—PROPHETS AND KINGS   LESSON 32

Rehoboam and Jeroboam
1 Kings 9; 11–12

Background

In one sense, the biblical account you will explore with your students in this lesson focuses on political decisions and intrigue not all that different from what we see on today's political landscape. The events in 1 Kings 12, however, carry graver import because they concern the people through whom the Lord had promised to send the world's Savior. Now, yet again, the sins of God's people sent that promise careening off track. Or seemingly so. This was not politics as usual. This was the work of Satan, tempting the leaders of God's people to idol worship, pride, and arrogance in order to destroy the plan of salvation. But God's plans cannot be deterred. God continued in mercy and grace to call His people back to repentance. Time and again, He sent prophets with warnings against sin, welcoming a return to faith, and offering the assurance of the promised Messiah for all who believe.

As you teach this lesson, you will focus on sin's consequences. But you will focus even more sharply on the grace of Christ who bore those consequences for us and who makes it possible for us to "rend our hearts" in repentance and faith, living as His holy, baptized children.

Central Truth

Sin is unacceptable and has consequences; God allows these consequences, using them to move us toward repentance.

Objectives

- Acknowledge that we sin, and that God continues to call us to repentance and faith.
- Recognize that sin has consequences—ultimately ending in death; Jesus chose to suffer the punishment, taking the eternal consequences of our sin to the cross to save us.
- Praise God that salvation is a free gift to all who believe in Him.

Materials

- A piece of cloth to wear/rip
- Hymnals and music CDs
- Web Resource 32a
- Reproducible 32

Bible Prep

Post in advance so students can bookmark references before class time.
- 1 Kings 9; 11–12

Devotions

When you are dismayed, when fear and pain overwhelm you, how do you show it? (Let volunteers suggest responses.) **During Old Testament times, people often ripped their clothing.** (If possible, wrap an old sheet around yourself like a robe and, at this point, suddenly rip it in two for emphasis.) **Imagine seeing someone actually do this! Quite dramatic!**

Sometimes people tore their clothes when a loved one died. Sometimes they did so when they heard about a terrible disaster. Sometimes they did it in anger or grief. Sometimes they did it when they recognized some terrible sin they had committed, and sometimes they did it when they saw how terrible the sins of the whole nation were.

But sometimes they faked their grief and dismay. They tore their robes, but they felt no true contrition at all. They weren't sorry for their sins, and they had no plans to change. The prophet Joel wrote to God's people during a time like that. Here's what he said: "'Yet even now,' declares the LORD, 'return to Me with all your heart, with fasting, with weeping, and with mourning; and rend your hearts and not your garments'" (Joel 2:12–13a).

For a long time, God's people had been faking repentance. They told themselves they could fool God by pretending. But the Lord said, "Stop it! Return. Weep. Mourn. Mean it!" Sometimes we fake repentance too, saying "I'm sorry" but not really changing our ways. We might fool those around us, but we don't fool God. That's scary! But if you're frightened by it, God has good news for you today. Here's the rest of what Joel said: "Return to the LORD your God, for He is gracious and merciful, slow to anger, and abounding in steadfast love" (Joel 2:13b).

Close by singing thanksgiving to God for His many blessings to us, physical and spiritual, in the hymn "Sing to the Lord of Harvest" (*LSB* 893; recorded as *Hymn of the Season* for grade 6, Thanksgiving). Also praise the Lord by saying (or chanting) together Psalm 23.

INTO the lesson

Multiplied Sins

It is important to always look at the whole picture of King Solomon. He started off well; God was pleased with him. Solomon even wrote some of the books of the Bible, such as some of the wisdom we find in the Book of Proverbs. But not even kings—not even very wise kings—get away with sin. There are always consequences. Solomon was half-hearted in following the Lord. That is not enough. God calls on us to love Him with our whole heart! Read aloud these verses from the psalms: Psalm 9:1; 86:12; 111:1; and 119:2.

Divided Kingdom

The Student Book gives a "big picture" look at the divided kingdom. More of the details will be explored in lessons to come. Emphasize God's continual mercy, reaching out to the people through the messages of the prophets. Have students turn to the table of contents of the Bible and read through the names of the books from Isaiah to Malachi. Except for the Book of Lamentations, these are all names of prophets sent by God during the period of the divided kingdom. God was persistent; some people believed, but more did not; and there were consequences. The Lord used these consequences to bring His people back to faith and to await the coming of the Messiah. This discussion continues in the "Covenant Connection."

Ripped Apart

Today's lesson and this map are crucial to understanding the remaining portions of Old Testament history, particularly in regard to the kings and prophets. Study this map. Determine what happened at the various locations. And return to this page often. Use the map on Web Resource 32a to help students find locations on their individual maps and to focus attention on specific locations.

Rehoboam's Foolishness

Rehoboam was a weak and foolish king, but it should be noted that we know of at least two times that he repented and listened to the word of the Lord. In 1 Kings 12:21–24, Rehoboam had gathered an army to fight Jeroboam. God sent the prophet Shemaiah to tell them not to fight against their relatives—the people of Israel. This time, they listened to the word of the Lord and did not fight. Life was a rocky road with Rehoboam. In 2 Chronicles 12:1, we learn that as soon as he had established his rule, Rehoboam "abandoned the law of the Lord." So God allowed an enemy, Shishak from Egypt, to attack them. Again, God sent the prophet Shemaiah to say, "Thus says the Lord, 'You abandoned Me, so I have abandoned you to the hand of Shishak'" (v. 5). The princes and the king humbled themselves and said, "The Lord is righteous" (v. 6). When God saw their repentance, He delivered them. But there were consequences—the king of Egypt looted many of the golden treasures from the temple. However, the end result for Rehoboam and the kingdom of Judah was that "the wrath of the Lord turned from him, so as not to make a complete destruction. Moreover, conditions were good in Judah. So King Rehoboam grew strong in Jerusalem and reigned" (vv. 12–13).

Jeroboam's Foolishness

Ask, **What was Jeroboam's motivation for inventing new gods, new places to worship, and phony festivals?** (He wanted to keep the people close so they would remain loyal to him; he wanted to counteract any desire to go to Judah to worship and be influenced there.) **Why would the people accept the king's phony gods, phony priests, phony sacrifices, and phony feasts?** (Possibilities: Some may have been afraid to disobey the demands of the king. Some may have liked it that their worship sites would be closer to home, even though they were not close at all to the truth. There were familiar ties with the past—the golden calves, as in Egypt, and familiar feast days celebrated at the same time as before—sort of like having Christmas without Christ. This plan made them more like the neighboring nations they often sought to imitate. It was an easier religion without all God's laws. Many of the new practices were immoral, which would also appeal to those forsaking the Lord.)

Lesson 32

Rehoboam and Jeroboam

Multiplied Sins

We begin this story with a sad ending. Unfortunately, even though Solomon dedicated the temple, he did not dedicate himself to the Lord. He did not show a lifetime commitment. (See 1 Kings 11:1–8.) His sin was egregious (flagrant, outrageous). He turned away from God and worshiped idols. He ignored the Word of God (1 Kings 9:1–7). God gave King Solomon more wisdom than anyone else. Yet, all his wisdom didn't stop him from committing terrible acts of disobedience.

The Lord told Solomon that as a consequence of his sin, his kingdom would be ripped apart. Read 1 Kings 11:9–13. As you do, find the word *tear* three times. What would be torn? Answer on the lines below.

1. God would tear the kingdom away from _____Solomon_____.
2. God would tear it away during the reign of _____Solomon's son_____.
3. God would not tear away _____the whole kingdom_____.

Divided Kingdom

After Solomon died, the kingdom that David had united as one was torn in half. This was a pivotal point in the history of the nation. Throughout the remainder of the Old Testament, there were two separate kingdoms ruled by two different kings. King Rehoboam, Solomon's son and David's grandson, ruled over one tribe in the south. It was later called "Judah," or "the Southern Kingdom." King Jeroboam ruled the territory in the north. It was sometimes known as "Israel," or "the Northern Kingdom." Though the people in both kingdoms were all descendants of Abraham, they warred with each other. Worst of all, they no longer worshiped together, and many of them worshiped false gods. The Northern Kingdom of Israel never had a king that was faithful to the Lord; the Southern Kingdom of Judah had some kings who loved the Lord, but many did not and led the people astray. God was very patient with the people, continually sending prophets to warn them about their sins and bring them to repentance. Eventually, however, God allowed the Assyrians to take the Northern Kingdom captive, never to return. Some time after that, God allowed the Babylonians to take the Southern Kingdom captive. After seventy years, God allowed a faithful *remnant* (a fragment, or small part) to return to Judah. Descendants of this remnant were Joseph, Mary, and baby Jesus.

Review

Covenant Connection

Why didn't God simply reject the whole nation? Why did He continue to allow the royal family to reign over one tribe—Judah? The answer is God's faithfulness. He had promised that the Savior-Messiah would come from Abraham's family, the tribe of Judah, and David's royal line. God maintained the existence of the land of Judah in order to carry out His promises and because of His love for all people. As God promised, through Christ Jesus, all the people of the world have been blessed. The salvation He obtained is anyone's and everyone's by faith in His redeeming death and resurrection.

70

140

Ripped Apart

Rehoboam's Foolishness

King Solomon harshly multiplied the taxes of the people to support his luxurious lifestyle. When Solomon died, the people asked Rehoboam to rule with kindness. Rehoboam said he needed to think about it. What was the advice of his older counselors (1 Kings 12:6–7)? **If the king served with goodness, the people would always be loyal to him.** What advice did Rehoboam get from his young, rich friends (vv. 9–11)? **He should be even harsher and meaner than his father.** Rehoboam took the wrong advice, multiplying even higher taxes. All this multiplication resulted in division. The nation was torn apart, split in two.

Jeroboam's Foolishness

Even before Solomon died, Jeroboam knew that he would be king of part of the kingdom. (Read 1 Kings 11:29–38.) But Jeroboam was also foolish. He did not listen to the advice of the Lord. He was afraid that if his people went to worship at the temple in Jerusalem, they would support the king of the Southern Kingdom. Jeroboam's solution was to create phony gods, phony priests, phony sacrifices, and phony feasts. Read 1 Kings 12, verses 25–33. Jeroboam's great sin was in leading so many people to idolatry.

Both kings were foolish, and this led to the foolishness of war (1 Kings 14:30). The nation that should have been united as family (as the descendants of Abraham) and united in faith (as the children of God) was ripped apart, turning its people against each other and destroying itself.

This story that started sadly is ending sadly, except for the continuing presence of God as He calls His people back to repentance and faith.

Remember

"Return to the LORD your God, for He is gracious and merciful, slow to anger, and abounding in steadfast love." (Joel 2:13)

and sometimes not. While we're sorry for some of our sins, we enjoy other sins and aren't always willing to walk away from them. This is evidence of original sin at work in us.

4. *Sins rips up relationships.* This is true, even when we don't see evidence of it—and usually, there's plenty of evidence!

5. *Some sins have no consequences.* This is false, even though Satan and the world system around us want us to believe we can do what we want, and that we're safe as long as we don't get caught.

6. *There's no way to stop the consequences of sin in my life.* This could be true or false, depending on how students read it. There is no way we ourselves can stop sin and its consequences in our own lives or in the lives of others, even when we want to very, very much! But Jesus can! **Jesus has taken our guilt onto Himself. He died for us so we will escape the consequence of eternal death. He also helps us confess and make amends to those whom we have hurt by our sins.**

Encourage the group to talk about what it's like to know the unimaginable love of Jesus who endured our eternal consequences in our place. Discussion around this question could be especially meaningful if students share authentically. To encourage that kind of transparency, give everyone time to think. The silence may be a bit uncomfortable at first, but if one or two class leaders rise to the occasion and speak up, the results could prove extremely helpful to everyone. Share your own thoughts as that seems appropriate, but work hardest at drawing out the students.

INTO our lives

Consequences (in Your Life)

The Student Book is filled with biblical history, so continue now with today's life applications as they are presented on Reproducible 32. Begin by noting the many consequences of sin that were taking place in the Bible story. Say, **Let's consider now our own sins and their consequences.** Ask students to complete the brief true/false exercise on their own. Then talk about it.

1. *Sin angers God.* This is true. Lead students to conclude that we often grossly underestimate God's anger, which is right and just because of His holiness. His anger also stems from the fact that He loves us so much, and He hates what He sees our sins doing to us and to the people around us.

2. *Sin rips at God's heart.* This is true, again because of His love for us and His anguish in seeing us walk away from the good He wants us to enjoy. The Bible talks about this in terms of "grieving" God (as in Ephesians 4:30).

3. *Sin rips at my heart.* Sometimes this is true

Remember

You may want to sing this Bible verse using the melody found on *LSB* 157 or 173. *Option:* Some students may like to try writing their own melody for this verse. One way to do this that also ensures success is to use the pentatonic scale—the five black keys in an octave on the piano. All notes in the pentatonic scale blend well together, so there is no wrong way to do it. (Students might note a somewhat Asian sound to this.)

Critical thinking

As we teach, especially as we teach the Scriptures, no lesson stands alone—at least, it shouldn't. Each lesson we teach fits into a bigger picture. Keep that bigger picture in mind, and help your students see it as you teach the faith. Connect the Bible stories you study to the doctrines they illustrate. Today's account, for example, points to the First Commandment and the consequences that accrue when we break it. We, too, rely on false gods, just as Solomon, Jeroboam, and their people did. They may look different (comparing their golden idols with our own false gods of placing our own will, possessions, and money first in our lives). Satan has tweaked his temptations to capture our hearts today. Tell students that it's easier to understand Israel's idol worship when we remember what the calf idols meant. They were gods of prosperity, sex, and power. They promised worshipers "the good life." With that as background, ask students to work together to identify Satan's use of the same temptations today. Suggest that students think about the entertainment industry, sports, or shopping/commerce. In and of themselves, these things are neutral and can be good gifts from God. But they become problems when they begin to displace the time, commitment, trust, and value that rightly belong only to our Lord. Keep both Law and Gospel in mind. We, too, need the Savior whom God promised. Always point your students to the cross of Christ as the consistent touch point in their relationship with the Lord.

Curriculum Connection

Rehoboam made his big mistake under the influence of his younger advisors, who were his friends and peers. This lesson might be a good time to introduce the ideas in section 6.3.1.5, Behaving in a Safe and Healthy Manner When Confronted with Negative Peer Pressure. You can find it in the sixth-grade Physical Education volume of the Concordia Curriculum Guide series.

HANDS TO SERVE

Good government matters! Pray for the leaders in your town, state, and nation because God commands it. Refer students to 1 Timothy 2:1–4, where Paul connects good government and civil peace with opportunities for evangelism. Wicked government, like the government of King Jeroboam, leads to false belief and many other evils. Work with your students to find a way to contribute to good government in your local municipality. This could be as simple as picking up trash in a local park. On the other hand, you might write letters or e-mails to public servants, encouraging them in their work and telling them of your prayers for them. You might consider a field trip to the local office of your congressional representative or inviting the mayor to visit your class. (They might be more willing to communicate if you suggest using e-mail or Skype, since these methods would take less time from their busy schedules.) Ask that person to share the top three concerns faced by local or state government right now and why. Have students write a three- or four-paragraph response after the visit, including a prayer for God's blessings on the government and its leaders.

Technology

As you look at the map on Web Resource 32a, ask, **Why do you think King Jeroboam chose Dan and Bethel as locations for the two golden calves he set up?** (He put them in locations that would be a convenient distance for his people to travel—more convenient than Jerusalem, the location of the true temple, where the true priests offered true sacrifices and worshiped the true God.) Consider: **Do we ever make choices for worship based on convenience?**

Reaching Every Child

Research has shown the importance "background knowledge" plays as students learn. Old Testament accounts, in particular, can present students with difficulty in this regard. If your class includes students who are new to Lutheran schools, you may need to find ways to fill in the gaps for these new students before they will be able to catch up to their more informed classmates. One helpful strategy would include involving parents and perhaps your pastor in identifying suitable resources for daily devotional use at home. Appropriate materials will vary with both the students' needs and family characteristics. Suggest using the book *One Hundred Bible Stories*, available from Concordia Publishing House. This gives a good overview of important Bible narratives from the Old and New Testaments, using an abridged text taken from the Scriptures themselves.

UNIT 3—PROPHETS AND KINGS

LESSON 33

The Prophet Elijah
1 KINGS 16—19

Background

The widow's oil and flour did multiply daily to provide bread for her, her son, and Elijah. Elijah did raise the widow's little boy from death. But God was at work in even more remarkable and gracious ways here. King Ahab, Elijah's nemesis, reigned over the Northern Kingdom. King Jeroboam had claimed this territory for idolatry in a shameless political plot to keep his people out of Jerusalem and away from the temple—despite the fact that Yahweh had explicitly commanded every male Israelite to worship there three times each year (Deuteronomy 16:16). Jeroboam and the kings who followed him feared that if their people spent so much time in Jerusalem, they might eventually plot reunification and, after all, a single kingdom would need only one king—a son of David! As a consequence of gross idolatry, the people of the Northern Kingdom would one day go into exile, never to return.

From His omniscient perspective, the Lord knew all this. And yet, in love, He reached out to one of the Northern Kingdom's most wicked kings—Ahab. Multiple chapters of 1 Kings detail all God did to bring Ahab to repentance. Neither Ahab nor any of his people would be ancestors of the Messiah; the Savior would come from the tribe of Judah. But the covenant God had made with Abraham was so strong, He refused to let *any* of Abraham's wayward children go without a fight—a battle to save them. So great is His grace, in fact, that it reached *beyond* the covenant people—even to the Gentile widow and her son in Sidon. That great grace still reaches out to you and me today. It reaches out to your students too. Pray that they will be drawn ever closer to the Lord of love.

Central Truth

The stories continue, repeating again and again examples of God's deliverance for His people and His call to repentance and faith in the promised Messiah-Savior.

Objectives

- Recognize that humankind's sin with its consequences does not change God's love and faithfulness.
- Affirm that God intends His warnings through the Law and prophets to lead us to repent and to see our need for the Savior.
- Praise God that His promised blessings in the Messiah-Savior, fulfilled in Jesus, have remained constant throughout all history and will remain so into eternity.

Materials

- Hymnals and music CDs
- Web Resource 33a
- Reproducible 33

Bible Prep

Post in advance so students can bookmark references before class time.
- 1 Kings 16–19
- Matthew 17:1–6

Devotions

Our Bible verse to remember today is from Psalm 145: "The eyes of all look to You, and You give them their food in due season. You open Your hand; You satisfy the desire of every living thing." This is a very appropriate Scripture passage to learn at this time of the year, when we give special thanks for all our blessings. At Thanksgiving, we think a lot about the food we appreciate. Today's Bible story tells of several amazing ways God provided food for the prophet Elijah. We will see that God blessed Elijah in some amazing ways, but that He also blessed him in some simple ways. God also blesses us in amazing ways and simple ways—but too often, we don't notice either one. When we are blessed amazingly, we often say we were "really lucky" rather than give God the credit. When we are blessed in simple ways, we may expect and even *ignore* the simple things that are blessings.

The most amazing way God blesses us is through Jesus. It is amazing that God is so forgiving of our sins and so patient with our weaknesses. It is even more amazing that He seeks us out, coming to us with His Word and Sacraments, and gives us the gifts of salvation and eternal life for free!

Let's pray that God will open our eyes to see His blessings surrounding us, leading us to respond with gratitude, giving Him all glory. If we look at the blessings around us with open eyes, we will see the Lord working in all things in our lives.

Sing two songs of gratitude and appreciation. First, sing "Sing to the Lord of Harvest" (*LSB* 893; recorded as *Hymn of the Season for grade 6, Thanksgiving*) to praise God for the many blessings, such as food and care and protection, that surround us. Second, sing "Open Our Eyes" (*AGPS* 195; recorded on *JPS*) to especially express thanks for all that we receive through Jesus' death and resurrection.

INTO the lesson

While King Ahab was the most wicked king of Israel, we could also say that Jezebel was the most wicked queen. It was her influence that led Ahab to bring in Baal and to commit atrocities, including the sacrifice of children and temple prostitution—a religion exactly opposite of the grace and mercy of God. Baal's "wife" was worshiped in areas where Asherah poles were built—poles with wooden carvings of the goddess. (Look at the "Covenant Connection," which gives evidence of Elijah being the opposite of Ahab.)

This lesson will focus on several *quandries*. Explore the meaning of this word in a dictionary and thesaurus. A quandry is a perplexing problem. It involves a dilemma, difficulty, and uncertainty. It brings up the question, "What should I do?" The illustrations show several times that Elijah was in a quandary, and each time his help came from the Lord. The lesson continues by exploring these three quandaries and also explores some of the quandaries in our own lives that are best met with the same conclusion: "What should I do? Go to the Lord in prayer; He hears and helps in the best way at the right time!"

Lesson 33
The Prophet Elijah

Introduction

The Northern Kingdom (Israel) always had wicked kings, but the very worst was King Ahab. This is not just an opinion. What does the Bible tell about him (1 Kings 16:30–33)? **He brought in worship of the idol Baal; he angered and provoked God.**

God countered this by sending in one of His strongest prophets—Elijah. This was followed by a series of *quandaries* (difficult situations) that God solved miraculously!

Food Quandary

The Lord gave the prophet Elijah courage to stand before wicked King Ahab and confront him with the message that there would be famine and no rain in the land for years. This was also an affront to Ahab's god Baal, who was supposed to be the god of rain and growing crops. During the next three years, God provided for Elijah.

1. How did God miraculously provide food for him? (See 1 Kings 17:1–7.) **Ravens brought him bread and meat twice a day.**

2. When that source ended, how did God miraculously provide food (1 Kings 17:8–16)? **While he lived in the widow's home, she baked bread for him, for her son, and for herself using flour and oil that never ran out.**

Covenant Connection

We saw biblical evidence that Ahab was one of the worst kings. Look now for biblical evidence that Elijah was one of the strongest prophets. See Matthew 17:1–6. When Jesus was transfigured in all His glory, the three disciples heard the voice of God the Father, and they saw Jesus talking to two great prophets—Moses and Elijah. This is a strong connection between the Old and New Testaments. It emphasizes that Jesus is true God who came to fulfill the Father's promises about the Savior-Messiah.

INTO the Word

Food Quandary

God's message through the prophet Elijah started the drought and famine, and three years later, God's message through the prophet Elijah ended the drought and famine. This alone should have shown King Ahab and all of Israel who the true God is. The god Baal was powerless, even though he supposedly ruled over the weather and agriculture. A god who can do nothing is no kind of god. On the other hand, we see Jesus centuries later in a boat, with the disciples marveling in wonder, saying, "Even the winds and the waves obey Him."

God miraculously provided food for Elijah. It is contrary to the nature of ravens to share food and to do so regularly. Ravens are scavengers that are more likely to take food away than bring it. Look at the map in Lesson 32 (or the Student Book Appendix or Web Resource 32a). Find Shechem, where the king lived; find the ravine of Cherith, across the Jordan River, where ravens fed Elijah (point out that there are several different spellings for some of these ancient locations); and then find Zarephath, which is significant because the widow who helped Elijah was a Gentile. God had to send His prophet out of the land of Israel to find help; and, even more significant, this shows that God's love extends to all people, even Gentiles like you and me. God never forgot this widow. In fact, nine centuries later, Jesus mentioned her as an example of God reaching out in love to people who had not descended from Abraham (Luke 4:25–26). What does that tell you about His purposes from all eternity? Note that in the Student Book this section extends to the top of the next page.

Fire Quandary

The question was "Who is the true God?" Elijah challenged the people, saying, "'How long will you go limping between two different opinions? If the LORD is God, follow Him; but if Baal, then follow him.' And the people did not answer him a word" (1 Kings 18:21). The challenge Elijah set up was "the God who answers by fire, He is God" (v. 24). When God answered the question, or quandary, by miraculously sending fire, the people finally spoke, saying, "The LORD, He is God; the LORD, He is God" (v. 39).

3. What extra blessing did God graciously give the widow and her son (1 Kings 17:17–23)? When the son died, Elijah prayed, and God brought him back to life.
4. What extra blessing did God graciously give the widow's heart (1 Kings 17:24)? She came to faith in the true God.

Fire Quandary

After three years, God decided it was time to send rain again. But first, God sent Elijah to confront Ahab once more. The king called Elijah a troublemaker. How did Elijah courageously answer him (1 Kings 18:18)? Elijah said something like "I'm not the troublemaker. You are, because you abandoned God's Law and worshiped idols!"

Then Elijah challenged the king to a contest.

1. What did the prophets of Baal do (1 Kings 18:22–29)? They set up an altar and prayed to Baal for hours, but "no one answered; no one paid attention."
2. What did the prophet Elijah do (1 Kings 18:30–37)? He soaked his altar and filled a trench around it with water and said a short prayer.
3. What did God do (1 Kings 18:38–39)? God immediately answered Elijah's prayer, sending fire to consume the sacrifice, stones, and water, showing the people He is true God.
4. What extra blessing did God graciously give the people (1 Kings 18:42–45)? From a tiny cloud in the distance came a heavy rainstorm.
5. What extra blessing did God graciously give Elijah (1 Kings 18:46)? God gave Elijah the power to run down the mountain faster than Ahab in his chariot with horses.

Faithfulness Quandary

When Queen Jezebel heard about all of this and that the prophets of Baal had been killed, she threatened to have Elijah killed too. To escape Jezebel, Elijah ran away into the wilderness and settled in a cave. He was depressed. He felt he was a failure, and he was ready to give up.

God was still with him. What did God ask him (1 Kings 19:9)? "What are you doing here?" Elijah felt that in all the land, he was the only one left who was faithful to the Lord. God passed by Elijah, but God was not in the wind or the earthquake or the fire. God came to Elijah in a low whisper (1 Kings 19:11–12). In that still, small voice, the Lord told Elijah to go and get back to work. What surprising information did God give Elijah to encourage him (1 Kings 19:18)? There were still seven thousand people faithful to the Lord in Israel.

Remember

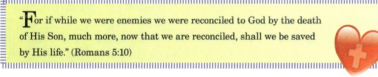

"For if while we were enemies we were reconciled to God by the death of His Son, much more, now that we are reconciled, shall we be saved by His life." (Romans 5:10)

INTO our lives

Today's Quandaries

Jesus has solved our biggest quandary (dealing with sin, death, and the devil) through His death on the cross. He empowers us now through the Holy Spirit to live as people of God in all that we do. Use Reproducible 33 to discuss God's personal love and individual care for each of us in Christ. It highlights an encouraging, challenging worldview. We can legitimately see our life as an adventure of faith and ourselves as playing a significant part in what our Savior wants to do in the lives of people around us. The discussion could dovetail tightly with the doctrine of vocation. (Explain that *vocation* is your work, or your purpose. For comparative purposes, to help student understanding of the term, you could note that sometimes, "people take a vacation from their vocation.") See "Searching Further" on the Lesson Support page for more detail.

Faithfulness Quandary

Emphasize that when Elijah gave up, God did not give up on Elijah. The Lord came after him, questioning him, and also encouraging him. The Lord had worked in surprising and mighty ways in Elijah's life; but now, in the low whisper, God was also saying that He could work in simple ways. God encouraged Elijah with the information that there were still seven thousand faithful believers in the land. As wicked as Israel was, the faith of the believers could not be extinguished. God's Word endures.

An example of one of these hidden believers is mentioned in 1 Kings 18. This man, Obadiah, was not the prophet of Judah who later wrote a book of the Bible. This Obadiah lived in Israel and was actually very close to the king, serving as Ahab's chief servant—the head of the king's household. Obadiah worked for the king but was not influenced by his evil ways. In fact, when the king tried to put an end to the word of the true God in the land by killing God's priests and prophets, Obadiah rescued one hundred prophets, hiding them in caves and feeding them. *Option:* Use Web Resource 33a to review Elijah's life story. Ask students to tell what is happening in each picture. Save the last picture to show at the end of Lesson 34 or the beginning of Lesson 35.

Hands to Serve

Consider asking your class to organize a canned food drive at your school. Or set up a time when they and their families can serve at a local soup kitchen. Feeding the hungry in some way ties in naturally with this lesson. Consider working with your class to bake homemade bread and send it with the pastor when he makes shut-in calls. Include notes and cards from the students with words of encouragement and appropriate Scripture verses.

Searching Further

If you haven't already talked with your class about the doctrine of vocation, this would be an excellent time to do so. Ahab sinned against God in his vocation as king by continuing the idolatrous practices of his ancestors and encouraging his people in them. The widow served God in her vocations of mother by caring for her son and of neighbor by caring for Elijah. Elijah served God in his prophetic vocation by speaking God's Word to the widow and her son, raising the son from the dead, and calling Ahab to repentance.

Some of the things we do in our various vocations seem mundane: for instance, the widow gathered sticks. Some of the work God gives us in our vocations seems spectacular: Elijah raised a dead person! But no matter how we see our vocation, our Lord Jesus considers it service to Him. It's as though we do it for Him. We honor Him in it and serve our neighbors (Matthew 25:31–46).

The Table of Duties in Luther's Small Catechism could make a good starting point as students begin to name their vocations and think about ways God wants to use them to make a difference in their world.

Bringing it home

Have students print out a verse of thanks from a psalm. Ask that they take it home and use it with their families as a mealtime blessing for the next several weeks.

Check it Out

There is an interesting side event that is tucked away in the section of Scripture studied in this lesson. Look at 1 Kings 16:34. This single verse speaks of the rebuilding of Jericho. It mentions that the man who rebuilt the city did so at the cost of the lives of two of his sons. One died at the beginning, when the foundations were laid, and the other died at the end, when the gates were set in place. So what is significant about this? This fulfilled the word of the Lord spoken through Joshua centuries earlier. Read Joshua 6:26. Two small verses show the omniscience and constancy of the Lord.

UNIT 3—PROPHETS AND KINGS

LESSON 34

Naboth's Vineyard
1 Kings 21

Background

From the beginning, Ahab lived as if God didn't matter and as if what Ahab wanted mattered most. Jezebel, Ahab's wicked queen, goaded him on in his wickedness, acting even more wickedly than her husband. The narrative you and your students will address today illustrates all that. It also serves as a kind of case study into which we can read the consequences of our own greed and sinful self-focus (if we're honest with ourselves and with our Lord, that is).

As king, Ahab had enough and more than enough to support his body and life. Still, from the moment he began to covet Naboth's vineyard, he couldn't get it out of his mind. He wanted it, and nothing else would satisfy him. Such is the power of sinful thoughts. Idolatry. Coveting. Bearing false witness. Murder. Theft. The list of Ahab's sins goes on and on. Yet, in an astonishing turn of events, 1 Kings 21 ends with Ahab hearing God's Law and showing what appears to be sincere sorrow. However, this sorrow (perhaps sorrow over being punished) does not appear to have led to repentance because Ahab continued in his unfaithful and unbelieving ways. How different was the response of King David when the prophet accused him of covetousness and murder (the same sins as Ahab)! David responded with repentance and a plea for God's mercy and forgiveness, and then David went on to ask God to create a new spirit in him that would live for the Lord.

Central Truth

God is unwavering in His desire to call all people to repentance and faith—speaking through the prophets, through Scripture, and especially through the Word made flesh, Christ Jesus.

Objectives

- Identify King Ahab's poor choice of friends, his selfishness, and his pouty tantrum; identify that these traits also appear in our own lives.
- Acknowledge the unrelenting patience of God through the ages, His continuing efforts to bring wayward sinners to repentance.
- Praise God that He remains faithful, constant, and consistent in His Word and promises.

Materials

- Hymnals and music CDs
- Web Resource 34a
- Reproducible 34

Bible Prep

Post in advance so students can bookmark references before class time.
- 1 Kings 21
- Matthew 15:18–19
- 2 Kings 2:1–15

Devotions

Here's a thought experiment. Imagine that tomorrow morning, when you wake up, you focus your very hardest on not sinning, on not disobeying God or hurting other people in any way. Imagine trying very, very hard to do every good thing God sets in front of you. What would happen?

I know you know the "right" answer is "I wouldn't get very far." But think harder. What would happen if you tried really, really hard? Pause.

When God gave His people the Law on Mount Sinai, they responded: "All that the Lord has spoken we will do" (Exodus 19:8). They really meant it! They really thought they could do it! But just like us, they didn't get very far. Not forty days later, for example, they all were falling down to worship a golden calf!

They thought they had an excuse. Moses had left them, and they didn't know where he was. How could God expect them to obey if their leader was dead? When Moses returned, they grumbled about being hungry and thirsty. How could God expect them to obey while they were wandering around in the desert? So God brought them into the Promised Land and gave them ready-made homes, towns, vineyards, orchards, and much more. But they didn't have a king. So how could God expect them to obey? "If we only had a king like the peoples around us," they said in essence, "we'd be good!" (1 Samuel 8:4–9).

So God gave them a king. But as we have seen, they did not obey *then* either. Not even their kings obeyed! Instead of making excuses, they needed to make confession, repent, and change their ways. They didn't need a king; they needed a Savior. And so do we. Jesus is that Savior, and I'm so glad! I pray you are too.

Read together David's words of confession and repentance in Psalm 51:1–12. Sing "God of Grace and God of Glory" (*LSB* 850; recorded as *Hymn of the Month* for grade 6, November).

INTO the lesson

Lots of Stuff

Give students time to create a list of their "Top Ten All-Time Greatest Possessions" in their Student books. The list need not be in rank order, but it should include the possessions they treasure most. If someone asks permission to name people, give it, but tell them they should name only physical things, not spiritual, emotional, or social things.

When everyone's list is finished, direct students to cross one thing off their list. Some students may press you for more details, asking why, but resist responding. Just repeat the direction you gave: "Cross one thing off your list."

Then ask them to cross off two more items. Again, resist responding to questions.

Continue in this way, asking that students cross off one or two items at a time until they have only one item left. At this point, many of them will likely feel quite uncomfortable. Ask about this. How did it feel to cross the first item off? Later items? How did they decide what to cross off?

Point out that all you asked them to do was to make a line through words on a paper. So what made this exercise so frustrating or threatening or anger producing? The problem occurs when these things become too important in our lives, replacing things like compassion for others and obedience to parents and other authorities, and even hindering our love and respect of God, His ways, and His will.

Covetous Thoughts

Help the group understand that we sometimes get very, very attached to our possessions. The things and people God places in our lives bring us joy. There's nothing wrong with that. God intends that we receive His good gifts thankfully and take pleasure in them. But it's so easy to forget the Giver and to look at these gifts as what we deserve or expect or have a right to own. It's easy to forget that all our stuff is really on loan from our Lord. Additionally, Satan often tempts us to think that having more stuff, especially other people's stuff, would make us happier or more secure. This is the sin of coveting, and it can lead to all kinds of other sins, such as lying, theft, and even murder. Discuss why God places such an emphasis on not having sinful thoughts. (Our thoughts lead to actions, so they are often the origin of other sins. While we can hide our sinful thoughts from other people, we can never hide them from the Lord or from our own conscience, which condemns us when we hear God's Law. Coveting also affects attitudes and relationships. Discuss instances that show this.)

INTO the Word

Whose Stuff Is It?

Before working on this section of the Student Book, show Web Resource 34a after introducing it with these thoughts. Point out, **One of the big problems of discontentment is that people always want more; they are never satisfied, and they are never happy. This is what happened in the Bible narrative we will explore. King Ahab had palaces and wealth, but he wanted more. And he made a fuss until he got what he wanted.** Look at slides of some of the extravagant things that people sometimes covet, like a penthouse in Manhattan; a yacht on the French Riviera of the Mediterranean Sea; a villa in Tuscany in Italy; and a vineyard in California's Napa Valley. This last item is similar to what King Ahab wanted—a lush vineyard in a prosperous, beautiful valley. Continue to display the vineyard picture as you explore the Bible narrative in the next activity.

Have students use Reproducible 34 to survey the account in 1 Kings 21. Ask them to make a storyboard, summarizing the events in the three settings in the Bible narrative. Have students work on their own or in small groups to complete the outline. When everyone has finished, compare re-

Whose Stuff Is It?

After studying the Scripture account in 1 Kings 21, answer these questions.

1. Why wouldn't Naboth sell his vineyard even after the king offered him a good deal?
   It was not just a piece of land; it was his family's heritage.

2. Why do you think God told Elijah he would find Ahab in "the vineyard of Naboth" (1 Kings 21:18), even though Naboth was already dead?
   Ahab did not have a right to the land, so it still belonged to Naboth's family in God's eyes.

3. When you remember that God gave you everything you have and that it's really His, how does that change the way you think about it, use it, care for it, and share it? _____
   Answers will vary.

Epilogue

Because of their wickedness, Ahab and Jezebel died dishonorably, as God had said they would (see 1 Kings 22:34–37; 2 Kings 9:30–37). Elijah, however, departed this world in an amazing way. Read about it in 2 Kings 2:1–15.

1. In what way did God take His faithful prophet to heaven? _____
   In a fiery chariot in a whirlwind

2. What showed that Elijah had passed on his *vocation* (his purpose) to Elisha? _____
   Elisha took the cloak Elijah left behind and used it to perform a miracle at the Jordan River, as Elijah had done.

"Keep your life free from love of money, and be content with what you have, for He has said, 'I will never leave you nor forsake you.' . . . Do not neglect to do good and to share what you have, for such sacrifices are pleasing to God." (Hebrews 13:5, 16)

---

sults. Accept responses students can defend. Allow students to make additions or corrections at this time. (*Note:* If someone asks why Ahab is accused of murder when Jezebel is the one who caused Naboth's death, point out that this was not the first time Ahab had pouted about something with the result that Jezebel did something cruel. Ahab was manipulating her to get what he wanted. He knew what she would do. They were both wrong.)

Then continue with the discussion questions in the Student Book. Talk through the questions. Again, emphasize: **God brings material blessings into our lives for our use and, often, for our pleasure. He just doesn't want the things we own to become false gods, idols. This happens when we expect God's material blessings to make us secure or bring us lasting joy. Only Jesus can do that.**

A good test of whether that is happening or not is to consider whether we could give away a treasured possession without becoming pouty, jealous, selfish, annoyed, or enraged, as King Ahab did.

When we remember that **everything we have has come to us as a gift from God, when we unselfishly look for ways to use our things to help the people around us, we honor our Lord. That only**

INTO our lives

Epilogue

Explain that an *epilogue* tells what happened after the story. Briefly mention that we see that God's prophecy through the prophet Elijah was fulfilled. Ahab and Jezebel both died dishonorable deaths. God delayed some portions of the prophecy, giving Ahab yet another chance to go beyond contrition (he was sorry about what happened—or about getting caught) to true repentance. But Ahab continued in his unfaithful ways to the end.

Focus more on the unique departure of one of God's unique prophets. Look again at Elijah's unique career (using Web Resource 33a), and add the final illustration of the fiery chariot coming to take him to heaven.

happens when the Holy Spirit reminds us that Jesus gave up everything for us—even His life. He died on the cross to wash away our selfishness, our covetousness, and even our tantrums.

In Baptism, God anointed us as His servants. We are caretakers of all the riches He entrusts to us, and it brings us joy to use them as He intends. Sing together "We Give Thee But Thine Own" (*LSB* 781; recorded as *Hymn of the Month* for grade 3, March).

Lesson Support

Celebrating GROWTH

With this lesson, Unit 3 comes to an end. Take a few moments to look back over the unit with your class. What highlights do they remember? What patterns have they seen? In what ways do God's dealings with His Old Testament people differ from the ways He deals with us today? What has stayed the same?

Consider asking students to select the one event from the unit they would most like to have seen or participated in. Ask that they write a one-page paper explaining why. As an alternative, ask that they prepare a three-minute video presentation (similar to YouTube), answering the same question. If they choose that approach, suggest that they work in pairs, one person acting as an interviewer and the other answering. Then, switch roles.

Music Connection

Point out that the old spiritual "Swing Low, Sweet Chariot" is based on the story of Elijah's ascent into heaven. If possible, listen to a recording of the song. Explore further this spiritual that was sung during the shameful period of slavery in American history. Emphasize the fact that hope in the Lord was often the only hope slaves had, but it was a hope of redemption and eternal life in Jesus. Explore some of the profound lyrics of some of these songs. Also encourage students to explore the hidden meanings in some of the spirituals that became messages about escaping to freedom.

Reaching Every Child

Elijah served God as one of the most colorful prophets in Old Testament times. Fiery, fierce, committed to God, and not afraid to show emotion, he appears seemingly out of nowhere and performs miracles that no one before or after him replicates—until our Lord Jesus Himself appears on the scene.

Perhaps you could talk your pastor or a male DCE into donning a robe and sandals and bursting into your classroom at a prearranged time, a time when the students are engaged in math or language arts, for instance. "Elijah" could tell about his ministry in the Northern Kingdom, lead a map review, and share some of his emotions during the spiritual roller coaster ride he experienced during the reign of Ahab and Jezebel.

Bringing it home

Encourage students to talk to their parents about today's lesson, especially today's memory verse. Perhaps they could work with family members to sort through their closets and take outgrown clothes, shoes, toys, and the like to a local "free store" that serves the poor or homeless.

Curriculum Connection

Although God wanted Ahab to respect Naboth's ownership, Ahab and Jezebel used their advantage in power to destroy Naboth and seize his property. Something similar can happen in the world of plants and animals. Make a creative connection to science by using section 6.2.2.2, Competition and Mutuality among Organisms, in the sixth-grade Science component of the Concordia Curriculum Guide series. Explore with students: **What are examples of plants and animals that work together to meet each other's needs (symbiosis)? Which ones simply take without giving anything in return (parasitism)?**

Ideas for the Gifted

Suppose Elijah stepped out of the pages of the Bible and into our world today. Where would he go? What would he do? To whom would he speak? What would he say? How would people respond?

Ask gifted students to create a story speculating about this, relying on what they have learned in this unit and on other accounts from 1 Kings as background.

Unit 4—Collapse and Captivity

Theme

As we approach (and perhaps are even overwhelmed by) the holiday season, you may wonder about the unit title for our Bible study of the Old Testament—"Collapse and Captivity." That doesn't seem to fit with the season. But actually, it really does! During this time in biblical history, God was using events to prepare His people for the coming promised Messiah. God prepared their hearts by ridding them of idolatry and replacing that with repentance and reliance on the Lord. The Advent season is a time of preparation. God prepares our hearts as we hear His Holy Word. He is leading us to repentance of our sins and reliance on Him for our hope and salvation. We, too, are looking for the promised Messiah. We look back at the coming of Jesus at the first Christmas; we ask Him to come into our hearts today and transform our lives; and we look forward to His second coming on the Last Day, when He will return in glory and rejoicing to take all believers to our heavenly home! As the people of old yearned with hope for the Savior, we, too, yearn with hope, knowing the certainty of our Savior's promises of forgiveness, life, and salvation. Live in that hope! Celebrate that hope! It is a certainty in Christ Jesus! May you share the many joys of this season of hope!

Worship

Each lesson in this curriculum includes Devotions. If you already have an established plan for your opening worship, you can use the Devotions suggested in the Teacher Guide as an introduction to the lesson instead. The theme for this unit has such a strong connection to the season of Advent. Help your students discover the language of so many Advent hymns that speak of yearning for the coming of the Messiah. (Note that the *Hymns of the Season* for this unit and this month have both Advent and Christmas hymns because you are likely to want to choose from both listings.) Instead of a suggested psalm to read this month, the Devotions suggest that the class say together the words of Luke 2:1–20, which speak of the fulfillment of the promise of the Messiah in the birth of Jesus. (Saying these words each day, many students will find that they soon know them by memory—a treasure to keep in their hearts. Also, as we repeat words and they become familiar to us, there is a tendency to speak them with more intensity and earnestness.)

Resources

Among the many resources you can find on the One in Christ Portal are family letters that are printed in Spanish. You may have children in your classroom who know English as a second language, but whose parents still struggle with English and are more comfortable speaking and reading Spanish. Because these letters share a Gospel message with the home, we want to do what we can to facilitate this communication. If you subscribe to the One in Christ Portal, you will find that the unit tests are presented in a self-correcting mode, if you choose to use them that way. The tests are not too difficult because it is important for students to experience success, not failure, in studying God's Word. The tests are also intended to be discussion starters, as together you talk about why one answer is wrong and another is correct. Unit 4 test answers are (1) c; (2) b; (3) d; (4) c; (5) a; (6) c; (7) b; (8) a; (9) c; (10) c. Note that the titles of this unit's lessons are listed in the column at the right to give you an overview of the material covered in this unit.

Unit 4

35. The Prophet Elisha
36. Joash
37. Hezekiah Prays
38. Josiah
39. Jonah
40. Jeremiah
41. Daniel and His Friends
42. Three Men in the Fiery Furnace
43. Daniel and the King's Dreams
44. The Writing on the Wall
45. Queen Esther Saves Her People

Bulletin Board

This Bulletin Board is available, ready to cut out and pin up, from Concordia Publishing House. There will be a Bulletin Board that focuses on the unit's theme available for each unit/month. As you study Old Testament Bible history, you can see a succession of kingdoms rising to power and falling in defeat. The pattern continues throughout history because the pattern is put in place by people—all sinners, with a human nature that is contrary to God's will. Yet throughout all of these events, we see that God's will remains predominant. God works through history and its people and kingdoms, always for the purpose of fulfilling His promises to His faithful people. And God's main promise focuses on preparing the people and place for the coming of the Messiah. Jesus Christ—that Messiah—is the fulfillment of God's promise of salvation. While earthly powers change, Jesus is constant. He is unchanging in His loving grace and mercy, demonstrated in His death on the cross and resurrection, offering us forgiveness, life, and salvation. "Jesus Christ is the same yesterday and today and forever" (Hebrews 13:8).

Bible Book Overview

The Student Book Appendix has a valuable feature that gives a summary of each book of the Bible. Looking at the summaries of sixty-six books can be overwhelming, so it is suggested that each month/unit, your class look at the summaries of just a few of these books. During Unit 4, introduce the Scripture's books of poetry—Job, Psalms, Proverbs, Ecclesiastes, and Song of Solomon. Point out that Hebrew poetry differs from our usual standards. We look for rhymes and rhythms in the words of poetry. But Hebrew poetry focuses on comparing ideas—concepts that repeat an idea with different words, concepts that are opposites in character, or concepts that gradually build in emphasis. Also point out that poetry in the Bible is not limited to these five books. Hebrew poetry can be found in other places in Scripture, such as Isaiah 12. Read together and discuss the summaries of these five books in the Student Book Appendix when you have available time. (Note that a copy of the Student Book Appendix is included in the back of this Teacher Guide.)

UNIT 4—COLLAPSE AND CAPTIVITY

LESSON 35

The Prophet Elisha
2 Kings 4–6

Background

You are probably entering the Advent season. The prophets of old and the prophet John the Baptist provide significant Advent themes as we look forward with hope and yearning to Christmas, the celebration of the Messiah's first coming, and also to the second coming of that Messiah at the Last Day. The prophets of the Old Testament pointed to the coming Messiah. Many also pointed to John the Baptist, who would, in turn, point to the arrival of that Messiah. Matthew 3:1–3 says, "In those days John the Baptist came preaching in the wilderness of Judea, 'Repent, for the kingdom of heaven is at hand.' For this is he who was spoken of by the prophet [Isaiah 40:3] when he said, 'The voice of one crying in the wilderness: "Prepare the way of the Lord; make His paths straight."'"

"John wore a garment of camel's hair and a leather belt around his waist, and his food was locusts and wild honey" (Matthew 3:4). A similar outfit was worn by Elijah. In terms of being unusual and even unpopular, the prophet Elisha was also like him. Elisha was bald-headed (2 Kings 2:23) and strong enough to drive a team of twenty-four oxen (1 Kings 19:19). Such an imposing man was sure to draw attention. Elisha, like the prophets before and after him, proclaimed God's message of repentance, in his preaching and in the marvelous acts God empowered him to do.

Spiritually, our world today is similar to the world of Elijah and Elisha. Satan and our sinful nature continue to cause us to forget God's will for our lives. Your preteen students are already encountering attacks on their faith. God gives powerful ammunition to fight these attacks in both His Word and in His daily forgiveness and renewal in their lives, begun at Baptism. As you share these truths with your students, pray that God would keep and preserve them as they grow in Him.

Central Truth

Sometimes God uses unusual and even unpopular people to do His will; it is the message, not the messenger, that is important.

Objectives

- Recognize that following the ways of the world and what everybody is doing rather than God's ways will lead to sin and tragedy.
- Rejoice that in Christ, we have forgiveness and the perfect example of God's will and ways.
- Be imitators of Christ Jesus in all our ways and days, as we are empowered by the Holy Spirit.

Materials

- Hymnals and music CDs
- Reproducible 35
- Web Resource 35a

Bible Prep

Post in advance so students can bookmark references before class time.
- Luke 2
- 2 Kings 4–6

Devotions

"Oh, no!" groaned Luis as he looked at his class schedule for the new quarter. "I've got Mr. Lang for science." "What's wrong with Mr. Lang?" asked his older brother, Juan. "I learned a lot from him." Luis replied, "Everyone I know who's been in Mr. Lang's class said he's the strangest teacher ever. He wears really weird ties. He sometimes dresses up like a mad scientist and talks in a crazy voice as he teaches the lesson." Juan chuckled. "That's what's so cool about him, Luis. People may say Mr. Lang is strange, but I bet they remember the facts he taught them. Give him a chance. You might be surprised at all you'll learn."

The prophets God selected to preach His Word and to lead His people back to Him sometimes looked unusual. We've learned about some of the remarkable events in the life of Elijah. Today we'll learn about his successor, Elisha, who often spoke harshly to those who were unrepentant. Other prophets, like Ezekiel and Jeremiah, often did and said unusual things to catch the attention of the people so that they would listen to the message from the Lord. They each proclaimed the message of God's salvation of the world through the Messiah, Jesus, our Savior.

Throughout Advent, we reflect on God's promise to save us, on His fulfillment of that promise through Jesus, and on His future return on the Last Day. Whenever we stray from Jesus through sin, we can be certain that our Good Shepherd searches for us, finds us, and brings us back to safety in Him.

Let's reflect on the second coming of Jesus as we sing the Advent hymn "The King Shall Come" (*LSB* 348; recorded as *Hymn of the Season for grade 6, Advent*). Then say, **To keep in our minds the focus of the prophets and the focus of this Advent season, let's read together the words of Luke 2:1–20.**

INTO the lesson

This lesson is primarily a Bible study that shows striking similarities in the events of the lives of the prophets Elijah and Elisha. Point out the following: **There are at least three reasons that these similarities are not surprising: (1) They basically lived in the same environment in the Northern Kingdom of Israel during times of turmoil in the reigns of wicked and idolatrous kings; (2) Elijah was Elisha's mentor and teacher, and both served the true God in proclaiming a message of repentance; and (3) Elisha asked for and received an inheritance from Elijah as a blessing from God, receiving a double portion—or firstborn's portion—of Elijah's spirit. (Elisha was an heir by faith in the same Lord.)**

INTO the Word

Comparing Ministries

This Bible study will help to distinguish the two prophets as you first review an event in Elijah's life and then read a biblical account of a similar, though unique, event in Elisha's life. You are likely to need two days to cover all of this information. You might also consider dividing into two, three, or six groups that share the stories in a culminating discussion.

The message the prophets proclaimed from God to the people was often unpopular. The prophets' messages required the people to stop following idols and to stop becoming wealthy through dishonest means. In these situations, God never forgot His prophets, and He protected them. He continued to train up spokesmen so that His Word, especially concerning the coming Savior, Jesus, would not be forgotten.

Look at the three illustrations in the Student Book. They show what Elijah and Elisha might have looked like based on biblical descriptions. Then ask, **Who do you think that third guy is? He looks kind of rugged and "outdoorsy" like Elijah, and he spoke a message of warning and of repentance as did both Elijah and Elisha.** Continue then with Reproducible 35 and the "Into Our Lives" section as you look at the prophet John the Baptist, again relating this to an Advent theme.

LESSON 35
The Prophet Elisha

Comparing Ministries

Elisha took over Elijah's role as prophet when Elijah went to heaven. However, before he left, Elijah asked what he could do for Elisha, who was reluctant to see his teacher and mentor leave. Elisha said, "Please let there be a double portion of your spirit on me" (2 Kings 2:9). In other words, he asked for the same blessing that would be given to a firstborn son. We can see that God blessed Elisha's ministry. In fact, God worked through Elisha in many ways that were similar to the way God worked through Elijah. Let's explore some of these similarities.

1. God blessed the widow of Zarephath with an unending supply of oil and flour to provide food for herself, her son, and Elijah. What happened to Elisha, a widow, her sons, and a supply of oil in 2 Kings 4:1–7?
   A widow came to Elisha for help; her sons were going to be sold as slaves; God miraculously gave her an unending supply of olive oil for her to sell to pay off her debts.

2. When the poor widow of Zarephath's son died, Elijah prayed and God restored the boy to life. What differences and similarities are there in Elisha's story in 2 Kings 4:1–20 and 30–37?
   A wealthy Shunammite couple built a room for Elisha to stay in when he was traveling; they were blessed with a son; when the son died, God worked miraculously through the prophet to bring the boy back to life.

3. God worked through fire to demonstrate His power in answer to Elijah's prayer and sacrifice. How did God work through water to demonstrate His power in 2 Kings 5:1–16?
   God worked through the waters of the Jordan River and the message of the prophet Elisha to heal Naaman of his leprosy.

Review

Covenant Connection

The time of Elijah, Elisha, and other prophets of the divided kingdom showed God's patience and love for His people as He continued to send a message of warning and repentance to prepare their hearts for the coming of the Messiah. God was faithful to His Word. Those who faithfully believed lived in yearning and in hope for the fulfillment of God's promises, which came in Christ Jesus. God calls us to repentance also, preparing our hearts for the hope we have of Christ's second coming, knowing He will be as faithful to that promise as to the first.

76

INTO our lives

As you begin this section of the lesson, using Reproducible 35, ask, **What interesting or unusual qualities have you noticed about Elijah, Elisha, and John the Baptist?** (Students will likely focus on the prophets' unusual apparel as well as on the miraculous ways in which God enabled them to share His message.) **Do you think the life of a prophet would have been an easy one?** (Not often. Prophets had to confront people with sometimes unpopular messages that focused on behaviors that went against God's Law and His will. Prophets often found themselves hated by the leaders of their times, even to the point of being hunted down and murdered. Prophets probably felt lonely and isolated. They needed God's encouragement and strength to carry out the work God had for them to do.)

Probably the most surprising messengers God uses to share the Gospel are you and me! Even through our imperfections, God can work for good. He uses ordinary people like us to go and tell the most important message of all: Jesus died and rose to save us from our sins.

Consider, **In what ways, positive and negative, have you noticed people your age being influenced by other young people?** (Responses will likely include influences on

154

4. Elijah spoke harsh words of warning to the wicked King Ahab, calling him a troublemaker and idol worshiper. What harsh words did Elisha say to Israel's wicked King Jehoram as they met with the godly King Jehoshaphat of Judah in 2 Kings 3:9–14?
Elisha didn't want to have anything to do with Jehoram and said he should go back to his false prophets. Elisha said that if it weren't for good King Jehoshaphat, he wouldn't look at or even notice Jehoram.

5. Elijah had to deal with covetous Ahab, who wanted Naboth's vineyard. What covetous person did Elisha have to deal with in 2 Kings 5:19–27?
Elisha's covetous servant Gehazi lied and schemed to get the money that Elisha had refused to take from Naaman.

6. Chariots of fire took Elijah to heaven. What were the circumstances when Elisha saw chariots of fire in 2 Kings 6:8–23?
The king of Syria was fighting Israel and wanted to especially capture God's prophet, who kept revealing his sneak attacks. The Syrians surrounded the city where Elisha lived, but God surrounded the Syrians with His angels and chariots of fire.

Elijah   Elisha

Remember

"Repent and turn from all your transgressions." (From the prophet Ezekiel 18:30)

---

behavior, attire, activities, language, purchase of products, and on the practice of their Christian faith.) **In what ways can the comments of your peers strengthen your faith? In what ways can the comments of your peers undermine your faith?** (Their comments will give you a window into the kinds of pressures, both positive and negative, your students experience.) **In what ways can you be a positive influence on the faith of others?**

Read Ephesians 5:1–21, using Web Resource 35a to focus on individual verses. Ask, **What does it mean to "imitate God"?** (To follow His ways; to act in a way that pleases God) **We know that we are sinful people. How is it possible for us to imitate God?** (We can follow God's will and ways only by the power of the Holy Spirit working in us.) Point out that these words written roughly two thousand years ago address pressures that people face today: sexual sins and inappropriate physical behavior (vv. 3–5); the need for love and kindness to combat violence and hatred (vv. 1, 2, 11, 21); false teachings (v. 6); drug and alcohol abuse (v. 18).

You've probably already experienced peer pressure in your life. If you've ever been influenced to buy a particular product, dress a particular way, or become involved in an activity, these things have happened because of either positive or negative peer pressure.

Look again at Ephesians 5:2 and ask, **What does it mean to "walk in love, as Christ loved us"?** (Responses include to love others unselfishly; to put the needs of others before our own; to be kind, patient, and forgiving.) **How can following the truth of these verses help improve your relationship with your parents and with your friends?** (When we put the needs of others before our own, we think about others first. We try to see things from their perspective. We speak to them in kind and caring ways. We approach differences and disagreements with calm, thoughtful responses. We treat others with respect and do not allow problems to escalate into arguments that result in hurtful words. We pray and ask Jesus for help and strength to "walk in love.")

God constantly works to lead us to repent of our sinful ways. Through His Word and Sacraments, He turns us back to Him with forgiveness and love for Jesus' sake. In Jesus, we have the perfect example of God's will and ways. Each day, through the renewal the Holy Spirit gives us that began at our Baptism, we have a fresh start and a new chance to honor God in all that we do and say.

Option: You may also wish to develop some role-playing activities that initially define the behavior that needs to change and then give students opportunities to role-play acceptable behavior. Use this role playing to address behaviors that you have witnessed in the classroom and that have caused students increased stress. Be sure to design the activities so that they do not call attention to any specific students in your class.

Role-playing ideas might focus on how to respectfully take turns in class discussions and ways to show respect for the comments and ideas of classmates, especially when you disagree; how to include everyone in activities; how to deal with bullies; and how to show respect to one another in your speech.

Lesson Support

Bringing it home

Sixth grade is a time when peers play an increasingly important role in the lives of young people. Preteens and teens begin to develop friendships that are closer and more constant than in earlier years. These friendships are important. They are places where youth can explore their identity and feel accepted, and where they can develop a sense of belonging. Friendships allow youth to practice and foster social skills that are crucial for future success in everyday life and in the workplace.

This time in a young person's life can be a challenging one for parents, as their once-dependent child moves toward greater independence. Parents worry that their child may fall into the wrong circle of friends and be negatively influenced by his or her peers. Parents fear that they will forever lose a close relationship with their child.

Research shows, however, that these fears are generally unfounded. Although the original parent-child relationship may seem to be lost, in actuality, preteens and teens are shifting the original relationship to include their increasing independence and maturity. Youth still consider their parents to be the most influential people in their lives. If parents and teens work together to keep the lines of communication open, their relationship can remain close. (Information is based on the article "Friendships, Peer Influence, and Peer Pressure during the Teen Years" by Maria R. T. de Guzman, *NebGuide* [© 2007, The Board of Regents of the University of Nebraska on behalf of the University of Nebraska Lincoln Extension. All rights reserved.])

Faith in Action

Work with the first- through third-grade teachers in your school to allow willing students from your class to serve as mentors for younger students. You will want to select students from your class who exhibit Christlike behavior and who would be positive role models. These students could help their younger friends with classroom assignments, eat lunch with them, play basketball, soccer, or kickball with them on the playground, or plan special activities for them, such as a field day. As they befriend these younger children, your students have an opportunity to practice being imitators of Jesus (and also do some mentoring, as Elijah did for Elisha).

Music Connection

This unit provides such an appropriate connection to the season of Advent. Use this time of study to look at Advent hymns that are related to this season of hope and yearning, which focuses on the coming of the Messiah. The Bible's central message is Jesus saves. Throughout all of Scripture and by all of God's servants, we are reminded that Jesus would come, did come, and will come again.

Reaching Every Child

A good method to help preteens and teens combat negative peer pressure is to have them prepare "mental scripts" so they will have ready responses when pressured to engage in an activity they know is wrong. Discuss possible responses to these scenarios.

Pressure Point 1: You and a group of friends are hanging out after school at the park. One person pulls out a pack of cigarettes. "I found these in my dad's dresser drawer. C'mon, try one." Possible "imitator of God" responses: "No, thanks. I don't want to wreck the good health God's given me." Or, "No way! I'm on the basketball team, and I don't want to ruin my chance to play."

Pressure Point 2: You and your classmates are sitting at your lunch table, eating lunch. A new student walks up to your table and asks, "Mind if I eat lunch with you?" One of your table mates replies, "Sorry, this table's already full." There is an empty seat next to you. Possible "imitator of God" responses: "I guess my friend didn't notice the empty seat next to me. C'mon and sit here." Or, get up from the table with your lunch tray and say, "This table's kind of full, but why don't you and I sit together over here? I saw you come in during math class. It's great to meet you."

Pressure Point 3: "Hey!" the coolest kid in class whispers to you. "I don't want to take that science quiz after lunch. Let's just cut class and hang out behind the school until it's time for P.E." Possible "imitator of God" responses: "No, thanks. I'm not ready for the quiz either, but I'd rather take a chance with a bad grade than get into trouble for cutting class." Or, "Sorry, but if I do that and my parents find out, I'll be grounded for a month."

Searching Further

If you divide the class into groups to study this lesson, consider having each group present their information to their classmates in the form of a skit, biography-type report, or PowerPoint presentation. Provide some Bible commentaries on 2 Kings such as *The People's Bible Commentary, 1 & 2 Kings* (CPH, 2005) to help students research and understand some of the more difficult Bible stories about Elisha. Also have several copies of *The Lutheran Study Bible* (*TLSB*) available for exploring the notes.

Unit 4—Collapse and Captivity

Lesson 36

Joash
2 Chronicles 22–24

Central Truth
God blesses us with Christian leaders to guide us in faith through His Word.

Objectives
- Admit that we sometimes resent those in authority when we want to do things our own way.
- Acknowledge that being a part-time or half-hearted disciple of the Lord is not acceptable to God.
- Recognize that following Jesus is a life-long commitment—a commitment based on His giving of His life for us.

Materials
- Hymnals and music CDs
- Web Resource 36a
- Reproducible 36

Bible Prep
Post in advance so students can bookmark references before class time.
- Luke 2:1–20
- 2 Chronicles 22–24
- 1 Peter 5:6–9
- Luke 9
- Philippians 2

Background

For some time now, the number of teens and young adults attending church following their confirmation has been plummeting. The most disturbing fact concerning this statistic is that at a time in their lives when they are experiencing great changes, encountering new people and ideas, and facing often difficult challenges, these young people are not partaking of the gifts of strengthened faith and forgiveness that God gives through the study of His Word and through Holy Communion.

King Joash can be viewed as a "poster boy" for the disastrous effects of half-hearted discipleship. Joash was raised by the priest Jehoiada to love and fear God, and the early years of his reign showed the fruits of this faith as well as the God-pleasing leadership of Jehoiada. But once Jehoiada died, Joash ignored God's will and His commands and instead followed the ungodly ways of the princes of Judah. The temple was abandoned, and the people returned to their idolatry.

The young people you teach will soon be confirmed. Through you and other Christian teachers and pastors, God has laid the groundwork for their faith. Before you continue your preparation of this lesson, pray for your students. Ask that God would continue to powerfully work in their hearts to give them the joy and desire to follow Jesus with their whole heart all the days of their lives. Pray also that God would continue to give them faithful Christian leaders who meaningfully proclaim and apply the truths of the Word to their lives. Ask God to help your students to always "[look]" to Jesus" (Hebrews 12:2) as the one true source of forgiveness and eternal life.

Devotions

"No! I don't want to go!" Jonas and Darin could hear the little girl's cry over their bouncing basketball. Darin said, "That girl should listen to her babysitter."

After their game of one-on-one, Jonas and Darin walked home. Suddenly, above the roar of the city traffic, they heard a woman's voice. "Look, Officer, I don't care what you say. I was only going five miles over the speed limit. I don't deserve a ticket!" Jonas said, "Oh, man! She's going to get fined for that!"

"See you tomorrow, Jonas," said Darin as they entered their apartment building. As Darin opened the apartment's door, he saw a mess in the living room. His mom was busy in the kitchen. "Hi, Darin," she said. "I'm glad you're home. Would you do me a favor and pick up the mess you left behind this morning?" "Aw, Mom," Darin cried, "give me a break! I want to relax and watch TV."

Three floors up, Jonas's dad was folding laundry. "Hi, son," he said as Jonas came in the door. "Would you grab a few towels and give me a hand so I can finish this before your mom gets home?" "Dad!" yelled Jonas. "I've got a ton of homework to do! Just leave me alone!"

What similar behavior did the little girl, the woman, Jonas, and Darin show? (Each person did not show obedience or service; they evidenced self-interest rather than a commitment to God's will.) **In Old Testament times, how did God's people often treat the spiritual leaders, such as the prophets and priests?** (They often treated them with disrespect, which meant that they were also showing disrespect to God.) **What have you noticed about the behavior of many of the kings themselves?** (Many were poor leaders who did not follow God's commands either.)

Christian leaders are gifts from God. Our sinful natures often rebel against even the very best leaders and against God Himself. Jesus, our Good Shepherd, our perfect Leader, and our eternal King, seeks us to rescue us from our sins. He forgives us and guides us. He does all of this out of a love so great that He gave His life to save ours. Let's thank and praise **Jesus for His perfect guidance and love as we sing "The King of Love My Shepherd Is"** (*LSB* 709; recorded as *Hymn of the Month for grade 6, December*). Then say, **To keep in our minds the focus of the prophets and the focus of this Advent season, let's read together the words of Luke 2:1–20.**

157

INTO the lesson

Use Web Resource 36a to review some of the kings of the divided kingdom. The title asks, "Why Are There So Many Bad Guys?" Point out that when the kingdom split after the reigns of David and Solomon, the Northern Kingdom of Israel never had a good king. They all were wicked and violent; they all were unfaithful to God and worshiped idols (especially the idols Baal and Asherah, whose worship encouraged immorality). As we have seen in previous lessons, King Ahab was the worst of these kings. However, before piously accusing them, we need to realize that conditions in the world today are still dominated by sin. Look at the TV news and you will hear about tragedies around the world caused by ruthless leaders. Coming closer to home, we recognize that our cities are filled with deceit and crime and violence. So we can ask again, this time about our society, "Why Are There So Many Bad Guys?" We get the same answer today—sin.

Take a brief look now at some of the kings of Judah. This is especially significant because this is the royal line of David from which the promised Messiah would be born. The Southern Kingdom of Judah got off to a bad start with two bad kings. But then the people were blessed with two kings who were faithful to the Lord. However, they were followed by a quick "nose dive" as things got worse and worse. That is where we pick up today's Bible narrative.

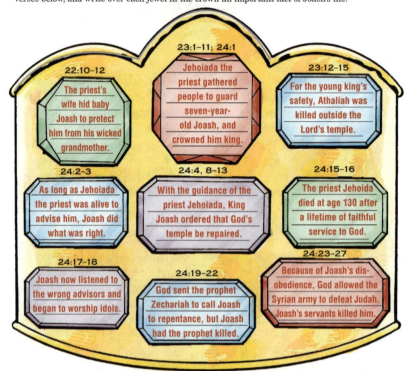

INTO the Word

ALMOST . . . a good king

Talk about the title in the Student Book. Discuss why the word *almost* is often not a good thing. Ask students to give examples of situations where *almost* is not enough, and not enough is no good. (For example, he *almost* escaped from the crocodile; she *almost* got into the house before the rain poured down; he *almost* avoided being hit by the ball; she *almost* kept the milk from spilling.) Work together on the Student Book activity, having volunteers read the Scripture verses aloud, and discussing how Joash made a good start as king but did not finish the job well at all; how he was not reliable or faithful to the Lord; how he did not make a lifelong commitment to God.

You may want to add some of the following points to your discussion: Athaliah was the queen of Judah, but we can trace her wicked ways back to Israel because her parents were King Ahab and Jezebel. Athaliah brought her evil ways with her when she married into the royal family of Judah. Eventually her husband and son died, and she took over as ruler. Ask, **Why did she want to kill everyone in her family?** (So no one could take her power away. That is why the rescue of Joash was so important.)

Joash was a grown man with a family when he ordered that the temple be restored, so he had had many years to learn from the priest Jehoiada about the ways of the Lord. (Jehoiada lived to the age of 130.) Joash's commitment to the Lord, however, was not strong. He soon followed the ways of wicked friends and princes. The Bible says in 2 Chronicles 24:17 that these princes paid *homage* to the king. The original language indicates bowing low in worship, so Joash was probably flattered to be treated almost as if he were a god. However, he was soon led astray by personal vanity and self-interest. The evidence of his total downfall is that he refused to listen to God's prophet Zechariah. (This is not the biblical author Zechariah, who lived after the time of the Babylonian captivity.) The sins kept piling up as the king had Zechariah killed; shamefully, this was done in the very courtyard of the house of the Lord. Consider that Joash showed no appreciation for Jehoiada, who had rescued and guided the king himself so many years before, when Joash now had Zechariah, Jehoiada's own son, murdered.

Influences

List things that positively and negatively affected Joash. List things that negatively and positively can affect people in today's world.

	POSITIVE INFLUENCES:	NEGATIVE INFLUENCES:
KING JOASH	The priest Jehoiada taught him God's Word; the priest's wife raised him from infancy.	Ungodly friends flattered him and led him to worship idols.

	NEGATIVE INFLUENCES:	POSITIVE INFLUENCES:
PEOPLE IN 20___	Ungodly friends, violent video games, X-rated media, materialistic advertisements, selfish interests	God's Word and Sacraments, Christian friends, Christian parents, teachers, and pastors, a kind heart that imitates Jesus

Commitment

A true commitment is a trustworthy promise, a reliable pledge, a sincere intention to follow through and act on your resolution and responsibility. Faithful people of God make a true commitment to the Lord. We can't do this without the help that God gives to us by the power of the Holy Spirit working through God's Word!

Name three other things in life to which a person might make a commitment.
Possible answers: to be faithful in marriage; to perform a job well; to practice a musical instrument; to pay back a loan of money; to help a sick friend; to follow Jesus.

According to Luke 9:23, what commitment does Jesus expect of His followers?
That a person "deny himself" (put Jesus first) and "take up his cross daily" (daily serve and even suffer).

What kind of commitment did Jesus make for us? See Philippians 2:5–8.
He gave up life in heaven to become one of us; the King of kings became a servant; He became nothing for us, humbling Himself to the point of death on a cross.

Join in praising Jesus by reading aloud together Philippians 2:9–11.

Remember

"Be ___**faithful**___ unto ___**death**___, and I will give you the ___**crown**___ of ___**life**___." (Revelation 2:10b)

INTO our lives

What If . . . ?

For a change of pace, distribute Reproducible 36, and discuss some of the things that influence our health, broadening the discussion to consider factors that influence our attitudes and our lives. (You may need to guide the discussion of the health questions; if you wish students to use Internet resources to answer them, bookmark appropriate sites before class begins.)

As you discuss the "What if . . . ?" question concerning confirmation, realize that it may be difficult for your students to imagine not attending worship and Bible study on a regular basis if it is an integral part of their lives right now. Direct them back to the story of Joash and how he fell away from faith in the true God. Remind them of the discussions you had in the previous lesson concerning peer pressure and the powerful influence it can be. Joash was influenced by negative peer pressure from the princes of Judah. (This is an appropriate time to explore the purpose of confirmation and of making a pledge to God of lifelong commitment in faith.)

As time permits, direct students to 1 Peter 5:6–9. Even the most faithful of God's servants can fall for Satan's traps and deceptions. As we remain in the Word and regularly partake of the Lord's Supper, God strengthens us and keeps us close to Him.

Say, **A faithful Christian teacher taped a tag to the top of her Bible and printed on it, "God's Vitamins." Why is this title a good description of God's Word?** (Just as vitamins found in foods strengthen our bodies physically, when we read, hear, and ponder the truths in God's Word, the Holy Spirit works in our hearts to strengthen us spiritually and to help us grow in Christ.)

Influences/Commitment

Use the next two sections of the Student Book to expand on the importance of positive influences and of positive lifelong commitment.

Point out that a commitment should not be taken lightly; failing a commitment reflects negatively on a person's reliability, integrity, and honesty. A commitment takes effort and can even become difficult, but we can always go to God in prayer, asking Him to strengthen us in our faith and faith life, and enabling us to live more as true children of God.

The motivation for our commitment to the Lord flows out of Jesus' total commitment to us. With unfathomable love for us, Jesus gave His life so that we might live. By the power of the Holy Spirit, when we deny our own wants and desires to follow Jesus, we do not lose anything. Instead, we gain the greatest riches ever: forgiveness and eternal life.

Through His death and resurrection, Jesus fulfilled God's covenant promise to save all people. Our commitment to follow Jesus for our entire lives is based on the truth that Jesus gave His life for us. In love and gratitude, we are empowered by the Holy Spirit to live our lives for our Lord.

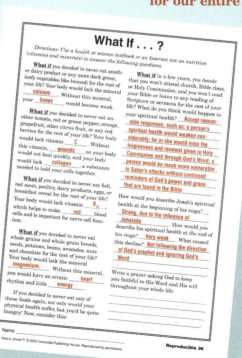

Lesson Support

Celebrating GROWTH

Ask, **Is it easy to follow Jesus?** (Not always. It takes the strength that only God can give to withstand the attacks of our sinful flesh, the world, and Satan. We need God's constant direction and redirection so that we can always "[look] to Jesus, the founder and perfecter of our faith" [Hebrews 12:2].)

Baptism and Holy Communion are two of God's Means of Grace for us. They are ways in which God gives to us some very marvelous blessings.

At Baptism, God began an eternal relationship with you. As the very best friend you will ever have, Jesus promises, "I am with you always" (Matthew 28:20). From the moment the water and Word are applied, the Holy Spirit daily works in your heart to cleanse, renew, strengthen, and grow your faith.

At Baptism, God gives us a new, eternal life in Him. The process of remaking and renewing us in God's image begins. Through faith in Jesus, by God's grace, we receive salvation, forgiveness, eternal life, and a home in heaven.

Read together the Bible words in Revelation 2:10. This indicates Jesus' desire for lifelong faithfulness to Him and beautifully states what awaits all believers who remain faithful.

Then ask, **Why is "the crown of life" a fitting way to describe what we receive through faith in Jesus?** (A crown symbolizes an item of great worth. Eternal life is the greatest blessing God gives us. It is a symbol of the triumph over sin, death, and Satan that we receive through faith in Jesus.)

Searching Further

Compare and contrast the orders of service for Baptism and Confirmation found on pages 268–274 in *LSB*. Discuss how God uses confirmation instruction as a way to strengthen our faith relationship with Him and increase our understanding of what it means to be a Christian. Pose this question: **Why might it be a good idea for people to reaffirm the pledge they make at confirmation at various points throughout their life?**

Working in Groups

Select groups of students to explore the importance of a firm commitment to following Jesus in each of the following phases of their lives: high school; college; on the job; in dating relationships; marriage; family; retirement. First, have students list the joys that God gives at each stage in our lives (e.g., friends, learning opportunities, careers, a spouse, children, a time of rest from work and for new opportunities to serve Him). Also challenge students to think of situations that could be problematic in each of these life stages. Help them consider how peer pressure, loneliness, fear, worry, and other issues can be a part of each life stage.

Then challenge students to think of ways that firmly following Jesus would influence each of these stages in a positive way. How would a committed walk with Jesus help when problems arise? Why is it important to be connected to the Lord through Word and Sacrament?

Finally, for whatever life stage they are exploring, have each group develop a list of Bible passages that express the joys and the strength that God gives as we face challenges. This is a good opportunity for students to practice their skills using a Bible concordance.

Curriculum Connection

Many people behave like Joash: when they are under the influence of Christian friends and family, they do well; but when they come under negative peer pressure, they begin to do evil. Refer to section 6.3.1.5, Behaving in a Safe and Healthy Manner When Confronted with Negative Peer Pressure. You'll find this in the sixth grade Physical Education volume of the Concordia Curriculum Guide series. Discuss with students: **How can we help one another stay strong in the Lord?**

Faith in Action

Use current newspapers, news magazines, and reliable Internet news resources to make a list of challenges that currently face those who are in positions of authority in our society. Then spend time in prayer for parents, teachers, principals, police officers, those serving in the military, politicians, and national leaders and ask God for His help and strength for them as they face those challenges that students discovered.

UNIT 4—COLLAPSE AND CAPTIVITY

LESSON 37

Hezekiah Prays
2 KINGS 18–19

Background

The prophet Isaiah began his ministry in 740 BC. He lived in Jerusalem and preached to the people about the coming of the kingdom of God. He foretold the work of John the Baptist in Isaiah 40:3, saying, "A voice cries: 'In the wilderness prepare the way of the LORD; make straight in the desert a highway for our God.'" He foretold the birth of Christ, with specific details about the Virgin Mary and Christ's suffering, death, and resurrection.

During his ministry and counsel to the king, Isaiah provided a glimpse of God's judgment to those who were disobedient. But he also gave hope for salvation to those who loved the Lord.

The Book of Isaiah offers a message of hope for the Messiah along with warnings to the people about their idolatry. Its theme points to God's judgment and salvation.

During King Hezekiah's reign, Isaiah assured the king that God would hear his prayers. He foretold the fate of King Sennacherib, yet warned the people of Judah that they would fall into captivity at the hands of the Babylonians. He predicted their deliverance and redemption, thus revealing God's mercy and forgiveness.

Hundreds of years later, in Luke 4:14, Jesus read from Isaiah's scroll, proclaiming Himself as the fulfillment of God's promise for the Messiah. God's Word is truth, and His prophecies were and will be fulfilled.

Central Truth
Even in times of trouble, God is with His faithful people and blesses them.

Objectives
- Confess that we are all sinners, undeserving of God's grace, yet He is merciful to us and blesses us through Christ Jesus.
- Recognize that God's power is greater than any king, army, disease, or other evil; He has triumphed over sin, death, and the devil.
- Go to God in prayer; He hears and He answers in the way He knows is best.

Materials
- Hymnals and music CDs
- Reproducible 37
- Web Resource 37a

Bible Prep
Post in advance so students can bookmark references before class time.
- Luke 2
- 2 Kings 18–20
- The Book of Isaiah

Devotions

Show Web Resource 37a. **What does the phrase "strong as an ox" mean to you?** Have you ever seen a real, live ox? It looks like a huge, muscular cow. Oxen are used to perform work because of their great strength. They can be trained to respond to signals, and they often work in pairs while wearing a large harness called a "yoke." They are used to plow farmland, thresh grain, haul wagons, and any other duty that requires hard work. The word *yoke* is often used to indicate a difficult job, heavy burden, or stubborn problem.

Do you ever feel like your problems in life are just too hard to deal with? Do you ever feel as though you are trudging along, pulling a wagonload of trouble? Today we will hear about the troubles of a king; but people your age can have heavy burdens too, such as difficulties from an accident or illness, or problems in the family like divorce, or even death—and sometimes, just the day-to-day troubles of homework and peer pressure can seem overwhelming.

In Matthew 11:28–30, Jesus says, "Come to Me, all who labor and are heavy laden, and I will give you rest. Take My yoke upon you, and learn from Me, for I am gentle and lowly in heart, and you will find rest for your souls. For My yoke is easy, and My burden is light."

It's very clear in these verses that we still need to do the work. Jesus does not say that He will take the yoke from us so we don't have to work. The yoke must be worn in order to do the work of living a godly life, and Jesus asks us to take *His* yoke upon us, not ours. God will give us even greater strength than an ox. A yoke joins two together, which means we will never have to do our life's work alone. Jesus says we should learn from Him. Learning involves active work on our part. We will still be faced with work, trouble, problems, and sin in this life. But God's undeserved grace offers us rest for our souls. God is merciful to us. God has the power and strength to take our burdens and be gentle and humble at the same time. It's important for us to go to God in prayer and let Him lead us. He will hear our prayers, lighten our load, and give us the rest we need to continue our work in this life. He blesses us with the help of Jesus Christ, who shares our burdens. We need not be afraid of what life has to offer. God knows what is best for us.

Sing about our heavenly King in the hymn "The King of Love My Shepherd Is" (*LSB* 709; recorded as *Hymn of the Month for grade 6, December*) or "The King Shall Come" (*LSB* 348; recorded as *Hymn of the Season for Grade 6, Advent*). Remembering the "reason for the season," read together Luke 2:1–20.

161

INTO the lesson

Relief from a Good King!

After reading about so many wicked kings, it is good to read about a God-fearing king like Hezekiah. Point out, however, that Hezekiah was a sinner like everyone else. His goodness came from the Lord, who forgave his sins, transformed his heart, and led him to live as a child of God. The relief mentioned in the subtitle is the rescue that God gave to Hezekiah from Sennacherib and the Assyrians and also from an illness (which you may choose to explore through several articles in the "Lesson Support" section).

INTO the Word

A Chain of Events

This is a Bible study that leads students through the main events in Hezekiah's difficulties with the Assyrians, who were "the world power" at that time, conquering one country after another. Point out that this narrative follows two good methods of writing. First, the events are given as a chain of events with one thing leading to another (not randomly or out of sequence). Second, a good method for active writing is showing actions and reactions and thus showing the interplay of these events. (We could also speak of this as "cause-and-effect" writing.) Point out to students that we see a common pattern in this story: God continued to send a prophet to speak His message to the people, whether the king was a faithful king or not. The prophet at the time of this faithful king was Isaiah, whose message spoke to Hezekiah and to Judah—and to people of all time because of Isaiah's many messianic prophecies.

Tell the students that by looking closely at this confrontation, we can learn how important it is to stand firm in our faith and call on God in times of trouble. **We will always be under attack from outside influences in this life. The devil continues to try and capture our hearts, demanding more with every conquest if we give in to sin. God, however, is far more powerful and will triumph through Christ Jesus.**

A Model Prayer

Read together Hezekiah's prayer from 2 Kings 19 in the Student Book. Then have a volunteer read aloud God's answer to that prayer in verses 31–37.

LESSON 37

Hezekiah Prays

Relief from a Good King!

Hezekiah, from the royal family line of David, was twenty-five years old when he became king of Judah. He trusted God completely and obeyed His Commandments. The good king mentioned in the title, however, is the Lord, the King of kings, who gave Hezekiah relief from enemies and illness, and the courage to face them.

A Chain of Events

For each action, write the letter of the reaction that followed it. (See 2 Kings 18–19.)

__b__ 1. Action: The Israelites were worshiping the ancient bronze serpent that Moses made. (18:1–7)

__a__ 2. Action: Assyria had taken the Northern Kingdom (Israel) prisoner and now attacked the cities of Judah. (18:11–16)

__e__ 3. Action: The king of Assyria sent his supreme commander, his chief officer, and his field commander with a large army to King Hezekiah for negotiations. (18:17–18)

__c__ 4. Action: Assyria's commanding officers mocked and ridiculed the people of Jerusalem, urging them to turn against King Hezekiah. (18:28–30, 33, 36)

__f__ 5. Action: King Hezekiah tore his clothes and sent for the prophet Isaiah. (19:1–2, 6–7)

__d__ 6. Action: Sennacherib sent a letter of warning, ridiculing the power of Hezekiah's God. (19:9–11, 14)

a. Reaction: Hezekiah turned over all he could find in the palace treasuries in the temple of God and even gave the king of Assyria the temple doors and the doorposts that were overlaid with gold.
b. Reaction: Hezekiah destroyed all idolatrous shrines and smashed the ancient bronze serpent.
c. Reaction: The people of Jerusalem remained silent, just as their king had commanded them.
d. Reaction: King Hezekiah went into the temple, spread Sennacherib's letter before the Lord, and prayed.
e. Reaction: King Hezekiah sent the son of his palace administrator, the secretary, and the son of his recorder out to meet the commanders of the Assyrian army.
f. Reaction: Isaiah responded with words from the Lord that God would save them.

Review

Covenant Connection

The Northern Kingdom of Israel never repented of its idolatry and wicked ways. God allowed the Assyrian enemy to take them captive, never to return. Because there still remained a small remnant of the faithful in Judah, God continued to be with them, calling for repentance, and offering the promise of the Messiah.

A Model Prayer (2 Kings 19)

(14) Hezekiah received the letter from the hand of the messengers and read it; and Hezekiah went up to the house of the Lord and spread it before the Lord.

(15) And Hezekiah prayed before the Lord and said: "O Lord, the God of Israel, enthroned above the cherubim, You are the God, You alone, of all the kingdoms of the earth; You have made heaven and earth.

(16) Incline Your ear, O Lord, and hear; open Your eyes, O Lord, and see; and hear the words of Sennacherib, which he has sent to mock the living God. . . .

(19) So now, O Lord our God, save us, please, from his hand, that all the kingdoms of the earth may know that You, O Lord, are God alone."

READ GOD'S ANSWER TO THE PRAYER IN 2 KINGS 19:31–37.

What Can You Learn about Prayer . . .

From verse 14? Take your troubles directly to God in prayer.
From verse 15? Begin prayer with praise to God.
From verse 16? Honor and speak up for the name of God.
From verse 19? Trust the Lord and give Him the glory.

Remember

"Come to Me, all who __labor__ and are __heavy__ __laden__, and I will give you __rest__." (Matthew 11:28)

INTO our lives

What Can You Learn about Prayer . . .

Use this section of the Student Book to analyze Hezekiah's prayer (which is also printed on the Student Book page). Have students consider what the various portions of his prayer teach us about our own prayers. Remind students that God doesn't give rules about the format of prayer. He just asks us to pray in faith in Christ Jesus. However, we can look at prayers in the Bible to guide our own prayers.

Continue then by using Reproducible 37 to take a closer look at the significant message of the prophet Isaiah. His message from the Lord spoke of Jesus' birth, death, and resurrection, so it is an important message for all times. These prophecies have a special tie to the Advent season as we join the people of long ago in looking for the coming of the Savior. We see Christ's coming as it was at Christmas, as it is now as He comes to us in faith, and as He will come again on the Last Day to take us to heaven.

Note that the last two hymns discussed can be sung as recorded for *Hymn of the Season for grade 3, Advent* and *grade 6, Christmas*.

Lesson Support

Searching Further

Learn about another event in Hezekiah's life that involved troubles (a fatal illness), earnest prayer, the prophet Isaiah, and God's good answer. Emphasize God's power (triumph over disease) and forgiveness and Hezekiah's faith and acceptance of God's will. Ask the students to interpret the course of events found in 2 Kings 20:1–11.

Did God turn back time? Did the backward steps of the shadow mean that the earth was actually rotating backward on its axis? Whatever the cause, we know that the only explanation is that it was a miracle of God. He created the universe and has power over it.

What is the significance of Hezekiah being healed and going to the temple on the third day? Allow students to make connections by accepting a variety of responses through this discussion. (Also look at the "Background" section in the story of Jonah, Lesson 39.)

As an art extension, create a sundial. Research sundials on the Internet for information and for pictures of a variety of styles. When this craft project has been completed, students should take their sundials outside to see them in action. Have students look for their shadows to make a connection to the story, keeping in mind God's power and complete control over all things.

Check it Out

Research the portion of Scripture from 2 Kings 20:20–21 and the importance of the pool and tunnel that Hezekiah built for the benefit of the city. Refer to the footnotes in a study Bible in order to understand that the fresh water supply aided Jerusalem's independence. Stress the idea that King Hezekiah was a good and successful king. God blessed his reign, and the people benefited from this blessing in numerous ways. An Internet search may also provide a look into the history of aqueducts during this period. This will provide a better understanding as to just how innovative the aqueduct was for that time.

Faith in Action

Tell students to write a prayer about their troubles, asking God for help. **Boldly pray for His healing hand, for His triumph over sin and evil, for His mercy, grace, and forgiveness. Ask Him to strengthen your faith like that of King Hezekiah who believed he would be healed. Pray that His will be done and that you may understand that He always answers prayer.**

Teacher Tips

This particular lesson will involve a longer segment of time in which to read the Bible story. The teacher may choose to read a portion aloud to the class in order to move the lesson along. Use discretion to decide if the students work better reading independently, in small groups, or as a whole class. Explain portions of the story if needed. If students are working in groups, circulate the room in order to monitor their progress. By breaking down the lesson into thematic events, students are better able to understand and recall the story of Hezekiah's reign.

Reaching Every Child

Hezekiah was given a medicinal concoction containing figs, but the power of healing was from the Lord. Have students use a concordance to look up the word *fig* in the Bible and read aloud the references to this fruit as it is mentioned several times in Scripture. Look for pictures and information about figs on the Internet or in library books. For a treat, provide cookies that have a fig jelly center so students may experience a fruit that was very common in Bible times.

Ideas for the Gifted

Hezekiah seems to have been suffering from an infection of some sort. Help your students learn more about infections and the germs that cause them by using section 6.1.7, Pathogens, found in the sixth grade Health volume of the Concordia Curriculum Guide. Focus on basic health practices (such as handwashing) that can prevent infections among your students. Also discuss: How can you avoid passing germs around in your classroom? Are there any simple steps you could take (for example, having tissues readily available in the classroom)?

164

UNIT 4—COLLAPSE AND CAPTIVITY

LESSON 38

Josiah
2 Chronicles 34–35

Background

It seems incredible that the people of Josiah's time could have forgotten and lost the Scriptures. Yet, many Christians in today's society seem to have done the same thing.

Sadly, it often doesn't take long for this neglect to begin. Members of a high school youth group were recently asked to take out their cell phones. Twelve out of twelve students quickly did so. When asked to take out their Bibles, not one person had one with them. While not one of these young people would ever think of leaving home without a cell phone, not one of them carries a Bible with any regularity. The disconnection between Christians and the Scriptures is far more serious than any dropped call on a cell phone could ever be.

It is not a coincidence that Psalm 119 is found close to the center of the Bible. In verse after verse, the psalmist extols the wonder, beauty, and life that is found in God's Word. Ten times the psalmist declares the "delight" he takes in God's Word. Eleven times he states his "love" for the Word. God's Word is indeed a delight and something to be loved, for in the Word, we are "[made] wise for salvation through faith in Christ Jesus" (2 Timothy 3:15).

As you teach this lesson, show your students your own love for God's Word. If you mark passages in your Bible, explain to your students why you do this. Share verses and sections of Scripture that you frequently call to mind in times of joy, sorrow, worry, fear, and thankfulness. By the power of the Holy Spirit, lead your students to see that the Holy Scriptures are a precious gift and are given to us by God as the source of truth for all the callings He gives us in our lives.

Central Truth

God promises that those who are faithful unto death will receive His promised gift of eternal life through Jesus.

Objectives

- Know that the Law of God shows us our sinfulness and directs us to heartfelt confession and true repentance.
- Rejoice that God is eager to give us the joy of forgiveness and salvation we have in Jesus.
- Dedicate our lives now and in the future to serving God and sharing God's love with others.

Materials

- Hymnals and music CDs
- Web Resource 38a
- Reproducible 38

Bible Prep

Post in advance so students can bookmark references before class time.
- Luke 2
- 2 Chronicles 34–35

Devotions

The students of St. John Lutheran School in Norwood Young America, Minnesota, recently had an exciting opportunity to follow God's calling to share the Good News of Jesus. When the school received a large amount of money from a former student, the school board divided this money into two funds. One fund is designated to help the school with ongoing needs. The other fund is designated for mission outreach. Students, parents, and members of St. John Lutheran Church were asked to submit mission project ideas. From the list of ideas, student representatives had the privilege of selecting which projects to support.

One of the chosen projects is the Guinea Training Pastors Project from LCMS World Mission. This project is currently training five men to become pastors. These five men will serve forty-eight villages in the West African country of Guinea. The pastors will train church leaders in each village about the truths of God's Word. The leaders will then teach the people in their villages. The monetary gift the Minnesota students donated will pay for bicycles, raincoats, and boots for the five pastors. Some students were so excited about the project that they wanted to give even more.

On a world map or globe, help the students find Guinea. Ask, **What do bicycles, raincoats, and boots have to do with sharing God's Word?** (If the pastors don't have transportation and proper clothing for the weather conditions, they will have many difficulties getting to the people who need to hear about Jesus.) **There are still many people in the world who live in sin's darkness. They don't know about the light of salvation found in Jesus alone. God works in us in many different ways so that Jesus might be known by all people. Let's consider today how blessed we are to have such easy access to God's Word. Do we make use of that easy access, or do we take it for granted? How can we open God's Word to more people?**

Hold an open Bible and say, **The Messiah, King of kings, came at Christmas. Let's speak together God's Word from Luke 2 about that advent of our King.** Speak together Luke 2:1–20. Then say, **Jesus comes to us today in God's Holy Word. From that Word we can learn more about the next coming of Jesus—on the Last Day, when He will take all believers to heaven. Let's sing about that glorious advent that is still to come.** Sing "The King Shall Come" (*LSB* 348; recorded as *Hymn of the Season for grade 6, Advent*).

165

INTO the lesson

If I Were King . . .

Use this creative writing activity to help students get an idea of what it would be like to lead a country before even reaching their teen years (as Joash and Josiah did). The fact that God worked through both Joash and Josiah shows that God works in us at every age to serve Him. Encourage willing students to share their thoughts.

INTO the Word

King to King: Joash to Josiah

To get an overview of the two boy kings, read aloud their similarities and differences. Point out that even though they are often referred to as boy kings, some of their most important work was done when they were adults; it was when they were grown up that both worked to restore the temple. **Why do you think that restoring the temple was such an important task in both of the kings' reigns?** (Both Joash and Josiah were preceded by very wicked kings; during those periods the temple was neglected and fell into disrepair; during those periods it is likely there were also desecrations of the temple as idol worship was prominent.)

Then ask, **What was the major difference between the reigns of Joash and Josiah?** (Josiah remained faithful to the Lord for his entire life while Joash allowed himself to be led away from God after the death of his advisor, the priest Jehoiada.)

An interesting side point to bring up involves Manasseh, Josiah's grandfather. Manasseh was one of the most evil kings. He undid what his father, good king Hezekiah had done. Manasseh brought idols into God's temple; he killed his own sons on idol altars; and Judah become more evil than the other nations around them (2 Chronicles 33:1–9).

Amazingly, and by God's power and grace, Manasseh became a remarkably changed man. When troubles came, he humbled himself before the Lord and prayed for God's help. He removed all the idols and idol altars, and he led the people to serve the one true God (33:12–16). Manasseh's life was the opposite of Joash's because he returned to the Lord. (We could compare him to the thief on the cross who returned to the Lord at the end of his life.)

Sadly, Manasseh's son Amon was thoroughly wicked and God's Word and God's house were again neglected. This led to the reign of his son, Josiah, whose life will be explored more in the next section.

LESSON 38

Josiah

If I Were King . . .

In recent lessons, we've studied both good and bad rulers. Have you ever thought about what you would do if you were given an opportunity to be the head of a government? Here's your chance! Finish the following statement with at least three ideas: If I were king or queen of a country, I would . . .

_____
_____
_____
_____

King to King: Joash to Josiah

People sometimes confuse the two kings of Judah named Joash and Josiah because in some ways, they were similar. However, in the most important way, they were different.

Similarities
- Both were very young boys when they became king.
- Both faithfully followed God in the early years of their reign.
- Both purged idols from Judah.
- Both worked with the Levites to restore the temple.

Differences
- Josiah's reforms stretched from Judah and also into Israel.
- Josiah observed the Passover with the people, according to God's Word.
- Josiah remained faithful to God for his entire life, whereas Joash fell away from faith.
- When Josiah died, he was buried in the tombs with the other faithful kings, but Joash was not.

Review

Covenant Connection

God's Word is the only source for truth about God Himself, the Messiah, and the plan for our salvation. Jesus is God's Word made flesh (John 1:14), and for that reason, He could say, "I am the way, and the truth, and the life" (John 14:6).

A Profile of King Josiah

Work on this Bible study together. (All verses are from 2 Chronicles 34–35.) This will give an outline of the key events in Josiah's life.

As you discuss part a, ask students, **What does it mean that Josiah "did not turn aside to the right hand or to the left"?** (Josiah followed the ways of the Lord and kept his focus on God's will.) Note the significance of Josiah clearing out idols from his own country, Judah, and also from Israel. At this point in time, the Northern Kingdom had been totally conquered by the Assyrians, who captured the people of Israel, and took them as prisoners to captivity in another land. Israel was basically a "no man's land" that was devastated. Only the weak, ill, and very old might have been left behind. Therefore, it would have been easier for Josiah to send his people into the Northern Kingdom to remove the idols and altars from that area as well.

As you discuss part b, point out that this portion of the narrative is associated with the illustration in the Student Book. Ask, **Why was Josiah so upset when he heard the Law read from the Scriptures that had just been found?** (The Law made him realize how very sinful the nation was and how far they had turned from the Lord. As the nation's leader, he called to God for mercy for himself and also for his people.)

As you discuss part c, **emphasize that God gives us the Law so that we realize our sins, confess them, and repent of them. When we are humble and contrite before God,**

A Profile of King Josiah

Read the following verses and write what significant event happened in the life of King Josiah.

a. 2 Chronicles 34:1–7 — Josiah rid all of Judah and Israel of idols.

b. 2 Chronicles 34:8–21 — When the Book of the Law was found among the ruins in the temple, Josiah was terrified because he realized how far from the Lord the people had strayed. He repented to God for this sin.

c. 2 Chronicles 34:22–28 — Huldah the prophetess condemned those who continued their wicked ways, but she assured Josiah of God's forgiveness for those who do repent.

d. 2 Chronicles 34:29–33 — Josiah publicly read the Scripture (God's Law) to the people. He made a covenant with God to follow His Law; he led his people to do the same.

e. 2 Chronicles 35:1, 16–19 — Josiah showed his faithfulness to God as they kept the Passover as no other king had done since the time of Samuel.

Remember

"For by grace you have been saved through faith. And this is not your own doing; it is the gift of God, not a result of works, so that no one may boast. For we are His workmanship, created in Christ Jesus for good works, which God prepared beforehand, that we should walk in them." (Ephesians 2:8–10)

83

He is quick to offer the Gospel message of forgiveness. This was true in Josiah's time and it is true for us today. (This concept will be explored further in this lesson.)

As you discuss part d, emphasize that Josiah was a positive role model for his people, leading them by reading God's Word and (in part e) by celebrating the Feast of the Passover as it had not been celebrated since the time of Samuel. (In other words, during the whole period of the kings, the celebration had not been like this.)

As a footnote to this biblical narrative, in 2 Chronicles 35:24–25, we see that Josiah eventually was killed in a battle with the Egyptians. Included among the people mourning his death is mentioned the prophet Jeremiah, who we will hear about again in coming lessons.

INTO our lives

Law and Gospel

Say, **King Josiah loved God's Word and lived God's Word. God's Word contains two main doctrines or teachings—the Law and the Gospel.** King Josiah's reaction upon hearing God's Law is a perfect example of the Law's power to show our sins. The comforting words God gave to Josiah through Huldah the prophetess perfectly show God's grace and proclaim the Gospel message. Josiah confessed and repented his sin of not knowing God's Law. Because of God's love for him through the promised redemption of Jesus, God forgave Josiah and the people of Judah.

Use Web Resource 38a to explore this concept further. The resource distinguishes between Law and Gospel; then students are asked to identify if a statement is Law or Gospel; and it concludes with several statements from the Book of Romans (which has a thorough exploration of Law and Gospel).

Also look at the Bible verse to remember in the Student Book. This statement from Ephesians is very much a Gospel statement, but within it are reminders that we are not saved by the Law and our good works. It closes in verse 10 with a sanctification statement that shows the correct use of the Law in the life of redeemed and justified Christians—as a guide for following God's will. In our sanctified lives, we can do good works because our sins have been removed and the Holy Spirit empowers us to live as people of God. We live transformed lives. **We don't do good works in order to be saved; instead, because we are saved, we do good works.**

Good works in our sanctified lives are not a cause of, but rather a result of salvation in Christ Jesus! This is a very important concept to develop. Our justified life is about Jesus removing our sinful past and it is continued with our sanctified life, today and in the future, as we live for Him, through the power of the Holy Spirit working in us.

Conclude with Reproducible 38. Say, **King Josiah loved the Word of God and lived according to the Word of God. At the very center of our Bible is Psalm 119, which is about the Word of God. This is a constant reminder to us that God's Word should also be the center of our hearts and lives.** Explore the excerpt from Psalm 119, highlighting the various terms that are used to refer to the Word of God. (Note that in this case, the word *Law* refers to the books of Moses—God's Word in Genesis, Exodus, Leviticus, Numbers, and Deuteronomy—not just to the commandments.)

God has led you into the vocation of Christian teacher. Teaching is a demanding profession, but also one filled with many blessings. Take some time at the end of your school day today to make a list of blessings you've received as an educator. Tape the list inside a desk drawer or closet door that you frequently open to remember during those challenging days why you are a Christian teacher.

In frustrating times, remember this promise from your Heavenly Father: **For as the rain and the snow come down from heaven and do not return there but water the earth, making it bring forth and sprout, giving seed to the sower and bread to the eater, so shall My word be that goes out from My mouth; it shall not return to Me empty, but it shall accomplish that which I purpose, and shall succeed in the thing for which I sent it.** (Isaiah 55:10–11)

Technology

Before class, bookmark Internet Web sites for LCMS World Mission, Concordia Seminary-St. Louis, Concordia Theological Seminary-Ft. Wayne, and for the Concordia University System. Encourage students to find information about career opportunities as church workers as they surf these sites. As they explore information about the Concordia University System, help the students see the opportunities and advantages of being trained for non-church work careers within a Christian university.

The archives of *The Lutheran Witness* also contains several excellent articles about our seminaries, our seminarians, and our universities. Articles that can be found online include, "Pastoral Profiles: Snapshots of Service," Roland Lovstad and Sandy Wood, May, 2010, and "Learn More About the Concordias," Roland Lovstad, April, 2009. To view these articles, go to www.lcms.org, click on *The Lutheran Witness* logo, then click "search archives."

Curriculum Connection

The discovery and reading of God's Law was a turning point in Josiah's attempt to lead his people back to worshiping the Lord. It sparked repentance and a new commitment to the Lord that extended even into neighboring Israel. Explore the role of communication and technology today in spreading the Gospel. Use the ideas and activities in section 6.3.2.6, Cultural Change by Diffusion, Invention, Innovation, and Communication. You'll find it in the sixth grade Social Studies volume of the Concordia Curriculum Guide.

Searching Further

Read more about Christians in various vocations who actively share their faith through their work. Some articles to supplement this activity found in the archives of *The Lutheran Witness* include: "Sharing Individually, In Community, At School," January, 2008, by Diane Srzelecki and Roland Lovstad; "In the Public Eye," September, 2009, by Sandy Wood; and "Seeing Creation from a Spaceship Window," August, 2010, by Sandy Wood.

Reaching Every Child

"We are God's workmanship." This phrase from this lesson's Bible verse is an important one to remember as you work to reach every child in your classroom with Jesus' saving love. Look for ways that you can involve the quiet student, the new student, the lonely student, the academically challenged student so that they discover skills and talents with which God has blessed them and through which He desires to work. As you identify talents, give these students opportunities to successfully use them.

Unit 4—Collapse and Captivity Lesson 39

Jonah
The Book of Jonah

Background

It seems that God must love numbers. He is a God of order and logic. He is a being of brilliance and an intelligent designer of creation. We can look to the Old Testament and the New Testament and see the special significance of the use of certain numbers. The number *three* is noteworthy, especially in regard to the Holy Trinity, the Father, Son, and Holy Spirit. God always was, is now, and always will be. It was on the third day of creation that God made dry ground appear out of the water and the land produced seed-bearing plants and fruits. This is an early foreshadowing of the resurrection and the eternal life given through God's gift of Jesus Christ.

We see patterns of threes in Holy Week. Our vision of the crucifixion includes the three crosses on Mount Calvary. Before Jesus' death, Peter denied Him three times. On the third day following Christ's death, He rose again to new life.

We can certainly see there is significance to the three-day waiting period that Jonah experienced when he was swallowed up by a great fish and remained in its belly for three days. During that time, Jonah prayed as if "out of the belly of Sheol . . . and You heard my voice" (Jonah 2:2).

Jonah is the only Old Testament prophet to be compared to Christ. In Matthew 12:40, Jesus Himself told the Pharisees, "For just as Jonah was three days and three nights in the belly of the great fish, so the Son of Man will be three days and three nights in the heart of the earth." Jonah's incident was not just a coincidence; God used it as a preview of things to come in the life of the promised Messiah.

In spite of our shortcomings, whether as a prophet of old or a twenty-first-century teacher, the Holy Spirit empowers our lives, strengthening our faith and blessing us.

Central Truth

God wants all people to be saved and to come to the knowledge of the truth.

Objectives

- Recognize that God demands confession of our sins and repentance; and that He rejoices in offering believers the forgiveness and salvation we have in Christ Jesus.
- Understand that God commissions us to share the Good News of the Gospel with all people and all nations.
- Live a repentant life, changed and transformed, a new life as a child of God.

Materials

- Hymnals and music CDs
- Reproducible 39
- Web Resource 39a

Bible Prep

Post in advance so students can bookmark references before class time.
- Luke 2:1–20
- Jonah 1–4

Devotions

Today we will study the prophet Jonah. Other than being swallowed by a great fish, Jonah has a lot in common with each of us, especially when we are facing difficult situations. Have you ever been faced with a very tough decision, when you knew what should be done, but it was not what you wanted to do? Life is filled with tough choices. Sometimes when we make the wrong choice, we feel as though God is tapping us on our shoulder, reminding us to go back and make the right choice. If you feel sometimes like your conscience is bothering you, God may be trying to teach you something.

When we don't do what is right, one bad decision can turn into a series of unfortunate events. One poor choice then becomes a serious mistake. One mistake can then turn into another mistake, and things may spiral out of control. Then our world feels like it has just collapsed, and we feel like we have become captives of our own bad decisions. That's how Jonah felt—his bad decision led to a downward spiral of troubles until he was at his lowest point, captive, and pleading to God for help.

We, too, may be at our lowest point when we call upon the Lord for help and forgiveness. Even when we are submerged in a sea of trouble, tossed about by waves of sin and darkness, and sinking to the bottom of an ocean of problems, God can come to our rescue. He can prevent us from being swallowed up by a whale of despair. No one likes to feel like they are all alone with their troubles, sitting next to a rotting pile of big mistakes. There is forgiveness and salvation, but we need to confess our wrongdoings, which might involve admitting our mistakes to other people in addition to praying to God for forgiveness. He can provide a way out of our mess. How can we avoid or at least cope with many of our troubles? Listen to His voice. God speaks to us in His Word. He says, "I, the Lord your God, hold your right hand; it is I who says to you, 'Fear not, I am the one who helps you' " (Isaiah 41:13). Point out that this picture of God leading us by the hand is very similar to the image of Jesus guiding us as the Good Shepherd. Sing about it in the hymn "The King of Love My Shepherd Is" (*LSB* 709; recorded as *Hymn of the Month for grade 6, December*). As you say together Luke 2:1–20, think about the shepherds who worshiped the Baby born in Bethlehem who is the Good Shepherd of all.

169

INTO the lesson

Where Is God?

Point in opposite directions as you introduce today's Bible narrative by saying, **In today's Bible lesson we will hear about the prophet Jonah. God told Jonah to go to Ninevah, but Jonah didn't want to do that. So he went in the opposite direction, taking a ship to Tarshish. Why was it not a very smart thing to try to run away from God?** (God is everywhere; you can't run away from Him.) To indicate this, have students look in their books at the arrow pointing left and ask, **Is God to the left of us?** Have them draw a symbol there of God (such as a cross, a heart with a cross on it, a triangle, or three interlocking circles on a triangle). Then have students look at the arrow pointing to the right. **Is God to the right of us?** Have them draw a symbol of God to the right; and then also draw the symbol in the center because God is right here with us in the middle of things. Say, **What was Jonah thinking? He must have been crazy to think he could hide from God! On the other hand, what are we thinking when we ignore God, when we think He doesn't see or care about the wrong things we do, when we act as if God is far, far away instead of right here with us. What are we thinking!? As we look further into Jonah's story, keep in mind how very much we are just like him (minus the whole fish-swallowing thing!).**

LESSON 39

Jonah

Where Is God?

← OVER THERE?   OVER THERE? →

Details of a Dilemma

Directions: Tell what happened in the four parts of Jonah's story

Chapter 1: A Bad Decision
Tell about God's request. Jonah heads the other direction on a ship; a terrible storm comes up; and when he is tossed into the sea, the storm stops.

Chapter 2: A Time to Think
Tell about Jonah being swallowed by a fish. For three days he prays, and then the fish spits him out onto dry land.

Chapter 3: A Hostile Helper
Tell about Jonah now doing what God commands; the reaction of the people; and look ahead to chapter 4:1–2 to see Jonah's reaction.

Chapter 4: An Attitude Check
Tell about Jonah pouting; the plant shading him and then dying; and how God used the plant to teach Jonah a lesson.

Review

Covenant Connection
Jesus Himself made a connection with the Old Testament story of Jonah. Jesus noted that Jonah, in the belly of the fish for three days, was a foreshadowing, or preview, of Jesus being buried for three days in the tomb. This is called "the sign of Jonah." Jesus said, "For just as Jonah was three days and three nights in the belly of the great fish, so will the Son of Man be three days and three nights in the heart of the earth" (Matthew 12:40). And in verse 41, Jesus added, "And behold, something greater than Jonah is here." Jesus would arise on the third day, defeating death, and winning life eternal for us!

84

INTO the Word

Details of a Dilemma

Consider working in small groups on this Student Book activity. If possible, have two or even three separate groups for each oval section. In the groups, students will read aloud the chapter assigned from the Book of Jonah and then tell in their own words what happened, writing the shared information in their assigned section. Then meet together and have the groups read their summaries. Listen to every group that had the same chapter to see differences in perspective or differences in choices of facts presented. After all reports on a single chapter are made, allow two minutes for other group members to write down what they learned. Continue in this way with all four chapters.

Discuss, **Why do you think Jonah was so opposed to preaching repentance to Ninevah?** (Ninevah was the enemy of his country. Ninevah was the capital of Assyria which at that time was the most powerful nation in that part of the world. The Assyrians had been ruthless in starting wars, stealing money, and capturing people as slaves. Jonah had no compassion for these evil people and probably felt any punishment they received was their due.) **In what ways did God show His power over His creation?** (The storm stopped as soon as Jonah was thrown into the sea—the waters obeyed God's will. Also, the fish followed God's timing and commands.)

Even though the fish story "gets the most publicity," chapter four is probably the most significant part of the story. Point out that in verse 2, Jonah is actually angry at God for being kind and caring. **Listen to Jonah's words as he angrily accuses God of being** who He is: "I knew that You are a gracious God and merciful, slow to anger and abounding in steadfast love." It is almost laughable that he used those words to *complain* about God. Have you ever heard before those words that Jonah said? He was quoting exactly from Psalm 145:8. (See today's Bible words to remember.)

The final message to Jonah and to us is that God loves and cares for all people. He wants all people to be saved. Jonah felt sorry for the plant, which God created. By comparison, God said, "Should not I pity Nineveh" where 120,000 people, whom God created, needed the message of God's forgiveness. **As Jesus centuries later stated, He did not come to save the self-**

170

righteous who didn't think they needed Him to be saved, He came for the lost, the sick, the sinners, for all who repent and believe in Him.

Diary of a Fish Dweller

Encourage students to be creative and have some fun with this section. You may want to give guidance to the class, providing these statement starters to help motivate their thought processes. Pause after each starter statement, allowing time for students to write their responses.

Day 1: What a storm! I can't believe I've been swallowed up by a fish. I feel . . .

Dear Lord, forgive me for running away. Please help me to . . .

Day 2: Today is my second day in the whale's belly, and there is seaweed everywhere! I wonder . . .

Dear Lord, I am in great despair. Will I ever get out of . . .

Day 3: I feel my life is ebbing away. I am so hungry that I could eat . . .

Dear God, I vow to make good on Your command. I promise to . . .

When the work is finished, allow students to share their ideas with the class. Then return to Jonah 2:2–9 to read exactly what Jonah did say. Select seven readers, asking them to read their verses very dramatically. Most likely Jonah was earnestly pleading with God to get him out of there!

INTO our lives

One Step Forward, Two Steps Back

Jonah made some wrong decisions, which took him farther away from God, not in location (for God is everywhere), but rather away from God's will. Illustrate how this can happen in people's lives today by having the group try "One Step Forward, Two Steps Back." Place a Bible in a prominent place in the classroom and have the students face it. Allow space for them to take steps forward and backward as you have volunteers read the situations on Reproducible 39. Students should listen and decide if the character made the right decision or the wrong decision. If they believe the character made the right decision, they should take one step forward. If they believe the character made the wrong decision, they should take two steps backward. Lead the students to understand that **God does not move away from His people, but people often move away from God. Bad decisions can separate us from God, taking us further away from Him. By distancing ourselves from the Lord, it becomes harder to hear His voice and know what He wants us to do in life.** A discussion may ensue about what the characters should have done instead.

Conclude your lesson with Web Resource 39a, which guides a discussion on several interesting relationships and connections between people in the Bible.

Curriculum Connection

God used unwilling Jonah to bring about a major change in the Ninevite society. God continues to use people to bring about change today. Explore this topic with your students using section 6.3.2.8, Ideas That Promote Change. You can find it in the sixth grade Social Studies volume of the Concordia Curriculum Guide series.

You may want to check with the fifth-grade teacher at your school to see if the skit in the Appendix of the fifth-grade Performing Arts volume of the Concordia Curriculum Guide series was used last year with the class you have now. If this was not used, don't pass up the opportunity to have your class act out this play about Jonah, which focuses mostly on Jonah 4.

This is a serious story, but it does lend itself to some interesting visuals. Let students enjoy drawing a picture of Jonah crawling onto the beach covered in seaweed. (Jonah 2:5 says, "Weeds were wrapped about my head.") It might be fun to draw a starfish attached to his tattered robe or a crab pinching one of Jonah's toes.

Another artistic approach is creative drama. Form groups of three or four students to create an eyewitness account, acting as if they are the inhabitants of the city of Nineveh and Jonah has just approached them. Encourage them to react to Jonah's appearance along with his message to repent. Assign one group to be the king and the royal court of Nineveh. This group should use Jonah 3:7–9 to issue the king's proclamation.

HANDS TO SERVE

Celebrate Jonah Day! Be creative with a box of fish crackers, blueberry yogurt, and larger, round crackers. Students can celebrate Jonah Day by preparing a "pool" for the fish. Spread the blueberry yogurt on the round crackers and top with a fish cracker. Create snack plates for the other grades and plan a delivery of a tray of treats along with a variation of this message: "Our classroom has just finished a study of Jonah. We wish to share this Jonah Day snack with you. Remember that even though God provided a great fish to swallow Jonah up, God was forgiving and rescued Jonah so he could continue to preach the good news of God's mercy and grace."

Technology

Use BibleGateway.com to do a keyword search for the number *3*, where students will find over three hundred matches. Have students take special note of the significant way in which the number *3* is used in the passage of time, along with the appearance of men and angels. Have them make connections to the resurrection and the Old Testament prophecies. As they view passages from the books of the Old Testament, have them cross-reference verses from the New Testament that refer to the destroying of the temple in three days. Have them make inferences as to what this means. Follow up this activity with a Google search of the Grammy Award-winning Christian rock band Third Day.

Working in Groups

Encourage class discussion by asking these "What if . . . ?" scenarios:

What if Jonah had not boarded a ship to run away, but instead set out on land to another city?

What if God had not sent a great storm to stop Jonah?

What if the sailors had not been afraid of the Lord?

What if the sailors had not thrown Jonah overboard?

What if the sea had not grown calm after the sailors threw Jonah overboard?

What if Jonah had not been swallowed up by a fish?

What if Jonah had only been inside the great fish for one day instead of three?

What if Jonah still did not go to Nineveh after his three-day ordeal in the belly of the whale?

What if Jonah had gone to the city of Nineveh immediately upon God's request?

Encourage students to think of additional "What if . . . ?" scenarios. Help them understand that because Jonah fled from his mission, he created bigger problems for himself and others. Allow them to make the conclusion that out of something bad, something good came about. God allowed Jonah and the sailors to suffer during the storm so that they would have greater respect for the Lord and come to believe in His might and power. God also provided an opportunity to show the sailors the need for repentance. The sailors made vows to God and realized that He was in control and deserved sacrifice and worship

Unit 4—Collapse and Captivity

Lesson 40

Jeremiah
The Book of Jeremiah

Background

We've made his name into a word: *jeremiad*. It refers to a long, mournful lament or complaint. It characterizes Jeremiah's message perfectly. This "weeping prophet" could not have been called at a darker time in the nation's history. Into this milieu Jeremiah plunged, headlong, perhaps as young as a teenager. (See Jeremiah 1:6.) From a human point of view, he was destined for failure. The common people mostly ignored him. Priests and false prophets hated him. Kings persecuted him. People from his hometown plotted his murder! Later in his career, Jeremiah would watch as the Babylonian army dragged most of Judah's defeated inhabitants into a captivity that would last seventy years, just as he had predicted, from the word of the Lord.

Why? What purpose did Jeremiah's ministry and Judah's misery in captivity serve? In it all, judgment fell for the sake of the Gospel. The plan of salvation that the Lord had announced to Adam and Eve in Eden, to Abraham and Sarah in Canaan, to David in Jerusalem—that plan would not fail. For our sake, it could not fail! The Savior would be born from the descendents of Abraham. He would be the "Lion of the Tribe of Judah," just as God had promised (Genesis 49:9, Revelation 5:5).

But for that to happen, idolatry and rebellion had to be purged from the nation. Repentance and faith had to be reignited. The task of keeping that spark alive—albeit with green wood and damp kindling—fell to Jeremiah. And in God's timing (seventy years), a faithful remnant would return, cleansed of idolatry.

Central Truth

Sin is serious; God is patient, but He is also just and holy and must punish sin; Jesus suffered our punishment on the cross.

Objectives

- Confess that God calls all to repentance through His Word; the unrepentant will be punished at the time God chooses.
- Rejoice that God calls all to repentance through His Word; through faith in Christ Jesus, the repentant receive the blessings of salvation.
- Live a life of repentance, in faith, empowered by the Holy Spirit, looking for the second coming of the Messiah.

Materials

- Hymnals and music CDs
- Reproducible 40
- Web Resource 40a
- Web Resource 40b

Bible Prep

Post in advance so students can bookmark references before class time.
- The Book of Jeremiah
- 2 Chronicles 36
- Lamentations 3:22–2

Devotions

Back in 2009, a student at the University of Alberta in Canada decided to wear the same pair of jeans for fifteen months without washing them! He wanted to know how much bacteria would grow in the creases. Would it pose a health risk? After almost seven months, the jeans began to stink so bad that the student couldn't stand it. Unwilling to give up on his experiment, he began tossing them into the freezer overnight. Almost magically, the cold killed the stench.

What kills the stench of sin? You don't think sin stinks? Then listen to what God told the prophet Jeremiah about Judah's idolatry: "They have polluted My land with the carcasses of their detestable idols, and have filled My inheritance with their abominations" (Jeremiah 16:18). We don't often think of sin as being that serious—a complete mess of stinking junk. But Judah's idols offended our holy God!

What if Jeremiah peeked into our lives today? What would he see? Would he catch us forgetting about God? Would he catch us living as though God didn't matter and as if *we* mattered most? It's likely! And it's dangerous. We won't get by with a thing! God is patient, but He is also holy and just. He must punish sin.

No freezer on earth is cold enough to stop the stench of our sin. The only cure is the cross of our Savior. In His cross, all our sins—our cursing, our hatred, our cheating, our selfishness, our unkindness, and all the rest, *all* of it—are washed clean. Let's pray: Thank You, Lord Jesus! You forgive my sins so I can receive God's blessing. Show me the changes You want me to make. Then work those changes in me through true repentance. Let my life honor You, Lord. Amen.

Sing "God of Grace and God of Glory" (*LSB* 850; recorded as *Hymn of the Month for grade 6, November*).

INTO the lesson

Warning by Warning

As you work through the opening Student Book discussion ask, **How dangerous was Judah's condition?** (The people not only continued to sin, they arrogantly ignored Jeremiah's predictions, which as he always announced, were the words of the Lord. Jeremiah gave them exact details about who would conquer them, what exact devastation would take place, and how long the captivity would last. Even with such details presented, the people just laughed at Jeremiah or tried to get rid of him so they wouldn't have to listen to him. They seemed to feel that the temple was almost like a "good luck charm," as if the presence of the temple would keep them safe.) Also ask, **How dangerous is *our* nation's condition today?** (Point out that too many people consider that the name "Christian" makes them safe, or that sitting in a church makes them saved. Too many people do not see the need to recognize and confess their sins. Too many people do not understand that a repentant life means a changed life, living not for what we want, but rather, according to God's will as He enables us in Christ Jesus.)

INTO the Word

Pay Attention!

Emphasize that the people of Judah refused to pay attention to Jeremiah, so, as suggested by the Lord, he began to do unusual things to capture their attention and to make it difficult to avoid hearing his message. Use Web Resource 40a for visuals related to the techniques Jeremiah used. (Though Scripture references are listed, you can summarize each of these events.)

Emphasize the last sentence of this section. Note that this is a common reaction even of people today. No one likes to be told they have done wrong; people don't like to hear about laws and rules and disobedience. People like to justify themselves and blame others. Very often, the person they blame or attack is the one who accuses them and requires consequences or a punishment. Ask, **Have you ever thought your parents were mean when they took away a privilege because you did something wrong? Who is the guilty person in that situation? Who deserves punishment? Who needs to admit they were wrong and try to change their actions and attitude? Or did you ever get mad at a teacher who took away your recess or gave you a detention because you disobeyed a rule? Whose fault was it? How can you avoid detentions? Who is in authority? You or your parents and your teachers (whom God has placed in positions of authority and responsibility)? This is not a simple matter. When we try to be the authority of our own lives, we are rejecting the authority of God to rule in us! That is a serious matter! What can make a difference? Repentance—sorrow over sin, faith in forgiveness, and life dedicated to the Lord.**

Reactions

As Jeremiah escalated his warnings, the people escalated the arrogance and violence of their reactions. Read about the two unique situations that are pictured in the Student Book. The king was openly defying God's Word, which God gave to Jeremiah, who dictated the words to his assistant, Baruch. The king desecrated God's Holy Word by tearing it into strips and showed he didn't care what God said as he had those strips burned in a fire. It is important to note that, as God promises, His Word will endure. After this, Jeremiah had Baruch write down God's message once again, adding that the king's actions would not stop the punishment of the Lord through the Babylonians.

In Jeremiah 36:15 and 23–24, we see two different reactions to the reading of God's Word. Ask students, **If you were one of the many impenitent people in Judah, what would you have thought when you heard**

LESSON 40
Jeremiah

Warning by Warning

The prophet Jeremiah was one of the many people who mourned the death of good King Josiah. He found he had even more reason to mourn when the people of Judah went back to worshiping idols. (Jeremiah was known as "the weeping prophet.") He served God as a prophet, warning the people of their sins and of the coming punishment; and he saw this judgment take place when the Babylonian armies invaded and devastated their territory. In a series of raids, the Babylonians would soon carry off Judah's wealth. They would also take all the leaders, all the educated people, and all the rich people into captivity. Everyone except the poorest and the weakest was exiled to live in Babylon. The enemy, King Nebuchadnezzar, would burn Jerusalem, tear down the city walls, and demolish the temple.

Before all this happened, though, Jeremiah warned the people. God wanted to show them mercy if they would just repent. Yet God would not put up with the terrible sins His people were committing. What three responses did the people give to Jeremiah's warnings in 2 Chronicles 36:15–16? __They kept mocking God's messengers, despising His words, and scoffing at His prophets.__

Pay Attention!

In Jeremiah 18:18, the people said, "Come, let us make plots against Jeremiah . . . And let us not pay attention to any of his words." So Jeremiah began to do unusual things to get people to pay attention.

Jeremiah made a wooden yoke like the ones oxen wore to pull a wagon. He put it on his own neck and walked among the people, warning that they would wear the yoke (or bear the burden) of slavery, serving the Babylonian king, Nebuchadnezzar (Jeremiah 27:1–2, 4, 8).

Another time, Jeremiah took clay pots and threw them down before the people, shattering the pots to pieces. Similarly, the Lord would break the people of Judah and the city of Jerusalem into pieces that could never be mended (Jeremiah 19:1–2, 10–12).

Jeremiah stood in the courtyard of the temple, shouting to people passing by that unless they repented, God would destroy the temple (Jeremiah 26:1–8). After that, Jeremiah was not allowed to go into the temple again. (Instead of blaming themselves for their own sins, the people blamed their accuser.)

Review

Covenant Connection

Much of the prophet Jeremiah's message was harsh and sad. On the whole, Judah would not repent and believe. God's judgment would fall. But after 70 years of exile in Babylon, God would bring a cleansed and restored people back home, and the Messiah would come at God's appointed time. Jeremiah 23:5–6 tells about this. We often read and think about this passage during Advent. Can you see why?

86

174

Reactions

Jeremiah 36:1–4, 21–23, 27–28

Jeremiah 38:4–13

Discuss what is happening in each of these illustrations. What was the result of these unheeded warnings? (See 2 Chronicles 36:16–20.) **As God had said, the Babylonians killed or captured the people and destroyed the walls, buildings, and the temple.**

Not without Hope

As bad as things were, God still offered hope to those who remained faithful and to those who would come to repentance. Jeremiah spoke the word of the Lord that the captivity would last 70 years. Then, a faithful remnant would return to Judah, and from this remnant would come the promised Messiah.

What great promise did God give in Jeremiah 29:11 that is also an important promise for you and me? **God has good plans for His people to give them a hope and a future.**

In Jeremiah 31:10–14, God promises that His people will be gathered together again, rejoicing in the comfort and blessings of the Lord. And in that same chapter, God gives His people, including you and me, the most important promise of all. Read verses 33–34, and write what that promise is. **God said, "I will forgive their iniquity, and I will remember their sin no more."**

How can you be sure that those promises are for you? **Jesus did all things for our salvation; we are made people of God by grace, in faith, through His unfailing power and mercy.**

Remember

"The steadfast **love** of the LORD never **ceases**; His mercies never come to an **end**; they are new every **morning**; great is Your **faithfulness**." (Lamentations 3:22–23)

INTO our lives

Not without Hope

Emphasize that the purpose for all of God's actions was to lead the people back to Him in faith. So along with all the messages of warning and destruction, God continued to offer hope to those who were faithful. **These promises of God are also meant for us. The forgiveness the Messiah would obtain for the faithful in Judah is the forgiveness the Messiah has obtained for the faithful in the twenty-first century!**

As you talk about the believing people in Jeremiah's time, stress the fact that they longed for and waited for the Messiah whom God had promised to send. They must have wondered about whether God really would keep His promises, especially after they were herded off to captivity in Babylon. But they continued to wait in hope; we, too, can remember that as we wait for Jesus to come again to take us to heaven. Advent reminds us that God kept His promise to send Christ the first time and helps us focus on Christ's promised return in glory.

Note: As you look at the words of hope in the Bible words to remember, point out that the book of Lamentations was also written by Jeremiah.

The hope in Jeremiah 31:10–14 is the basis for the song "Listen! You Nations of the World" (*AGPS* 164). Use Web Resource 40b as you join in singing this song.

---

about this incident? What would you have felt? If you were one of the few repentant believers in Judah, what would you have thought? felt?

In the second incident, enemies hoped to kill Jeremiah by dropping him into the muddy mire of an empty well. The significant part of this event is that the prophet was rescued by an Ethiopian man from Africa who worked in the king's house. It was dangerous for him to rescue Jeremiah because he would be defying a dangerous mob, and even more dangerous, he courageously brought this matter up to the king himself. This man, Ebed-melech, was risking his job and also his life.

Point out that **God had been patient and for many years had tried to bring His people to repentance, but now, as the Bible states, the king "stiffened his neck" and "hardened his heart." God saw that there was no remedy. He took action. Only by bringing the people to their knees in despair would they return to the Lord for help.** Read aloud together the result in 2 Chronicles 36. By taking impenitent Judah into exile, the Lord brought about sorrow, contrition, and repentance. Seventy years later, He brought a remnant (a small group) of them home again, purified and eager for good works. Jesus, our Savior, was born into this nation, this family of believers. Not all of the people in Jesus' time were faithful, of course. (The scribes and Pharisees were two large groups of mostly self-righteous unbelievers.) But the worship of Canaan's gods was gone, the temple had been rebuilt, and worship in the temple—particularly the sacrifices—once again pointed to God's promised Messiah. We care about this because Jesus is our Messiah and Savior too!

Lesson Support

Celebrating GROWTH

Jeremiah 1 describes the day God called Jeremiah to serve Him and His people. It indicates that the prophet was young; some scholars think he may have been only a teenager.

Ask students to think and write or tell about a time God used them in an ordinary or a special way. Was it fun or hard—or both? Why does the Lord use sinners like us to accomplish His purposes on earth? (He does so in grace toward us, His forgiven children in Jesus. He also does so in grace toward those who need our help.)

Curriculum Connection

Jeremiah is sometimes called the weeping prophet because the message he brought from the Lord was almost completely bad news. God's unrepentant people would go into captivity and their land would be desolate. Consider using section 6.4.2.2, Tone, Mood, and Emotion Conveyed in Oral Communication, found in the sixth grade Language Arts volume of the Concordia Curriculum Guide. Working through the activities there will help your students learn more about how speakers convey mood and emotion in a variety of situations.

Critical thinking

The key factor in the Book of Jeremiah is the Word of God. Jeremiah listened to and then repeated the word of the Lord. Baruch wrote it down; Jehoiakim tore it up; and Baruch wrote it down again. The Book of Jeremiah is filled with phrases like "the word of the Lord came to me saying" or "hear the word of the Lord" or "so declares the Lord." Explore this by assigning one chapter of Jeremiah to each student. Tell them to quickly scan their chapter and highlight any similar references to God's Word. Then let students report on their findings. If they are still interested at this point, there are enough chapters in the book that you can probably assign a second chapter to scan, highlight, and share. Continue with the discussion about the Word of God that is on Reproducible 40. Option: *What happened to Baruch, Jeremiah's assistant?* Have your students work as teams of detectives to find the answer to this question. The Book of Jeremiah itself gives some clues. Encourage students to find out what they can and report back to the class.

Music Connection

Look at several Advent and Christmas hymns that relate to this message. The people of Judah would indeed go into captivity. (Explain that *captivity* means being captured and taken prisoner.) The people would indeed go into exile. (Explain that exile is being forced from your own home to live elsewhere, and usually under servile or at least unpleasant conditions.) Look at stanza 1 of "O Come, O Come, Emmanuel" (*LSB* 357), which speaks of these key words. Today as we look for the Savior's second coming, we sing of captivity to sin and exile on earth, away from our heavenly home. These thoughts of salvation and our heavenly home continue in stanzas 4 and 5, which also refer to the Messiah as a branch on the family tree of Jesse and his son David. Similar concepts can be found in "Lo, How a Rose E'er Blooming" (*LSB* 359). (If you choose to sing these hymns, they are found in the *Hymns of the Season* CD collection for Advent and Christmas.)

In one way, Jeremiah's ministry failed. The people of Judah did not repent. Babylon attacked Judah in three invasion waves. All but the poorest people were taken to live five hundred miles away. Yet, God did not give up on His people or His promise. The faithful people remembered Jeremiah's words and kept looking toward the coming Messiah. Advent and Christmas remind us that the Messiah came. Advent and Christmas also remind us that Jesus, the Messiah, will come again to take us to live with Him in joy and glory forever! We live in repentant faith, looking forward to that day!

UNIT 4—COLLAPSE AND CAPTIVITY

LESSON 41

Daniel and His Friends

DANIEL 1

Background

Babylon was a rising power in the Fertile Crescent in the seventh century BC. Nineveh, the Assyrian capital, fell to the Babylonians in 612, and the Assyrians fell back toward northern Syria. In 605, Nebuchadnezzar of Babylon defeated Pharaoh Neco at Carchemish and advanced southward to the coastal plain of Philistia.

King Jehoiakim spared Judah from attack during this campaign by pledging himself as a vassal to Nebuchadnezzar. But in 601, Jehoiakim rebelled, and Nebuchadnezzar ordered and attacked Judah. Late in 598, Nebuchadnezzar besieged Jerusalem. The campaign was swiftly concluded; Jehoiachin, son of Jehoiakim, surrendered the city to Nebuchadnezzar in 597. Jehoiachin and other government officials were deported to Babylon.

In 589, Zedekiah, Judah's last king, rebelled against Nebuchadnezzar. Early the next year the Babylonian army returned to Jerusalem. Nebuchadnezzar sealed off Jerusalem with siege works and devastated the surrounding countryside. The Book of Lamentations gives a vivid picture of the horrors of life in Jerusalem: "How lonely sits the city that was full of people!" (Lamentations 1:1) . . . "All her people groan as they search for bread; they trade their treasures for food to revive their strength." (1:11) . . . "Happier were the victims of the sword than the victims of hunger, who wasted away, pierced by lack of the fruits of the field." (4:9) The next lessons will look at the life of several of the Judeans living in exile, who were blessed by God for their faithfulness to Him.

Central Truth

God is active throughout history, guiding and caring for His people.

Objectives

- Know that God warns patiently about disobedience and does punish the unrepentant.
- Believe that though faithful believers suffer the consequences of living in a sin-filled world, God is with us and blesses us, even in the midst of difficulties.
- Pray that our faithful God will lead us to be faithful to Him.

Materials

- Hymnals and music CDs
- Web Resource 41a
- Reproducible 41

Bible Prep

Post in advance so students can bookmark references before class time.
- Luke 2:1–20
- Daniel 1
- Jeremiah 24:6–7

Devotions

How do you handle waiting? Are you patient, or do you get frustrated easily? Do you focus on what you are waiting for, or do you get distracted and lose interest?

Tom and Jason were both waiting. Their father had promised to take them to the movies to see the new science fiction epic after he came home from work. It was still early afternoon, and the boys had hours to wait. And waiting was so hard. Tom slouched on the couch as he flipped through the television channels for the third time. "There's nothing on but soap operas and talk shows," he groaned, turning off the television. "And it's only been an hour since lunch. I think the clock has stopped."

"I know," said Jason. "But I'm really looking forward to the movie. Dad will come, just like he promised." Jason looked around the messy family room. "I think I'll get busy and clean up this room while we wait—maybe even reorganize the DVD collection." "Whatever," mumbled Tom as he drifted toward the door. "I'm going out. Who knows? Dad might not even come." "Not come?" thought Jason. "Of course he'll come. And when I finish cleaning up the family room, I'll make myself a sandwich to eat before we go to the movies."

God promised Adam and Eve that He would send a Savior. For thousands of years people waited for the Savior to come. Some waited patiently, believing God would keep His promise. Others got tired of waiting and turned to other gods. Finally God kept His promise and sent His own Son, Jesus, to save all people who believed in Him from sin, death, and the power of the devil. We are waiting too—waiting for Jesus to come again to take us to be with Him in heaven. While we wait, we are busy doing God's work here on earth—helping the poor and needy, being a friend to the lonely, bringing a smile to the sick and the sad, and telling the Good News about Jesus our Savior to everyone we know.

Sing several Advent songs, especially "The King Shall Come" (*LSB* 348; recorded on *Hymns of the Season, grade 6, Advent*). Point out the tone of yearning, waiting, and watching that fills the words and music of so many Advent hymns. What were people yearning for in Old Testament times? Speak together Luke 2:1–20 to hear about the first coming of the Messiah. We yearn today for His second coming and the eternal life in heaven He has won for us.

INTO the lesson

God's Promised Punishment and Mercy

Our modern culture often portrays God as a kindly grandfather who looks the other way when we disobey His rules. The Bible—particularly the Old Testament—is full of evidence that God is a God of justice. He does not tolerate sin, and He carries through on the punishment He has promised. Point out that Judah was devastated. A land that once had about 200,000 people was reduced by wars, disease, and famine. The Babylonians deported only the educated, wealthy, healthy, and strong, which was about 20,000 people. The few who were weak, sick, old, or had disabilities were left behind to fend for themselves.

God is a just God, but He is also a God of mercy. In His mercy, God provided for the people of Judah who were taken into exile in Babylon. When the people of Israel were taken into exile by Assyria in 721 BC, they were scattered throughout the vast Assyrian empire, where they vanished from history. By contrast, God directed matters so that the Babylonian officials settled the captured people of Judah in Babylon itself, mostly in villages and towns along the Chebar River (actually an irrigation canal), ensuring the survival of the Jewish people. In addition to being allowed to live together in communities, the Jewish exiles were allowed to farm and engage in other useful work. God's mercy to His exiled people included the promise that, at the end of seventy years, "I will . . . gather you from all the nations and all the places where I have driven you . . . and I will bring you back to the place from which I sent you into exile (Jeremiah 29:14).

As the exiles waited with hope for God to keep His promise to return home, so believers waited for God to send the Savior He had promised. This promise was fulfilled in the birth, life, death, and resurrection of Jesus Christ. We recall this time of waiting as we celebrate Advent. With your students, discuss ways in which we can make this time of waiting more meaningful during this Advent season (special devotions, Advent wreath, service projects in the congregation and community).

Lesson 41
Daniel and His Friends

God's Promised Punishment and Mercy

Finally the time for punishment had come. In a series of deportations, about 20,000 people of Judah were exiled; but God did not forget His chosen people in far-off Babylon. The Lord gave His special promise to the faithful (see Jeremiah 24:6–7). Today we look at four of these exiled people who were blessed by God for their faithfulness to His will.

The Résumé of Four Friends

Personal Background
- Born in Judea.
- Follower of the true God.
- Relocated to Babylon in 605 BC, along with many members of the royal family and other nobility.
- Endowed by God with good appearance, wisdom, skills, and understanding.

Education
- Chosen for special training in the language and literature of the Chaldeans.
- Entered three-year course of study.
- The classmates Daniel, Hananiah, Mishael, and Azariah were given the Babylonian names Belteshazzar, Shadrach, Meshach, and Abednego.

Review

God used the Babylonian captivity to transform His people, to bring them to contrition and repentance and to a renewed faithfulness to God and His Word. And as He said, God would return the faithful to the land of Judah after 70 years; they would be a changed people who never again reverted to idol worship. These were part of the preparations, getting Judah and the people of Judah ready for the coming of the Messiah, Christ Jesus.

INTO the Word

The Résumé of Four Friends

Be sure to explain the term *résumé* and how to pronounce it (with the emphasis on the first syllable, noting that the first *e* has a short *e* sound, and the final *e* sounds like a long *a*). Explain that a résumé gives a person's background, including his or her personal, educational, and employment history. This is an interesting way of looking at Daniel and his friends.

Also explain that in Babylon at that time, most written materials were written on clay tablets, not paper. The clay of a tablet would be moistened and the characters etched using a stylus (a type of pointed stick). Later, the tablet could be "erased" by moistening the clay and smoothing out the etchings; or, if a permanent record of the information was wanted, the clay would be baked in a kiln, making the tablet as hard as pottery or stone. You may want to search the Internet for photos of ancient tablets retrieved from archaeological digs. Also see Web Resource 41a.

Help your students read the account from their Bibles in Daniel 1. Then focus on each point of Daniel's résumé, discussing the ways in which God showed His mercy to Daniel and his friends.

Conditions of Service

- Trainees to receive the same food and wine served to the king.
- The food and wine were refused because they conflicted with Jewish dietary laws; even worse, the king's food and wine usually were part of a sacrifice or offering to an idol god.
- Ten-day trial period agreed upon during which Daniel and his friends would consume only vegetables and water.
- God blessed the young men of Judah with greater health and strength than the other students, who consumed the king's food and wine.
- God blessed the young men of Judah with learning and skill in literature and more.

Present Employment

- After completing their studies, they were named advisors to King Nebuchadnezzar or governors of his provinces.
- By God's grace and favor, they were rated ten times higher in wisdom and understanding than all the magicians and enchanters in Nebuchadnezzar's kingdom.

God Blesses His People

God calls us, as His justified and sanctified people, to put Him and His will first in our lives; He will take care of the rest. As Jesus stated in the Sermon on the Mount, "Therefore do not be anxious, saying, 'What shall we eat?' or 'What shall we drink?' or 'What shall we wear?' . . . But seek first the kingdom of God and His righteousness, and all these things will be added to you" (Matthew 6:31, 33).

Remember

"For I know the plans I have for you, declares the LORD, plans for welfare and not for evil, to give you a future and a hope."
(Jeremiah 29:11)

INTO our lives

God Blesses His People

After reading the statement in the Student Book, continue with Reproducible 41. Discuss how God has blessed each of us in the areas of personal background, education, and service experience. Encourage students to think about God's blessings in their future plans. Daniel and his friends didn't sit idly and wait for the seventy-year exile to end. They understood that they were "blessed to be a blessing." How will your students use the blessings God has given them to be a blessing to their family, their community, and their world?

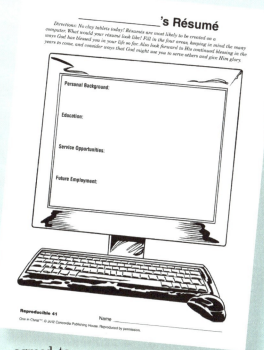

Personal Background: Daniel and his three friends were born in Judah, members of God's chosen people and of the tribe from which the promised Savior would come. They were followers of God, and their faith in God was strong enough to keep them from following the ways of the Babylonian court. They had been relocated to Babylon along with other members of the Jewish aristocracy. God had blessed them with pleasant appearance, wisdom, and understanding that were apparent even to their Babylonian captors. Why were these young men a part of the punishment through exile? We will see that God had a purpose for their lives and for His people.

Education: God blessed Daniel and his three friends, Hananiah, Mishael, and Azariah, by giving them the opportunity for three years of special training in Babylonian language and literature. Their education probably also included mathematics and astronomy and maybe even natural history and architecture, which were commonly studied by the very educated. These young men were "blessed to be a blessing" and would speak for God to Nebuchadnezzar and his court. We can see from this section that they were willing to immerse themselves in the culture of Babylon, and they were even willing to adopt Babylonian names. However, they refused to accept the gods and religions of Babylon, as we will see in the next section.

Conditions of Service: When Daniel and his friends were offered food and wine from the king's table, God gave Daniel the courage to refuse food that was not in keeping with the Jewish dietary laws. An even greater problem with the food from the king's table was that it was usually presented first before their idol gods. These four young men took a stand, refusing to accept something that was in defiance of the true God. The chief eunuch agreed to give the men only vegetables and water for ten days. (Note that commentators say that "vegetables" would include growing plants like wheat and other grains, from which bread and the like would be made.) The ten-day experiment worked. God blessed Daniel and his friends with physical health and strength and with learning and skill.

Present Employment: At the end of the three-year training period, Daniel and his friends became advisors to King Nebuchadnezzar. By God's grace and favor, the four men were rated ten times higher in wisdom and understanding than Nebuchadnezzar's magicians and enchanters.

Teacher Tips

What a great hero Daniel was! And then he had the courage to face down those hungry lions! It would be easy for the children in your classroom to see Daniel as the hero of these stories. But these stories are really accounts of God's saving grace as shown to Daniel and to each of us. By God's grace, Daniel and the other Jewish exiles were preserved in Babylon. By grace, God endowed Daniel with good looks, wisdom, skills, and understanding. By grace, God had Daniel and his friends chosen by Nebuchadnezzar for special training, and by grace God preserved them in their time of testing, giving them health and strength in addition to knowledge and understanding. By grace, God gave Daniel the power to interpret dreams. Who is the hero of this story? Make sure your students understand that God is the hero of every story in the Bible. Pray that your students will also see the Lord as the hero of their own lives; He is the one who daily blesses them, and also blesses them eternally through Christ Jesus.

Bringing it home

The Jewish exiles in Babylon had to wait for seventy years for God to keep His promise of deliverance. In the same way, Old Testament believers waited for centuries for God to keep His promise of deliverance from sin, death, and the power of the devil—the promise that came true in the birth of Jesus. We remember this time of waiting and hope each year as we celebrate the season of Advent. Encourage students and their families to work together to plan a special Advent devotion time this year. Many excellent resources are available, from *Portals of Prayer* to the Lutheran Hour Ministries devotions available online every day. Students and parents can make or buy a simple Advent wreath and light the appropriate number of candles each day. Family members can take turns reading the devotion and Scripture, then discuss what has been read, and close with prayer and a blessing.

Ideas for the Gifted

Many of the exiles taken from Judah to Babylon viewed their captivity as God's punishment for their nation's idolatry. While many followed God's direction through the prophet Jeremiah to build houses and raise families while they waited for God's promised deliverance, others were consumed by bitterness and despair. In captivity, they mourned for their sin and its consequences. Read the words of Psalm 137:1–6. The "waters of Babylon" refer to the Chebar River—actually an irrigation canal—along which most of the Jewish exiles had been settled. The canal ran through the heart of lower Mesopotamia from Babylon to Erech, a distance of more than one hundred miles.

The real danger to the Jewish community was the temptation to be assimilated into Babylonian life. To preserve their identity, the religious Jews of Babylon faithfully observed the Sabbath and circumcised their male children—practices that set them apart from their neighbors. Daniel and his friends observed the Jewish dietary laws instead of accepting the king's food and wine. Today we are surrounded by a culture that tempts us away from our Christian values and way of life. How can we resist the forces of that culture and remain strong in our faith and practice?

Technology

Nebuchadnezzar built many beautiful buildings in his capital city of Babylon. The exiles from Judah would have marveled at the magnificent Ishtar Gate in the city's walls. This gate was discovered by archeologists and brought to Berlin, Germany, where it now stands in the Pergamum Museum. Have students search the internet for pictures of and information about the Ishtar Gate.

UNIT 4—COLLAPSE AND CAPTIVITY

LESSON 42

Three Men in the Fiery Furnace
Daniel 3

Background

"Who's in charge here?" is a question pervading every area of our lives. Do we follow the example of media celebrities who abuse drugs or alcohol? Do we go along with society's "everybody's doing it" attitude toward sexual promiscuity? Do we remain silent when we perceive the government's actions to be contrary to God's will for our lives?

Who's in charge in the Church? Congregational leaders complain that their pastors are domineering, using their sacred office as an excuse to force their own agenda on the congregation. Pastors insist that the lay leadership is trying to run the congregation like a business, forgetting that the Church is the Body of Christ. Who's in charge in the Church?

The pastoral office is a divine institution—a gift from God for His Church. Jesus has given us this office and its qualifications because He loves us and desires what is best for us. He Himself is our Chief Shepherd (1 Peter 5:4). He has laid down His life for us (John 10:11) and gives us eternal life (John 10:28). The pastor has been called by God and, by the power of the Holy Spirit, by the congregation to preach the Word of God, forgive the sins of the repentant, and administer the Sacraments. In following the example of Jesus Christ, the pastor humbles himself to be the servant of all. "Shepherd the flock of God that is among you, exercising oversight, not under compulsion, but willingly, as God would have you; not for shameful gain, but eagerly; not domineering over those in your charge, but being examples to the flock" (1 Peter 5:2–3).

The people of the congregation make up the Church, the Bride of Christ for whom He gave His very life. St. Peter writes, "You are a chosen race, a royal priesthood, a holy nation, a people for His own possession, that you may proclaim the excellencies of Him who called you out of darkness into His marvelous light" (1 Peter 2:9). So who's in charge in the Church? Jesus Christ, of course.

Central Truth
God is King of kings and Lord of lords.

Objectives
- Recognize that it often seems that the easiest way to live is to pretend we don't know God, to ignore Him, or to abandon Him; God never said being a Christian would be easy.
- Rejoice that God forgives our weakness when we repent; the strength we need to stand up for Jesus comes from Jesus Himself and His Word.
- Sometimes God's ways are miraculous, sometimes they are inscrutable—whatever His will, praise the Lord!

Materials
- Hymnals and music CDs
- Reproducible 42

Bible Prep
Post in advance so students can bookmark the reference before class time.
- Daniel 3

Devotions

There is an old story about a young college student who took a summer job at a lumber camp. When he came home at the end of the summer, he spoke about how awful it was to be around that group of people because they spoke filthy language, told dirty stories, were rough and vulgar, and acted like God was just a joke, so they felt they could do whatever they wanted. One of his friends said, "That is awful. What did they do when they found out you are a Christian?" The young man laughed and said, "Oh, they never knew!" What does that reply tell you about how the young man spent his summer? No one could tell by his actions or his words that he was a Christian. He fit in with the behavior of the other men. He did not live as a Christian; he didn't even stand up to claim the name *Christian*. He took the easy way out. He followed their lead rather than following Jesus. Living the life of a Christian takes faith and obedience (as we are empowered by God), but it also takes strength and courage. When we don't feel strong and brave, God invites us to go to Him in prayer, knowing He is with us and will hear us. What happens when we ask for wisdom to live as a child of God? Listen to what Scripture tells us: "The wisdom from above is first pure, then peaceable, gentle, open to reason, full of mercy and good fruits, impartial and sincere" (James 3:17). And "if any of you lacks wisdom, let him ask God, who gives generously to all without reproach, and it will be given him" (James 1:5). One definition of wisdom is the "ability to reach and implement proper decisions when facing challenges" (From *The Lutheran Study Bible* © 2009 Conordia Publishing House, note on James 1:5, p. 2135). **Pray for God to strengthen you and give you the wisdom to follow Jesus and live for Him; He will not turn you away!** Sing together "Stand Up, Stand Up for Jesus" (*LSB* 660; recorded as *Hymn of the Month for grade 7, April*).

181

INTO the Word

Hot Times in Babylon

Briefly review the setting of the Babylonian captivity. Remind students that Shadrach, Meshach, and Abednego were the three friends who, along with Daniel, were chosen by Nebuchadnezzar for special training to serve as advisors in his government. Like Daniel, they had been brought to Babylon in the first group of exiles. Like Daniel, they refused the king's food and wine and abided by the Jewish dietary laws. By God's grace and favor, they remained healthy and strong and increased in knowledge, understanding, and skills.

Help your students read the text from Daniel 3. Then read the three newspaper articles that retell the story. You may wish to assign three students to serve as "radio or television newscasters" who read the stories to the class.

The golden statue was probably an image of the Babylonian god Bel. The writer mentions several times that the statue was "set up," emphasizing that it had no power to make or present itself. The fiery furnace was probably a smelting kiln, with openings on the top and side. Burning was an ancient method of execution.

Students may wonder why the Chaldeans turned in Shadrach, Meshach, and Abednego. It is possible they were jealous because these Judean exiles had been given positions in the government. They may also have been seeking favor with Nebuchadnezzar. They phrased their accusation in personal terms: "These men, O king, pay no attention to you; they do not serve your gods or worship the golden image that you have set up" (Daniel 3:12).

Nebuchadnezzar offers the Judeans another opportunity to worship the statue; they explain: "Our God whom we serve is able to deliver us from the burning of the fiery furnace, and He will deliver us out of your hand, O king. But if not, be it known to you, O king, that we will not serve your gods or worship the golden image that you have set up" (Daniel 3:17–18). Although God is always able to rescue His people, there are times when it is not God's will to rescue believers from danger or death. Real faith trusts God whether or not He preserves believers when they face trials. Faith trusts that God has a good purpose for His good plans.

The furious king orders the furnace to be made hotter, and the three men are bound fully clothed and thrown into the fire. Imagine Nebuchadnezzar's astonishment when he sees four men walking about in the flames, and one appears to be an angel. Nebuchadnezzar recognizes that God has saved Shadrach, Meshach, and Abednego in the fire and praises God.

His decree makes worship of the Jewish God legal in Babylon, paving the way for a vital Jewish community even after the exile has ended. God worked through the Babylonian king to protect His people.

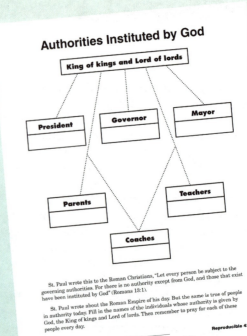

So Who's in Charge Here?

You may think the answer to that question depends on where you are. In your community, it's the mayor or the police chief. At school, it's the principal or your teacher. At home, it's your parent or the caregiver your parent has left in charge. When your parent asks you to watch your little brother, it might even be you.

Think a little deeper. People who are "in charge" have the power to influence your actions and even your thoughts and beliefs. Are you influenced by what the popular kids in your school might think about you? Do movie or television personalities, sports figures, or popular musicians influence your thoughts and actions?

Who's in charge here? For the Christian, the answer is easy. God's in charge. It's His world. He made the universe and everything in it. He keeps the planets in their proper orbits and tells the lilies when to bloom. He even gave us written instructions on how He wants us to live—the Ten Commandments. All we have to do is obey them.

The answer is easy. But living it? Not so much. No matter how hard we try, we cannot obey God's Commandments perfectly. The one we break most often is the first one—"You shall have no other gods"—the one that acknowledges that He's in charge. But "God so loved the world, that He gave His only Son, that whoever believes in Him should not perish but have eternal life" (John 3:16). When we repent of our sins, God forgives us for the sake of His Son, Jesus.

So how do we live as if God is in charge when popular kids, the media, and even governments try to influence us in other ways? Jesus has promised to stand beside us—"I am with you always, to the end of the age" (Matthew 28:20)—and one believer plus Jesus always makes a majority. He strengthens us through the study of His Word as we face the challenges of the world around us.

Remember

> "Hear, O Israel: The LORD our God, the LORD is one. You shall love the LORD your God with all your heart and with all your soul and with all your might. And these words that I command you today shall be on your heart. You shall teach them diligently to your children, and shall talk of them when you sit in your house, and when you walk by the way, and when you lie down, and when you rise." (Deuteronomy 6:4–7)

91

INTO our lives

So Who's in Charge Here?

Distribute Reproducible 42 and help your students make a list of the people who are in charge of the various aspects of their lives. Ask, **Why is it important to understand who's in charge? How does our behavior show who we really acknowledge as being in charge?** We are talking about who is in authority. Help students understand that while God has delegated authority to people, He still remains the King of kings and Lord of lords—the ultimate authority. Unfortunately, too often, we want to be the one in charge. How often people say, "I have a right to do this" or "It's my life; I can do with it what I want." These types of statements actually place self will above God's will.

Continue with the section in the Student Book, leading the class discussion from the obvious authority figures in the students' lives (government officials, police, parents, teachers, principal) to those who are less obvious, such as celebrities in the entertainment field, sports figures, classmates, and friends. Point out that **People can be "in charge" by exerting influence that makes us act in a certain way. Sometimes these influences are positive, but often they are negative and result in behavior that is contrary to God's will for our lives.** For instance, drug and alcohol abuse and sexual promiscuity by entertainment celebrities may make this behavior seem acceptable; cheating and steroid use by sports figures may lead young athletes to use any means to win or get ahead; pressure to be accepted by classmates or friends might make someone gossip, lie, or disobey their parents.

Expand on the concept of acknowledging God as being "in charge" in our lives with the following discussion starters about what happens next.

1. Your soccer team starts tournament play next week. But all of your practices this week were rained out. Coach has scheduled a practice for Sunday morning, and he says that anyone who misses practice will have to sit out the tournament.

2. You and your friend Jake were throwing rocks at the windows of an old abandoned garage. You had just left to find more rocks when a police officer arrived. When you came back a minute later, the officer had Jake by the arm. "I'm taking this young man to talk to the owner of the garage. I know you weren't involved, so just run along home."

3. You really want a new CD that all your friends are listening to, but you already spent your allowance, and your bank is empty. You ask your parents if they would buy the CD for you. "Why buy it?" your dad asks. "Can't you just borrow it from one of your friends and make a copy on your computer?"

4. The most popular girl in your class has invited you to a sleepover at her house. "Just don't tell Sophia about it," she whispers. "We wouldn't want her to show up in those ugly clothes she wears."

Help students understand that while our lives are influenced by all of these forces, God is truly the one who is in charge. (This is true whether we believe it or not—Nebuchadnezzar thought he was in charge, but found out differently.) The Bible calls God "the blessed and only Sovereign, the King of kings and Lord of lords, who alone has immortality, who dwells in unapproachable light" (1 Timothy 6:15–16). Jesus' reign extends even over those earthly rulers who wield great power and exercise control.

The King of kings and Lord of lords has given us clear, simple directions for how He wants us to live. But no one is able to follow those directions completely. Remind your students that we are born with the condition of original sin, which makes it impossible to keep from sinning. But **God in His mercy sent His Son, Jesus, to take the punishment for our sin. When we come to God in repentance, He forgives our sins for Jesus' sake.** Jesus promises to be with us and help us withstand the influences of those who would like to be in charge of our lives instead of Him. Through His Word, He works in us to give us the power to resist temptations.

Lesson Support

Critical thinking

We acknowledge God as King of kings and Lord of lords. But what does the Bible say about His kingdom? The Bible says that God rules the universe and everything in it (Psalm 66:7; Daniel 5:21). The phrase "kingdom of God" (or "kingdom of heaven") appears nearly one hundred times in the New Testament. All but a few of the occurrences are in Matthew, Mark, and Luke. God opens His kingdom to all people, not just a few. Jew and Gentile, wealthy and poor, men and women are all welcomed into God's grace (Galatians 3:26–28). However, not all people enter the Kingdom. Human pride and self-righteous attitude reject the work of the Spirit. We enter the Kingdom as helpless as children (Mark 10:13–16), born anew by water and the Spirit (John 3:1–6). When Pontius Pilate asked Jesus if He was a king, Jesus answered, "My kingdom is not of this world. If My kingdom were of this world, My servants would have been fighting, that I might not be delivered over to the Jews. But My kingdom is not from the world." The kingdom of God continues to advance in the world through the work of the local congregation and the witness of every Christian. Wherever the Gospel is preached and the story of Jesus is shared, the Holy Spirit works to expand the rule of grace through faith in God's Son.

Searching Further

When Nebuchadnezzar ordered Shadrach, Meshach, and Abednego to worship his statue or be thrown into the fiery furnace, they answered, "Our God whom we serve is able to deliver us from the burning fiery furnace, and He will deliver us out of your hand, O king. But if not, be it known to you, O king that we will not serve your gods or worship the golden image that you have set up" (Daniel 3:17–18). There are times when it is not God's will to rescue believers from danger or death. Genuine faith trusts God whether or not He preserves believers when they face trials. Consider how both the wicked and the righteous suffered when God used Babylon to overthrow Judah. All of the apostles except John were put to death for their faith. Stephen, the first Christian martyr, was stoned in Jerusalem (Acts 7:54–60), and countless other martyrs have followed him through the centuries. Point out that there are many present-day people who are persecuted for living as Christians. Perhaps we are not always aware of this fact because much of this is taking place in parts of Africa and Asia and may seem distant from our circumstances. However, we need to be concerned about these people who are our brothers and sisters in the faith. Write a prayer asking God to give strength and peace and deliverance to all people who are being persecuted for their faith.

Ideas for the Gifted

According to Daniel 3:4, Nebuchadnezzar's herald proclaimed that everyone should fall down and worship the golden statue when they heard the sound of the horn, pipe, lyre, trigon, harp, bagpipe, and every kind of music. Three of these instruments—the horn, pipe, and bagpipe—are wind instruments. The other three—the lyre, trigon, and harp—are stringed instruments. The Old Testament contains many references to musical instruments. Some of these instruments are still used today; others have evolved into modern instruments, while still others have disappeared. Learn more about music and instruments in the Bible on page 993 of *The Lutheran Study Bible*. Construct one or more of the instruments, and use it to accompany the reading of a psalm.

Curriculum Connection

The king's golden image was a sculpture, a piece of art—but it was put to a bad use when he ordered people to worship it. Today, too, art can be used in both good and bad ways. Together with students, come up with a list of ways that art can be used both for good and for bad in your community. Section 6.5.2.2, Art in Daily Life in Communities and Cultures, may be helpful. Also look at section 6.5.2.1, Tactics Used by Advertisers to Sway Thinking. You'll find both of these in the sixth grade Visual Arts volume of the Concordia Curriculum Guide.

Faith in Action

This lesson's Bible words to remember from Deuteronomy are very much like an Old Testament creed. It is very likely that Shadrach, Meshach, and Abednego repeated these words once or twice a day, as the faithful would in their close-knit community in exile. Jesus Himself quoted from this in the New Testament when speaking of the top priority in our lives—to love God above all. We join in speaking these great words with the faithful over the centuries, over millennia.

UNIT 4—COLLAPSE AND CAPTIVITY

LESSON 43

Daniel and the King's Dreams
DANIEL 2 AND 4

Background

How long does a kingdom or empire or civilization endure? History gives us a variety of answers. The Mesopotamian civilization, in one form or another, endured for almost 3,500 years—long, but not unusual in the ancient world. Then it ended. Civilization in ancient Egypt lasted 1,000 years longer. But it ended. The civilizations of Southern Asia endured for 3,500 years, and the dynasties of China for 2,220 years. They, too, ended. The glories of Greece lasted over 1,000 years, and the Roman Empire 1,400 years. They lasted a long time, but they ended like the others.

How long is long to God? Moses said, "You return man to dust and say, 'Return, O children of man!' For a thousand years in Your sight are but as yesterday when it is past, or as a watch in the night. You sweep them away as with a flood; they are like a dream, like grass that is renewed in the morning: in the morning it flourishes and is renewed; in the evening it fades and withers" (Psalm 90:3–6).

So what's the point? Does nothing endure? The prophet Isaiah answers, "The grass withers, the flower fades, but the Word of the Lord will stand forever" (Isaiah 40:8). While human beings and their institutions—governments and civilizations, kingdoms and empires—are unfaithful, God is faithful forever. These words of the Lord through the prophet Isaiah brought comfort to the Judean exiles in Babylon. Our own country is still in its infancy compared to these empires of ancient history. Whether it endures for another decade, century, or millennium, it will one day end. However, our Lord Jesus Christ and His Word endure forever.

Central Truth

Earthly kings and kingdoms rise and fall, but the Word of the Lord endures forever.

Objectives

- Confess that as was the case in days of old, the biggest temptation for people today is to focus all we do on ourselves—what we like, and what we want, breaking the First Commandment, making ourselves our own ruler, decision maker, and god.
- Look to Jesus as the center of your life and His blessings of forgiveness, life, salvation, and more will overflow.
- Proclaim the works of the Lord as enabled by the Holy Spirit to witness to those around you.

Materials

- Hymnals and music CDs
- Reproducible 43
- Web Resource 43a

Bible Prep

Post in advance so students can bookmark references before class time.
- Daniel 2 and 4
- Psalm 90

Devotions

Annie loved to visit her great-grandmother, Edith, in the nursing home. Edith had grown up in France, and Annie loved to hear her stories about her homeland. Some of the stories were funny, while others were sad. Great-Grandma Edith said, "Growing up in a village in France was so much fun. My brother Pierre and I played in the park and went to school, of course. On Sundays we went to church with our family, and sometimes we went to the city and attended a concert or visited a museum. When World War II came, everything changed. The Nazis invaded our country and we lived in fear. We stayed in our village and in our little house. The Nazi leader, the *Führer*—Hitler, himself—was on the radio. He said that Germany had established the Thousand Year Reich—a kingdom that would last for ten centuries or more. We did not want to be a part of that kingdom so we prayed every day for God to send help for us. Help did not come quickly; we had to be patient and trust the Lord. I was especially frightened when Pierre would leave our little house late at night. He was sixteen and in the French resistance. One day we heard that a Nazi tank had been blown up by a homemade bomb; we never saw Pierre again after that day. In 1944 we heard a rumor that help was on the way; we could hear the noise of battle in the distance. Finally, soldiers from England and America came into our village and we were free again! God blessed us through those people from across the sea. The war finally ended, Hitler killed himself, and the Thousand Year Reich was no more. His kingdom of a thousand years did not even last twenty years." Great-Grandma's story ended, but her thanks to the Lord for their rescue never stopped. We know that no "kingdom" made by human beings will last forever. Men make promises they cannot keep; they lead in paths we should not follow. God is our dwelling place, a refuge for all generations. Only the Word of the Lord endures forever."

Read Psalm 90 responsively by whole verse. Sing "O God, Our Help in Ages Past" (*LSB* 733; recorded on *Hymns of the Month, grade 3, November*).

INTO the Word

Nebuchadnezzar's Journal (Dream 1)

The account of Nebuchadnezzar's dreams and how God gave Daniel the interpretation of the dreams is told from Nebuchadnezzar's point of view in the form of journal entries. Read and discuss each of the entries separately. Because of the journal format, events are not told in the same order as in the account in Daniel 2. For this reason, you may want to delay having students read the Bible account until the end of the lesson.

Discuss Nebuchadnezzar's first dream with your students. Nebuchadnezzar ordered his wise men to explain the dream. They answered that no man could do what he asked; only a god would be able. Nebuchadnezzar sentenced all of the wise men to death. Then Daniel enters the story. He acknowledges that the dream and its interpretation could indeed be answered—by his God, the true God. Daniel 2:14 says that Daniel approached the captain of the king's guard "with prudence and discretion." Discuss those terms with students. Note that Daniel's request to delay the execution showed mercy like that shown by his God.

At this time, Daniel sought the support of his friends and more importantly, he sought God's help. Read Daniel's prayer in 2:20–23. God, who reveals mysteries, made known events secular and political that would happen in the near and also distant future, as kingdoms would rise and fall. Nebuchadnezzar honored Daniel and acknowledged that Daniel's God was greater than all other gods—not really faith, but an important step away from idolatry.

Use Reproducible 43 and Web Resource 43a to explore this interpretation that we can now put names to, because the events happened in history as God decreed. Students may color or label the various sections of the statue. The golden head stands for Nebuchadnezzar and the glories of his kingdom (which included one of the Seven Wonders of the Ancient World—the Hanging Gardens of Babylon). The dream showed his kingdom would end and be replaced by another, though inferior kingdom, which is represented by the silver chest and arms. (We will study this takeover in the next lesson, when his heir would be conquered by the Medes and the Persians.)

Eventually the power of the Persians was broken by Alexander the Great who spread the Greek culture and influence far and wide through his successful military campaigns. This is suggested by the bronze middle and thighs of the statue (bronze being inferior to silver in value, but used often in weaponry). Then came the iron legs to represent the strength of the Roman civilization that would conquer the known world at that time. However, note that the feet of iron are mixed with clay as a reminder that Rome had its strength, but also serious weaknesses, which eventually led to its downfall.

The stone not formed by human hands represents Christ, conceived without a human father. (Point out that Jesus was born during the reign of Roman Emperor Caesar Augustus.) The stone destroyed all of the other kingdoms so completely that they were like chaff or dust blown away by the wind. Christ's kingdom is unlike the others; it can never be destroyed; it is a heavenly kingdom that will last forever. **Christ the King offers His people forgiveness of sins, life in Him, and salvation, now and eternally.** (For further study, look at the *People's Bible Commentary, the Book of Daniel,* Concordia Publishing House, 2005.)

Nebuchadnezzar's Journal (Dream 2)

It's like déjà vu all over again! This dream is driving me crazy, and my wise men are clueless as to what it means. So today Daniel came in, and I told him the dream, because I know the spirit of God is in him. My dream is this: A mighty tree stood in the middle of a field, with its top reaching to heaven. Its leaves were beautiful and its fruit abundant, and in it was food for all. Animals lived in its shade, and birds lived in its branches. Then a messenger came from heaven and said to chop down the tree, cut up its branches, and scatter its leaves and fruit, but leave the stump and roots in the earth amid the grass of the field. The stump would be wet with dew, like the grass in the field around it, and the mind of a beast would be given to him. Seven periods of time would pass, so that everyone would know that the Most High rules the kingdom of men and gives it to whomever He wills. Daniel said that I am the strong, beautiful tree in my dream. My greatness has grown, and my dominion reaches to the ends of the earth. But it is the decree of the Most High that I will be driven from among men and dwell with the beasts of the field. I will eat grass like the oxen and be wet with dew for seven periods of time, until I recognize that the Most High rules the kingdom of men. As the stump was left in the field to sprout again, so my kingdom will be returned to me at the time I acknowledge that heaven rules.

So much has happened in the years since my last entry. Twelve months after my dream, I stood on the roof of the palace and boasted about my great kingdom. Immediately I heard a voice from heaven telling me the kingdom had departed from me and my dream was about to come true. I don't remember the next seven years, but people tell me I went insane, living out in the fields with the animals, eating grass like an ox. My hair grew as long as eagles' feathers, and my nails were like bird claws. Finally I lifted my eyes to heaven, and my reason returned to me. I praised and honored the Most High God who lives forever, for His kingdom is an everlasting kingdom. My kingdom was restored to me with even more greatness. Now I praise and honor the King of heaven, for all His works are right and His ways are just. Those who walk in pride, He is able to humble.

Remember

"The grass withers, the flower fades, but the word of our God will stand forever." (Isaiah 40:8)

Nebuchadnezzar's Journal (Dream 2)

Nebuchadnezzar's second dream came at a time when everything was going well, and it terrified him. Again he tried his Chaldean wise men; when they failed, he sent for Daniel. He recognized that Daniel was specially blessed by God, although his own knowledge of the true God was limited. He told Daniel he had dreamt about a mighty tree, its top reaching heaven, whose leaves were beautiful and whose fruit provided food for all. A messenger from heaven ordered the tree to be cut down, its branches, leaves, and fruit scattered. The stump remained, bound with iron, in a grassy field, wet with dew. His mind changed from that of a man to that of a beast; seven periods of time would pass over him. God gave Daniel the interpretation of the king's dream, which had a personal rather than political interpretation. The tree represented Nebuchadnezzar himself. God had decreed that Nebuchadnezzar should be driven from society, with a mental illness in which he had the mind of a beast (possibly what is known as lycanthropy). The stump shows that after seven periods of time he would be restored.

Nebuchadnezzar's boasting from the palace rooftop shows that he honored himself more than God, a sin against the First Commandment. Insanity struck him instantly, and he spent seven periods of time (probably years) living like a mad dog who has been chained out in a field because people couldn't stand his presence. At the end of the prescribed time, Nebuchadnezzar had learned his lesson. He turned to the Lord, and his reason returned to him. He praised God as the Most High, whose kingdom endures forever. Read more about this in Daniel 4.

"We need constantly to be reminded that, although earthly kingdoms have great power and authority, the Most High rules. Thankfully, He rules mercifully . . . and for the benefit of His Church" (From *The Lutheran Study Bible* © 2009 Concordia Publishing House, footnote on Daniel 4:4–18, p. 1404).

Technology

Some of the kingdoms of the ancient world lasted for a very long time, but eventually they perished. Use a calculator to compute the length of time each of these kingdoms or civilizations endured. Remember: If the time period begins in BC and ends in AD, you will need to make two calculations and add them together.

Mesopotamia	4000 BC — 539 BC
Ancient Egypt	5000 BC — 332 BC
Civilizations of Southern Asia	3000 BC — AD 500
Civilizations of Southeast Asia	2000 BC — AD 1500
Dynasties in China	2000 BC — AD 220
Age of Ancient Greece	1100 BC — 31 BC
Rise and Fall of Rome	900 BC — AD 500
Development of African States	3000 BC — AD 1500
Mesoamerican Civilizations	1500 BC — AD 1521

When you have finished your calculations, use the computer to make a graph comparing the length of each kingdom or civilization.

Searching Further

Although the Word of the Lord endures forever, the political history of God's chosen people is a story of the rise and fall of one kingdom after another. The patriarchs lived in a family/feudal system among the small desert kingdoms of their time. During and after the Exodus, Israel was a theocracy, ruled by God through Moses, Joshua, and later the judges. When the people of Israel demanded a king, Samuel anointed first Saul and then David to rule over them. After the death of David's son, Solomon, the land was divided into the Northern Kingdom (Israel) and the Southern Kingdom (Judah). While the Northern Kingdom was carried off by the Assyrians in 721 BC, the descendants of David ruled Judah until the Babylonian captivity in 587 BC. After that time the Jewish people were always subject to some foreign government—Babylonians, Medes, Persians, Greeks, Romans. In spite of this political instability, the direct line of God's Word endured—the Word was made flesh in the form of Jesus, God's Son, a descendant of King David, King of kings and Savior of all. "But when the fullness of time had come, God sent forth His Son, born of a woman, born under the law, to redeem those who were under the law, so that we might receive adoption as sons" (Galatians 4:4–5).

Teacher Tips

The psalmist tells us, "He who dwells in the shelter of the Most High will abide in the shadow of the Almighty. I will say to the Lord, 'My Refuge and my fortress, my God, in whom I trust'" (Psalm 91:1–2). Fortresses were important in the time of King David, during Nebuchadnezzar's reign, and in medieval times. Use the Internet or a book on world history to learn more about fortresses. Check your library for a copy of *Castles* by David Macaulay. Then turn your Lego-maniacs loose to create one or more fortresses from various time periods.

Include the following message in your regular letter home to your students' families. *In this week's religion lessons, your student has been studying the account of Daniel and the Dreams of Nebuchadnezzar. We have learned that we need to put our trust in God rather than in earthly institutions, because earthly kings and kingdoms rise and fall, but the Word of the Lord endures forever. The psalmist tells us, "A day in Your courts is better than a thousand elsewhere. I would rather be a doorkeeper in the house of my God than dwell in the tents of wickedness" (Psalm 84:10). In setting priorities for your family, remember to put "the house of my God" at the top of the list. Worship together regularly in the Lord's house. Make time for family devotions every day. Study God's Word individually at home and together with your fellow believers.*

Curriculum Connection

The statue in the king's dream was a mixture of several metals and of clay. As Daniel points out, metal and clay do not bond well, and fall apart easily. For a fun science connection, consider using section 6.1.1.18, Processes to Separate Mixtures, found in the sixth grade Science volume of the Concordia Curriculum Guide. Together with students, find as many mixtures as you can. Which would be easiest to separate? Which hardest? What procedures would work the best?

UNIT 4—COLLAPSE AND CAPTIVITY

LESSON 44

The Writing on the Wall
Daniel 5

Background

Daniel's career as God's servant in foreign governments spanned perhaps eighty years. The Lord used Daniel to influence the rulers of Babylon and, later, Medo-Persia for the good of His people. Quietly but surely, the Lord preserved the Jewish nation and kept His promises to (1) cure them of their propensity toward gross idolatry; (2) bring them safely home to Judah after seventy years; and (3) send the world's Savior as a descendant of Abraham, Judah, and David. Today's Bible narrative details a key event in that process.

The year was 539 BC. Babylon's last king, Belshazzar, held power. He and his court were celebrating a festival, perhaps the new year. Babylon's capital city, though under siege by the Persians, seemed impregnable. So despite the Persian army at their gates, the king and his courtiers ate and drank themselves into oblivion. During the banquet, a mysterious hand appeared as if from nowhere and wrote their doom on a wall of the banquet hall. Daniel interpreted the script and watched as the prophetic word came true—within hours!

That very night, in a surprise move, Cyrus the Great diverted the Euphrates River into nearby irrigation channels. It lowered the level of the river enough so that his armies could storm the city walls from the riverbank.

Cyrus's subsequent reign was marked by his willingness to tolerate and even support religious beliefs other than his own. Just as Isaiah had predicted nearly two hundred years before, Cyrus released the Jewish captives to return home. (There's some evidence that Cyrus saw himself described by name as Judah's liberator and signed the order releasing the Jews. See Isaiah 44:28; 45:1–7.)

While relatively few took advantage of this opportunity, those who did leave were ably shepherded by leaders like Ezra and Nehemiah. The Lord's ultimate purposes for His people in exile were fulfilled—repentance, faith, and worship of the true God were restored.

Central Truth

Throughout the history of the world, God is present, powerful, and reigns supreme.

Objectives

- Recognize that whatever is most important in your life becomes your god (even if the most important thing is yourself).
- Acknowledge that God commands that we love and honor Him above all things.
- Be assured that God is active in our lives today; He forgives the sins of the repentant and guides them to live for Him through Christ Jesus.

Materials

- Hymnals and music CDs
- Web Resource 44a
- Reproducible 44

Bible Prep

Post in advance so students can bookmark references before class time.
- Luke 2:1–20
- Daniel 5
- Ephesians 2:13–16

Devotions

Write these words on the board: "The handwriting is on the wall."

We've imported this saying into our language from the Bible narrative we will study today. Later, we'll see how it got started. For now, does anyone know what the statement means? (It is a warning; there is no escape from the consequences.) **When "the handwriting is on the wall," something is sure to happen. For example, if you use your dad's tools or your mom's mixer to do a school project and you break it in the process, well, "the handwriting is on the wall!" There are bound to be consequences! When Adam and Eve fell into sin in Eden, "the handwriting was on the wall," and all kinds of trouble and death were unleashed into our world.**

Both of these examples are examples of Law and judgment. When God promises to punish sin, He keeps that promise. "The handwriting is on the wall," and it's bad news for us. But "the handwriting is on the wall," too, when it comes to the Gospel. God promised Adam and Eve that He would send a Savior to rescue them from sin's guilt and power. God would keep that promise to them and to you and me.

During Advent, we remember God's faithfulness to His promise. We remember that baby Jesus was born in Bethlehem as *Immanuel,* **"God with us." We also remember Jesus' promise to come back to earth to take His children (that's us!) home to Himself in heaven, where it will be "us with God," forever! The handwriting is on the wall! God has a glorious future in store! I'm glad, and I pray you are too!**

Let's pray together: Dear Lord, before You created us, You loved us! You purposed to save us! Forgive us for the times we ignore Your Word, disobey it, or even despise it. Teach us to live with Your promise to return always in our hearts. We know it will happen—the handwriting is on the wall! Amen. Sing "The King Shall Come" (*LSB* 348; recorded as *Hymn of the Season for grade 6, Advent*). Say together the words of fulfillment of the promise of the Messiah from Luke 2:1–20.

189

INTO the Word

Babylon Will Fall

Read the introductory paragraph in the Student Book, and then have the class turn to Daniel 5. Use the following outline of key verses to tell the Bible narrative.

Verses 1–4: A successor to King Nebuchadnezzar insults and blasphemes the Lord.

Verses 5–6: A supernatural warning is given for all to see. (Note the king's reaction.)

Verses 13–16: The king calls in Daniel for an interpretation of the message.

Verse 17: Daniel refuses the gifts of the king, knowing the credit belongs to God.

Verses 23–28: The judgment and warning are announced.

Verses 30–31: Swift justice takes place.

(*Note:* If anyone asks about the last word given as both *Parsin* and *Peres* in the Bible, point out that one seems to be the plural form of the other.) Continue by using Web Resource 44a, which further examines the message, giving a summary of its meaning and a more complete explanation. The three lines can be summarized as "Numbered" (your days are numbered), "Weighed" (you've been measured and weighed and found empty), and "Divided" (you will be divided between the Medes and the Persians).

These events are significant because the new rulers (Medes and Persians) were much more inclined to respect other people's religion and to allow them to return to their homeland. God was preparing to bring a restored and faithful people home to await the coming of the Messiah.

Lesson 44
The Writing on the Wall

Babylon Will Fall

It's possible we'll meet King Nebuchadnezzar in heaven. Nebuchadnezzar may have come to faith through the witness of Daniel, Shadrach, Meshach, Abednego, and others. His words in Daniel 4:37 seem to indicate a better understanding of the Lord. We don't know for sure, of course. But it's interesting to think about. However, the Babylonian rulers who followed had no relationship with the true God. King Belshazzar (who was either the son or grandson of Nebuchadnezzar) blasphemed the Lord our God in both his words and actions. Judgment was about to fall!

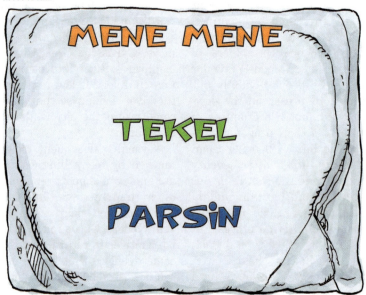

Review

Covenant Connection

The Old Testament is not a series of random stories. Together, they form a coherent picture of God at work to bring our Savior into the world. As the events in today's Bible narrative take place, the people of Judah have been in Babylon for 70 years, just as Jeremiah had foretold. Now, God is getting events ready for their return to the Promised Land. Baby Jesus would be born—not in Babylon, but in Bethlehem. Inspired by the Holy Spirit, Micah foretold it in Micah 5:2.

INTO our lives

Take a break in the lesson now to work together on Reproducible 44. Allow students to work in pairs or triads so they can discuss and reflect on the activity. If they have trouble estimating how much time they spend in each activity on a typical day, have them create a one-day schedule on another sheet of paper. They should break down their waking hours on weekdays into thirty-minute time slots and think about where they usually are at that time. Then have them create a similar schedule for Saturday and one for Sunday.

Using these schedules, they should be able to come up with a fairly reliable time budget. In the column on the far right of the chart, ask that they log the approximate amount of time they spent last week in each of the activities listed. When that is complete, ask that they fill in the left-hand column. This is a straightforward process. The activity that took up more time than any other activity was their first priority, the activity to which they devoted the next most time was their second priority, and so on. After a few minutes of discussion among partners, ask the whole class: **How satisfied are you with the results? Do you think this exercise identifies your true priorities or not?** *Option:* You

The Writing on the Wall—for Me!

Belshazzar's actions revealed what was in his heart—disrespect for the Lord and a total focus on himself. He and his thousand guests thought they were safe. They thought nothing would disrupt their priorities, power, and pleasure. But judgment was sure. The handwriting was on the wall! The warning was set in stone. If God wrote on *your* wall, what would He write? Where do you see evidence in your life that God's will doesn't matter most to you? What would God tell you, ask you to do, or ask you to change? On the wall below, record God's directive to you according to His Law and will.

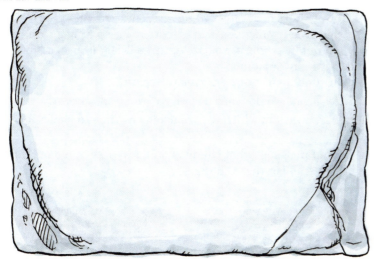

Breaking Down Walls

Sin builds walls between you and other people. More significantly, sin builds a wall that separates you from God. The handwriting is on the wall. The consequences are eternal death and damnation. However, we *can* be rescued from these circumstances. There is an answer for breaking down that wall. Read about it in Ephesians 2:13–16. Only Christ Jesus can reconcile us, breaking down walls and reuniting us with the grace and mercy of God. On your wall, demonstrate this by drawing a large yellow cross over the very middle of the wall.

Remember

"By my God I can leap over a wall. This God—His way is perfect; the word of the LORD proves true; He is a shield for all those who take refuge in Him." (Psalm 18:29b–30)

95

---

may want to discuss that several of the categories could be considered service events if they give glory to God. For example, willingly helping the family is serving others; however, helping out begrudgingly and grumbling does not give God glory.

Now continue with the section *The Writing on the Wall for Me!* Consider what all of this means for our lives today. Say, **You have taken a few minutes to examine how you spend your time. As God looks at you as His child, what warning might He give you? What command might He give you? Think about what God would say if He wrote on your wall! Perhaps He would say, "Honor your father and your mother." Maybe He would say, "Don't use texting and social media to hurt someone's feelings." Or would the message say, "Do your homework more accurately and on time"? As you think about this, get as specific as you want—you can make it about a personal concern in your life or a general comment for all kids your age. These "warnings" are really about obedience to God's Law (such as the Fourth and Eighth Commandments) and following His will, rather than our own, for our lives.**

Then ask students to fill in the wall on the second page of the lesson with a message God could write to them. What words *should* a just God write on it? It may be best to keep this activity private and personal, unless some volunteers want to share what they wrote.

Breaking Down Walls

Continue by reading aloud the Student Book text for this section. Then you can comment: **The Law and its warnings can seem serious and difficult, but remember that in repentance, we can rely on the forgiving and transforming power of God. Because of the reconciliation and redemption we have in Jesus, we can now leap over the demolished wall of hostility, receiving the grace of God and moving toward each other in love and peace. Christ made it all possible!**

Continue now with a group project to build a wall—a wall of praise and thanksgiving to God! Set aside a designated area on a bulletin board or piece of poster paper to create this wall. Provide sticky notes on which students can write praise, thanks, and prayer statements. (Consider using a variety of colors.) Students are to place their responses next to each other, row by row, starting at the bottom of the designated area, and gradually building up a wall of praise to the Lord! (This can be done over a period of several days.)

191

Lesson Support

Bringing it home

Have students create a more detailed weekly schedule (or buy a small calendar from an office supply store). Ask that they track their time for two, three, or four weeks, noting especially the ways in which they spend/invest their spare time. After the appointed time, ask students to analyze the data they recorded. (Gifted students might be able to create a simple spread sheet in Excel and then transfer the data to a pivot chart to create a visual presentation.)

Ask that students show their schedules/charts to a grown-up at home and talk about what it shows. You might send a set of two or three brief discussion questions home to help scaffold these conversations:
- Do our calendars accurately reflect our priorities? Explain.
- Are these the priorities Jesus would want us to have? Why or why not?
- How can we celebrate the ways in which we are using our time to honor our Savior?
- Knowing we are forgiven in Jesus, what changes would we like to make? How will we help each other establish those changes?

Searching Further

Refer students to Isaiah 44:28 and 45:1–7. Tell them that Isaiah wrote these words 150 years or so before Cyrus was even born! God was working through His prophet Isaiah in foretelling the role Cyrus would play in the history of His people. God used Cyrus (as He has used earthly rulers—both the evil and the pious) to accomplish His purposes. Still today, God uses rulers in the government for the good of His Church. How do Ephesians 1:19–22 and Proverbs 21:1 both express this? What comfort can this truth provide when world events seem out of anyone's control?

Teacher Tips

Not all Bible narratives are equally well known. Today's narrative, for example, finds its way into children's Bible story books and Sunday school curriculum much less often than, say, "Noah's Ark" or "Daniel and the Lions." While inductive learning has its place in Christian education, especially as your students' reasoning abilities mature, there's also a place for what educational psychologists call, "direct instruction." It's a time-honored approach and its efficacy is supported by solid research. In addition, direct instruction often saves time. However, teachers who use this methodology need to make sure students have the necessary background information if direct instruction is to be as meaningful as possible. The biblical material for Lesson 44 (and for Lesson 45—Queen Esther) will likely be more unfamiliar to your students than some previous lessons in this course have been. Check the Internet for resources. Also check your sixth grade social studies text; if there is a unit on this part of the world, you may want to move it in your schedule so that you can teach it at this time, relating the two curriculum areas.

Ideas for the Gifted

Have your gifted students research Cyrus the Great and the kingdom he established. Rather than asking for a written or oral report, have them work together to create a mini-museum filled with artifacts that replicate those that might be found in an antiquities collection focused on the Medo-Persian Empire. After they have developed the collection, have them lead "tours" for classmates, describing the artifacts and explaining the major achievements, beliefs, and leaders of the empire.

Technology

Look back at Web Resource 44a and God's three-word message (considering that the first word is given twice, for emphasis) to Belshazzar. Call attention to the ways this message is something like the abbreviated messages often sent as text messages on cell phones and other electronic communication devices today. Challenge students to create a text message that accurately communicates today's Bible memory verse (Psalm 18:29b–30).

Check it Out

Have students work with a partner to read Jeremiah 25:8–14 and 29:4–14. Ask that they list as many prophesies as they can find that God fulfilled. These passages indicate that the Babylonian exile will last seventy years. They also indicate God's judgment on Babylon because of the violent, hurtful ways the Babylonian rulers treated Judah in exile. Furthermore, Jeremiah 29 includes promises of God's plan for good for Judah; that "good" included, especially, the coming of Jesus, the Savior and Messiah.

UNIT 4—COLLAPSE AND CAPTIVITY

LESSON 45

Queen Esther Saves Her People
THE BOOK OF ESTHER

Background

Here's one of Scripture's most profound synopses of the Christmas story—and you're in it:

Blessed be the God and Father of our Lord Jesus Christ, who has blessed us in Christ with every spiritual blessing in the heavenly places, even as He chose us in Him before the foundation of the world, that we should be holy and blameless before Him. In love He predestined us for adoption as sons through Jesus Christ, according to the purpose of His will, to the praise of His glorious grace, with which He has blessed us in the Beloved. In Him we have redemption through His blood, the forgiveness of our trespasses, according to the riches of His grace, which He lavished upon us, in all wisdom and insight making known to us the mystery of His will, according to His purpose, which He set forth in Christ as a plan for the fullness of time, to unite all things in Him, things in heaven and things on earth. (Ephesians 1:3–10)

In one breathtaking sweep, Paul sums up all of salvation history. From "before the foundation of the world," our heavenly Father chose to adopt us as His heirs, chose to redeem us through the precious blood of His own Son, Jesus, and then chose to unite all His people of all time to Himself.

Pause for a moment to think back on the Old Testament history your class has studied. Then think ahead to the Christmas celebration you're about to enjoy. All of it—all of it!—ties together! Today, you will read how God used Esther to preserve His people and to encourage them to trust His love. As God's children in our generation, we now carry that baton. Mordecai's words to Esther belong to us too: "Who knows whether you have not come to the kingdom for such a time as this?" (Esther 4:14).

Central Truth

We are saved and blessed, not because of who we are, but because of who God is—our loving and forgiving Lord.

Objectives

- Acknowledge that God calls us to live as His people in all circumstances.
- Remember that God can use us as His tool to bless other people.
- Confess that God gives purpose to our lives; that purpose includes worshiping Him and serving others.

Materials

- Hymnals and music CDs
- Reproducible 45
- Web Resource 45a
- Web Resource 45b

Bible Prep

Post in advance so students can bookmark the reference before class time.
- The Book of Esther

Devotions

Roger and his friend Wallace wandered their neighborhood with shovels. Last night, the sky had opened up and dumped twenty-four inches of snow on their town. School was cancelled, and the two friends had found plenty of work, clearing driveways and sidewalks.

Just as they were ready to head to Wallace's house to play a game on his Wii, a door opened and a woman stuck her head out. "Are you boys clearing driveways? If you do mine, and the sidewalks too, I'll pay you sixty dollars."

"You bet!" Roger shouted. "Yes!" echoed Wallace. It was more than double what they had been charging. Roger and Wallace were in the right place at the right time. Has something like that ever happened to you?

Today, we will see that God placed Queen Esther in just the right place at just the right time. Her life was no accident. Neither is yours! Esther's uncle told her, "Who knows whether you have not come to the kingdom for such a time as this?" (Esther 4:14). Esther had "come to the kingdom" at just the right time to save her people from annihilation.

As we celebrate Christmas, we remember all the things God has done to preserve His covenant people. Like Moses, Joshua, Ruth, Deborah, David, and many others before her, Esther made a big difference in the history of Christ's kingdom—the real and eternal kingdom to which our heavenly Father has called us too.

Do you dream big dreams for your life? You can, because God has brought you to His kingdom for such a time as this! Let's pray: Lord Jesus, because of Your cross, I belong to Your eternal kingdom. Forgive me for not always honoring You, my King, in my words and actions. Teach me to stay alert for opportunities You give me to serve You by serving others, especially in the vocations you have given me. Amen. Sing "Lo, How a Rose E'er Blooming" (*LSB* 359; recorded on *Hymns of the Season, grade 6, Christmas*). Say together the words of the promise fulfilled in Luke 2:1–20. Then sing of that baby Messiah in "Infant Holy, Infant Lowly" (*LSB* 393; recorded on *Hymns of the Season, grade 3, Christmas*).

193

INTO the lesson

Distribute Reproducible 45. Point out: *Vacations are breaks in the routines of daily life. Vocation includes everything in our daily lives* from a Christian perspective. Every Christian has a particular calling from God. With the doctrine of vocation, ordinary relationships, the nine-to-five routine, doing school work, taking care of the family, the work-a-day world—the way we spend most hours of the day—are touched and blessed with the presence of God. **In your vocation, with the Lord at the center of your life, you humbly serve others and glorify God in all that you do in response to the forgiveness, life, and salvation He offers through Christ Jesus.** Today we will hear about Hadassah, also known as Esther, who found unusual changes in her daily life. And more importantly, she discovered how she could use this new life to serve and even rescue others while also serving and glorifying God.

Discuss the reproducible activity together and then say, **We never really take a vacation from our God-given vocations. That's a good thing! Wherever we go, our Savior wants to make a difference in the lives of other people through us. It gives great meaning and purpose to our lives.**

INTO the Word

Introduce the story of Esther by giving this background information: **As the Book of Esther opens, some of the Jewish people have returned to Jerusalem with Ezra and Nehemiah. Many Jews stayed in Persia, including a young woman named Esther. Her parents may have died, because Esther's uncle Mordecai is taking care of her. Why would many of the Jewish people, like Daniel, remain in Babylon? Perhaps because their families had lived there for more than seven decades and had set down roots. Many had started businesses and grown wealthy and didn't want to give up their rebuilt lives for the hardships of rebuilding Jerusalem, which had been thoroughly devastated. Then, too, it's likely some stayed because of the calling God had placed on their lives. Esther and Mordecai probably fall into this category.**

No one knows who wrote the Book of Esther, but many scholars think Nehemiah may have done so to encourage the people he led as they encountered many problems and dangers on their return to their homeland. Hearing about the protection God gave Esther and her people in Persia would

INTO our lives

Use the Web Resource 45b link to learn more about Christian people who share the love of Jesus as their vocation in the many and varied occupation they have. Continue with a discussion, asking students what are their favorite things to do, and how they can do these things in a Christian way, living a Christian lifestyle. Also discuss what future occupations your students are interested in; discuss ways that their life in Christ can be part of all that they do.

have encouraged all the Jewish people that God continued to love and care for them.

Use Web Resource 45a to tell Esther's story. You may want to briefly go through the text on the slides to give an overview of the events and then go through it again, adding details to the narrative as you read from the selected Bible verses. The illustrations in the Student Book are an exact replication of the Web resource. It can be used as a review of what was learned, perhaps focusing this time on the symbols and pictures and having students explain how they relate to the story.

The last frame poses a question. Provide key Scripture verses for students to research and then have them make summary statements that answer the question. Suggest these readings: Esther 8:1–2 (Mordecai received Haman's house and signet ring); 8:3–8 (the king allowed Esther and Mordecai to make an edict to save the people); 8:9–14 (messengers rushed through the land, saying that the Jews could defend themselves on the two days that people were pledged to harm them); 8:15–17 (Mordecai increased in power, and the Jewish people rejoiced); 9:1–4 (there was a reversal of events as the Jews gained mastery over the people who intended to harm them); 9:20–22, 26–28 (it was declared that each year, the Feast of Purim should be celebrated to remember God's care of His people at this time); and 10:3 (Mordecai was ranked second only to the king; the people liked him because he worked for their peace and welfare. Note that this last phrase is a good description of Mordecai's vocation.)

Lesson Support

Searching Further

The Book of Esther explains the origins of the Feast of Purim. Have interested students research this festival and perhaps even plan a Purim celebration for the class. (Purim falls in late February or early March each year.) A room parent or two may be willing to bring the traditional sweet Purim pastry for students to enjoy. It's called "Hamantaschen." (Recipes are readily available online.) Jewish children often wear costumes during Purim, much as many children do at Halloween. If your class wants to dress up, you might assign parts based on the story of Esther and have the class dress up like the characters and reenact the account. *Note:* If you ask students to research Purim traditions online, give them a list of approved Web sites to use, as is advisable in all cases of Web research, because some sites students might find on their own might have inappropriate content.

Check it Out

King Ahasuerus is sometimes called King Xerxes or Xerxes the Great. Why did he have more than one name? What do historians tell us about him? Students interested in early Greek and Spartan history may want to research the part Xerxes played in the Battle of Thermopylae. His accomplishments later in life, particularly in architecture, may be of interest as well.

Queen Esther also had another name; her Jewish name was Hadassah, which means "star." As you learn about this "star" who led her people to safety, think about the greater star that led the Wise Men to little Jesus, the promised Messiah, who came to rescue all people to the safety that He provides in His gifts of forgiveness, life, and salvation.

Technology

In recent years, several well-done movies have been made about the life of Esther. If you do consider showing portions of any of these, first watch the film yourself to determine if it is biblically and historically accurate. Also watch to see that it is age-appropriate. As is true of the Book of Esther itself, these movies are unlikely to mention God's purposes, provision, and protection, so be sure to conclude with comments on the most important role in the story—the role of our Lord and Savior.

Critical thinking

Tell students that more than four hundred years elapse between the last book of the Old Testament and the first book of the New Testament. What happened during these so-called "silent years"? Was God still watching over His people or not? Encourage students to find out all they can about those four centuries. The history is quite exciting. One good resource of the "intertestamental period" is the article in *TLSB* entitled "The Time Between the Testaments" (pp. 1551ff).

Curriculum Connection

The Book of Esther is a wonderful part of Scripture; it is also a great story dealing with the universal theme of danger and deliverance. Discuss with students: Who is the "underdog" in this story? Who is powerful but finally gets what he deserves in the end? What series of coincidences (actually, the hand of God) leads to the happy ending? Can you think of other stories that share a similar pattern? For more ideas, see section 6.2.3.3, Universal Plots, Patterns, or Themes, found in the sixth grade Performing Arts volume of the Concordia Curriculum Guide.

Teacher Tips

Discussion often improves in quality and overall participation when learners have a few minutes to think and write before they speak. This lesson includes several opportunities in which you can take advantage of this phenomena. Consider using the technique more often in the future—in all the classes you teach.

Reaching Every Child

Today's narrative focuses on ten chapters of biblical text. In addition, it includes material based on a culture and customs very different from our own. Consider using a Bible storybook or a Bible paraphrase as you present it to your class. Concordia Publishing House has many such materials available; check the Web site at www.cph.org.

UNIT 5—THE PROMISED ONE IS HERE!

Theme

It's Epiphany! If you are studying this unit in January, you are in the Epiphany season of the Church Year. If you take a close look at the lessons in Unit 5, you will see how they connect—it's *an* epiphany! An *epiphany* is that "aha moment" when you recognize and realize something important. The Bible narratives we will be studying provide that epiphany—leading us to see who Jesus is, to understand His purpose, and to comprehend what He has done for us. An epiphany is an "eye-opener" in which you can finally see clearly. We're not talking about vision; we're talking about insight and perception—that "I see! I get it now!" type of vision. The people of God had waited a long time for the promised Messiah, and when He came, it took a while to understand who He was and what His purpose was. In Scripture, we see that Jesus was sent by the Father (Lesson 50); He is true God (46) and true man (47). He came with the purpose (48) of winning victory over Satan (51). This was pointed to by John the Baptist (49), and that message was carried on by the disciples (52). Jesus came for the young (55) and the old (53), for individuals (54) and for large groups (56). He came for all because we are all sinners needing rescue. His purpose was completed in His death and resurrection, which give us forgiveness, life, and salvation! (Note that the titles of this unit's lessons are listed in the column at the right to give you an overview of the material covered in this unit.)

Worship

The hymn for Epiphany for grade 6 carries on the theme of the unit, revealing who Jesus is—"You Are the Way; through You Alone" (*LSB* 586). This hymn and all of the Epiphany hymns on the *Hymns of the Season* CD continue the unit theme of identifying who Jesus is. Always feel free to use hymns that are suggested for other grade levels. The more these hymns are sung, the more they will become familiar to students, and the more students will enjoy singing them to worship the Lord! The grade 6 *Hymn of the Month* for January is "Take My Life and Let It Be" (*LSB* 783), which encourages our response to the goodness of our Savior, Jesus—He lived and died for us, and we respond by living our new lives for Him! The psalm for the month is Psalm 121.

Resources

If you subscribe to the One in Christ Portal, you will find additional resources, such as interactive whiteboard activities, slides, and more to enhance your lessons. The unit tests are presented in a self-correcting mode online, if you choose to use them that way. The tests are not too difficult because it is significant for students to feel success, not failure, when studying God's Word. The tests are meant to also be discussion starters, as together you talk about why one answer is wrong and another is correct. (Unit 5 test answers are: 1-a; 2-e; 3-c; 4-b; 5-a; 6-c; 7-d; 8-c; 9-c; 10-b.)

UNIT 5

46. God's People Return Home
47. Jesus Is Born
48. The Boy Jesus in the Temple
49. John Prepares the Way
50. The Baptism of Jesus
51. The Temptation of Jesus
52. Jesus' First Disciples
53. Nicodemus Visits Jesus
54. Jesus and the Woman at the Well
55. Jesus and the Children
56. Sermon on the Mount

Bulletin Board

This Bulletin Board is available, ready to cut out and pin up, from Concordia Publishing House. This Bulletin Board connects to the unit theme (as discussed on the previous page). Display the entire visual, connecting the shapes with yarn or paper strips to show the developing revelation of who Jesus is. Throughout the unit, refer back to this display, relating individual sections with individual Bible narratives that are being studied. This could be called an "Epiphany Flow Chart," which culminates in the final line of shapes that declare God's good gifts to us in Jesus Christ as He offers us forgiveness, life, and salvation.

Bible Book Overview

The Student Book Appendix has a valuable feature that gives a summary of each book of the Bible. Looking at the summaries of sixty-six books can be overwhelming, so it is suggested that each month/unit, your class look at the summaries of just a few of these books. During Unit 5, introduce the Scripture's books of the Major Prophets—Isaiah, Jeremiah, Lamentations, Ezekiel, and Daniel. Why are they called the "major" prophets? Perhaps it's because these books are longer than the books of the "minor" prophets; but it is more likely due to the powerful prophetic statements about the Messiah found in these books. Note especially Isaiah 53 and Jeremiah 31. Read together and discuss the summaries of these five books in the Student Book Appendix when you have time. (Note that a copy of the Student Book Appendix is included in the back of this Teacher Guide.)

Unit 5—The Promised One Is Here! Lesson 46

God's People Return Home
Ezra and Nehemiah

Background

The story of God's people returning from exile can be confusing. Few Bible story books include anything from Ezra or Nehemiah, and the Bible books themselves do not always follow a clear chronological sequence. It takes some work to understand what is going on.

So as you prepare to teach this lesson, focus on three main concepts: *return, rebuild, restore.* Each has an earthly meaning for the Jews during the fifth century before Christ and a spiritual meaning for both them and us at the same time.

Return. The people of Judah returned to the Promised Land. By God's grace at work in them, they also returned to the true worship of Yahweh. Returning to the Lord always involves repentance and forgiveness, for them and for us.

Rebuild. Led by Ezra, the people rebuilt the temple. Led by Nehemiah, they rebuilt the walls of Jerusalem and began to repopulate the capital city. Both of these outward actions were key to the nation's worship life and physical protection. At the same time, God was rebuilding His people, gathering them to worship Him and to live under His protection. The Holy Spirit continues this same construction work in our hearts today, building us up as the Church of Christ, the future citizens of the New Jerusalem (Revelation 21).

Restore. Little by little, God restored the fortunes of His people. Very soon, the long-promised Messiah would come to rescue, forgive, and restore both Jews and Gentiles to God's kingdom. Together, both Jews and Gentiles would become His witnesses to the nations (Isaiah 43:9–11). They would declare His glory, especially His grace toward sinners.

Central Truth

God's promises are sure—we see that in the Old Testament, and we know it to be true in our own lives.

Objectives

- Admit that we all fall and are taken captive by sin, needing to return in repentance to the grace and mercy of God.
- Celebrate that our relationship with God as His people has been rebuilt through the death and resurrection of Jesus.
- Enjoy the comfort and peace of salvation that is restored to us in faith through our Savior, Jesus.

Materials

- Hymnals and music CDs
- Reproducible 46
- Web Resource 46a
- Optional: Lego building blocks

Bible Prep

Post in advance so students can bookmark references before class time.
- Ezra 1; 3; 6:16–22
- 2 Corinthians 7:10–11
- Isaiah 30:15
- Nehemiah 2:11–19
- Nehemiah 4:1–23
- Nehemiah 6:16
- Nehemiah 8:8–12

Devotions

Advance preparation: Write the words *return*, *rebuild*, and *restore* on separate pieces of poster paper. You will display these words during the devotion. Begin by singing together stanza 1 of "Take My Life and Let It Be" (*LSB* 783; recorded as *Hymn of the Month* for grade 6, January). **What does the first sentence of this hymn mean? When we ask God to "consecrate" our lives, what are we asking Him to do?** (Let volunteers comment.) **The word *consecrate* is something like the word *dedicate*. It means that we want God to set us apart for His service. We want Him to use every minute of our lives to serve Him by serving others. When I hear the first sentence of the hymn, though, I sometimes think about a different way I might want to phrase it: "Take my life and let *me* be. . . ." In other words, "Don't bother me, God! Let me be. Let me do what I want to do." If we're honest, these are the words we'd prefer to sing, aren't they? Like all sinners, we're focused on ourselves. Life is all about us. Or we wish it were! God's ancient people thought like that too. Their lives showed it. And finally, when they wouldn't repent and change their ways, God allowed the Babylonian armies to take them into exile. But that exile didn't last forever. By God's grace, the Jewish people *returned* home to Jerusalem. They worshiped in** a *rebuilt* temple, inside the safety of rebuilt city walls. Their position as God's faithful people was *restored*. (Display each of these words as you say it, holding up or writing them on the board, one at a time.) **God works these three gifts in our lives too. When we sin, He makes it possible for us to *return* to Him in repentance and faith. He helps us *rebuild* the relationships damaged by our sin. And He *restores* us to our position as His consecrated, holy children because of what Jesus did for us on the cross. Let's sing stanza 1 of the hymn again.**

INTO the lesson

Return

Before having students begin work in their Student Guides, distribute Reproducible 46 and/or use Web Resource 46a. Guide them in using the timeline.

When you finish, talk about what students see. Ask questions like these:

- **What surprises do you notice?**
- **How many years are depicted on this timeline?** (167) **How does this compare with history with which you are more familiar—U.S. history, for example?**
- **How many different groups returned from Babylon/Persia to the Promised Land?** (Three)
- **How long did the Jewish people live in Jerusalem, unprotected by city walls?** (Over 90 years)
- **How does this timeline illustrate God's continuing faithfulness to His people?**

Then move into the Student Guide. Have students pair up to answer the questions on the first page and to read the Bible texts. Note that answers will vary. Accept comments students can defend, based on the Bible text itself.

Review

Read through this brief article with students. While Herod the Great is credited with building the temple that stood at the time of Christ, in reality, he just renovated the temple built and dedicated at the time of Ezra. King Herod indeed made the building much larger and ornate, turning it into a magnificent structure. But the true fulfillment of Haggai's prophecy (2:9) came when the Lord Jesus, God's promised Messiah, entered there.

LESSON 46
God's People Return Home

Return

God's people returned in two ways: (1) They returned to the land God had promised to Abraham. (2) They also returned to faith in the true God and to proper worship. Another word for this second kind of returning is *repentance*.

1. Read about the people's *physical return* to the Promised Land from Ezra 1; 3; and 6:16–22. Then list the evidence you find in these texts of the people's *spiritual return*, their repentance.
   Possible answers include the following:
   - People responded to the call to return home, specifically to rebuild the temple (Ezra 1:3, 5).
   - The people willingly began to observe the festivals God had commanded and to bring offerings (3:4–5).
   - They reestablished the priesthood and laid the foundation of the temple with great joy (3:8, 11).
   - They finished the temple, dedicated it, and observed the Passover once again. The Lord had made them joyful (6:16, 19).

2. The word *repentance* in the New Testament means "a change of mind." What change of mind had to happen before the Jewish people came back to the Promised Land? See 2 Corinthians 7:10–11.
   - When God changes our minds, we become sorry for our sins. Then we're eager to do what pleases Him.

Review

Covenant Connection
Between the time God's returning exiles laid the foundation for the rebuilt temple and the time the temple reconstruction was finished, some twenty years passed. Enemies interfered with the construction, and the people became discouraged. God sent two prophets, Haggai and Zechariah, to support them. Through Haggai, God made this promise: "The latter glory of this house shall be greater than the former. . . . And in this place I will give peace" (Haggai 2:9). God kept that promise when Jesus Himself taught in the temple the returning exiles built! He is the Prince of Peace.

98

INTO the Word

Rebuild

Work through this section with the class, again asking that students work in pairs. Alternatively, read the texts to them from a Bible and work through the questions with the class. Refer back to the timeline on Reproducible 46 to set the events in context. To make the story even more concrete, choose one of the following activities after students have completed question 1:

1. Allow students to work in small groups, each with their own set of Lego building blocks and figures with weapons. Encourage students to build a section of a city wall, but to focus on the feelings and dialogue of the Jewish people, who remained vigilant despite the taunts and attacks from their enemies.

2. Have the class pretend to be a group of Jewish people gathered after the evening meal, discussing Nehemiah's plan, either before work has begun or after they've started and have begun to encounter opposition. Encourage the students to choose a role (e.g., mother, father, child, priest, noble, official) and a position, either for or against the rebuilding of the wall. Students will begin to see that there were many

200

Rebuild

The temple was rebuilt, despite the opposition God's people encountered. But humanly speaking, the people were still vulnerable. Thieves, vandals, and bands of looters could easily attack them. Through Nehemiah, a high-ranking official in Persia, the Lord fixed this problem. Almost eighty years after the dedication of the rebuilt temple, Nehemiah brought a group of Jewish people back from Persia to Jerusalem.

1. Summarize the task Nehemiah set for himself and his people and the way they went about it. Base your answer on Nehemiah 2:11–19 and 4:1–23.
   Responses should focus on Nehemiah's leadership in rebuilding the walls of Jerusalem, despite the opposition of dangerous and shrewd enemies. In the end, the people worked side by side, weapons in one hand and trowels or mortarboards in the other.

2. Consider Nehemiah 6:16 and 8:8–12. Besides the wall around Jerusalem, what else was being rebuilt?
   The people were slowly gaining confidence in the Lord and in His protection. They were also learning about Him from the Scriptures, seeing their sins, and confessing them. All this is evidence of the growth and rebuilding of true faith.

Restored

God restored Judah, both physically and spiritually. Despite their sin, the nation would provide a home for the world's Savior less than four centuries later. They had been faithless, but the Lord remained faithful.

When has God shown His faithfulness to you? Tell about a time you've experienced His goodness even though you didn't deserve it. What can you learn from that experience?

When has He made it possible for you to return and rebuild as His restored child? Do you feel that God has given you a second chance in some area of your life? What New Year's resolution will you make this year as you return again to the Lord? What area in your life could use a little rebuilding and restoration right now?

Remember

"Do not be grieved, for the joy of the LORD is your strength." (Nehemiah 8:10b)

Restored

Use this section of the lesson to help students personalize the main points.

Read the questions in the second paragraph to your students, and ask that they jot some notes to themselves on a separate sheet of paper. Then, depending on the trust level in your classroom, you may (1) ask students to share thoughts with a partner; (2) lead a discussion with the whole group; or (3) have students write a one-page essay based on the questions.

Consider a combination of these three options, asking students to first share thoughts with one another and then commit their experiences and learnings to paper, perhaps as an assignment.

Remember

Point out the context of today's memory verse. God's people had gathered to hear the Word of God as they began to celebrate the Feast of Tabernacles (also called the "Feast of Booths"). It came right after Passover and was a joyous celebration. As they heard the Scriptures read, though, they became more and more aware of the many ways they had offended our Holy God. Alarm and sorrow overtook them. In the words of today's memory verse, Nehemiah comforted the people with the Good News of God's forgiveness and His assurance that He wanted to restore to them the joy of His salvation (Psalm 51:12). Remind your students that if they've gotten into some bad habits in the past year, God gives forgiveness and second chances. He continually calls us to return in repentance. Pray that God gives your class joy in keeping their New Year's resolutions and forgiveness when they fail. **Through faith in our Savior, Jesus, we can enjoy the comfort and peace of salvation.**

---

reasons for the people to oppose the rebuilding of the wall. After the creative dramatic scene, reiterate that in the Bible, we see how the people did respond. Together as a class, complete question 2, stressing the spiritual rebuilding that was taking place. Discuss how the attitude of God's people reflects their faith. They were taunted, despised, and attacked, but they still trusted in God to make them prosper. If time permits, refer students to Isaiah 30:15 and discuss how God's people calmly trusted in Him to keep His promises. Note on the timeline on Reproducible 46 how God brought about good for His people, despite the odds. What had appeared impossible earlier became easy because of God's plan (e.g., not only did Cyrus allow the Jewish people to go home, but he also let them return with the temple goods; at first, King Artaxerxes said there would be no building of the temple, but then King Darius said yes).

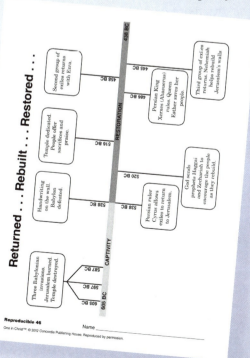

Check it Out

Haggai and Zechariah are both *postexilic prophets*. What does this term mean? In this lesson, we looked at the encouragement Haggai offered God's people (2:9). How would Zechariah 2:6–12 have been an additional encouragement to God's people as they decided whether or not to return to Jerusalem? How would it have encouraged them as they rebuilt and dedicated the temple?

Curriculum Connection

The exiles' return home was bittersweet; they could not help comparing what Jerusalem and God's temple used to look like with what it was now. Yet, in some ways, the new temple would be even greater, for Jesus Himself would come to it. Make a math connection to this lesson using section 6.1.4, Comparing Values on a Number Line. You'll find it in the sixth-grade Math volume of the Concordia Curriculum Guide series.

Bringing it home

In a country filled with families that seem to move constantly, the biblical story of the exile and return may have personal meaning for your students. Some of your students will be the children or grandchildren of immigrants; many will have personal memories of moving to a new house, community, state, or even country. Allow students to share those stories. They may wish to interview parents or grandparents to ask where they came from (whether overseas or out-of-state) and how things are different here. What do they miss? What are they glad to escape? Students could share these stories through posters, writing assignments, or oral presentations.

Teacher Tips

Sixth graders have a developmental need to move. Getting up after each fifty-minute class to change classrooms isn't enough. Effective instruction incorporates movement approximately every fifteen minutes. How can you accommodate this?

- Ask students to get up to turn in papers. Don't have one student collect them all.
- Have students stand up and move their chairs or desks to sit next to a friend for partner or group activities.
- Re-create today's timeline, enlarging it to develop a physical demonstration. Tie a clothesline across the front of the room. Have individuals or small groups of students create posters illustrating each key event. Clip these posters to the clothesline using clothespins in the correct sequence. Have students who are good at math figure out the correct spacing.

Ideas for the Gifted

Encourage students to learn about displaced people in the world today. How many are there? Why do people leave their homes in the first place? Are they ever able to return? What is the difference between a refugee and an internally displaced person? What parts of the world have the most refugees and displaced people? What needs do these people have? Who is helping? Is there a way that students can get involved in helping?

Searching Further

Interested students might explore the history of Ezra's temple. Key points might include the desecration of Ezra's temple by Antiochus IV Epiphanes, its rededication by Judas Maccabaeus, and its destruction by the Romans in AD 70. King Herod the Great was renowned for his architectural achievements. What renovations did he introduce, and what did the temple look like when he finished his work? (See the comments of Jesus' disciples and our Lord Himself in Mark 13:1–2.)

Students might create a scrapbook to document what they find. Some might prefer to make models or draw pictures—perhaps dividing the work among three groups of students: Solomon's temple, Ezra's temple, and Herod's temple.

UNIT 5—THE PROMISED ONE IS HERE!   LESSON 47

Jesus Is Born
Luke 2:1–20

Background

"But when the fullness of time had come, God sent forth His Son, born of woman . . ." (Galatians 4:4). Why did God choose that time and place for Jesus to be born? There are several possible reasons.

Jesus was born near the beginning of the Pax Romana ("Roman peace") in Judea, a conquered remnant of the old nation of Israel. This was a time when the Roman Empire had conquered the Mediterranean world and remained in strong control of it. Although the conquered nations chafed under Roman rule, they received benefits as well. The Romans enforced peace and put down uprisings and local violence. They built excellent roads and had a sophisticated postal system. Perhaps most important, they brought with them a common language—Koine Greek—which was used by people across the empire in addition to their own local languages. Greek was the international language of trade and commerce, much as English is today.

All of these things meant that the Good News of Jesus' salvation spread incredibly fast. Missionaries were able to travel with more freedom and safety than ever before, as we see from the Book of Acts. They could count on finding Greek speakers in virtually any city, which made it much easier to tell people about Jesus. All the books of the New Testament were written in Greek, which meant that even more people heard the Gospel. (There was already a Greek translation of the Old Testament—the Septuagint—which prepared the hearts of many people to hear about the promised Messiah, who had finally come.)

Central Truth
God knows the right time and right way to carry out His plans and promises.

Objectives
- Recognize that the only substitute who could take away our guilt and punishment was someone born like us but without sin (which is our human condition).
- Affirm that the birth of Jesus, our Savior, is significant at all times of the year.
- Glorify God, who daily offers peace on earth and joy eternal to all believers.

Materials
- Hymnals and music CDs
- Reproducible 47
- Web Resource 47a

Bible Prep
Post in advance so students can bookmark references before class time.
- Luke 2:1–20
- Psalm 121
- Galatians 4:4–5

Devotions

"I wanna go *now*," whined Lily. "Go, go, go!"

Brian made a face at his little sister and said, "If you don't stop whining about going to Grandma's house, I'm going to stick a stamp on your head and drop you in the mailbox. Then you can get there first, okay?"

"Go NOW!" shrieked Lily, dancing in a circle until she fell over.

"Dad!" called Brian. "Lily's making me crazy. Why can't she ever wait for anything?"

Their father came in and looked at Lily on the carpet and Brian with his head in his hands. He picked up the little girl and said, "She's only three. She doesn't understand that it's not the right time yet."

Brian said, "Why can't she just grow up? And isn't it her bedtime, anyway?"

His dad laughed and sent Lily off to brush her teeth. "Now it sounds like it's *you* that's having a hard time waiting," he said.

"Well, yeah," Brian answered. "I wish I could just push a button and turn her off when she starts screaming that way. I can't even do my homework. Can't they invent something?"

Brian's dad smiled. "Little kids are like that. We just have to teach them and wait for them to grow up more. It'll happen in God's time, don't worry."

"God's time!" Brian frowned. "How come God's time always takes so *long*?"

"Well, it sure seems like that," said his father. "I mean, it took thousands of years before God kept His promise and sent Jesus to be our Savior, and it's been two thousand years now, and we're *still* waiting for Jesus to come back. But God knows the right time for everything."

"I guess," said Brian. He looked hopeful. "So—is it the right time for me to go on the computer yet?"

"That depends. Did you finish your science?"

Brian pretended to scowl, and his father chuckled and went off to put Lily to bed.

Sing "Savior of the Nations, Come" (*LSB* 332; recorded as *Hymn of the Season for grade 7, Advent*). Say together Psalm 121. Then pray, **Father, You sent Your Son, Jesus, at the right time to save us. Help us to trust You even when we don't understand what You are doing, and to wait for You patiently. In Jesus' name we pray. Amen.**

INTO the lesson

Time vs. Timing

Move from today's devotion into a discussion about two kinds of time. Introduce this discussion by having students read through the five bulleted statements in the Student Guide. **Which statement differs from the rest? How so?** (*Number 4 has the sense of* kairos *rather than a numerical time.*)

Ask that students make up sentences of their own, one using *time* in the sense of *chronos* and the other in the sense of *kairos*. (Some students may benefit from working with a partner as they do this.)

After learners' examples demonstrate a clear understanding of the differences, call attention to today's memory verse on the next page. Have students highlight the word "time." **Which meaning for** *time* **would Jesus have had in mind as He spoke these words?** The Greek New Testament uses *kairos* in this context. Events converged to make this just the right time for God's Messiah to come into the world.

Then ask students to turn to Galatians 4:4–5. Here the Greek New Testament uses *chronos*. However, it adds a phrase to this word—"*the fullness* of time." Time was full. Events were just about to come together in just the right way. Just as water can gradually be added to a glass until it reaches the brim, events in the past gradually led up to this pinnacle moment, all for our salvation.

Have students consider what things have to be in place for an Olympian to break a world record and receive a gold medal. From the very beginning, the child needs to be born with the "right" genes and body composition to give him or her some natural talent. Most likely, the child will need good practicing facilities, the right training gear and equipment, and the best coaches. As the Olympics approach, the athlete cannot be too young or too old, cannot be nursing any serious injuries, and most likely cannot be distracted by any issues that might arise in his or her family (e.g., the death of a loved one). To "make" an Olympic gold-winning athlete, circumstances have to come together in just the right way.

What had happened to get things ready in Judah? Help students review the centuries of Old Testament history in which God had acted, preparing His people to see their need and receive the Savior He had promised. Use Reproducible 47 to understand how not only the people's hearts were ripe to receive their Savior, but how the political environment of the first century made the region ripe for dispersing the Gospel.

Also note that **Sometimes people talk about a "perfect storm." That refers to an event when weather conditions converge with just the right temperature, just the right moisture, and just the right winds coming together to create amazingly terrible weather conditions—a "perfect" storm. With Jesus, something amazing but wonderful happened as events converged, and at just the right time—according to** *God's* **timing—Jesus created the "perfect peace." He brought peace between God and humankind. He brought peace on earth!**

Lesson 47

Jesus Is Born

Time vs. Timing

When we use the word *time*, we don't always mean the same thing. Think about the stories below. One of them uses *time* differently from the others. Which is it? Explain.

- "Sure, you may go to Roberta's house to work on your report, Kim. But be home in time for supper at 6," said Mom.
- "The eclipse will occur right on time, 1:42 p.m. today," said the weather forecaster on the early morning broadcast.
- "At 3:10, I'll call time. At that point, everyone will put their pencils down," said the teacher as she handed out the year's first achievement test.
- "Jacob joined the team just in time," remarked Coach Winters. "I thought we might lose every game, but now we have a fighting chance!"
- "What time did you get to bed last night, Jana?" asked her dance instructor. "That's the fourth time you've yawned this hour!"

In the Greek language of the New Testament, two different words for "time" appear:

Chronos (**krō**-nos) refers to time as measured by clocks, calendars, schedules, seasons, and appointment books.

Kairos (**kī**-ros) refers to the point at which circumstances are just right for something to happen. Everything is ready. Events are converging toward one conclusion.

Read today's memory verse on the next page. Highlight the word *time*. Which of these meanings for *time* do you think Jesus had in mind as He spoke about "time" to His first listeners? Explain your reasons for thinking so.

Review

Covenant Connection

"While we were still weak, at the right time Christ died for the ungodly" (Romans 5:6). This Bible verse tells us two important things about Christmas: (1) Jesus was born as a little baby at Christmas so He could die on the cross on Good Friday, and (2) you and I are the reason Jesus came at Christmas—so He could rescue us, the weak and ungodly. And why did He do this? Verse 8 of the same chapter in Romans tells us, "God shows His love for us in that while we were still sinners, Christ died for us." This is why Christmas is so important, any day and every day!

100

The Fullness of Time

Malachi was the last of the Old Testament messengers, or prophets. After he put down his pen, God did not speak directly to His people again until John the Baptist began preaching and baptizing at the river Jordan. Malachi was the last of the Lord's messengers for more than four hundred years! (To put this in perspective, remember that one of our nation's first settlements, Jamestown, was founded about four hundred years ago, in 1607.)

If you had lived in Jerusalem or Bethany or Nazareth, would you have wondered about God's promise to send the Messiah? Would you have wondered why He was taking so long? What if during those four hundred years, foreign armies had invaded your land? What if they imposed heavy taxes? What if they despised your faith and desecrated your temple—the temple Ezra and the returning exiles had built after so much effort and during a time of danger? Would you have wondered about God's promise then? Would you have asked, "What is He waiting for?"

Maybe some people did wonder, but God had not forgotten His promises. He was waiting for His *kairos*—"the fullness of time." Then, one day, the time arrived. Jesus waited not one second longer to begin His earthly mission—His rescue mission. As He left heaven, He had you in mind!

With God's promises and His timing in mind, read or say Luke 2:1–20. Try to put yourself into the picture. You weren't at the stable in Bethlehem. Still, in what ways did you play a part in the events of the first Christmas? __God knew you before you were born, and He knew you would be born with a sinful condition and would need a Savior. God sent Jesus for you. See Psalm 71:5–6; Galatians 4:4–5.__

Taking Time

At Christmas, Christians sometimes get so busy with the externals (concerts, shopping, decorations, gift wrapping, and the like) that we don't take time for the things in the list below. Maybe that happened to you this past Christmas. It's not too late! Make a plan to do two (or more) of these thank-You's this week in honor of Jesus coming at Christmas. The time is right!

Tell what God has done for you: _____

Pray for God's continuing help: _____

Show kindness wherever you are: _____

Serve others without being asked: _____

Remember

"Jesus came into Galilee, proclaiming the Gospel of God, and saying, 'The time is fulfilled, and the kingdom of God is at hand; repent and believe in the Gospel.'" (Mark 1:14–15)

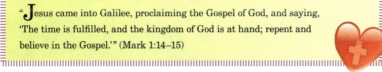

Into the Word

The Fullness of Time

To consider how God knows the right time and the right way to carry out His plans and promises, use Web Resource 47a or, together as a class, read the introductory information about Malachi (which means "messenger") in the Student Book. Malachi, the last of the postexilic prophets, wrote his book around four hundred years before Jesus was born. To help students put the time period into perspective, mention the fact that one of our nation's first settlements, Jamestown, was founded in 1607—about four hundred years ago.

Ask, **Why a Christmas story when the calendar says that the Christmas season is over?** For Christians, Christmas Day is every day because every day, we need our Savior! People waited a long time for His coming. We continue to wait, but now for His second coming, when He will take all believers to heaven! Continue through this section of the Student Guide, discussing with the class the part *they* played in the first Christmas. Have students consider all the time and energy that is spent planning a party, maybe even a Christmas party. Usually a party is not thrown together at the last minute. How does a thoughtful host take into account his or her guests as the party is planned (e.g., "I'll serve cupcakes because I know Kendra likes them" or "I won't serve nuts because Dylan's allergic to them.")?

Have your students ever considered the fact that God had each of them specifically in mind as He planned the first Christmas and then put this part of His plan of salvation into practice? How could recognizing that fact change the way we look at the Scriptures that describe the first Christmas?

After talking about that briefly, have students turn to Luke 2:1–20. As they read the account from their own Bibles, ask that they put themselves into the picture. To capture this one special, significant moment in time, have students work in small groups to create a tableau scene (frozen characters) of either the shepherds in the fields hearing about their long-awaited Savior's birth or the shepherds meeting their Savior for the first time. Students can pretend they are a photograph shot at a dynamic moment. Have students consider the thoughts and feelings of the shepherds (their expressions) and the pleasing, interesting arrangement of the characters (their composition), each group placing themselves, as it were, on their own life-size Christmas cards.

How does reading this text today differ from reading it on December 24? Why is it good to study the "Church festival" texts during those seasons? Why is it good to study them at other times of the year too? (When read during the appropriate seasons, the Bible texts remind us of the events we commemorate and the reasons we worship. When read at other times during the year, we may be able to see and think about things we don't notice during the flurry of activities that often accompany Christmas, Lent, and Easter.) Christmas is significant each day!

Into our lives

Taking Time

The preceding conversation leads logically into this section. Work with students to brainstorm endings for each of the four sentence starters. Record all the ideas suggested on the board. Encourage students to be as specific as possible.

When you have five or six ideas for each sentence starter, let students choose which they would like to follow up on. They should jot these in their books. Ask that they complete at least two, but encourage them to do more.

Lesson Support

Ideas for the Gifted

Encourage gifted students to research the use of *BCE* and *CE* by scholars today when they reference time (dates). These abbreviations for the terms "Before Common Era" and "Common Era" may slowly be replacing *BC* ("Before Christ") and *AD* ("anno Domini," which is Latin for "the Year of Our Lord"). **What could lie behind this change? Why would Christians resist it? How could we do that?**

Curriculum Connection

The birth of Jesus is meaningful even to some non-Christians because it embodies one of the universal themes of human storytelling—the story of a tiny, insignificant beginning that turned out to have a worldwide impact. Discuss universal themes with your students using section 6.2.3.3, Universal Plots, Patterns, or Themes. This can be found in the sixth-grade Performing Arts volume of the Concordia Curriculum Guide series. Discuss: **Why do you think God chose to record this humble beginning to His Son's earthly life?** Read the answer to this question in Philippians 2:5–11. Let students choose a song that celebrates the name of Jesus.

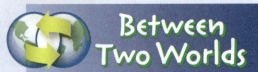

Between Two Worlds

Many students learning English have trouble with the fast pace of English speech. One man compared the sound of English to a group of birds twittering; the words went by so quickly he could not catch them. You can help your immigrant students by slowing down your speech and using short, simple sentences—especially when giving directions. Repeating yourself and making sure they can see your lips also helps. Keep in mind that most of these students are having to mentally "translate" what you say into their own native language before they can comprehend and act on it. If you speak too quickly, they will miss what you say next because they are still translating the last part.

You can also help children who are learning to speak English by making sure that important matters are communicated in two ways, both spoken and written. For example, give assignments in written form instead of asking students to write down your oral directions. Write instructions on the test itself, and give them orally as well. If you are asking students to bring something the next day, hold the item up as you tell them. Students (and parents trying to help them at home!) will be grateful. (Note that the unit Family Letters available on the One in Christ Portal are also available in Spanish.)

Taking Note

Use a Venn diagram to help students compare and contrast the gifts we receive from other people and the gift of Jesus, given by God. Note the suggested answers below, but be aware that responses may vary, depending on the nuances students have in mind. Accept responses they can defend.

Label one circle "God's Gift." Phrases that belong in that section include: Lasts forever; priceless; planned from all eternity; intended for everyone; invisible, but real.

Label the other circle "Our Gifts." Phrases that belong in that section include: Break, wear out, or get lost; sometimes cheap, sometimes expensive; sometimes given from a sense of obligation (because they "have to").

Phrases that belong in the overlapping section include: Given in love; creates joy; sometimes unappreciated; sometimes received gratefully.

After you've worked through the exercise together, ask, **What insights did you gain from this activity? What observations do you have?**

Critical thinking

Either in class discussion or as a writing assignment, encourage your students to think through some "What if . . . ?" scenarios. For example, what if Jesus had been born in a palace as part of a royal family? What effect would that have had on His life? His work? our faith? What if He had been born today to a poor woman in an inner city? What if God had chosen to make Him Eve's son or grandson—to send our Savior almost immediately after the fall of mankind? (Note that this is just another way of asking why God chose to allow the human race to wait so long for our Savior.) **What benefit was there for us in making us wait?**

There will be no right answers for these questions—only an opportunity for careful thinking. Pray that your students will conclude this exercise with a greater appreciation for God's wisdom in choosing the time and place He did for Jesus' birth, life, and work.

UNIT 5—THE PROMISED ONE IS HERE!

LESSON 48

The Boy Jesus in the Temple
Luke 2:41–52

Background

Jesus visited Jerusalem with His parents at age 12—the beginning of young manhood. It also might have been the first time His parents felt safe bringing Him back to Judea. After their return from Egypt, the family decided to go back to Nazareth rather than return to Bethlehem, where Herod Archelaus had become ruler and was known for his cruelty. Deposed in AD 6, Archelaus was no longer a threat to Jesus' life. Jesus' devout parents therefore took Him along as they went to Jerusalem to worship.

Families from one area would often travel together in large groups for safety and for company. This explains why Mary and Joseph didn't notice Jesus' absence until a day had passed—they doubtless thought He was with His friends. Discovering their mistake, they returned to Jerusalem and turned the city upside down, looking for their lost son.

It is rather surprising that they didn't think to look first at the temple. Perhaps Jesus' childhood had been so normal that they had temporarily lost sight of what made Him different from others—His identity as the Son of God.

The temple was a favorite spot for teaching and debate. Jesus Himself taught there on many occasions as an adult. As a child, His precocious understanding and love for the Lord must have pleased some teachers and baffled others. And yet, after all was over, Jesus went home with His parents "and came to Nazareth and was submissive to them" (Luke 2:51). The incarnate Son of God still had a lot of growing to do. And He faithfully honored His parents, keeping the Fourth Commandment.

Central Truth

God leads us to grow in faith, fed and refreshed by His Word, throughout our entire lives.

Objectives

- Acknowledge that people often see "being a Christian" as a part-time thing (part of the day, just on Sunday, or a few years of your life); however, God expects a lifelong commitment.
- Appreciate that when we do stray from the Lord, He calls us back to repentance, and He will strengthen us for a commitment to living for Christ.
- Dedicate ourselves to continuing in His Word and will throughout our lives.

Materials

- Songbooks and music CDs
- Reproducible 48

Bible Prep

Post in advance so students can bookmark references before class time.
- Luke 2:41–52
- Psalm 121

Devotions

Note that the Student Guide refers to today's devotion, so be sure to use it as class begins.

Do you know anyone who would say, "Well, it's Sunday morning. I think I'll have a drink of water. Then I won't need another drink until next Sunday morning"? That sounds foolish, yet some people think of God's Word in just that way. They take in the water of life—God's Word—once a week and think it's enough.

Or think about what will happen when we finish this school year. That doesn't mean we take a summer break from God! Would you ever say something like "I drink plenty of water in school. I don't need to drink anything more till the next school year starts"? Of course not. You're not that silly!

But some people *are* that silly about God's Word. Even worse, some people think that after confirmation, they will never need to read the Bible again and they'll stop going to church. They would never say, "Well, I'm done drinking water for the rest of my life." But they don't see that they're making that same foolish mistake with something much more important.

We need water every day to be physically healthy. We also need God's Word to stay spiritually healthy. Water makes things grow, and our faith won't grow without God's Word. A dip in a pool of water makes us feel better on a hot summer day; a dip into Scripture strengthens our hearts, bringing us peace in times of trouble. Water cleans us up when we get dirty; God's Word reminds us that Jesus cleanses us of our sins.

Jesus said, "Whoever drinks of the water that I will give him will never be thirsty again. The water that I will give him will become . . . a spring of water welling up to eternal life" (John 4:14). That's Jesus' promise to all of us. Let's thank Him!

Sing "I've Got Peace like a River" (*AGPS* 139; recorded on *JPS*). Say together Psalm 121. Pray: **Lord, You refresh us with Your Word and promises. Keep us always thirsty for the Word of life You give. Amen.**

207

INTO the lesson

Designs on the Future

Based on the opening devotion, ask the class to consider a hypothetical case of someone who once worshiped regularly and always came to Sunday School, but now no longer does so.

Then ask, **Do you suppose that person just decided one day to walk away from Jesus? Maybe so, but probably not. What's a more likely scenario?** Invite one or two volunteers to comment. Then ask the class to keep this question in mind during the lesson. You will return to it later.

Move from here into the first page of today's lesson. Let students work individually to fill in the four "designs" as directed. As they do so, walk around the classroom, asking individuals about their responses. On what evidence have they based their answers? Encourage them to think back to specific Scriptures they have memorized or Bible narratives they have studied.

When everyone has finished, ask for observations. Guide the conversation with these questions:

- **Have you ever considered the idea that your teachers, pastors, and the other Christian adults around you care about your future? Which of them especially encourages you in your faith? Have you ever thanked them for it?** (It would encourage *them* if you did!)
- **Have you ever considered the idea that Satan cares about your future and that he's already scheming to derail God's purposes for you? Why is it in Satan's best interests to keep you from thinking about his schemes? How does that add a more serious tone to this discussion?**
- **When you think about your Lord's will for your future, what thoughts and feelings come to mind? How do His strength, His promises, and His purposes help comfort you in light of Satan's schemes?**

LESSON 48

The Boy Jesus in the Temple
Designs on the Future

A blueprint is a plan and a design telling what something will be like when it is built. There are blueprints for houses, bridges, skyscrapers, rockets, and gyms. Many people have a blueprint for their lives—plans that they hope will happen in the future.

You may think a lot about your future. Or you may not. Either way, others are thinking about it. They have designs on it. That expression does not mean they have your life planned out step-by-step for you. It does not mean they can force you to do this or that or the other thing. It does mean, though, that they care about you, have hopes and dreams for your future, and may even want to influence the outcome.

What designs do your parents or grandparents have on your future? What have they said or done that leads you to think that?

What do your teachers, coaches, and pastor want for your future, especially your faith life?

Answers will vary.

What designs does Satan have on your future, especially your faith life? How do you know?

What does your heavenly Father want for your future, especially your faith life? How do you know?

Review

Covenant Connection
Already at the age of twelve, Jesus was beginning to understand the plans that God had designed for His life. In Luke 2:49 in the King James Version of the Bible, Jesus asks His parents, "[Didn't you know] that I must be about My Father's business?" The heavenly Father's business is our salvation through Jesus, the promised Savior. What plans does God have for your life? Jeremiah 29:11 tells us, "I know the plans I have for you, declares the LORD, plans for welfare and not for evil, to give you a future and a hope." Praise God!

102

INTO the Word

Designs on Jesus' Future

Use the opening paragraph in this section to spark student thought regarding Mary and Joseph's relationship with Jesus as He grew to manhood. Point out that as today's Bible narrative opens, Jesus is about the age of your students. His parents likely thought about His future even more than our parents have considered our futures, simply because of all the unusual events that occurred during the first months of Jesus' life.

When they thought about their Son's future, what do you think they imagined? We don't really know, but surely chapters like Psalm 22 and Isaiah 53 in the Hebrew Scriptures came to their attention! They must have remembered the words of Simeon when the baby Jesus was brought to the temple. See Luke 2:25–35. Lead from here into vv. 41–52. When you've finished reading, ask students to return to the questions:

- Mary and Joseph's immediate hopes for Jesus involved getting Him safely back to Nazareth. No doubt, they wanted Him to grow up to do the important work God had in mind for Him. Even the name they gave their Son at Gabriel's command hinted strongly at His future. *Jesus* means "the Lord is salvation."

Designs on Jesus' Future

Jesus' mother, Mary, and His earthly father, Joseph, must have thought a lot about Jesus' future. They may have thought about it more than most parents think about their children's prospects. Just think! They had heard the angel Gabriel—God's personal messenger—speak about that future. They had listened as shepherds reported the words of the angelic chorus the night Jesus was born. They had watched as the Wise Men worshiped the Christ Child and presented expensive, exotic gifts to Him.

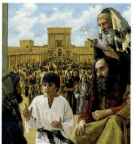

What hopes do you suppose Mary and Joseph had for Jesus' future? What was Satan hoping? What future did the heavenly Father have in mind for His Son? Think about those questions as you read Luke 2:41–52. Then talk about whose designs on Jesus' life were accomplished.

Design Your Own Future?

When we think about the relationship we want to have with our heavenly Father in the future, we have to admit there's a lot we can't control. We cannot make ourselves believe or keep ourselves in the faith. Only the Holy Spirit can do that.

On the other hand, God does promise that when we keep on drinking the "living water" Jesus talked about in today's opening devotion (John 4:14), it will strengthen the new life He gave us in our Baptism. In that sense, we have choices to make. We may have the best intentions. Even so, many distractions clamor for our attention. In the list below, check the three distractions you think are most likely to derail the faith life and spiritual commitment that you and those who love you want for your future.

- ❏ Screen time (electronics)
- ❏ Athletics
- ❏ Studying to get good grades
- ❏ Earning money for college
- ❏ Parties
- ❏ Music
- ❏ Clubs and organizations
- ❏ Volunteering
- ❏ Sleep
- ❏ Leadership roles at school
- ❏ Drama—either acting or working behind the scenes
- ❏ Earning money for a car
- ❏ Hobbies
- ❏ Other _____
- ❏ Other _____
- ❏ Other _____
- ❏ Other _____
- ❏ Other _____
- ❏ Other _____

None of the activities in this list is wrong or evil. In fact, they are all gifts from God—when prioritized properly. Since you now have a good idea what your top three potential distractions are, you can talk with your Savior about them and then make a plan to keep the main thing—God's Word—the main thing in your life. What will that plan look like?

Who could help you stick to your plan? _____

Remember

"I will meditate on Your precepts and fix my eyes on Your ways. I will delight in Your statutes; I will not forget Your word." (Psalm 119:15–16)

- Satan hoped to delay and eventually derail God's will for Jesus. It's interesting to consider the fact that the devil must have actually believed he could accomplish this. Otherwise, why would he have worked so personally and persistently in Jesus' life?
- **Ephesians 1:3–10 shows us that from all eternity, the heavenly Father agreed with the Son and the Holy Spirit that we would be saved through the death of Christ Jesus.**

The plans of God for Jesus' life were fulfilled, just as He had promised from all eternity.

Temple or Synagogue? What's the Difference?

As you read the New Testament, you will notice that Jesus sometimes worshiped in synagogues and sometimes at the temple in Jerusalem. What was the difference? Read each text and use the information to discern what happened there.

Text	Temple	Synagogue	What happened there?
Matthew 13:54		X	Jesus taught there in Nazareth.
Matthew 21:12–13	X		The temple was to be "a house of prayer."
2 Chronicles 7:1	X		Burnt offerings and sacrifices were made. The glory of the Lord filled the temple.
Matthew 21:15	X		Children cried out, praising Jesus, saying, "Hosanna to the Son of David!"

My Summary of the Distinction

The Old Testament doesn't mention synagogues. They seem to have been started when the people were captive, in exile far from Jerusalem. Use a concordance and Bible dictionary to learn more about the temple and synagogues. Write a brief paragraph explaining what you understand the differences and similarities to be.

The temple, located in Jerusalem, was the only place in Judah where sacrifices could be legitimately offered. Jewish males were required by God to come to the temple three times each year for worship at the major feasts. Synagogues, on the other hand, were located in the towns and villages scattered throughout Israel. No sacrifices were offered there. Instead, people came together in synagogues on the Sabbath to hear the Scriptures read and to be taught.

INTO our lives

Design Your Own Future?

Say, **In one sense, no one can design his or her own life. There are too many variables. Take one example—someone who wants to play professional baseball. That person may eat only the most healthful food, make it a habit to get plenty of sleep, practice all the right skills, and study endless video replays of famous games. But one injury can derail the plan in a split second.**

Have a volunteer read the first two paragraphs in this section in the Student Book. Then, based on them, ask students to summarize what we can and cannot control about our lives of faith. **What does God ask of us?** (To put ourselves in a position to receive the Means of Grace—hearing God's Word with other Christians and reading and meditating on God's Word on our own each day, receiving the Lord's Supper when it is offered, remembering our Baptism daily) **For what is God responsible?** (Using His Word—the written Word, the spoken Word, and the visible Word in the Sacraments—to sustain and strengthen our faith, just as He has promised) Then remind students of the question you asked earlier about Christian teens or young adults who walked away from the faith. **It's not likely that most of them just woke up one morning and decided they no longer wanted or needed Jesus' friendship. What's a more likely scenario?** (That they gradually stopped using the Means of Grace. Subtly, Satan tempted them with other priorities, and their faith weakened.)

Perhaps Satan even used some of the distractions listed on this page to ease these teens away from the Savior. Reiterate the truth that nothing on this list is evil or wrong. But any and all of these things can take on a priority that crowds out the Means of Grace in our lives. After everyone has checked three distractions, talk together about what you have learned and write out a plan for defeating Satan's designs. Look at today's Bible verse to remember. Ask, **Do you think the psalm writer kept this promise?** No, he did not. No sinner could. We can't either. **But there is forgiveness for us and others who have strayed from God and His Word, because Jesus kept the promise perfectly for us; He obeyed God's Law in our place. Now, when God considers our use of His Means of Grace, He sees that we always and fully treasure the Word and obey it—not in ourselves, but in Jesus, who did all this for us.**

Close by singing "Open Our Eyes" (*AGPS* 195; recorded on *JPS*).

Lesson Support

Searching Further

What was the difference between the synagogues of Jesus' day and the temple in Jerusalem? Now that your students have wrapped up the lessons focused on the Babylonian exile, they are in a position to understand this distinction. Use Reproducible 48 to guide their exploration of this question.

Bringing it home

Consider placing this in a note to parents:

Will our children continue in the faith? Will they continue to grow in Christlikeness? Will they continue to treasure the Word and Sacraments? Or will the "tribulations" of life and the "persecution" that "arises on account of the Word" draw them away from their Savior (Matthew 13:3–23)? As with many such questions, we recognize a two-part answer—God's part and our part.

We sinful human beings cannot bring ourselves to faith or keep ourselves in the faith. Only the Holy Spirit can do that. He works through means—the Means of Grace. Through the life-giving, life-preserving Word and Sacraments, God is always at work, transforming human hearts. There and only there, He promises to convey His forgiveness to us. There and only there, He has promised to create in us clean hearts and renew our spirits (Psalm 51:10).

This, then, brings us to our part in the process. As God's redeemed, dearly loved children, we need to be open and receptive to His gracious Word of life. We need to resist Satan's Sunday-morning temptations to reverse priorities. We need to have a time, a place, and a plan to read God's Word daily and talk with Him in prayer about what He is teaching us. We need to encourage one another in these spiritual exercises.

Of course, the desire and energy to do even that much must come from God Himself. And He willingly provides these things. Place your child in the Lord's hands, trusting Him to shepherd your child, just as He has promised.

Check it Out

Your students could learn from other adults who already have a Bible study plan in place. You may want to invite a panel of three to five congregation members to visit your classroom and answer questions about their experiences, such as what they participate in at church, what personal Bible study they do and when and where they do it, what value they place on studying God's Word, and what difference it makes in their lives. Perhaps one of the participants could even be an alumnus of your school and could encourage students that a Christian education is of value even when you're older. Students may be interested in doing an Internet search of Bible studies available (from Concordia Publishing House or other Christian publishing companies) at different phases in life. Students will begin to see that at every stage in life, there are resources available to grow in the faith as we are fed and refreshed by God's Word.

Curriculum Connection

A great connection to use with your class is section 6.3.3.4, Changes in Families, which is found in the sixth-grade Social Studies volume of the Concordia Curriculum Guide series. Discuss how Mary, Joseph, and Jesus interacted with one another. **What seems familiar and predictable to you? What surprises you, and why? For example, would your parents allow you to travel in the same group but out of their sight for a whole day? Why or why not?**

Critical thinking

Mary and Joseph found Jesus "in the temple, sitting among the teachers, listening to them and asking them questions" (Luke 2:46). Say, **Jesus was about your age at the time. What do you suppose He was asking? If He were here in your class, what would you ask Him? What would He ask you?** Point out that He *is* here with us now; we can talk to Him in prayer; we can hear Him speak in Scripture.

210

UNIT 5—THE PROMISED ONE IS HERE!

LESSON **49**

John Prepares the Way
MATTHEW 3:1–11; LUKE 3:1–1

Background

God Himself was going to visit His people; it was time to get ready!

God sent John the Baptist to prepare Israel to receive its promised Messiah and King. But John's work was not to build new roads, plan state dinners, or repaint guest rooms. It was through repentance that God's people would be made ready. They needed to recognize their sin, confess their guilt, and see their need for the Savior.

The coming King was not the Savior they expected. He would not drive out the Roman armies and restore the ancient kingdom of David. Instead, He would be crowned with thorns and conquer by way of a cross. He would be the final sacrifice who would take away their sins.

Through John's preaching, many people recognized their sins and repented. John the Baptist also identified Jesus as the promised Messiah who came to save His people. God reveals His Son to us today in His Word, giving us faith in "the Lamb of God, who takes away the sin of the world!" (John 1:29).

Devotions

Sarah's cousins were coming to visit! She could hardly wait. Ruth and Lisa were both close to Sarah's age, and they had been best friends forever. But they had moved away a year ago, and this was their first visit back.

Sarah was already making plans. They would walk to the park every day. They would go skating. Maybe Mom would take them to a movie, and then they could go out for pizza. Sarah eagerly helped her parents prepare for the visit. She folded clean sheets and towels. She found her favorite movies to watch with them. She helped her mother make peanut butter cookies—her cousins' favorite.

Then her mother asked, "What about your room—is it ready?"

"Um, yeah, I guess so," said Sarah. "Why?"

"Ruth and Lisa will be sleeping in there, so make sure it's neat. I'll help you put sheets on the bed, and then . . ."

Sarah interrupted her mother. "Sleeping in *my* room? Why not in Vicky's?"

"You know your room is bigger," said her mother. "And besides that, it was just painted. Your cousins will like the way you've decorated it. You'll be sleeping with Vicky while they're here."

Sarah walked slowly upstairs and sat down on her bed with a thump. "Well, that's okay, I guess," she thought. "They *are* my favorite cousins. I guess I can put up with Vicky's snoring for a while. But I've sure got a lot of extra work to do, getting ready."

Today we will learn about preparing for a much greater guest. John the Baptist came to prepare the hearts of the people for the coming of Jesus. This was John's purpose even from the time he was a little baby, when his father, Zechariah, said, "You, child, will be called the prophet of the Most High; for you will go before the Lord to prepare His ways, to give knowledge of salvation to His people in the forgiveness of their sins" (Luke 1:76–77).

Central Truth

The Law prepares hearts for the Gospel by accusing us of sin, directing us to repentance, and directing us to the need for a savior; through our Savior, Jesus, the promised Messiah, we are freed from the Law and the punishment of our disobedience, as He offers us forgiveness, life, and salvation.

Objectives
- Confess that we sinners can do nothing to earn or deserve salvation.
- Recognize that Jesus is our substitute, who wins the victory for us.
- With transformed and grateful hearts, live for the Lord.

Materials
- Hymnals and music CDs
- Web Resource 49a
- Reproducible 49

Bible Prep
Post in advance so students can bookmark references before class time.
- Matthew 3
- Luke 3
- John 1
- Ephesians 4:25–32
- Romans 12:9–21
- Galatians 5:16–26

We, too, need to have our hearts prepared by repenting of our sins, hearing the Gospel message of salvation, and honoring Jesus as the first priority above all other things in our lives. Sing about John's preparations and proclamations in "On Jordan's Bank the Baptist's Cry" (*LSB* 344; recorded as *Hymn of the Season* for grade 4, Advent).

211

INTO the lesson

Get Ready!

Work together on the opening section of the Student Book, which emphasizes the importance of preparing in advance for special or important circumstances. Say, **God had been preparing the way for the Messiah for centuries and millennia. The time was near—the fullness of time—so God prepared by sending one more prophet. Even this prophet had been prophesied!** The last prophet of the Old Testament, Malachi, told of this messenger (John) four hundred years before he was born, as the prophet told this word from the Lord: "Behold, I send My messenger, and he will prepare the way before Me. And the Lord whom you seek will suddenly come to His temple; and the messenger of the covenant in whom you delight, behold, he is coming, says the Lord of hosts" (Malachi 3:1). "For you who fear My name, the sun of righteousness shall rise with healing in its wings. . . . Behold, I will send you Elijah the prophet before the great and awesome day of the Lord comes" (4:2, 5). Then continue with the Review section, which details this message further.

Review

The Old Testament prophet Isaiah wrote about John preparing the way for the coming of Christ. What do we hear John's voice crying out? Read Isaiah 40:3. Ask, **What do you think is meant by the phrase "in the desert"? What kinds of situations did the Israelites face at the end of the Old Testament and the beginning of the New Testament period?** (The desert of captivity in Babylon, the desert of oppression by the Romans) **What do you think the phrase "a highway for our God" means?** (The way of salvation; nothing will get in the way of God's plans and promises.)

Read Isaiah 40:4. Ask students to close their eyes and think about racing video games with challenges that get in the way of your car or motorcycle. **How is repentance like building a straight, level road?** (We don't want any obstacles to get in the way of God redeeming us through His Son.) **God comes to us, takes our sins away, and restores our relationship with Him through Christ.**

LESSON 49

John Prepares the Way

Get Ready!

Some things just happen, and that's okay. If you were planning a picnic and it rains, you can just have the picnic inside your house. But there are times when it can be a mess if you aren't prepared. If you are in a mountain cabin and there is three feet of new snow outside and you forgot your skis, boots, and a shovel, that could ruin your day. Consider these special circumstances that go better with preparation.

What would a coach do to prepare for a basketball tournament? _____

What would you do to prepare to see your favorite movie star or singing group in person? _____

What would your grandmother do to prepare for a big family dinner? _____

What would a highway crew do to prepare to build a faster, safer super-highway here? _____

The time was ready for Jesus to begin His ministry and fulfill His mission. God had been preparing the way for centuries and centuries through His covenant promises and prophecies. Now it was time to send one more prophet—John the Baptist. John announced the coming of the Messiah, proclaiming:

The time is near!

Review

Covenant Connection

The Old Testament prophet Isaiah prophesied about John the Baptist, saying, "A voice cries: 'In the wilderness prepare the way of the Lord; make straight in the desert a highway for our God. Every valley shall be lifted up, and every mountain and hill be made low; the uneven ground shall become level, and the rough places a plain. And the glory of the Lord shall be revealed, and all flesh shall see it together, for the mouth of the Lord has spoken'" (Isaiah 40:3–5). The prophets of old proclaimed, "The time is near!" John roused up the people by proclaiming that "The time is now!" (Change the bold purple statement above this box by crossing off the word "near" and changing it to "now.")

104

INTO the Word

Repent

As you read together the following sections about John's message, encourage students to read dramatically and forcefully, reflecting the earnestness of John, which called out to some and was rejected by others. Use Web Resource 49a as a background, showing the setting of the Bible narrative.

Read Matthew 3:1–6. What do these verses tell us about John? What did he do? What did he look like? What did he tell people? (John preached in the wilderness of Judea. John was dressed in rough clothing of camel's hair and a leather belt. God's promised Messiah was coming, the Lord Himself, and John was the one who would prepare people for His coming. People came to listen to John preach, and John baptized them in the Jordan River.) **Can you see why John the Baptist was often compared to the prophet Elijah?** (In appearance, both were rough outdoorsmen who wore camel hair clothing. God led both to speak courageously, accusing people boldly of their sins. Neither would stop when threatened by the unbelieving. God blessed the powerful message He gave to each to speak.)

Luke 3:3 says that John "[proclaimed] a baptism of repentance for the forgiveness of sins." What does that mean?

Repent

Luke 3:3 says that John proclaimed "a baptism of repentance for the forgiveness of sins." What does that mean? **John's Baptism was a baptism of repentance, a sign that the people being baptized were sorry for their sins, that they were ready to change their lives, and that they had faith in God.**

Read Luke 3:7–9. Some of the people who listened to John did not think they needed to be sorry. What did John tell the Pharisees and Sadducees? **He called them children of snakes, a "brood of vipers!"**

John the Baptist told the people to repent of their sins. They were to change the way they lived, showing that they were truly sorry for their sins. The people asked John how they should live. Read the Bible verses for each group of people, and write down John's reply to them.

To the Pharisees and Sadducees (Matthew 3:8): **Bear fruit in keeping with repentance.**

To the crowds of people (Luke 3:10–11): **Share clothing and food with the poor.**

To the tax collectors (Luke 3:12–13): **Collect only the money you are supposed to collect.**

To the soldiers (Luke 3:14): **Don't threaten people, and be content with your pay.**

In what way would the Messiah, Jesus, be different from John (Matthew 3:11)? **Jesus would be greater; the Baptism of Jesus would be more than a baptism of repentance because it would have the Holy Spirit and power ("fire").**

Fruitful Results

Some people ignored John's message; some arrogantly thought they were good enough; some preferred to do whatever they wanted to do. This happens today also, but God calls to us through His Word to repent of our sins, preparing our hearts to welcome the Messiah. How can we live as people redeemed by the Messiah? John told tax collectors not to cheat and soldiers not to threaten people. What might John tell you today? What then shall *we* do?

Read these Bible verses for some ideas:

Ephesians 4:25–32: _____
Romans 12:9–21: _____
Galatians 5:16–26: _____

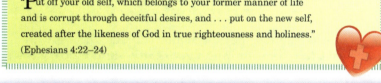

Remember

"Put off your old self, which belongs to your former manner of life and is corrupt through deceitful desires, and . . . put on the new self, created after the likeness of God in true righteousness and holiness." (Ephesians 4:22–24)

105

Students will use their Student Books to write down what John told the crowd. **Read Luke 3:7–9. Some of the people who listened to John did not think they needed to be sorry. What did John tell the Pharisees and Sadducees?** The Pharisees and Sadducees were very religious people. They may not have thought they needed to repent or change how they lived. They believed that as descendants of Abraham, they already enjoyed God's favor. What did John say to that? He told them God could turn stones into children of Abraham. Sinners can't do anything to earn or deserve salvation. We can never be good enough to earn forgiveness. Forgiveness of sins is a free gift of God because Jesus paid the price. The Pharisees and Sadducees needed to repent, desiring to change their sinful lives, or they would face judgment like a bad fruit tree that is destroyed.

Other people asked John how to "bear fruit in keeping with repentance." Have students compare in their minds the image of a desolate desert landscape (the sinful world) with an oasis of growing plants (our new lives) fed by living water (Christ Himself). The Holy Spirit strengthens our faith so that with transformed and grateful hearts, we live for the Lord. **How should they live to show they were sorry for their sins? Read Luke 3:10–14. What did John tell them?** Have students complete the rest of the section in their Student Books.

INTO our lives

Fruitful Results

Use the Student Book passages to discuss what God tells *us* about living as His forgiven people. You may wish to have the students work in three groups to answer the questions, assigning a Bible text to each group.

The people were curious about John. They were waiting for the Christ, the Messiah, to come. John told them he was not the Messiah. It was his job to prepare the people of Israel to receive the Messiah. Right now, we are in the season of the Church Year—the season between Christmas and Lent—called Epiphany. *Epiphany* **means "to make known" or "to reveal." In today's Bible lesson, we saw how John the Baptist revealed the Savior—revealed God's glory—and made Him known to the people of Israel. Read Luke 3:15–17.** (Use Reproducible 49 to record notes.) **How did John describe the Christ? How would the Messiah be different from John?** (The Christ was so powerful and mighty that John was not even worthy to untie His sandals. John baptized with water. The Messiah would baptize with the Holy Spirit and with fire. He would judge the people.) **Read John 1:29–31. What did John reveal about Jesus?** (Jesus was "the Lamb of God" who came to take away the sins of the world.) **He came to take away the sins of the people who listened to John, and He came to take *our* sins away.**

Remember

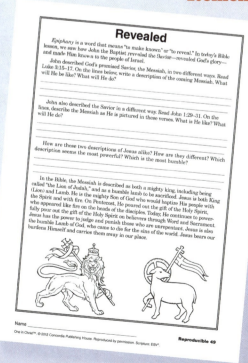

Talk about how the Holy Spirit renews our hearts and minds in Christ through Baptism. The Spirit is at work in the believer's heart, leading us away from living fruitless lives or lives with bad fruit to living fruitful lives and lives with good fruit— the fruit of the Spirit!

213

 Faith in Action

The people who were baptized by John asked him what they could do to "bear fruit" to show their repentance: "What then shall we do?" John said, "Whoever has two tunics is to share with him who has none, and whoever has food is to do likewise" (Luke 3:10–11). There are many ways in which your students can bear fruit as God's redeemed children, but they might want to follow John's suggestion to share clothing and food. Plan a project to collect clothing and food to be donated to a local shelter or another organization that helps people in need. Students can design posters, write announcements for school and church newsletters, and arrange for collection boxes. They might also include notes, cards, or pamphlets with their donations that proclaim Jesus as the Savior of the world.

Curriculum Connection

Make an art connection using section 6.5.1.3, Artwork Containing Visual Metaphors That Express Cultural Traditions and Myths, from the sixth-grade Visual Arts volume of the Concordia Curriculum Guide series. Bring in a variety of pictures of John the Baptist, particularly those from Renaissance art. Discuss with students: **Why is John so often shown pointing to Jesus? Why is he sometimes shown as a man at Jesus' Baptism, and sometimes as a small child with the even younger baby Jesus? What does the reed cross found in many of the pictures stand for? And the lamb?** Encourage students to draw on their knowledge of the Bible to answer.

Searching Further

John came to get people ready for the first coming of Jesus. Discuss with students: **What are we Christians doing to get ready—and help others get ready—for the second coming of Jesus?** List as many specific things as you can. Then consider adopting one idea as a special class project. Your students can help to prepare the way for Jesus as John did!

Critical thinking

Soldiers asked John the Baptist how they could "bear fruits in keeping with repentance" (Luke 3:8). John told them, "Do not extort money from anyone by threats or by false accusation, and be content with your wages" (v. 14). First-century soldiers sometimes acted like bullies, and many modern students do too. Discuss the problem of bullying with your students. (Emphasize that bullying happens in words and attitudes, as well as in physical threats and assaults.) Why do some people act that way? What can your students do if they see someone teased or threatened by another student? Help them to understand that they can and should talk to an adult about the problem. Talk about ways to encourage and support the student who has been frightened or hurt. Showing kindness to others is a way to "bear fruit in keeping with repentance."

UNIT 5—THE PROMISED ONE IS HERE!

LESSON 50

The Baptism of Jesus
MATTHEW 3:13–17; JOHN 1:32–34

Background

When Jesus went to the Jordan River to be baptized, John tried to stop Him, saying, "I need to be baptized by You, and do You come to me?" Since Jesus was sinless, He had no need to be baptized—in fact, it would have made more sense for Him to baptize John! But Jesus does the unexpected. As the innocent Lamb of God, He stepped into the Jordan River to receive John's Baptism and "fulfill all righteousness" (Matthew 3:15). He stood in the river in the place of sinners, identifying with them, although without sin Himself. Just three years later, Jesus would hang on the cross, again in the place of sinners, this time suffering the penalty of death in our place.

In this wonderful miracle at the beginning of Jesus' earthly ministry, all three persons of the Holy Trinity reveal themselves. As the Son of God rises from His Baptism, the Holy Spirit comes in the form of a dove to rest on Him, and the Father's voice announces that He is pleased with His beloved Son.

Anointed with the Holy Spirit, Jesus began His public ministry. We begin our life in Jesus anointed by the Spirit in the Word and water of Holy Baptism. In that wonderful miracle, the Father, the Son, and the Holy Spirit are present as we are baptized into God's name. Our sins are forgiven for Jesus' sake, and we are brought into the kingdom of God.

Central Truth

Jesus is much more than a good example—He fulfilled the Law and all the prophecies for us, taking our sin and punishment so that we receive His righteousness for eternal life.

Objectives

- Acknowledge that we are sinners and that Jesus promises to wash our sins away in Baptism, one of the ways—a special way, a sacramental way—that He offers the gift of forgiveness.
- Rejoice that Jesus is true God and we are baptized in His name, with the Father and the Spirit—one in Trinity.
- Live each day as a child of God, celebrating when we were or when we will be baptized.

Materials

- Hymnals and music CDs
- Web Resource 50a
- Reproducible 50

Bible Prep

Post in advance so students can bookmark references before class time.

- Matthew 3:13–17
- John 1:32–34
- Colossians 3:12–15

Devotions

When Mark got home from school, he found his father fixing the lawn mower. "Was I ever baptized?" asked Mark.

"Of course," said Dad. "You were baptized at St. Timothy's, the same church we go to now. Why do you ask?"

"I don't remember anything about it. Are you sure?"

"That's because you were just a baby," explained his dad. "When you were a few weeks old, Pastor Allen poured water over your head and baptized you in the name of the Father, Son, and Holy Spirit. I remember it well because I was baptized on that same day! On that day, God put His name on you *and* on me. We are still wearing that name today."

Mark frowned and looked down at his jacket. "The only name I see is the name of my baseball team," he said.

"I remember when you got that jacket. You didn't want to take it off," said Mark's dad.

Mark started to laugh. "I slept in it the first night, and it got all wrinkled."

"You wanted to wear your team name all the time," said his dad. "God's name on your life is like that. God put His name—the name of the Father, Son, and Holy Spirit—on you at your Baptism, and you still wear that name. You can't see it, but it is there. You are called a Christian, a child of God. This is who you are all the time. Other people can see by your words and actions that you belong to God."

"Maybe they'll want to be a part of God's team too!" said Mark.

Let's sing about the Holy Spirit, who works through God's Word, which is connected to the waters of Baptism, giving us faith in the forgiveness we have through Jesus. Sing "Holy Spirit, Light Divine" (*LSB* 496; recorded as *Hymn of the Season for grade 3, Pentecost*).

INTO the lesson

Baptism? When?

Begin the lesson by having students read aloud the narrative of Jesus' Baptism from Matthew 3:13–17. Continue with a few questions about Baptism in order to assess the background knowledge of your students. Ask, **Is Baptism a sacrament? What is a sacrament?** See what the students understand, but be sure to include the following points: It's something holy, begun by God Himself, in which God has joined His Word with something visible. **What are the two Sacraments?** (Baptism and the Lord's Supper) **Why did God give us the Sacraments?** (They are ways or means through which God distributes His forgiveness in Christ Jesus; and where there is forgiveness, there is also life and salvation. The Sacraments have the Word of God as an essential element in them, and along with the Word of God, the Sacraments are called "the Means of Grace." God chose to express Himself in more than one way as He offers His many gifts to us, touching our lives with the assurance and certainty of His grace.)

Look at the illustrations in the Student Book and ask which picture shows the correct age to be baptized. Then emphasize that *Any* and *all* **ages are appropriate. Jesus Himself was thirty years old when He was baptized. In Scripture, we often see whole families being baptized, which would indicate a variety of ages. Paul and Silas baptized the jailer of Philippi and his family (Acts 16:30–33). Lydia and her whole household were baptized in verses 14–15; it is likely that her household also included servants as well as family. In Baptism, we are all children—children of God!** "See what kind of love the Father has given to us, that we should be called children of God; and so we are" (1 John 3:1).

Baptism? What's Happening?

This section reviews several key concepts about Baptism. Discuss these thoroughly because you may have students who are unfamiliar with them. (*Note:* The order of answer placement in each row can vary; it is shown in a traditional manner.)

LESSON 50
The Baptism of Jesus

Baptism? When?

At what age are people baptized? Only infants? Only adults? People your age? All of these? What does Scripture tell us? "Repent and be baptized every one of you in the name of Jesus Christ for the forgiveness of your sins, and you will receive the gift of the Holy Spirit. For the promise is for you and for your children and for all who are far off, everyone whom the Lord our God calls to Himself" (Acts 2:38–39).

Baptism? What's Happening?

Directions: Use the following words to fill in the answers on the chart:

| Holy Spirit | life | Father | forgiveness | Holy Spirit | salvation |
| death | water | sin | Word | Satan | Son |

1. In whose name are we baptized?	Father	Son	Holy Spirit
2. *Who* works through *what* that is connected to *what* in Baptism?	Holy Spirit	Word	water
3. Baptism in the name of Jesus defeats what?	sin	death	Satan
4. Baptism in the name of Jesus offers what?	forgiveness	life	salvation

Review

Covenant Connection

Jesus is called "the Messiah," a Hebrew title that means "the Anointed One." The title "Christ" is the Greek word for "the Anointed One." In the Old Testament, when a person was made king, he was anointed with oil as a sign that God had chosen him for special work. As Jesus began His earthly ministry, He was anointed with the Holy Spirit. Isaiah prophesied about the Messiah in the Old Testament, saying, "The Spirit of the Lord God is upon Me, because the LORD has anointed Me to bring good news to the poor; He has sent Me to bind up the brokenhearted, to proclaim liberty to the captives" (Isaiah 61:1).

Review

One of the many significant factors of Jesus' Baptism is that John had been told by God that the Spirit descending from heaven like a dove would be the sign of the Savior, who would baptize with the Holy Spirit. John recognized this and attested to who Jesus was, saying, "And I have seen and have borne witness that this is the Son of God" (John 1:34). Until this time, it appears that John did not know Jesus was the Messiah (v. 33), but God revealed this to him. After this, John pointed directly to our Lord Jesus, saying, "Behold, the Lamb of God, who takes away the sin of the world!" (v. 29). Jesus was "the Chosen One" and "the Anointed One" spoken of by the prophets and sent from God. Use Web Resource 50a to look at additional Scripture verses that relate to this concept.

Baptism? Why Jesus?

Read Matthew 3:13–17. Why was John so surprised? __Jesus wanted to be baptized, but John thought Jesus should instead baptize him.__

What did Jesus tell John? __Jesus said that it was "fitting," or right, that He be baptized, "to fulfill all righteousness" (v. 15).__

Jesus did what we couldn't do—He lived a perfect life for us. Now He calls us to follow His example. "Therefore be *imitators* of God, as beloved children. And walk in love, as Christ loved us and gave Himself up for us" (Ephesians 5:1–2).

Baptism? Once?

You are born (physically) one time. You probably celebrate that event each year. But things keep happening daily after your birthday.

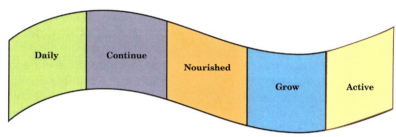

Spiritually, you are reborn—in Baptism—one time. Celebrate that event each year—it's your "rebirthday"! These important things keep happening daily after your rebirthday:

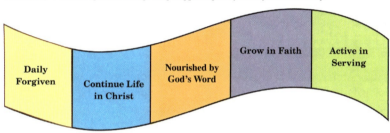

Remember

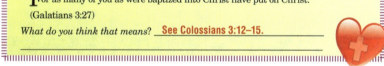

"For as many of you as were baptized into Christ have put on Christ." (Galatians 3:27)

What do you think that means? __See Colossians 3:12–15.__

INTO our lives

Baptism? Once?

Emphasize that though we are only baptized once, it is an important part of our daily lives—we live as baptized people of God. (Compare this to someone who becomes a U.S. citizen, or an actor who wins an Academy Award: the special event occurs once, but for the remainder of his or her life, this tells who the person is—an American citizen, an Oscar-winning actor. The daily significance of Baptism is obviously much greater, as daily we receive forgiveness as God's redeemed people!)

Work through the Student Book activity as a reminder of the daily significance of being a baptized Christian. Be very specific in identifying the terms on the second line: we are daily forgiven; we continue life in Christ (it's not just something in the past); we are nourished by God's Word (we need nourishment/food to live); growing is a constant in life, and growing in faith (through the Means of Grace) is part of our Christian life; and an active life as a Christian involves things such as serving others and giving glory to God in all things.

Remember

Read the suggested Scripture section to learn more about "putting on Christ." We put on clothes each day; "putting on Christ" means to be clothed or covered in His love, showing compassion and kindness to others.

INTO the Word

Baptism? Why Jesus?

Use the questions in this section to review the biblical account and to discover the purpose of Jesus' Baptism. Jesus was perfect in every way, following God's commands, doing all things for us, and living as an example for us to follow (as we are enabled by the power of the Holy Spirit). Say, **Jesus did not have any sins for which to repent. But it was right for Him to join sinners in the water for a Baptism of repentance, just as three years later, He would again take the place of sinners—including you and me—on the cross.**

Use Reproducible 50 to explore this concept. It is a simple story about little children; but the story explores several important concepts about Baptism. Have students highlight statements that tell a significant truth about Baptism. Then suggest that your class work together or in groups to present this skit to younger children in your school. This will provide them the opportunity to share the message of our Savior with others. There are a variety of ways this can be presented. It could be given as a puppet play, or it could be acted out by costumed actors (volunteers). Let students suggest other presentation models; for example, presenting this on film or via Skype to another class could be an interesting project. It would also be interesting to see the variety of ways different groups could present the same skit.

Lesson Support

Celebrating GROWTH

With your students, read through the service of Holy Baptism on pages 268–271 in *LSB*. Talk about the meaning of each part of the service, and explain things that might be difficult or unfamiliar. Show how the Apostles' Creed is used in the questions and answers. If possible, take your students into the church and show them the baptismal font and its decorations and symbols. Ask your pastor to talk to the class about the importance of Baptism and about Baptisms he has performed. Find out if there is going to be a Baptism in an upcoming service so that your students can, if possible, plan to attend that service. Also discuss the subject of Confirmation as a renewal of their baptismal vows.

Just for Fun

Ask your class if they have ever watched the ceremonies for the Olympics on television. **Do you remember what the symbol on the Olympic flag looks like?** (There are five interconnecting rings, representing the five land masses of the world—the Americas, Africa, Asia, Australia, and Europe.) **The Olympic symbol reminds us of the relationship we have with people of other lands.**

Continue, **Find a symbol of the triune God that has three interconnecting rings. These represent the Father, Son, and Holy Spirit, in whose name we are baptized. We have a relationship with the true God because Jesus has reconciled us to God through His death and resurrection, and the Holy Spirit has worked faith in our hearts through the Means of Grace—God's Word and the Sacraments.**

You may want to create your own classroom baptismal remembrance ceremony by letting each student make and wave his or her own flag of the trinitarian symbol (three intertwined circles). For each flag, provide students with a permanent marker to draw the symbol on a rectangle of white fabric, and then provide glue or a stapler to attach the fabric to a thin dowel rod.

Curriculum Connection

A great art connection for this lesson would be section 6.1.1.5, Variations on the Same Theme with Different Media and Styles. This appears in the sixth-grade Visual Arts volume of the Concordia Curriculum Guide series. The Baptism of Jesus has been a favorite subject for artists throughout history. Gather a dozen or so representations of this event from different cultures and historical periods. (Try art books or an Internet image search.) Explore with students: **What is the same in all of them? What things differ, and why?**

Bringing it home

Encourage students to ask their parents about their own Baptism. Families can talk about where and when the Baptism took place, the names of sponsors or godparents, and how the event was celebrated. Families may want to plan a special celebration of their children's Baptism birthdays. If students have not yet been baptized, encourage families who might be interested to talk to the pastor about this important gift of God. Always affirm the faith the students have, which the Holy Spirit worked in their hearts through the Word of God; encourage those who have not been baptized by telling them they can look forward to the day when they will share in that gift of God also.

Reaching Every Child

Ask your pastor or church secretary for a sample of the baptismal certificate used in your congregation. Ask students to bring in their own baptismal certificates or those of parents or grandparents. Students can work together or in groups to create a baptismal certificate. They can use the words from sample certificates and use existing designs or develop new designs and symbols as illustrations. A scallop shell with three drops of water beneath it is a common symbol of Baptism (a shell was sometimes used to apply the water, and even today, some churches use a shell or a silver shell to pour water during a Baptism).

UNIT 5—THE PROMISED ONE IS HERE!

LESSON 51

The Temptation of Jesus
MATTHEW 4:1–11

Background

The temptations of Jesus have been explained in many ways, but it is worth noting that all of them involve the devil suggesting to Jesus that He do things the devil's way rather than the Father's way. This is the essence of sin—to turn away from God, to make oneself and one's own wishes a god instead. Every human being has fallen to this temptation at one time or another—every man but Jesus.

As a true man, Jesus could certainly be tempted. This was no play-acting. The suffering was real. And for that reason, all of us can find hope and trust in Jesus, who suffered the strongest temptations, just as we do, and yet resisted. He can help us also when we are tempted.

Be sure your students notice how Jesus countered temptation: by using the Word of God. He did not argue or debate with the devil, as Eve did—and lost. Instead, Jesus relied on the same protection available to all of us: God's Word in the Scriptures. As long as we hold fast to the Word, we are safe. Of course, this requires that we *know* that Word—so students need reminding, once again, about how important Bible reading and study is. No soldier lets himself get caught without a weapon. Neither should we allow ourselves to be ambushed by temptation without the Word of God stored up in our hearts and minds.

Central Truth

The devil tempted Jesus, but Jesus resisted the temptation; He guides us to pray "lead us not into temptation" (or "lead us away" from it).

Objectives

- Be aware (and beware) that we are tempted by the devil, people, and things in the world around us and by our own sinful will (sinful nature); we are tempted to sin in physical and spiritual matters, by omission and by commission.
- Rejoice that God is in this battle with us, equipping us with the Word, strengthening us in faith, and giving us the ultimate victory in Jesus.
- Give glory to God in all that we do, think, and say.

Materials

- Hymnals and music CDs
- Web Resource 51a
- Reproducible 51

Bible Prep

Post in advance so students can bookmark references before class time.
- Matthew 4:1–11
- Luke 4

Devotion

David was in sixth grade. He really, *really* wanted his own computer to keep in his room, but his parents would only say, "Not now. You're not old enough. Maybe someday."

But his older brother, Philip, didn't want to wait for "someday." He had his own special wish. Phil already had his driver's license, and he wanted his own car—*now*.

But every time the boys asked, their parents said no to both of them. "You two need to show more responsibility," they said. "And Phil, we can't afford to pay for your insurance, so you'll need to get a job too."

Phil argued with his parents. "I'm responsible!" he said. "More than David, anyway. And how can I get a job if I don't have a car?"

His father suggested the bus. Phil scowled and slammed the door as he left.

Later that evening, their mother got a phone call. "Hi, this is Vernon, Scott's dad," the voice said. "I don't know exactly how to tell you this, but Scott and Phil borrowed my car without asking, and they've had a wreck. They're both okay, but . . ."

David's parents flew out of the house so fast that he barely saw them leave. David took a deep breath and sat down.

"Boy, is Phil ever in trouble," he said to himself. "I know he really wanted a car, but I never thought he'd be tempted to take somebody else's. I am *so* glad it's not me. I hope it never *is* me." He shook his head. "Maybe I'd better stop bugging Mom and Dad about the computer for a while, no matter *how* tempting it is."

Let's pray together: Lord, help us to listen to Your Word and turn away from things that tempt us. Amen. Sing "I Want to Walk as a Child of the Light" (*LSB* 411).

219

INTO the lesson

Types of Temptations

Emphasize that some of the temptations around us are not bad in themselves. **Food is good, but following the devil's way to get it is wrong. Likewise, electronic games are not always bad, but whining to your parents and ignoring other duties because of them is wrong. Often the sin comes in how a person gets what they want, such as using bad language in order to appear "cool." And let's face it, if you are bullying other kids or you disobey your parents, it is often a power issue where *you* want to control what you do. This is not only an issue with people; you are also struggling against God when you give in to these temptations. Let's learn more about the devil's clever ways.** *Note:* The three types of temptations relate to the Bible narrative. You may want to point out that the devil has many more weapons in his arsenal. For example, the devil uses doubts and disasters to tempt people to not trust the Lord and to be unfaithful.

Tactics

As you work through the Student Book, encourage students to give real-life examples. Here are several possibilities: In what way can sin be appealing? You really want the new MP3 player or music CD, and taking money from Mom's purse is the only way you can get it. Or, to be "cool," it seems fun to laugh at and make jokes about the clumsy new kid at school.

Jesus was in the wilderness for forty days. Where do your students often find themselves when temptations strike? When are they most vulnerable and weak, like a small, wounded animal, perfect prey for a prowling predator? As students discuss temptations that come their way, help them to be realistic in what they suggest. They will not likely be tempted to rob a bank, but they may be tempted to take a small amount of money from someone. They may not be tempted to physically hurt someone, but they may like to gossip and hurt the reputation of another student. Discuss the fact that there are different ways of sinning. We sometimes sin by *doing something wrong*. These are called "sins of commission." But sometimes we sin by *not doing something we should do*. These are called "sins of omission." For example, we sin against the Eighth Commandment by speaking badly or lying about someone; but we also sin when we fail to speak up to defend someone. Say, **We have painted a very gruesome, nasty picture. And the worst part is that we have painted a picture of ourselves! We know that there is only one answer—Jesus.** Use Web Resource 51a and read aloud the Scripture's summary of this situation (1 Peter 5:8–11).

LESSON 51
The Temptation of Jesus

Types of Temptations

The devil is very clever; he tempts us with our own will and wants. He knew exactly what Jesus wanted—food, after forty days without it (Matthew 4:1–4). The devil also tempted Jesus with an easy way to get people's attention and show He was the Son of God (vv. 5–7). The devil knew it would be appealing to get all the power and glory in the world without having to suffer and die (vv. 8–11). The devil is also clever with you and me. In what ways does the devil use these same types of temptations on people today? Give examples in the boxes.

WANTS	POPULARITY	POWER
Possible answers: Wanting the latest electronic games	Trying to always act "cool" and better than others	Trying to use any means to become the group leader

Tactics

The *tactics* of the devil are his plans and schemes. He pulls you (and maybe even some of your friends) into the process. He knows what you want, and he knows how to use that to make you sin. Here are some of the devil's tactics. Write an example for each temptation tactic.

1. He makes sin appealing. **Answers will vary.** _____

2. He makes sin seem like the easy way out. _____

3. He makes sin seem fun. _____

4. He makes sin seem necessary. _____

Review

Covenant Connection

The name *devil* means "slanderer." The name *Satan* means "adversary." He is the tempter, the father of lies, and our enemy who will stop at nothing to get us to seek our own glory. Just as Israel in Old Testament times had been tested in the wilderness, Jesus was tested in the wilderness, but He did not fail as the Israelites had. Jesus is our substitute who lived a perfect life in our place, defeating Satan for us and setting us free from the devil's power as He suffered the punishment for us on the cross.

INTO the Word

Fight Back!

Emphasize these key factors: Too often, we don't even *try* to fight back; too often, we ignore God and even turn away from Him. However, we *can* fight back, but only through Jesus, who sends the Holy Spirit to empower us through the weapon Jesus Himself used—the Word of God. Explore the four key words that are shaded in purple. 1-God calls us to *confess* our sins; this means to admit when we have done wrong. Sometimes a general confession is too easy; are you really ready to admit specifically when you are wrong? 2-God calls us to confess *sorrowfully*; that means to be sad and contrite about what we have done. God does not want empty words. (Have you ever said to someone "I'm sorry" just so they will leave you alone or let you go without a consequence? That won't work with God; He knows our hearts, and He looks for a contrite heart.) **3-God calls on us to *receive* His forgiveness, trusting that all Jesus did is finished and complete for our salvation, relying totally on what He has done rather than on what we do.** 4-God calls us to *repentance*, which involves a change of mind, heart, and behavior. True confession and repentance do not turn back immediately to the same sin. We will sin, but with Jesus working in us as the Spirit transforms us, we will change and grow.

Fight Back!

The Bible tells us to resist, fight back, and stand firm against Satan, temptation, and sin. The problem is, we aren't strong enough to do that—but Jesus is! "For He who is in you is greater than he who is in the world" (1 John 4:4). God calls us to CONFESS SORROWFULLY, RECEIVING REPENTANTLY. Write a prayer about this! _____
_____
_____
_____

Boot Camp Training

Ephesians 6:10–18 compares fighting back against Satan to a soldier in battle, saying, "Put on the whole armor of God, that you may be able to stand against the schemes of the devil" (v. 11). The weapon provided (which Jesus used) is "the sword of the Spirit, which is the word of God" (v. 17). A soldier goes into training at boot camp. Can you design your own "spiritual fitness boot camp" to prepare yourself for combat with temptation? Be your own drill sergeant and try to form some spiritually healthy habits, especially if you're bored with your regular plan—or if you don't have one.

Time: Will you train early in the morning, as they do at many fitness boot camps? right when you get up? after school? before bedtime?
Location: Will you train at home or school? outside? indoors?
Frequency: Can you train at least once a week, such as adding an extra opportunity for worship during Advent or Lent? Can you do extra chores at least three times a week at home?
Duration: Four to six weeks is similar to the forty-day period Jesus spent in the wilderness. Do you want to continue it longer?
Participant(s): Will you try an individual plan? Will you work with others who will hold one another accountable? Will participating in a group help you to learn new strategies or help you to role-play tempting situations, asking yourselves, "What would you do if . . . ?"
Goal: Will you try to read a certain book of the Bible by the end of the boot camp? Will you try to memorize a certain number of Bible verses? Keep in mind that the ultimate goal is not only to gain "head knowledge" from spending more time in God's Word, but also to strengthen your relationship with the Source of our strength to fight temptations: God the Father—the One who cares for us and protects us; our Savior, Jesus—the One who won the battle over sin and the devil; and the Holy Spirit—the One who strengthens our faith.

Remember

"Let us also lay aside every weight, and sin which clings so closely, and let us run with endurance the race that is set before us, looking to Jesus, the founder and perfecter of our faith." (Hebrews 12:1–2a)

109

INTO our lives

Boot Camp Training

Fitness boot camps are intense physical training programs with the purpose of helping people to lose weight, increase strength and cardiovascular efficiency, and get into a routine of regular exercise. There are some similarities between fitness boot camps and military basic training, such as the intensity of the program, the social component, and the four- to six-week length of the program. Especially in military training, recruits are trained to be mentally prepared so that they will be reliable in a combat situation. If we are battling the devil, then we need a battle plan. **What were Jesus' tactics? Can you use the same ones?** Jesus used God's Word to fight the devil. Sing "Thy Strong Word" (*LSB* 578; recorded as *Hymn of the Month for grade 6, October*). Ask students, **What do you think "spiritual fitness" could mean? How can we stay in good spiritual health?** Help your class to recognize that just as people need to exercise several times a week to stay in shape, they will need to be in the Word regularly in order to be prepared for the challenges that the devil will throw our way. Discuss a "spiritual health and fitness plan" using the questions in the Student Book. Point out that the Bible passage to remember gives another picture of where training is needed—in a race. Just as you can't run a marathon if you haven't been in training, you'll have a difficult time enduring the pressures of temptation if you're not in the routine of finding strength in God's Word.

Sing the words of the repentant thief from the cross: "Jesus, Remember Me" (*AGPS* 146; recorded on *JPS*; *LSB* 767). To reinforce the concept of God calling us to repentance and faith, sing "Listen, God Is Calling" (*LSB* 833; recorded as *Hymn of the Month for grade 5, January*).

Read the story of Jesus' temptation in Luke 4. Read verses 1–2. How does Jesus get into the wilderness after His Baptism? How long was He there? (Led by the Spirit, Jesus now spends forty days in the wilderness before He begins His earthly work and takes up His path to the cross.) In the Bible, the number *40* often means a time of preparation and testing. **The devil tempts Jesus three times to follow selfish desires instead of doing what God wants Him to do.**

Read verses 3–4. How does the devil tempt Jesus? (Jesus is hungry, and Satan tempts Him to turn stones to bread.) **How does Satan make this look like a "win-win" situation?** (Jesus could satisfy His hunger *and* prove He is the Son of God at the same time!)

How does Jesus resist the temptations? What is Jesus' tactic in spiritual battle? Each time, Jesus says, "It is written." Jesus uses the Word of God from the Old Testament to resist the devil's suggestions. He uses Deuteronomy 8:3, "Man does not live by bread alone, but man lives by every word that comes from the mouth of the Lord."

(Important note: Continue this study with the "Critical thinking" section on the Lesson Support Page.)

221

Lesson Support

Critical thinking

Read verses 5–8. How does the devil tempt Jesus here? (The devil offers Jesus all of the world's glory and authority if He worships Satan.) **Just like the first temptation, how does this one try to put what Jesus might want in front of what God the Father wants?** (It attacks Jesus' pride and destiny as messianic king. Instead of going through all He would have to endure on the cross, Jesus could have immediate power and fame as a political ruler.) **Read verses 9–13. How did the devil tempt Jesus?** (The devil tells Jesus to challenge God's protection and throw Himself from the high point of the temple, most likely a hundred-foot drop.) **What tactics does the devil use?** (He casts doubt saying, "If You are the Son of God" [v. 9].) He copies Jesus by quoting Scripture (although he leaves off part of the verse).

Each time Jesus resisted temptation by quoting God's Word. Jesus followed God's will, not His own desires. The devil could not tempt Jesus into receiving fleeting glory for Himself (e.g., "Did you see the man who just turned rocks into bread? Who just dropped from the temple without getting hurt? Our new political leader?") Jesus followed His Father's will and died on the cross for us. When Jesus died and rose from the dead, He defeated Satan's power. Through faith in Jesus, we have forgiveness for our sins, and the devil cannot separate us from God forever.

Curriculum Connection

We, too, face temptations in our lives, and we need God's help to overcome them. Sometimes God uses other Christians to help us make good choices. Consider using section 6.7.2, Supporting Others' Choices, with your students. You'll find it in the sixth-grade Health volume of the Concordia Curriculum Guide series.

Reaching Every Child

Do you have a very gifted child in your classroom? This can be both a blessing and a challenge. Without a chance to stretch their abilities, gifted children may become bored and may even start acting out. There are several things you can do for such children. If you have enough of them, your school might start a special program for them, either after school or during a special period of the day. If not, you may encourage parents to enroll them in a local para-school program such as your city's gifted resource council. Consider enlisting students as teachers' aides for short periods. If you are concerned this may cause social problems with their peers in your own classroom, you might be able to "lend" such a child to the teacher of a younger class who would welcome an extra tutor or reader for a period. Or allow him or her to "staff" the computer room, answering basic questions and providing help. Gifted students entrusted with such responsibilities often grow tremendously.

Check it Out

Jesus, our Savior, resisted every temptation of the devil, but in our sinful weakness, we give in daily to temptation. We ask God for forgiveness for the sake of Jesus Christ. The *LSB* has two services of Confession and Absolution, one for group use (pp. 290–291) and one for individual use (pp. 292–293). Ask your pastor to talk to your students about confession and absolution and what these terms mean. He might want to go through one of the services with the students and explain what is happening and what the words mean.

Faith in Action

Through our Baptism, we know that we are God's children; His love can encourage us. In the Lord's Prayer, Jesus teaches us to ask for His help in fighting the temptations of the devil, the world around us, and our own selfish desires by praying, "Lead us not into temptation."

Reproducible 51 has an optional Bible study that explores more information about our enemy, the devil. There are many Bible verses to look up, so it would be best to work on this in groups to divide up the tasks.

UNIT 5—THE PROMISED ONE IS HERE!   LESSON 52

Jesus' First Disciples
MATTHEW 4:18–22; JOHN 1:35–51

Background

Make sure that students know the difference between disciples and apostles. *Disciples* are followers—students, learners. All who believe in Jesus are His disciples. (John the Baptist and the Pharisees also had disciples, students who followed them and learned from them.) In the New Testament, "the disciples" may refer to the original twelve, or it may refer to any group of Christians. *Apostles* are missionaries, those "sent out" by Jesus to bring the Good News to people everywhere. When we speak of "the apostles," we are usually talking about the original twelve—but Paul also carries this title, as do Barnabas and some others.

The original twelve people Jesus picked as apostles were a motley group—mostly Galileans, none of them rich or learned or powerful as far as we know. They included several fishermen, a former tax collector, a revolutionary (Simon the Zealot), and two former disciples of John the Baptist. All were Jews, though Philip and Andrew bore Greek names. Several had nicknames, or received new names from Jesus (for example, Levi was renamed "Matthew"). There are also two Judases, two Jameses, and two Simons. All of this can make it difficult to compare the different lists in the Gospels.

The one thing they all had in common was a willingness to leave their former lives and follow Jesus. During the roughly three years they lived with Him, they learned from Him and they carried out His commands. At times, they taught and worked miracles in His name. Often they misunderstood Jesus and showed themselves completely clueless about His plans to die at Jerusalem and rise again. But in the end, these men (barring Judas, who betrayed Him) became the foundation for the Christian Church Jesus was building.

Central Truth

Jesus graciously calls us to help in His work of spreading His Gospel and His loving kindness to all; He empowers and enables us to do the tasks He gives to us.

Objectives

- Perceive that as sinners, we can do no good and cannot even help ourselves to make things right.
- In thanksgiving, appreciate that Jesus has done all things for our salvation and empowers us to live as His people.
- Diligently serve God and others, knowing that God chooses even the weak for His purposes and blesses them so they may do His will.

Materials

- Hymnals, songbooks and music CDs
- Reproducible 52
- Web Resource 52a

Bible Prep

Post in advance so students can bookmark references before class time.
- Matthew 4; 9; 10
- Luke 6
- John 1
- 1 Peter 2

Devotions

"Just. Leave. Me. *Alone!*" said Jacob through gritted teeth. "Stop following me everywhere!" Little Ryan stuck out his tongue and kept following. Jacob walked as fast as he could, but he couldn't shake off his young brother.

They both made it back to the picnic blanket out of breath. Uncle Miles looked at Jacob's red face and sent Ryan off to the playground. "Go on," he said. "I want to talk to your brother." Ryan sulked, but he wandered away toward the swings, and Jacob flopped down onto the blanket. "He's driving me crazy!"

Uncle Miles looked amused. "I can see that," he said. "Does he follow you everywhere at home too?" "Yes!" said Jacob. "It's like having a shadow, but a lot noisier!" Uncle Miles laughed. "I know. Your dad used to do the same thing to me." "What?" asked Jacob, sitting up suddenly.

"He did. Little brothers are like that. Ryan follows you around because he wants to be just like you. He's watching what you do, and he wants to do it too." Jacob made a face. "You make it sound like a *compliment*." "Well, it is, sort of," said Uncle Miles. "You've got yourself a little disciple." "*What?*" said Jacob. "I'm not Jesus!" "Of course not," said his uncle. "But disciples are students. They follow their teachers everywhere and listen and watch everything their teachers do. That's what the twelve disciples did with Jesus, right?" "Yeah, I guess so," Jacob replied. "And that's what we do, too, when we read the Bible and pray and find ways to serve God. We're following Jesus." "Well, yeah. But I hope I'm not as annoying as Ryan!" Uncle Miles laughed. "I think Jesus will put up with us just fine. In fact, He wants us to follow Him as much as we can. Maybe you can ask Jesus for help and patience in dealing with Ryan."

Sing "You Are the Way; through You Alone" (*LSB* 526; recorded as *Hymn of the Season* for grade 6, Epiphany).

INTO the lesson

Making the Cut!

Discuss the types of experience and character traits the class thinks would make a good disciple for Jesus. Do your students think a doctor might be able to help Jesus with healing? Could a religious leader help Jesus with teaching? Could a great orator help Jesus with preaching? Brainstorm ideas together and list them on the board. You might even want to give students time to develop an audition video, telling in what way a person today might try to qualify as a disciple. Finally, look at the experience of the disciples Jesus *did* choose, as described in Scripture and the Student Book. Give students time to consider what *their* résumé would look like, and help them to perceive that as sinners, we can do no good and cannot even help ourselves to make things right. There is no way that on our own, we could become qualified. Emphasize: **No matter what our experience is, we are all disqualified by sin; but by His loving grace, God chooses us anyway.**

Read Luke 6:12–16. What did Jesus do before choosing the men who would be His helpers and closest companions over the next three years? Hold auditions or tryouts? (It appears that Jesus sought guidance from His heavenly Father before a big decision.)

Say, **Today's lesson teaches us how God chose twelve very special followers to help carry out His message of love, forgiveness, and eternal life for all believers. But He didn't choose them because of any merit or worthiness on their part. The disciples were simple, unqualified men who admitted that they were sinful. They weren't looking for a career change; Jesus approached *them*.** He knew they were just the right men for the job, and He blessed them so they could do His will.

He knows that *you* are just the right person to be His disciple too. Jesus empowers *you* to live as His child. Together, read the first two paragraphs of Luther's explanation of the Third Article of the Apostles' Creed (in the Catechism in the Student Book Appendix). On our own, we can't believe in Jesus or come to Him. Through the Gospel, the Holy Spirit invites us to "Come!" and be a part of God's family and receive all the blessings that includes. **Read 1 Peter 2:9. Who are we? What is our "job"?** Jesus graciously calls us to help in His work of spreading His Gospel and His loving kindness to all; He empowers and enables us to do the tasks He gives to us. *That's* how you made the cut!

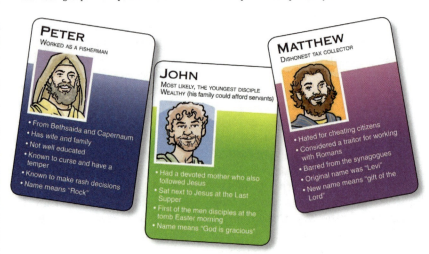

INTO the Word

Making the Connection

Point out that John the Baptist had his own disciples, or followers. Andrew is identified in John 1:40. The other man mentioned is presumed to be John. **Read verses 37–38.** Ask, **Why would John and Andrew be familiar with the phrase "Lamb of God"?** (John the Baptist had been preparing people for Jesus' coming.) **The next day, Jesus went to Galilee. What did He do there (v. 43)?** (He called Philip, who was from the same town as Andrew and Peter.) **In verse 45, why did Nathanael ask what good could come from Nazareth?** (It was a small, insignificant town, even despised; certainly not a place one would expect the Messiah to come from.) **How did Jesus encourage Nathanael that exciting times were ahead? Read vv. 50–51. Do you think Nathanael needed extra prodding to follow Jesus, or was he excited enough to follow Jesus just knowing that Jesus knew who he was?** (Accept responses.) **In Matthew 4:18–22, was Jesus a stranger to these men?** (No, Andrew and most likely John had followed Jesus for a day. Andrew had introduced his brother to Jesus, so when this authority figure called them, they listened.)

What did Jesus do after that? Read vv. 23–25. (Jesus went all

Making the Connection!

Read about Jesus calling the disciples to follow Him in John 1:35–51 and Matthew 4:18–22; 9:9–13; and 10:1–4. Then answer these questions.

1. Andrew was so thrilled to follow the Lamb of God, what did he do first?
   He brought Peter to Jesus.
2. How did Andrew describe Jesus to his brother?
   "The Messiah"—the Son of God and Son of Man, the way to heaven.
3. Philip was so thrilled to follow the Messiah, what did he do?
   He told Nathanael, who was doubtful that anything good could come out of Nazareth.
4. Did Philip give up, even after Nathanael didn't share his excitement?
   No; he encouraged Nathanael to "Come and see."
5. When did Nathanael believe?
   When Jesus made it clear that He had seen Nathanael even before Philip told him about Jesus; Nathanael was amazed at Jesus' divine knowledge.
6. How did Matthew respond?
   He rose and followed Him immediately. He made a great feast.

Making the Catch!

After much prayer and thought, Jesus called twelve disciples (followers and learners) and named them apostles (those sent to teach a message). Below, shade or color only the shapes that contain a name of one of Jesus' original twelve disciples. (Some have their second name listed.)

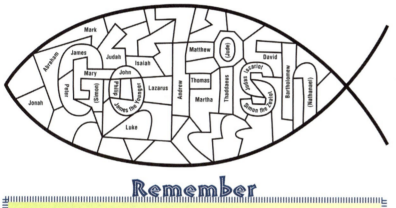

Remember

"And ___He___ said to ___them___, '___Follow___ ___Me___, and I will make you ___fishers___ of ___men___.' ___Immediately___ they left their ___nets___ and ___followed___ ___Him___." (Matthew 4:19–20)

111

---

around Galilee, preaching, teaching, and healing.) When He passed on from Capernaum, possibly on the border between the territories of Philip and Herod Antipas, where commercial tolls were levied, He saw Matthew. **Read Matthew 9:9–13.** Jesus deliberately chose a tax collector as a disciple and shared the fellowship of the table with "sinners"—disreputable people. Eating a meal with someone meant that you were participating in a common thing together; it was a sign of friendship and companionship. The Pharisees would *never* affiliate with sinners like this, who they said stood outside the Law. This was scandalous behavior for Jesus, a rabbi!

INTO our lives

Making the Catch

Before working on the Student Book page, read Matthew 10:1–4. Shade or color only the shapes that contain a name of one of Jesus' original twelve disciples, which will form the words "Go Fish." (Note that some disciples have more than one name listed: Jude was also known as Thaddaeus; Bartholomew was also known as Nathanael. Some disciples had the same name so usually a defining name was added: Simon could be Simon Peter or Simon the Zealot; James could be James the son of Zebedee or James the son of Alphaeus, who was also called James the Younger or James the Less.) After completing the puzzle, ask, **What do those words have to do with today's lesson?** Suggest that they look at the Bible words to remember for clues. Jesus wanted the disciples to "fish" for—to gather in—people to hear the Gospel message of salvation.

If you could characterize these men, what would you say they all have in common? (They were all sinners. They all left everything to follow Jesus.) **You've already been called to *be* a disciple. When you're called to *live* as Jesus' disciple, what is your response?**

- First tell me what I have to do. I need to know all the details: what's involved, when, where, how long will it take, and so on.
- Let me think about it awhile.
- What?! And give up what I'm doing *now*?
- Let's go!

God calls us, too, by His grace for the sake of Jesus, the Messiah. The Crucified and Risen One stretches out His nail-pierced hands and summons us to follow Him and become fishers of men. At once, drawing on the power He provides, we can follow without question. Read Ephesians 3:8. Say, We are in no way worthy to be disciples of God, but He uses us anyway. **What a privilege it is to be entrusted with such a wonderful job of carrying His message to other people!** Close by singing "Sent Forth By God's Blessing" (*LSB* 643; recorded as *Hymn of the Month for grade 8, May*) and "Who Was the Man" (*AGPS* 268; recorded on *JPS*).

Remember

Following Jesus and being a fisher of men means letting *Him* lead; it means being open to all He has to teach you in His Word and to follow His leadership through worship, people, and experiences. It means joining in His work of sharing the Good News.

Reaching Every Child

We hope it will never happen, but the reality is that some children come to school hungry on a regular basis, even in Lutheran schools. These may be children from families in financial trouble (temporary or long term), or they may have parents who are unable to take proper care of them due to illness, either physical or mental. Others are malnourished because their families can't afford the healthy foods young children need.

Keep an eye out for children who appear to be much shorter or thinner than others, or who appear to be tired, ill, or cold much of the time. Watch what happens at lunchtime. If students bring their lunches, what are they bringing? If lunch is served at school, are there certain children who appear to be "stocking up," eating more than you would expect, or going back for multiple servings?

If you suspect one of your students may be going hungry at home, talk with your school administration and especially the school nurse. The family may be eligible for food assistance of some kind. If you discover that this is a widespread problem in your school, you might be able to start a "breakfast club" to ensure that needy students have a good start to their day.

Curriculum Connection

Jesus and His disciples did a lot of traveling together as they told the Good News of the kingdom of heaven. For a fun connection to this lesson, try using the game Traveling Together found in the Appendix (p. 74) of the sixth-grade Physical Education volume of the Concordia Curriculum Guide series.

Working in Groups

Divide the students into groups of two or three. Give students large pieces of bulletin board paper and have students make large comic strips that depict Jesus first calling Simon, Andrew, James, and John (Matthew 4:18–22); Matthew (9:9–13); and Philip and Nathanael (John 1:35–51). Allow them to divide the stories any way they choose as long as they present the scenarios in a logical manner. Encourage them to be neat and to use bright colors that will be appealing to viewers. Caution them to especially write the words clearly in dark ink first and then add a speech bubble around the words so that the words remain visible and legible. When all are finished, display them on the walls in the hallway. Be sure to invite students, teachers, the principal, and other staff to stop by and view your class's creations!

Searching Further

Have students do more research on the disciples, using Reproducible 52 to take notes. Take time to share and discuss the information. Discuss which comments are based on Scripture. Also note that some of the information we have is based on historical tradition and narratives of the times, so the accuracy needs to be examined. Some information may be just legend, and though it may be interesting, it should be ignored unless there is data to support it. Be sure students recognize that tradition and legends may not be historically accurate. For the only concrete facts about the disciples' lives, we must refer to the Bible.

See also Web Resource 52a.

Faith in Action

As you talk about what it means to be disciples of Jesus, brainstorm with your students to come up with a list of simple, disciplelike things you can do together in the next month. Because disciples learn, your list might include learning activities, such as Bible reading and memory work. Because disciples follow in Jesus' footsteps of service, you might include practical helping activities such as picking up trash, tutoring younger children, or any community service project.

UNIT 5—THE PROMISED ONE IS HERE!　　　　　　　　　　　　　LESSON 53

Nicodemus Visits Jesus
John 3:1–21

Background

Nicodemus was a Jewish leader and a member of the Sanhedrin (equivalent to the Supreme Court). He visited Jesus at night, possibly because he was afraid to have anyone find out that he considered Jesus to be sent from God (John 3:2). Later, he became bolder, speaking up for Jesus in the Sanhedrin and suffering for it (7:50) and finally helping Joseph of Arimathea give Jesus' body decent burial (19:38–42).

Nicodemus struggles to understand what Jesus means by being born *anōthen* (a Greek pun; it can be translated either "born again" or "born from above," that is, from God in heaven). We understand Jesus to be talking about the Spirit's work in Baptism, a spiritual rebirth. Emphasize that Baptism is not something *we* do—it is an act of God. That is why it has power; it is efficacious through God's Word. The power in Baptism is the power of the Gospel message of salvation through Jesus' death on the cross and resurrection at Easter. It is important to emphasize that Baptism is not a "get-into-heaven ticket." The action is God's, but we receive it by faith. Turning away from faith is also turning away from baptismal vows and promises.

(Regarding the phrase "born again," we see this term differently than some other churches do. In some church bodies, the phrase means a conversion experience that would rely on personal thoughts and emotions. The truth is that we are born again in Baptism through *God's* action as He adopts us into His family.)

Central Truth
Heavenly things are beyond earthly understanding, but God reveals all we need to know about salvation through Christ Jesus.

Objectives
- Acknowledge that faith is not based on our knowledge or intellect, but on the certainty of who God is and what He says and does.
- Confess that Jesus forgives our weakness, doubts, and questioning; He leads us through the Holy Spirit, in the Word, to strengthen our faith and to trust Him unconditionally, just as He loves us unconditionally.
- Proclaim that all questions are answered and all promises are fulfilled in Jesus (2 Corinthians 1:20).

Materials
- Hymnals and music CDs
- Reproducible 53

Bible Prep
Post in advance so students can bookmark references before class time.
- Psalm 121
- John 3:1–21
- Romans 1:16
- Ephesians 5:8–21
- 1 Peter 2:9

Devotions

"You were so little when your mom died. Do you remember much about her?" Dana asked, taking a bite of her pizza.

"Yeah. Pretty much everything." Kelly's eyes were distant. "I still think about her every day."

Dana hesitated. "Do you ever get angry that she's not here anymore?"

"Well, for a while I was angry, but now I'm more . . . just . . . sad," said Kelly, looking down. "And I have lots of questions."

"Like what?"

"Like why she will never get to see me play volleyball, or see the pictures I paint, or be there when I get married someday. And why do I have to wait so long to see her again?" The tears had started, and Dana looked uncomfortable.

"She has a lot of questions, doesn't she?" said Kelly's dad as he walked into the room for a moment. He put a drinking glass on the table in front of his daughter and left again. Kelly picked it up, realized it was empty, and started laughing through her tears. "What are you laughing at?" Dana asked curiously.

"My dad and I have a family thing where when one of us gets sad, the other one gets out this glass that's all fogged up—see? We weren't supposed to put it in the dishwasher because the water was too hot for it. Now the glass is clouded over, and you can't see through it anymore." Kelly handed it to Dana. "Anyway, it reminds us of that place in the Bible where it says that now we understand or see dimly, but then someday, in heaven, we will be with God face-to-face. And even though we have questions and we can't see why God let something happen, we can trust Jesus to take care of us. *And my mom too.*"

"For sure!" Kelly replied. Then she called out, "Thanks, Dad!" "Sure, sweetheart," Dad replied.

Let's pray together. Dear Lord, thank You so much for being my strong support when I am weak. Help me to trust in You when I don't understand what's happening in my life. In Your name I pray. Amen. Say together Psalm 121. Then sing "You Are the Way; through You Alone" (*LSB* 526; recorded as *Hymn of the Season* for grade 6, Epiphany).

INTO the Word

A Breath of Fresh Air

Discuss the opening paragraphs of the Student Book with your class. Guide them to see what the wind can teach us about the Holy Spirit. (1) You cannot box up the wind; you cannot contain the Holy Spirit. The Holy Spirit brings us to faith in the salvation we have in Jesus, but He is not confined to a church building. The Holy Spirit works through the Means of Grace: God's Word and the Sacraments (Holy Baptism and the Lord's Supper). And as Jesus, true God, said, "Where two or three are gathered in My name, there am I among them" (Matthew 18:20). (2) The people long ago could see Jesus in person, but we cannot see the Holy Spirit. We hear Him, however, in God's Word, His message to us. (3) The Holy Spirit comes and goes without our direction. We don't choose Him; He chooses us and brings us to faith. "No one can say 'Jesus is Lord' except in the Holy Spirit" (1 Corinthians 12:3). We don't bring other people to faith; we can only be tools, telling them about God's Word; only the Holy Spirit works to bring people to faith. (4) Wind changes things by blowing them over or moving them. The Holy Spirit changes us—transforming our lives and enabling us to live as people of God. Through the Holy Spirit, we are something new; the old has gone away (2 Corinthians 5:17)! (5) When the troubles of this world get us down, the Holy Spirit lifts us up and refreshes us through the Word of God. "Restore to me the joy of Your salvation, and uphold me with a willing spirit" (Psalm 51:12).

While we cannot see the Holy Spirit, we can see the work He is doing as He brings people to faith, strengthens their faith, and keeps them in faith! The Spirit is active in our lives today! Have student volunteers read aloud John 3:1–9, which contains portions of the actual conversation between Nicodemus and Jesus. Ask if students learned any additional information as this was read. Especially note Nicodemus's question, "How can these things be?" Just as we sometimes don't understand everything in God's Word, Nicodemus didn't understand either. So Jesus continued to explain.

A Splash of Water

Discuss the very significant concepts presented in the Student Book. Each statement tells something additional about Baptism.

Point out that the three water drops pictured can stand for the fact that we are baptized in the name of the triune God—Father, Son, and Holy Spirit. However, in this case, we want to consider three of the benefits (or blessings) that God gives to us in Baptism. Turn to the Student Book Appendix, Luther's Small Catechism, the section on Holy Baptism. Have a volunteer read the first section, which tells what Baptism is.

Then look at the second section, where you will find three benefits of Baptism. Have students write those on the three lines on their Student Book page. Then continue by looking at the third section on the power of Baptism, which emphasizes that the Sacrament's power does not come from the water. Also point out that a Bible verse from this section of the Catechism is given as today's Bible verse to remember.

228

A Blast of Power

What is the source of all this power we are talking about? What is the source of power that brings forgiveness, life, and salvation? We read about this power source in the Gospel, where we hear about Jesus' death on the cross and His resurrection for us. What does Romans 1:16 tell about the power of the Gospel? __"It is the power of God for salvation to everyone who believes."__

Read about the powerful love of God that Jesus spoke of to Nicodemus—and to you and me—in John 3:14–17. Then indicate that power of the Gospel by adding a black cross to the red "blast of power" on the left.

A Burst of Light

Sometimes cartoons show a character with a shining light bulb above his head to indicate that the "light came on" and he finally understands. Like Nicodemus, sometimes our earthly knowledge is not wise enough to comprehend heavenly things. In His infinite mercy, however, God shines light on our dark, sin-filled world and forgives us for these times of doubt and ignorance. He helps us place our trust in Jesus, even when we don't fully understand.

However, John 3:19–21 goes beyond our own understanding as it talks about Jesus as the light of the world. This light shows us the way to heaven—through Him who is the light. (See 1 Peter 2:9.) Jesus calls on us to reflect His light, showing His love toward others as lights in this world, serving others and sharing the Gospel message of this light of the world. What is our life like as we live and walk in the light of the Lord? See Ephesians 5:8–21.

Jesus shines on us and leads us to walk in His light, following what is good and right and true, avoiding the darkness of sin, and praising and giving thanks to God. We are able to do this only because we are empowered by the Holy Spirit.

Remember

"He saved us . . . by the washing of regeneration and renewal of the Holy Spirit, whom He poured out on us richly through Jesus Christ our Savior, so that being justified by His grace we might become heirs according to the hope of eternal life. The saying is trustworthy." (Titus 3:5–8)

113

INTO our lives

A Burst of Light

In Jesus' conversation with Nicodemus, we see yet another "word picture" of Jesus, this time as the "light of the world." As you work through this section of the Student Book, emphasize that if we try to "follow our own path," doing what we want and following our own will, we will wander in darkness, blindly stumbling through life. There is only one true light, and that is Jesus; we are either in the light or in darkness. The Holy Spirit brings us to the light, giving us faith in Jesus; and then the Holy Spirit enables (makes us able) to walk in the light, leading us to do good deeds that manifest, or attest to, the presence of God in our lives. (See John 3:21.)

Use the concordance in the Student Book Appendix to find other key Scriptures verses that speak of light. Then sing "I Want to Walk as a Child of the Light" (*LSB* 411; recorded as *Hymn of the Season for grade 7, Epiphany*).

A Blast of Power

Use the "Review" section to lead into the second page of this lesson, in which we **speak about the power of Baptism, and point out that the source of all this power is in the redemptive work of Jesus as He died on the cross and arose for us at Easter.** This part of the conversation (John 3:14–17) is the most important part of Jesus' message to Nicodemus—and to the whole world!

Was this Gospel message efficacious? Did these words have power to transform Nicodemus? We see him mentioned two other places in Scripture when he boldly stood up, even before the Pharisees, the Sanhedrin (governing council of the church), and before the Roman governor, Pilate. In John 7:43–52, Nicodemus spoke up for Jesus before the chief priests and Pharisees; it also says that Nicodemus was "one of them," meaning one of the followers of Jesus. In 19:38–42, Nicodemus and Joseph of Arimathea bravely aligned themselves as followers of Jesus, asking permission to bury Him; and note that they buried Him with seventy-five pounds of myrrh and aloes, which is the amount used for the burial of a king.

229

UNIT 5—THE PROMISED ONE IS HERE!   LESSON 54

Jesus and the Woman at the Well
JOHN 4

Background

Jesus encountered the woman at Jacob's well while traveling from Judea back to Galilee. The most direct route meant traveling through Samaria, which was something most Jews avoided due to prejudice and a belief that the Samaritans were religiously unclean. It is characteristic of Jesus that He not only visited Samaria several times, but He ate and drank there, spent the night, and taught the people.

The Samaritans of Jesus' day were the descendants of Israelites left behind after Samaria's destruction in 722 BC and of foreigners imported by Assyrian kings (2 Kings 17:24–28, 33–34). The two groups intermarried. The residents of Samaria blended the worship of Israel's God with the worship of their familiar idols, a practice known as "syncretism." They also altered other Jewish teachings, such as worshiping on Mount Gerizim in their own territory instead of at the temple in Jerusalem.

The woman in this story may have been looked down upon not only by the Jews but by her own people as a result of her personal life. She visits the well during the hottest part of the day instead of early in the morning, when other women would be there, socializing. Yet Jesus treats her with courtesy and kindness, and He refrains from saying anything about her sins until she in effect invites Him to do so (John 4:15). He also honors her by making her the first person to hear the truth—that He is the Messiah—directly from His own lips: "I who speak to you am He" (John 4:26). Recognizing the joy of forgiveness, she immediately shares the Good News with the whole village.

Central Truth

God wants all people to be saved, of every race, gender, nation, culture, and background.

Objectives

- Acknowledge that God doesn't measure us according to who's less or more sinful—we are all sinners who are dead to righteousness.
- Declare that Jesus gives living (continuously flowing) water as He washes away our sins; He offers living water that springs up to eternal life.
- Especially when we feel spiritually dried up, rely on the restoring power of the Gospel of salvation.

Materials

- Hymnals and music CDs
- Reproducible 54
- Optional: plain M&M's candies
- Web Resource 54a

Bible Prep

Post in advance so students can bookmark references before class time.
- John 4 and 7
- Genesis 22
- Psalm 67
- Psalm 121
- Revelation 21

Devotions

Megan was so excited to be traveling by airplane for the first time. She sat with her face glued to the window, watching the landscape unfold below her. "Look at all those bright green circles down there," she said to her father. "What are they?"

Father craned his neck to look out the window. "Hmm," he said. "The pilot said we're over Kansas now, and I'm pretty sure those circles are fields where they're growing crops."

"But why are they so green when everything else is brown?" asked Megan.

"Because the farmers irrigate them," said her father. "This part of Kansas doesn't get a lot of rainfall, so everything dries out and dies. But not the crops—they have a special sprinkler system."

"But why are the fields round?" asked Megan.

"Well," said her father, "the farmers use these really long sprinkler pipes that ride above the field on big wheels. They go around and around in a circle because they're connected to the pivot in the center of the field. That's where the water comes from."

"I'd like to see one of those close up," said Megan. She looked at the brown parts again. "So I guess water means life. No water, no life."

"You sound like something out of the Bible," her father said with a laugh. "Like the living water Jesus promised to give everyone who believes in Him."

Megan giggled. "Well, it's true," she said. "The water down there makes the plants alive, and Jesus makes us alive too! In fact, Jesus gives us life forever. I can see why we say that He gives us *living water*."

Let's pray: Jesus, we thank You for the living water You give us. Help us to grow and live for You in all we do. Amen. Say together Psalm 121. Sing "Take My Life and Let It Be" (*LSB* 783; recorded as *Hymn of the Month for grade 6, January*) or "I've Got Peace Like a River" (*AGPS* 139; recorded on *JPS*).

INTO the lesson

Diversity

Talk about ways a variety of experiences, like diversity in people, makes life interesting. Ask students to consider what life would be like if everyone had the same interests, talents, and personality.

Option: Pour a large bag of plain milk chocolate M&M's into a bowl, or distribute individual snack-size bags of the candy to each student. Challenge students to name all six colors without looking. Then ask several students to name their favorite color of the candy and tell why they like that one the best. Would they refuse to eat M&M's that are not this color? Proceed with this experience by eating the M&M's. Students will soon discover that there really is no good reason to choose one color over another; all of the M&M's taste exactly alike because they are all exactly alike on the inside.

Continue through the first Student Book page, and then distribute Reproducible 54. Explain that although God made each person unique, all people have three kinds of basic needs: physical, emotional, and spiritual. Many of these needs are listed on the bottom of the page. Read Luther's Explanation of the First Article of the Apostles' Creed. Categorize the needs, and then explore how each of these needs is met. God often accomplishes this through people. For example, He usually provides food, clothing, and shelter through our parents. Love and acceptance come through family and friends, while opportunities for achievement occur at home, at school, in sports, in the arts, and in our work. While our family members and friends may or may not forgive us for the wrong things we do, only God's forgiveness truly *removes* the sin. **Through faith in Jesus, God gives us eternal life. He gives faith and comfort through the gift of the Holy Spirit.**

Review

Remind students that all people need forgiveness because all people sin. We are all sinners who are dead to righteousness. Sin is sin, just like chocolate is chocolate. While we are tempted to view the sins of someone else as greater than our own, God counts all transgressions alike. And "the wages of sin is death" (Romans 6:23). The ax murderer, the bank robber, and the sixth grader who angrily shoves his sister all stand before God equally guilty and equally in need of His forgiveness. Yet all are forgiven through faith in Jesus, the long-awaited Messiah, who washes away their sins. Have students fill in the blanks in the "Remember" section on the next page of the Student Book. God wants all people to be saved, of every race, gender, nation, culture, and background.

LESSON 54

Jesus and the Woman at the Well

Diversity

The normal bag of plain M&M's (not the ones with peanuts or pretzels or some other special variety) contains six colors of candy. While red may be your favorite color in clothing, or green may be the color of your favorite football team, you don't choose which M&M's to eat on the basis of color, because everyone knows the color doesn't make any difference in the taste. While M&M's look different on the outside, inside the colored shells they are all exactly alike—delicious milk chocolate.

Like M&M's, people look different from one another on the outside. They come in a variety of sizes and shapes, with hair, eyes, and skin of different colors. Some people are outgoing; others, shy. Some learn easily, while others struggle to understand their lessons. Some excel at sports; others play the violin or paint or dance. The differences in people make life interesting, just like the colors in a bag of M&M's.

But inside, all people are alike. They were created by God, with nervous systems, skeletal and muscular systems, skin, and sensory organs. All people have the same basic needs: air, water, food, love, acceptance, and a sense of achievement.

All people are alike in another way too. All people sin. It's their nature—their human nature. Ever since Adam and Eve's first sin, all people have inherited the condition of sinfulness. We call that *original sin*. Just as one M&M isn't more or less chocolaty than another, in God's eyes, one person isn't more or less sinful than another. Chocolate is chocolate; sin is sin. And the penalty for sin is death. God sent a Savior to meet the most important need of all people. Through Jesus, God gives the gift of eternal life to all who believe in Him. God's grace and forgiveness is for all people.

Review

Covenant Connection

Throughout the Old Testament, the Lord worked His purposes through the people of Israel while emphasizing that through His plans, the whole world would be blessed. (See Genesis 22:15, 18 and Psalm 67.) God's loving plan of salvation through the Messiah was for all people. But many people, especially the priests and Pharisees (and even some of Jesus' disciples), thought the true God belonged to them exclusively. Jesus continually emphasized that He came for all people ("For God so loved the world . . . ," John 3:16). He did that in today's story when He surprised the disciples by speaking to a sinful woman—and not only that, but a woman from *Samaria*, a land that many Jewish people would not even walk through. We today can be especially thankful that Jesus came even for Americans, Canadians, Mexicans, Chinese, and all the people of the world.

114

INTO the Word

Looking for Living Water

The text of the Bible story has been set as a skit with only two characters. Give pairs of students the opportunity to present the story to each other as a readers theater. After partners have read and presented the story twice (switching parts), invite them to open their Bibles to John 4. "Play detective" to find what's unusual about this story. Provide whatever background is necessary regarding the relations between the Jews and the Samaritans. Be sure to mention that many Jews avoided any contact with Samaritans for fear of contamination by the Samaritans' unorthodox religious beliefs. Look at a map from the Student Book Appendix.

Help students to discover the following:

En route from Jerusalem to Galilee, Jesus passed through Samaria rather than bypassing it (v. 4).

The woman came to the well to draw water around noon instead of early in the morning (vv. 6–7).

Jesus asked the woman for a drink, ignoring the usual hostility between Jews and Samaritans and the common denigration of women (vv. 7–9).

Jesus offers "living water"—flowing water. In John 7:37–39, this expression refers to the gift of the Holy Spirit, who creates new life (John 4:10). Jesus explains that anyone who drinks His living water will never thirst again, and that this water will lead to eternal life (vv. 13–14).

Looking for Living Water

(The setting is midday at Jacob's well, located near the city of Sychar in Samaria. Jesus is seated at the well when a woman approaches to draw water.)

Jesus: Give Me a drink.

Woman: How is it that You, a Jew, ask for a drink from me, a woman of Samaria?

Jesus: If you knew the gift of God, and who it is that is saying to you, 'Give Me a drink,' you would have asked *Him*, and He would have given you living water.

Woman: Sir, You have nothing to draw water with, and the well is deep. Where do You get that living water? Are You greater than our father Jacob? He gave us the well and drank from it himself, as did his sons and his livestock.

Jesus: Everyone who drinks of this water will be thirsty again, but whoever drinks of the water that I will give him will never be thirsty again. The water that I will give him will become in him a spring of water welling up to eternal life.

Woman: Sir, give me this water, so that I will not be thirsty or have to come here to draw water.

Jesus: Go, call your husband, and come here.

Woman: I have no husband.

Jesus: You are right in saying, "I have no husband"; for you have had five husbands, and the one you now have is not your husband. What you have said is true.

Woman: Sir, I perceive that You are a prophet. Our fathers worshiped on this mountain, but You say that in Jerusalem is the place where people ought to worship.

Jesus: Woman, believe Me, the hour is coming when neither on this mountain nor in Jerusalem will you worship the Father. You worship what you do not know; we worship what we know, for salvation is from the Jews. But the hour is coming, and is now here, when the true worshipers will worship the Father in spirit and truth, for the Father is seeking such people to worship Him. God is spirit, and those who worship Him must worship in spirit and truth.

Woman: I know that the Messiah is coming. When He comes, He will tell us all things.

Jesus: I who speak to you am He.

Jesus promised the woman at the well "living water." He said, "Whoever drinks of the water that I will give him will never be thirsty again. The water that I will give him will become in him a spring of water welling up to eternal life" (John 4:14). Read John 7:37–39 and Revelation 21:1–6 to learn more about the "living water" that wells up to eternal life. The water that Jesus gives is living water, continuously flowing as He washes away our sins each day. Through this life-giving, life-renewing water, we are empowered to serve God and our neighbors and to share the Good News of salvation with others. The Holy Spirit continues to work faith in our hearts each day. And through faith in the saving power of Jesus' death and resurrection, we will live with Him eternally in heaven.

Remember

"For _____ have _____ and fall short of the glory of God, and are _____ by His grace as a _____, through the _____ that is in Christ Jesus." (Romans 3:23–24)

The woman asks Jesus for living water so she will not have to come to the well again (v. 15).

Jesus tells her to bring her husband to Him; she says she has no husband (vv. 16–17). Jesus reveals that she has had five husbands and is now living with a man who is not her husband (vv. 17–18).

The woman recognizes that Jesus is a prophet, but she tries to involve Him in an argument over the proper place to worship (vv. 19–20).

The returning disciples are shocked to see Jesus speaking to a woman, because Jewish custom did not allow a rabbi to speak to a woman in public (v. 27).

The woman was so anxious to tell her neighbors that she forgot her water jar at the well (vv. 28–29).

The woman's Samaritan neighbors believed in Jesus because of the woman's testimony (v. 39).

Jesus stayed two days with the Samaritans, and many believed His words (vv. 40–41).

To understand the significance of Jesus' conversation with the woman, look beyond the facts in verses 6–7, 17–18. The Samaritan woman had been married five times and was now living with a man to whom she was not married. Adultery is a sin against the Sixth Commandment, and the woman could have been stoned to death for her sin (Leviticus 20:10; Deuteronomy 22:22; John 8:4–5). Instead of coming to the well early in the morning with the other women, this woman came alone at midday. She had apparently been judged and ostracized by her neighbors in Sychar. Jesus led her to see her sin and need for a Savior who could wash away her sins. Jesus reached out to her with acceptance—hating the sin, but loving the sinner.

Continue by looking at the closing paragraph of the Student Book lesson. Say, **Jesus reaches out to us with living water, just as He reached out to the woman at the well. He knows our need for love and acceptance as well as He knew hers. How far have you gone to receive acceptance? Have you lied to your friends or parents about achieving something you didn't? Have you put someone else down or gossiped, just to build yourself up? Have you given in to peer pressure and done something you know you shouldn't have, just so that group of people would accept and include you? Jesus knows our sins, He hates our sin, but He loves us and forgives us. He drowns our sinful nature in the living water of Baptism. Through the power of the Holy Spirit, He helps us to live lives that are pleasing to Him, trusting in God to meet all our emotional (and physical and spiritual) needs. God wants *all* people to rely on the restoring power of the Gospel of salvation, especially when they feel spiritually dried up—and that includes each of you.**

From another viewpoint, also discuss if they have ever been the ones who reject and ostracize others, such as people of other ethnic backgrounds or religious beliefs, people with disabilities, or people whose lifestyle we may judge as sinful. Remind students that Jesus reached out to people regardless of race or gender, culture or background. Through the power of the Holy Spirit—the living water He gives us—He empowers us to follow His loving example. "For I have given you an example, that you also should do just as I have done to you" (John 13:15). Close by reading the stanzas of "In Christ There Is No East or West" (*LSB* 653; *AGPS* 135).

Lesson Support

♥ Faith in Action

Jesus' disciples were shocked to find Him reaching out to the Samaritan woman at the well. Like the disciples, we often forget that Jesus' love extends to people who are "not like us," including people of other ethnic and religious backgrounds. Use the Internet to learn more about one of the organizations sharing the Gospel with other ethnic or religious groups. For example, People of the Book Lutheran Outreach (POBLO) ministers in Jesus' name to Muslims, and the Apple of His Eye Mission Society brings the living water of the Gospel to Jewish people. You will find other similar ministries listed under "RSOs" in *The Lutheran Annual*. Request materials to make a classroom display about the ministries. Encourage your pastor to invite a representative of one of these organizations to make a presentation to your congregation.

✋ Hands to Serve

"Water, water, every where, Nor any drop to drink," wrote the poet Samuel Taylor Coleridge. Today, natural disasters such as floods and hurricanes often provide too much water. Homes are uninhabitable, livestock die, and diseases flourish. This water can't be used for drinking, growing food, or staying clean. In other regions, drought kills crops and livestock; when rain finally comes to the parched ground, it is too late. Access to clean water makes the difference between sickness and health, death and life. In 2010, 1.2 billion people had no access to affordable clean water. By 2050, this figure will have risen to 4 billion. Contact LCMS World Relief and Human Care to find out how your class or school can raise money to provide water filters for a school or a community.

📚 Curriculum Connection

A good connection for this lesson might be 6.4.2.19, Prior Understandings and New Information, found in the sixth-grade Science volume of the Concordia Curriculum Guide series. The woman at the well had certain information about God and about the coming Messiah; Jesus' words and, even more, His caring actions changed her understanding completely. Discuss with your students: **What new information did she have after interacting with Jesus? What effect did this have on her actions? When, in science or in other areas of life, have you gained new information and changed your actions as a result?**

🔍 Searching Further

Help your students explore these other examples of love and acceptance of people who were not accepted by their neighbors. Assign the following texts to individuals or groups of students, and have them report their findings to the class.

Matthew 8:1–4 (Jesus heals a man with leprosy); 15:21–28 (Jesus heals the daughter of a Canaanite woman); 20:29–34 (Jesus restores the sight of two blind men); Mark 2:13–17 (Jesus dines with tax collectors and sinners); Luke 7:36–50 (a sinful woman anoints Jesus' feet); 8:26–39 (Jesus heals a man possessed by demons); 19:1–10 (Jesus reaches out to Zacchaeus and forgives him); 23:39–43 (Jesus forgives the dying thief on the cross); John 8:1–11 (Jesus forgives the woman accused of adultery).

Finally, read Isaiah 53:3. Who was not accepted? Jesus Himself! Surely Jesus understands how the woman at the well felt. Surely Jesus understands how we feel when we thirst for attention and acceptance. In fact, when Jesus was on the cross and spoke the words "I thirst" (John 19:28), perhaps not only was He expressing His human nature, but also His divine nature. On the cross, Jesus took upon Himself the sins and the spiritually parched feeling of all people from all times. Jesus truly knows how we feel because He bore that pain for us.

❓ Critical thinking

Check out the importance of water to living plants. Conduct an experiment with three identical houseplants. Water one plant twice a week, the second plant once a week, and the third plant every other week. Record the growth and condition of each plant. Some plants require more water than others. How often do ferns and other tropical plants need water? How much water does a cactus require? Although plants such as cacti can exist with limited water, they will eventually die with no water at all.

UNIT 5—THE PROMISED ONE IS HERE! LESSON 55

Jesus and the Children
Mark 10:13–16

Background

It may be difficult to grasp what it meant to be a child in Jesus' day. We live in a world that idealizes and sentimentalizes childhood to a degree that was unknown in the ancient world. Children then were marginalized legally and socially—they were loved but considered of low status, similar to slaves, foreigners, and women. Many died very young, and it was a rare family that saw all its children survive to adulthood. Except in wealthy families, children could expect to begin supporting the family by working hard at an early age. They had few rights but many responsibilities compared with modern children in developed countries.

With this background, it's not surprising that the disciples thought dealing with children was a waste of Jesus' time. Jesus corrected them in an astonishing way: "Do not hinder them, for to such belongs the kingdom of God" (Mark 10:14). God loves the littlest and least, and He has given them high honor in His kingdom. They represent all Christians who are saved by grace, for especially in the case of children, it is obvious that they receive God's blessings as a free gift. And especially in the case of infants and young children, there is no question of them earning it.

Central Truth

God is never too busy or too far off to care about each of us individually and personally.

Objectives

- Recognize that the disciples wrongfully thought that Jesus was concerned mostly for adults; it is just as wrong to think He is there just for children.
- Respect the fact that God loves, cares about, and saves people of all ages and throughout all their lives.
- Commit to serving God and giving Him glory all through our life, knowing He is always with us.

Materials

- Hymnals and music CDs
- Reproducible 55
- Web Resource 55a

Bible Prep

Post in advance so students can bookmark references before class time.
- Mark 10:13–16
- 1 Peter 2:2

Devotions

Do you remember a favorite outfit you wore last year? You loved that outfit so much that you couldn't wait to get it out and wear it again this year. But when you put it on, you discovered the pant legs ended above the tops of your socks, and you could barely get the shirt on at all. You had outgrown your favorite clothes.

Some things are best outgrown. St. Paul wrote, "When I was a child, I spoke like a child, I thought like a child, I reasoned like a child. When I became a man, I gave up childish ways" (1 Corinthians 13:11). Your parents were glad when you outgrew diaper rash and temper tantrums. You were probably happy to outgrow training wheels and compulsory naps.

One thing you will never outgrow is your relationship with God. Through Baptism, God washed away your sins and made you His child. He has clothed you in Jesus' perfect righteousness—and this type of clothing you will never outgrow. While you may have left behind the finger plays and coloring pages of your preschool Sunday School classes, you continue to study God's Word as you "grow in the grace and knowledge of our Lord and Savior Jesus Christ" (2 Peter 3:18).

As you grow in that grace and knowledge, you will need a guide and an example to follow. St. Paul wrote, "Therefore be imitators of God, as beloved children. And walk in love, as Christ loved us and gave Himself up for us, a fragrant offering and sacrifice to God" (Ephesians 5:1–2). Jesus loved all people, from the little children He held in His arms to the adults whom He healed and taught. He died to pay for their sins. He included all of them in His kingdom of grace.

Even someday when you are an adult, your mom and dad will always see you as their child. Pray that throughout your entire life—now, and someday as a teenager, as an adult, and as an elderly man or woman—God will continue to call you His child. In 1 John 3:1, the writer says, "See what kind of love the Father has given to us, that we should be called children of God; and so we are."

Sing both "Children of the Heavenly Father" (*LSB* 725; recorded as *Hymn of the Month* for grade 5, November) and "Father Welcomes" (*LSB* 605; recorded as *Hymn of the Month* for grade 3, April). Close by saying, God calls us to repentance and faith. He calls us to walk with Him, trusting Him, as He says in Isaiah 41:13: "For I, the LORD your God, hold your right hand; it is I who say to you, 'Fear not, I am the one who helps you.'"

INTO the lesson

...and Children of All Ages

"Ladies and gentlemen, boys and girls, children of all ages!" This traditional cry of the ringmaster has greeted circus goers for decades. Toddlers, parents, and grandparents watch elephants, lion tamers, and acrobats with the wonder of little children. Together they gasp at the daring of the trapeze artists and laugh at the antics of the clowns. For as long as the circus lasts, they have all become childlike.

All people, even the elderly, possess some childlike qualities. The circus brings out the sense of wonder in almost everyone. Ask students to think of other occasions that make older people think or act like children. Students may recall watching a grandparent blow out the candles on his or her birthday cake or helping an older relative trim the Christmas tree. Other possibilities might include fishing, riding bicycles, or eating a favorite childhood treat.

Jesus said, "Whoever does not receive the kingdom of God like a child shall not enter it" (Mark 10:15). Make sure students understand that He did not say *"as a child."* This statement would exclude everyone who comes to faith as an adult. The account of the thief on the cross and the story of the conversion of St. Paul prove that the Holy Spirit can work faith in persons of all ages. Instead of limiting the Kingdom to people of a particular age group, Jesus was talking about the *qualities* of children that are typical of all who are part of the kingdom of God. These qualities include trust, humility, and faith.

Read the example of trust on the first page of Lesson 55 in the Student Book. Ask students to give other examples of trust involving young children. These might include learning to ride a bike without training wheels. A young child also trusts his parents to provide for his needs and to take care of him in every situation. The young boy with the loaves and fish trusted Jesus to be able to use his lunch to provide for the dietary needs of five thousand people. Challenge students to think of other biblical examples of trust. These might include young Isaac on the trip to Mount Moriah; Shadrach, Meshach, and Abednego in the fiery furnace; Daniel in the lions' den; and Peter stepping out of the boat to walk on the water to Jesus. Through the power of the Holy Spirit, these people of various ages demonstrated trust in God.

Read the example of humility in the Student Book. Children are aware that they are not powerful enough to take care of themselves. They know they must depend on others for everything they need. Young Mary acknowledged her dependence on God and submitted to His gracious will for her. Other biblical examples might include Moses, who originally felt unqualified to lead God's people, and Jeremiah.

Read the example of faith in the Student Book. Simeon displayed that childlike faith, believing that the poor infant before him was the promised Messiah. Another biblical example would be Abraham, who left his homeland and traveled to the land God had promised him. For a complete list of people who believed even when they couldn't see, direct students to the "Hall of Faith" in Hebrews 11.

A young boy who trusted Jesus to use his lunch to provide for five thousand people, Mary as a young woman who humbly submitted to God's will, and ancient Simeon believed in the Savior God had sent and shared their faith with others. Being a "child" has nothing to do with age. The boy, Mary, and Simeon received the kingdom of God with the childlike qualities Jesus was talking about.

Review

The parents brought their children to Jesus so He could lay His hands on them and bless them. This laying on of hands and blessing was associated with inheritance rights in the Old Testament (Genesis 48:14–18). This blessing signified that the children were inheritors of God's kingdom of grace. As His children, they are heirs of the riches of their heavenly Father's kingdom—eternal life, forgiveness, and salvation.

Lesson 55
Jesus and the Children
...and Children of All Ages

Jesus said, "Whoever does not receive the kingdom of God like a child shall not enter it" (Mark 10:15). But what qualities of a little child was Jesus talking about?

A little child **trusts**. Have you ever watched a little child and her father in a swimming pool? "Jump," calls the father. "I will catch you." The child runs and jumps into the father's arms. She trusts her father to catch her, just as he said he would. The Gospel writer John tells how a crowd of more than five thousand people followed Jesus to hear Him teach (John 6:1–14). When dinnertime came, a little boy offered his lunch—five barley loaves and two fish—trusting Jesus to provide what the people needed. Jesus took the food, gave thanks, and provided enough food for everyone.

A little child shows **humility**. He understands that others are bigger, more powerful, and more experienced than he is. The child knows he must depend on others for all that he cannot do for himself. The Gospel writer Luke relates how the angel Gabriel appeared to a young woman named Mary and told her she would be the mother of the Savior (Luke 1:26–38). Mary didn't argue or propose a better plan. She demonstrated great humility in her response: "Behold, I am the servant of the Lord; let it be to me according to your word" (v. 38).

A little child has **faith**. She believes what she has been told. Luke gives us an example of this kind of childlike faith in an older person. The Holy Spirit had revealed to an old man named Simeon that he would not die until he had seen the Christ. Simeon had faith in this promise. When he saw baby Jesus in the temple with Mary and Joseph, he took the baby in his arms and said, "Lord, now You are letting Your servant depart in peace, according to Your word; for my eyes have seen Your salvation" (Luke 2:22–38).

These are the attributes God wants to see in His children of all ages—trust, humility, and faith.

Covenant Connection

When Jesus laid His hands on the children and blessed them, it showed that the children received the inheritance associated with being in God's family. We share in this inheritance described in 1 Peter 1:3–4 (see "Remember" on the next page). We share this inheritance as children of God with Abraham, David, Jeremiah, and all other believers in Jesus Christ. By faith we will inherit eternal life!

116

The Day the Children Came (Mark 10:13–16)

"I don't get it. Can't these people see Jesus is too busy to talk to children? I don't get it. Doesn't Jesus realize He has more important things to do?"

"I thought You were just another teacher, but now I realize that You are the promised Messiah! More than anything, I want my children to be part of Your kingdom."

"What a joy to bless the children! Truly, I say to you, whoever does not receive the kingdom of God like a child shall not enter it. My most important work is to share God's love with *all* people."

"We had to walk a long way to get here, and it was hard to see You, Jesus, in the big crowd. I'm so glad You welcomed me and my baby sister. I know for sure now that You came for all people, young and old and in between."

Childlike (Not Childish)

What about you? Is your faith childlike—or just childish? How does a person receive the kingdom of God like a child? As children receive everything they need from their parents, so you received faith as a gift of the Holy Spirit through God's Word and in Baptism. Through the witness of your parents and teachers, your faith has grown. As you continue to study God's Word and worship with other Christians, your faith will grow and mature. How does 1 Peter 2:2 describe us (believers at any age)? **Like newborn infants, hungry for the pure spiritual milk that nourishes us so that by it, we may grow up into salvation.**

It is an interesting paradox that childlike trust, humility, and faith in Jesus actually show great maturity of faith. Pray that the Holy Spirit will continue to grow such faith in us.

Remember

"Blessed be the God and Father of our Lord Jesus Christ! According to His great mercy, He has caused us to be born again to a living hope through the resurrection of Jesus Christ from the dead, to an inheritance that is imperishable, undefiled, and unfading, kept in heaven for you." (1 Peter 1:3–4)

117

INTO the Word

The Day the Children Came

Your sixth-grade students may think they are too old for this story about Jesus and the little children. But Jesus was talking about believers who are like children in their attitudes, not their years. Through the study of this lesson, help your students to understand that faith is ageless; we never outgrow it. **No matter what age we are, we depend upon God our entire lives. No matter how mature we become, salvation is always a gift of grace through faith in Christ, without any merit or worthiness on our part.** Remind them that they are just at the very beginning of their study of God's Word; there is a lifetime of things to learn about God, and even that lifetime will not tell all, not until we see the Lord Himself in heaven. This short story covers only four verses in Mark (10:13–16). The concept is discussed in a similar text in Matthew 18:1–6. In Matthew, these verses follow one of the disciples' frequent inquiries about who would be greatest in the kingdom of heaven. Jesus placed a child before them and used him as an object lesson in humility: "Unless you turn and become like children, you will never enter the kingdom of heaven," Jesus told them (v. 3). A child's humility is evident in his dependence on others. Greatness in the kingdom of heaven is characterized by humble dependence on God.

INTO our lives

Childlike (Not Childish)

Children become part of human families through birth. Review the story of Nicodemus visiting Jesus (John 3:1–20) from Lesson 53. Remind students that they became a part of God's family through this new birth in faith through the Word of God and the waters of Baptism. Just as infants and children need proper nutrition to grow into healthy adults, so young Christians need the nourishment that comes through the study of God's Word. The students' maturing faith will show itself in the way they live. Children are great imitators of their parents. Paul encourages us to be imitators of God. In Ephesians 5:1–2, Paul tells us, "Therefore be imitators of God, as beloved children. And walk in love, as Christ loved us and gave Himself up for us, a fragrant offering and sacrifice to God." We are enabled to walk in love because Jesus loved us enough to die on the cross for us.

Also use Reproducible 55, which focuses on Paul's discourse on love in 1 Corinthians 13 to contrast childlike faith with childish behavior. It's childish to crave everyone's attention and to desire to be the center of everyone's universe. Young children often tell their parents, "Watch me!" In contrast, a childlike faith acknowledges that *God* deserves all the attention and praise. God is the one who grants us our blessings and successes. On our own, we have no power or control over events. A childlike faith recognizes God's power and gives *Him* the glory throughout our life.

237

Lesson Support

Celebrating GROWTH

We love to watch the preschool children praise Jesus with their finger plays and simple songs. But as children grow older, their spiritual lives need to mature along with their minds and bodies. Help your students get into the habit of daily Bible reading by setting aside a fifteen-minute period each day for that purpose. Let students decide what they are going to read. Encourage students to keep track of their reading, listing the date, the passage read, and a one- or two-sentence summary of the day's reading. At the end of each week, invite students to share what they have read with their classmates. Ask them to tell (1) something new that they learned from the week's reading, or (2) something they already knew but were glad to read again.

Faith in Action

Children are humble because they have to depend on others for all they need; childlike faith is characterized by humble trust in the Lord. Children and adults with developmental disabilities are more dependent than other people of their chronological age. Learn more about your church's ministry to the developmentally challenged by contacting Bethesda Lutheran Home in Watertown, Wisconsin. Over many years, the Holy Spirit has brought many residents and clients of Bethesda to trust Jesus as their Savior from sin, death, and the power of the devil.

Working in Groups

Divide into groups to make Bible story books for the preschool or kindergarten children in your school. Ask each group to choose a story for their book. Encourage students to think of stories that would appeal to young children. Some favorites would include the creation of the world, the flood, baby Moses in the basket, Daniel in the lions' den, the birth of Jesus, the feeding of the five thousand, the Palm Sunday entry into Jerusalem, and the crucifixion and resurrection of Jesus. Working together, write, illustrate, and assemble the books. Use a word processing program on the computer to produce the text, leaving space on each page for illustrations. When the pictures have been added, use a color copier to make the final pages for the books. Bind the books with cardboard covers. When all of the books are finished, arrange for students to visit the preschool classroom. Let them read their stories to the children and present the books to them for their class library.

Check it Out

Have the children work with partners; one student will be the "clay" and the other will be the "sculptor" in creating the expressions that the disciples, Jesus, and the children would have had in the Bible narrative. In a gentle, appropriate way, the "sculptor" will move ("mold") the "clay" into a new position and give the student a new facial expression. Or the "sculptor" could model the facial expression, and the "clay" could mimic it. First, have the sculptor create a rebuking and unkind face and body language. After a certain work period, tell all the sculptors to stand back and admire the sculptures, as if viewing an art gallery. Point out certain common characteristics of the sculptures. Ask, **Where else have you seen that type of face? Have people shown that expression to you? When?** Then let the other student assume the sculptor role and "mold" his or her partner into a welcoming and kind face and body language. Participate in the same review and discussion.

Searching Further

The Apostle Paul wrote to Timothy, "Let no one despise you for your youth, but set the believers an example in speech, in conduct, in love, in faith, in purity" (1 Timothy 4:12). Learn more about Timothy: his family background (2 Timothy 1:5); his early growth as a young Christian (3:14–15); and Paul's challenge to him (1 Timothy 6:11–16). Discuss: How is Timothy's life like your own? How is it different? Who serves as a spiritual leader in your life? As you have time, use Web Resource 55a to review the actions of other faithful young people in the Bible.

Curriculum Connection

The social status of children in Jesus' day was very low, which may have been why the disciples didn't want them to bother Jesus. Take this occasion to help your class work through the ideas and information found in section 6.3.3.6, Social Status. You'll find it in the sixth-grade Social Studies volume of the Concordia Curriculum Guide series.

UNIT 5—THE PROMISED ONE IS HERE!

LESSON 56

Sermon on the Mount
MATTHEW 5–7

Background

Matthew is the only one of the evangelists to record the entire Sermon on the Mount, although Mark, Luke, and John each include some of the same words of Jesus. The sermon is notable for the way it cuts through human misunderstandings of God's Law and forces us to face the fact that we have not kept it, even the apparently easy commandments like "Do not murder." The Sermon on the Mount holds a mirror up to our lives, and the picture we see is not pretty.

For this reason, Matthew 5–7 makes uncomfortable reading. It is designed to do what God's Law always does—cause us to flee for help to Jesus, our Savior. Jesus forgives us, restores us, and gives us everlasting life as God's children. Then we can read the sermon again—not to cringe this time, but rather to discover the many ways the Holy Spirit is reshaping our lives to resemble Jesus' own.

Devotions

A black beaver gnawed at the trunk of a young aspen tree. With a soft thud, it fell to the ground, like many other trees in this Colorado mountain valley. The beaver dragged the fallen tree to the nearby stream and wedged it in with the others to build a dam, blocking most of the water's flow. Soon a pond formed behind the dam. The beaver will bring more logs to build a lodge in the pond. The entrance will be under water so predators can't get in. In this lodge, she will give birth to her babies and nurse them until they can safely go out into the pond.

The beaver didn't fell the aspen trees and build the dam in order to become a beaver. She won't build her lodge and raise her babies so that she will be a better beaver. She already is a beaver. God made her a beaver. She does these things because she is a beaver. She is only doing what God created her to do.

You and I were created by God as His precious children. When we were lost in sin, God sent His own Son, Jesus, to redeem and forgive us. God made us His children through water and His Word in Baptism. Through the power of the Holy Spirit, He calls us to live as His disciples, serving as salt and light in our world. With the Spirit's help, we love our enemies, we pray and help others, and we trust God to supply everything we need. We don't do this to become Jesus' disciples—God has already made us His children through Jesus' death and resurrection. Now the Holy Spirit helps us to live lives that honor God. Let's pray together: Lord Jesus, You gave Your life for me. Through the power of the Holy Spirit, help me live my life for You. Amen.

Praise God's love and action in your life by responding with love and service to Him and others. Sing "Lord, Be Glorified" (*AGPS* 165; recorded on *JPS*) and "Make Me a Servant" (*AGPS* 174; recorded on *JPS*).

Central Truth

We have been redeemed and forgiven by Jesus Christ; He calls on us to live sanctified lives of discipleship, empowered by the Holy Spirit.

Objectives

- Recognize that we have been forgiven and redeemed through Christ Jesus, who calls us to live as His disciples, moving beyond the letter of the Law, exceeding the Law in kindness, as we are led by His love for us.
- Understand that we are able to live as Jesus' disciples not by our own efforts, but as we are empowered by the Holy Spirit, who works in us through God's Word and Sacraments.
- Dedicate our lives to discipleship, guided by Christ Jesus in following God's will.

Materials

- Hymnals and music CDs
- Reproducible 56
- Web Resource 56a

Bible Prep

Post in advance so students can bookmark references before class time.
- Matthew 5–7

INTO the lesson

"So That" or "Because"?

Read the story about Jake. Help students understand that Jake's motivation was Law. He felt he needed to work hard to earn his parents' love. He worried that he had not done enough, and he tackled extra chores to try to make his parents love him more. When Jake fell short of his mother's standards by leaving his video games on the family room floor, he was afraid of being punished. Remind students that God gave His people the gift of His Law. He intended the Law to be used as a curb to keep order in the world and restrain rebelliousness; as a mirror to show us our sins; and as a guide to show us how to live God-pleasing lives. But our sinful nature makes perfect obedience to the Law impossible. No one can be saved by the Law, for the Law condemns everyone.

Only Jesus Christ obeyed the Law perfectly; then He died to pay the penalty for our disobedience. God offers the forgiveness of sins only in the Gospel, the Good News that we are freed from the guilt, punishment, and power of sin, and that we are saved eternally because Christ kept the Law and suffered and died in our place.

Go on to the story about Jackson. The actions in both stories are the same, but the motivations are very different. Jackson knows the unconditional love of his parents. His actions are motivated by his love for them and his desire to please them in response to their love. He doesn't worry that he hasn't done enough, but wants to do more than is required for his parents who love him so much. When Jackson fell short of his mother's standards by leaving his video games on the family room floor, he was confident of her love and forgiveness. This confidence motivated his efforts to do better in the future. **Which boy is happier? Who has a better relationship with his parents? Who is likely to continue serving his parents, and who may finally give up his efforts?** Have students personally consider, **Why do you do what you do? So that you don't get in trouble? So that you earn love? Because you want to make others happy?**

Sanctified Living

Having been justified through Christ Jesus, we are now sanctified by the power of the Holy Spirit, and we respond to God's redeeming love by living in ways that will please Him. The love of Christ motivates and enables us to do the will of God. Read aloud Galatians 2:20. Emphasize that we can live godly lives because of the power of God working in us! Living a Spirit-led life is called *sanctification*. It is a life of new obedience, a life lived in faith in Christ. Our faith gives a believer's mind a new attitude, with Christ as its focus.

LESSON 56
Sermon on the Mount

"So That" or "Because"?

Jake raised the garage door and pushed out the lawn mower. "I know mom and dad will be grocery shopping this morning," he told himself. "I'll get the grass cut before they come home so that they will love me." Jake was careful not to miss a single patch of grass. Then he found the weed whacker and trimmed around the trees. "I hope my parents will love me for working so hard," he worried.

Jake thought back to yesterday. He had left his video games all over the floor, and his mother was angry. "I'll never let that happen again," Jake had promised his mother. He was scared of what she might do to punish him. "From now on, I'll always put my games away so that you will love me."

Jackson raised the garage door and pushed out the lawn mower. "I know mom and dad will be grocery shopping this morning," he told himself. "I'll get the grass cut before they come home, because they love me and take such good care of me." Jackson was careful not to miss a single patch of grass. Then he found the weed whacker and trimmed around the trees. "I don't mind working this hard, because I appreciate how much my parents have done for me," thought Jackson.

Jackson thought back to yesterday. He had left his video games all over the floor, and his mother was angry. "I'm sorry I left such a mess," Jackson had told his mother. He smiled when his mother forgave him and gave him a big hug. "Next time, I'll make sure I put the games away because I know you love me."

Sanctified Living

Like Jake, many people try to please God "so that" He will love them. They work hard to obey the Ten Commandments. But because they are human, they eventually fail. They cannot earn God's love by what they do. Jackson did exactly the same things Jake did—but for a different reason. Jackson knew that his parents loved him. As Christians, we know that God loves us so much that He gave His own Son to die in our place and forgive all our sins. "Because" God loves us so much, we want to please Him in everything we do. Through the power of the Holy Spirit through Word and Sacraments, we are called and enabled to live sanctified lives as Jesus' disciples today.

Covenant Connection

God tells us that He made a new covenant with His people. Jeremiah 31:33–34 says, "I will put My law within them, and I will write it on their hearts. And I will be their God, and they shall be My people. . . . I will forgive their iniquity, and I will remember their sin no more." Through Christ, we are forgiven. And through the Holy Spirit working faith in our hearts, we are empowered to live as God's people. We have new, clean, sanctified hearts; our faith in Christ gives us a new attitude. The sanctified life is the message of the Sermon on the Mount.

118

INTO the Word

Job Description for a Disciple

Read the first paragraph of this section with your students. Be sure students understand that Jesus is teaching His disciples in this sermon. These people already believe in Him. Jesus is not telling them how to earn entrance into His kingdom. He is teaching them about their motivation in their new lives—they are led by the love of Jesus rather than the Law. Because of this, in our sanctified lives, we are led by Jesus to go beyond the Law, to do even more than the Law asks. (For example, if someone hits you, turn the other cheek. Look for more examples of this.)

Explain that the Pharisees believed and taught that salvation came from obedience to the letter of the Law. In addition to the Ten Commandments, this included all of the requirements in the Torah, the Law given to the Israelites in the wilderness. For further insight into the legalism of the Pharisees, read Matthew 12:1–14; 15:1–20; and especially 23:1–36. Their reliance on their own works was similar to Jake's thinking in the first section.

In the Sermon on the Mount, Jesus turns the teachings of the Pharisees upside down. He explains what life is like in the kingdom of God, where believers who have been redeemed live sanctified lives in response to God's grace.

240

Job Description for a Disciple

One day, Jesus took the disciples up on a mountain and began to teach them about the way people who believed in Him would live. These teachings are known as the "Sermon on the Mount," and they make a complete job description for a Christian disciple today—one who has been forgiven and redeemed by Christ Jesus. The old covenant was based on the Law, but no one can keep the Law because we are all sinners. So Jesus came to fulfill the Law for us. Now, as justified and sanctified people of God, we are called to live a life of love that surpasses and exceeds the Law! Romans 13:10 says, "Love is the fulfilling of the law." Here is part of the "job description" Jesus gives for our lives in the Sermon on the Mount.

- **Benefits:** Disciples will enjoy God's blessings in the kingdom of God, here on earth by faith and in heaven forever. (Matthew 5:3–12)
- **Role:** Disciples will be salt and light, effecting change in the world around them. As light, disciples will do good works that will lead others to glorify God. (Matthew 5:13–16)
- **Understandings:** Because of God's redeeming love for them, disciples will go beyond the requirements of the Law, doing more than the Law demands. Disciples refrain from anger as well as murder, and they turn the other cheek instead of getting even. Disciples love their enemies as well as their friends. (Matthew 5:17–48)
- **Attitudes:** In response to God's love, disciples will be God-centered instead of self-centered. They will not seek public attention when they help the needy, pray, or show kindness, but will do good works to glorify the Father in heaven. Disciples trust in God and place Him first in their lives, rather than seeking earthly treasures or worrying about their physical needs. (Matthew 6)
- **Actions:** Disciples are called to live out their faith in Jesus, their Savior. Jesus assures them that He will answer their prayers for help in sanctified living. He warns them to examine themselves before judging others and to treat others as they would like to be treated. Disciples cling to their Savior in faith that cannot be shaken by the storms of life. (Matthew 7)
- **Required Education and Experiences:** None; just faith in Christ Jesus.

My Job Description

You have been redeemed and forgiven through Jesus' death and resurrection. God made you His child in Baptism and has called you to live as His disciple. Through the power of the Holy Spirit in Word and Sacraments, He enables you to live a sanctified life.

Scan Jesus' Sermon on the Mount in Matthew 5–7. Then write three ways in which your life can show Jesus' love for you and lead others to glorify your Father in heaven.

Because Jesus loved me so much that He gave His life for me, I will . . .

1. _____
2. _____
3. _____

Remember

"Let your light shine before others, so that they may see your good works and give glory to your Father who is in heaven." (Matthew 5:16)

Believers go *beyond* the Pharisees' obedience to God's Law, and they do it joyfully because of God's love for them.

The word *disciple* means "learner" or "apprentice." Read "Job Description for a Disciple" in the Student Book. Then divide the three chapters of text—Matthew 5, 6, and 7—according to the topical headings in the students' Bibles. Assign one or more sections to small groups or individual students. Ask students to study their texts and report to the class about what Jesus was saying about the sanctified life of a believer. Use Reproducible 56 to study the Beatitudes. **Was Jesus' teaching the same as or different from the teachings of the Pharisees? How was it different?** (Jesus taught the same, and more. This "more" was based on the motivation of love.)

Option: When all students have reported, ask individuals or groups to make a poster illustrating Jesus' teaching in the section of the Sermon on the Mount that they studied. Hang the posters in a school hallway where other students may see them. Or ask each group to put together a skit demonstrating Jesus' teaching in their section of the sermon. As time permits, you can also have students review the Beatitudes by completing the crossword puzzle on Web Resource 56a.

INTO our lives

My Job Description

Ask your students to put themselves in the place of the disciples on that hillside in Galilee. They had been raised to believe that they must please God by obedience to the Law. Now Jesus says that He has come to fulfill the Law, and that their righteousness must exceed the righteousness of the Pharisees. But God regards us as righteous because of the suffering and death of Jesus in our place. In the kingdom of God, we live in *response* to God's redeeming love for us.

Help students scan Matthew 5–7 by reminding them of the reports in the previous section of the lesson. Encourage them to choose a topic that is meaningful to them personally—for example, anger, retaliation, loving your enemies, giving to the needy, prayer, laying up treasures in heaven, or worrying. Help them to compose statements that show understanding of Jesus' teaching. Encourage them to put the phrase in their own words. Instead of "not worry," the student might write, "Trust God for all I need instead of worrying."

Remind students that our sinfulness often gets in the way of sanctified living in response to God's love for us. When we confess our mistakes and shortcomings to God, He promises to forgive us for Jesus' sake. Through the power of the Holy Spirit, He empowers us to live for Him.

Jesus' teachings in the Sermon on the Mount are so demanding that even the most dedicated disciples fail to live up to them all the time. It is good news that Jesus kept the Law perfectly in our stead (Hebrews 4:15). It is good news that Jesus does not merely command long-suffering, forgiveness, and love of enemies. He puts them into practice Himself—lovingly bearing with *us* and forgiving *us*!

Remember

Remind students that the purpose of good works is so that others will glorify God. How does this verse relate to Matthew 7:15–20? How does this verse sum up the entire Sermon on the Mount?

Lesson Support

Curriculum Connection

Make a literature connection by using section 6.2.1.1, Purpose, Point of View, Tone, Style, Audience, and Message; this is found in the sixth-grade Language Arts volume of the Concordia Curriculum Guide series. Together with students, identify these elements in the Sermon on the Mount. Especially discuss these questions: **Why did Jesus use so many parables and vivid examples? Why did He teach so briefly on so many different subjects? What is the one main point Jesus was leading up to—and why do you think He chose that point of emphasis? Do you think Jesus would have taught in a different style if He were, say, in a private room with only His disciples present?**

Searching Further

The Pharisees of Jesus' day believed and taught that salvation came through strict obedience to the Law. This Law was contained in the Torah, the five books of Moses, and was given to the people of Israel through Moses about 1450 BC. The Hebrew word *Torah* means "teaching," "instruction," or "doctrine." God's Law quickly became surrounded by human rules intended to further explain it and prevent people from breaking it unknowingly. Thus, the law regarding rest on the Sabbath was elaborated into a long list of permitted and forbidden activities, even specifying how far a person might walk on that day. Challenge students to find more examples of these extra rules. **What is the difference between them and God's Law? Why did Jesus object to these extra rules?**

Teacher Tips

Expand on this lesson's memory verse (Matthew 5:16) with the following illustration. In John 8:12, Jesus said, "I am the light of the world. Whoever follows Me will not walk in darkness, but will have the light of life." In the Sermon on the Mount, He says, "You are the light of the world. A city set on a hill cannot be hidden" (Matthew 5:14). Use science to illustrate the concept. Light a candle and set it on a table or desk at the front of the darkened classroom. Tell the students that this candle represents Jesus, the light of the world. Then invite several students to place small mirrors around the candle. Ask: **How many lights do you see now? Do these mirrors produce any light on their own?** Remind students that we, like the mirrors, are reflections of Christ's light to the world around us. Or study how the moon reflects the sun's light. Read Ephesians 5:1–2. When others see the light of our faith through the way we live, they will glorify our Father in heaven.

Hands to Serve

Fold your hands in prayer. In Matthew 5:44, Jesus tells His followers, "Love your enemies and pray for those who persecute you." Jesus Himself was the best example of this teaching: "God shows His love for us in that while we were still sinners, Christ died for us" (Romans 5:8). As He hung dying on the cross, He looked at His executioners and prayed, "Father, forgive them, for they know not what they do" (Luke 23:34). Ask each of your students to think of someone who has done something to hurt them. Invite them to pray for that person each day.

Check it Out

Many favorite Bible verses are included in the Sermon on the Mount. Ask students to choose their favorite verses from these three chapters and write them on strips of paper. Place these treasures of Scripture in a box or treasure chest in your classroom. Invite students to choose a verse from the treasure chest to read at the close of school each day.

Working in Groups

Many of Jesus' sayings in the Sermon on the Mount have become favorite Bible passages of Christians. Make a set of greeting cards featuring appropriate verses from Matthew 5–7 to be sent to shut-ins or other congregation members in need of an encouraging message. Choose verses that would be suitable for various occasions (be sure to double-check your students' choices for appropriateness). Then design cards on your computer, using a program such as Microsoft Publisher. Print your cards on heavy paper or cardstock. Envelopes may be purchased at an office supply store. Your pastor can provide you with a list of names of people who would appreciate a card. He may even offer to hand-deliver your cards when he makes his regular visits.

Unit 6—The Ministry of Jesus

Theme

In this unit, we look at Jesus' ministry. We will look at many of Jesus' miracles, such as the healing of a man who is paralyzed and the ten men with leprosy. We will see Jesus feeding five thousand or more people in a miracle providing for daily needs and also a miracle of protection as Jesus calms a storm. His teachings will be explored in the parable of the sower and the parable of the rich fool. Recognition of Jesus as true God is studied in the narratives of Peter's confession, the Roman centurion's faith, and Christ's Transfiguration. And Christ's main mission—to bring forgiveness and life—is studied in the story of the woman who is judged and the raising of Lazarus. So this unit gives an overall picture of Jesus' ministry, leading into the next unit, which focuses on His death and resurrection. As you know, the curriculum has nine units to roughly correspond to the nine months of a school year, so Unit 6 is suggested for use in February, which is usually the beginning of Lent.

Worship

As you are approaching or have entered the Lenten season of the Church Year, you will be emphasizing the main purpose for Jesus' life on earth: to suffer and die to take away our sins and to rise again at Easter, winning the victory of salvation and eternal life for us. The *Hymn of the Month* (February) is "By Grace I'm Saved" (*LSB* 566) and the *Hymn of the Season* (Lent, Part A) is "Come to Calvary's Holy Mountain" (*LSB* 435). These are recorded on the CDs with the same name. Always feel free to make additional hymn choices, including songs from *All God's People Sing!* (with fifty of these songs recorded on *Jesus' People Sing!*). Consider frequently reviewing hymns learned in previous years also. The psalm choice for this month is Psalm 130, which appropriately is a plea for God's mercy and forgiveness. Use this in your daily devotions to increase familiarity with this important psalm. Later in the unit, a Web Resource is available on the One in Christ Portal to become acquainted with and try chanting the psalm.

Resources

Though the Teacher Resource Book provides many extra materials to use with this curriculum, these resources are also on the One in Christ Portal, which includes links to other Web sites, interactive whiteboard (IWB) applications, slide presentations, and other resources for the lesson of the day. Quizzes can be printed out or taken online (with a self-checking feature!). (Unit 6 printed test answers are: 1-a; 2-c; 3-b; 4-c; 5-e; 6-b; 7-c; 8-e; 9-b; 10-c.) Note that the titles of this unit's lessons are listed in the column at the right to give you an overview of the material covered in this unit.

Unit 6

57. The Faith of the Roman Centurion
58. Friends Bring a Man to Jesus
59. Ten Men with Leprosy
60. The Parable of the Sower
61. Jesus Is Transfigured
62. Jesus Feeds a Crowd
63. A Woman Is Judged
64. Peter's Confession
65. Stormy Seas
66. The Parable of a Foolish Rich Man
67. Jesus Raises Lazarus from the Dead

Bulletin Board

This bulletin board is available, ready to cut out and pin up, from Concordia Publishing House. There will be a bulletin board available for each unit/month that focuses on the unit's theme. Here is a list of Bible references that you can explore to expand on the concepts presented in each of the sections of the bulletin board, which answers the question "Who Is Jesus?" **My Prophet**—John 1:1, 14; Matthew 5:1–7:29; Mark 16:15. **My Priest**—Galatians 4:4–5; Hebrews 7:26–27; John 17:20–26. **My King**—1 Corinthians 15:25–27; Revelation 17:14; John 14:1–3. **True God**—John 1:1–3; Hebrews 13:8; Matthew 28:18; John 21:17; Matthew 28:20. **True Man**—John 1:14; John 11:35; Luke 4:1–13; Hebrews 4:15; Mark 15:21–39. **My Savior**—Hebrews 2:14–15, 17; 1 Peter 1:18–19; 2 Corinthians 8:9; 1 John 2:1–2; 1 Corinthians 15:57.

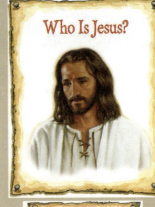

Bible Book Overview

The Student Book Appendix has a valuable feature that gives a summary of each book of the Bible. Looking at the summaries of sixty-six books can be overwhelming, so it is suggested that each month/unit, your class look at the summaries of just a few of these books. During Unit 6, introduce the Minor Prophets of the Old Testament (minor not in significance, but rather in the size of the books). Often their prophecies look to the coming Messiah, and in Unit 6, we will see the Messiah, Jesus, fulfilling the prophecies. Read together and discuss the summaries of these twelve books (Hosea through Malachi) in the Student Book Appendix when you have available time. (Note that a copy of the Student Book Appendix is included in the back of this Teacher Guide.)

UNIT 6—THE MINISTRY OF JESUS

LESSON 57

The Faith of the Roman Centurion
Matthew 8:5–13; Luke 7:1–10

Background

After a while, Jesus' healing miracles might all start to sound alike to our students—and maybe even to us! However, a close examination of each account reveals new and wonderful truths the Holy Spirit wants us to know. Today's account is no exception. (Note that today's Bible narrative is explored in the light of two other events, one that is the opposite and one that is similar.)

Great crowds had swarmed Jesus from all Judea and Jerusalem. Jews and Gentiles alike, they had come to hear and to be healed. Jesus teaches them, and when He finishes, an unlikely candidate for healing steps forward. Or, to be precise (according to the account in Luke), his representatives step forward. The leaders of the synagogue in Capernaum had come to our Lord, representing a Gentile, a centurion whose slave is in great pain and about to die. These few facts convey so much!

- Being a centurion, this man has authority, prestige, and in some cases, the power of life and death.
- Being a Roman and a member of the foreign army that occupied Israel, this man would have been hated on sight by the Jews.
- Synagogue leaders in Capernaum spoke well of the centurion in today's Bible narrative and wanted to help him. This would have been extremely unusual! Because the synagogue leaders represent the centurion, we deduce something quite drastic has changed their minds about him.
- The centurion's message ("I am not worthy to have You come under my roof") speaks volumes about his humility of heart.
- The centurion asked nothing for himself, but pleads for Jesus to help his slave! Startling! A slave in Roman culture held the value of livestock. But this centurion has compassion on his slave as a person.

God has been at work in the centurion's heart. If even a Roman centurion can come to faith, then the Father has flung the doors of life open to anyone and everyone! Even Jesus Himself marvels at the humility and faith of this man.

Central Truth

No one is worthy to come to the Lord, but He graciously makes us worthy through Jesus.

Objectives

- Acknowledge that Jesus came for all people who are sinners—and that includes everyone.
- Celebrate that Jesus takes away our sins and gives us His righteousness, claiming us to be children of God.
- Trust in the gracious ways and will of God, who works always for our good.

Materials

- Reproducible 57
- Web Resource 57a
- Hymnals and music CDs

Bible Prep

Post in advance so students can bookmark the references before class time.
- Psalm 130
- The Gospel of Matthew
- Revelation 5:12–13

Devotions

One Sunday, a homeless man left the park where he had slept the night before and entered the church down the block. He sat in the back row, hoping no one would notice him or his ragged clothing. But one of the ushers saw him and sat down next to him and spoke quietly. The usher said, "I'm afraid you will have to leave. We dress respectfully when we are in God's house. You are welcome to come back when you have a clean shirt and tie. In fact, I will give you twenty dollars so you can buy a clean shirt." The homeless man left and never came back again. The usher thought to himself, "I knew giving him that twenty dollars was just a waste of money. He probably came here just to get a hand-out." Meanwhile, the homeless man sat at an outdoor table of a fast-food restaurant and thought to himself, "I haven't eaten in four days. I just couldn't spend money on a shirt when I am so hungry. I don't know why I thought a worthless person like me could go into such a nice church."

In God's eyes, which of these men is worthy? Actually, no one is, but God loves us anyway—that's why He sent Jesus to rescue us. Jesus took our sins to the cross and He gives us His righteousness in return—Jesus makes us worthy so that in God's eyes we are "blameless and innocent, children of God without blemish" (Philippians 2:15). Through this "great exchange," Jesus has made us worthy to be called children of God! (1 John 3:1). This has nothing to do with a clean shirt and tie!

In today's world, people are considered valuable and worthy if they have lots of money, power, or fame. But Jesus turns the world upside down. He leads us to humility and compassion—He leads us, showing the way by His own life! Dear Lord, help us to recognize that we are unworthy of Your love and forgiveness. Help us to look at others with the same compassion that You look at us. Amen.

In today's Bible lesson, we will learn more about humility and worthiness. Sing "Jesus Sinners Doth Receive" (*LSB* 609; recorded on *Hymns of the Month, grade 7, January*). Read Psalm 130 in your Bibles or hymnals. This fits well with today's theme of humility and as we approach Lent.

INTO the lesson

What Do They Deserve?

The Bible narrative today looks at three events in the Book of Matthew. We begin with the saddest of the stories. The young man in chapter 19 shows pride instead of humility. He says he has kept God's Law entirely. Now he wants to "seal the deal" by doing a good work that will ensure that he goes to heaven. He trusts in himself and what he can do. He does not see his own sin; he does not see a need for the Savior. He proudly tells others why he is worthy—but it is exactly this self-righteous attitude that makes him unworthy. His love and reliance on himself has turned him away from relying on the love of God. That is why his story is so sad.

In the second narrative, we see a woman who is so humble that she asks only for the leftovers and little crumbs of blessings that no one else seems to need. Jesus testifies to all about her great faith and then offers her abundant blessings. God loves us not because we are lovable, but because He is love. (If someone asks why Jesus almost seems rude to her, point out that Jesus knew what was in her heart and in the hearts of His followers; Jesus was using her faithfulness to teach others that God's love is there for all people. He does not "look down" on people; instead, He "lifts them up.")

In the third narrative, we see a centurion who in the eyes of the world has wealth and power. But his faith in Jesus had turned his life upside down. Instead of making commands and demands, the centurion is humble and says he is unworthy before the Lord. He shows compassion for his servant (whom others would see just as a piece of property) and depends totally on the grace and power of Jesus. Many factors make this event astonishing. First of all, the power of Jesus to heal a dying man from a distance astonishes us! Also astonishing is the humility the centurion showed—this humility was a gift from God. Finally, the faith of the centurion in the one true God is astonishing. We know the centurion had come to faith in the true God because Jesus tells us so and marvels at it! Through this Gospel message, the evangelist accents Jesus' saving power at work for all people. The miracle illustrates Jesus' divine power. It shows His concern for people from every nationality and social class.

The wall between the centurion and his slave also appears to be crumbling. While slavery was an accepted institution in the Roman world, the spread of Christianity eventually led to its decline. Christians who owned slaves began to reevaluate this practice in light of their faith and saw how wrong it was to consider any human being as a "possession." The centurion in this account cared for his slave as he might have cared for a family member. Of course, we might hope he would later release the slave, but that would be mere speculation. However, that is exactly what Paul asked Philemon to do in the case of Onesimus, an escaped slave.

Review

Discuss the concept of "ignoring God by *keeping* the Law." These were people who trusted in their own good works to make them righteous and deserving of heaven. They did not recognize the need of the Savior God had promised. They were holy in their own eyes, loving and trusting in their own "goodness" rather than in the mercy and grace of God.

What Do We Deserve?

The hymn "Jesus Sinners Doth Receive" says "we deserve but grief and shame" (*LSB* 609:2). However, Jesus intervenes:

God Gives Mercy: He does not give us the punishment we do deserve.
We deserve punishment, but God says NO.

God Gives Grace: He does give us the love that we do not deserve
We don't deserve love, but God says YES.

Humility's Best Example

Do nothing from rivalry or conceit, but in humility count others more significant than yourselves. Let each of you look not only to his own interests, but also to the interests of others. Have this mind among yourselves, which is yours in Christ Jesus, who, though He was in the form of God, did not count equality with God a thing to be grasped, but made Himself nothing, taking the form of a servant, being born in the likeness of men. And being found in human form, He humbled Himself by becoming obedient to the point of death, even death on a cross.

Therefore God has highly exalted Him and bestowed on Him the name that is above every name, so that at the name of Jesus every knee should bow, in heaven and on earth and under the earth, and every tongue confess that Jesus Christ is Lord, to the glory of God the Father. (Philippians 2:3–11)

Remember

"Put on then, as God's chosen ones, holy and beloved, compassionate hearts, kindness, humility, meekness, and patience." (Colossians 3:12)
"Far be it from me to boast except in the cross of our Lord Jesus Christ." (Galatians 6:14)

121

INTO the Word

What Do We Deserve?

Emphasize: In true humility and repentance, we recognize that we are children of God not by who we are or by what we do; we are children of God because of who Jesus is and by what He has done for us as our Savior.

The grace and mercy of God toward us leads us to respond with grace and mercy toward others. The word *mercy* can also mean kindness shown to people in need. Check the lcms.org website to find current video clips on what our church organization is doing to show mercy around the world. Follow this logical path on the website: *what we do/help people/mercy medical teams.* These people are giving their time as a gift of mercy; they are giving their skills as a gift of mercy; they are giving their compassion as a gift of mercy. They are able to do this as they are led by Jesus and His perfect example of compassion.

INTO our lives

Humility's Best Example

The story of Jesus washing the feet of the disciples in John 13 would have been appropriate for this section. However, the Philippians 2 reference shows Jesus' humility to an even greater extent—He became nothing as He became one of us. Philippians 2 relates to Luke 2 for when Jesus was born at Christmas, He was demonstrating His great humility.

Give students a moment to highlight three phrases that they especially appreciate in the Philippians 2 section. Discuss what are their favorites and why. Perhaps list the phrases on the board and keep a tally of those phrases that were selected.

You might also point out the organization of these verses. The beginning portion is a message to each of us about our response of discipleship (following Christ's example, enabled by the Holy Spirit). The middle portion speaks of Christ's humiliation. The last part speaks of His exaltation.

Read about who is truly worthy in Revelation 5:12–13. Then sing "The Lamb" (*LSB* 547; recorded on *Hymns of the Season, grade 5, Lent*) and/or "Jesus, Name Above All Names" (*AGPS* 145; recorded on *JPS*).

Remember

Point out that the verse from Colossians is like a guideline for discipleship. Also point out the role of humility in these various terms. In order to show compassion, kindness, meekness, and patience, you must also have humility, not seeing yourself as better than others, but rather putting the welfare of others above your own.

In connection with the Galatians verse, read aloud 2 Corinthians 10:17–18. This emphasizes that rather than bragging about or elevating ourselves, leave it to the Lord to commend us and bless us.

Listen to Web Resource 57 and then ask students to sing along.

247

Lesson Support

Searching Further

Have interested students research Roman centurions and report back to class. These professional soldiers figure prominently in many New Testament accounts. The report might involve a poster display or a PowerPoint presentation. Or perhaps students will want to create costumes to display for a visual reference as they report orally to the class, perhaps even while "in uniform."

Ideas for the Gifted

Ask gifted students to create a graphic device—perhaps a chart—to illustrate the similarities and differences in Jesus' miracles of healing. Limit their search to Luke's Gospel, explaining that as a physician, Luke took special interest in our Lord's healing ministry.

Students might find each miracle using an online Bible, block the text, copy it into a word processing program, and print it out. After finding all the examples Luke records, students might tape each to its own note card for easier sorting and categorizing.

What headers will the students use on their chart? What symbols would make the chart easier to read? What do all the miracles have in common? What do the miracles teach us about our Savior?

Celebrating GROWTH

Use the game from Reproducible 57, "'I Never Knew That!' Bingo" as a way to help your students learn more about one another, your similarities and your differences.

After two or three people have called "Bingo!" gather the group and debrief, using questions like these:
- What did you learn about your classmates that surprised you?
- Was it easy or hard to begin talking with each other about topics like these? Why?
- Did it get easier as you went along? Explain why that might have been.
- In what ways are the members of this class alike? In what ways do we differ?
- Could any of the characteristics on the game sheet create walls between people? How?
- In this class, how can we keep our differences from creating walls between us?
- Outside of class, how can you avoid letting differences create walls that prevent you from showing Jesus' love and speaking about that love to other people?

Curriculum Connection

"I say to one, 'Go,' and he goes, and to another, 'Come,' and he comes," said the centurion to Jesus (Matthew 8:9). For fun, give your students the opportunity to practice "coming and going" at your word using section 6.3.2.3, Cooperation and Collaboration in Leading/Following, Mirroring, Imitating, Echoing, and Sequence Building. You'll find it in the sixth grade Performing Arts volume of the Concordia Curriculum Guide in the dance section.

HANDS TO SERVE

Middle school students often have a great deal of compassion for people who are sick, poor, troubled, or hurting in any way. Capitalize on this by asking the class or a group of volunteers to research various national and international human care agencies (such as LCMS World Relief and Human Care). In what ministries are these agencies currently involved? Are there ways for middle schoolers to get involved? If so, how? What might your class do? What might you encourage your whole school to do?

Check it Out

Compare Matthew 8:5–13 with Luke 7:1–10. In one, the centurion comes to Jesus himself; in the other, the centurion sends a delegation of leaders. Is this a contradiction? Point out similar uses of language today. For example, the president might send an aide to Congress saying, "The president will veto the bill unless you make changes." The Speaker of the House might later say, "The president told me to make the changes." Is the Speaker lying? No, the president's aide had communicated the president's wishes. Similarly, Matthew knows the centurion sent the synagogue leaders in his place to speak for him. He understands that the synagogue leaders deliver, not their own request, but the request of the centurion.

UNIT 6—THE MINISTRY OF JESUS

LESSON 58

Friends Bring a Man to Jesus
MATTHEW 9

Background

The synoptic evangelists, Matthew, Mark, and Luke, all record this miracle of our Lord. It occurred early in Jesus' ministry and set off a firestorm of controversy. "Who *is* He?" everyone, especially the religious leaders, wanted to know.

The man whom the Lord healed suffered from debilitating paralysis. It took four friends and drastic measures to get him into the Lord's presence. Removing tiles from the roof of the home where Jesus was teaching, the friends lowered the patient on a stretcher. The ruckus interrupted everything and riveted attention on what Jesus would do next. Those in the crowd had already seen or at least heard about several miracles on His part. However, here was a case that might prove more difficult.

Almost everyone at that time would have believed you could draw a straight line from a specific personal sin to a specific personal problem. This man must be guilty of some horrendous offense! (See John 9:1–2.) Immediately, though, Jesus corrected this thought, at once absolving the man, and offending the scribes and Pharisees. "Blasphemy! Only God can forgive sins," the religious leaders thought to themselves. But Jesus—true God—knew their thoughts and challenged their objections. Claiming a title the Old Testament ascribes to the coming Messiah ("Son of Man"; see Daniel 7:13), Jesus asserted His divine authority and underscored it by performing a miracle that left every mouth open in awe.

"We have seen extraordinary things today," the onlookers said (Luke 5:26). And indeed, they had! They had seen . . .

- God's Messiah teach God's Word and then claim God's authority.
- Jesus of Nazareth release one of their peers from all guilt and heal him from terrible paralysis.
- A clue about the victory over sin, sickness, death, and Satan the Savior would shortly win.

They had seen extraordinary things. And so have we.

Central Truth

Jesus came to heal hearts and heal health (healing spiritually and physically).

Objectives

- Confess that there is sin in us and around us causing consequences that affect all people and our environment.
- Recognize that Jesus provides for our greatest needs, which are spiritual, but also blesses us physically.
- Dedicate all that we are—body and soul—to the glory of God.

Materials

- Chain with a lock and key
- Web Resource 58a
- Reproducible 58
- Hymnals and music CDs

Bible Prep

Post in advance so students can bookmark the references before class time.

- Matthew 9
- Matthew 28:20
- Romans 8:28
- Revelation 21:3–4
- Psalm 130
- Romans 3:23
- Romans 8:18–23

Devotions

Before class, wrap a sturdy chain around your classroom globe and padlock it. Tape the key to the back of a cross in your classroom. As the devotion begins, show students the globe and chain. Ask what this might symbolize. If necessary, have a volunteer read 1 John 5:19 as one clue. Lead students to conclude that the chain represents the world's slavery to sin and Satan.

Sin opened the door to many other evils as well. What were some of these? Brainstorm together, listing sin's consequences on the whiteboard as students mention them (such as accidents, tornados, pests like mosquitoes, sickness, birth defects).

God didn't want to abandon us, enslaved and suffering. He covenanted to provide the key that would release earth from bondage, but at great cost. Hold the cross where students can see it. Then, reveal the key, unlock the padlock, and unwrap the chain.

The cross was the key to our release. The guilt of our sins is gone. The power of death to harm us is gone. Our new lives of freedom and joy have begun! While there are more troubles to face, there are also more blessings to come. One day, because of what Jesus did on the cross, all the consequences of sin that plague our universe will be gone. We will enjoy at last what our Lord had in mind for us from the beginning!

Together look at the first five stanzas of "Dear Christians, One and All Rejoice" (*LSB* 556). Ask students to find what they feel is the key phrase in each stanza that summarizes its message. (Note that there may be more than one possibility.) Call attention to the word picture with which the second stanza begins ("Fast bound in Satan's chains I lay." Note that this uses the meaning "fasten tightly" for the word *fast,* rather than the common meaning of "quick.") You may want to play the melody of this hymn as you discuss it. Use the accompaniment version of "On Christ's Ascension I Now Build" as is recorded on *Hymns of the Season, grade 6, Pentecost*.)

INTO the lesson

Authority?

After reading the text from Matthew 9 aloud, emphasize that **Jesus has the authority to heal both physically and spiritually.** Have students list in the boxes some of the blessings Jesus gives to make our bodies physically healthy and our souls spiritually healthy. Then ask, **From where does Jesus get the power and the authority to do this?** Listen to John 12:49, as Jesus said, "I have not spoken on My own authority, but the Father who sent Me has Himself given Me a commandment—what to say and what to speak." Then ask, **Why does Jesus have this power and authority that no ordinary human being has?** (Because He is true God.) **Listen to the words of Jesus in Matthew 28:18, "Jesus came and said to them, 'All authority in heaven and on earth has been given to Me.'"** How did Jesus show His power and authority in the Bible narrative? (He forgave the man's sins and Jesus healed the man's body.)

INTO the Word

Why Heal?

Continue by reading the selected verses from Matthew 9 to see some of the many things that Jesus has authority over. **Of all these examples in Matthew 9, the most important is that Jesus has authority to forgive our sins because He is true God, who came to take our punishment for sin on the cross and arose at Easter, proclaiming His authority over death and the devil!**

A "by-product" of the events in Matthew 9 is that Jesus' fame spread throughout the area and large crowds came to see and hear Him. But this was not Jesus' reason for performing miracles. He did it to give glory to God and because He felt compassion for people in need and wanted to help them. We will see later that these are also our reasons for helping others (not to show off or get a reward or praise, but rather to glorify God and to share His kindness and blessings).

Review

Point out that the Covenant Connections in our study of the Old Testament always looked to the future and the coming of the Messiah. Now, in the New Testament, as the Messiah/Savior/Jesus has arrived, the Covenant Connections focus on how Jesus has fulfilled the promises and prophecies of God.

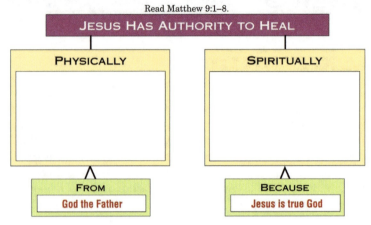

Who's to Blame?

When someone is suffering a tragedy, who should be blamed?

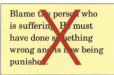 Blame the person who is suffering. He must have done something wrong and is now being punished.

or

 Blame someone else, anything else, but certainly don't blame the victim.

or

 Blame it on God. Why did He let it happen?

Perhaps a better question to ask is "Who will help?"

Matthew 28:20 — God will be with us even in the middle of our problems.

and

Romans 8:28 — God works to bring good into our lives.

and

Revelation 21:3–4 — God will take us to heaven where there will be no more troubles.

Respond—Befriend

The focus of every Bible lesson is on Jesus as our Savior. But we can also learn something from the four friends in the story. They showed mercy (kindness to someone in need). Here are three ways they showed mercy. Write how you could do these things to show mercy to someone today.

   Being persistent.

Give two reasons for showing mercy. _To glorify God and to show compassion to someone in need_.

Why are you able to show mercy to others? _The Holy Spirit is working in us, guiding us to live as people of God_.

Remember

"Behold, the dwelling place of God is with man. He will dwell with them, and they will be His people, and God Himself will be with them as their God. He will wipe away every tear from their eyes, and death shall be no more, neither shall there be mourning nor crying nor pain anymore, for the former things have passed away." (Revelation 21:3–4)

123

Who's to Blame?

Guide students through the three perspectives given in the Student Book concerning who is to blame for the troubles a person has. The first statement has been a common explanation for ages and ages. **In John 9:1–2, the disciples saw a blind man and asked Jesus who was to blame—who had sinned, he or his parents, causing the punishment of blindness.** Ask class members if any of them have ever encountered someone who had this idea about sickness and trouble, a kind of "God's gonna get you for that" philosophy. Let volunteers respond. **It's a very common, but incorrect belief that there is immediate punishment when we do wrong. However, God punished Jesus for our sins. That doesn't mean we won't have troubles. Problems surround us because we live in a sin-damaged, sin-tarnished world. We suffer the consequences of our environments. Sometimes, we will suffer the natural consequences of doing wrong (like getting a broken bone when being reckless on a skateboard). But that is not God striking us down in vengeance—Jesus suffered that for us on the cross. Read John 9:3–4 to see Jesus' response to the disciples' question.** (He said that this would be used to glorify God, and then Jesus healed the man.) Have students make a large X on the first box.

The middle statement certainly describes our society today. Everybody likes to see themselves as the victim, placing the blame on someone else. Even when someone does something wrong, excuses pop up to place the blame elsewhere. For example, consider this scenario: *As they reached the school, Jake purposely crashed his bike into Martin, who was riding a shiny new bicycle. While Jake sat waiting in the principal's office, he was angry, "I blame my parents; if they had gotten me the new bike I wanted, I wouldn't have felt so jealous about Martin. And I blame Martin too. I just couldn't stand that smile on his face any longer, so a few dents on his bike took care of that. I'm not at fault here. If our teacher did her job, we would all get along better. Actually, I'm the victim here. I feel sorry for me—if I was rich I wouldn't even care about Martin's new bike. It's just not fair."* Ask, **Do you think Jake has forgiveness for what he did?** (Point out that he doesn't see it as a sin, he isn't sorry, he doesn't recognize that he needs forgiveness. There is not contrition or repentance.) Cross off the second box with an X.

The third one is another common response—blaming God. God has promised complete relief from pain and problems in heaven, but He never promised that on earth. Becoming a Christian is not like a "good luck charm" that will keep all troubles away. We can trust that God will do what is best for us and at the right time—and His judgment on that can be different than what we had in mind. (Cross off the third box.) **So instead of looking for someone to blame, let's look for someone who will help when we have troubles—and that will be our Lord and Savior. Read the Bible references in the next line of boxes and write down some of the ways God helps us even as we are right in the middle of a problem.**

Look at Web Resource 58a for another way of looking at the many ways God can help us when we are in trouble. Then read together about God's great care for us in Psalm 130.

Respond—Befriend

Discuss together this section in the Student Book. Then move to a discussion of the vignettes in the "Digging Deeper" section on the Lesson Support Page, Ask students to comment on the troubles or possible reactions to these troubles based on what they have learned in this lesson. Use Reproducible 50 in connection with these concepts.

Curriculum Connection

The four friends in the Bible narrative had to cooperate to bring the paralyzed man to Jesus. For a fun connection to this story, use section 6.3.2.1, Role of Each Individual in a Cooperative Physical Activity. It has ideas and an activity students will enjoy. You'll find it in the sixth grade Physical Education volume of the Concordia Curriculum Guide.

Teacher Tips

It's possible, and even probable, that your class includes one or more students who struggle with a chronic disease or some other, ongoing and life-altering problem. Some of these children may be wondering about God's promises or His care for them. They may want help in connecting their faith with what's happening to them. Be sure to keep the door open to a conversation like that. Maintain an invitational attitude, but don't push. You might say something like this in private: "Josh, I think you might be going through some hard times right now. If you ever need someone to listen and to pray with you, I want to be here for you. But no pressure." In any case, be sure to pray for specific spiritual challenges in the lives of your students.

Critical thinking

Tell students that some churches teach that any Christian who has enough faith and prays hard enough can overcome any disease or sickness here on earth. If you're not healed, it's a sign you don't have enough faith or that you don't really want to be healed. Ask how students would counter this teaching in light of Romans 8:18–23.

As the class discusses this, point out how destructive this "blame the victim" approach can be. Someone who is not healed right away might even begin to doubt the Savior's love! Help the class understand the pervasive corruption sin has worked on earth. Human beings have only a limited capacity for understanding sin's destructive power. When we finally see the new heaven and new earth, we will likely be awestruck, finally realizing how terribly sin damaged God's first creation. In our present world, believers and unbelievers alike fall prey to sin's ravages in our bodies, as Romans 8 clearly indicates.

Christians, though, have a blessing and a hope others do not enjoy. We know Jesus' comfort and strength in our troubles, through our troubles, and after our troubles end. When we're ill or face dangers or problems of any kind, we can always ask Jesus for help. He always will help us! Sometimes, He will bring an end to the trouble or heal the illness right away. In some cases, we will find release only in heaven. But we can always trust the promise of Romans 8:28 that God is working right now in everything that happens, using it to bring about our ultimate good.

DIGGING DEEPER

1. Miriam's family lost their house in a hurricane last summer. Jana's house was right next door, but it withstood the storm. Does Miriam's family sin more often or sin worse sins than Jana's? No, for all have sinned and fallen short of the perfection God rightly demands of us. See Romans 3:23. The damage to Miriam's home occurred because we live in a fallen, broken world. This kind of pain and suffering is not what God intended for His good creation. Instead it is an opportunity for Jana's family to show compassion to their neighbors.)

2. Richard was riding his bike to the store to get some diapers for his baby brother. He was in a hurry. At one intersection, a truck slowed down, but didn't see Richard and hit him. Now he has a broken arm and won't be able to finish out the basketball season. (Who is at fault? Rather than try to fix blame, we should remember that troubles are a natural consequences of living in a world damaged by sin.)

3. When she was twelve, Malika developed leukemia. She spends a lot of time at the hospital getting treatments for it. Sadly, we live in a fallen world where even kids sometimes get cancer. In this situation, Malika and those who care about her might focus on fixing blame and become more and more bitter as they do so. They might even blame God and grow angry at Him. However, human beings are the ones who brought sin into the world and who continue to multiply disobedience on earth. The evil we've unleashed, sometimes manifests itself in the form of terrible diseases. No one is to blame and yet, all of us, as sinners, are to blame.)

4. Autumn's mom and dad got divorced. Autumn lives with her mom. About a year later, Mrs. Seasons lost her job and couldn't pay the rent. This weekend, Autumn and her mom have to move out of their apartment. They have no place to go. (Again, the attempt to fix blame in this situation is counterproductive and will likely lead to bitterness and anger. Many sins on the part of many people have no doubt led to this distressing situation. Focus instead on trust in God's help and reliance on the kindness of God's people.)

Discuss how God could bless and bring good out of each situation. Close by reading Romans 8:18–23 discussing the hope that these words offer.

UNIT 6—THE MINISTRY OF JESUS

LESSON 59

Ten Men with Leprosy

LUKE 17:11–19

Background

In this lesson, you will examine yet a third healing miracle chronicled by Luke the evangelist. As with the healing of the centurion's servant (Lesson 57) and the healing of the paralyzed man (Lesson 58), the healing of the ten men with leprosy illustrates Jesus' divine power to heal. But as with the other two healing miracles in this unit, this account makes its own unique point and carries its own unique accents. First, we see from Luke 17:11 that Jesus was "on the way to Jerusalem." We know what awaits Him there—rejection, betrayal, suffering, death, and resurrection. He intends, not simply to heal the many individuals who come across His path asking for mercy, but to bring about the kingdom of God in all its fullness through the sacrifice of Himself. He intends to draw countless penitent believers to God, making it possible for us to "live before God in righteousness and purity [and in perfect health], forever"! Second, we notice that the ten ask Jesus for "mercy" (verse 12). Word of Christ's miracles has spread far and wide, so far, in fact, that the news has reached even these socially untouchable lepers! They shout out to Jesus, begging Him to do for them what they cannot do for themselves—and trusting Him to do it! (Point out that *mercy* can mean "not getting the punishment we deserve," but in this case the definition of *mercy* is "showing kindness to those in need.") Third, Luke emphasizes not so much the miracle itself, but the response Jesus' compassionate act evokes from one sufferer. One of the ten—a Samaritan—comes back, exclaiming praises to the God of Israel. A "foreigner" has found a home among God's people, in the arms of the Savior whose mercy is for all.

Central Truth

No one is worthy to come to the Lord, but He graciously makes us worthy through Jesus.

Objectives
- Acknowledge that Jesus came for all people who are sinners—and that includes everyone.
- Celebrate that Jesus takes away our sins and gives us His righteousness, claiming us to be children of God.
- Trust in the gracious ways and will of God who works always for our good.

Materials
- Web Resource 59a
- Reproducibles 59a and 59b
- Hymnals and music CDs

Bible Prep

Post in advance so students can bookmark the references before class time.
- Leviticus 13:45
- Luke 17:11–19
- Philippians 4:8

Devotions

Have you ever felt you didn't belong? Maybe your family moved and you had to switch schools, leaving all your friends behind and walking as a stranger into the new school on your first day. Maybe everyone in your circle of friends went out for a sport, but for some reason you couldn't or didn't want to. (Ask volunteers to talk about how that feels.)

Outsiders. Outcasts. The Holy Spirit led the evangelist Luke to include many examples of Jesus' love for people like that—outcasts, outsiders, strangers.

Luke wrote about the shepherds who came to worship baby Jesus. (People thought of shepherds as smelly and treacherous—outsiders.) A day or two ago, we talked about Jesus healing the slave who belonged to the Roman centurion; both the centurion and the slave were outsiders. Luke includes many other examples of God's mercy on outsiders too. Many thought of them as "throwaway people," disposable people who were not needed; but Jesus loved and accepted them.

Still today, Jesus cares about every person, especially the "throwaways." Prisoners. The homeless. The elderly in nursing homes who can no longer walk, talk, or feed themselves, or those who never had those abilities in the first place. Jesus hung and bled and died on the cross for them, even though He knew many of them would reject His love.

Our love isn't like Jesus' love. We look down on certain people. We sometimes reject others. Maybe Jesus loves them, but we don't! In part, we act that way because we think (deep down) that we ourselves somehow deserve Jesus' love. We are smart and nicely dressed. We go to church and memorize Bible passages. We are good (at least, part of the time)! This is the sin of self-righteousness. It's deadly! (Pause.) Or maybe we only care what our friends think, especially if they think—we're cool. That is a sin of pride. It's deadly! (Pause.)

The Good News is that Jesus died for these sins too! We can confess them and trust Jesus to keep on including us inside the circle of His love. And we can ask Him to help us welcome others, even outsiders.

Sing "Father Welcomes" (*LSB* 605; recorded on *Hymns of the Month*, grade 3, April). Speak together Psalm 130.

INTO the lesson

Out! Far Out!

The opening paragraphs here reiterate a few of the main themes of today's devotion and make a transition into basic background information necessary for a thorough understanding of today's Bible narrative. Read them to the class or have a volunteer do so.

Discussion 1: If your students enjoy working with partners, have them pair up and talk about this question. After a minute or two, ask volunteers to summarize their conclusions for the whole class. Answers will vary, but will likely focus on the hardships such a lifestyle must have posed.

Discussion 2: Use Web Resource 59a to guide the discussion. Encourage students to suggest any additional ideas they have. Draw attention to the titles on the Venn diagram, emphasizing that Jesus has the power to help us physically (such as with "skin disease"), and He has the power to help us spiritually (such as with "sin disease").

INTO the Word

Very Far Out—But Clearly In

To introduce the Bible story, read aloud the paragraphs in this section. If the class paired up earlier in the lesson, have them work with their partner to read Luke 17:11–19 and answer the question. (If needed, point out that being a Samaritan made the one man a double outcast because Jewish people did not like or trust Samaritans, considering them to be among the lowest of the lowly; his ethnic background had a social stigma. As necessary, explain that Jews and Samaritans hated each other. The Samaritans of Jesus' day were descended from the foreigners who settled in the region after the Babylonians deported most of the Jews into exile. The Jews left behind were among the poorest and least educated. They intermarried with the foreigners.

When the exiled Jews and their descendents returned to their homeland, they refused to consider these "Samaritans" (inhabitants of Samaria) true Jews. Samaritans were not permitted to offer sacrifices at the temple in Jerusalem, so they set up an alternative worship site on Mt. Gerazim. They accepted only the five Books of Moses as divinely inspired Scripture, and they had a somewhat corrupted version of even those. In the eyes of most Jews, Samaritans were outcasts, outsiders.

LESSON 59
Ten Men with Leprosy

Out! Far Out!

In his Gospel, Luke the evangelist includes many events to show Jesus' love for the outcasts of His day, such as tax collectors, Roman soldiers, slaves, and other sinners. It's hard to imagine a group of people who lived further outside society, though, than people with leprosy.

This disease was almost certainly not the disease we call leprosy today. The term *leprosy* was used at that time for any highly infectious and contagious skin disease. We do know that it brought terrible consequences into people's lives. It often devastated their families too, as victims were separated out and sent away (quarantined) to protect family and friends from catching the disease. People infected with this skin disease:

- Could not be around healthy people, even for worship.
- Had to leave their home, village, and family.
- Usually lived in caves and other wilderness areas outside the towns.
- Formed groups that stayed together for protection and companionship.
- Had to warn others to stay away, shouting out "Unclean! Unclean!"

What effect do you suppose this kind of lifestyle had on people? Put yourself in their sandals. What effect would being such an outcast, living away from family, friends, and the comforts of home have on you? **Answers will vary.**

The Old Testament Law of Moses called for many of the rules listed above. (Also see Leviticus 13:45.) These rules applied to no other sickness. Only leprosy made someone an outcast. Many Bible experts believe that God used leprosy to symbolize sin. On a separate piece of paper, create a Venn diagram to show ways sin and leprosy are alike and different.

Review

Covenant Connection

When someone was healed of leprosy in Bible times, they were pronounced "clean" and were welcomed back into the community. Jesus not only has power over the disease of leprosy, He also has power over the "leprosy of sin." Sin cast us out from God, making us outcasts to Him; but Jesus forgives and removes our sin through His death and resurrection. Because our sin has been taken away, we are declared "clean" and holy (Philippians 2:15). We are welcomed into the family of God! (1 John 3:1).

But **Jesus looks at all people with eyes of love and forgiveness, calling all people to Himself.** Read aloud Acts 2:39—a very significant verse! How did Jesus show that the Samaritan leper was clearly "in," clearly loved by God? (Jesus healed him. When the Samaritan saw what had happened, he came back to thank Jesus, who commended the man's faith.)

Very Far Out—But Clearly In

As Jesus' reputation for compassion and healing power spread, more and more people came to Him for help. Even outcasts with leprosy came!

In Luke 5, we see Jesus touching (shocking!) and healing one such person. Later, Luke tells about a whole group of people with leprosy who came to Jesus. Read about it from Luke 17:11–19. As you read, look for one person who fits the description: "very far out, but clearly in." Who is he?

In what way was he "very far out"? In what way was he "clearly in"? **The Samaritan was a double outcast because of leprosy and also because of prejudices against Samaritans; he was clearly in the family of God because of the faith Jesus recognized in him.**

In—Completely and Forever

As kids grow from their preteen years to becoming teenagers, one concern they usually have is about "fitting in" with everyone else. As you look around, you might think that most kids your age seem to feel comfortable with "who they are" and at peace "in their own skin." You may wonder if you are "in" or "out" when you look at the popularity others have or how they look. You may wonder:

The more we think about these things, the more nervous and insecure we get. We convince ourselves that we're outsiders. In your community or school, what makes someone an outsider? What does it take to be an insider? Answer briefly in the spaces below. Then follow your teacher's directions as you finish the diagram.

OUT   IN

Think about this: Jesus calls all people in to Himself. In discipleship, what can you do to bring someone who is outside in? Then read Philippians 4:8 for clues, and pray for God's help and blessing.

Remember

"I am the LORD your God, the Holy One of Israel, your Savior. . . . You are precious in My eyes, and honored, and I love you." (Isaiah 43:3–4)

INTO our lives

In—Completely and Forever

The better your rapport with your students and their respect for one another, the more helpful this section will likely be as your students grow in their personal discipleship.

You may find your students reluctant to express their true feelings about this subject. They may feel more comfortable with projecting their ideas in a generalized way on an anonymous, fictional person. If you can share some personal example from your own preteen years, it, too, will likely make an impact.

As students answer the question about what makes people outsiders and insiders in your community or school, jot their suggestions inside two circles on your classroom whiteboard, one labeled **Out** and one labeled **In**. These should mirror the circles in the Student Book. Ask students to copy the responses in the correct circles in their books too.

When you've noted a dozen or so suggestions, draw the outline of a cross to connect both circles, illustrating the idea that in the cross of our Savior, God offers everyone His forgiveness and love. **Whether we see ourselves as insiders or outsiders, we belong to God and to one another because of what Jesus did. Some people will reject that love and will walk away. Some will never be thankful for it. But for those of us who believe, it's the very best news we will ever hear. All who believe receive eternal life.**

Ask that students draw a similar cross across the two circles in their own books.

Remember

Today's memory verse reinforces the truth of God's intense love for us. Imagine that the holy God would consider us sinners "precious"! He cares about us individually and personally. It's amazing!

Lesson Support

Hands to Serve

Sometimes, preteens, in order to prove they are growing up, reject giving attention to younger children, making them feel as outcasts. Encourage your students to be a good friend to younger children. Young children often respond very positively to the attention of a child who is a few years older, so your students have a responsibility to be a good example and a good encourager with younger kids. Reproducible 59b provides a visual way that your students could share today's Bible narrative with a younger sibling, young neighbor, or a younger classroom group. The picture can be, but doesn't have to be colored in. Tell students to fold the page in half like a card. Then fold the outer quarter sections back. Begin telling the story by holding up the picture of Jesus. Then open the illustration up by folding the outer flaps back, revealing just the healed men rushing back to Jerusalem to show themselves to the priests. Then push the two outer flaps together so that they meet in the middle to show the Samaritan kneeling in thanks before Jesus. (Having an evangelism tool like this in their hands equips your students so they feel motivated to share the Bible narrative with others.)

Bringing it home

Have students ask a parent or grandparent about experiences with fitting in, with being an insider or an outsider. Reproducible 59a introduces the conversation, offers several questions to guide it, and provides space on which students can record answers.

As you distribute it, point out the "tear off" section at the bottom. The person each student interviews should place his or her initials on that line, verifying that the interview took place. Only this section needs to be returned; it is of more value for the student to keep the interview personal and just between the two involved. Then how can you be certain the interview took place? Emphasize the trust factor that you are investing in your students.

Celebrating GROWTH

Ask that in the next week, students look for an opportunity to befriend someone who might be feeling like an outsider. Caution them not to do this as an experiment. Our Savior never used other people for His own purposes and He wouldn't want us to do that, either!

Instead, they should consider it an occasion to show Jesus' love in a thoughtful, sincere way. They might offer to play checkers with a lonely neighbor or great-grandparent. They might help younger siblings do chores or read to them. (See "Hands to Serve.") They might ask other members on their soccer team to stop calling names or putting down a less skillful player. (Caution them to choose something they know is safe. If they are not sure, they should get a parent's permission first.)

Afterward, ask that they write about the experience. Was it easy or hard? Scary or boring? Why? How does including outsiders benefit the other person? How does it benefit us? Are there outsiders in our class? If so, who decided to make them that? How can we change it?

Searching Further

Have students read about Father Damien, a Roman Catholic priest who served among people with Hansen's Disease (what today is considered leprosy) on the island of Molokai in Hawaii for sixteen years until he himself succumbed to the disease. He is considered the patron saint of Hawaii. The story of his life and his selfless service is quite moving. Several children's books tell his life story, as do many articles online. Ask students to think about how God might want to use their lives to befriend outsiders by making them insiders.

Curriculum Connection

The ratio of people who returned to thank God in this story is 1 to 9—a disappointing number! Help your students learn more about ratios using section 6.1.7, Ratios, found in the sixth grade Math volume of the Concordia Curriculum Guide. Also discuss with them: How can we improve the ratio of thankfulness to unthankfulness in our own lives?

In Romans 1:18–23, the apostle Paul describes God's anger at human sin. One of the first of the terrible sins he mentions is unthankfulness (verse 21). We don't usually consider this such a terrible sin. Why does God think of it as so serious? What does it reveal about our hearts? Trusting in the forgiveness Jesus won for us on His cross, how can we become more thankful? What could we ask God to do for us? What reminders might we create? How else might the Holy Spirit want to help us grow into His amazingly thankful people?

UNIT 6—THE MINISTRY OF JESUS

LESSON 60

The Parable of the Sower
MATTHEW 13:1–23

Background

Called *Rabbi (Teacher)* by His disciples and friends (John 1:38; Mark 9:5; John 20:16), Jesus is the ultimate Master Teacher. A *master teacher* is a term used to identify exceptional instructors. These are some of the qualities and skills a master teacher exhibits:
- knows the students, who they are and how they learn
- connects subject matter to real life
- encourages a love of learning in students
- teaches how to build positive relationships with others
- creates environments conducive to learning
- inspires and motivates students to change, grow, and achieve

Jesus perfectly exemplifies every master teacher quality. He has a personal relationship with every believer. His teaching style, especially when telling a parable, uses real-life situations that are understood by those with open hearts. Jesus teaches the ultimate guide for building relationships with others: "Love one another: just as I have loved you" (John 13:34). Jesus is passionate about His message—so passionate that He gave His life to show it! As He continually communicates with us through His timeless Word, the Holy Spirit inspires us to serve Him and others.

As you teach this lesson, point out Jesus' masterful teaching to your students. Continue to use the teaching skills with which God has blessed you. Pray that the Holy Spirit will continue to work through them and through the Word so your students may grow in faith.

Central Truth

God comes to us through His Word, offering the message of salvation in Christ Jesus.

Objectives

- Confess that we do not always listen to the Word of God and live according to it.
- Rely, in repentance, on the transforming power of the Holy Spirit to guide us to live and grow as God's people.
- Proclaim the Word of God and its message in all aspects in our lives.

Materials

- Web Resource 60a
- Reproducible 60
- Hymnals and music CDs

Bible Prep

Post in advance so students can bookmark the references before class time.
- Matthew 13
- Psalm 78:1–7
- 2 Timothy 3:14–16
- Galatians 5:22–23

Devotions

"Hey, Jake! Roll that wheelbarrow over to me!"

"Okay, Dad." Jake rolled the wheelbarrow to the garden's edge. "Ew! What is this smelly stuff?"

"That's compost. The food scraps your mom saves and the decayed plants from last year's vegetable garden make good fertilizer for the soil. Now, hand me that pitchfork so I can work the compost into the dirt."

Jake handed the pitchfork to his dad. He tipped the wheelbarrow so the compost spilled out on the freshly-tilled soil. "The soil already looks dark and rich enough to me," Jake said. "Why don't we just plant the seeds now?"

Dad explained, "Compost adds lost nutrients back into the soil. With the right nutrients, the seeds will grow into stronger and more fruitful plants."

Clunk! The tine of the pitchfork hit a rock. Jake's dad bent over and chucked the rock to a small pile at the edge of the garden plot.

"Another rock, Dad?"

"Unfortunately, yes. Rocks block the seedlings' growth as they push up out of the soil."

Jake lowered the wheelbarrow and reached down to pull out a thistly weed.

"Good job, Jake. We don't want those weeds either. They take control and choke out the vegetable plants."

Ask the students, **Have any of you ever helped to plant a garden? What did you do to get the soil ready for planting?** (Let the students explain.)

What did Jake and his dad do to get their garden soil ready for planting? (They added compost to the soil to give it the necessary nutrients. They picked out the rocks and weeds so the plants could more easily sprout and grow.)

In this lesson's Bible story, Jesus tells about a farmer who planted or *sowed* some seeds. As we study the story, see if any of the things that Jake and his dad encountered in their vegetable garden were also encountered by the farmer in today's Bible story.

Sing "Listen, God Is Calling" (*LSB* 833; recorded on *Hymns of the Month*, grade 5, January).

INTO the lesson

The Master Teacher

Though students may like the idea of a teacher letting them do whatever they want, it has nothing to do with being a good teacher. This approach would leave students where they are without encouraging improvement or progress. Jesus is the Master Teacher; He would not leave us where we are—in our sins. **His concern is for our transformation, becoming the forgiven and redeemed people of God. This happens, not through our own efforts, but through the power of the Holy Spirit working in us through the Word of God. This happens through the processes of justification and sanctification, with the result that we are now a new creation in Christ Jesus!**

Have a volunteer read out loud the paragraph about Jesus as a Master Teacher. Ask, **In the Bible stories we've studied, what have you noticed concerning the way that Jesus teaches?** (Let the students respond. Comments may include how Jesus positioned Himself to teach effectively to large groups of people, how He was able to effectively teach in many different environments from the temple to a hillside to the middle of the Sea of Galilee, and how He incorporated the people's experiences and backgrounds into His examples and lessons.) Use this information as a bridge to the activity that analyzes the parable of the sower.

LESSON 60
The Parable of the Sower

The Master Teacher

A good teacher lets you do whatever you want to do. What is wrong with that statement? The best example of a teacher is Jesus, the master Teacher. He didn't necessarily tell people what they wanted to hear, but rather, what they needed to hear. Jesus' *classroom* was wherever the people were—sometimes in the temple courtyard, or on a country hillside, or in a discussion at dinner. His lessons are timeless. Let's look at a parable Jesus told about a sower (planter, farmer) planting seeds—a story that actually is a message about listening to God's Word. Jesus encourages us in lifelong learning and a lifetime of Bible study so that we can continue to grow in Him.

Digging into the Story

Symbols: Seed = the Word   Sower = the Teacher   Soil = the Learner

Matthew 13	What happened in the story?	What does that mean?
vv. 3–4	The path was too hard for the seeds to take root, so the birds ate them.	vv. 18–19 This is a person who either doesn't listen to God's Word or rejects it altogether.
vv. 5–6	The seed sprouted, but the root could not go very deep. It couldn't get the water and nourishment it needed to grow.	vv. 20–21 This person listens to God's Word at first, but because the Word does not take firm root in his heart, when troubles come, the person immediately falls away.
v. 7	Thorny plants grew quickly, crowding and choking the plant.	v. 22 This person hears God's Word, but other things around him are bigger and more important. They take over his life.
v. 8	These grew into mature plants that yielded fruit (results).	v. 23 This person hears the Word, continues to learn and and understand it. By the power of the Holy Spirit, the Word works in the person's heart and bears fruit (good works, empowered by God in us).

Review

Covenant Connection

The Gospel writer, in Matthew 13:35, says of Jesus' teaching, "This was to fulfill what was spoken by the prophet: 'I will open my mouth in parables; I will utter what has been hidden since the foundation of the world.'" Once again, we see Jesus fulfilling God's covenant promises about the Messiah. Read the Old Testament section referred to (Psalm 78:1–7). This has an interesting past, present, and future relationship as Jesus at that present time, fulfills the words of the prophet from centuries earlier, who speaks of future generations being taught God's Word. You are that next generation who hears the Word of God from your teachers, pastors, and parents!

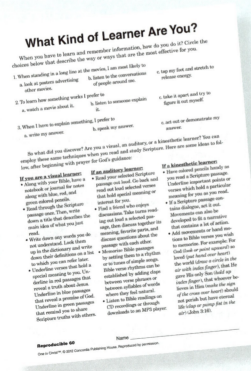

INTO the Word

Digging into the Story

Work together on this activity as a group. Introduce the parable by looking at the "classroom" setting. Note also that in a parable, one object is meant to represent something else, like a symbol. So the symbols listed are clues for understanding the story.

Take one row across at a time as you work together on the chart. Point out that Jesus' parable involved a grain like wheat or barley, but the Student Book pictures show a watermelon plant. Ask if anyone can see a connection. (Jesus chose objects that the people of that day were familiar with. If Jesus talked to people today in a city setting, He might use a more familiar object to you and me, like a garden plant, such as a watermelon.)

Use Web Resource 60a to review what students have learned from this activity. Point out that this resource is something they saw last year in the grade 5 level of One in Christ, but hopefully they are all growing in their understanding and intelligence, and will have more background information that will help them to understand this resource even better this year. Emphasize that studying the Bible is a lifelong activity—there is always something more to learn about our Savior and our salvation!

Feeding and Weeding

Plants can dry up and wither away. They need nourishment (fertilizer and water) so they can grow. The Word of God is what the Holy Spirit uses to nourish, feed, grow, and strengthen our faith. Plants must continually be fed and watered. What do we continually need? (See 2 Timothy 3:14–16.) We need the power of the Holy Spirit working in our hearts to keep us focused on God's Word and the truth it holds for salvation.

Listed below are some distracters (weeds) that can overcome and choke out the seed of faith. Opposite these are Bible verses that speak of the power of God that combats and conquers those "weeds." After reading each Bible verse, match it to the "weed" that is overcome by the Word.

THE WEEDS		THE WORD
1. Worry/doubts	__3__ a.	"Be strong in the Lord and in the strength of His might. Put on the whole armor of God, that you may be able to stand against the schemes of the devil." (Ephesians 6:10–11)
2. Earthly pursuits (hobbies, friends, sports, jobs)	__1__ b.	"Trust in the LORD with all your heart." (Proverbs 3:5)
3. Weakness/temptation	__4__ c.	[Jesus said,] "But the Helper, the Holy Spirit, whom the Father will send in My name, He will teach you all things and bring to your remembrance all that I have said to you." (John 14:26)
4. Difficulty understanding	__2__ g.	"Seek first the kingdom of God and His righteousness, and all these things will be added to you." (Matthew 6:33)

What Kind of Learner Are You?

Visual: **S**ee with **U**nderstanding.

Auditory: **L**isten **O**ften to **G**od's **W**ord.

Kinesthetic: **T**ake **A**ction by **S**erving.

Above **A**ll: **L**isten, **L**earn, and **L**ive in **F**aith.

Remember

"Faith comes from __hearing__, and hearing through the __word__ of __Christ__." (Romans 10:17)

"He said, 'Blessed . . . are those who __hear__ the word of God and __keep__ it!'" (Luke 11:28)

127

INTO our lives

Feeding and Weeding

As you work through this activity, emphasize the work of the Holy Spirit through God's Word that brings us to faith, keeps us in faith, and strengthens our faith. As Martin Luther says, we "need the Holy Spirit to begin and sustain this faith in [us because] by nature [we are] spiritually blind, dead, and [enemies] of God" (*Luther's Small Catechism with Explanation*, Christian Question 157). Luther says in the explanation to the Third Article of the Apostles' Creed, "I believe that I cannot by my own reason or strength believe in Jesus Christ, my Lord, or come to Him; but the Holy Spirit has called me by the Gospel, enlightened me with His gifts, sanctified and kept me in the true faith." For further biblical connections, see 1 Corinthians 2:14 and 1 Corinthians 12:3.

What Kind of Learner Are You?

Distribute Reproducible 60. Direct the students to read the statements at the top of the page and circle the choice that best identifies the way they learn.

When the students have done so, say, **The way that people learn is called their *learning style*. Not everyone learns information in the same way. Some people learn better when they see something in a drawing or chart or when they read it in print. That person is a *visual learner*. Others learn best when they hear something read or presented with music rather than when they see or read it. That person is an *auditory learner*. Hands-on activities that involve motion help a *kinesthetic learner*. Others learn best when they employ a combination of these techniques.**

If you marked choice "a" for all of your answers, you are mostly a visual learner. If you marked choice "b" for all of your answers, you are mostly an auditory learner. If you marked choice "c", you are mostly a kinesthetic learner. If you marked a variety of choices, you use a combination of learning styles.

Why is it important to understand how you learn? (Knowing your learning style helps you find the most effective way to study and improves your chances of remembering important information.)

The Bible is the most important book you will ever read. Using techniques that teach to your learning style can help you in your personal Bible study. Direct students to look over the column in the chart that addresses their individual learning style.

Then read through the summary statements in the Student Book. Close by referring to Acts 17:11, "They received the word with all eagerness, examining the Scripture daily to see if these things were so." Explain that this refers to the Christians in Berea. They combined learning styles—they listened to the Gospel preached by the apostle Paul, and then they read the Scriptures themselves, combining auditory and visual learning, as they searched for truth in God's Word.

259

Lesson Support

Celebrating GROWTH

Plan a trivia night with its proceeds going toward a project that shares the written Word of God. Have your students write the trivia questions to show their growth in knowledge with which the Holy Spirit has blessed them. Possible groups to support include LCMS World Relief and Human Care and Orphan Grain Train, organizations that feed both body and soul. Have the students select categories and questions based on the lessons they have studied in this year. Assist students as they write the questions, prepare PowerPoint slides for presentation, publicize the event, and organize the evening. Enlist the help of parents.

Curriculum Connection

Jesus' parable was based on practical farming problems that His hearers were very familiar with—seed that was lost to ground that was too hard, rocky, or weed infested. Today, we still face similar problems. Help your students explore them using section 6.1.2.5, Human Interaction with Physical Environment found in the sixth grade Social Studies volume of the Concordia Curriculum Guide. Consider focusing on your own geographic area—what environmental problems are most pressing where you live? Consider issues with land, water, weather, and pollution.

Technology

Use Internet resources and books to search for information about farming techniques used in New Testament times as well as farming techniques used in our country today. Be sure to bookmark before class any Internet sites the students will view to keep students and your computers safe. A helpful printed resource is *Everyday Life in Bible Times* (CPH).

The comparisons can even include farming techniques used today in developing countries. In many impoverished areas of the world, the only farming tools a family has available are a hoe for breaking up the soil and a machete that is used to poke holes in the ground for seed planting. These are the same kinds of tools they have used for hundreds of years.

Note that many students who live in urban areas may have no idea how the food they eat reaches the supermarket. If this is the case in your classroom, include an investigation of this topic as a part of this project. Have students compile their findings using charts, graphs, and PowerPoint slides.

Working in Groups

Plan and plant a community vegetable garden on your school property. This will involve getting permission from your school board and congregation. It will also involve the expertise of adults who support your school and have the time and energy to help with this long-term project, helping the students learn how to prepare the ground for planting, the planting of the seeds, and the continued care of the plants. These adults will also need to be willing to provide the proper equipment and to be supervisors as the students plant, weed, water, and harvest. Once permission for the project has been secured, decide whether the students will grow and care for all of the vegetables, or if the plot will be divided into small areas that will be rented out to area residents who would like to have a place of their own to garden. Mature produce can be donated to a food pantry or community meal programs may welcome your donations. The produce can also be sold at a stand near your garden with the proceeds going to defray costs of seed, water, and other materials as well as to a mission project your class selects.

Critical thinking

Study some of the other parables Jesus taught, which are recorded in Scripture but will not be studied this year. Select four parables. Compare them on points such as these: What truths of God are taught in each parable? What real-life examples are used in each parable? Do any parables have similar themes? What over-arching truths do you see between the parables? Encourage students to develop charts or Venn diagrams which illustrate the comparisons.

Ideas for the Gifted

Write a modern-day version of one of Jesus' parables. Keep the same main point, but use more familiar comparisons. Some ideas: The parable of the prodigal son (Luke 15:11–32): Include ways that teens and young adults today can lose their way (drugs, pornography). The persistent widow (Luke 18:1–8): Use one of today's courtroom television shows as the setting. The hidden treasure (Matthew 13:44–46): instead of finding the treasure buried in a field, use the idea of a safe, attic trunk, safety deposit box, or bank vault as the place the treasure is hidden.

Unit 6—The Ministry of Jesus

Lesson 61

Jesus Is Transfigured
Matthew 17:1–13; Mark 9:2–13; Luke 9:28–36

Background

What do Moses and Elijah have to do with it? Handpicked by God, and asked to leave heaven's gates behind them, they came down to earth to do God's bidding. Meeting with Jesus on the mountain, they talked. What was that conversation about? Luke 9:30–31 tells us that they talked about the task awaiting Jesus in Jerusalem to complete our salvation. Prior to the trip up the mountain, Jesus spoke to His disciples of His impending death. Jesus' work on earth was nearing completion and He would leave them, but not before great suffering. Naturally they were depressed and afraid. Peter even took Jesus aside and expressed his disapproval, to which Jesus responded, "Get behind Me, Satan! You are a hindrance to Me. For you are not setting your mind on the things of God, but on the things of man" (Matthew 16:23). Truly a slap in the face, to be called Satan. Poor Peter! So why did Elijah and Moses meet with Jesus on the mountain? Both of these men had been given someone to train and carry on their work. Moses was given Joshua, and Elijah was given Elisha. Jesus was giving His disciples the task of continuing His work. Jesus knew that they would need encouragement. This glorious day provided a glimpse that all would work out according to God's will and plan. When the disciples came down from the mountain that day following the Transfiguration of Jesus, it was with certainty that they were changed men. They had just heard the voice of God which said, "This is My beloved Son, with whom I am well pleased; listen to Him!" (Matthew 17:5).

Central Truth

Jesus is true God and true man, who is the only one who could be our substitute, taking the punishment for our sins.

Objectives

- Acknowledge that our sinful human nature makes us unable to do anything to obtain forgiveness and salvation.
- Believe that Jesus, holy and all powerful, willingly took our sins on Himself and gave us His righteousness.
- Honor Jesus as our eternal God and Savior.

Materials

- Web Resources 61a and 61b
- Reproducible 61
- Hymnals and music CDs

Bible Prep

Post in advance so students can bookmark the references before class time.
- Luke 9
- Luke 24
- Revelation 5
- Galatians 4
- John 10

Devotions

When something outstanding or extraordinary happens, people often call it a *peak experience* or a *mountaintop experience*. (Ask students if they can name a time that was very special or exciting for them.) When Colin Firth received an Academy Award for Best Actor, he said, "I think my career just peaked." He felt that he had reached the top as an actor. One of the top two finalists on *American Idol* said, "I'm only seventeen years old, and this is the best thing that's ever happened to me." That sounds almost like the ninety-year-old woman thinking back to the birth of her daughter a half-century earlier and saying, "It's the best thing that ever happened to me." Colonel Jeffrey Williams had a mountaintop experience that was much higher than a mountain—he viewed the Earth from outer space as an astronaut. (The photos he took and his words of praise to God are in his book titled *The Work of His Hands*, available from Concordia Publishing House.) Peak experiences don't have to be that grand, however. One little five-year-old girl, standing in line to march on stage for the school musical commented, "It's the most exciting day of my life." She probably felt as much joy at that moment as the winner of the Super Bowl. Hopefully, that was just the first of many more mountaintop experiences for her.

Today, we will hear about a mountaintop experience of several of Jesus' disciples. This high point helped prepare them for some of the low points that would follow; but it would also prepare them for even greater peak experiences. We can share what the disciples learned from this because we share a faith in the same Lord Jesus, the Lord of Glory. We thank God that He is with us in the low points in our lives and we praise Him for the high points He gives to us, knowing that the ultimate peak experience will be when we see Jesus face-to-face in heaven.

In your hearts give praise to God as stated in 1 Timothy 1:17, "To the King of ages, immortal, invisible, the only God, be honor and glory forever and ever. Amen." Sing "Immortal, Invisible, God Only Wise" (*LSB* 802; recorded on *Hymns of the Month, grade 6, April*) or "Glory Be to God the Father" (*LSB* 506; recorded on *Hymns of the Season, grade 5, Christian Education month, September*).

INTO the lesson

Say, Today's Bible lesson is about Jesus' Transfiguration. It is an unusual story—but it is also very important. First, we will look at the story from a *western* perspective. Westerners, like Europeans and Americans, like to look at things directly, straight, in order, just like it happened. Then we will use an *eastern* perspective like the Greek philosophers, who liked to circle around an event and analyze it from several perspectives.

So, first, we will take a direct look at the event from three sources in the Bible. At this point, choose three volunteers to step to the front of the class to read from Scripture. You will be giving one reader verses to read from Matthew 17, another will read from Mark 9, and the third from Luke 9, as follows. You will announce the subject of the verses and then announce which verse each volunteer should read. (Caution: Not all verses are in order.)

SUBJECT	MT 17	MK 9	LK 9
Travel to the mountain	v. 1	v. 2	v. 28
Jesus' appearance	v. 2	v. 3	v. 29
Moses & Elijah	v. 3	v. 4	v. 30
Peter's response	v. 4	v. 5	vv. 32–33
God the Father speaks	v. 5	v. 7	vv. 34–35
Disciples are terrified	v. 6	v. 6	----
A return to normal	vv. 7–8	v. 8	v. 36

As you listen to these verses, you may want to add some of these comments. Note that the travel time in Luke says eight rather than six days, as the other two mention. Does this mean that the Bible made a mistake? No. For one thing, Luke says *about* eight days. Perhaps he included preparation time for the trip and perhaps the others ended their calculation upon getting to the mountain rather than climbing on it. Some commentators think this was Mount Hermon, which is ten thousand feet high and has snow at the top year round. So there are many factors that weigh into these figures.

Note that the description of Jesus is of an unusual radiant light, similar to descriptions of angels at other events. This was truly an extraordinary, spiritual experience. It was so outstanding that Peter wanted to stay there—once again speaking before thinking. Jesus needed to move on because He had so much to accomplish yet for our salvation.

Note that Luke didn't even bother to mention that the disciples were terrified. So often we see in Scripture that the human reaction to angels and to Christ in His exalted state was to be afraid. That is why the first words from Jesus (and from angels, usually) are "Fear not."

LESSON 61
Jesus Is Transfigured

A Quick Glance

A Glimpse of the Past. Moses represented the Law. Elijah represented the prophets. What was significant about those two appearing at Jesus' transfiguration? (See Luke 24:44.) *Jesus came to keep the Law for us and to fulfill the prophecies.*

A Glimpse of the Present. What was significant about the conversation Jesus had with Moses and Elijah? (See Luke 9:30–31.) *The time was soon approaching for Jesus' death and resurrection. The two faithful prophets spoke with Jesus about what He would accomplish at this time.*

A Glimpse of the Future. This was a brief glimpse of Jesus' glory. When would the disciples again see Jesus exalted and in His glory? *At Easter and at His ascension; and we will all see Him in glory in heaven.*

True Man and True God

Jesus set aside the glory He had in heaven when He came to be born on earth. Jesus was born, lived, and died as a true man. This is called His state of humiliation. Why did Jesus have to be true man? (See Galatians 4:4–5.) *So that He could be our substitute, obeying the Law and also taking its punishment for us.*

The transfiguration also showed that Jesus is true God at the same time. Jesus revealed all His divine powers, His state of exaltation, when He arose at Easter. Why is it so important to us that Jesus is true God? (See John 10:25–27.) *Because He is God, He has the power to give us eternal life.*

In the following verse, underline the words that speak of Jesus as true man (state of humiliation). Circle the words that speak of Jesus as true God (state of exaltation).

"The Word became flesh and dwelt among us, and we have seen His glory, glory as of the only Son from the Father, full of grace and truth." (John 1:14)

Review

Covenant Connection

In His Transfiguration, Jesus revealed Himself as true God. He fulfilled the words of the Old Testament prophet, who said, "Arise, shine, for your light has come, and the glory of the LORD has risen upon you. . . . The LORD will arise upon you, and His glory will be seen upon you. And nations shall come to your light" (Isaiah 60:1–3). Jesus was living up to His name, as was stated in Matthew 1:23, "They shall call His name Immanuel' (which means, God with us)."

As with most *peak experiences* a return to normal followed. Follow this discussion by reviewing the Bible narrative using Web Resource 61a. Continue then with the Student Book by analyzing the Transfiguration from four different perspectives.

A Quick Glance

Peter was hoping they could stay longer on the mountain, but this was just a glance or glimpse of what could and would be. It gave a brief look at important considerations from the past, for that present time, and for the future glory of heaven. Read together the song of glory to God, and especially the Lamb, Christ Jesus, in Revelation 5:11–13. You may also want to sing it (see *LSB* 155 or 171).

Note: There are a lot of Scripture references to look up in this lesson. You may want to assign them to individual students rather than having everyone look up every verse (which can sometimes slow down the pace of a lesson).

True Man and True God

One of the best expositions of Christ's states of humiliation and exaltation is in Philippians 2. Use Reproducible 61 as you examine these concepts.

Christ's state of humiliation can be compared to a "diamond in the rough." The diamond is there, the value is there, but it is not revealed because it is hidden in the rock. Christ willingly set aside His glory, becoming *nothing*, so that we might become children of God. See Philippians 2:5–8.

Purpose? Preparation!

What was the purpose of Jesus' transfiguration? We get clues by looking at the context (surrounding information) of the Bible narrative.

- What was Jesus talking about before the transfiguration? (See Luke 9:21–23.) _Jesus told the disciples He would suffer and die, and arise on the third day._
- What did Jesus talk about during the transfiguration? (See Luke 9:30–31.) _He talked about what would soon happen to Him in Jerusalem to accomplish our salvation._
- What did Jesus talk about after the transfiguration? (See Luke 9:43–45.) _Jesus again foretold His capture and death, but the disciples didn't understand and were afraid to ask Him about it._

Jesus knew that difficult days were ahead of Him and He wanted to prepare His disciples. He wanted to encourage them to trust in Him as the Lord God, having seen His glory. However, the disciples did not fully understand until Jesus' death and resurrection had been completed. After Easter, Jesus was with them for forty days helping them to understand His purpose. Read aloud these important words of Jesus in Luke 24:44–49.

Years later in his second epistle, Peter spoke boldly about being a witness of Christ's glory, saying, "We were eyewitnesses of His majesty. For when He received honor and glory from God the Father, and the voice was borne to Him by the Majestic Glory, 'This is My beloved Son, with whom I am well pleased,' we ourselves heard this very voice borne from heaven, for we were with Him on the holy mountain" (2 Peter 1:16–18).

Transfiguration and Transformation

In a general way, both of the words in this title mean "a change." However, when we relate these words to who Jesus is and to what Jesus does in us, there are several differences.

Jesus' Transfiguration is about *who He is*. Jesus is both God and man. He didn't change into God and then change back into man. However, He did choose in His state of humiliation to not use or reveal all of His divine power and glory. He did this willingly. Once He had accomplished all things for us, He was exalted and remains so.

Our transformation is about *who we are becoming*. Our transformation through Christ Jesus is a change from sinner to saint (2 Corinthians 5:21). Jesus justified us, changing us by taking away our sin and giving us His righteousness. The Holy Spirit sanctifies us, enabling us to live as people of God. In Him, we are a *new creation* (2 Corinthians 5:17). Because of Jesus, our transformation one day will be perfect and complete—when He takes us to heaven! (Philippians 3:20–21).

Remember

"The LORD bless you and keep you; the LORD make His face to shine upon you and be gracious to you; the LORD lift up His countenance upon you and give you peace." (Numbers 6:24–26)

Christ's state of exaltation can be compared to a polished, shining, faceted diamond—all its glory can be seen. Philippians 2:9–11 rejoices in His exaltation. Also, in the Apostles' Creed, note that the turning point is when Jesus descended into hell. He is no longer in the state of humiliation—He is declaring His victory—**He has conquered sin, Satan, and death. His state of exaltation continues from there, with the certainty and hope of our joining Him in glory!**

Purpose? Preparation!

This section of the Student Book emphasizes what Jesus was focusing on at this time. His focus was on the cross and our redemption. He talked about it before, during, and after the Transfiguration. This brief episode of glory would provide hope and comfort to Himself and His disciples in the days ahead.

It is significant to also note the affirmation of God the Father. Ask, **At what other time had God the Father said the same thing about His Son, Jesus?** (At Jesus' Baptism) Jesus' Baptism occurred at the beginning of His ministry and now He was nearing the end of His ministry. At both times, the beginning and ending of His ministry on earth, He was blessed and affirmed by the words of the Father. He was not alone, even though not long after this, He would feel alone on the cross. All of this was part of God's plan for our salvation so that we will never be alone—Jesus promises to be with us always and to be reunited with us eternally in heaven.

INTO our lives

Transfiguration and Transformation

This section is called "Into our Lives," but <u>all</u> that Jesus did is about our lives. He did all things for our salvation! He transforms us through the power of the Holy Spirit so that we can now live for Him!

Point out that the Bible words to remember are the Benediction that we often hear at the end of a worship service. Ask, **What phrases remind you of Jesus' glory and exaltation?**

Also explore the word *transformation*. **We don't transform ourselves. The Holy Spirit changes us as He works through the Word and Sacraments, bringing us to faith in Christ Jesus. This transformation involves change. To *believe* in Jesus is not just head knowledge—it is not just a matter of knowing Bible facts. To *believe* as a Christian is to *be* a Christian. *Being* is who we are. It defines us as people—we are people of God. To *believe* as a Christian is also to *live* as a Christian. *Living* as a Christian defines our actions, what we say, and what we do. It is a total commitment. It is a lifelong commitment.** Use Web Resource 61b to reinforce these concepts.

Jesus: True God and True Man

Jesus Christ is both true God and true man. But He willingly set aside His divine glory to become one of us as a true man, so He could become our substitute. Jesus remained true God, but did not reveal that part of who He is except at certain times. Jesus as true man is called His state of humiliation. The Apostles' Creed describes it this way: He was "born of the virgin Mary, suffered under Pontius Pilate, was crucified, died and was buried." Philippians 2:6–8 says:

This is a diamond in the rough. You can't see the beauty of the diamond that is in this rock, but the value is there. The worth of the diamond is there even though it is not revealed because it is covered with ordinary stone.

Christ Jesus, "who, though He was in the form of God, did not count equality with God a thing to be grasped, but made Himself nothing, taking the form of a servant, being born in the likeness of men. And being found in human form, He humbled Himself by becoming obedient to the point of death, even death on a cross."

At the Transfiguration, Jesus gave a glimpse of His glory as true God. Once He had fulfilled and completed God's plan of salvation for us through His death and resurrection, He revealed His full glory as true God. The Apostles' Creed describes it this way: "He descended into hell (to proclaim His victory). The third day He rose again from the dead. He ascended into heaven and sits at the right hand of God the Father Almighty. From thence He will come to judge the living and the dead." Philippians 2:9–11 says:

This is a diamond that has been polished and faceted to show its true glory. It is a strong and valuable stone that reflects light, shining brightly, with clarity and perfection.

"Therefore God has highly exalted Him and bestowed on Him the name that is above every name, so that at the name of Jesus every knee should bow, in heaven and on earth and under the earth, and every tongue confess that Jesus Christ is Lord, to the glory of God the Father."

Critical thinking

As you study the three accounts of the Transfiguration, you may note that the three Gospel writers described things in a slightly different way. For example, Matthew says Jesus' clothes became as white as the light, Mark says that Jesus' clothes became more dazzling white than anyone could bleach them, and Luke compares Jesus' clothes to a bright flash of lightning. Skeptics like to criticize the Bible's accuracy by pointing to such differences. However, the truth is that the three descriptions do not contradict one another. They are just different ways of saying the same thing. People speak and write with a variety of words and a variety of perspectives. It makes reading all three accounts more interesting. While skeptics may try to disprove Scripture, they are not considering that if the three writers were so unscrupulous as to invent the story, they would also have been unscrupulous enough to copy one another's exact words. The variety of descriptions of the same event tends to prove that these were eyewitness accounts. Skeptics also fail to take into account the fact that the writers were inspired by the Holy Spirit in their writings. As 2 Peter 1:21 states, "No prophecy was ever produced by the will of man, but men spoke from God as they were carried along by the Holy Spirit." God used these writers as His writing tools and instruments, but the words are the Word of God.

Encourage students to be strong in their faith. Remind them again that they, too, can be transformed by the forgiveness of Jesus. Ask students to think about what they see when they look in a mirror first thing in the morning. While for some it may not be a pretty sight that early in the day, remind all of your students that Jesus steps in as our substitute so that God sees only Jesus when we ask for forgiveness for our sins. In today's Bible narrative, it said that Jesus' face shone like the sun. With the transformation He makes in us, taking away our sin and making us blameless before God, we now can shine like lights in this world. Have the students write out on a note card Philippians 2:15 and Matthew 5:16. Tell them to post this on their bathroom mirrors, reminding them that they, too, are transformed into shining lights through the power of God and for His glory. Encourage them to meditate on these words each morning, which can offer hope in an uncertain, self-conscious, middle-school world.

Teacher Tips

Students that have not grown up in the church may be unfamiliar with the story of the Transfiguration. Help them to understand that Jesus' ministry was for the blessing and benefit of masses of people, but it was also a blessing and benefit for Jesus' closest friends, the disciples, whom He was equipping to carry on His work after He was gone. Lead students to understand that God works in very personal yet miraculous ways in each of our lives. God so loves the world in general, but He also loves you in particular, individually, and personally. The affirmation of God the Father was strengthening for Jesus, assuring for His disciples, but is also a message for you and me. Also refer to the last sentences in Matthew 17:5; Mark 9:7; and Luke 9:35, which clearly state God's message in reference to His Son, Jesus, "Listen to Him!"

Jesus' Transfiguration was characterized by light—brilliant, glorious light revealing Him as the Son of God He truly is. Make a science connection to this story by using any of the activities and information in section 6.1.6, Light Energy, found in the sixth grade Science volume of the Concordia Curriculum Guide. Discuss with students: Why is light so often associated with God's glory? When they think of light, what feelings, emotions, and ideas come up for them? Use a Bible concordance to find key verses using the word *light*, such as 1 Peter 2:9.

Unit 6—The Ministry of Jesus

Lesson 62

Jesus Feeds a Crowd
Matthew 14:13–23; Mark 6:30–46; Luke 9:10–17; John 6:1–14

Background

We sometimes wonder if we have an impact in the lives of our students. It's important to remember that Jesus fed this large crowd through the humble beginnings of a boy with a meager lunch. The boy's barley loaves indicated this was cheap bread, the food of the poor, a humble offering, from a mere child. Sound familiar? Humble beginnings are Jesus' style.

Perhaps, this can put things into perspective in your own life. Do you think you have only a little bit to offer? Doesn't matter; Jesus will multiply it. Take your number of years of service and multiple that by the number of students typically found on your class list. Have you fed God's message to twenty students this year? Take that times five years of teaching. One hundred children may have been influenced by your words. Do you encourage them to talk about Jesus to their parents? Add that number into the equation, be it a single parent or both parents. Are you the first source of God's Word for a child in your classroom? for a parent sitting at the conference table?

Throughout the rest of your teaching career, remember who your audience is. Feed them the Word of God. Encourage them to feed their own families. Read the passage about the feeding of the five thousand often in your teaching. Be compassionate. Be concerned about meeting the very basic needs of your students. Is hunger one of them? Do your students come to school with physical or emotional hunger? Do your students hunger for the Word of God? Do you ask God to take what you have to offer and multiply it?

And when your classroom of students sometimes feel like five thousand, remember the words of Jesus found in Mark 6:31 (NIV), "Come with Me by yourselves to a quiet place and get some rest."

Central Truth

Jesus has the power to feed us physically and spiritually because He is true God, the bread of life.

Objectives

- Perceive that often we look to God to supply our daily needs while neglecting His spiritual blessings.
- Appreciate Christ's physical blessings while recognizing the great, far-reaching, eternal blessings of forgiveness, life, and salvation.
- Demonstrate gratitude by caring for the gifts God gives and by sharing those gifts with others.

Materials

- Reproducible 62
- Hymnals and music CDs
- Web Resources 62a and 62b

Bible Prep

Post in advance so students can bookmark the references before class time.
- Psalm 130
- John 6:15, 22–40
- John 20:31

Devotion

Distribute Reproducible 62. Say, **Today we are going to study a familiar story. Many of you know about Jesus feeding the five thousand people. But today, maybe we will learn some new thoughts about this event. Let's begin by thinking about how different our lives are today than their lives were in Bible times. At the top of the page, make a list of ten things we have today that the people in ancient times did not have.**

After most students have had time to complete this, gather the group's attention again. Take the list of a volunteer and say, **I'm going to slowly read this list. If you have a similar item on your list, draw a line through that statement.** After that have students read off items they have not crossed off, while others continue crossing off similar items. Once all the items have been read say, **That was quite a list. We live in abundant times. We have more things than most people in previous centuries ever had!**

Now let's switch our thinking. List five things that people needed in ancient times that we also need today. Follow the same process.

Then say the following (reinforcing an idea that someone has probably mentioned by now), **Let's focus on the one thing that all people need, from ancient times to today and to eternity.** Have students fold their papers twice to make a card shape. Tell them to use one hand to hold the corner where the folded edges meet (with folded corner edge at the bottom and the left side). Use the other hand to tear off the extra space so that an L-shape that is about one-inch thick is left behind. Open the L-shape and it will form a cross. Sing "When I Survey the Wondrous Cross" (*LSB* 426; recorded on *Hymns of the Season*, grade 8, Lent). Say together Psalm 130.

265

INTO the Word

A Scavenger Hunt

Divide the class into four groups, assigning one of the Bible readings listed in the Student Book to each group. Have students circle the assigned reference in their books and choose a group leader. The leader of each group will guide them through the statements in the Student Book as the group scans their reference to find the exact verse related to each statement. Group members are to work together, sharing what they find, and recording the information. (This will provide students with the opportunity to study the Bible narrative; the next activity provides supplemental information that analyzes the data.) After the groups are finished, gather together and tally the data collected. List the numbers 1 through 18 and place a tally mark for each student group that found a verse that gave that particular information. Discuss the findings. Did any group have all of the information in its source? How many zeros did each group have (indicating where a piece of information was not given in that particular source)? Analyze this and come to some conclusions. For example, different authors see different information as significant. (If you have four people witness the same event, they will notice different things.) Point out that the various sources align and do not contradict each other; to get the whole picture, it is good to read from each source. Also note that some authors write for different purposes; that is why some may be more brief or more detailed than others. Review the Bible story, using Web Resource 62a.

Review

Because bread is such an important item and concept in this lesson and because bread is such an essential necessity around the world, consider sharing different kinds of bread with your students or have students plan a group project to share different kinds of bread from around the world. Point out that there are many differences in flavors, shapes, textures, and colors of bread from culture to culture. While we often like white, fluffy bread, other cultures may have heavy dark bread as a mainstay. Mexican tortillas and Greek pitas are flat breads that have also become very popular in our culture too.

Lesson 62

Jesus Feeds a Crowd

A Scavenger Hunt

Read Matthew 14:13–23; Mark 6:30–46; Luke 9:10–17; or John 6:1–14. List the Scripture verse where the following information is found. If it is not mentioned in your chosen reference, write a zero.

_____ 1. It was almost time for the Passover.

_____ 2. Jesus went by boat to a quiet place on the other side of the sea to rest.

_____ 3. People from the towns heard where Jesus was and ran to meet Him.

_____ 4. When He saw the crowds coming, He felt compassion for them.

_____ 5. The people seemed like sheep without a shepherd.

_____ 6. He welcomed them.

_____ 7. He healed the sick and injured.

_____ 8. He taught them many things about the kingdom of God.

_____ 9. As evening approached, the disciples said Jesus should send the people away.

_____ 10. Jesus astonished the disciples when He told them to feed the people.

_____ 11. The only food to be found was a boy's lunch of five loaves of bread and two fish.

_____ 12. Jesus had the people sit on the green grass in groups of 50 and a 100.

_____ 13. Jesus prayed, blessing and thanking God the Father, before the bread was distributed.

_____ 14. The fish were also divided and passed out to the people.

_____ 15. Everyone ate until they were satisfied.

_____ 16. There were five thousand men in the crowd, not even counting all the women and children.

_____ 17. Afterward, twelve baskets of leftovers were gathered up.

_____ 18. After Jesus dismissed the people, He went up the mountain to pray.

Review

Covenant Connection

How does this event relate to the Old Testament? Jesus Himself pointed to a connection with God providing bread (manna) to eat for the Israelites traveling in the wilderness centuries earlier. Bread is a basic necessity. If you don't have the income or supplies to at least have bread, you probably have nothing and will starve and die. When Jesus called Himself the bread of life, He was saying that He is a basic necessity for eternal life. Without Jesus, we have nothing, and we will starve spiritually and die eternally. Praise God that He offers Himself and His salvation freely to all who believe!

Do a taste test, using plastic gloves to tear the different types of bread into small pieces to sample. (Point out that the tearing the bread into pieces is like the "breaking of the bread" mentioned in the Bible narrative.) Perhaps place a label naming the bread and country of origin for each type. Students who are not bringing bread could bring paper plates, make labels, or bring a topping (such as pressurized cheese, for quick application). As you consider different shapes of bread, point out that some types of bread are like what we might call crackers or biscuits (which are probably what the loaves in the Bible narrative were like).

Lessons to Learn

Directions: There are many things we can learn from this Bible story. Briefly write some of these ideas on the loaves of bread at the side.

- God gives abundantly.
- Pray before meals.
- Don't waste food.
- Quiet time is good.
- Jesus cares about our needs.

The Main Point

The four Gospel writers (Matthew, Mark, Luke, John) had different styles, perspectives, and purposes in their writings.

- Matthew wrote mainly to Jewish people, emphasizing that Jesus fulfilled the Messianic prophecies of the Old Testament.
- Mark, a helper of Simon Peter, wrote mostly to Roman Christians in a Roman style that was brief, direct, and active.
- Luke was a doctor who focused on Jesus' compassion through His miracles and through the parables He used to teach the people.
- John wrote often to Greek Christians. The Greeks tended to be very philosophical, so John wrote more about Jesus' preaching and theology.

This miracle of the feeding of more than five thousand people is the only miracle, other than Jesus' resurrection at Easter, that is recorded in all four Gospels. What did all four evangelists (Gospel writers) see that was so important about this event? The main point of the narrative comes <u>after</u> the miracle. Read John 6:15, 22–40.

a. What did the people want from Jesus? **They wanted to make Jesus king so He would give them whatever they needed and solve their problems here on earth.**

b. What did Jesus want them to know? **That He is true God, who came to save them, but not from hunger. He came to save them from sin and give them what they truly need most—eternal life in heaven, which lasts forever.**

c. What is the main reason the Gospel writers wrote? (See John 20:31.) **"These are written so that you may believe that Jesus is the Christ, the Son of God, and that by believing you may have life in His name."**

Remember

"Truly, truly, I say to you, whoever believes has eternal life. I am the bread of life." (John 6:47–48)

131

---

was going to the new big action movie and you want to hear about it. So you run up to your friend and ask, "How was the movie? Tell me all about it!" And your friend answers, "The popcorn and soda were great!" That's not much of a reply. The main point was totally missed.

Jesus didn't come to give away bread; He came to BE the bread—THE BREAD OF LIFE. That was the main point that the people were missing! Ordinary bread is a necessity; if you are hungry and eat, you will live another day. By comparison, Jesus is the bread of life—He is a necessity for the spiritually hungry and starving soul; if you have Jesus, you will live more than just another day, you will live forever in heaven. Jesus, the bread of life, brings eternal life!

Work together on the questions. Then look at Web Resource 62b. This song pulls together the main idea of today's lesson. First, read through the stanzas of "Who Was the Man" (*AGPS* 268). Stanza 1 is about Jesus calling His disciples and stanza 2 is about Jesus healing and helping the crowds of people. But stanzas 3 and 4 focus on Jesus' main purpose—He came for our eternal salvation. He came to win the victory over sin, death, and the devil through His death on the cross and resurrection at Easter. Join in singing the song together.

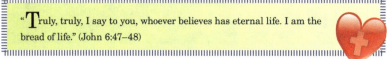

Lessons to Learn

Say, **This is an interesting Bible story because there are so many different things we can learn from it. In your books, write briefly some of the things you learned from this story.** Allow time for the activity and then let students share their ideas. Several possibilities are listed on the sample page in red.

The Main Point

Read together the beginning portion of this section of the Student Book and the Bible reading from John 6:15, 22–40. Then say, **So many of the five thousand and more people missed the main point. After Jesus had talked to them all day about God's love, the main thing they thought of was free food. Their reaction is very much like this modern-day scenario: You see your friend who**

What Do You Have? Want? Need?

Directions: Make a list of ten things people have today that no one had in Bible times.

1. _____
2. _____
3. _____
4. _____
5. _____
6. _____
7. _____
8. _____
9. _____
10. _____

Directions: Make a list of five things people needed in Bible times that we also need today.

1. _____
2. _____
3. _____
4. _____
5. _____

Reproducible 62

Lesson Support

Ideas for the Gifted

Use a map to locate the Sea of Galilee (the northeast shore) and Bethsaida the possible sight of the feeding of the five thousand to plot out and discuss the logistics of this lesson. (See the maps and pictures in the Student Book Appendix.) By seeing places on a map, the story becomes more real to the students. If a scanner is available, these maps could be scanned and projected on an interactive whiteboard or copies could be made for students to pinpoint locations and highlight Jesus' travels. A travel log could be created for subsequent lessons. Sing together a song that embodies the main point of the lesson, based on the words of Matthew 6:33: "Seek first the kingdom of God and His righteousness, and all these things will be added to you." God does provide for our physical needs; but it is His desire that our main focus is on Christ and salvation through Him. Sing "Seek Ye First" (*AGPS* 207; recorded on *JPS*).

Working in Groups

Search the Scriptures and make an inference about the weather on the day Jesus feeds the crowd. Can we assume it was a nice day? Can your group provide proof that it was in fact a great day for a picnic? (Prior to the feeding of the five thousand, Jesus and His disciples took a boat ride to the far shore of the Sea of Galilee. A great crowd gathered because they saw the miraculous signs He had performed on the sick. The day must have been clear enough for a boat ride and clear and warm enough for sick people to venture out. There was plenty of green grass to sit on. The people stayed on into the evening hours, therefore the weather must have been cooperative.) What more does this say about our generous and gracious God? (This miraculous picnic shows that Jesus, the bread of life, supplies our needs as well as providing sunshine, warm weather, and gentle breezes. He leads us beside still waters and restores our souls.) Provide water colors and work together to create the scene that day, visualizing the surrounding countryside.

HANDS TO SERVE

Have a continuing project to give students a sense of the large number of people that Jesus fed on that miraculous day. Display a green sheet of poster or bulletin board paper to represent the grassy hillside where the people sat on that day long ago. Set out tape so students can make tape rolls to attach pennies to the paper. Each penny represents one person. Suggest that they group the pennies in groups of fifty, as Jesus grouped the people on that day. (Perhaps use a black crayon to circle a completed group of pennies/people.) So what can you do when the goal is reached and you have five thousand pennies (fifty dollars)? What makes the most sense is to give the money to a food bank that feeds people in need! (Option: Increase the challenge: What if at least half of the men were married and each of those had three children? How much more will you need to collect?)

DIGGING DEEPER

Discuss the last portion of John 6, verses 51–57. Ask, **What is Jesus giving a preview of in these verses?** (The Lord's Supper) He is relating the miracle, where people ate the bread, with receiving Himself as the bread of life, in a supernatural, spiritual way. When Jesus gave the Lord's Supper, He spoke of eating bread and drinking wine in a natural way that at the same time was receiving His own body and blood in a supernatural way—we call this the *Real Presence* of Christ in the Sacrament. The Lord's Supper is not just bread and wine that symbolize Jesus; the Lord's Supper is not bread and wine changed into body and blood. We believe that the Real Presence of Christ's body and blood is in and with and under the bread and wine—there is a real presence of all of these. Believing in this miracle, as in the other miracles of Jesus, He is in us and gives us life—life forever. It is a miracle. It is a mystery. It does seem abstract—but what is more real than bread and what is more natural than a living Savior!

Critical thinking

In today's Bible narrative, Jesus said and did things to show His deity—He is true God. That is probably why the Gospel writers all felt compelled to report this event. The miracle demonstrated His power as true God. Yet the next day, some of the people asked Jesus, "What sign do You do, that we may see and believe You? What work do You perform?" (John 6:30). He had just fed five thousand people! What more proof did they need? Doesn't that just make you want to scream? Wait a minute—aren't we often just as dense about recognizing God's action in our lives and just as hardheaded about trusting God for our needs today and to eternity? Aren't we just as shortsighted about focusing on earthly concerns, wanting a quick and easy solution? Instead of criticizing those people long ago, we need to see ourselves in them and go repentantly to God, thanking Him for His grace and goodness!

UNIT 6—THE MINISTRY OF JESUS

LESSON 63

A Woman Is Judged
John 8:1–11

Background

As Jesus teaches in the temple, the Pharisees come and bring a woman to Him, a woman caught in the act of adultery. The Pharisees do not believe that Jesus is God's promised Messiah. They want an excuse to arrest Jesus and bring charges against Him. If they can make Jesus speak against the Law of Moses, they could prove to everyone that He cannot possibly be sent from God. Jesus, however, turns their plan around, catching the Pharisees in their own trap. The woman is a sinner, but so are they. They are forced to admit that they are sinners, but they turn and walk away from the source of their forgiveness. The woman is left alone with Jesus. He does not condemn her but sends her away, forgiven, with the command, "From now on sin no more."

Just as Jesus confronted the Pharisees, the Law of God confronts us with our sin. There is no one without sin who can pick up that first stone. It is a trap from which we cannot escape. The good news for us is that the trap attempted by the Pharisees finally closed in on Jesus. He was arrested, tried, and condemned to death on the cross. Innocent of any sin of His own, He died for our sins and rose from the dead. Through Jesus' death and resurrection, the Law lost its power to accuse and condemn us before God. Death itself was trapped and destroyed, losing its hold on us. According to God's plan, Jesus endured the trap that had been set for Him and triumphed over it. Our sins are forgiven, and in Baptism, we are raised to new life. Our risen Lord says to us, "Neither do I condemn you; go, and from now on sin no more."

Central Truth

Jesus uses the Law not to angrily punish us but, in love, to direct us to contrition and repentance.

Objectives

- In repentance, confess (admit) our sins with contrition (sorrow).
- In repentance, believe in Jesus as our only Savior, trusting His promise of forgiveness.
- In repentance, live changed lives as we are transformed by the Holy Spirit.

Materials

- Web Resources 57b and 63a
- Reproducible 63
- Hymnals and music CDs

Bible Prep

Post in advance so students can bookmark the reference before class time.
- John 8:1–11

Devotions

Sandy came home from school and went straight to her room. Her worst fears had come true. All the popular kids were going to a party next Friday, but she was not invited. Sandy was sure she knew the reason she wasn't invited. She walked over to the mirror on her dresser and studied her reflection. She did not like what she saw. The popular girls were pretty and she was not. "If I looked different," Sandy thought, "I would be popular at school! People would want to invite me everywhere." She turned away from the mirror, wishing she was someone different but knowing she could never be anyone but who she was.

Sandy's mother knocked on the door, looking for her. "You didn't come into the kitchen when you came home. Is everything all right?" Sandy answered. "I'm not all right. I'm all wrong!" She told her mother about the party and the reason she wasn't invited—at least the reason she imagined. Sandy walked to the mirror again. "Look at me," she said. "Who would invite me anywhere?" Sandy's mother looked in the mirror with her. "A mirror shows you the person God made you to be. Sometimes, you like what you see and sometimes, you don't. But the mirror can't show you everything. It can't show you how much you are loved—by me, and by your dad. I know you have friends at school and the mirror can't show how much they care about you. The mirror can't show how much God loves you." Her mother picked up a small cross necklace from the dresser and put it on Sandy. They looked in the mirror again. "This cross shows how much God loves us. He sent Jesus to be our Savior. You are more than all right. You belong to Jesus!"

Those of you who have ever felt this way after not being invited, or not making the team, or not getting the lead part, know that there is something else to this story. What we really want is to have both—the love of Jesus and popularity with friends. Pray about it and understand that God has a good plan for you. Trust His ways and also trust His timing. Look for the good, often surprising, blessings He gives to you. Remember His words in Jeremiah 29:11, "For I know the plans I have for you, declares the Lord, plans for welfare and not for evil, to give you a future and a hope."

Sing "Come to Calvary's Holy Mountain" (*LSB* 435; recorded on *Hymns of the Season, grade 6, Lent*) or "Make Me Like You" (Web Resource 57b). Listen to the chanted version of Psalm 130 (Web Resource 63a).

INTO the Word

What's Going on Here?

Together read aloud John 8:1–8 to find out the story behind the picture. Then say, **The picture shows angry Pharisees, a crying woman, and Jesus writing something on the ground. But there is much more going on here than that. We need to dig deeper to find out all the many things that are going on. They say a picture is worth a thousand words; but in this case, it will take a thousand words to explain the picture.**

The woman in this Bible narrative was an outcast. She came face-to-face with the Law and with her sin of adultery. According to Jewish law, she deserved to die for what she had done. But she also came face-to-face with her Savior. The Law confronts us too; and praise God that our Savior, Jesus, is in "our picture" too.

Lesson 63 — A Woman Is Judged

What's Going On Here?

John 8:1–8

Accusing and Blaming

There is a lot more going on here than catching a woman who committed adultery. In fact, we won't talk about her till much later. The main problem here is the self-righteous people who are accusing and blaming her. They were trying to make themselves look good in comparison to how bad she is. They were building themselves up by tearing someone else down. They were justified in their own eyes by their contrast with her. Shameful!

We wouldn't do that. Or would we? Or do we? Have you ever laughed at someone else's mistake to make yourself feel smarter than that person? Have you ever talked to a friend about the dorky, totally out-of-style clothing someone else has so that you would feel "cool" by comparison? Have you ever called someone a name because of "something stupid" they did in a game so that you could feel much more skilled than that person is? Pointing out the faults of others is a popular habit today (or should we call it a common sin). This sin seems even "safer" when we do it anonymously (over the social network) or if we are a distance away (watching it on TV). But the sin is still a sin. And no matter what, there are two who know about it—you in your heart and God who is right by you. You might try to excuse yourself by saying, "I'm just telling it like it is." But that doesn't make it right—that sounds just like one of those Pharisees so long ago. So what is expected of us? Look to Jesus—His way is mercy.

Review

Covenant Connection

Once again, we see Jesus fulfilling the promises of grace in God's covenant to be with and to save His people. The Pharisees were quick to point to the Law in Scripture. But they overlooked the many portions of grace recorded in the Old Testament. Psalm 79 says, "O God of our salvation, for the glory of Your name; deliver us, and atone for our sins, for Your name's sake! . . . Let the groans of the prisoners come before You; according to Your great power, preserve those doomed to die! . . . We Your people, the sheep of Your pasture, will give thanks to You forever; from generation to generation we will recount Your praise" (vv. 9, 11, 13).

INTO our lives

Accusing and Blaming

Say, **Let's begin with the accusations. The Pharisees felt they were right in doing this because they stood behind the Law of Moses. However, Jesus knew that it was not God's Word that filled their hearts, but rather pride and self-righteousness. They did not understand that "love is the fulfilling of the law" (Romans 13:10). And Jesus came to share His love and forgiveness with all people.**

When we look carefully into the mirror of God's Law, our sins show up much more clearly. The Law accuses all of us of doing wrong. We are all guilty! So Jesus came to put Himself between us and the accusations of the Law. Jesus obeyed all of the Commandments. He never sinned. His life perfectly reflected God's Holy Law. Jesus was innocent but He suffered the punishment we deserve for our sins. **Because Jesus died in our place, God forgives our sins. He looks at us and says, "Not guilty!" Yet whenever we look into the mirror of God's Law, we see that we are still sinners. We confess our sins and receive God's forgiveness. As His forgiven people, each day we rise to a new life in Christ as the Holy Spirit helps us to follow God's commands.**

It's a Test

Actually, this event was not really about the woman. It was about Jesus. Scripture tells us that the Pharisees and scribes came to Jesus, hoping to trap Him into making a mistake so they could bring charges against Him. They hoped to use Jesus' own goodness and mercy to bring Him down. They didn't look so good next to the perfect grace and mercy of Jesus. They wanted to build themselves up by tearing Him down. They were trying to justify themselves in their own eyes. Shameful!

We wouldn't do that. Or would we? Or do we? Have you ever spread the news when you overheard a pastor say a bad word? (You know a pastor isn't perfect like Jesus, but you still seem to enjoy seeing a "good" person do "bad.") Have you ever watched the self-righteous anger of the news media when a government leader has misappropriated funds or the way people gobble up magazine articles about a famous religious leader caught in a scandal? For some sad reason, we don't feel so bad about our own sins if we can point to the wrongs of others. While their actions should be acknowledged as wrong, we should not "delight" in the sin and the suffering it causes. The Pharisees were hoping to accuse Jesus of doing wrong, but it didn't happen because Jesus is true God and He knew what was in their hearts. Jesus didn't shout and accuse them in anger; He simply posed a question for them to examine their own hearts. So what is expected of us? Look to Jesus—we are justified only through Him.

Judgment—Forgiven!

This is the part we like. She sinned—she was forgiven—end of story. Or is it? People like to think that forgiveness is a quick and easy way to "clean the slate" and go back to whatever it was you were doing, because there is always more forgiveness. As if forgiveness is a "free ticket," take it, and then go on with your life. Is this what Jesus teaches?

We would never think that. Or would we? Or do we? How often have you lost your temper, asked for forgiveness, but then failed to control your temper the next time you were angry? How often have you used bad language with the excuse that other people do it too? How often have you said to your mom "I'm sorry" when you didn't clean your room, but the same thing happened the next week and the next and the next? What did Jesus say when He forgave the sins of the woman? He said, "Sin no more!" That is His message to us too. He is ready with His grace and mercy for all who repent and believe in His name. The word we tend to overlook is *repent*. God calls us to repentance, to be sorry about our sin and receive His forgiveness <u>and</u> *to turn away from that sin and live as a child of God.* We have a responsibility to change; the problem is we can't do it on our own. So what is expected of us? Look to Jesus—we are sanctified through His gift of the Holy Spirit. Jesus knows what we need and gives it to us so that we can be empowered to live changed, transformed lives. Pray that the Holy Spirit will guide you on this path to *sin no more*, which is not an easy one and which is filled with setbacks. But don't give up because God is not giving up on you. He says, "I, the Lord your God, hold your right hand; it is I who say to you, 'Fear not, I am the one who helps you' " (Isaiah 41:13).

Remember

"Repent and be baptized every one of you in the name of Jesus Christ for the forgiveness of your sins, and you will receive the gift of the Holy Spirit. For the promise is for you and for your children and for all who are far off, everyone whom the Lord our God calls to Himself." (Acts 2:38–39)

It's a Test

When Jesus lived on earth many people believed that He was the Savior and God's promised Messiah. But there were also many people who did not believe in Him. Some of the Pharisees, the Jewish religious leaders, did not believe. They thought Jesus was a false prophet and they wanted to find an excuse to have Jesus arrested and killed. What was their plan? **The Pharisees were testing Jesus. They want to trap Him into saying something wrong so that they could bring charges against Him.** If Jesus didn't agree that the woman deserved to die, the Pharisees could accuse Him of speaking against the Law of Moses. For that crime, Jesus would deserve to die! The Pharisees would have an excuse to arrest Him and put Him on trial.

We don't know what Jesus wrote on the ground; the Bible never tells us that. But when Jesus stood up He had the perfect answer for the Pharisees. What did He say? (He said the person without sin should throw the first stone at the woman.) **Jesus knew that the woman caught in adultery was guilty. It was a grievous sin. But the Law accuses everyone because everyone is guilty of sin. The Pharisees were sinners too. They also sinned against the Law and they knew it. They tried to trap Jesus, but Jesus instead trapped them. What did the Pharisees do?** (The Pharisees left, one by one, until only the woman was left standing in front of Jesus.) **Her accusers were gone. There was no one to condemn her.**

Judgment—Forgiven!

At the end of the story, the woman was forgiven yet she was still a sinner. The Pharisees were still sinners. Jesus came to die for sinners—for the woman and even for the Pharisees who tried to trap Him. According to God's plan, when the time was right, Jesus' enemies succeeded in arresting Him. He was innocent but He was put on trial, falsely accused, and sentenced to death. Jesus died on the cross in the place of sinners, for the woman caught in adultery, for the Pharisees, and for you and me. Because Jesus suffered the punishment we deserve for our sins, God declares us not guilty. Jesus asked the woman, "Has no one condemned you?" The woman said, "No one, Lord." Jesus forgave her sins. He said to her, "Neither do I condemn you." Because of Jesus, we are not condemned. In Romans 8:1, the apostle Paul wrote, "There is therefore now no condemnation for those who are in Christ Jesus." And He says to us, through the enabling power of the Holy Spirit, to sin no more!

Lesson Support

Curriculum Connection

Make a literary connection to this story using section 6.2.1.3, Character Development through Revealed Thoughts, Words, Actions, and Narrator Description. This appears in the sixth grade Language Arts volume of the Concordia Curriculum Guide. Read the story with students, and then ask them what words they would use to describe the character of Jesus based on this story only. Also ask them to describe what it is in the story that causes them to choose those words to describe Him. As much as you can, try to go beyond the obvious (e.g., forgiveness). For example, ponder this question: Why did Jesus choose to write on the ground instead of directly confronting the leaders? What does this say about His character? Speculate what Jesus might have been writing on the ground and why.

DIGGING DEEPER

The Law plays a significant role in this lesson. You may want to explore further the mirror of the Law using Reproducible 63. Say, **God does not condemn us; we are His forgiven, blameless, and therefore holy people. Yet we know that we are still sinners. When we look at ourselves in the mirror of God's Law, we can see that we sin every day. We do not obey God as we should and the Law still accuses us. We are sorry for our sins. We confess our sins to God and receive His forgiveness.**

God's Law is a mirror and shows us our sins. It shows us that we need our Savior. But the Law also shows us God's will for our lives. When Martin Luther explained the Commandments, he used each commandment to show not only what we *should not* do but also what we *should do* to live as God's holy people, what we should do to "sin no more." Use the activity to find ways to follow God's commands in your thoughts, words, and actions. Even as we study the Law, we will see that we are still sinners. Remember that we have forgiveness because of Jesus, our Savior!

Teacher Tips

As Lutherans, we often talk about the three uses of the Law. Sometimes, the three uses of God's Law are compared to a curb, a mirror, and a guide (or to a leash, a mirror, and a map). The first use of the Law is like a curb that keeps cars on the street or a leash that controls a dog on a walk. The Law of God in this first use restrains or holds back evil in the world. All people, even unbelievers, have the Law of God written on their hearts. Although people still sin, God uses His Law in their hearts to keep the evil in check as their consciences tell them that certain behaviors are wrong. In its second use, the Law is a mirror that reflects our sins back to our sight and shows us our need for the Savior. The Law in its third use is a guide or map that shows us God's will for our lives. The Holy Spirit is at work in our hearts to help us in leading a God-pleasing life.

Bringing it home

The challenges of peer pressure make it very difficult for teens and preteens to "sin no more" as they seek to follow Jesus in their daily lives. Send a letter to parents explaining your classroom lessons about God's Law, sin, and the free gift of forgiveness we have in Christ. Ask parents to talk to their children about the difficulties of friendships and about the social situations in which they may face temptation. Encourage parents to talk to their sons and daughters about following Jesus each day, even when that may not seem like the most "popular" thing to do. Invite parents to bring their children to church and Sunday School. All of the family members can grow stronger in faith and in their relationships with each other through the study of God's Word.

Celebrating GROWTH

The Pharisees tried to use the woman caught in adultery to trap Jesus into speaking against the Law of Moses. It's likely they did not care about the woman or what might happen to her. They only wished to use her sin to find a way to condemn Jesus. Jesus, however, forgave the woman and encouraged her to live a God-pleasing life and "sin no more." Talk to your students about people who are used and bullied by others. They may know fellow students who are not considered popular. Perhaps no one sits with them at lunch time, talks to them at recess, or invites them to join in social activities. How can they help and encourage those students? What can they say to the students who are hurt by unkind words and actions? How can they stop students who mistreat others? When should they talk to an adult about the situation? In helping others, they are serving the Lord Jesus.

UNIT 6—THE MINISTRY OF JESUS   LESSON 64

Peter's Confession
Matthew 16:13–18

Background

What kinds of things do you know to be true? You know your age and your name; you know you work in a certain place and live on a particular street. As Christians, we know many things to be true about God. According to Scripture (Romans 1), even unbelievers know some things to be true about God as Creator; that is, they would know it if they did not deny the evidence displayed before their eyes each day.

What do we know to be true about Jesus? People in today's society believe many things about Him. Some people think Jesus was a great teacher or even a prophet. Others may think of Him only as a first century Jewish rabbi who was killed by the Romans. Because the Holy Spirit has called us to faith through the preaching of the Gospel, we know much more to be true about Jesus. We know that He is the Son of God, God Himself in human flesh. We know that He is the Savior and that He came to give His life as a sacrifice for the sins of the world. The Spirit also reveals the truth to us about ourselves—we are sinners in need of a Savior. We believe and confess to others the wonderful truth that forgiveness and eternal life are found only in Jesus' name.

When Jesus lived on earth, people had many different opinions about Him. Some thought He was the murdered John the Baptist, returned to life. Others thought He was an Old Testament prophet who had come again to Israel. But God the Father revealed the truth to the disciples. Jesus is the Christ, the promised Messiah of Israel, the Son of the living God!

Central Truth
God's Word leads us to confession of sins and to confession of faith.

Objectives
- Contritely tell what we know is true, confessing that we are sinners.
- Firmly tell what we know is true, confessing our faith in the triune God—Father, Son, and Holy Spirit.
- Boldly declare our trust in Jesus' promise of forgiveness, life, and salvation to all who believe in Him.

Materials
- Web Resources 64a and 64b
- Reproducible 64
- Hymnals and music CDs
- Option: rocks, paint, twine

Bible Prep
Post in advance so students can bookmark the reference before class time.
- Matthew 16:13–18

Devotions

It was the first day at summer camp. To help the kids get to know one another, the camp counselor asked everyone to bring one item that told something unique about who they are. When it came to Willis's turn, he held up a picture. One boy said, "It's a baseball card. So are you a baseball card collector?" Willis replied, "Yes, but there's more to it." "Okay," said one of the girls, "you must like to play baseball, right?" Willis replied, "Yes, but there's more to it. Do you know who this is?" Someone shouted out, "He was last year's MVP in the final World Series Game!" Willis replied, "Yes, but there's more to it." Another person said, "I know, he's announcing now on television for the Saturday afternoon big league games." Willis replied, "Yes, but there's more to it." One of the girls said, "I heard that people are hoping he will be the next governor of our state." Willis replied, "Yes, but there's more to it. I think the best thing about him is that he is my dad!"

If you hold up a picture of Jesus to a group of people today and ask who that is, some might say that He was a great teacher. Some might say He was a prophet who spoke about showing love and kindness to people. Some might say He was a great humanitarian who helped the sick and the poor. These things are not wrong, but they don't go far enough. Jesus is so much more than a teacher or a prophet or a nice guy. What is most important to know is that Jesus is true God who became one of us to take away our sins, to win the victory over death and the devil, and to give us the certainty of eternal life in heaven. If you don't know that, you don't know Jesus! In this Bible narrative, we have an opportunity to listen in on a conversation about who Jesus is. Read Matthew 16:13–18.

Sing "You Are the Way; through You Alone" (*LSB* 526; recorded on *Hymns of the Season, grade 6, Epiphany*). Say or chant Psalm 130.

INTO the Word

Who Do You Say I Am?

Luke 9:2 tells that Jesus had sent out His disciples on a mission trip. Now He asked them (Luke 9:18) what the crowds of people were saying about Him, and the disciples gave their report. As you read through the answers, have students draw a line through the incorrect responses (a, b, c, d). After students write Peter's response (which they have heard in devotions, read in the Bible, and written on the line), have them draw a fish shape around Peter's words, using two simple, curving lines that connect at one end (head), and cross over each other at the other end (tail).

A Confession of Faith

After reading through the paragraphs in this section of the Student Book, point out that the key words mentioned here are *rock* and *truth*. Use a Bible concordance (such as the online resource BibleGateway) to find other related Bible verses to aid their understanding.

Emphasize that the *rock* that Jesus is referring to is not Peter, but rather the truth that Peter spoke as He was led by the Holy Spirit. Consider singing "My Hope Is Built on Nothing Less" (*LSB* 575; recorded on *Hymns of the Month*, grade 5, October).

Option: Provide a smooth, small rock for each student. **What could we paint on this rock to make it a symbol of the faith we have in Jesus?** The most readily recognizable symbol would be a cross. Provide paint, or even better, finger nail polish (which dries to a hard finish) so students can paint a cross on their rocks—a symbol of their faith in Jesus. You may want to take this a step further by connecting the cross to Easter by noting that the rock can also stand for the stone that was rolled away from Jesus' grave to reveal that He had arisen. These two concepts give a very complete expression of our faith. An additional option is to provide twine (or cord or string) that can be wrapped around the stone (many times), with additional lengths of twine at both ends so that this can be tied at the neck and worn as a necklace. **If someone asks you about your unusual necklace, you can give them a confession of your faith!**

Review

This section helps to clarify two different types of confession. It also introduces an Old Testament confession of faith and mentions the Apostles' Creed as a confession of faith. This would be a good time to turn to the Appendix of the Student Book to read together the Apostles' Creed.

LESSON 64

Peter's Confession

Who Do You Say I Am?

Jesus had healed many people, done many amazing miracles, and preached to thousands about the kingdom of God. One day, He asked His disciples this seemingly simple question: "Who do people say that I am?" (Mark 8:27). These are the answers He was given:

a. Some people say John the Baptist.
b. Others say Elijah.
c. Some say Jeremiah.
d. Others say a prophet from of old.
e. Peter said, in Matthew 16:16,
   "You are the Christ, the Son of the living God."

A Confession of Faith

A *confession* is *stating what you know to be true*. Jesus said that Peter's confession was like a solid rock—it was solid truth! Jesus said that Peter didn't figure this out by himself, for this truth was revealed to him by "My Father who is in heaven" (Matthew 16:17). For "no one can say 'Jesus is Lord' except in the Holy Spirit" (1 Corinthians 12:3).

Peter called Jesus *the Christ*, which is not just a name; *Christ* means "the Anointed One," "the Messiah," "the Promised One from God." Peter called Jesus *the Son of God*, declaring Jesus to be more than a man and more than a prophet—He is true God, sent from the Father. Peter said He is a *living* God—not an idol or idea created by man, but the Creator, Provider, Savior, and Comforter of all. Peter's rock solid statement is full of truth. It is a confession of faith.

Some time after this, Pontius Pilate, the Roman governor, asked Jesus, "What is truth?" We know the answer to that question, as Jesus Himself said, "I am the way, and the truth, and the life" (John 14:6).

Review

Covenant Connection

In most worship services, we have two types of confessions. In our *confession of sins*, we state the truth about our condition as sinners, declaring that we have done wrong and are desperately in need of a Savior. In our *confession of faith*, we state the truth about God the Father who sent His Son, Jesus, to be our Savior, and the Holy Spirit who brings us to this faith and keeps us in faith. We join in the Old Testament confession of faith, "Hear, O Israel: The LORD our God, the LORD is one" (Deuteronomy 6:4), Peter's confession of faith, and the words of the Apostles' Creed in declaring the truth we know and confess about the one true God!

134

INTO the lesson

A Symbol of Our Confession

After discussing this section of the Student Book, tell your class about two additional ways to make this symbol. These are shown at the top of Reproducible 64. The first uses your fingers: Extend the thumb and index finger on both hands, while tucking the remaining fingers down. Have the tips of your thumbs touch each other. Cross the index fingers at the middle knuckle. This will make the simple fish symbol from two curving lines.

Another ancient version of this symbol is a circle that is evenly divided into eight sections. On this shape, you can trace over the overlapping letters of the Greek word ΙΧΘΥΣ.

Continue then with the remainder of the reproducible page, which looks at the beliefs of some people and compares these to what we believe based on what we know from Scripture.

A Symbol of Our Confession

Today, the most common symbol of our Christian faith is a cross. But in the early days of the Christian Church, crosses were still too evident as signs of Roman cruelty, torture, and death. So the earliest symbol that was used was a fish. Our word *fish*, is *ichthus* in Greek, the language commonly used in New Testament times. The Greek letters for ichthus are ΙΧΘΥΣ. These letters can be used as an acrostic, with each letter beginning a word in this confession of faith: *Jesus Christ, God's Son, Savior*. Notice how similar this is to the words of Peter's confession.

Greek Letter	Name of the Letter	Initial of the Word . . .
Ι	Iota	Jesus
Χ	Chi	Christ
Θ	Theta	God's
Υ	Ypsilon	Son
Σ	Sigma	Savior

My Confession of Faith

In two or more sentences, say what you believe to be true about God.

_____
_____
_____
_____
_____
_____

Remember

"If you confess with your mouth that Jesus is Lord and believe in your heart that God raised Him from the dead, you will be saved." (Romans 10:9)
"In your hearts honor Christ the Lord as holy, always being prepared to make a defense to anyone who asks you for a reason for the hope that is in you." (1 Peter 3:15)

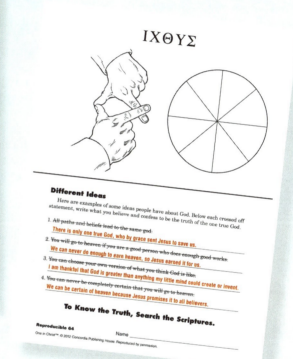

My Confession of Faith

After students have completed the Student Book activity, use Web Resources 64a and 64b to sing two songs that proclaim and confess Jesus as our solid rock in whom we have faith.

You could have students share their confessions of faith with the class. However, consider trying this method instead. During the day, let students key in their personal statements on a computer file, so that you have a collection of all of their thoughts. Each student should begin by keying in their own name and then key in the statement they wrote in the Student Book. (If this is not feasible, have them copy their names and statements on sheets of paper to be handed in.)

This will provide two opportunities for you. First, as you read over the statements, you can evaluate if something is clearly not accurate. Then talk to the student privately about it, giving them the opportunity to make changes. (Later on, you can bring up some of these mistaken concepts in a general way. But do so in a way that does not identify, single out, or embarrass the student.)

Second, you can choose from the phrases the students have given you to make a "Classroom Statement of our Christian Faith." (This will be easier to do if their statements are already on the computer; then you can do a quick cut, paste, and delete.)

Check it Out

When Jesus told His disciples about His coming arrest, death, and resurrection, Peter did not want to hear about it! He did not want Jesus, his Lord and Master, to suffer such terrible treatment and certainly He did not want Jesus to die. Peter said, "This shall never happen to You" (Matthew 16:22). Peter and the other disciples did not yet understand that Jesus had to go to Jerusalem to be crucified. He was the Lamb of God who came to take away the sins of the world (John 1:29). The Old Testament prophets had described how the Messiah would be crucified (Psalm 22), buried in a rich man's grave (Isaiah 53:9), and raised from death (Psalm 118:17–18; Isaiah 53:10–11). The prophet Isaiah said that the Messiah would take our sins on Himself (Isaiah 53:5). When the Spirit of truth was poured out on the disciples on Pentecost, Peter finally understood. In his sermon on the day of Pentecost, it was Peter who said that Jesus' suffering and death happened "according to the definite plan and foreknowledge of God" (Acts 2:23).

Curriculum Connection

We confess our faith assertively, and at times, we must also refuse to compromise what is right assertively. Jesus did so when Peter attempted to turn Him away from the road to the cross. Your students can learn this skill as you use section 6.6.5, Negotiation Skills, found in the sixth grade Health volume of the Concordia Curriculum Guide. There you will find ideas and information to help your students say yes to what is good and no to what is not.

Reaching Every Child

Not every student may feel ready to become involved in role-playing situations about sharing Jesus with others. Let the students know that there are many ways to witness to their faith in Christ and share His love. Some students may feel more comfortable reading stories or letters that they have written about their faith. Artistic students can draw and paint pictures about Jesus. They may wish to design personal symbols representing their salvation, perhaps on a flag, a shield, or a shirt, and then explain those symbols to the class. You might help the class plan a service project for the school, church, or community. Students can explain that they are cleaning, picking up trash, or raking leaves because they love Jesus and want to share His love.

Searching Further

The people who saw Jesus thought He might be John the Baptist or an Old Testament prophet. King Herod was mistaken about Jesus too. When the king heard about Jesus' fame, he said, "This is John the Baptist. He has been raised from the dead; that is why these miraculous powers are at work in Him" (Matthew 14:2). No doubt Herod was worried because he was responsible for John's death. The people who believed that Jesus was Elijah were thinking of the words of the Old Testament prophet Malachi, "Behold, I will send you Elijah the prophet before the great and awesome day of the Lord comes" (Malachi 4:5). They knew that Elijah was supposed to return before the Messiah came. We know from the words of Jesus that it was John the Baptist who fulfilled this prophecy (Matthew 17:10–13).

Faith in Action

During this lesson, your students have discussed ways to answer questions about Jesus. Look for additional opportunities for "witnessing practice." Students might prepare beaded or braided bracelets to use in telling the story, with different color beads or threads representing the life of Jesus (yellow for the star at His birth; green for His earthly ministry and miracles; red for His suffering and death; clear or gold for His resurrection; and blue for heaven where He reigns). The bracelets could be used as gifts for friends or relatives who may not know Jesus as their Savior.

Technology

As Christians, we know that Jesus is the way, the truth, and the life. He said, "No one comes to the Father except through Me" (John 14:6). We know that "there is salvation in no one else, for there is no other name under heaven given among men by which we must be saved" (Acts 4:12). Have students work individually or in groups to research other religions such as Judaism, Islam, Buddhism, and Hinduism. How is salvation found in those religions? What do other religions teach about sin and forgiveness?

Most world religions acknowledge that Jesus lived on earth, but what do they teach about Him? Ask the students to present their research to the class. What questions might people of other religions ask about Jesus? How would you answer?

UNIT 6—THE MINISTRY OF JESUS

LESSON 65

Stormy Seas
Matthew 8:23–27; 14:22–33

Background

In the previous lesson, Jesus asked the disciples what other people were saying about Him. Some people (including the guilty King Herod) thought Jesus was the murdered John the Baptist returned from the dead. Others thought that Jesus was Elijah or another Old Testament prophet. None of these theories was correct. Jesus then asked His disciples, "But who do you say that I am?" God the Father revealed the truth to Simon Peter and he answered, "You are the Christ, the Son of the living God" (Matthew 16:16). Jesus was not simply a good rabbi, a prophet, or a kind man! Jesus was, and is, the Messiah of Israel, God in human flesh. He is true God and true man, the God who created all things walking the earth as a man.

Today's Bible narrative illustrates more than Jesus' compassion for protecting the lives of the disciples. As you look at their response in the two situations, you can see that they are growing in faith. That is the great miracle—that God condescends to save us through the redeeming power of Jesus and to bring us to faith and strengthen us through the Holy Spirit.

In this lesson, we will also review several Bible narratives, looking at the big picture of how Jesus uses His divine power to help us. With the Son of God, in whom we "find grace to help in time of need" (Hebrews 4:16), we can proclaim what the world needs to hear: the Good News of salvation in Jesus Christ.

Central Truth

Jesus has power over all things because He is true God and Creator and Preserver of all things.

Objectives

- Repent when we have doubts about God's power, love, or care for us.
- Trust that God always does what is best for us in the time and way He knows is best.
- Praise God that He blesses us in big ways and also in small ways, as we glorify His name.

Materials

- Web Resources 65a, 65b, 65c
- Reproducible 65a and 65b
- Hymnals and music CDs

Bible Prep

Post in advance so students can bookmark the references before class time.
- Matthew 8:23–27; 14:22–33
- Psalm 107:23–29

Devotions

Kelly's school was holding fund-raisers to help a boy in third grade. Brad had cancer and everyone in the school was trying to raise money to help his family. Kelly organized a bake sale for her brother's baseball game. She found people who volunteered to bring cookies to sell. Kelly and her mother baked many cookies for the sale, such as peanut butter, sugar, and Kelly's favorite, chocolate chip. On the day of the sale, Kelly and her two friends Liz and Ann went to the park early to set up a table, signs, and a cash box. Then things started to go wrong. A few people brought their baked goods, but a lot of volunteers never arrived with the items they promised. The girls had hardly anything to sell. A few people at the game came over to the table, but most wandered away without buying anything. How would they raise any money for Brad like this? Kelly prayed silently, "Jesus, help our sale do better so we can help Brad!" As the three girls looked at their nearly empty cash box and watched the game, Kelly heard her name. "Kelly, I'm so sorry. I almost forgot the sale! I've brought the cookies you asked me to bake," said Mrs. Anderson. Three more of Kelly's volunteers came by to drop off cupcakes and brownies. Mrs. Kim brought a big container of ice cold lemonade and plastic cups. "I thought people might buy more cookies if they had something cold to drink!" she said. The people watching the game saw all the activity by the sale table and started coming over. They bought handfuls of cookies and big cups of lemonade. Some people even donated extra money when they read the sign about Brad and his family. "We did better than I hoped," thought Kelly. "Jesus, thank You for helping us!" This story is an example of how God can bless us in small ways or big ways. It also reminds us that God can use us to be a blessing to other people. The volunteers who came late were God's answer to a prayer, and Kelly, Liz, and Ann were a blessing to Brad's family. Let's recognize God's action in our lives and pray that He may use us to bless someone else.

Sing "Beautiful Savior" (*LSB* 537; recorded on *Hymns of the Month, grade 4, September*).

INTO the Word

Two Storms

Read aloud the two Bible accounts from Matthew. Then, use the chart to analyze the two events, comparing similarities and differences of the two events. Emphasize the difference in the response of the disciples. It is evident that they are growing in faith. After the first event, they wonder who this man is, and after the second event, they proclaim Jesus as true God. That is the most significant part of these stories. This also reminds us of God's actions in our lives. **Jesus blesses us and cares for us because He has compassion on us and loves us. And above all, Jesus works in our lives to bring us to faith, to grow and strengthen that faith, and to keep us in faith.** He works in many ways through the Holy Spirit, working through the Means of Grace. Jesus said, "I came that they may have life and have it abundantly" (John 10:10). Praise God for His abundant blessings!

Continue now with Web Resource 65a, "I'm in the Same Boat with Jesus," which is a song based on these events in Matthew. (You might want to discuss the idiom *being in the same boat*, which means that you share the same problem.) The first time, turn off the audio and have students read the words with you. Then listen to the audio recording. Then play it again with students singing along. Follow this by singing "Our Hero," which is on Web Resource 65b. This would be a good time to read aloud together the Bible verses mentioned in the Covenant Connection (Psalm 107:23–29).

LESSON 65
Stormy Seas

Matthew 8:23–27 and Matthew 14:22–33

Two Storms

	Matthew 8	Matthew 14
Where is Jesus?	v. 23 **In the boat**	vv. 22–23 **On a mountain**
Surprisingly, Jesus . . .	v. 24 **was asleep.**	v. 25 **walked on water.**
Amazingly, Jesus . . .	v. 26 **stopped the storm.**	v. 32 **stopped the storm.**
The disciples' response:	v. 27 **What sort of man is this?**	v. 33 **Truly you are the Son of God.**

Review

Covenant Connection

Psalm 107:23–29 foreshadows the events in this lesson's Bible story. In Matthew 8 and 14, Jesus fulfills the prophecies of the psalm. Reading these verses in Psalm 107 is like reading the New Testament accounts, especially as the people's courage melts away and they cry out for help. The strongest connection though is in Psalm 107:29, which says, "He made the storm be still, and the waves of the sea were hushed." God's Holy Word again shows us God's holy plan through Christ Jesus, our Savior!

Types of Miracles

Jesus' miracles proved that He truly is the Son of God. However, His main purpose in doing them was not for proof but out of compassion. Jesus also shows His compassion to us today in many ways. Look at this review of some of Jesus' miracles, which we are studying. It is interesting to consider His wonders by categorizing them into four main types. Then, respond on the blank lines, writing how Jesus works to supply those same needs in your life today.

1. **Daily Needs.** (Recall Jesus feeding 5,000 people. Respond.) _____
_____
_____
_____.

2. **Protection.** (Recall Jesus stilling the storm. Respond.) _____
_____
_____
_____.

3. **Health.** (Recall Jesus healing the man who was paralyzed. Respond.) _____
_____
_____
_____.

4. **Life.** (Look ahead to the raising of Lazarus. Respond.) _____
_____
_____
_____.

And the greatest miracle of life is the eternal life we have through Jesus' victory. By His death on the cross and resurrection at Easter, He has conquered sin, death, and the devil. And miracle of miracles, He gives His victory to us— giving us forgiveness, life, and salvation!

Remember

"These are written so that you may believe that Jesus is the Christ, the Son of God, and that by believing you may have life in His name." (John 20:31)

INTO our lives

Types of Miracles

This section is just one of the ways to analyze Jesus' miracles. It is a very concrete approach that should be helpful for young students. First, allow time for students to work on this individually or in pairs. Point out that though God can work miracles in our lives, He often blesses us in ordinary and even special ways that we might not even recognize. Have them list ways that God helps us today with our daily needs, protection, health, and life, emphasizing that there are many possibilities.

Take time for students to share their answers. After each of the four sections, ask if there are any volunteers who will lead the class in prayer. (You may want to point out that sometimes we read prayers, sometimes we write prayers, but throughout our lives, we will find that most of the time our prayers come straight from the heart and out of our mouth!) Sing together the song on Web Resource 65c.

Reproducible Activity

Reproducibles 65a and 65b review the portion of the lesson on the types of Jesus' miracles. They consist of poem verses about the Bible stories reviewed and also about God's action in our lives today. Students are to place each verse on a separate sheet of paper and illustrate the verse in order to make a book titled "Miracles of Jesus." Give students several choices on how to approach this project. It can be done individually or by pairs or in groups. The verses can be cut apart and taped to each page or they can be rewritten. The illustrations can be drawings depicting the verse (which might be from Bible times or from modern times). Another choice could be that students design a symbol to represent what is happening in each verse. Or they could create a collage of pictures cut from magazines, Sunday School leaflets, or other sources. Another possibility, which would require group work, is to take photos of a staging of each verse—these could be photos of dioramas students make or this could be photos of tableaux, which would be still shots of students acting out a scene. Another possibility, again probably requiring group work, would be to create an online book, with the verses keyed in and possibly a video instead of an illustration for each page. Discuss whom these books may be shared with.

Working in Groups

Ask your students to design bookmarks or door hangers as gifts to members of your congregation or for residents in a local nursing home. Decorate the gifts with Bible verses that speak of God's promises to help His people. Illustrations might include the cross which is certainly a symbol of God's love, or a rainbow, a design often used as a reminder that God keeps His promises. Use heavy cardstock for the bookmarks or door hangers and laminate the finished designs. Arrange for students to hand out the finished designs to church members on a Sunday morning or plan a trip to the nursing home to deliver their gifts (contact the nursing home to see if students might include other small items, such as hand lotion, soap or socks, with their gifts).

DIGGING DEEPER

Say, **When our plans are going well or if there are no serious problems in our lives, we don't worry so much. At such times, we feel very sure that God cares for us. But when trouble comes, big problems or small problems, we start to worry and feel frightened. We often experience fear and doubt, just as Kelly did, in the devotion, when her bake sale was not going well. We are not sure what will happen next. That is when we may start to doubt that God really cares for us. "Where is God?" we ask. "Why doesn't He do something? He promised to help!" Can you describe some times in your life when you felt worried and doubted God's care?** Let the students discuss difficult times when they have had doubts. If your students do not feel comfortable discussing personal stories of fear and worry, ask them to suggest possible reasons for doubting God's love and care—sickness, loneliness, worry about grades, family problems, or friendship worries. **God's help does not always come to us in the way we think it might. He may not help us at the time we think is right, but His help will come at the right time, in His time. Sometimes, we may think that God does not answer our prayers at all. Read Romans 8:28. What does God promise?** (He promises that all things work together for good for those who love Him.) **God answers our prayers in His time and for His glory.**

We don't ever have to worry about God's love for us. He loves us and He will help us but His timing is not the same as ours. We might think He is not doing anything, but He acts when the time is right. When the time was right, God did the most wonderful thing for us that He could ever do. God sent His Son to die on the cross so our sins can be forgiven. Jesus rose from the dead and we know that sin and death can never separate us from God. If God took care of us and defeated the greatest trouble of all—sin and death—He can help us with all of the other problems in our lives too. Romans 8:31–32 says, "If God is for us, who can be against us? He who did not spare His own Son but gave Him up for us all, how will He not also with Him graciously give us all things?" When you are tempted to doubt God's love and help, remember what He has already done for you. Remember that Jesus died on the cross and rose from the dead. Your sins are forgiven and you have the gift of eternal life! God can help you in ways you cannot imagine.

HANDS TO SERVE

Kelly, the girl in this lesson's devotion, organized a bake sale to help a family in need. Talk to your pastor and to other teachers to find out if there are families in the congregation, school, or local community that may need financial assistance during difficult times. Help your class organize bake sales, garage sales, car washes, or other events to raise money for those in need. Ask parents, church members, or teens in your church's youth group to help. Other service projects might include collecting canned food for a local food pantry or clothes and toys for a homeless shelter. Your students can share God's love and care as they work together to serve others in the name of Christ.

Teacher Tips

God blesses us in big and small ways. We have the great blessings of forgiveness and eternal life in the name of Jesus, our Savior. We have the blessings of church, school, home, family, and friends. Decorate a classroom bulletin board with raindrop shapes on which students write about blessings God showers or pours on them. Blessings might include the names of family members and friends, things in God's creation, or life events and times of trouble in which students or family members experienced God's help.

UNIT 6—THE MINISTRY OF JESUS

LESSON 66

The Parable of a Foolish Rich Man
LUKE 12:15–34

Background

Today's text is a wonderful springboard for a discussion on worldly desires! Many sixth graders are entering the stage where they look to their peers to define their worldly status. They are looking at brands of clothing and shoes, amounts of allowances, sizes of houses, numbers and types of family cars, and so forth, and starting to judge people accordingly. They often collaborate on what television shows are watched, trips that have been taken, and people they have "hung out with" and define one another's worth by peer-made standards. This lesson provides a timely opportunity to make students aware of the dangers of worldliness. In your studies, point students to the "one thing needful!" Instill in them the amazing impact of Jesus, their greatest treasure! While it is far more important to desire heavenly treasures than earthly treasures, God, in His mercy, provides for both our physical and spiritual needs in spite of our weaknesses. With your students, praise Him for being such an amazing God! Also discuss the concept of tithing. Emphasize that tithing is about the whole, the one hundred percent! It is not just about money, but it is about their time and talents (as well as their treasures) too!

Central Truth

While there are many things people may want in life, there is only one thing that lasts forever—the grace of God who lovingly sent Jesus to obtain forgiveness, life, and salvation for all who believe.

Objectives

- Confess that too often we get caught up in our desire for possessions, money, fame, power, and other worldly acquisitions.
- Rely on God's transforming power, working in us through the Means of Grace, to set our eyes on Jesus, following Him as our priority in all things.
- Increase in discipleship as we are enabled by the power of the Holy Spirit.

Materials

- Web Resource 66a
- Reproducible 66
- Hymnals and music CDs

Bible Prep

Post in advance so students can bookmark the references before class time.
- Luke 12:15–34
- Luke 10:38–42
- 2 Timothy 1:2

Devotions

"Mom, why does our house have to be so small?" Lexi shoved her suitcase into her crowded closet and shouted, "Don't even think about falling out, you suitcase!"

"Well, let me know if talking to your suitcase helps!" Lexi's mom chuckled.

"I just wish our house wasn't so small. Everybody else I know has a big house with big closets," Lexi reasoned.

"I see. Let me guess, at your sleepover last night you went and measured Abby's closets."

"Mom! No! I didn't have to measure them; I can just tell they're a lot bigger!" Lexi tried to keep from smiling.

"And how do bigger closets help Abby's life?" Lexi's mom asked intently.

"Well, she doesn't have to shove her suitcase anywhere."

"Mmm. Okay, what else?" asked her mom again.

"And, and, well she can keep more clothes in her room!"

"Okay. What else?" her mom persisted.

"What do you mean?" Lexi was getting impatient now.

"I mean, does having a bigger house and bigger closet make her closer to God? Does it keep her faithful? Will that closet last forever?" It was clear that Lexi's mom wanted her to think.

"Well, I guess . . . no." Lexi sighed as she got on her knees and started digging around in her closet. "I just wish I could find some buried treasure in here."

"Okay. Maybe someday we'll be blessed with a bigger house, but for now, let's focus on the treasures we do have."

"What treasures?" Lexi looked puzzled.

"The ones we have in the Lord; the treasures of forgiveness and eternal life through Jesus," her mom answered.

"I hate to admit it, Mom, but you're right," Lexi smiled. "If I had a bigger closet, I'd probably just have a bigger mess."

"Now, let's work together to clean your closet so you don't try to talk us into moving the next time you put your suitcase away!"

"Okay," said Lexi, "but be careful you don't start an avalanche in there!"

Lexi's mother ducked into the closet and teased, "I'm going in! And if I'm not back in ten minutes, call your father!" They both laughed and got to work.

Read together stanzas 1, 3, and 6 of "Jesus, Priceless Treasure" (*LSB* 743). Then sing "Come to Calvary's Holy Mountain" (*LSB* 435; recorded on *Hymns of the Season, grade 6, Lent*).

INTO the lesson

A Short Survey

Where we spend much of our time and money is often an indication of what is important to us. The two questions in the survey are meant to encourage students to begin thinking about what they truly value. (For example, if you have an extra hour after school and can choose between going outdoors to practice basketball or sitting on the couch to play a video game or playing a silly game to make your baby brother laugh, your choice will tell something about you and what is important to you.)

Lost Treasures

Read Luke 12:15–21 and note that the man in the picture and the parable Jesus told valued his money and his possessions. When he died suddenly, none of these things could be of value to him. (See James 1:11, which is almost a summary statement of the parable.)

In your discussion of the questions in the Student Book, be very real with the students. (They know what the answers "should" be; encourage them to think carefully and be honest about how they really feel.) Emphasize that we all have things we want; wanting is not always wrong. It is wrong, though, when it becomes the most important thing in our lives or if we break God's Commandments in order to get or keep those things we want. (This is serious—God gave both the Ninth and Tenth Commandments about coveting, which is wanting what is not ours and scheming to get it in an unethical way.)

The amazing thing is—if God's way is our priority, He blesses us with things we need and want anyway. It might not be exactly what we had in mind, but it will be a blessing because God knows what is best for us and the right time to give it to us. Sing together "Seek Ye First" (*AGPS* 207; recorded on *JPS*), relating this song to Luke 12:31. Also sing "Have No Fear, Little Flock" (*LSB* 735; recorded on *Hymns of the Month, grade 3, December*), relating it to Luke 12:32.

To further explore that "one thing that is most needed," turn back a few chapters in your Bibles to Luke 10:38–42. Ask, **What one thing is necessary? (God's Word of salvation through Jesus) Why is this so necessary? (It is our only hope; it lasts forever; there is no other way to eternal life.)**

Lasting Treasures

By now, many of your students will know the "expected" answers to give when you talk about the riches of blessings that God gives to us. This activity provides the opportunity to hear how Scripture talks about these rich treasures. If you have access to the One in Christ Portal, use Web Resource 66a at this time. This resource motivates students to listen carefully to the Bible passages that are recorded and read.

If you do not use the Portal, you can read the following verses, having students listen carefully to what you say to identify the key words: Ephesians 1:7; Colossians 3:16; Philippians 4:19; Titus 3:5–6; James 2:5; Colossians 1:27; Ephesians 1:17–18; and Ephesians 2:4–5.

Have students look up 2 Timothy 1:2 and read it aloud together because it is like a summary statement that lists off many of the immeasurable riches we have received from the Lord.

Giving It Away

Discuss the two situations presented in this section, which show selfishness and ingratitude. Discuss the implications of this in our own lives as we consider that everything we have is a blessing from God. Do we claim these blessings as "what's mine is mine" or do we share with others, motivated by the kindness and compassion that God is working in our hearts?

The passage from 2 Corinthians 9:7 is mentioned ("God loves a cheerful giver"). Point out that God knows our hearts and intentions. He does not want us to give because we have to or to impress someone. The first part of this verse says, "Each one must give as he has decided in his heart, not reluctantly or under compulsion" and an earlier verse says that it should be a "willing gift, not as an exaction [forced,

Lasting Treasures

The lasting treasures of the kingdom of God are the "immeasurable riches" He offers us through Jesus Christ (Ephesians 2:7). What kind of riches are we talking about? Listen as several Bible verses are read to you and write down the types of riches that are mentioned.

Grace	Faith
The word of Christ	(The hope of) glory
All you need	(A glorious) inheritance
(Blessings of the) Holy Spirit	Mercy

What makes you rich? Who you are, not what you have.
And who are you? A child of God!

Giving It Away

At the park, Sheila's grandmother bought her a two-dip ice cream cone with sprinkles. Grandma asked for a small taste. Six-year-old Sheila stubbornly shouted, "No! This is mine. You get your own." Comments? _____

Fourteen-year-old Robert was playing with the new video game his parents had given him. His dad came in the room and asked if he could try it out too. "Nope," said Robert. "This is mine and I don't want anyone else messing up the controls or the program." Comments? _____

- God blesses us in so many ways. Do we ever, like Sheila, selfishly think, what's mine is mine? Do we become stingy, like Robert, about sharing these blessings? Since our blessings are from God, are we adding unthankfulness to this list of wrongs?
- God doesn't ask much for Himself (wanting just our faith-filled hearts). God does ask that we share with the Church and with those in need. So what are your priorities? In 2 Corinthians 9:7, we are told "God loves a cheerful giver." (This is not just talking about money, either.)
- Here's an amazing thought from Luke 6:38. It says that what we give away is not really gone, because God returns a like measure (or similar portion) of what we give away. Not only that—His measure of blessings to us is "running over." You just can't outdo God when it comes to kindness, serving, and compassion!

Remember

"For where your treasure is, there will your heart be also." (Luke 12:34)
"My God will supply every need of yours according to His riches in glory in Christ Jesus." (Philippians 4:19)

139

---

required]." These Scripture verses are telling us that the offerings we give to church and the things we share with others are also matters of heart and attitude.

Continue examining what we give away by using Reproducible 66. Point out that the title could have said "My Offerings" or "My Donations." Why is "My Gifts to God and Others" a better title? (It helps focus on the purpose—to show loving kindness to God and other people. It also implies that this sharing involves more than money.)

Have students write 10 percent in the first section of the chart. Then look to the right side of the chart and have students indicate 20 percent for saving, which many consider a good habit to develop in consideration of your own future needs. Ask, **How much does this leave for you to spend?** (A whopping 70 percent) Add, **Keep in mind that 100 percent of what we have actually belongs to God. Are you using what He has given you according to His will and for His glory?**

Be sure that the students understand that the first section is a guideline. Recall that 2 Corinthians 9 said that our gifts should not be forced or required; they should be willing. However, it is good to evaluate the guideline of a tithe, begun in Old Testament times. Point out that the chart seems to indicate even divisions between the three categories, which would be fine, but is not what is expected. Even divisions would be 33 percent for each category. A tithe is only asking to give away 10 percent. Point out that 10 percent is actually a smaller amount than the tip many people give a server in a restaurant. And it certainly is less than the amount that the government takes for taxes.

The remainder of the reproducible page explores some of the gifts we can share with others—gifts of time, talents, and treasures. Actually, start at the bottom of the list and point out, **The treasures that we share can be either money or possessions. Write down examples of treasures you could share with others, and include who these "others" might be.** Discuss some of the possibilities students thought of, perhaps including things like food and clothing collections for the poor.

Continue working backward and consider talents that the students might have that they could share with others. Point out that at first, when we think of talents, we might think of singing or drawing or pitching a baseball. These can be special talents, but this category includes much more. Your talents are all sorts of things that you do well, such as being friendly, telling good jokes, being able to explain new computer programs, and much more. What is important is using what you can do to help others.

Finally, look at the gift of time. In our busy, hurried lives today, this is often the gift we are least willing to give up. Between a busy schedule and the time we want to spend with the latest communication and digital technology, we too often don't want to take time for someone else. Yet this is often what other people need most. Discuss possibilities such as taking time to help mom do the dishes (which may also give you some time to talk together); taking time to visit an elderly grandmother who is lonely and feels as if no one cares .

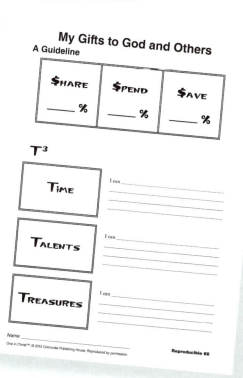

283

Lesson Support

Curriculum Connection

The foolish rich man thought he was well-off, not realizing that in God's eyes he was desperately poor, spiritually sick, and miserable. It is important for your students to learn to assess their lives accurately, including the area of health. Consider using section 6.3.7, Health Assessment, with your class. It appears in the sixth grade Health volume of the Concordia Curriculum Guide.

Hands to Serve

Christians who have lived a long life and who are even possibly near the end of their lives often realize what life's true treasures really are! Coordinate a field trip for students to visit and volunteer at a Christian nursing home. Encourage students to interview the residents and ask them about the treasures in their lives. Additionally, have the students ask them about the difference between worldly and heavenly treasures, and be sure they record their answers to share with the class when they return from the field trip. Upon returning, discuss the results of their interviews and assign students to each write a paragraph or two about what they learned. Post the writings in the hallway so others may read!

Faith in Action

Allow students to demonstrate that even imperfect people can share the treasure of the Gospel by having them brainstorm creative ways to share the Good News of Christ Jesus. Perhaps they could each make a place mat for one or more of the dinners held before or after a Lenten service. Students could chose a part of the passion story and illustrate it, including a Bible reference. They could also share their favorite Bible story and illustrate it, or they could use fancy handwriting and decoratively write their favorite Bible verse to share with someone. In addition to sharing God's Word with others outside the classroom, set up a classroom mailbox system and allow students to send Bible passages to each other. Encourage students to try to send verses to a variety of students so that *all* students receive the Good News of Jesus and no one feels left out! Look at the hymn "Take My Life and Let It Be" (*LSB* 783; recorded on *Hymns of the Month, grade 6, January*) and determine if a stanza is talking about our time, talents, or treasures. (For example, stanza 1 is talking about our time; stanzas 2 and 3 are talking about the things we do, so that would be our talents; and the first portion of stanza 4 is talking about our treasures.) Sing the song together.

Bringing it home

Assign students to bring two identical worksheets home. One worksheet should be completed by a parent or guardian and the other worksheet should be completed by the student. The worksheet should be simple and ask each person four basic questions: What are some physical blessings you have experienced in the past and at the present time? What are some spiritual blessings you have experienced in the past and at the present time? Are there any blessings you have experienced that you did not realize were blessings at first but later realized they were? What is your greatest blessing? Encourage students to share their answers with their family member and then bring them back for sharing with the class.

Searching Further

Just how much do birds have to work to get their food and to build their nests? How long does it take for a flock of birds to fly south in the winter, and what would happen if they didn't fly south? What percentage of birds actually survive the entire round-trip migration? How long does it take for grass to grow? What are the factors that determine whether grass lives or dies? How can drought-ridden grass be rejuvenated? What do lilies and other flowers need to thrive? What is the best type of plant food? What causes some people to be allergic to grass or flowers? Research these and other questions students may have regarding birds, grass, and flowers such as the lilies mentioned in today's Scripture lesson, and then compare God's love for nature with the love He has for you—His most precious creation! Throughout your studies, emphasize the fact that God's love for nature is far less than the love He lavishes upon His children. We are the crown of His creation, and if He loves nature enough to take care of it, how much more does He love us! What a wonderful God we have!

UNIT 6—THE MINISTRY OF JESUS   LESSON 67

Jesus Raises Lazarus from the Dead
JOHN 11:1–54

Background

Jesus raised Lazarus for the glory of God (John 11:4b), to help His disciples believe (John 11:14), and to prove His absolute power over life and death. While we, even as Christians, often have difficulty accepting God's allowance of death in our world, knowing and believing in Jesus' power over death gives us the hope of an eternal resurrection. While the Pharisees believed and preached of "the resurrection on the last day," the Sadducees did not believe or preach of such a hope. Today, many people still do not believe in the resurrection! Stir up a sense of urgency in your students to pray for and to reach out to those who need to hear about and be assured of the hope we have in the resurrection.

Today's text mentions that after this miracle, the Pharisees were afraid people would start following Jesus on a regular basis. It is then that Caiaphas, the high priest, said that it is better for Jesus to be put to death so that He doesn't cause the Romans to come and destroy their land and their life. Little did Caiaphas know that he was also uttering the very words of God and prophesying about Jesus' upcoming death and resurrection. The story of Lazarus being raised from the dead is an important prelude to the events that lead to Jesus' crucifixion and resurrection, our redemption and hope in life everlasting!

Central Truth

As true God, Jesus has power over life and death.

Objectives

- Acknowledge that the consequence of our sins is physical and spiritual death.
- Rejoice that Christ has won the victory over death and gives that victory to us.
- Trust with certainty that we will go to heaven because of what Christ has done for us, and we will live there with Him eternally, just as God planned according to His good and gracious will.

Materials

- Reproducible 67
- Web Resource 67a
- Hymnals and music CDs
- Yellow highlighters

Bible Prep

Post in advance so students can bookmark the references before class time.
- 1 Corinthians 15:54–57
- John 11:1–54
- Jeremiah 29:11
- Romans 8:28
- Revelation 21:3–5

Devotions

"So, how long do you think I have to live?" Grandpa asked, his hand holding Grandma's.

"It will all depend on how you respond to the treatment," Dr. Grunewald picked up his clipboard and asked if they had any more questions. Grandma and Grandpa shook their heads. "Okay, I'll see you back in my office in two weeks."

"Thank you, doctor." Grandpa's voice wobbled. Looking at Grandma, he tried to sound comforting, "Well, I think it's what we expected to hear, isn't it?"

"Yes. I think so. But it sounds so terrible when you actually hear the words you were terrified to hear!" Grandma began to cry now.

"Terrified? What's terrifying about dying when you know you're going to heaven?" Grandpa again tried to sound assuring.

"What will I do without you?" Grandma tried to wipe her tears.

"Well, that's what you have the girls for and all of your Bible study friends. Besides, I'm not dead yet!" Grandpa teased. "I'm going to fight this!"

"But what if you can't win?" Grandma sniffled.

"Win or lose on this earth, because Jesus has already won the battle for me, I win no matter what!" Grandpa put his arm around Grandma.

"You always have such a way with words!" Grandma smiled.

"One day at a time is all we can do," Grandpa replied.

"As I said, you have a way with words!" Grandma chuckled.

"Now, let's go see if our little grandchild is crawling yet!" Grandpa took Grandma by the hand as they walked toward their car.

Pray together, **Lord, You have all power over life and death! Thank You for sending Your Son, Jesus, to fulfill all of Your promises through His death and resurrection! May we always radiate joy in the hope of the resurrection on the Last Day. In peace we pray to You, O Lord! Amen.** Read together 1 Corinthians 15:54–57 and then sing together the first few stanzas of "I Know That My Redeemer Lives" (*LSB* 461; recorded on *Hymns of the Season, grade 4, Easter*). Point out that this hymn is based on today's Bible words to remember from the Old Testament in Job 19:25–27. (The Old Testament—the New Testament—it all ties together in Christ Jesus!)

INTO the Word

The Plot

Read together John 11:38–44. Look at the outline in the Student Book. Point out that the verses just read are at the center of the Bible narrative, but a lot more is going on here. The next sections of the lesson look at the other portions of John 11 and the subplots that were going on in connection with the raising of Lazarus.

A Subplot—the "Why" Question

Dealing with death has always been difficult and continues to be so today. Even Jesus cried at the death of Lazarus (John 11:35), though He knew that He would soon raise Lazarus from the dead. So why did Jesus cry if He knew this? Why do Christians cry when another Christian dies, even though they know that on the Last Day Jesus will raise all believers to new life—life eternal in heaven? (Death is still sad because we feel sorrow for the surviving family and friends; we feel sad because we will miss the person who is gone; the changes caused by someone's death can often bring difficult circumstances that are hard to face.)

So the "why" question always pops up. **We know death is a consequence of living in a sin-filled world. Death does remove a person from the tragedies and problems of this life. However, death is not an end point because God promises that our souls are taken directly to heaven by the angels, and our bodies will have a resurrection on the Last Day, and with body and soul reunited, we will live forever in heaven. These are truths, but we still ask why and why now and why in this way. The only real answer to this is: trust God. Trust God's timing, trust God's wisdom, trust God's plans. This is not easy, but it is our only hope and answer.**

Lesson 67
Jesus Raises Lazarus from the Dead

The Plot

1. Lazarus died and was buried in a tomb.
2. Jesus said, "Lazarus, come out."
3. Lazarus came alive again.
   End of story?
   I don't think so!

A Subplot— The "Why" Question

Here is an interesting twist in this story. At the beginning of the Scripture narrative, Jesus was told that his good friend Lazarus was seriously ill. John 11:6 says, "So, when He heard that Lazarus was ill, He stayed two days longer in the place where He was." Why didn't Jesus rush to heal His friend? Why did He wait around for a couple days before going to help? Why did Jesus let His friend die? Why? Why? Why? Other people were asking the same questions, as verse 37 states, "Some of them said, 'Could not He who opened the eyes of the blind man also have kept this man from dying?'"

Even today, people ask these same questions. When a young child dies, people ask, "Why did this happen to someone so young?" When a family is killed in an auto accident, people ask, "Why did God let this happen?" If a doctor gives someone a tragic medical report, the person might ask, "Why is this happening to me?"

The answer to the why question is that God knows, even though we may not understand till later or maybe never. It is never an easy question, but we can trust that God can bring blessings to us even in the middle of a difficult situation. "Trust God" is the answer to the why question. Read Jeremiah 29:11 and Romans 8:28. Keep these words in your memory and in your heart so they will be ready to comfort and strengthen you when you need them. Perhaps the best answer to the why question is "Don't ask the question! Trust God."

Jesus did have a plan. What was the reason for Lazarus's death? See verse 4.
that Jesus could give him life—for the glory of God

Review

Covenant Connection

The story of Jesus raising Lazarus from the dead has a direct connection to the messianic prophecy in Isaiah 25:8–9. "He will swallow up death forever; and the Lord GOD will wipe away tears from all faces, and the reproach of His people He will take away from all the earth, for the LORD has spoken. It will be said on that day, 'Behold, this is our God; we have waited for Him, that He might save us. This is the LORD; we have waited for Him; let us be glad and rejoice in His salvation.'"

140

Review

After reading the Covenant Connection in the Student Book, read the related, yet-to-be-fulfilled, New Testament prophecy in Revelation 21:3–5. We can be certain that this prophecy will be fulfilled because of the faithfulness of God in the many promises He has already fulfilled through Jesus. **We can be certain we will go to heaven because that promise relies not on what we do or who we are, but it relies on all that Jesus has done for us in His death and resurrection!**

A Subplot—Preparation

The raising of Lazarus is a foreshadowing of events to happen in just a few days. Jesus has divine power over life and death and raises Lazarus, foreshadowing Jesus' coming death that He willingly approaches and foreshadows His power as true God over His own return to life at Easter.

The raising of Lazarus was not the first time Jesus had raised someone from the dead. (He raised a young man to new life in the city of Nain [Luke 7] and He raised Jairus's twelve-year-old daughter from the dead [Luke 8]). However, the timing of this miracle is significant as it not only prepares the

A Subplot—Preparation

When Jesus traveled to Bethany to accomplish this miracle, He knew that it would soon be time for Him to suffer and die. He had His eyes on Jerusalem and Calvary. His disciples warned Him about the danger of going to Judea at this time. Read John 11:7–8. But Jesus knew that it was necessary for Him to accomplish all things for our salvation.

Jesus also knew that the coming days would be difficult for His followers. The raising of Lazarus from the dead would give them the assurance of His divine power and the hope of the resurrection. This may not have been understood by the disciples yet, but one day they would look back at this and recognize how Jesus was preparing them so that they could spread the Gospel message of the forgiveness and life we receive freely from Jesus.

This was also a time of preparation for Jesus' enemies. Why did the priests and Pharisees want to get rid of Jesus? **They did not like it that Jesus had confronted them with their own sins; they did not like it that people were following Jesus instead of listening to them; they thought killing Him was the only way to stop Him.**

Jesus' enemies were so anxious to stop Him and to stop people from talking about His message, they even considered killing Lazarus too. Read John 11:45–57 and 12:9–11.

A Subplot—Martha Was Listening

There are a lot of things going on in this Bible narrative, but the most important part is the conversation between Jesus and Martha. At an earlier visit, Martha had been so busy with her work that she failed to listen to Jesus; but she was listening now and spoke boldly of her faith in the Lord. Highlight key phrases in this conversation that show this story is about life, not death.

> Martha said to Jesus, "Lord, if You had been here, my brother would not have died. But even now I know that whatever You ask from God, God will give You." Jesus said to her, "Your brother will rise again." Martha said to Him, "I know that he will rise again in the resurrection on the last day." Jesus said to her, "I am the resurrection and the life. Whoever believes in Me, though he die, yet shall he live, and everyone who lives and believes in Me shall never die. Do you believe this?" She said to Him, "Yes, Lord; I believe that You are the Christ, the Son of God, who is coming into the world." (John 11:21–27)

Remember

> "I know that my Redeemer lives, and at the last He will stand upon the earth. And after my skin has been thus destroyed, yet in my flesh I shall see God, whom I shall see for myself, and my eyes shall behold, and not another." (Job 19:25–27)

Lazarus, Come Out! (Readers Theater)

Match the words spoken (indicated with letters) to the name of the speaker (with numbers). Then assign ten volunteers speaking in order from 1 to 10, saying the name of the character and then reading the appropriate quotation.

1. Messenger — b
2. Jesus (response) — i
3. Disciple — f
4. Thomas — c
5. Mary — a
6. Martha — d
7. Mourner — h
8. Jesus (command) — j
9. Pharisees — g
10. Caiaphas — e

a. "Lord, if You had been here, my brother would not have died."
b. "Lord, he whom You love is ill."
c. "Let us also go, that we may die with Him."
d. "I believe that You are the Christ, the Son of God, who is coming into the world."
e. "You know nothing at all. Nor do you understand that it is better for you that one man should die for the people, not that the whole nation should perish."
f. "Rabbi, the Jews were just now seeking to stone You, and are You going there again?"
g. "What are we to do? . . . If we let Him go on like this, everyone will believe in Him."
h. "Could not He who opened the eyes of the blind man also have kept this man from dying?"
i. "This illness does not lead to death."
j. "Lazarus, come out."

The Bible narrative does not include any words said by Lazarus. If you were Lazarus, what would you have said just after you were raised from the dead? **Answers will vary.**

The most important words in this Bible story were spoken by Jesus. Write them here (John 11:25): **"I am the resurrection and the life. Whoever believes in Me, though he die, yet shall he live."**

Reproducible 67

A Subplot—Martha Was Listening

Martha so often is remembered for being scolded because she was too busy to listen to Jesus, while her sister Mary listened to the one thing needed (Luke 10:38–42). Yet Martha gave one of the most significant testimonies of faith in Scripture at the time of the death of her brother. Instead of judging Martha's mistake, we see that she did listen and learn and Jesus made a significant difference in her life. Pray that God will do the same in our lives as we hear His Word!

After working through the Student Book section, take time to review. Use Reproducible 67 to review the Bible narrative by looking at the dialogue presented. The Bible narrative is filled with many quotations. Have students identify who said each statement. Then assign the parts and read through it, much like a choral reading or readers theater. Then use Web Resource 67a to review some of this unit's key Bible words to remember.

Lesson Support

Teacher Tips

In this lesson, you are doing some very important preparation. As you know, people of all ages face circumstances involving death. For some children, their first close association with death may be that of an elderly grandparent or great-grandparent. But we know that death touches all ages. Therefore, it is important to discuss concerns children may have about death. Look at John 11:11–15, where Jesus spoke of death by saying that Lazarus was sleeping. His disciples thought that meant he was getting a good rest and would soon recover his health. So Jesus had to be more direct and say that Lazarus had died. Discuss the implications of death being like sleep. (When we sleep, we are unaware of the passage of time. Sleep is usually healing and healthy; when we are resurrected on the Last Day, we will have perfect healing and health. Do you need someone or something to wake you up from sleep? On the Last Day, Jesus will wake us up Himself and with the sound of trumpets.)

Discuss some "modern" spins on death that are not true, such as saying that the person who died is watching you from heaven or is beside you watching over you or has turned into an angel. These are human interpretations of what people might want to believe, but they are not scriptural and they are not true. *Luther's Small Catechism with Explanation* is a good handbook and reference for learning truthful information and finding Bible verses about both death and eternal life. Look at the catechism's questions and answers that are numbered: 144–152; 187–192; 253–260.

Curriculum Connection

Lazarus's resurrection took on a deeper, more significant meaning after Jesus Himself rose from the dead. At first, it was simply another miracle, a little more impressive than most; but after Jesus' resurrection, it was clearly seen as a foreshadowing of that great event and of our own general resurrection at the end of the world. Consider using section 6.2.2.14 with your class, Perception of Events (Change over Time), from the sixth grade Social Studies volume of the Concordia Curriculum Guide. Often the true significance of an event becomes clear only years or decades later. Challenge students to name historical events of this kind, and explain how people's understanding of them changed over time.

Digging Deeper

Point out that the New Testament Scriptures were written in Greek, which was the common language of the day that most people could speak, at least as a second language. Today, especially in our country, English is the main language that is common to most people, and Spanish may be the other language that some people know. Using the language common to most people makes the Scripture accessible to more people.

In the Greek language, there are many ways to say the word *love*. Each of these words for love have a specific meaning. Love is mentioned at least twice in today's Bible narrative, but in both cases it is *not* a romantic type of love (such as between husband and wife) and it is *not* the over-expression of liking something (such as I love eating cookies). The word *filial* is used for love in John 11:3, which means the love of a good friend. In verse 5, an *agape* type of love is mentioned; this is a godly love of care and compassion.

Bringing it home

Ask students to interview someone in their family who has experienced the death of a loved one/friend or someone who has endured a traumatic experience. Have students ask the "Who, What, When, Where, Why, and How" of the situation. For the "How" question, ask how Jesus was with them during this difficult time. Have students write or type up their reports and share them with the class.

Searching Further

As a class, research what Jerusalem was like during Bible times. Search the Internet, encyclopedias, magazines, Bible reference books, Bible atlases, commentaries, and the like, to answer questions such as: How far is Bethany from Jerusalem? What was a burial cave/tomb like? How big was a typical stone in front of a burial cave/tomb? What spices were used in burial preparation? What role did a high priest have? Perhaps you could assign the students to be part of a research team of two or three people and assign each team to cover many or all of the questions using one resource, or each team could answer one or two questions using as many reference tools as possible to "flesh out" their answers. When all of the groups have researched and learned the answers to their questions, have each group share its findings with the rest of the class. Encourage each group to include visual examples such as pictures and maps. As the teacher, work with the class and help the different groups synthesize the results of their research into one integrated report.

Unit 7—Jesus Completes Our Salvation

Theme

This unit is not only the focal point of our studies of our Christian faith this year, but it is also the focus of the entire Bible—and by God's grace, it is also the focus of our entire life! Our studies in math and science and social studies are essential for daily life, but it is in our study of Scripture that all these blessings find their true purpose and meaning through life in Christ. God blesses us with intelligence and abilities and talents, and He guides us to use these for our personal welfare—this is true. But He also desires that we use these blessings for the good of others and for the glory of the Lord.

Our focus in this unit is on Holy Week and the events surrounding it. Here we see God's covenant promises coming together and being fulfilled in Christ Jesus. We cannot save ourselves; only Jesus could do that for us, because He is the sinless Son of God. Amazingly, He is also our substitute! He gives His victory to us!

Jesus suffered all things, died on the cross, and arose at Easter to complete our salvation. It is finished! He offers us the gifts of forgiveness and eternal life through His loving grace and mercy. May the comfort and assurance of God's grace be the center of your life!

Worship

As you know, this curriculum has nine units, which roughly correspond to the nine months of the school year. Unit 7 is suggested for use in March, which usually falls during the latter part of Lent. (Exact correspondence to the liturgical Church Year cannot be expected because it changes from year to year. So you may find Easter lessons during Lent, which are significant in explaining the purpose of Lent. In fact, the lessons on Christ's suffering and death should always include the promise of Easter.) The *Hymn of the Month* (March) is "Crown Him with Many Crowns" (*LSB* 525), and the *Hymn of the Season* (Lent, Part B) is "O Sacred Head, Now Wounded" (*LSB* 450). These are recorded on the *Hymns of the Month* and *Hymns of the Season* CDs. Always feel free to make additional hymn choices, including songs from *All God's People Sing!* (*AGPS*); fifty of these songs are recorded on the *Jesus' People Sing!* (*JPS*) CD. Both hymn choices for this month have deep meaning and significance. If they are unfamiliar to your students, have students simply listen and meditate on the words the first few days before trying to sing along. The psalm choice for this month is Psalm 51:1–12, which appropriately is a plea for God's mercy and forgiveness. Use this in your devotions to increase familiarity with this important psalm. Web resources will also be available for chanting the psalm and for singing portions of it from the liturgy (*LSB*, Divine Service 3).

Resources

Though the *Teacher Resource Book* provides many extra materials to use with this curriculum, these resources are also on the One in Christ Portal, which includes access to links to other Web sites, interactive whiteboard applications, slide presentations, and other resources for the lesson of the day. Tests can be printed out or taken online (with a self-checking feature!). (Unit 7 test answers: 1-d; 2-b; 3-c; 4-b; 5-d; 6-a; 7-a; 8-c; 9-b; 10-e.) Note that the titles of this unit's lessons are listed in the column at the right to give you an overview of the material covered in this unit.

Unit 7

68. Banquet Parables
69. Zacchaeus
70. The Pharisee and the Publican
71. A Woman Anoints Jesus
72. Jesus Rides into Jerusalem
73. Jesus in the Temple
74. The Last Supper
75. Peter Denies Jesus
76. Jesus on Trial
77. Jesus Dies and Is Buried
78. Jesus Rises from the Dead

Bulletin Board

This Bulletin Board gives an overview of Holy Week and also an overview of this unit. None of the pieces of the mural can be isolated from the rest. They all tie together to reveal God's fulfillment of His promise of salvation through Jesus Christ. Across the top, we see an illustration of Jesus riding into Jerusalem on Palm Sunday; children singing praises to Jesus in the temple; and Jesus offering His body and blood in the Sacrament of the Lord's Supper on Maundy Thursday. The lower portion continues with Jesus praying in Gethsemane; His trial before the Roman governor Pontius Pilate; and His death on the cross on Good Friday. All of these events center on Easter, as Jesus arose from the dead, exalted in all His power and glory. Easter Sunday is just the beginning of the forty-day Easter season, during which Jesus time and again appeared to individuals and groups of people. He assured them of His victory, and He taught them how all these events had been prophesied throughout the Old Testament and were now fulfilled in His victory over sin, death, and the power of the devil. He gives this victory, offering forgiveness, life, and salvation, to all who believe.

Bible Book Overview

The Student Book Appendix has a valuable feature that gives a summary of each book of the Bible. Looking at the summaries of sixty-six books can be overwhelming, so it is suggested that each month/unit, your class look at the summaries of just a few of these books. During Unit 7, introduce the first five books of the New Testament. Explain that the first four books are called "The Gospels" because they tell of all that Jesus did on earth for our salvation through His birth, ministry, death, and resurrection. (Point out that Gospel messages of salvation can be found throughout all of the Bible. The four Gospel books give the story narratives and details of how Christ fulfilled God's promises.) This would be a good time to teach students how to quickly find the most important portions of Scripture; the accounts of Jesus' suffering, death, and resurrection can be found in the last three chapters of each of the Gospels. Also explain that the book we often call "Acts" is actually called "The Acts of the Apostles" because this is a book of narratives about the apostles spreading the message of Jesus and salvation and about the growth of the Early Christian Church, all through the empowering of the Holy Spirit. Read together and discuss the summaries of these five books in the Student Book Appendix when you have available time. (Note that a copy of the Student Book Appendix is included in the back of this Teacher Guide.)

UNIT 7—JESUS COMPLETES OUR SALVATION

LESSON 68

Banquet Parables
Luke 14:7–24

Central Truth
Jesus invites all people to His heavenly feast; only those who reject Him will not enter.

Objectives
- Confess our sin when we put other things first before the gracious will of God.
- Rejoice that Christ's invitation for forgiveness, life, and salvation is given according to His open and unconditional love for all people.
- In humility, serve others and give glory to God.

Materials
- Hymnals and music CDs
- Web Resource 68a
- Web Resource 68b
- Reproducible 68

Bible Prep
Post in advance so students can bookmark references before class time.
- Luke 14
- Philippians 2
- Genesis 22:18
- Isaiah 60:1–3
- Matthew 22:2
- Revelation 19:9
- Ephesians 2:4–10

Background
Jesus' parables teach truths about God's kingdom. These excerpts from the article "Longing for a Kingdom" (*The Lutheran Study Bible* [*TLSB*], pp. 1565–66) can help our understanding.

"God opens His kingdom to all people, not just a few. Jew and Gentile, wealthy and poor, men and women are all welcomed into God's grace (Gal 3:26–28). Not all people enter the kingdom of God, however. Human pride and a self-righteous attitude block the work of the Spirit. Only after the Law has stripped away all pretense of personal merit can a sinner come to know the grace of God in Christ Jesus. . . .

"Only Jesus, crucified for the sins of the world and raised again for the justification of sinners, can create the Kingdom that leads to eternal life. Anchored in the cross of Christ (a past event) and actualized in the present through the proclamation of God's Word and the administration of His Sacraments, the kingdom of God also awaits its fulfillment in the visible [future] return of Jesus Christ in glory.

"As the messianic King, vested with complete divine authority, Christ Jesus commissions His followers to make disciples by baptizing and by teaching (Mt 28:18–20). He promises to be with His people always, even to the end of the present age, to accomplish this purpose.

"The reign of God continues to advance in the world through the work of the local congregation and the witness of every Christian. Wherever the Gospel is preached and the story of Jesus shared, the Holy Spirit works to expand the rule of grace through faith in God's Son."

Devotions
The dining room table had been extended to seat as many people as the table could hold. A crisp white tablecloth, the good china, gleaming silverware, and several bouquets of flowers adorned the tabletop. Delicious smells of roast beef, mashed potatoes, and gravy wafted out of the kitchen. It was certainly going to be a special eightieth birthday feast for Grandma Rose's celebration.

Megan walked around the table and read the names of the invited guests from the name cards that marked each person's place at the table. "Hmm," murmured Megan. "I wonder who Doris and Marie are. They're not members of our family."

Just then, Megan's mom walked into the dining room and placed several serving bowls on the table. "Did you say something, Megan?" she asked.

"Yes, Mom," Megan replied. "Why are there places set at the table for Doris and Marie? I've never heard of them. Why would we want them here at Grandma Rose's party?"

"Doris and Marie are friends of Grandma's from the Senior Center. I wanted to make sure that everyone who loves and cares about Grandma was invited and included at her special banquet."

Have you ever been invited to a banquet? How did it feel to be included in such a special occasion? When we are invited to attend a banquet or dinner for a loved one or good friend, we usually make every effort to attend.

Jesus told several parables about a banquet. These stories reveal important truths about God's kingdom and whom He invites to His banquet in heaven. As we study these parables, consider what they say about God's mercy and grace for you today. God invites us to share in the blessings of our loving Savior, Jesus. Let's sing about that in a song based on Song of Solomon 2:4, which says, "He brought me to the banqueting house, and His banner over me was love." Sing "His Banner over Me Is Love" (*AGPS* 118; recorded on *JPS*). During the season of Lent, it is suggested that you say together Psalm 51:1–12 in your devotions. Point out that this is a great psalm of confession of sins, forgiveness from Jesus, and new life as we are transformed through the sanctifying work of the Holy Spirit renewing us. (The chanted version of this psalm is available on Web Resource 68a. After a few days of reading the psalm, you may want to have the class listen to the recording several times before attempting to chant it themselves.)

INTO the Word

Humility at the Banquet Feast

Ask, **Why is it difficult for us to be humble?** (As sinful human beings, we are self-centered. We like to feel important. We like to be well regarded. We are often filled with false pride in our own accomplishments. We forget that all we are and all we have are blessings from God. Our human pride also makes it difficult for us to admit our sinfulness. This is why we need instruction on the importance of humility, especially before God.)

Jesus teaches that we should act humbly. Instead of promoting ourselves, we should allow others to do so. Praise is so much more rewarding if it comes from someone else. In fact, praise that comes from yourself would have to be called "bragging." Relate the connection between Jesus' parable in the Bible, the illustration in the Student Book, and the following modern parable:

It was a warm summer day at the ballpark. Up to the plate stepped one of the batting heroes of Major League Baseball. He waved his hat to the cheering crowd, flexed his muscles, and then shook his finger at the pitcher as if to say, "Watch out! I'm going to hit a home run off you."

The pitcher threw the ball, but there was no home run—just a little blooper that barely reached the outfield. On the way to first base, the runner tripped over his own feet and fell to the ground. It was an easy out. There was no flexing of the muscles or tipping of the hat as he headed to the dugout.

The next person up was a rookie. It was his first time at bat; he could hardly think, he was so scared. The crowd was silent, wondering who this guy was. The batter could hear murmurs of disgust when he swung at the first pitch and missed by a mile. But he hit the next pitch, which meant he had to run on those shaky legs. He just hoped he didn't throw up on his way to first base.

Amazingly, his coach kept waving him on. The rookie hadn't even realized he had hit a home run! When he finally tagged home plate, he ran straight for the dugout and sat down, stunned at what had just happened. But the manager came over to him and said, "Can't you hear that crowd cheering? Get out there and take a bow!"

Say, The lesson Jesus teaches in His parable is basic common sense: those who think they are great will be brought down low, and those who are humble will be lifted up in praise. However, as Christians, our motivation is different from that of other people. Our motivation is not just "common sense." We are motivated by our gratitude for all that Jesus has done to forgive us, save us, and make us His own. We are motivated to show our love and gratitude by following His example, living as His disciples, and doing everything for the glory of God. That is our reason for following this good advice! In this way, we are putting the will of God first, rather than putting ourselves first.

The Student Book mentions Philippians 2:5, which tells us to follow the example of Jesus. Have students turn to Philippians 2 to see exactly the model that Jesus lived for us. In verses 6–8, we see the humility of Jesus; in verses 9–11, we see how God the Father exalted Him. (*Note:* verses 9–11 are also this lesson's words to remember.)

Kindness at the Banquet Feast

As you discuss Luke 14:12–14, ask, **Can you think of a time when you helped another person and did not receive any recognition for it?** Accept answers. Students may mention doing chores or favors for others for which they have not been thanked, or performing service projects to benefit people whom they will never meet. **When we serve someone, should we expect thanks and recognition?** It is proper and polite to thank someone when they do something for you. It is heartwarming to be thanked for service we have performed. But true Christian service is not performed with the expectation that we will be thanked. It is done out of love and honor for God and

---

LESSON 68
Banquet Parables

Humility at the Banquet Feast

Jesus was having dinner at the home of a Pharisee. Some of the Pharisees were His enemies, some were His friends, and some were just curious or unsure. Luke 14:1 says, "They were watching Him carefully." Jesus spoke to them in parables. Read Jesus' story in Luke 14:7–11.

What was Jesus teaching in this story? See verse 11. **"Everyone who exalts himself will be humbled, and he who humbles himself will be exalted."**

In what ways did Jesus demonstrate this kind of humility? **He became one of us; He washed the disciples' feet; He touched people with leprosy; He died the death of a criminal.**

In what ways did God the Father exalt Jesus? **In Jesus' resurrection, ascension, and as He is now enthroned in heaven**

Philippians 2:5 says, "Have this mind among yourselves, which is yours in Christ Jesus."

Kindness at the Banquet Feast

Jesus' first story was told from the viewpoint of a guest. Now He tells another parable, this time from the viewpoint of the person giving the banquet. Read Luke 14:12–14. In this story, Jesus is saying that it is easy to be kind to people who are kind to you. So, how can you demonstrate unselfish kindness? See verse 13. **Be kind to people who can't repay your kindness; give to the poor and needy. You won't be losing out, because God sees your heart and will bless you.**

Jesus is teaching that discipleship involves serving others.

Covenant Connection

As usual, Jesus' parables taught about the kingdom of God. Unfortunately, many people at that time thought the kingdom of God was meant only for descendants of Abraham. They overlooked the many times in the Old Testament when God gave His promises to all people. Even to Abraham, God said that through his family (in Jesus), all the nations of the world would be blessed (see Genesis 22:18). Many psalms speak of this, as does Psalm 65:5: "O God of our salvation, the hope of all the ends of the earth." And prophets, too, spoke of all nations being blessed through the Messiah (see Isaiah 60:1–3).

What Is This Feast?

Recall that a parable is an earthly story with a heavenly meaning. So Jesus wasn't just talking about behavior at a dinner. This banquet feast has a spiritual significance. To what is God inviting us? See Matthew 22:2 and Revelation 19:9. **Heaven, which is God's kingdom of glory**

While it may be some time before we attend that banquet feast, we are privileged to be invited here on earth to another one where God's grace is freely offered. What is this other banquet? **The Lord's Table, Holy Communion, which is part of God's kingdom of grace here on earth**

R.S.V.P.

"R.S.V.P." is often found on invitations. It is the abbreviation for a French phrase that means "please reply."

In today's Bible narrative, Jesus tells yet another banquet parable. In this parable, the people gave excuses for not accepting the invitation. The significance for us and the world today is that God invites all people to hear the Gospel message of salvation through Jesus. He invites us to come to faith and receive the forgiveness and eternal life He offers to all who believe in His name. Yet people today have lots of excuses for not putting Jesus first in their lives. Read Luke 14:16–24; then fill in the chart below.

EXCUSES FOR REFUSING THE INVITATION

IN THE PARABLE	IN OUR WORLD TODAY
Verse 18 **Needed to check out his new property**	**Possibilities: Too busy**
Verse 19 **Needed to care for new a possession (ox)**	**Need the time to make and spend money**
Verse 20 **Needed to spend time with family (new wife)**	**Rather spend time with friends and family**

All of these excuses show the people's priorities, revealing what is more important to them than their relationship with the Lord. They break the First Commandment, which is explained, "We should fear, love, and trust in God above all things" (Luther's Small Catechism).

God has a right to be angry when we consider earthly goods, earthly relationships, and earthly responsibilities and activities to be more important than He is. But He continues to call us to repentance. Read Ephesians 2:4–10. What does it say that assures you that you do indeed have a seat at God's great banquet table in heaven? **Answers may vary, but basically, focus on the love and grace of God.**

Remember

"God has highly exalted Him and bestowed on Him the name that is above every name, so that at the name of Jesus every knee should bow, in heaven and on earth and under the earth, and every tongue confess that Jesus Christ is Lord, to the glory of God the Father." (Philippians 2:9–11)

143

---

to receive in faith the body and blood of Jesus in, with, and under the bread and wine. This is a mystery and a miracle. It is an invitation extended to all who are part of God's kingdom of grace here on earth. *Option:* Read together the first two stanzas of the Communion hymn "Jesus Comes Today with Healing" (*LSB* 620). Note especially the last phrase of both stanzas.

R.S.V.P.

This section focuses on Law and Gospel. In the parable and in our lives, we are confronted by the Law, which points to our basic sin—placing other things and placing our will first in our lives rather than loving and trusting the Lord above all else. The excuses in the parable are basically like excuses in our world today, which place possessions and relationships above our relationship with God. People have all sorts of excuses for not going to church, for ignoring God, for living just for themselves, for living just for pleasure or success. Anytime those excuses become most important to us, they overshadow Christ in our lives. This is a sin against the First Commandment.

The Law points to our unfaithfulness; the Gospel points to the faithfulness of God. He does not abandon us; He continues to call us to repentance. In Ephesians 2, we see the greatness of God's grace and mercy. Not only does He bring us to faith and forgiveness, but He also enables us to grow in faith and in our faith life through the empowering work of the Holy Spirit in us. Ask, **What tools does the Holy Spirit use to work in us?** (God's Word and the Sacraments of Holy Baptism and the Lord's Supper) **By grace, He helps us to serve Him and to follow His will for our lives.**

Conclude the lesson by praising the name of Jesus, whom God has exalted on high, by reading the Bible words to remember. Then sing "How Majestic Is Your Name" (*AGPS* 122; recorded on *JPS*) and "Jesus, Name Above All Names" (*AGPS* 145; recorded on *JPS*).

---

as a response to all that He does for us. Our reward for service will be given to us when we reach our heavenly home through faith in Jesus Christ. Be sure that students understand that "serving others" means helping others and showing kindness. **Jesus' parable instructs us to be generous to others and to share the good things God has given us with those who are in need. The humble service of believers will be rewarded in heaven.** Sing about the glorious heavenly feast for the Lamb of God to which we are invited in the hymn "This Is the Feast" (*LSB*, p. 155 or 171; recorded on Web Resource 68b).

What Is This Feast?

While we can look at these parables for lessons in humility and kindness, there is an even deeper spiritual significance. The heavenly banquet, the Lamb's feast to which we are invited, is the eternal life we have through the mercy and grace of our Redeemer, Jesus Christ. We will enjoy that celebration in heaven in God's kingdom of glory. But the Lord also extends an invitation to us here on earth to come to His Table, the Lord's Supper,

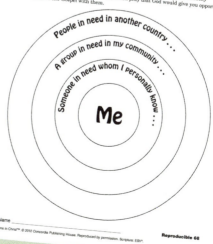

293

Lesson Support

Critical thinking

Many people in Judah thought the Messiah would come only for them, so they were not interested in mission work, as evidenced in their prejudices against Samaritans and Romans. A similar type of separatism or isolation has occurred in more modern times. For example, some nineteenth-century mission efforts viewed people in other lands as "lesser Christians," partly because their worship customs and languages were different. Also, the evil of segregation in our nation's history often included the separation of "white" and "black" churches, which Scripture does not affirm (see Galatians 3:7–9, 28). As John 3:16 tells us, God's love and salvation through Christ Jesus are for everyone.

Curriculum Connection

When you remember the fact that the people who had been invited to the banquet in the parable had *already accepted* the invitation before the actual day arrived, their rude change of plans at the last minute is astonishing. Use the ideas and information in section 6.3.1.10, Voice and Language Appropriate for the Audience and Purpose, in the sixth-grade Language Arts volume of the Concordia Curriculum Guide series to examine their excuses. Why is each excuse not a proper thing to say to someone who is expecting you to keep your promise and come? What excuses might be accepted, and why? Would any of these excuses be acceptable in another situation (for example, when first receiving an invitation to an impromptu party you hadn't known about beforehand)?

HANDS TO SERVE

Distribute and discuss Reproducible 68. Then plan an activity or an event with your class, grade level, or school that involves a banquet or meal and opportunities for service:
- Gather volunteers to help serve a weekend meal at a local soup kitchen or homeless shelter.
- Make table decorations that feature encouraging Scripture passages for use at a local nursing home or women's and children's shelter.
- If your congregation participates in a Meals on Wheels program in your community, obtain permission for students to ride along with adult volunteers to help deliver meals one day during lunch.
- Help plan a lunch for Grandparents Day. Set up a banquet table in an area of the lunchroom. Make cheerful decorations and place mats. Have students serve the guests as waiters and waitresses.
- Prepare a special snack break for the people who prepare meals in your school cafeteria to express your appreciation for the work they do for you.
- For a local food pantry, prepare baskets that contain a complete nutritious meal for a family.

Technology

Use technology to produce a video version of the banquet parables. Involve students as scriptwriters, actors, costume designers, directors, videographers, and computer techs who will download the finished video to the computer for viewing.

Faith in Action

Ask a representative of your church's outreach group to visit your class to discuss the ways in which they invite people to worship and other congregational events. Have your class work with this individual to develop and produce invitations that can be used for this purpose. Or work with this individual to design an invitation directed at children, to be used in conjunction with this summer's Vacation Bible School program.

As the students brainstorm ideas, ask them to think about aspects of their faith life that interest them (e.g., service projects, choir and music ministry, Vacation Bible School, preteen youth activities, drama ministry, Bible study opportunities). Use photos and Bible truths from these activities as focal points on the invitation. Be sure a Scripture verse is featured prominently. When the copy is written, proofread it well to make sure that all times, dates, and phone numbers are accurate. Use a desktop publishing program and other computer resources to design and print your invitation. Plan how the invitation will be distributed.

UNIT 7—JESUS COMPLETES OUR SALVATION

LESSON **69**

Zacchaeus
LUKE 19:1–10

Background

Money—is it really the root of all evil? Friends will tell you that money isn't everything, but it's certainly ahead of whatever's in second place. Zacchaeus the tax collector was good at acquiring lots of money; he defrauded his countrymen for financial gain. But he's not the only character in the Bible whose life was ruled by greed. Abraham's nephew Lot chose the productive land watered by the Jordan River—and found himself among the evil men of Sodom and Gomorrah (Genesis 13). Achan kept some of the spoils of war at Ai, and he and his family were executed by the Israelites (Joshua 7). Ahab and Jezebel conspired to take the vineyard of Naboth and were cursed by the prophet Elijah (1 Kings 21).

However, there were wealthy Bible characters who pleased God by faith. Abraham possessed enormous flocks and had many servants. But "Abraham obeyed when he was called. . . . He was looking forward to the city that has foundations, whose designer and builder was God" (Hebrews 11:8, 10). Joseph of Arimathea, a rich disciple, buried Jesus' body in his own new tomb.

According to 1 Timothy 6:10, "*the love of money* is a root of all kinds of evils" (italics added). For professional church workers, possessing too much money is rarely a problem. But worrying about money and material possessions is a great temptation when finances are tight. Focus instead on Jesus' reminders to "Look at the birds of the air" (Matthew 6:26) and "Consider the lilies of the field. . . . Seek first the kingdom of God and His righteousness, and all these things will be added to you" (vv. 28, 33).

Central Truth

Jesus Christ came to save sinners, like you and me.

Objectives

- Ask forgiveness for any pride we feel in what we do as Christians, recognizing that we are saved by what Christ did for us.
- Appreciate that Jesus came for all people, even those who we may sinfully think don't deserve His grace.
- Respond by following Jesus by imitating His ways, empowered by the Holy Spirit.

Materials

- Hymnals and music CDs
- Reproducible 69

Bible Prep

Post in advance so students can bookmark references before class time.
- Luke 19:1–10
- Luke 23:39–43
- Matthew 9:9–13

Devotions

In today's Bible narrative, we will hear about Zacchaeus, a lost sinner whom Jesus came to save. We can see many other lost sinners throughout history. In 1725, when America was still just a group of small colonies, John Newton was born in London, England. His mother died when he was seven years old; when he was eleven, he went to sea as a sailor with his father. By the time he was twenty, he had deserted from the English navy and was in all sorts of trouble. He constantly rebelled against authority, and he eventually ended up sailing on ships that transported slaves from Africa to the West Indies.

On one of these trips, he went too far as he mocked the captain, created obscene poems, and fought with the other sailors. As punishment, he was imprisoned on the ship, chained like the slaves the ship carried, and later imprisoned in Sierra Leone in Africa. After several months, his father intervened, and he was released. On the voyage back to England, his ship was overtaken by a violent storm that nearly sank the unseaworthy craft. The experience brought Newton to his knees in prayer and repentance, and he became a Christian by conviction—not just in name, but in active faith.

Back in England, he became involved in his church, serving as a lay preacher. Eventually he decided to study for the ministry. Later in his life, Newton worked to abolish the English slave trade in which he had once taken part. With his friend William Cowper, a gifted writer, Newton wrote many hymns, including "Amazing Grace." This hymn's words tell the story of the prodigal son ("I once was lost but now am found") and of the blind man healed by Jesus ("Was blind but now I see"). But they also tell the story of Newton's own life and of your life and mine—lost sinners saved by Jesus' suffering and death in our place. Read together and then sing "Amazing Grace" (*LSB* 744; recorded as *Hymn of the Month for grade 5, December*). Say or chant Psalm 51:1–12.

INTO the Word

A Sinner's Story (Luke 19:1–10)

Read the story from Scripture and then review it from the three viewpoints stated in the Student Book. Most people viewed tax collectors as traitors to the Jewish people because they collected taxes for the hated Romans and their Jewish puppets (like King Herod). A tax collector, they believed, was no longer a true Jew—not a "son of Abraham" (Luke 19:9). Many were probably jealous of Zacchaeus's wealth, ill-gotten at their expense.

Zacchaeus was painfully aware of his neighbors' attitudes. He lived in his elegant house, but he was isolated from the social and religious life of his community. He sought inclusion and the sight of Jesus, but his neighbors pushed him away from the road Jesus would travel. Notice that Zacchaeus didn't argue or fight with the crowd; he knew his place. Instead, he ran ahead and climbed a tree—a perch no one else wanted.

Zacchaeus was looking for Jesus, but it was Jesus who found Zacchaeus. Stopping under the tree branch, Jesus looked up and called Zacchaeus to come down, saying, "Zacchaeus, hurry and come down, for I must stay at your house today" (Luke 19:5). Jesus' words were a sign of acceptance, fellowship, and forgiveness to Zacchaeus. Zacchaeus hurried down and received Jesus joyfully. His reaction shows that he recognized Jesus' love and mercy in contrast to the hatred of the religious leaders and his neighbors who felt no need for a Savior.

Remind students that some of the people of Jericho would have thought that by eating with a "sinner" such as Zacchaeus, Jesus was becoming a partner with him in his sin (refer to Matthew 9:9–13). In fact, Jesus had come to deliver Zacchaeus from that sinful life and, through forgiveness of sin, lead him to a new life lived for the Lord.

Zacchaeus's encounter with Jesus changed his life. The coming of Jesus meant that the lost Zacchaeus had been sought and now was found. Jesus declared Zacchaeus a true son of Abraham by faith in Him. Paul wrote, "That is why it depends on faith, in order that the promise may rest on grace and be guaranteed to all his offspring—not only to the adherent of the law but also to the one who shares the faith of Abraham, who is the father of us all" (Romans 4:16).

The Jews of Jesus' day viewed tax collectors as traitors to their Jewish countrymen and unworthy of Jesus' love. But Jesus repeatedly reached out to tax collectors with acceptance, love, and forgiveness. Direct students again to Matthew 9:9–13 and review the account of the calling of Matthew, another tax collector, to be Jesus' disciple. The Pharisees intended to find fault with Jesus over His association with tax collectors. Jesus quoted Hosea 6:6: "I desire steadfast love and not sacrifice." Hosea condemned Israel for supposing that God desired obedience to ritual laws (sacrifice) more than the practice of mercy. The Pharisees were equally guilty of this sin. **What did Jesus mean by the words "Those who are well have no need of a physician" (Matthew 9:12)? Consider the following saying, seen on one congregation's bulletin board: "A church is not a museum for saints; it's a hospital for sinners." How does this quote fit with Jesus' words and actions? How does it fit your congregation? How does it apply to your own life?**

Zachary's Story

Read the first paragraph of Zachary's story, and discuss Stacey and Alex's reaction when they first saw Zachary in their church. Why did they think Zachary didn't belong there? Ask students if they have ever reacted that way to people who don't seem to "belong" in church. What groups of people might provoke that kind of reaction in your church today? Students may mention people who are homeless, mentally challenged, or handicapped. They may be people who seem different because of their clothing, race, ethnicity, language, or behavior. None of these is a reason to reject someone. On the contrary, these are all reasons to reach out to them with the loving care of Jesus.

Read Zachary's story aloud and discuss Zachary's early life, listing the

Zachary's Story

The pastor told the congregation that they would have a special speaker that day. Stacey and her friend Alex stared at the man walking slowly up to the front of their church. Stacey whispered to Alex, "What is somebody like that doing here in our church?"

"You are so right," whispered Alex. "He looks kind of scary to me. What could he possibly have to say to people like you and me?"

Everyone in the church was quiet as the stranger began to speak. "Good morning, brothers and sisters," he said with a shy smile. "My name is Zachary, and I'm here to tell you my story. It started when I was a little kid. I can't remember a time when I wasn't getting into trouble—skipping school, breaking windows, stealing from the neighborhood store. As I got older, I just got into bigger trouble, hanging out with the wrong friends. I was going down a path of destruction." He pointed at his tattooed arms and said, "I joined a gang, and things just got worse and worse. I was in and out of jail for fifteen years.

"After I was released from prison, I was required to participate in a rehabilitation program. One of the supervisors in the program was a beautiful woman named Grace. It was easy to see that Grace was filled with an inner peace and joy, and I wanted to know why. Grace told me that her joy came from knowing Jesus as her Savior. She said Jesus had given His own life to take away her sins. This sounded like a good deal to me, but Grace's sins were nowhere near as bad as mine. I wondered how Jesus could ever forgive me. I felt hopeless.

"Grace took me to Bible classes at her church. I learned that Grace was right—Jesus' death and resurrection took away the sins of all people, even sins like mine. His forgiveness filled me with a peace and joy I had never known before. My life had a new purpose: loving and serving God and sharing His good news so others don't make the same mistakes I did.

"Recently, I saw somebody I knew long ago. He wondered why I had changed so much. He was trying to ridicule me when he asked, 'What happened to you, brother? Did you find Jesus?' I answered him, 'No, Jesus was never lost. I am the one who was lost. And Jesus found me!'"

A Hopeless Story?

Read Luke 23:39–43. Talk about a hopeless situation—one man dying on a cross, asking another dying man to help him.

What did he ask of Jesus? **"Jesus, remember me when You come into Your kingdom."**

What was Jesus' answer? **"Truly, I say to you, today you will be with Me in Paradise."**

What about you? What's your story? Your story may not be so extreme, but remember that sin is sin. If you are lost, you are lost. There is no such thing as being "less lost" than someone else. What difference does Jesus make in *your* life? **Answers will vary.**

Remember

"[The Lord says,] I dwell in the high and holy place, and also with him who is of a contrite and lowly spirit, to revive the spirit of the lowly, and to revive the heart of the contrite." (Isaiah 57:15)

the facts about His birth, life on earth, death, and resurrection, or was it more? Grace's "knowing" meant believing completely that Jesus' life, death, and resurrection were for her. It meant staking her life, here and in eternity, on that belief—in other words, faith. Zachary wanted that kind of faith and life for himself, but he knew he didn't deserve it.

Grace took Zachary to the source—God's Word—through personal and group Bible study. There he learned that Jesus' death and resurrection paid for his sins too. Ask students what Bible stories or verses they think Zachary might have studied. Point out that Zachary had searched for peace and joy on his own and hadn't found it, but God reached out to Zachary through His Word and found him. How did confessing his sins fill Zachary with peace and joy?

A forgiven Zachary was a changed Zachary. Discuss the "fruits of faith" now visible in Zachary's life—visiting families of gang members and helping released prisoners adjust to life outside prison.

various kinds of trouble in which he was involved. How did Zachary's first infractions—skipping school, breaking windows, stealing—lead to his later, more serious crimes? Students should notice the influence of Zachary's bad choice of companions. How did these companions encourage his misbehavior and keep him from breaking free from his destructive way of life? Point out that his alcohol and drug use leading to addiction complicated Zachary's problems and made it almost impossible for him to change his life on his own.

Zachary understood that he was hurting his family by his behavior. Ask students to pretend they are Zachary's brothers and sisters. How would they describe their feelings toward Zachary? These emotions may range from unconditional love to worry to shame to hatred. If Zachary understood he was hurting the people who loved him, why didn't he change? He didn't care about himself—so how could he care about anybody else? On his own, Zachary was powerless to change his behavior. Consequently, he spent fifteen years—what should have been the most productive years of his life—in and out of prison.

Zachary encountered Grace in his rehab program, where she served as a supervisor. Note that what first attracted Zachary was her obvious peace and joy—qualities he had searched for but never found in his own life. Grace told Zachary that her peace and joy came from knowing Jesus as her Savior. Discuss what "knowing Jesus" meant to Grace. Was it just knowing

A Hopeless Story?

At first appearances, the dying thief asking for help from a dying Jesus would seem hopeless. It would be similar to a drowning man asking another drowning man for help. But the thief recognized that there is hope in Jesus—an eternal hope that only He can give. In fact, Jesus died to give us that hope and that life! Sing together (several times) the words of the thief on the cross, making them your words and your plea, knowing already the answer we have from our Savior. Sing "Jesus, Remember Me" (*LSB* 767 or *AGPS* 146; recorded on *JPS*).

Lesson Support

Celebrating GROWTH

Many of Zachary's problems were caused by having chosen the wrong friends. Friends have a strong influence on us, particularly on young people. This influence can be for good or for evil. Common beliefs and values form a strong basis for a good friendship. The most important of these beliefs is faith in Jesus as Savior. But choosing good Christian friends doesn't mean avoiding all contacts with unbelievers. Zachary came to faith through his friendship with Grace. He was first attracted to Grace by the peace and joy that came through her personal faith in Jesus. Grace never put aside this faith in her dealings with Zachary; it was this faith that led to their friendship. Jesus calls us to be light and salt in a world that desperately needs our light and saltiness. Teach your children to "let your light shine before others, so that they may see your good works and give glory to your Father who is in heaven" (Matthew 5:16).

Working in Groups

Jesus sought out, loved, accepted, and forgave Zacchaeus. How can the people in your congregation seek out, love, and accept people who need Jesus' forgiveness? Divide your class into groups of four or five students. Ask each group to think of ways your congregation could reach out to others, particularly to people who might seem different from most of your members, people who are excluded or are outcasts. Students should start by identifying the groups of people not being effectively reached by your congregation. Would changes in the type of worship offered, kinds of music, or service times and locations make your ministry more relatable to the groups identified? Could your congregation provide greeters to meet strangers as they enter your church and seat them with someone who will help them find their way through the service? Is someone assigned to follow up with people who have visited your church? Discuss the work of all of the groups; compile the results, and present them to your pastor, your board of elders, and your evangelism board.

Bringing it home

Consider sending home this note to parents: *Your child has been studying the story of Zacchaeus, the tax collector who was found, loved, and forgiven by Jesus. The Jews viewed tax collectors as traitors and terrible sinners and, therefore, unworthy of Jesus' love. Have your words and actions ever indicated that you believe certain individuals or groups of people may have more weaknesses or faults? Children learn what they live, and attitudes are more often caught than taught. Confess your sins of pride, and ask for God's forgiveness. Then ask for His help in teaching your children to love all people, regardless of their behavior, their background, or their station in life. A powerful CEO said that he evaluates his employees not on how they relate to him or their supervisor, but on how they treat the waitress in the restaurant, the custodian who empties their wastebasket, and the clerk who delivers their mail. Teach your children by example to recognize and respect each individual as a person created by God and redeemed by God's Son.*

BEYOND THE CLASSROOM

Reproducible 69 provides a tool that your students can use to tell friends and family the story of Zacchaeus. Distribute copies and have your students fold the sheet down the center, like a greeting card. Open the sheet and fold both side pictures back. Have students practice with a partner using this visual aid to tell the story of Zacchaeus, starting with the two center sections. Suggest that they give the setting: Jesus was walking past Jericho on His way to Jerusalem where, within a week, He would be welcomed, then captured, tortured, and killed. He wasn't running away; He was walking willingly toward Jerusalem, knowing this was necessary in order to save us.

Students may then fold the sheet to view just the first section, pointing out that Zacchaeus climbed the tree because he was short, but also because he was disliked and no one in the crowd would welcome him through to see Jesus. Emphasize that Jesus found *him*, not the other way around. We don't go looking for Jesus. He is near, and He comes to us.

Then flip the sheet over to show the single picture of the happy Zacchaeus. Talk about why he was so happy and what a difference forgiveness made in his life. Note that Jesus didn't say, "I forgive you. Now go back to whatever you were doing before." He expects that true love and faith will show in hearts that are also open to the new life we have as His disciples.

UNIT 7—JESUS COMPLETES OUR SALVATION

LESSON 70

The Pharisee and the Publican
Luke 18:9–14

Background

Jesus sometimes used humor and hyperbole (intentional exaggeration) to get across the point of His parables. Satire—an oral or literary device that ridicules someone's vices or foolishness—was particularly effective. In the parable of the Pharisee and the tax collector, Jesus purposely overstates the Pharisee's haughty gestures and arrogant pride. The Pharisee's prayer is nothing more than a song of praise to himself. In comparing himself with his fellow men, the Pharisee singles out the meanest, most hated sinners (showing himself to be judgmental and prejudiced). His practice of fasting twice a week is not commanded in Old Testament law. If this man was like other Pharisees, he may even have tithed on his garden spices (Luke 11:42), while still neglecting justice and the love of God.

The humility of the tax collector stands in stark contrast. He stands afar off, beating his breast, and he won't even lift his eyes to heaven. His prayer is simple and heartfelt: "God, be merciful to me, a sinner!" Jesus says that the tax collector went down to his house justified, rather than the Pharisee, who thought he was already righteous.

Why did Jesus tell this story? Luke 18:9 states that Jesus' audience included "some who trusted in themselves that they were righteous, and treated others with contempt." Overstating the Pharisee's vices might have made the self-righteous listeners see these onerous characteristics in themselves. The satire made it easier to see the contrast between the Pharisee's pride and the tax collector's humility, between the Pharisee's reliance on himself and his deeds and the tax collector's dependence on God's grace.

Central Truth

Our forgiveness and salvation are based solely on what Christ Jesus has done for us.

Objectives

- Recognize that there is no good in us that deserves or earns our salvation.
- Celebrate that Jesus forgives us and covers us with His righteousness.
- Enabled by the transformation Jesus makes in our lives, do good works for His glory and to help others.

Materials

- Hymnals and music CDs
- Reproducible 70
- Web Resource 70a
- Web Resource 70b
- Crayons or pens for underlining

Bible Prep

Post in advance so students can bookmark references before class time.
- Luke 18:9–14
- 2 Corinthians 5:21
- Isaiah 53:5b

Devotions

Have you ever been in a situation that felt hopeless? Perhaps you disobeyed your parents and didn't want them to find out what you had done. Maybe you hurt one of your friends by betraying a confidence. You tried to cover what you had done—to make things right by yourself—but all of your efforts only made the situation worse.

Then you can understand the hopelessness felt by Derek, a young sailor on Lake Michigan. Derek usually went sailing with his dad. But one day, he ignored the small craft advisories on the radio and took the family's small sailboat out on the lake by himself. Soon, dark clouds loomed on the western horizon, and the wind whipped the cold gray water into towering waves. Derek lowered the sail and held on for dear life. Finally, an enormous wave crashed over the deck, and the little boat capsized. Derek knew that he could save himself by clinging to the hull of the boat. But he saw to his dismay that the wind and waves were pushing the overturned boat away from him. He tried to swim after it, but the water was cold and the waves were powerful. Soon he was exhausted. His efforts to save himself had failed.

As Derek was about to give up hope, a Coast Guard rescue boat approached. Derek swam with all of his strength toward the life ring that was thrown to him, but the waves kept pushing it out of his reach. Finally, a Coast Guardsman in a wet suit jumped into the water, put his strong arms around Derek, and pulled him to the boat, where he was rescued. Derek was saved by someone else's efforts.

Like Derek, we are drowning in sin. No matter how hard we try, we cannot save ourselves. But Jesus came into our world and saved us. All of our hopes of forgiveness, new life, and eternity in heaven rest on Him. We, too, are saved by someone else's efforts: Christ did all things to redeem us and to make us children of God. Sing together of God's great grace and mercy in the hymn "Just As I Am, without One Plea" (*LSB* 570; recorded as *Hymn of the Month* for grade 4, March). Speak or chant Psalm 51:1–12.

INTO the lesson

How to Become Righteous

The journal entries of Justin, Sophie, Maya, and Robert reflect common sense. We learn early in childhood that "being good" results in a favorable reaction from those in charge. Doing chores earns us extra allowance or additional privileges. Being cheerful and getting along with siblings puts smiles on our parents' faces. Community service brings recognition and Boy Scout badges. Satisfactory schoolwork gets us promoted to the next grade and maybe even the honor roll. These attitudes affect adults as well as children. Few adults would report for work every day without the promise of a paycheck; they are especially motivated when service above what is required results in a bonus check as well. In almost every aspect of our lives, our rewards are based on what we do and how well we do it. The exception, of course, is our relationship with God. We can define *righteous* as "being in a right relationship with God," but God demands perfection, saying, "You shall be holy, for I the Lord your God am holy" (Leviticus 19:2). God sees into the heart; He knows that, because of original sin, none of us is capable of meeting His standard. In His great love, He provided the solution for our hopeless situation: **through faith in Jesus, we are justified—declared righteous—by grace. This is not something we do. It has been done for us!** Mrs. Parker's students had many ideas about what makes a person righteous. Trying to obey the Ten Commandments, helping people in need, attending church regularly, and protecting the environment are all good things to do. But because we are born sinful, we cannot make ourselves righteous before God by the good things we do. St. Paul was quoting the Psalms when he wrote, "None is righteous, no, not one. . . . No one does good, not even one" (Romans 3:10, 12). Paul knew God's answer to our problem of sin: "But now the righteousness of God has been manifested apart from the law," Paul wrote, "although the Law and the Prophets bear witness to it—the righteousness of God through faith in Jesus Christ [is] for all who believe" (vv. 21–22). Robert knew he couldn't make himself righteous. Every night, he confessed his sins to his heavenly Father, knowing his sins were forgiven for Jesus' sake. Only through faith in Jesus can believers be found righteous before God. The "Covenant Connection" explains this further: **When God looks at you and me, He sees the righteousness of Jesus because He has poured it on us, covered us with it, and clothed us in Jesus' righteousness. He enables us (makes us able) and empowers us (gives us power) to do good things, which we do—not for our salvation (we are already saved), but rather in gratitude and service, to glorify God.**

Lesson 70
The Pharisee and the Publican
How to Become Righteous

Mrs. Parker often challenged her class to write in their journals. Because they trusted Mrs. Parker, they felt free to express their real feelings about whatever topic she gave them for the day's journal assignment. One day, she said, "Today's journal word is *righteous*. Write about what being righteous means to you." The students thought about the assignment and began to write.

Justin: I learned in Boy Scouts that it is important to respect your country and your parents. Boy Scouts work hard to serve other people, especially those who are less fortunate. I organized a coat drive this winter to help poor kids at my school, and I collected canned goods for people who needed food. I know I'm doing good things for other people, so God must be pleased with me. That's what righteous means, isn't it?

Maya: My family and I are dedicated to taking care of God's world. We reuse, recycle, and reduce our carbon footprint to help preserve our natural resources. Last year, we collected money to help save animals that were in danger of extinction. I think my family's work for the environment makes the world a better place, and that makes us righteous.

Sophie: My family hasn't missed church in years! We always sit up in the front row. When we were little, my parents taught us how to behave in church—not to talk or fool around like other kids, when to stand up and sit down, and all that stuff. And we always put a generous offering in our church envelope. I'm sure this makes God happy with us. That's what being righteous means.

Robert: I know how God wants me to live. I make it my goal to obey Him. But before breakfast, I usually have already sinned. Sometimes I get things right, and sometimes I'm all wrong. I tell God I'm sorry for all the times I have disobeyed Him. I know that He forgives me. When God looks at me, He sees Jesus' righteousness instead of my sin.

What does the Bible say about our righteousness? See 2 Corinthians 5:21. _____
"[God] made [Jesus] to be sin who knew no sin, so that in [Jesus] we might become the righteousness of God." (The Great Exchange)

Review

Covenant Connection
The Old Testament prophet Isaiah said, "I will greatly rejoice in the Lord . . . for He has *clothed me* with the garments of salvation; He has *covered me* with the robe of righteousness" (Isaiah 61:10, emphasis added). Isaiah's prophecy is fulfilled in Jesus, who gives us His righteousness and salvation, as is stated in the New Testament: "He saved us, *not because of works done by us in righteousness*, but according to His own mercy, by the washing of regeneration and renewal of the Holy Spirit, whom *He poured out on us* richly through Jesus Christ our Savior" (Titus 3:5–6, emphasis added).

146

INTO the Word

A Parable about Righteousness

Note: Be sure that students understand that *publican* was another title for tax collectors in Bible times, probably because they dealt with the public on a daily basis. *Publican* has nothing to do with a political party.

Have students share some of their words and phrases that describe the two men (using terms from the Bible and/or their own word choices). Then give them the answers for the blanks below the pictures. The Pharisee was "self-righteous" because he was righteous in his own eyes, and he felt what he had done himself was what would save him. The publican was "redeemed-righteous"; that is, he was righteous in God's eyes because his sins had been taken away by Jesus. With his sins removed and his soul redeemed, he was indeed holy and blameless before God.

The redeemed-righteous condition of the publican can be paraphrased using Luther's words that explain the Second Article of the Apostles' Creed: The publican was redeemed, "a lost and condemned person, purchased and won . . . from all sins, from death, and from the power of the devil; not with gold or silver, but with [Christ's] holy, precious blood and with His innocent suffering and death" (Small Catechism).

A Parable about Righteousness

Jesus used a parable to teach people who thought that the good things they did made them acceptable to God. The parable showed the true righteousness that God desires. Read Jesus' story in Luke 18:9–14. Write words or phrases that describe the Pharisee on the stripes of his robe. Write words or phrases that apply to the publican (tax collector) on the stripes of his robe.

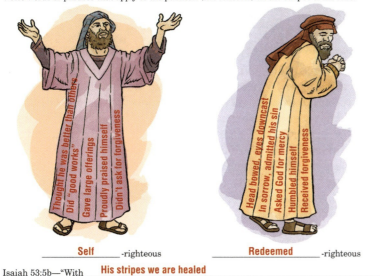

_____**Self**_____-righteous   _____**Redeemed**_____-righteous

Isaiah 53:5b—"With **His stripes we are healed**_____."

Put on Righteousness

To "put on righteousness" is to be covered or clothed in what Christ Jesus has done for us. Read about this in a translation that describes righteousness in this way.

- Romans 13:14 (NIV): "Clothe yourselves with the Lord Jesus Christ."
- Galatians 3:27 (NIV): "All of you who were baptized into Christ have clothed yourselves with Christ."
- 1 Peter 5:5 (NIV): "All of you, clothe yourselves with humility toward one another, because, 'God opposes the proud but gives grace to the humble.'"
- Colossians 3:12 (NIV): "Therefore, as God's chosen people, holy and dearly loved, clothe yourselves with compassion, kindness, humility, gentleness, and patience."

Remember

"For by grace you have been saved through faith. And this is not your own doing; it is the gift of God, not a result of works, so that no one may boast." (Ephesians 2:8–9)

147

Note the final statement of this section. It is important to point out to students that this is a play on words. In the illustration, students wrote their answers on the stripes of each person's clothing. In the Bible verse, the word *stripes* refers to the wounds in the beatings Jesus suffered to heal us of our sin-sickness that would have led to eternal death without the healing and new life He gives to us.

This, however, is not the end of our story. Jesus has won salvation for us and has justified us by grace. But His actions continue in our lives: He continues to lead us and guide us to live new lives, following and serving Him in all that we do. He sends the Holy Spirit to sanctify us, continuing to work in us to enable and empower us to live as people of God. Our justification through Jesus is complete, but the sanctification process continues. Let's learn more about living in righteousness.

INTO our lives

Put on Righteousness

This Student Book section emphasizes that "putting on" the righteousness Jesus gives becomes part of who we are (not just something tucked away in a pocket to be brought out on Sunday morning). When you "put on" jeans and a T-shirt, you are clothed; what you put on is what people see. The same is true of "putting on" Jesus and His righteousness; if we are clothed in Him, this is what people will see when they look at us. Similarly, if you "put on" sunscreen, you are covered with it; "putting on" Jesus' righteousness means we are to be covered with it. It affects everything we do. Read the Bible verses aloud, emphasizing that this is how our lives look when we have "put on" the righteousness of Christ.

A Contrast in Motivation

Go back and look again at the journal entries of Justin, Sophie, Maya, and Robert. Ask your students to name all the good things these four students were doing. Point out that these good works didn't make them righteous before God. We don't do good things in order to become righteous; instead, because Jesus covers us in His righteousness, we now are able to do good things. **Good works don't save us, but good works are the natural outcome of being saved.** Read Ephesians 2:10, the verse that follows this lesson's Bible words to remember (Paul's famous statement on salvation by grace through faith): "For we are His workmanship, created in Christ Jesus for good works, which God prepared beforehand, that we should walk in them." The motivation is what is significant. Works done out of fear, to gain the favor of others, or to earn salvation are not "good." If the motivation is gratitude for what God has done for us, if God Himself is the origin, and if the power source is the Holy Spirit, then we truly can do "good" works. Use Reproducible 70 to further explore these concepts. Also use Web Resources 70a and 70b, which are recordings of Psalm 51:10–12 in two different settings. You will need to point out to students that there are slight variations in wording because these settings are taken from an older English translation of the Bible, the King James Version (KJV), from 1611. Though the version is more than four hundred years old, it is still a favorite of many people.

301

Lesson Support

Curriculum Connection

Consider using section 6.4.1.4, Characteristics of Effective Presentations, found in the sixth-grade Language Arts volume of the Concordia Curriculum Guide series. Both the Pharisee and the tax collector made "presentations" of a sort to the Lord. But the Pharisee forgot his audience as he made his prayer; his words were not a prayer to God, but rather were a boast to people around him. **Why do you think the Lord was moved to forgive the tax collector but not the Pharisee?**

Celebrating GROWTH

As your students near the age of confirmation, help them become familiar with the liturgy of the Divine Service. Invite students to turn to page 167 in *LSB*. Discuss the reason the service begins with Confession and Absolution: we need to confess our sins and be forgiven before we come into God's presence to worship Him. Read the words of confession together several times so the students will be familiar with them. **We tend to think of sinning as "what we have done." How do we sin through "what we have left undone"?** Explain that *absolution* is the "forgiveness." **By what authority does the pastor forgive sins?** Read "The Office of the Keys" in *Luther's Small Catechism with Explanation*.

Ideas for the Gifted

Hymnwriters have given us powerful word pictures of our reliance on Jesus' sacrificial death in our place for forgiveness of sins and salvation. Challenge your artistically gifted students to express these faith concepts in a favorite art form. Hymns that are particularly suitable are found in *LSB*'s "Justification" section (555–76), especially "Dear Christians, One and All, Rejoice" (556); "Drawn to the Cross, Which Thou Hast Blessed" (560); "The Tree of Life" (561); "Jesus, Thy Blood and Righteousness" (563); "In the Shattered Bliss of Eden" (572); "Before the Throne of God Above" (574); and "My Hope Is Built on Nothing Less" (575). Display students' artwork in the school or church hallways or libraries along with students' explanations of the meanings of their projects.

Bringing it home

Consider sharing this note with parents: *Every parent remembers the "I'll do it myself!" cries of a toddler. When the child's safety is not threatened, wise parents allow their children to try to be self-sufficient. But often the child's attempts to "do it myself" end up in spilled milk or backward clothes. Family therapists suggest that this insistence on self-sufficiency in the toddler serves an important purpose: parents would never allow their precious babies to grow up without this difficult period of normal behavior. In our spiritual relationship with God, we are often like those toddlers. We would rather "do it ourselves" than accept the free grace He offers us through Jesus Christ. But all of our efforts to save ourselves end badly. Only through faith in Jesus and the salvation He has won for us are we declared righteous before God. You can help your child learn to depend on God's grace by modeling unconditional love in your family relationships. When your child has done something wrong, always assure him or her that although you do not like what he or she has done, you will always love and forgive.*

Searching Further

Can anyone be considered righteous by the things they do? Could King David? Could the apostle Paul? Although both of these biblical characters were heroes of faith, their "true confessions" show that they knew they were sinners in need of God's forgiveness. Read the story of David and Bathsheba in 2 Samuel 11–12. When the prophet Nathan confronted David with his sin of adultery (compounded by lying and murder), David confessed, "I have sinned against the Lord." Nathan extended God's forgiveness: "The Lord also has put away your sin" (12:13). Psalm 130 conveys David's emotional desolation and confidence in God's forgiveness: "Out of the depths I cry to You, O Lord! . . . If You, O Lord, should mark iniquities, O Lord, who could stand? But with You there is forgiveness, that You may be feared" (vv. 1, 3–4). Changed by his encounter with Christ on the road to Damascus, Paul carried the Good News about Jesus all over Europe and wrote letters expounding on the Gospel to the churches he had started. Yet Paul's words about his own sinful condition and need for a Savior are clear: "For I know that nothing good dwells in me, that is, in my flesh. For I have the desire to do what is right, but not the ability to carry it out. For I do not do the good I want, but the evil I do not want is what I keep on doing" (Romans 7:18–19). He concludes, "Who will deliver me from this body of death? Thanks be to God through Jesus Christ our Lord!" (vv. 24–25).

UNIT 7—JESUS COMPLETES OUR SALVATION

LESSON 71

A Woman Anoints Jesus
Matthew 26:6–13; Mark 14:3–9; John 12:1–9

Background

What is the best gift you've ever received? Regardless of its monetary value, it is likely that this gift is precious because of the loving feelings of its giver toward you. Such a gift is priceless. Mary, sister of Martha and Lazarus, gave Jesus the gift of pure nard, an ointment of exceptional quality. It was contained in an alabaster bottle. Alabaster is a semiprecious stone that was often cut into beautiful containers to hold perfume. In order to dispense its contents, the neck of the flask had to be broken. The ointment Mary gave Jesus "could have been sold for more than three hundred denarii" (Mark 14:5). A denarius was a laborer's daily wage. Mary's gift was valued at nearly a year's salary. But Mary didn't just hand Jesus a flask of perfume. She took time to apply the ointment in a loving and serving way. Mary "poured [the nard] on [Jesus'] head" (Matthew 26:7). She also "anointed the feet of Jesus and wiped His feet with her hair" (John 12:3). Anointing was usually done on a person's head. Mary anointed Jesus' head *and* His feet. Mary's actions show her humble devotion to Jesus.

Mary's giving shows what it means to give from the heart. Jesus knows what our heart attitude is. He loves us with an unchanging and immeasurable love. He helps us repent of our ingratitude, and He fills us with the joy and desire to serve Him with gladness. Pray that the Holy Spirit would continue to increase your love and the love of your students for Jesus as you serve Him and others.

Central Truth

God desires that in our humility and for His glory, we express our love for all He has done for us.

Objectives

- Recall repentantly that too often, we focus on our own wants rather than bless the Lord.
- Affirm that Christ gave His life for us by living for Him.
- Use the various talents and treasures we have to give Him our best and to serve others.

Materials

- Hymnals and music CDs
- Reproducible 71
- Web Resource 71a
- Crayons or pens for underlining

Bible Prep

Post in advance so students can bookmark references before class time.
- John 12:1–9
- Ephesians 4:29–32
- Isaiah 53:3–9
- Psalm 116
- Luke 9:35

Devotions

Today we will hear about a woman who gave Jesus a gift that would be worth thousands of dollars today. At another time that week, Jesus recognized a woman who gave a gift of two very small coins, worth just pennies. What a difference in the size of the two gifts! Yet Jesus praised both of the women. Why? Because He knew what was in their hearts. Both of them gave what they were able; both gave willingly and from the heart; both were thankful for and trusted in God's gracious care and mercy. The gifts were different, but the hearts were the same. That is what made these gifts valuable to our Lord. Read Mark 12:41–44. This occurred when Jesus was in the temple during Holy Week. Say, **The size of the gift is not what is most important; the person giving the gift is. Here is another story about giving. Four cousins were sitting together in church. Their parents were seated in the row behind them. When the offering plate was passed, each cousin put a dollar in the plate. The gifts were the same, but God knows what is in each heart. The first cousin thought, as he put his dollar in, "This should impress all my cousins. I'm giving a whole dollar!" He was doing it to show off. The next cousin dropped a dollar in the plate and thought, "I'd rather keep this and spend it later, but my dad is back there and will see if I don't." This person gave grudgingly, feeling she was forced to do it. The next cousin thought, "I am so happy about the ten dollars my neighbor gave me for cutting his grass! I'm more than happy to share one of the ten to help someone else."** He gave thankfully and joyfully. The next cousin thought, "Wow, I was only going to give a quarter, but I'll feel like a jerk if I don't give a dollar like everyone else." She gave, thinking only of her self-image and what other people would think of her.

The gifts we give to God are returned with promises of blessings. We've heard it before: the measure or amount we give to God will be returned in like measure; and "still more will be added to you" (Mark 4:24). These are not just gifts of dollars, but also gifts of time and kindness and service to others. God says that we should not give "reluctantly or under compulsion, for God loves a cheerful giver" (2 Corinthians 9:7). We can never outgive the One who has given us all that we have.

303

INTO the lesson

This Day in History

This activity provides a context for the events in today's Bible narrative and those that follow. Tell students to print "Jesus at Bethany" below the first Friday. (You may want to point out that one narrative says six days before Passover and another says two days. This may seem like a time discrepancy, but it is actually just different ways the people then expressed time. While we talk about sunrise, they spoke of sundown as the beginning of a new day. Also, the Passover was a weeklong celebration, not just a single meal. The Feast of Unleavened Bread was celebrated at a single meal, but there were many additional celebrations throughout the week. So two days before Passover week and six days before the Passover meal could occur at the same time. This is similar to the way we refer to "Christmas" as both the month of December and the date of the 25th.) Continue labeling the special events surrounding "Holy Week": "Palm Sunday," "Maundy Thursday," "Good Friday," and "Easter Sunday." Point out that although Monday, Tuesday, and Wednesday of this week do not have special names, these were very busy times. Every day, Jesus was in the temple, preaching to the people and telling them parables about the kingdom of God. During this time, Jesus cleansed the temple, praised the trust in God displayed by the poor widow, and more. Students can write "In the temple" on the timeline in such a way as to include all three days.

INTO the Word

Why Anoint?

Have students work on this section of the Student Book and discuss each main point.

Point 1: Ask, **While it is true that Jesus was a special guest at this dinner, what special reason did Mary have for expressing her humble thankfulness to Jesus?** (Jesus had just raised her brother, Lazarus, from the dead.) Point out that Lazarus was one of the people at this dinner, and many people came just to see him.

Point 2: Have students look at Luke 9:35, where God the Father Himself called Jesus His "Chosen One." Ask, **For what special role or reason was Jesus chosen?** (To be the Messiah, the Savior of all) Also read the prophecy in Isaiah 61:1 and its fulfillment in Acts 10:38. (Acts 10:36–43 gives a total summary of this fulfillment.)

Point 3: In John 12:8, Jesus Himself points out that this act of anointing is like a preview, preparing His body for burial, because He knew that in one week, He would die on the cross. The oil Mary used was an amazing luxury, with a cost equal to a man's wages for an entire year. This is an amount that would be used for a royal burial, and as such, it implies Jesus' role as King—not just a member of David's royal family, but the King of kings!

Compare the Narratives

Before continuing in the Student Book, explore Reproducible 71 to look at the Bible narrative in John 12 in its entirety and to compare it with these events as recorded by other Gospel writers. Also, display Web Resource 71a. Begin by having students scan the three readings to find a fact that is mentioned by all three writers. Whenever students find such a phrase, have them share their response with the class. Then check it out on the interactive whiteboard by dragging the phrase to the white center of the diagram. If the phrase sticks there, it is correct, and students should underline that phrase (or the similar one) in all three readings.

After finding all possible matches from all three writers, begin looking for matches found in two of the three writers. Check each response on the diagram, and then underline both with the corresponding color of crayon. (For example, if Matthew and Mark are similar, the phrase goes in the green section and is underlined in green; a Matthew-John match is in purple; a Mark-John match is in orange.)

What remains? Phrases that are mentioned by just one author. (Remind students

Why Choose?

The disciples (especially Judas) where indignant and self-righteous over what they considered Mary's "waste of money." What did they think should have been done with that large amount of money? **Give it to the poor.**

Who had the right idea? Who was right and who was wrong? **There is no "right" or "wrong" if the gift is given from the heart for the glory of God. Both types of gifts are welcome; one is not better than the other. The only thing "wrong" here was that the disciples should not have judged Mary's gift.**

Giving Our Best

Mary's gift was very valuable, worth thousands of dollars in today's money. But Jesus didn't look at her gift's value; He looked at her heart. In Mark 4:24, Jesus spoke of measuring gifts of gratitude, saying, "With the measure you use, it will be measured to you, and still more will be added to you." We can see this same spirit of generosity in Exodus 36, when the people of Israel brought gifts to build the tabernacle. The people brought so many gifts—much more than was needed—that Moses had to ask them to stop giving! More than the gifts, it was the heartfelt attitude that was overflowing!

What can you and I give to Jesus? Check the answer in Psalm 116 and also in this portion of a poem by Christina Rossetti:

> What can I give Him, poor as I am?
> If I were a shepherd, I would bring a lamb.
> If I were a Wise Man, I would do my part;
> Yet what I can I give Him: give my heart.

Remember

"What shall I render to the Lord for all His benefits to me? I will offer the sacrifice of thanksgiving and will call on the name of the Lord. I will take the cup of salvation and will call on the name of the Lord. I will pay my vows to the Lord now in the presence of all His people, in the courts of the Lord's house, in the midst of you, O Jerusalem." (*LSB*, pp. 159, 176, based on Psalm 116)

149

INTO our lives

Giving Our Best

The explanation of the Second Article of the Apostles' Creed tells of Jesus' great gift to us—not of gold or silver, but His holy, precious blood and His innocent suffering and death. What does He desire from us? That we "may be His own and live under Him in His kingdom and serve Him in everlasting righteousness, innocence, and blessedness" (Small Catechism). He wants from us a godly heart that expresses itself in kindness and service to others and in giving glory to God! How do we characterize such gifts? We give our best joyfully, not because of who we are, but because of *whose* we are—the forgiven, redeemed children of God.

---

that the Gospel writers wrote to different audiences for different purposes as they were inspired by the Holy Spirit. Therefore, some facts will seem more significant to one writer than to another.) If only Matthew mentions something, underline it in blue; if only Mark, use yellow; and if only John, use red. Looking at all three narratives gives a complete picture.

Why Choose?

As you discuss this section of the Student Book, emphasize that **Jesus recognized the value of both types of gifts—those given for the poor and those given for God's glory. He pointed out that there will always be poor people who need our help and kindness. However, that does not limit our purposes in giving. What is most important is the heart of the giver. Rather than making a choice between two types of gifts, it is good to find ways to do both.** To illustrate this, have students draw a large plus sign at the center of the diagram in their Student Book. (Point out that this is an issue that continues in today's world. Members of some congregations have had ungodly arguments about whether to spend a lot of money on new art for the church sanctuary or whether that money should be put to practical use building a food pantry for the homeless. This is not a matter for argument; it is a matter of the heart. God desires to lead us to have generous hearts that desire to do both rather than to choose between gifts to be given. A truly heartfelt gift will consider God's will rather than a gift that serves what the giver wants.)

Jesus praised Mary for the gift she gave. Anointing His head with costly ointment was a recognition of Jesus as ruler over all things, even death. Mary's gratitude likely stemmed from the recent miracle of Jesus raising her brother from the dead. **Jesus' great gift to us was His very own life! Our gratitude stems from all that Jesus has done for us to bring us forgiveness, life, and salvation.** Anointing Jesus' feet was Mary's recognition of her own sinfulness and lowliness. Her gift was from the heart.

Lesson Support

Critical thinking

In today's lesson, the disciples did not have their hearts in the right place. They were wrong to judge what Mary had done. (In Matthew 7:1–2, Jesus said, "Judge not, that you be not judged. For with the judgment you pronounce you will be judged, and with the measure you use it will be measured to you.") Their heart attitude was not one of compassion for the poor; rather, they displayed an attitude of superiority, as they tried to appear more righteous than Mary. This is a significant factor to discuss. **Too often, people tear down someone else in order to build themselves up. This can really take a toll on teens and preteens. It is an attitude that harms all people involved.** The person who is tearing down or ridiculing someone else is harmed by developing a hurtful, vain attitude; the person who is the victim of this behavior becomes emotionally scarred with feelings of inadequacy. Neither of these is God's will. In 2 Corinthians 10:12, Scripture says, "When they measure themselves by one another and compare themselves with one another, they are without understanding." So what *is* God's will? Read aloud Ephesians 4:29–32.

Curriculum Connection

Mary showed her love and honor for Jesus by anointing Him. Learn about ways you and your students can show similar care for others using section 6.6.2, Communicating Care and Respect, in the sixth-grade Health volume of the Concordia Curriculum Guide series. Discuss with students: **Since Jesus is no longer visibly among us, what can we do to show our loving thanks for Him today?**

HANDS TO SERVE

Take time to thank those who volunteer in your classroom and school for their humble service to you and your students. Students can design thank-you cards, banners, and posters to recognize these individuals. Perhaps you could prepare a hymn of thanks to sing for the volunteers at an upcoming chapel service. "Lord, Help Us Walk Your Servant Way" (*LSB* 857); "Where Charity and Love Prevail" (*LSB* 845); "Listen, God Is Calling" (*LSB* 833); and "They'll Know We Are Christians by Our Love" (*AGPS* 237) are possibilities. Or set up a student-led event where students serve the volunteers. Include Bible readings, a devotion, some singing, and refreshments.

Ideas for the Gifted

Our Lutheran hymns are rich in biblical truths. Lenten hymns are especially descriptive concerning the suffering sacrifice of Jesus that redeemed us. The words used in many of these hymns are great vocabulary builders. Invite students to investigate the following Lenten hymns and list the descriptions of Jesus' Passion they find: "Christ, the Life of All the Living" (*LSB* 420); "My Song Is Love Unknown" (*LSB* 430); "In Silent Pain the Eternal Son" (*LSB* 432); "Alas! And Did My Savior Bleed" (*LSB* 437); and "O Dearest Jesus, What Law Hast Thou Broken" (*LSB* 439). Read rather than sing the lyrics of these hymns in devotions as another way to help students understand the truths of Jesus' sacrifice for us.

Searching Further

Have each student compose a thank-You note to Jesus for His daily and continual goodness. Have them write their notes on actual stationery cards. Collect the notes, and share them during this year's Good Friday chapel or at some point during Holy Week as part of a prayer that thanks Jesus for His sacrifice for us.

Working in Groups

Have students design and prepare a mural that illustrates the truths of the Second Article of the Apostles' Creed and its meaning. First, print the paragraphs of the Second Article and its meaning at various points along the mural. Then surround each paragraph with drawings that illustrate each phrase.

The Second Article itself can be illustrated with the crucial scenes from Jesus' life that it mentions, including His birth, arrest, crucifixion, resurrection, and ascension. The first paragraph of the meaning of the article can be illustrated with scenes that show Jesus both as true God (e.g., performing miracles) and as true man (e.g., eating with the disciples, walking, talking with people). The second paragraph of the meaning can be illustrated with a graphic that shows how Jesus redeemed us (e.g., something similar to drawings that show how the cross bridges the gap between us and God). The third paragraph of the meaning of the Second Article can be illustrated with scenes that show how we can serve Jesus. End the mural with a picture of Jesus on His heavenly throne, triumphant as our Lord and King.

UNIT 7—JESUS COMPLETES OUR SALVATION

LESSON 72

Jesus Rides into Jerusalem
MATTHEW 21:1–11

Background

"Blessed is He who comes in the name of the Lord!" sang the crowds (Matthew 21:9) as Jesus entered Jerusalem in fulfillment of the prophecy of Zechariah (Zechariah 9:9). Their words were those traditionally used to greet pilgrims coming to Jerusalem. These words of praise are drawn from the Hallel, Psalms 113–118. These six "Hallelujah psalms" were sung before and after Passover. The first part of the Hallel, Psalms 113–114, was sung after the Passover liturgy retelling the story of the exodus from Egypt. After this, a prayer of benediction was spoken over the unleavened bread, which was distributed and eaten. The Passover lamb was eaten, a third cup of wine was blessed and shared, and the meal was ended. The second part of the Hallel, Psalms 115–118, was sung at this time. Both Matthew (26:30) and Mark (14:26) record the singing of a hymn at the end of the Passover meal at which Jesus instituted the Lord's Supper; this hymn was probably the Hallel. Psalm 113 is a general call of praise, echoing Hannah's song of praise (1 Samuel 2:1–10) and anticipating Mary's Magnificat (Luke 1:46–55). It opens with a triple repetition of God's name, similar to the trinitarian invocation in Christian worship. Psalm 114 is the only one of the psalms sung at Passover that points directly back to the exodus. Psalm 113 taught that the Lord lifts the needy. Psalm 114 shows how He did this during the exodus. Psalm 115 urges Israel not to look to outward manifestations of strength, but to remember God's steadfast love. Psalm 116 reminds us that God cares deeply about our mortality and has released us from its permanent bonds through the suffering, death, and resurrection of His Son. Psalm 117 celebrates God's grace, which began in Israel but is extended to all nations through Christ. As the last psalm of the Hallel, Psalm 118 was used as thanksgiving for national deliverance.

Central Truth

Jesus, the Son of David, fulfilled the promise and covenant God made in the Old Testament.

Objectives

- When we get caught up in the concerns of this world, contritely go to Jesus with our hosannas, asking Him to help us.
- Identify Jesus as our heavenly King who wants to rule in our hearts, giving us the victory He has won.
- Proclaim openly and unashamedly who Jesus is and who we are as His people.

Materials

- Hymnals and music CDs
- Web Resource 72a
- Reproducible 72

Bible Prep

Post in advance so students can bookmark references before class time.
- Matthew 21
- Mark 11:9–10
- Luke 2:14
- Luke 19:38
- John 12:13

Devotions

Sing together "Hosanna, Hallelujah" (*AGPS* 121; recorded on *JPS*; it is also found in *Songs Kids Love to Sing 2*, p. 28, and is recorded on the CD by the same name). **This song gives a summary of the Bible narrative we will study today about Jesus' entry into Jerusalem on Palm Sunday. The title of the song has two important words that people sometimes mistakenly think mean the same thing. But they don't. The word *hallelujah* means "Praise the Lord!" The word *hosanna* means "Save us!" Though the words have different definitions, it is possible that the people mixed their hosannas with hallelujahs on that Palm Sunday so long ago.**

Many people thought Jesus was coming to save them from their Roman enemies. But Jesus came for a greater purpose. He came to save us from the greatest enemies—sin, death, and the devil. Only He had the power to overcome them because only He is true God and true man.

Another important word in this Bible story is the word *rex*, or *king*. Once again, there was a misunderstanding. Many people thought Jesus came to Jerusalem as an earthly king—as the king of the Jews. **But Jesus came for a greater purpose. Jesus came as the heavenly King—the King of kings. His kingdom is not of this world; it is an eternal kingdom, the kingdom of glory. Because of Jesus' suffering, death, and resurrection, we will join Him one day to live forever in His kingdom in heaven.**

Sing together "The King of Glory" (*AGPS* 227; recorded on *JPS*). This song gives another summary of what Jesus has done to win the victory for us. Say, **"Thanks be to God, who gives us the victory through our Lord Jesus Christ"** (1 Corinthians 15:57).

INTO the lesson

Triumphal Ending

Refer back to the timeline in Lesson 71. Point out that Jesus is riding into Jerusalem, knowing He will soon die on the cross. Read aloud Matthew 21:1–11, and then compare the two events in the Student Book. The answers in the Teacher Guide are suggestions for comparisons. Your students may find additional possibilities.

Then examine the title of this section. It may be the ending of the basketball season in the first picture, but the second picture is a beginning—the beginning of what we call "Holy Week." Jesus knew what was ahead of Him, and He went willingly, knowing all things must be done to accomplish our salvation. Have students cross off the word "Ending" in the title and change it to "Entry." **We usually speak of Palm Sunday as Jesus' triumphal entry into Jerusalem. It was a happy day, yet some of the biblical accounts speak of Jesus' sadness. He was sad because He knew that some of these same people would turn against Him by the end of the week and would change their shouts to "Crucify Him! Crucify Him!" He was sad because of the grumbling of His enemies in the crowd.** (In the first picture, some people grumbled because they were for the other team. In the second picture, some people grumbled because they saw masses of people following Jesus rather than their own leadership.) **Jesus was sad also because He knew some people in the crowd were expecting something different from the Messiah. Some thought He was coming as an earthly king to deliver the Jewish people from the Romans. But Jesus came as a heavenly King to deliver all people from sin, death, and the power of the devil.**

Have students print the word *VICTORY* in capital letters, vertically, in the space between the two pictures. **Both of these are victory parades. The difference is that in the first picture, the championship victory was over; in the second picture, the victory was still to come. Jesus knew that the victory would come at the end of the week through His death on the cross and His resurrection at Easter.**

LESSON 72
Jesus Rides into Jerusalem

Triumphal Ending

The state university had just won the national basketball championship. Everyone celebrated with a parade through the middle of town. Compare this parade with Jesus riding into Jerusalem on Palm Sunday. Compare ways that the parades are similar or different.

Shouts of "We're number one!"	Shouts of "Hosanna!"
Waving flags	Waving palm branches
Riding in cars	Riding a small donkey
Red carpet on road	Coats on path
Grumblers in crowd	Grumblers in crowd
End of basketball season	Beginning of season of suffering

Review

Covenant Connection

Jesus' entry into Jerusalem was the direct fulfillment of an Old Testament prophecy spoken hundreds of years earlier. In this, we see God's continuing grace and promises to all His people. In Zechariah 9:9, the prophet said, "Rejoice greatly, O daughter of Zion! Shout aloud, O daughter of Jerusalem! Behold, your king is coming to you; righteous and having salvation is He, humble and mounted on a donkey, on a colt, the foal of a donkey." The Lord is faithful to all His promises!

150

INTO the Word

The Story Summary

The Student Book activity is a unique way of taking a closer look and analyzing the text. The answers given in red in the Teacher Guide are just possibilities. Listen to other student suggestions, and ask them to explain their choices. Look again at Matthew 21:10 and the question that people in Jerusalem asked: "Who is this?" Sing the song with a similar title, "Who Was the Man" (*AGPS* 268; recorded on *JPS*; also recorded on CPH's *Super Songs for Christ's Kids*). This song is a summary of Jesus' ministry and of the events of Holy Week, and it is an answer to the question "Who is Jesus?"

The Cheers of the People

There are several interesting things to note after students have completed this section in their books. Have them compare the words of Luke 19:38 with 2:14. **The author Luke saw the connection between these events at the beginning and end of Jesus' life. This parallel emphasizes that Jesus came to bring peace between heaven and earth. He has reconciled us to God in heaven, bringing peace by taking away our sins.**

In the words of John 12:13, the people called Jesus "the King of Israel." On Good Friday, Pilate,

The Story Summary

Give a one-word summary of these verses in Matthew 21.

Verse 1 — request
Verse 2 — donkey
Verse 3 — needed
Verse 4 — fulfilled
Verse 5 — prophecy
Verse 6 — obeyed
Verse 7 — cloaks
Verse 8 — branches
Verse 9 — shouted
Verse 10 — wondered
Verse 11 — Jesus

The Cheers of the People

Write the words of the people as they greeted Jesus.

Matthew 21:9 "Hosanna to the Son of David! Blessed is He who comes in the name of the Lord! Hosanna in the highest!"

Mark 11:9–10 "Hosanna! Blessed is He who comes in the name of the Lord! Blessed is the coming kingdom of our father David! Hosanna in the highest!"

Luke 19:38 "Blessed is the King who comes in the name of the Lord! Peace in heaven and glory in the highest!"

John 12:13 "Hosanna! Blessed is He who comes in the name of the Lord, even the King of Israel!"

A Happy Ending

We like happy endings. Like the people of Jerusalem, we might have wanted the story to end on Palm Sunday, with cloaks and palm branches and shouts of "Hosanna!" But God's plan included a different ending. The crowd's reaction to Jesus convinced the Pharisees and other religious leaders that Jesus must be stopped. They grumbled, "Look, the world has gone after Him" (John 12:19). Their plotting led to Jesus' arrest in the Garden of Gethsemane, to His trials, and to His cross on Calvary.

Wouldn't it have been better to end the story on Palm Sunday, without the blood and gore that was to come on Friday? The writer of Hebrews explained why the rest of the story was necessary: "Indeed, under the law . . . without the shedding of blood there is no forgiveness of sins" (Hebrews 9:22). Palm Sunday seemed like a happy ending. But Jesus' triumphal entry did nothing to remove the wall of sin that separated us from God. Only Jesus' death and resurrection could accomplish that, as Paul wrote: "For in Him all the fullness of God was pleased to dwell, and through Him to reconcile to Himself all things, whether on earth or in heaven, making peace by the blood of His cross" (Colossians 1:19–20).

Jesus' suffering and death paid the price for our redemption; it set us free to be people of God, forgiven, and blessed with life eternal. For sinners like you and me, that is the happiest ending of all.

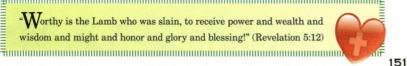

"Worthy is the Lamb who was slain, to receive power and wealth and wisdom and might and honor and glory and blessing!" (Revelation 5:12)

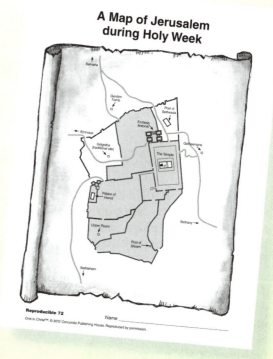

A Map of Jerusalem during Holy Week

---

the Roman governor, would take these words of the people and place them on a sign above Jesus' head on the cross, calling Him "the King of the Jews." Pilate was ridiculing the people of Israel who earlier in the week had cheered this King and then, at the end of the week, turned on Him to condemn Him. It was Pilate's ironic way of saying something like "See what these people do to their kings!?" Pilate did not realize the true enormity of this: **Jesus' crucifixion is what we *all* did to our King of kings! It was our sins that Jesus carried to the cross. We are all guilty! But thanks be to God, Jesus has removed all of our sin and guilt! We are at peace with God because Jesus has blessed us with His victory!**

A Happy Ending

Blood is not usually part of a happy ending. But the shedding of blood was always necessary for the forgiveness of sins. Remind students that Old Testament believers were forgiven by sacrifices that involved killing animals. Hebrews 9:22 points out that without blood, there was no forgiveness of sins. Jesus was the perfect sacrifice for our sins.

Point out the phrase "set us free to be people of God" in the third paragraph of the Student Book. This phrase is taken from the hymn "This Is the Feast" (*LSB*, pp. 155 and 171), based in part on today's Bible words to remember in Revelation 5:12. Choose one or both of the melodies on Web Resource 72a to sing this hymn together.

Direct students to the explanation of the Second Article of the Apostles' Creed. This can be found in Luther's Small Catechism, included in the Appendix of the Student Book (or in *LSB*, p. 322). This explanation provides an excellent summary of God's plan for our happy ending through Christ Jesus.

Option: At any point in the lesson, you may want to distribute copies of Reproducible 72, a map showing where events of Holy Week took place. Ask students to find the road Jesus took to Jerusalem. (That would be the road coming from Bethany and nearby Bethphage.) Mark 11:11 says that after entering Jerusalem, Jesus went to the temple. If you look at the map, you will see that the Bethany road leads right to the temple. This road was traveled frequently that week by Jesus and His disciples as He daily went to the temple and then stayed in the evening with friends in Bethany. Have students keep the map handy as a reference for the next lessons in this unit.

Technology

Prepare a radio drama of the story "Jesus Rides into Jerusalem" as recorded in Matthew 21:1–11. Assign one or more students to serve as narrator, one for the voice of Jesus, another for the prophet Zechariah, and others for the speakers in verses 10 and 11. Experiment with sound effects for the clip-clopping of the donkeys, the swishing of the palm branches, and the cries of the crowd, at a distance and also close-at-hand. When you are satisfied with your skit, record it and give a copy of the recording to a class of younger children. For a greater challenge, stage actors in poses for the various scenes in the story. Use a digital camera to photograph the scenes. Download the photos to the classroom computer, and import them into a program such as Microsoft's Windows Live Movie Maker. Then record your drama with sound effects as an audio track to accompany the pictures in your presentation.

Curriculum Connection

Consider the story of Jesus' triumphal entry with the help of section 6.4.1.9, Nonverbal Cues Used to Convey a Message, found in the sixth-grade Language Arts volume of the Concordia Curriculum Guide series. When you listen to the words, the people are hailing Jesus as King and Messiah, and Jesus is accepting their praise as He rides into Jerusalem, the capital city of ancient Israel. But what do the nonverbal elements of the scene say? Consider: Jesus is riding a young, untrained donkey, not a horse; the donkey is borrowed and must soon be returned; for a saddle, He has nothing but His disciples' cloaks; the "red carpet" laid out ahead of Him is made of more cloaks and palm branches torn from nearby trees; many of those praising Him are little children. Putting all of these things together, what kind of a king is this?

Working in Groups

As Jesus approached Bethphage on the Mount of Olives, He sent two of His disciples into the village to borrow a donkey and her colt. These disciples are never named. Jesus frequently paired workers for a task. After Jesus was rejected in Nazareth early in His ministry, He sent out His twelve disciples two by two and gave them authority over unclean spirits (Mark 6:7). Before the Last Supper, Jesus sent Peter and John to prepare the meal in the Upper Room (Luke 22:8). This support system works just as well today. Christians gain support from each other when sharing the Good News about Jesus. Encourage your students to work in pairs as they study the story of salvation as presented in God's Word. Verbalizing their faith to each other will give them valuable witnessing experience they can use throughout their lives.

Searching Further

The people of Jerusalem greeted the Messiah with a song normally sung during the Passover celebration—"Blessed is He who comes in the name of the Lord"—from Psalm 118, part of the Hallel. Try setting this line to music, or use the words as part of a cheer or a chant. Choose instruments to accompany your song. The Hebrew word *Hallel* is the root word of *hallelujah*, a joyful shout or song of praise. Search through *LSB* and *AGPS* for songs with "hallelujahs." Look at the liturgy for Holy Communion, particularly the Sanctus (*LSB*, pp. 161, 178, 195, and 208). Find the setting used most often by your congregation, and practice singing it together. Then listen to the most famous "hallelujah" of all—the "Hallelujah Chorus" from Handel's oratorio *Messiah*.

Faith in Action

The cheering people of Jerusalem recognized Jesus as the King prophesied by Zechariah (Zechariah 9:9). Days later, Pontius Pilate asked Jesus, "Are You the King of the Jews?" Jesus explained, "My kingdom is not of this world" (John 18:33–36). Soldiers twisted a crown of thorns and placed it on His head and clothed Him in a purple robe, saying, "Hail, King of the Jews!" (John 19:2–3). Jesus, who really is King of kings and Lord of lords, suffered this indignation as well as death itself to save us from our sins. Write a series of prayers about the events of Holy Week. Perhaps the prayers could be included in your church bulletins during Lent.

UNIT 7—JESUS COMPLETES OUR SALVATION

LESSON 73

Jesus in the Temple
Mark 11:15–19, 27–33

Background

Jesus had just entered Jerusalem with the honor and acclamation due Him as a king. Yet, the first place He went to do His work was not the palace, but the temple. Even as we recall how Jesus goes about the business of purifying the temple, it is important to keep in mind the purification of souls through His death and resurrection, which was His work at the end of the week. There is interesting contrast between the harshness with which Jesus deals with sin in this Scripture and the loving kindness with which He goes about healing the blind and the lame and accepting the praises of children. Our Lord hates sin, yet He provides gentle healing to those who humbly come to Him in need.

Jesus also establishes His authority in His own house in this segment of Scripture. The money-changers and buyers and sellers in the marketplace saw His judgment of their wrongdoing. Those still present in the temple witnessed His power to heal. They heard the praises of the children as well. All of these things pointed to the power and authority of Christ. They also angered the chief priests and scribes. While Jesus had avoided confrontation with the religious leaders several times in the past, He now placed Himself in their sights. The time had come for the ultimate fulfillment of Jesus' purpose on earth.

Central Truth

God calls us to confront the sin in our lives and to joyfully receive the gracious forgiveness and restoration He offers us through Christ.

Objectives

- Confront and confess the sin in our own lives and ask the Lord's mercy in getting rid of it.
- Recognize God's gracious forgiveness, spiritual healing, and loving restoration of relationship with His children.
- Respond to God's spiritual restoration with praise.

Materials

- Hymnals and music CDs
- Web Resource 73a
- Reproducible 73
- Web Resource 70a
- Web Resource 70b

Bible Prep

Post in advance so students can bookmark references before class time.

- Luke 2:49
- Mark 11
- John 12; 14
- Matthew 5; 21; 28
- 1 Timothy 1; 2
- Ephesians 2:18–19
- Hebrews 9; 10; 13

Devotion

"I'm going out to weed the garden," Grandma called. Caleb came into the room with a thoughtful look on his face.

"I thought you just weeded the garden a few days ago. Why would you need to do it again already? It seems like you are always weeding the garden. I've been here two weeks, and I think you've weeded six times—and I've helped you twice."

Grandma smiled and put down her gloves. "I love working in my garden," she replied. "But sometimes it even seems to *me* like I'm weeding all the time. The weeds keep growing, and if I didn't get out there and do something about them, they would take over the whole garden. Then the plants I'm trying to grow would die, and I'd be left with nothing but a weed patch."

"Yeah, I guess so," Caleb sighed.

Now it was Grandma's turn to look thoughtful. "In a way, it reminds me of sin in our lives," Grandma said. "If I just pretend it isn't there and hope it goes away, it can get out of control and choke out the fruits of faith that both God and I want in my life. I'm so thankful that Jesus died and rose so my sins can be forgiven! It's because of the power of Christ's love and grace that sin loses its power in my life." She turned to Caleb. "Why don't you think about that while you help me weed?" she laughed, patting him on the back.

Caleb sighed and pulled on his shoes. "Sure thing, Grandma," he said. "Let's go to war against those sins—I mean, *weeds*."

Let's pray: Lord, help us to confront the sin in our lives. Remove the sin through the forgiveness You freely give because of what Jesus did for us. We praise You for Your goodness and grace. **Amen.** Sing together "This Is He" (*AGPS* 239; recorded on *JPS*) or "Crown Him with Many Crowns" (*LSB* 525; recorded as *Hymn of the Month* for grade 6, March). Speak, sing, or chant portions of Psalm 51.

INTO the lesson

Confronting Sin in His House

To put today's Bible narrative into perspective, show Web Resource 73a, an overview of some of the events of Holy Week. It is important to remember where this event fits in the chronology of the ministry of Jesus. It is the beginning of Holy Week. Jesus knows He will take the sins of the world upon Himself and suffer and die at the end of that same week. He has just entered Jerusalem with honor and glory. He has been received as a king by the people who welcomed Him. It would have been tempting for most people to bask in the glory of that moment. But Jesus went right to the temple, where He belonged. He was not an earthly king. His realm of authority was reflected by His presence in the temple. It was quiet in His Father's house.

When Jesus returned the next day, He saw that dishonor had crept into His house through the front gate. Just as an earthly king would get rid of those who dishonored him, Jesus needed to get rid of those who were dishonoring the temple. He overturned their tables, and the money and goods they were using for their wrongdoing were thrown to the ground—where they belonged.

All four Gospels contain accounts of Jesus cleansing the temple. Matthew and Luke record it as the next significant event after His triumphal entry into the city, but Mark makes it clear that the temple cleansing took place first thing Monday morning. John's account of the temple cleansing is a bit different. John seems to place the event near the beginning of Jesus' public ministry. This could very well indicate that Jesus cleansed the temple both at the beginning and again at the end of His earthly ministry (like taking care of weeds that keep coming back). Despite His authority as God, Jesus chooses to refer to Scripture both to explain what the temple was supposed to be and to show what it had become. (Read aloud Mark 11:17.) Referring to the Scriptures was not unusual for Jesus. By His practice, He provides a model for us for using Scripture to guide our own words and actions. On this occasion, Jesus quotes from the prophets Isaiah (56:7) and Jeremiah (7:11). Those present at the temple—particularly the chief priests and scribes—would have been familiar with these writings.

LESSON 73
Jesus in the Temple

Confronting Sin in His House

When Jesus entered Jerusalem on Palm Sunday, He went to the temple. See Mark 11:11. It was late, and everything was quiet there.

The next day was a different story! Read about it in Mark 11:15–19. Why was Jesus so upset? _The temple courtyard had become a noisy marketplace. People were more interested in commerce and making money than in honoring God and using it as a house of prayer, as it was intended to be. They were breaking the Third Commandment, and they made it even worse by cheating people in their selling and trading._

Some people criticize Jesus for causing such a disturbance. Do you think Jesus should have ignored the problem and gone elsewhere to pray? Or do you think Jesus should have formed a committee to discuss the matter with the leaders of the temple? Do you think Jesus handled the matter in the right way? _Jesus, true God, would not accept or tolerate sin. He saw what was wrong and acted immediately to remove the sin, especially since the sin dishonored God Himself._

Showing His Authority

The chief priests and scribes questioned Jesus' authority. They wanted to know what right He had to control what was happening in the temple and to make commands. After all, *they* were considered the "temple authorities." Jesus was challenging their authority by His actions. Read Mark 11:27–33 to see how Jesus handled this situation. Why do you think Jesus refused to give them a direct answer? _He knew they were hoping to trick Him into saying something wrong so they could arrest Him; He had shown His authority many times before, and they had rejected Him. He would not "play their game" or "fall into their trap" until the time was right._

Jesus used His power and authority only for good. Read John 12:49 and 14:10. Where did His authority come from? _From God the Father (remembering that He and the Father are one)_

After Jesus had completed all things for our salvation through His death and resurrection, what did He say about His power and authority? See Matthew 28:18. _"All authority in heaven and on earth has been given to Me."_

Review

Covenant Connection

The prophet Jeremiah spoke God's message to the people of his day, saying, "Has this house, which is called by My name, become a den of robbers in your eyes?" (Jeremiah 7:11). Jesus referred to these words, which the chief priests and scribes would have known, and which should have been a warning to them. Instead, their reaction was to plan to "destroy Him, for they feared Him" (Mark 11:18). Jesus also spoke of the word of the Lord through the prophet Isaiah, who said, "My house shall be called a house of prayer for all peoples" (Isaiah 56:7). These Old Testament threads connected right to Jesus in the New Testament, especially the words in the same chapter, saying, "Soon My salvation will come, and My deliverance be revealed" (Isaiah 56:1).

152

INTO the Word

Showing His Authority

In the process of restoring honor to the temple, Jesus also demonstrates His authority there. The chief priests and scribes were used to being in charge at the temple, and they were not happy about what Jesus was doing. One can imagine them standing together, watching Jesus, unsure of what to do. As He healed, it had to be apparent that He had godly power and authority. It seemed it was the children's praises, however, that drove them to express their jealousy in words. Jesus defended the children and once again quoted Scripture to make His point—"Out of the mouths of infants and nursing babies you have prepared praise" (Matthew 21:16). He values the praises of the children. The praises that were flowing from the hearts to the mouths of the children had been put there by God. When the priests and scribes directly confronted Jesus about the source of His authority, He did not "play their game" in which they were trying to catch Him saying something wrong. Jesus was waiting until the time was right to willingly give Himself into their hands. The chief priests and scribes were dealing with a serious case of jealousy over the attention and respect Jesus was receiving. Satan used this jealousy to move them to plot to kill Jesus.

312

Putting His House to Good Use

During the remaining days of Holy Week, until Jesus was arrested on Maundy Thursday, He and His disciples continued to go to the temple and celebrate the Passover. During this time, Jesus honored God's house in three special ways.

1. **Helping.** How did Jesus help people while in the temple? See Matthew 21:14. **The blind and the lame came to Him, and He healed them.**

2. **Praising.** What was the song of praise the children repeated in the temple as Jesus listened? See Matthew 21:15. **"Hosanna to the Son of David!"**

3. **Teaching.** Jesus taught crowds of people who gathered in the temple. Sometimes, He spoke in parables (such as the parable of two sons, of talents, of a wedding feast). He answered questions about paying taxes to Caesar, about the resurrection, and about the final judgment on the Last Day.

In what ways do you see these same three things taking place in the house of worship that you attend? **Answers will vary.**

Jesus Cleans Your Heart

Jesus confronted and got rid of the sin in His house, the temple. Sin had worked its way in and needed to be cleansed so Jesus could concentrate on His good, loving work of healing and teaching and so the people could concentrate on praying and praising the Lord. God asks us to confront sin in our lives also, for we, too, are considered the temple of God: "Do you not know that you are God's temple and that God's Spirit dwells in you?" (1 Corinthians 3:16). God calls us through His Word to repentance—to confess our sins, receive His forgiveness, and turn away from sin in the future so that we can concentrate on letting the good things God wants for us to thrive in our lives.

In the following Scripture section, cross out the things listed that are sinful and should be confronted and cleansed from our lives. Put a circle around the things that thrive in a life committed to Christ.

"Let all ~~bitterness~~ and ~~wrath~~ and ~~anger~~ and ~~clamor~~ and ~~slander~~ be put away from you, along with all ~~malice~~. Be (kind) to one another, (tenderhearted,) (forgiving) one another, as God in Christ forgave you. Therefore be (imitators of God) as beloved children. And walk in (love,) as Christ loved us and gave Himself up for us, a fragrant offering and sacrifice to God" (Ephesians 4:31–5:2).

What do these things look like in your daily life? Consider some of the actions and characteristics that—with God's help—you want to cleanse from your life. Identify things that you want to grow in, through the Holy Spirit. Praise the Lord that Jesus cleanses us too! Pray that He will lead us to grow in faith and in our faith lives.

Remember

"If we say we have no sin, we deceive ourselves, and the truth is not in us. If we confess our sins, He is faithful and just to forgive us our sins and to cleanse us from all unrighteousness." (1 John 1:8–9)

Jesus Cleans Your Heart

While working through the exercise dealing with Ephesians 4:31–5:2, make sure the students understand the meanings of all the words. If time allows, have students look them up in the dictionary.

Point out that **since we are all sinful, we must rely on Jesus to take away our sin and enable us to live new lives. We can't do it on our own. It is only by the power of the Holy Spirit that we have changes in our hearts and lives.**

To take the lesson further and to emphasize the fact that it is only through Jesus, our Priest and Sacrifice, that we are free from sin and have access to God, work through Reproducible 73. Read the condition "Under the Law." Then read the verses and fill in the blanks to see how that changes through Christ. The last question for each part is more open-ended. Encourage students to talk about what it means for their lives while guiding their discussion.

Jesus, as our Mediator and Sacrifice, cleanses our hearts and sends the Holy Spirit to keep us in faith. Read together Matthew 5:8 and 1 Timothy 1:5, which speak about a cleansed and pure heart. Discuss: **What does that mean for our lives today?** Close by singing "Create in Me a Clean Heart, O God" (Web Resources 70a and 70b).

Putting His House to Good Use

After Jesus cleanses the temple of the money-changers, He goes further, restoring the honor of the temple. He begins healing the blind and the lame. This is work that certainly brings honor to the temple. It is a demonstration of Jesus' gentleness and love. It is also in marked contrast to how He dealt with what was bringing dishonor to His house.

Jesus not only listened to the children's praises, which brought honor to God's house, but He also defended their actions, quoting Scripture when the priests and scribes responded indignantly about the children's songs.

Throughout the week, Jesus continued to come to the temple, teaching more about the kingdom of God. The Gospels record many of His teachings, observations, parables, and answers to the questions that were brought to Him. He always focused on the mission His Father sent Him to fulfill. He spoke of repentance, forgiveness, living in faith, and of the final judgment.

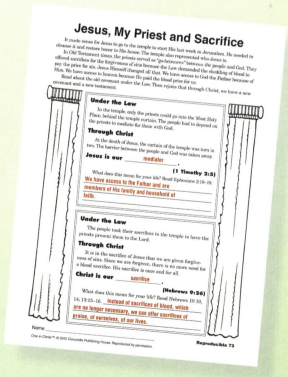

Technology

Have students use a digital camera to create a visual journal of this account. Have them use PowerPoint to create a presentation with descriptive captions. Talk about how using costumes and props (even basic ones) can contribute to the presentation. This activity could be done as a whole class or as smaller groups, depending on the size of the class.

HANDS to SERVE

Offer to go and teach a song to the preschool or kindergarten class. Ask them to sing one of their favorite songs for your class. When you return to your own classroom, ask students how the experience helped them picture and appreciate the children who praised Jesus in the temple.

Ideas for the Gifted

Encourage a discussion about how God's house may be used or misused today. Ask for opinions about church buildings that have been sold and turned into restaurants or museums. Some may say that the Church is the people, not the building. Others may say that a space that has been dedicated to God for worship should not be used for secular entertainment or other such purposes. Some may say that the religious decorations may witness to people who are visiting there for other purposes. Some may say that the religious decorations are being disgraced or dishonored, even when ignored. These are all comments that people must consider when repurposing a church building. The most difficult questions arise when a Christian church building becomes a worship center of another god (for example, the Hagia Sophia in Istanbul, Turkey, was used as a mosque from 1453 to 1931). These are issues that people continue to struggle with.

Searching Further

Using a map of the temple during the time of Christ from a Bible resource book, have students find out the names of the different courts in the temple. Have students report back to the class about how the different courts were used.

Working in Groups

Jesus healed the blind and the lame after He cleansed the temple of corruption. Have students work in groups to examine other times Jesus healed people during His ministry. Instruct students to note the circumstances surrounding the healing, any instructions or teaching Jesus gave to those who witnessed the healing, and how the religious leaders responded to the healing. What things were often represented when Jesus healed people physically? What other truths did He teach or show through healing? The following verses are among those that may be studied: Matthew 9:27–34; 12:9–14; Mark 1:29–34; 1:40–45; 5:35–43; 7:31–37; Luke 5:17–26.

Teacher Tips

To make teaching the lesson more visual, use paper or cardboard circles to represent coins. Write on them some of the wrong things Jesus found going on in the temple ("Becoming a marketplace," "Distracting from worship," "Cheating people who came," "Religious leaders letting it happen," and so forth). Throw the "coins" onto the floor or into the trash to demonstrate what Jesus was really getting rid of in the temple. Talk again about what Jesus *did* want the temple to be—a house of prayer and praise.

UNIT 7—JESUS COMPLETES OUR SALVATION

LESSON 74

The Last Supper
Matthew 26:17–29

Background

The Last Supper before the crucifixion was a solemn and significant meal shared by Jesus and His disciples. First, there was the observance of the Old Testament Law in the Passover meal, and then there was a celebration of the fulfillment of the Old Testament prophecy—in Christ's body and blood with the bread and wine of the Lord's Supper. First, Jesus is celebrating the deliverance of Israel from the plague of death and the exodus from slavery. Then He celebrates that He is the fulfillment of the Old Testament prophets, the deliverer of all people from death and the slavery of sin. He is the Lamb of sacrifice. Jesus institutes this as a new remembrance meal for His followers to celebrate often. Even more, however, He institutes it as a sacrament that offers forgiveness—and where there is forgiveness, there is also life and salvation. This event is an important connecting and turning point between the old covenant (Old Testament) and new covenant (New Testament). In the Lord's Supper, Christ Himself is with us, offering Himself and the blessings He brings. The Lord is not a vague, far-off presence; He is truly a real presence in His Supper as He nourishes our souls and touches our lives.

Devotions

In ancient times, it was sometimes the practice in royal courts to use a whipping boy. When a royal prince misbehaved or did something bad, he deserved to be punished—and according to the laws of justice, punishment had to be administered for wrong that was done. It wasn't considered proper, however, to punish someone of such high standing. That's where the whipping boy came in. It was his job to take the punishment that the prince deserved. So the one of royal standing would be naughty, and the lowly servant would be brought in for the punishment. Does that sound fair? Hardly. But the whipping boy didn't have much choice in the matter. He had to pay the price for his master's sins.

You may not have a whipping boy, but you do have someone who took the punishment for all your sins. Jesus Christ took the sins of the whole world on Himself, and He paid the required price of death for them. He Himself was our sacrifice. Yet, He *chose* to pay the ultimate price for us. He was not a lowly servant forced into service in place of a bratty prince. He was—and still is—a King, *our* King. The price He paid for us was not fair; it was done out of love. He was the ultimate substitute, the ultimate sacrifice of love for us.

Let's pray: Thank You, Jesus, for being the sacrifice and paying the price for our sins. Help us joyfully to remember every day what You did for us. Amen. Sing together "Crown Him with Many Crowns" (*LSB* 525; recorded as *Hymn of the Month* for grade 6, March). Say, sing, or chant portions of Psalm 51.

Central Truth

Jesus offered Himself as the sacrifice for our sins. His death instituted a new covenant, and He instructed His followers to observe a new remembrance Meal, the Lord's Supper.

Objectives

- Acknowledge that the price for sin has always been death.
- Recognize that Jesus was the sacrifice for our sins.
- Rejoice in the salvation we have through the sacrifice of Jesus and in the opportunity we have to participate in the remembrance celebration and the body and blood of Christ through the Lord's Supper.

Materials

- Hymnals and music CDs
- Reproducible 74
- Web Resource 74a
- Web Resource 68b

Bible Prep

Post in advance so students can bookmark references before class time.

- Matthew 26:17–29
- Romans 6:23
- John 1:29
- 1 Peter 1:19
- 1 John 1:7
- 1 Corinthians 5:7b

INTO the lesson

Background on the Passover

Introduce today's Bible narrative by reviewing the celebration of the Passover. As soon as sin entered the world, a Savior was needed. And a Savior was promised, because the shedding of blood was required to pay the price of justice for sin. In the Old Testament, under the old covenant, the bloodshed of the Savior to come was represented in the blood of the animals sacrificed to cover the people's sin.

The Passover sacrifice was a little different though. The people were to choose a perfect lamb for the sacrifice (that part was not unusual). The meat was to be eaten, perhaps to strengthen the people's bodies for the journey ahead. The blood was to be painted on the beams and crosspieces of their homes' doorways to mark them for deliverance. The covering provided by the blood of this lamb was a covering of deliverance from a very real and tangible death. Even as they could hear the wails of the Egyptians around them, the people of Israel could know that *they* had been spared. The next day, they were delivered from four hundred years of slavery in Egypt.

Distribute Reproducible 74 to review facts about the Passover. Work on this crossword puzzle together using Web Resource 74a to guide the process. (*Note:* the Bible references do not need to be examined at this time; they are listed only for reference if students are unable to determine the correct answers.) Discuss with students that each clue deals with the remembrance meal, the celebration of Passover that God commanded His chosen people to celebrate each year in very specific ways. These are ways God commanded the people of Israel to commemorate their deliverance from the plague of death. They also celebrated their deliverance from slavery in Egypt. The ways in which God commanded His people to celebrate helped them to look back at the faithful deliverance God had provided in the past. But they also pointed the people forward in anticipation of the faithful deliverance He would provide through the promised Messiah. Say, **Jesus and His disciples had come to Jerusalem for the weeklong celebration of the Feast of the Passover. Several of the disciples had made arrangements for the Passover meal to be celebrated together in an upper room. This was on Thursday of Holy Week, which we now call Maundy ("Command") Thursday. After the Passover meal, Jesus took some of the elements of the meal and dedicated them for a new purpose as He Himself was the fulfillment of the Old Testament covenant—He Himself would give His body and blood as the perfect Lamb and the perfect Sacrifice for all.**

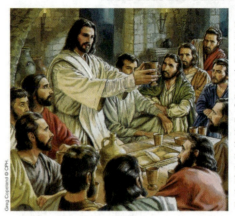

LESSON 74
The Last Supper
The Passover Sacrifice Fulfilled

As Jesus is celebrating the Passover meal with His disciples, He knows that He is about to become the Passover Lamb of sacrifice for the world. Jesus as true God knew the suffering He would have to endure as true man. In His perfect love, He chose to take our sins upon Himself and do it anyway. The Law demanded death for sin. The animal sacrifices of the Old Testament fulfilled that part of the old covenant for the people of Israel. Jesus, in this new covenant, became the perfect, ultimate sacrifice, not only for Israel, but also for all people. His death paid the blood price for all time. There was no more need for any other sacrifice.

Use the following Scriptures to fill in the blanks.

The price for our sin is **d e a t h** (Romans 6:23).

John the Baptist looked at Jesus and called Him "the **L a m b** of God, who takes away the sin of the world" (John 1:29).

We were ransomed from sin and death "with the precious blood of Christ, like that of a lamb without **b l e m i s h** or spot" (1 Peter 1:19).

"The **b l o o d** of Jesus His Son cleanses us from all sin" (1 John 1:7).

"Christ, our **P a s s o v e r** lamb, has been sacrificed" (1 Corinthians 5:7).

Fill in the numbered letters to complete the following sentence:

Because Jesus sacrificed His body and blood, **I   a m   s a v e d**!

Remember

"Our Lord Jesus Christ, on the night when He was betrayed, took bread, and when He had given thanks, He broke it and gave it to the disciples and said: 'Take, eat; this is My body, which is given for you. This do in remembrance of Me.'" (*LSB*, pp. 162, 179, 197, 209, 217)

INTO the Word

The Passover Sacrifice Fulfilled

Direct attention to the illustration in the Student Book. The related Scripture reference is the two-part section of words to remember (which appears on both pages). Have students read these two sections together aloud. Point out that these are the words the pastor says during that portion of the worship service in which the Lord's Supper is offered. Also read Matthew 26:17–29.

That very night, the night of the Passover feast, the body of Jesus (His flesh, not His bones) was torn and broken. His blood was spilled out in our place to spare us from the price that had to be paid. The price of justice for sin was blood, but it was His blood and not ours that was spilled. The next day, with His death, our deliverance from eternal slavery was complete. "Christ, our Passover Lamb, [had] been sacrificed" (1 Corinthians 5:7b). His sacrifice was so great that no other would ever be needed (Hebrews 9:15). With the sacrifice of Jesus came the establishment of the new covenant. Thank God that this new covenant was not only for the people of Israel, but for all people! (1 John 2:2).

God's People Share in the Celebration

People have different interpretations about what is happening when someone receives the Lord's Supper. Here are three of these interpretations:
* The bread and wine are symbols that remind us of Jesus' body and blood.
* The bread and wine are changed into body and blood.
* Christ's body and blood are in, with, and under the bread and wine.

How do we know which is accurate? We must look at Scripture to determine this. According to 1 Corinthians 10:16, the third interpretation is accurate, because the Bible says, "The cup of blessing that we bless, is it not a participation in the blood of Christ? The bread that we break, is it not a participation in the body of Christ?" So according to Scripture, all four elements are present, the visible (bread and wine) and the invisible (body and blood). We call this the "real presence" of Christ in the Sacrament.

How can we believe this? We believe this because Jesus said it is so. If Jesus says so, no other proof is needed. Luke 1:37 says, "Nothing will be impossible with God." Or to say it in another way, "With God all things are possible" (Matthew 19:26).

The Lord's Supper Is

A Mystery   A Miracle
God's Truth

The Lord's Supper Gives

Forgiveness   Life
Salvation

Remember

"In the same way also He took the cup after supper, and when He had given thanks, He gave it to them, saying: 'Drink of it, all of you; this cup is the new testament in My blood, which is shed for you for the forgiveness of sins. This do, as often as you drink it, in remembrance of Me.'" (*LSB*, pp. 162, 179, 197, 209, 217)

Continue by working on this section of the Student Book together (looking up the Bible references only if extra help is needed to determine the answer). Then sing together a hymn that summarizes key points of this lesson, especially the fact that Jesus is the perfect and complete sacrifice for the forgiveness of our sins—"The Lamb" (*LSB* 547; recorded as *Hymn of the Season for grade 5, Lent, part B*).

Also, be sure to discuss the parable in the Check It Out section of the Lesson Support page. This touching story can motivate a discussion about sacrificing for others and about the significance of Jesus as the ultimate sacrifice.

INTO our lives

God's People Share in the Celebration

Some of your students may already be participating in the Lord's Supper. Many will be looking forward to taking part in that celebration in the next couple of years. This portion of the lesson is meant to explore the meaning and purpose of the Lord's Supper in their lives.

In addition to discussing the Student Book, choose from among the following options to extend and enrich the lesson.

1. Together examine the questions and answers about the Lord's Supper in the catechism in the Appendix of the Student Book (this can also be found in the back of the Teacher Guide). It is especially significant to look at the question about the benefits of this Holy Meal.

2. Sing together "This Is the Feast" using Web Resource 68b. This song emphasizes Christ as the Lamb who was sacrificed to set us free to be people of God. He paid the ransom price with His own blood.

3. Together explore the "Service of the Sacrament" portion of the liturgy in *LSB* (found in various settings, beginning on pp. 160, 177, 194, and 208). The words spoken and sung in this portion of the worship service take us right through Holy Week. For example, the Sanctus ("Holy, Holy, Holy") calls to mind Palm Sunday. This is followed by the words Jesus spoke when He instituted the Lord's Supper on Maundy Thursday and by various prayers, recalling the time of prayer in the Garden of Gethsemane. The Agnus Dei ("Lamb of God") relates to Jesus' suffering and death on Good Friday, and the joy of "Thank the Lord" with its alleluia connects with the joy of Easter!

Working in Groups

Divide the class into three or four groups. Give each group a religious symbol connected to the Last Supper or Holy Week. Have each group look at the symbol and decide what they think it means based on the things they know. Encourage each group to write down several bullet points about the symbol and share their thoughts with the class. Look at each symbol as a class and talk about it briefly after each informal presentation. The Internet can be a valuable resource, but be sure to search Christian symbols and use discernment regarding the legitimacy of the site. Also explore the different names used for the Lord's Supper, such as "the Lord's Table," "Holy Communion," and "the Eucharist."

Bringing it home

Involve families by planning and hosting a Seder supper. Have students use the Internet to research the elements and ceremonies involved. Ask each family to come and bring a portion of the meal, either just enough so that everyone can have a taste of the different foods or a sufficient quantity to serve an actual meal. Serve the meal during the school day, or host it during late afternoon or evening so that more people can attend. As an alternative, if a church in your area is hosting a Seder supper, make arrangements with that church for your class's families to attend.

Curriculum Connection

Make an art connection to this lesson using section 6.1.1.5, Variations on the Same Theme with Different Media and Styles, in the sixth-grade Visual Arts volume of the Concordia Curriculum Guide series. The subject of the Last Supper has been portrayed thousands of times in painting and sculpture. Find a dozen or so different renderings, and discuss them with your class. On which moment has each artist chosen to focus? The foot washing? The betrayal? The institution of the Lord's Supper? What emotional mood is being conveyed, and how can you tell?

Look at a copy of Leonardo da Vinci's *The Last Supper*. Note the use of one-point perspective in the piece. Where do your eyes naturally come to rest, and why do you think the artist planned it that way? The whole painting points the viewer to Jesus. It can serve as a reminder to keep our focus on Him.

Check it Out

Say, **There is a modern parable about a young boy who had a very sick little sister. She was in the hospital and needed a blood transfusion. If she did not get the transfusion soon, she would die. The girl's brother was a match. His parents talked with him and asked if he would be willing to donate blood to save his sister's life. They explained that it would hurt a little, but not a lot. When the boy asked to have some time alone to think about it, his parents honored his request. A little while later, he came out of the room where he had been, tears still streaming down his face. He took a deep breath and said, "I've thought about it, and I know it will be hard, but I love my sister a lot, and I want her to live." His parents hugged him and thanked him for his bravery. The boy then added, "I just have one question: How soon will I die after they take my blood?" Of course, the boy didn't understand that the doctors wouldn't be taking *all* of his blood, just a little. The boy was certainly relieved when he found out the truth, but that didn't change the fact that he was willing to make the sacrifice, even when he thought he would have to die to do it. Jesus was a willing sacrifice for us. How do you feel about the sacrifice He made?**

Reaching Every Child

For an active learning connection, arrange to take the class into the sanctuary and have a pastor and/or a member of the altar guild talk with them about how the elements of the Lord's Supper are prepared. Show the Communionware and talk about any special practices or history regarding Communion that may be unique to the congregation. Find out how many members of the congregation need to have the Lord's Supper brought to them, either because they are homebound or living in a care center. Ask the pastor to show the portable Communion set he uses when taking the Sacrament to those people.

UNIT 7—JESUS COMPLETES OUR SALVATION

LESSON 75

Peter Denies Jesus
Matthew 26:30–35, 69–75

Background

Teenagers get themselves into trouble if they are unable (or unwilling) to think about the consequences of their actions. If their lack of wisdom or the possible dangers of their actions are pointed out to them, their response may be the confident statement "I know, I know. But that won't happen to *me*." This is not just true of teens; people of all ages easily fall into the same pattern of thinking. People use drugs, refuse to fasten seat belts, or make other careless decisions, giving the same excuse: "That will never happen to *me*."

We often have that same misplaced sense of confidence in spiritual matters. "I can withstand that temptation. I will never give in." Scripture warns us against such mistaken pride: "Therefore let anyone who thinks that he stands take heed lest he fall" (1 Corinthians 10:12). Jesus' disciples experienced the same misplaced confidence in their own courage and devotion. Jesus told them that they would all fall away. The Shepherd would be struck down and His flock scattered. Peter and the others immediately spoke up in fearless defiance. They imagined themselves standing firm, but instead, they fell very hard. Peter denied Jesus, swearing that he did not even know Him. The other disciples fled in terror. Before the night was over, Peter recognized the truth of Jesus' prediction and wept in repentant grief.

How often do we mistakenly trust ourselves in spiritual matters? We believe we can please God with our own efforts or earn His favor. Our trust must be placed only in Jesus, who was betrayed, arrested, and crucified for our sins. He carried the denials and the rejection in His own body to the cross. The disciples' sins—and ours—have been washed away in Jesus' blood. He is the one in whom we place our trust.

Central Truth

We cannot put our confidence in ourselves to live faithfully for the Lord; the only sure thing is the grace of God in Jesus.

Objectives

- Recognize that our sins separate us from God, but Jesus restores that relationship by forgiving and transforming us.
- Trust with confidence that Jesus is strong to forgive us where we are weak and to strengthen us in faith and faith-living.
- Express reliance in God's never-failing, unchangeable love for us through Christ Jesus.

Materials

- Hymnals and music CDs
- Web Resource 75a
- Web Resource 75b
- Reproducible 75

Bible Prep

Post in advance so students can bookmark references before class time.

- Matthew 26:30–35, 69–75; 28:20
- Psalm 51:12–13
- 1 Corinthians 10:12
- James 2:10
- Hebrews 3:12–13; 4:16
- Romans 12:17
- 1 Timothy 6:10
- John 14:3
- 1 John 1:9
- Ephesians 2:8

Devotions

Jennifer and Ashley stopped at their lockers between classes. Jennifer was wearing a new cross necklace that her aunt had given her for her birthday. Ashley noticed the cross and said, "That's a beautiful necklace. I really like it! But all of that faith stuff is just for Sundays." Jennifer didn't say a word as she watched Ashley pick up her books and walk to her next class.

After school, Kevin found Jennifer sitting alone in front of the gym. "You don't look very happy," he said. "Did you have a test today? Are you worried about something?" Jennifer said, "My friend Ashley doesn't go to church. I had a great chance today to tell her about Jesus, but I didn't say anything! I didn't know what to say." "What *should* you have said?" asked Kevin. "If you had another chance, what would you say?" Ashley liked the cross I'm wearing," said Jennifer. "She said it was beautiful. I could have told her the cross reminds me of Jesus and how He died for me." Kevin thought of some more questions. "What if she asks why He had to die? What would you say then?" "Well, He was punished for my sins so I can be forgiven," answered Jennifer. "See!" said Kevin. "There's your answer. Sometimes we are weak and afraid. We don't say the things we should, and we miss chances to talk about Jesus. But He died for those sins too. Jesus forgives you, and He will help you talk to Ashley next time." "You know," said Jennifer, "I'll see Ashley after school tomorrow at soccer practice. I could say, 'Do you remember when you said my new cross necklace was beautiful? My aunt gave it to me, and I think it's beautiful too. But I can tell you a reason that it's actually amazing!'"

Let's pray: Jesus, give us the courage and the right words to tell others about You! Amen. Say, chant, or sing portions of Psalm 51, confessing your sins, including those times you failed to speak up and stand up for Jesus. Sing "Lift High the Cross" (*LSB* 837; recorded as *Hymn of the Month for grade 4, April*).

INTO the lesson

Prologue

Point out, **Today's Bible narrative is about the disciple Peter. But there is more to the story than Peter's story, so we will begin with a** *prologue*, **which gives extra information before the story, and we will end with an** *epilogue*, **which follows up the story with extra information.** For the prologue, view Web Resource 75a, which has narrated illustrations of the Bible account of Jesus in the Garden of Gethsemane.

INTO the Word

Not Me! (Pride)

Read aloud the text in the Student Book. Ask students to describe Peter's attitude in the illustration. (Proud, sure of himself) Point out that **Peter's reply to Jesus was not about faithfulness to the Lord; it was about a vain certainty of himself. Peter had the nerve to argue and contradict Jesus' warning. In effect, he was saying that he knew better than Jesus. Self-confidence can be a good thing, but Peter had taken it to a ridiculous level, trusting himself more than the words of Jesus. Instead of listening to his Lord, he spouted off with his mouth. Peter spoke without thinking, just as we often do, and he later regretted it.**

Also note the reaction of the disciples. This, too, was not a testimony of faithfulness. It was more of the jealousy that kept popping up among the disciples. Luke 22:24 tells us that just minutes before this, "a dispute also arose among them, as to which of them was to be regarded as the greatest." The disciples were unwilling to let Peter incriminate them of weakness or act as if he were better than they were. Read more about this in Matthew 26:30–35.

Not Me! (Lied)

Before reading this section of the Student Book, point out, **Notice the similarity of the two titles, yet they mean very different things. Before, Peter was saying, "Not me! I won't leave Jesus." But now, circumstances have changed: Jesus has been arrested and placed on trial; His followers fear for their own safety. This time, Peter is reacting out of fear, and he lies, "Not me! I don't even *know* Jesus."**

Read aloud Matthew 26:69–75. Then read the paragraph in the Student Book that explores this part of the narrative. Note how Peter's denials escalate, becoming more vehement as his fear increases. Point out that the timing of the rooster crowing and Jesus passing by was no accident; it was a direct call to repentance from the Lord. Ask students about the significance of the last sentence and what it means for their own lives.

LESSON 75

Peter Denies Jesus

Not Me! (Pride)

After the Passover meal and the Lord's Supper, Jesus and the disciples walked to Gethsemane, a park or garden that was a favorite place for prayer and quiet meditation. Jesus warned the disciples that they would all fall away from Him that night. Peter, impetuous, bold, and boisterous, bragged that even if the others abandoned Jesus, *he* would never fall away: "Not me!"

Jesus gave Peter a special warning, prophesying that by the time the rooster crowed twice, Peter would deny Jesus three times. But Peter was so sure of himself that he contradicted what Jesus said, as if implying he knew more than the Lord Himself. The other disciples, not wanting to be outdone by Peter, all joined in, saying they would be faithful too. Yet, within a few short hours, each one of them would run away in fear as Jesus was led away as a prisoner.

Not Me! (Lied)

Peter followed from a safe distance to see what would happen to Jesus as He was led away and put on trial in the early morning hours. In the courtyard, a servant girl pointed to Peter and announced that Peter had been with Jesus. Peter denied this, saying, "I don't know what you are talking about." Yet another servant girl saw him and said to bystanders, "He is one of those disciples." Forcefully, using an oath, Peter said, "I am not!" One of the bystanders pointed out that Peter had a Galilean accent like many of Jesus' disciples. This time, Peter began to curse and swear and said, "I don't know the man!" Immediately the rooster crowed, and Peter remembered Jesus' words. He left, crying bitterly about what he had done. In Luke 22:61, we learn what was most convicting of all: "The Lord turned and looked at Peter." Jesus knew and saw what had happened—He always does!

Review

Covenant Connection

Jesus quoted the prophet Zechariah, who had said, hundreds of years before Jesus walked with His disciples to Gethsemane, "Strike the shepherd, and the sheep will be scattered" (Zechariah 13:7). This was fulfilled when Jesus was arrested in Gethsemane and all the disciples fled in fear for their lives. How did Zechariah know this would happen? Three times in that same chapter, the prophet says that these words are declared by the Lord. Zechariah recorded an even more important prophecy in the first verse of chapter 13, saying, "On that day there shall be a fountain opened for the house of David and the inhabitants of Jerusalem, to cleanse them from sin and uncleanness." Jesus on the cross is like a fountain, pouring out His blood to cleanse us from sin and to make us righteous!

Misplaced Confidence

Peter's pride was misplaced confidence in himself. Jesus warned Peter; He warns us too. Read each of the Bible verses below. What warning is found in each one?

1 Corinthians 10:12 — We should not be proud and think we can resist all temptations.

James 2:10 — We cannot keep God's Law perfectly.
Hebrews 3:12 — We must never fall into unbelief.
Romans 12:17 — Do not take revenge or repay evil with evil.
1 Timothy 6:10 — Don't let the love of money turn you away from God.

We have been warned. But if we rely on our own ideas and efforts, like Peter, we will fail. Despite what we may think, we are not wise enough or strong enough or good enough. Instead of looking to our own wants and self-will, we need to look to Jesus. We can have confidence in Christ because He is unfailingly wise and strong and good, and He uses all this to bless us! "Far be it from me to boast except in the cross of our Lord Jesus Christ" (Galatians 6:14).

Confidence in Christ

We can trust Jesus! Because He died for us, our sins are forgiven. He will be with us in times of trouble. In these verses, what does God's Word promise that we can trust with confidence?

Hebrews 4:16 — We can pray with confidence, knowing God will help us.
John 14:3 — Jesus has prepared a place for us in heaven.
1 John 1:9 — God will forgive our sins.
Matthew 28:20 — Jesus is with us always.
Ephesians 2:8 — We are saved by God's grace through faith in Christ.

Epilogue (Relied)

Eventually, Peter set aside his personal pride and instead relied on the power of the Holy Spirit rather than on himself. At Pentecost, the Holy Spirit empowered Peter, making him strong in faith to boldly stand up for Jesus. Later, in his epistle, Peter said, "In your hearts set apart Christ as Lord. Always be prepared to give an answer to everyone who asks you to give the reason for the hope that you have" (1 Peter 3:15 NIV).

The Holy Spirit works in us too, enabling us to live as people of God. The tools He uses to work faith and faithfulness in us are God's Word and the Sacraments—the Means of Grace. These are God's power tools, working to empower us to live in faith!

Remember

"He has said, 'I will never leave you nor forsake you.' So we can confidently say, 'The Lord is my helper; I will not fear.'" (Hebrews 13:5–6)

157

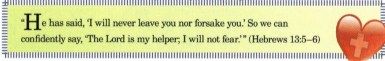

INTO our lives

Misplaced Confidence

Consider: **Why do you think this story about Peter is in the Bible? It is not there to accuse Peter, but to confront us! Peter is an example of the kind of weakness in our own lives.** So often, God warns us in Scripture, and we ignore those warnings. So often, we follow our own ways and will rather than the way of the Lord. The Student Book activity explores some of the warnings given in Scripture. These readings are available for presentation on Web Resource 75b.

We are like the disciples. We have confidence in our own ability to follow Jesus. We might wake up in the morning and say, "Today is a new day! Today I will follow Jesus in everything I do!" Then, suddenly, we begin to fall and fail. Already before breakfast, we argue with our parents or brothers and sisters. We arrive at school and begin to gossip and speak hurtfully about other students. Before long, all of our good intentions are gone. We follow our own desires instead of doing what God wants. **What are some other ways in which we fail to follow our good intentions?** Discuss with your students the kinds of sins we fall into so easily—gossip, lies, disrespect toward others, not showing kindness when we have the opportunity, or failure to witness about Jesus. Remind your students that we often do what is wrong and we also fail to do what is right. **We are thankful that Jesus came to change this situation, calling us to contrition and repentance as He offers forgiveness and new life in His name.**

Confidence in Christ

Explain, **Confidence can be a good thing, especially if it is based on a certainty. We have that certainty in Christ Jesus. Hebrews 13:8 says, "Jesus Christ is the same yesterday and today and forever." Of that we can be certain.** Work together on the Student Book activity, using the Bible references that continue on Web Resource 75b. Then look at the hymn "Jesus Lives! The Victory's Won" (*LSB* 490; recorded as *Hymn of the Season for grade 7, Easter*). Point out that each stanza ends with the words "This shall be my confidence." Have students scan the stanzas and tell in their own words what things we can be sure of. (For example, stanza one says we don't need to be afraid of death because Jesus will call us from the grave on the Last Day and things will be wonderful in heaven.) *Option:* Listen to the recording of this hymn, and perhaps sing along if students are comfortable with the words.

Epilogue (Relied)

The epilogue shows God's grace in forgiving Peter and strengthening him in faith so that he now served confidently—not because of his own efforts, but rather, relying on the power of God working in him. The verse from 1 Peter 3 is a stark contrast to Peter's words said in fear in the courtyard of the high priest. This change and the changes in our own lives are due to the grace and mercy of our Lord working in us. Work in groups on Reproducible 75, taking two words from the top box and two from the bottom box to complete each sentence. Have the groups share their responses, which are actually praise statements. Sing about God's "Amazing Grace" (*LSB* 744; recorded as *Hymn of the Month for grade 5, December*). Also consider singing or at least listening to the same hymn in Spanish (recorded as *Hymn with Spanish Lyrics for grade 6, track 10*).

321

Working in Groups

In the high priest's courtyard, Peter was confronted with questions and accusations about his relationship to Jesus. Out of fear for his own life, Peter denied being one of Jesus' followers. In the end, he even said of Jesus, "I do not know the man" (Matthew 26:74). Our lives are not in danger when we talk to others about Jesus, but still we may hesitate out of fear or worry. We may be afraid of looking foolish, or we may simply be unsure of exactly what to say. Have your students work in groups to discuss and practice ways in which they can witness to others. Help them list possible questions that others might ask about the Christian faith: Who is Jesus? Did Jesus really die on the cross? Why do you go to church? Isn't Christianity all about rules? Students can discuss and practice answers, find helpful Bible verses, and pray together, asking the Holy Spirit to help them as they witness. Teen books available from Concordia Publishing House can be useful resources and help students develop confidence in their ability to answer questions about their faith. Possible resources include *You Ask about Life: Questions Teen Are Asking* (2006); *You Ask about Faith: Questions Teens Are Asking* (2008); and *Life's Big Questions, God's Big Answers* (2010).

Curriculum Connection

Both Peter and Judas turned away from Christ that night in Gethsemane, but their outcomes were very different. Judas felt hopeless and despaired; Peter repented with the help of the Holy Spirit. When working with your students, consider using section 6.4.2.20, Advantages and Disadvantages of Possible Solutions to a Problem, in the sixth-grade Science volume of the Concordia Curriculum Guide series. Can your students name serious problems they face in their own lives and brainstorm good solutions?

Searching Further

As we look in this lesson at the great sins of Peter and Judas, it's only natural to compare ourselves with them, perhaps thinking that our own sins seem small by comparison. To emphasize that all sin condemns, no matter the size, assemble the following: a filthy item of clothing, a moderately smudged towel, and a tablecloth with one small spot. Place all of the items in a laundry bag or basket. Ask students which of the items need to be washed. Make sure they understand that regardless of the size of the stain, *all* of the items need to be washed. Explain that people are like the items in the laundry bag or basket. While some appear to be more soiled than others, none is clean. With David, we pray, "Wash me thoroughly from my iniquity, and cleanse me from my sin! . . . Wash me, and I shall be whiter than snow" (Psalm 51:2, 7). Forgiven by Jesus, we will one day stand before His throne and hear these words: "They have washed their robes and made them white in the blood of the Lamb" (Revelation 7:14).

Teacher Tips

In this lesson, our sinful weakness and misplaced confidence are contrasted with the grace and power of God. St. Paul suffered from a "thorn in the flesh," a physical difficulty not revealed in Scripture. Paul asked the Lord for healing, but he was told, "My grace is sufficient for you, for My power is made perfect in weakness" (2 Corinthians 12:9). Paul then boasted of the power of Christ at work in his physical weakness. God's ways are not our ways. Through the weakness and shame of the cross, Jesus delivered us from sin and defeated death and the devil.

Faith in Action

When Simon Peter denied Jesus, he "remembered the saying of Jesus, 'Before the rooster crows, you will deny Me three times.' And he went out and wept bitterly" (Matthew 26:75). Peter wept in repentant grief. Peter's reaction stands in contrast to the actions of Judas, who experienced regret at betraying Jesus and tried to return the money he received in payment. He said, "'I have sinned by betraying innocent blood.' [The priests told Judas,] 'What is that to us? See to it yourself.' And throwing down the pieces of silver into the temple, he departed, and he went and hanged himself" (Matthew 27:4–5). Judas felt regret and despair. Rejecting the Holy Spirit and unable to rid himself of guilt, he took his own life. By the power of the Spirit, Peter experienced a "godly grief" that turned him to find forgiveness in the Savior he had denied. The apostle Paul described the difference between godly grief and worldly grief: "As it is, I rejoice, not because you were grieved, but because you were grieved into repenting. For you felt a godly grief, so that you suffered no loss through us. For godly grief produces a repentance that leads to salvation without regret, whereas worldly grief produces death" (2 Corinthians 7:9–10). In repentant, godly grief, we look to our Savior for forgiveness.

UNIT 7—JESUS COMPLETES OUR SALVATION

LESSON **76**

Jesus on Trial
Matthew 27:11–31

Background

We sometimes hear news stories about people wrongly convicted and imprisoned for crimes they did not commit. The prisoner repeatedly protests that he is innocent, but no one believes him. Finally, after many years in prison, new evidence is found—often through DNA testing that had been unavailable in previous years—proving that the person truly is innocent. Justice is done, and the prisoner is set free. Those are dramatic events that do not happen often.

Have you ever been falsely accused of something? Perhaps there was a misunderstanding or an unintended error in communication. Or maybe someone wanted to hurt you and so gossiped and told lies about you. It is not a good feeling. Perhaps others looked at you as if you were guilty, when in reality you had done nothing to deserve those accusing stares and comments.

In today's lesson, we will read about the accusations made against our Savior, Jesus Christ. Jesus, who is without sin and truly innocent of all wrongdoing, stands in a Roman court, accused of blasphemy and treason. The sentence of death hangs over His head, yet Jesus does not speak up in His own defense. No one speaks up for Him except for the Roman governor's wife, who has suffered a bad dream about her husband's involvement with "that righteous man" (Matthew 27:19). As the trial progresses, a guilty man is released in exchange for the innocent man. Jesus is condemned, scourged, mocked, crowned with thorns, and led away to die. It was for us that Jesus endured the lies, the false accusations, and the shame. The innocent Lamb of God, bearing our sins and guilt in His own body, is sent to His death in our place. We, who are truly guilty, are released in exchange for the innocent man.

Central Truth

Our sins were the real cause of Jesus' suffering and death (not a Jewish mob or Roman soldiers); Jesus willingly suffered the punishment we deserve.

Objectives

- With contrition and sorrow, repent of the pain our sins caused our Lord.
- Recognize Jesus as the perfect sacrifice, carrying our guilt to set us free.
- Rely on the Holy Spirit to strengthen us when we suffer for the sake of the Gospel.

Materials

- Hymnals and music CDs
- Reproducible 76

Bible Prep

Post in advance so students can bookmark references before class time.
- Matthew 27
- Mark 14–15
- Luke 23
- John 18–19
- Colossians 1

Devotions

Danny tried to keep an eye on his little brother. Noah was four years old and had a special talent for getting into trouble. If anything was broken, scratched, or dented, Noah probably had something to do with it. One Saturday morning, Danny heard a crash in the kitchen. "Noah!" he thought and ran downstairs. There was Noah, surrounded by spilled milk, a broken glass bowl, and cereal flakes scattered like crunchy leaves on the floor. "Oh, Noah," sighed Danny, as he cleaned up the mess. He recognized the glass on the floor. "This isn't a cereal bowl! Why did you use one of Mom's good candy dishes?" "It looked like Christmas," said Noah, and then he started to cry.

Just then, the boys heard their mom's car pull into the driveway. "Maybe she won't notice that the dish is missing," said Danny. He gathered up the scattered glass and hid it at the bottom of the trash can. But as Mrs. Hansen came into the kitchen, she noticed some broken glass under the table. "What have you boys been up to?" she asked. She picked up the glass, looking first at Noah, who was trying not to cry, and then at Danny. "Are you trying to cover up what Noah did?" "I didn't want him to get in trouble," said Danny. "I wanted to help him." "I know," said Mrs. Hansen, "but it doesn't help to pile lies on top of wrongs."

"So who can make it right?" asked Noah. "Now *that* is the right question to ask," said their mother. "Only Jesus can. I knew the two of you were guilty as soon as I walked into the kitchen. I also know that you are both sorry by the look on your faces. Jesus sees this too. But He can do something about it. He takes away our guilt and sin, and He gives us His grace and mercy." "Yippee!" shouted Noah. "Grace and mercy are two of my favorite things! I need them every day!" "We all do," replied Danny and Mrs. Hansen. Confess your sins as together you speak Psalm 51:1–12. Then sing "By Grace I'm Saved" (*LSB* 566; recorded as *Hymn of the Month* for grade 6, February).

INTO the Word

Four Judges

Read the Student Book section aloud to get an overview of the trials of Jesus during Holy Week. Point out that it was bad enough that Jesus had four trials, one right after the other, with no chance to sleep, but He was also slapped, mocked, and beaten wherever they took Him. Take a closer look at the four trials by exploring Scripture. Note that different writers focused on different events, so it is necessary to look at all four Gospels in order to get the full picture.

Annas. Have a volunteer read John 18:12–13 and 19–24. Though Annas is called "the high priest," he is actually a *former* high priest. (This is similar to the way we speak of "President Bush," even though he is no longer in office.) Annas still had a lot of influence with the people, especially since the current high priest was his son-in-law. This trial was held secretly, though Jesus had always been open about all He said and did. Actually, this was just a pretrial, allowing the high priest time to get his people together.

Caiaphas. Have a volunteer read Mark 14:55–65. Note that Jesus spoke the truth, yet He was judged guilty of blasphemy—profanity against God. **Jesus knew His truthful answer would anger the judges, so why didn't He just continue to keep silent?** (Jesus knew that the time had come for Him to die, so He willingly allowed Himself to be taken and convicted.) The high priest's question was so essential—focusing on who Jesus is as true God—that Jesus could not ignore it. His answer was vital and relevant to all that would follow.

Pilate and Herod. The Jewish leaders may have condemned Jesus to death, but they could not carry out the sentence. Only the Roman officials could do that. The church leaders knew the Romans would not care about religious accusations, so they had to approach the Romans with political accusations, saying Jesus stirred up the people (Pilate would be afraid of that, knowing how rebellious the Jewish people could be) and that Jesus called Himself a king (Pilate would also be concerned about that because Caesar was the king/ruler of the Roman Empire). Use Reproducible 76 to take a closer look at Jesus before Pilate. Emphasize that Pilate tried many different approaches to resolve this incident with the Jewish people and Jesus. Sending Jesus to Herod was just one of his tactics, but it didn't work, and he ended up having to deal with the situation himself.

After completing this activity, listen to or sing together "O Sacred Head" (*LSB* 450; recorded as *Hymn of the Season* for grade 6, Lent, part B).

LESSON 76
Jesus on Trial

Four Judges

Annas. Annas was not the high priest and had no authority to conduct a trial. This pretrial was illegal—trials could not be held at night, and a prisoner could not be convicted the same day he was arrested. This trial was just a stalling tactic to give the high priest time to gather the Sanhedrin.

Caiaphas. False witnesses could not agree on anything Jesus had done wrong. The high priest hoped to catch Jesus with His own words, so he directly asked Jesus if He was the Son of God. When Jesus answered, the high priest tore his clothes in anger and said this was *blasphemy* (lies against God) and that Jesus deserved punishment by death. The council agreed. But they had no power to put Jesus to death, so they took Him to the Roman governor.

Pilate. Pontius Pilate could see that Jesus was innocent. But he was afraid that the people would rise up in anger if he set Jesus free. When he heard Jesus was from Galilee, he sent Jesus to Herod. When that and other tactics did not work, Pilate finally gave Jesus over to the people to be crucified.

Herod. Herod was curious about Jesus and wanted Him to perform a miracle. When Jesus was silent and did nothing, Herod was not amused and sent Jesus back to Pontius Pilate.

Review

Covenant Connection

Why was Jesus so quiet at His trials? Why didn't He defend Himself or speak out in anger or try to get away? No one could have captured and held Jesus unless He willingly set aside His power. Jesus did this willingly so that He could suffer the punishment for sin in our place. Hundreds of years earlier, the prophet Isaiah spoke of this, saying, "He was oppressed, and He was afflicted, yet He opened not His mouth; like a lamb that is led to the slaughter, and like a sheep that before its shearers is silent, so He opened not His mouth" (Isaiah 53:7). The entire chapter of Isaiah 53 gives an amazingly detailed account of what would happen to the Messiah and why: "The LORD has laid on Him the iniquity of us all" (Isaiah 53:6).

158

Guilty?

Work through the activity in the Student Book. Ask students to look at the title of this section and answer the question. Was Jesus guilty? No. Have students add the word *No* after the question mark. Ask, **So what do you think of this statement: "If Jesus had only had a good lawyer, He might have been set free"?** (First of all, Jesus had the power to save Himself at any time during this process. But He willingly gave Himself to be crucified so that He could save you and me! If Jesus had not done all things for our salvation, we would have no hope for eternal life.) In 1 Corinthians 15:17, 20, we read, "And if Christ has not been raised, your faith is futile and you are still in your sins. . . . But in fact Christ has been raised from the dead."

Guilty?

So who was guilty? Pilate? The Jewish leaders? The Roman soldiers? Judas? The truth is that *all* people are guilty because we are all sinners. Jesus took our guilt and suffered our punishment so that through faith we can live in Him eternally. Read Acts 2:22–24. **By whose plan did Jesus die?** (It was God's plan.) **What did Jesus say about His death in John 10:17–18?** (No one had the authority to take away His life. He laid down His life because God the Father sent Him to die for us.)

In his Pentecost sermon, Peter said that Jesus was arrested and killed "according to the definite plan and foreknowledge of God" (Acts 2:23). Jesus was innocent. He had no sins of His own for which He had to die. Read 1 Peter 2:24. **Who is really guilty?**

Guilty?

If you had been Jesus' defense lawyer at His trials, what could you have said to defend Him against each of these accusations?

Accusation 1: His enemies said that Jesus threatened to destroy the temple and rebuild it in three days.

Defense: **Jesus was talking about His own body (not a building), which would be destroyed (crucified) and arise in three days. See John 2:18–22.**

Accusation 2: His enemies said Jesus spoke blasphemy, making Himself equal to God.

Defense: **Jesus is true God. He and the Father are one. See John 14:8–11.**

Accusation 3: His enemies said Jesus stirred up and agitated the people.

Defense: **Jesus spoke kindness and peace, helping and healing people. See Matthew 9:35–36.**

Accusation 4: His enemies said Jesus opposed Caesar because He called Himself a king.

Defense: **Jesus said His kingdom is not of this world; He also told people to obey Caesar by paying taxes. See Matthew 22:17–21.**

Guilty?

If Jesus was not guilty, who is? We are! All people are guilty because we are all sinners. Read each Bible verse and explain it in your own words. Check off each statement that is true for you.

- ☐ "If we say we have no sin, we deceive ourselves, and the truth is not in us" (1 John 1:8).
  We are liars if we say we do not sin.
- ☐ "Against You, You only, have I sinned and done what is evil in Your sight" (Psalm 51:4).
  Our sins are committed against God.
- ☐ "Your iniquities have made a separation between you and your God" (Isaiah 59:2).
  Our sins separate us from God.
- ☐ "The wages of sin is death" (Romans 6:23).
  The punishment for sin is death.

This would be a grim story if it stopped here. But we know that Jesus took our guilt on Himself. He took our punishment on Himself. The Son of God makes us children of God. His righteousness makes us righteous. Draw a large cross over this whole section—and change its title too, because through the cross of Jesus, we are now judged not guilty! Jesus has reconciled us so that in God's eyes, we are holy, blameless, and above reproach!

Remember

"And you, who once were alienated and hostile in mind, doing evil deeds, He has now reconciled in His body of flesh by His death, in order to present you **holy** and **blameless** and **above** **reproach** before Him." (Colossians 1:21–22)

Whose sins did Jesus take to the cross? (We are guilty. **He carried our sins in His own body to the cross.) Jesus was the perfect Lamb who was sacrificed for the sins of the world.** He died for the people who accused and condemned Him. He died for the people who shouted for His death, and He died for the soldiers who nailed Him to the cross. He died for you and me.

Work together on the Student Book activity, changing the title of this section to *Not Guilty* and superimposing a cross over the text. Also, have students use dictionaries to find the meanings of words such as *alienate* and *reconcile* that are in the Bible words to remember.

Jesus before Pilate

Pontius Pilate, the Roman governor, knew that Jesus had done nothing wrong, but he was afraid that the angry crowd would become rebellious and riot. He tried several approaches and tactics to deal with the situation. Read the Bible verses and explain what happened during these events.

1. A conversation—John 18:33–38: **Pilate asked Jesus, "Are You the King of the Jews?" Jesus said His kingdom was not of this world; Pilate asked Jesus, "What is truth?"**

2. Herod—Luke 23:4–12: **Pilate hoped sending Jesus to Herod would relieve him of the problem; Herod was curious, wanting to see a miracle, but Jesus did not oblige him.**

3. Barabbas—Mark 15:6–14: **Pilate hoped to make a deal. The people could choose to set free either Jesus or the murderer Barabbas. Again, Pilate's tactic did not work.**

4. Pilate's wife—Matthew 27:19: **Even Pilate's wife became involved, asking Pilate to have nothing to do with this matter because Jesus was righteous and because she had had bad dreams about the whole situation.**

5. Punished—Luke 23:14–16; John 19:1–6: **Pilate had Jesus beaten, even though Jesus was innocent. He presented Jesus with a crown of thorns on His head, probably hoping the crowd would be satisfied, but that didn't work.**

6. Another conversation—John 19:7–11: **Pilate was frightened when he heard that Jesus called Himself the Son of God. They talked again, this time about authority.**

7. Presented again—John 19:12–15: **Again Pilate presented Jesus, saying, "Behold your King!" But the people shouted, "We have no king but Caesar" (which was actually a statement of treason against their own nation by acknowledging their Roman captors).**

8. Washed his hands—Matthew 27:24: **Pilate turned Jesus over to the people. He washed his hands to symbolize that he had nothing to do with the matter, but this could not wash away his guilt.**

9. Inscription—John 19:19–22: **Pilate gave in to the people, but he did get in the last word. He had a sign placed on Jesus' cross that read, "Jesus of Nazareth, the King of the Jews." This was written in Aramaic (the language of the Jews), Latin (the language of the Romans), and Greek (a universal language known by most people).**

Reproducible 76

Technology

Ask students to do research on other religions. We know Jesus shed His blood so that our sins can be forgiven. How do other religions around the world address the problem of sin? Do other faiths teach that it is possible to perfectly obey their own laws or rules? Are certain rituals or ceremonies necessary to earn forgiveness? Students should examine the teachings of major world religions such as Judaism, Islam, Buddhism, and Hinduism. What do they teach about sin? What do they teach about Jesus? Ask the students to report their findings to the class. Discuss with your students the differences between faiths. Help them to understand the wonderful grace of God and give thanks for the gift of the Savior.

Check it Out

Pilate washed his hands in front of the crowd, claiming to take no responsibility for shedding Jesus' innocent blood. The Bible tells us that as Jesus' trial progressed, Pilate "saw that he was gaining nothing, but rather that a riot was beginning" (Matthew 27:24). Pilate may have had good reason to fear a potential riot. As governor of the province of Judea, he had already had difficulties with the Jews. Pilate's Roman soldiers brought military standards (emblems and flags on long poles) into the holy city of Jerusalem. The standards were engraved with images of the Roman emperor, an offense against God's laws about idol worship. When the Jews protested and staged a "sit-in" and did not give in, even though Pilate threatened them with death, the Roman standards were removed. In another incident, Jewish citizens were killed in a riot protesting the use of money from the temple to build an aqueduct, or channel, to bring water into the city. After the Jews protested the use of golden shields honoring the emperor, the emperor himself warned Pilate to keep the peace. It is not surprising that Pilate feared another possible riot over Jesus' trial.

Critical thinking

Teen and preteen students are often hurt by lies and gossip, and they may easily inflict hurt on others in the same way. The use of social media makes it much easier to hurt others and to be hurt by harmful words. Talk to your students about ways in which words can be used to hurt or to help others, to tear people down or build them up. Discuss the Eighth Commandment and its meaning. The commandment forbids false testimony and tells us to use our words to defend our neighbor, "speak well of him, and explain everything in the kindest way" (*Luther's Small Catechism with Explanation*). When Jesus was put on trial, false witnesses were brought forward to tell lies about Him. Our Savior understands the hurt done by words. He died on the cross so that our hurtful speech can be forgiven.

Searching Further

The prophet Isaiah compared the promised Messiah to a silent lamb led to slaughter, and he said of Him, "But He was wounded for our transgressions; He was crushed for our iniquities; upon Him was the chastisement that brought us peace, and with His stripes we are healed" (Isaiah 53:5). When John the Baptist saw Jesus coming, he announced, "Behold, the Lamb of God, who takes away the sin of the world!" (John 1:29). The sacrifices in the Old Testament were a picture of the final, perfect sacrifice of Jesus, the Lamb of God. His blood was shed so that our sins could be forgiven. Speaking of the festivals and ceremonies observed since the days of the Old Testament, the apostle Paul said, "These are a shadow of the things to come, but the substance belongs to Christ" (Colossians 2:17).

UNIT 7—THE JESUS COMPLETES OUR SALVATION

LESSON 77

Jesus Dies and Is Buried
MATTHEW 27:27–66 AND RELATED GOSPEL ACCOUNTS

Background

Today's story is timeless, and yet, to middle grade students who have been raised in the faith, it can appear mundane at first glance because they've heard it all before. For this reason, the activities in the Student Book are designed to be catalysts that allow the students to either "do" or "discuss" the different scenes of such an important, life-changing biblical event! In teaching both the minor and major details, always emphasize the main point that only Jesus, God's Son, could have redeemed the world and saved us from sin, death, and the power of the devil. It had to be Jesus!

Another point to impress on students is that Jesus didn't have to do any one of these actions for His own good! He had a clean record as far as sins were concerned, but He did it because He loved us. Point out the word choice in the ESV translation of Matthew 27:50: He "yielded" His spirit. "Yielded" implies that something is given up—a right is forfeited. Jesus willingly gave up His right and became wrong so we could become right with God. Middle schoolers are at an age when they need to see that justice is being served. Remind your own students that they can certainly be happy that in God's eyes, justice is *not* served in the fair sense that they often seek. On the contrary, under God's justice, the Innocent One dies and the *guilty* are set free. Justice is on God's terms—and through His means alone—when it comes to our salvation. Thanks be to God!

Central Truth

Jesus, who was sinless, substituted for us, taking our sin and giving us His righteousness.

Objectives

- Confess Jesus as the true Son of God, who alone could ransom us from sin, death, and the devil.
- Call upon God to give us courage to proclaim Jesus as true God and to live for Him.
- Diligently learn, love, and live for our Savior.

Materials

- Hymnals and music CDs
- Reproducible 77
- Web Resource 77a

Bible Prep

Post in advance so students can bookmark references before class time.
- Isaiah 53:3–9
- Matthew 27:54

Devotions

"So did the car flip two times or three times?" The police officer started scribbling with his pen.

"Um . . . I think two times. And then it landed upside down and perpendicular to the direction it was headed." Krista was still trembling after witnessing the accident.

"And did you say the passengers got out of the car right after the crash?" the officer asked.

"Yes—almost immediately. It was such a miracle that no one was hurt!" Krista tried to look calm.

"You're right!" the officer agreed. "When I got the call, I was expecting it to be a lot worse. It really *is* a miracle that someone didn't get killed! Now we have to sort through all of the tricky details. I'm glad you stayed to report what you witnessed. It will really be helpful in dealing with the insurance companies involved."

"I'm happy I can help." Krista continued talking with the officer.

Eyewitnesses are indeed helpful when trying to figure out what really happened. What do you think it would have been like to be an eyewitness of Jesus' crucifixion? Would you have winced when they beat Him? Would you have tried to stop them from mocking and falsely accusing Him? Would you have wanted to bandage His bloody wounds? Would you have consoled Mary, His weeping mother? Perhaps *you* might have even been the one chosen to carry Jesus' cross! Would you—*could* you—have done it?

Needless to say, we weren't at Jesus' crucifixion. One fact, however, is sure: Jesus did carry our burdens to the cross, and regardless of how sinful we are, no blame whatsoever is assigned to us! We are completely forgiven; we are redeemed by the blood of Jesus Christ, who alone could suffer and die in our place. What joy we have in this sad story! What joy we have in Jesus!

Read aloud together the prophetic words in Isaiah 53:3–9. Then listen to and meditate on the Lenten hymn "O Sacred Head, Now Wounded" (*LSB* 450; recorded as *Hymn of the Season for grade 6, Lent, part B*).

INTO the lesson

Good Friday

Explore the timeline after pointing out that the time is tracked from sunrise until sunset. We know that the rooster crowed at dawn, as Jesus was led from the high priest's palace. So the first three hours of the day ("Journey to the Cross") would have included the trial before Pilate, beatings, and the trail to Golgotha. Point out that this was a hill outside the city wall of Jerusalem; it was also know as "Calvary" and "the place of the skull," perhaps because the rocks had a skull shape, or maybe because of all the people who died there.

Jesus was crucified at the third hour, 9 a.m. Point out that some people who were crucified lingered for more than a day, but Jesus had already been severely beaten. At noon, darkness covered the land, causing fear in many people. After six hours on the cross, Jesus died (at 3 p.m.). Even more fearsome events occurred: there was an earthquake, and the temple curtain tore in two, signifying that through Jesus, we now have direct access to God because we are His forgiven and redeemed people.

At sunset, 6 p.m., the Sabbath would begin, so Jesus' friends acted quickly to get permission to bury Him immediately. (Those honoring the Sabbath were not supposed to work on that day, but instead devote that time to worship and rest.) The men who saw to the burial were Nicodemus and Joseph of Arimathea. Both were wealthy, religious, powerful men who were not afraid to be recognized publicly as followers of Jesus. There were also several women attending the burial.

After discussing these facts, take a closer look at some of the events of the day.

Simon's Story

After reading aloud the opening paragraph of this Student Book section, sing together "Were You There" (*LSB* 456; recorded as *Hymn of the Season for grade 4, Lent, part B*). The repetition of certain words and phrases magnifies the nagging reality that Jesus did indeed die a physical death and that our sins did indeed put Him on that cross and result in His death! Then have students read through the script, which gives an idea of what it might have been like to be an eyewitness on that Good Friday. Continue with the "Covenant Connection," which asks students to answer the question "why?" Give students time to quietly write down responses; then ask volunteers to share what they wrote. Actually, we have been discussing the "why?" question in every lesson of this series. Why did Jesus suffer and die? He was fulfilling the covenant and promises God had made throughout time, ever since the first sin. **Only Jesus could pay the price; only Jesus could be offered as the blood sacrifice; only Jesus is the perfect, sinless Son of God who could be our substitute, taking away the guilt of our sin and offering us salvation.** The students' answers to the "why?" question are actually testimonies of faith.

Point out that we don't know much about Simon of Cyrene, but it is interesting that Mark 15:21 mentions his sons Alexander and Rufus, as if these are people with whom the readers of this Gospel may be acquainted. In Romans 16:13, Rufus is mentioned again (if it is indeed the same Rufus), as the apostle Paul says, "Greet Rufus, chosen in the Lord." We can only speculate that Simon took the message of Christ crucified back to his family in Cyrene (where Christianity flourished for some time). Imagine what it would have been like for Alexander and Rufus to be able to say, "Our father helped Jesus carry His cross."

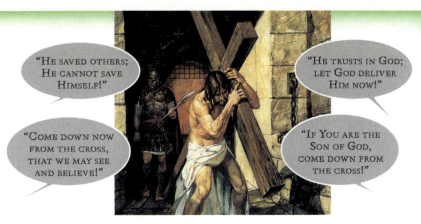

Seven Words

The words Jesus spoke on the cross were not only for those watching Him in His last hours, but also for you and for me! Write what each statement can teach us today.

"Father, forgive them, for they know not what they do" (Luke 23:34). **Jesus leads us to always think of forgiveness first.**

"Truly, I say to you, today you will be with Me in Paradise" (Luke 23:43). **Jesus promises that we, too, will live with Him in heaven.**

"Woman, behold, your son! . . . Behold, your mother!" (John 19:26–27). **Even though suffering, Jesus was concerned about the needs of others.**

"My God, My God, why have You forsaken Me?" (Matthew 27:46). **Jesus experienced separation from God so we will never have to.**

"I thirst" (John 19:28). **Jesus gave no thought for Himself until He knew He had completed everything for our salvation.**

"It is finished" (John 19:30). **I am certain I am saved; Jesus did it all!**

"Father, into Your hands I commit My spirit!" (Luke 23:46). **I trust all things to God's direction; my spirit is entrusted to God's care eternally!**

Remember

A Roman centurion spoke the amazing truth while standing at the foot of the cross. Write his words in large, bold letters. See Matthew 27:54.

"Truly this was the Son of God!"

INTO the Word

Seven Words

This section of the Student Book looks at the words spoken at the crucifixion. First of all, in the gray areas, read the mocking words spoken by enemies in the crowd as Jesus was hanging on the cross. As the day progressed, this mocking most likely turned to great fear as darkness covered the land and, as Jesus died, there was an earthquake and the temple curtain was torn in two.

Point out that what are usually called "the seven words of Jesus" on the cross are actually seven instances, or times, when He spoke during those six hours. Again, have students quietly respond, writing down what these words tell about Jesus and/or what the words mean for our lives today. Let volunteers share their answers.

Continue with Reproducible 77, which looks at the crucifixion from yet another point of view while also getting students further into the Scripture. Divide the class into four groups. Assign each group a different Gospel account: Matthew 27:24–66; Mark 15:16–47; Luke 23:24–56; or John 19:15–42. Tell students to read aloud their assigned Scripture passages and then work together on the reproducible page.

Let volunteers share answers. Look at the "Remember" section of the Student Book and the words of the Roman centurion. Then sing the words of the thief on the cross in the hymn "Jesus, Remember Me" (*LSB* 767 or *AGPS* 146; recorded on *JPS*). Close the lesson by using Web Resource 77a, which is an overview of Holy Week that ends with the essential telling of the resurrection.

Lesson Support

Technology

Allow students to use computers and work in pairs to create a PowerPoint presentation showing several sites around and near the place of Jesus' crucifixion (Golgotha, the Garden of Gethsemane, the temple, the tomb). Google images could be helpful in acquiring modern pictures, as could several other Web sites that offer pictures of the Holy Land.

Bringing it home

Ask if any of the students have ever seen a "Passion Play" reenactment of Holy Week. There are many famous ones, such as those in Oberammergau, Germany, and Spearfish, South Dakota. Check these locations on the Internet, adding the words "passion play" to the search bar, and learn more about these settings. Have students search to see if there are any local events that will be held or that students have seen. Have students inquire of family members if they have had such an experience.

Curriculum Connection

Some of the world's greatest music has been written on the subject of Jesus' suffering, death, and burial. Allow your students to listen to several pieces in a variety of styles; for example, you might consider using the spiritual "Were You There When They Crucified My Lord?"; Handel's "All We Like Sheep" from *Messiah* (note especially its startling emotional change at the end); and Bach's "Ruht Wohl" from the *St. John Passion*, which is a lullaby for the burial of Christ. Then use section 6.1.4.1, Aesthetic Qualities of Music Conveying Images or Emotions, to discuss what you've heard; you'll find it in the sixth-grade Performing Arts volume of the Concordia Curriculum Guide series.

Searching Further

Reading the story of Jesus' death and burial can seem pretty straightforward. However, as you read with your students, you can teach them to "dig deeper" as they read any footnotes or study notes available, and you can introduce them to using commentaries (such as CPH's *People's Bible Commentary* series or *TLSB*) and concordances as well. Internet searches provide plenty of information for inquiring minds, provided that the sites are deemed safe; remember to supervise students' Internet use at all times and use appropriate parental blocks and controls. Some crucifixion-related topics that students may want to research further for information could include earthquakes, the temple, the temple curtain, dyeing clothes in Bible times (which could account for Jesus' robe being described differently—purple vs. red—depending on the book of the Bible), ways they cast lots and what they used for lots, how they told time in Bible times, and the different names for the place where Jesus died (Golgotha, Calvary). Encourage students to first write down their questions, and then have them record the answers they find and where they found them. Additionally, ask students to evaluate whether the sources they used are reliable.

Working in Groups

Depending on its size, divide your class into groups, or allow the class to work as one group, as they plan and perform tableaux of various scenes that occurred on Good Friday. Emphasize that a tableau is a still scene, very much like a pantomime but without movement or narration. Encourage groups to carefully plan artistic placement and position of people and to show strong emotion through facial features and gestures. Each scene should be like a moment frozen in time or like a picture made with people instead of paint. When each group has had time to practice, call everyone together; then have one group at a time present their tableau for the rest of the class. For each reenactment, the teacher will say "Ready," and the group should take its positions; after counting silently from one to ten, the teacher will say "Rest"; then the group can sit down to watch the next group.

UNIT 7—JESUS COMPLETES OUR SALVATION

LESSON 78

Jesus Rises from the Dead
MATTHEW 28:1–15 AND RELATED GOSPEL ACCOUNTS

Background

The story of Easter is one of the most well-known Bible stories! Because most sixth graders will have heard this story several times before, be prepared for them to act as if they already know it all. So this lesson tries to explore the Easter story in unique ways, without abandoning a study of the actual Scripture texts. Provide ample opportunity for students to search the Scriptures and to engage in conversation regarding the resurrection. Rest assured that God says, "My Word . . . shall not return to Me empty, but it shall accomplish that which I purpose, and shall succeed in the thing for which I sent it" (Isaiah 55:11).

Help your students view the resurrection as one piece of a large puzzle that is absolutely necessary for the entire puzzle of God's plan to be accomplished. If the resurrection had not happened, eternal life would not have been won! "If the Spirit of Him who raised Jesus from the dead dwells in you, He who raised Christ Jesus from the dead will also give life to your mortal bodies through His Spirit who dwells in you" (Romans 8:11).

Some think Jesus' descent into hell was part of His humiliation, going to hell to be ridiculed and mocked. But 1 Peter 3:18–19 specifically states that Jesus went there to declare victory over sin, death, and the power of the devil: "For Christ also suffered once for sins, the righteous for the unrighteous, that He might bring us to God, being put to death in the flesh but made alive in the Spirit, in which He went and proclaimed to the spirits in prison." In hell, Jesus proclaimed His absolute victory. Christ is risen!

Central Truth

Jesus has claimed victory over death through His resurrection, and He gives that victory to us.

Objectives

- Acknowledge that because of the forgiveness, life, and salvation we have in Jesus, sin and Satan no longer have power over us.
- Identify the comfort we have—especially when facing our own or a loved one's death—in the hope and certainty Jesus won for us in His resurrection.
- Share the Good News of eternal life in Jesus so more people may be brought to the joy of life in Him.

Materials

- Hymnals and music CDs
- Web Resource 78a
- Reproducible 78
- Red pens or markers

Bible Prep

Post in advance so students can bookmark references before class time.
- Matthew 28:1–15
- Mark 16:1–7
- Luke 24:1–12
- John 20:1–18

Devotions

"I just wish I would have had a chance to say goodbye!" Mia's voice quivered as she stood by her brother Tom's casket.

"I know. This must be so hard for your family!" Mrs. Benson, Mia's teacher, gave her a big hug.

"Everything just happened so fast. He was running late for basketball practice, and I was studying my lines for the musical, so I really didn't pay much attention when he hollered goodbye to us and got into Mike's car. Then, only an hour later, we got the news about the accident! There were no real goodbyes . . . he was just . . . gone!" Mia began sobbing.

"I can't imagine how you feel, Mia! Just know that we are all going to help you through this. The most important thing is that Tom believed in Jesus, so we know he is in heaven."

Mia sniffled and tried to catch her breath. "It's just all so final! It makes me so sad to think that I won't see him again!"

"I know—and even though that hurt won't go away completely, as time goes by, God will help you to at least accept what has happened, and you will rejoice in Jesus' resurrection more than ever. Because Jesus lives, we will live also! Even though you will always miss your brother, you and he and *all* believers have the sure hope of eternal life because of Jesus' resurrection!" Mrs. Benson handed Mia a tissue.

Mia wiped her eyes and took a deep breath. "Thanks, Mrs. Benson. I'm going to need lots of reminders of that!"

"That's what I'm here for!" Mrs. Benson smiled and gave Mia another hug.

We all will have difficult times in our lives on this earth. Our main comfort is in our Lord Jesus. Let's sing about crowning Him, our King, with many crowns, remembering that He promises a crown of life—*eternal life*—to all who believe. Sing "Crown Him with Many Crowns" (*LSB* 525; recorded as *Hymn of the Month for grade 6, March*).

INTO the lesson

Putting the Pieces Together

Point out that in order to get the whole picture of what happened that first Easter, it is important to read the accounts given in each of the Gospels, because different writers emphasized different aspects of what happened on that busy day. See "Bible Prep" for a list of these accounts, and have volunteers read them aloud.

Say, **The events of Good Friday and Easter should not have been a surprise to the disciples because Jesus often told them what would happen. In the Book of Matthew alone, Jesus' predictions of His death and resurrection are recorded three times—in 16:21; 17:23; and 20:19. Jesus had given them all the "pieces of the puzzle," and now He had to help them put it all together so that it would make sense. That is why Jesus continued to teach and explain these things to His followers for forty days after Easter, assuring them—and us—of the certainty and confident trust we have in all that Jesus did for us.**

Continue with the activity in this section, saying, **In today's Bible story, there are several characters who, no doubt, had their own feelings about Jesus' death. Let's use the riddles in our Student Book to review what role each character played in Jesus' resurrection.** The information about Jesus' descent into hell may be unfamiliar to some students, so take time to explain it carefully. Explain that this was a victory proclamation. Jesus had already suffered "the pangs of hell" and had completed His sacrifice, saying it was finished, when He died on the cross. Read together the Apostles' Creed. Ask, **When Jesus descended into hell, was this an act of humiliation or of exaltation?** (Exaltation) Ask, **Do you know that some people teach that Jesus descended into hell to experience more mocking and ridicule—more humiliation? We, however, believe that Jesus' descent into hell is actually the turning point, the beginning of Jesus' exaltation!** Use Web Resource 78a, which diagrams the words of the Second Article of the Creed. (More information can be found in *TLSB* notes on 1 Peter 3:18–20 [p. 2155] and in *Luther's Small Catechism with Explanation*, question 143.)

As you look at the "Covenant Connection," emphasize the great significance of having a living Savior. Compare this with other religious beliefs; the Buddha, Muhammad, and Confucius are all dead, and idols were never alive in the first place. **Christianity is unique in having a kind and loving God who has saved us completely, without any merit or worthiness on our part, and who gives us forgiveness and eternal life. These are great gifts that others think they have to earn. But we know these are the free gifts of God through Christ Jesus.**

LESSON 78
Jesus Rises from the Dead
Putting the Pieces Together

When Jesus was buried, His disciples were fearful, confused, puzzled, and sad. Time and again, Jesus had told them He would die and arise on the third day, but they didn't understand, weren't paying attention, or both. (After all, the disciples were people like you and me.) After listening to the Gospel accounts of Easter morning, read the following riddles, placing the answers to "Who Am I?" on the puzzle pieces.

1.

2. We came to the tomb to anoint Him with spice.
   The changes we found made us really look twice!

3. This happened again as the tomb opened wide,
   Just like an event at the time Jesus died.

4. I rolled the great stone from the tomb on that morn
   As soldiers looked frightened and very forlorn.

5. An angel we saw, gleaming bright, toe to head.
   We fell down in shock, just as if we were dead.

6. These same words were spoken that bright Easter morn
   As angels told shepherds the night Christ was born.

7. I told all the women to tell all the men:
   In Galilee soon they would see Me again.

8. We bribed all the guards and then told them to say
   The dead corpse was stolen and taken away.

But wait! There is one empty piece. What was the first thing Jesus did that Easter morn? We learn in 1 Peter 3:18–20 that Jesus descended into hell to announce His victory over sin, death, and the devil's power. Write a riddle verse and its answer for number 1.

Then, using a red marker, pen, or crayon, write the following message in large print directly on the puzzle shapes: **Celebrate the Victory!**

Covenant Connection

Christ has risen! He has risen indeed! Jesus is our living Savior! A dead savior would be powerless to help us. As the apostle Paul states in 1 Corinthians 15:17, 20, "If Christ has not been raised, your faith is futile and you are still in your sins. . . . But in fact Christ has been raised from the dead." To assure us of this, Jesus continued to appear to His followers for forty days after Easter, appearing to individuals and to crowds of as many as five hundred people, teaching them the purpose of all that He had done. We can join in rejoicing: "I know that my Redeemer lives" (Job 19:25).

162

Why All the Running?

That first Easter morning, there was a lot of running going on, back and forth, between the walled city of Jerusalem and the open tomb. Write who was headed where and why.

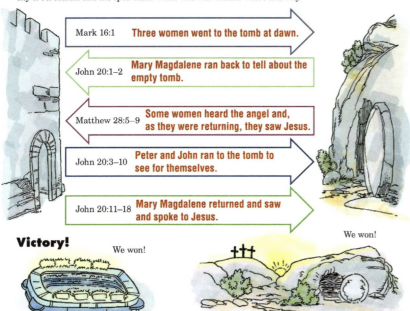

- Mark 16:1 — Three women went to the tomb at dawn.
- John 20:1–2 — Mary Magdalene ran back to tell about the empty tomb.
- Matthew 28:5–9 — Some women heard the angel and, as they were returning, they saw Jesus.
- John 20:3–10 — Peter and John ran to the tomb to see for themselves.
- John 20:11–18 — Mary Magdalene returned and saw and spoke to Jesus.

Victory!

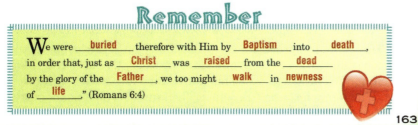

We won!   We won!

Look at the football stadium, where fifty thousand people are yelling, "We won!" Yet we know that there were only a few dozen people on the field who actually played the game. But everyone wants to claim the victory and claim the trophy.

Now look at the Easter picture. Millions of believers say, "We won!" Yet we know that it was Jesus alone who won the victory. We didn't do anything to deserve it. But in His great love for us, Jesus "gives us the victory" that He won (1 Corinthians 15:57). And amazingly, He also presents us with the trophy—eternal life! "Be faithful unto death, and I will give you the crown of life" (Revelation 2:10).

Remember

"We were **buried** therefore with Him by **Baptism** into **death**, in order that, just as **Christ** was **raised** from the **dead** by the glory of the **Father**, we too might **walk** in **newness** of **life**." (Romans 6:4)

INTO the Word

Why All the Running?

This activity gives an interesting picture of the frantic activities of Easter morning. People were running back and forth to tell other people about the empty tomb; some saw angels; some saw Jesus; and some still did not believe. (Discuss Mary Magdalene's reactions. She went to the tomb, but she did not stay long enough to hear the angel's message or see Jesus, as did the other women. However, on her return, following Peter and John, she was blessed to see and talk to the Lord.) That evening, even more people would see the risen Lord.

At this time, use Reproducible 78, asking students to again place themselves in the events of the day. They are to tell whom they would want to run to in order to share the news and what they would say. Then emphasize, **That message is just as vital today!** *Vital* means "necessary and life-giving." This message, that Jesus is alive, is *eternal* life-giving!

Sing about sharing the Gospel message with "Go into the World" (*AGPS* 101; recorded on *JPS*) and "Pass It On" (*AGPS* 196; recorded on *JPS*).

INTO our lives

Victory!

It is interesting how quickly people are ready to share in a sports victory that they had no part in except watching it. How much more exciting is Jesus' victory, because He *wants* us to share in His victory—He did it all for us, and yet He gives us the victory. Talk about the response a believer might have to this victory. Responses might include living for Him because He lives for us and offering prayers of thanksgiving, but we are likely to begin our response with songs of praise. Do so now, singing Easter hymns recorded on the *Hymns of the Season* CD 9.

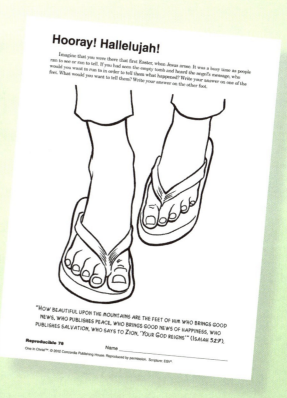

Curriculum Connection

Jesus' resurrection is both the guarantee and a foretaste of our own resurrection on the Last Day. His experience is similar to what ours will be, though His is greater because He is also God Incarnate. We could say that His resurrection is similar but not congruent to ours. Explore these mathematical concepts using section 6.4.7, Similar Not Congruent Shapes, in the sixth-grade Math volume of the Concordia Curriculum Guide series.

Working in Groups

If you have a picture of Easter that you don't mind cutting into pieces, use it to make a group mural. Cut the picture into squares. Give each student one square to redraw on a much larger square of paper (about 9 × 9 inches). When all of the larger squares are finished, assemble them to create a large Easter mural, taping the pieces together on the back after making sure of proper placement. If possible, display the mural in the hallway.

HANDS TO SERVE

Easter lilies are seen everywhere at Easter time, and they have become a symbol of hope. Have students trace around their hands onto craft paper (with fingers slightly separated) and cut them out. Have them gently curve each hand-shaped piece, rolling it from side to side, and glue or tape it to form a cylindrical Easter lily, with the fingers forming the petals. Then insert a pipe cleaner into the bottom of each lily, and tape it in place. If desired, bend an additional pipe cleaner to make two or more leaves; attach them to the center of the stem, pointing the leaves in opposite directions. To each stem, have students attach a piece of paper with their favorite Bible reference on it. Add these lilies to a bulletin board display.

Searching Further

Mary Magdalene and the other Mary were coming to the tomb with spices. Have students research what spices they might have brought. Additionally, have students find information about embalming by using reliable and safe Internet sites, periodicals, biblical commentaries, and other books. Emphasize that wrapping the body in cloth strips and putting fragrant spices on it was one way of honoring the dead (similar to people having flowers and a casket at a funeral today). The spices and wrapping were not intended to mummify the body or preserve it for reincarnation, as was the intent in many Eastern religions, when bodies were embalmed and preserved to protect them for the so-called afterlife.

Unit 8—The Spread of the Gospel

Theme

This entire unit is basically about the Great Commission, as Jesus prepared the people of the Church to carry on spreading the message of God's love and salvation. During the forty days following that first Easter Sunday, Jesus came to His disciples many times and for great lengths of time, preparing them for the tasks He was giving them. His appearances gave His followers the reassurance and certainty they needed to carry on this mission. But even more than that, Jesus continued to teach them, explaining how everything that had happened was in accordance with God's plan and had fulfilled the prophecies of the Old Testament. Jesus had told them these things before Holy Week, but the disciples had not understood. Now, with all things accomplished, He led them to a new understanding so that they could share the Gospel with the world. It is also our task to continue sharing God's love and His message of salvation with the world, for we are His disciples too!

Worship

The *Hymn of the Month for grade 6, April*, is "Immortal, Invisible, God Only Wise" (*LSB* 802), and the *Hymn of the Season for grade 6, Easter* is "O Sons and Daughters of the King" (*LSB* 470). These are recorded on the *Hymns of the Month* and *Hymns of the Season* CDs. Always feel free to make additional hymn choices, including songs from *All God's People Sing!* (*AGPS*); fifty of these songs are recorded on the *Jesus' People Sing!* (*JPS*) CD. You can use Psalm 98 this month, which is, appropriately, a psalm of rejoicing.

Resources

Though the *Teacher Resource Book* provides many extra materials to use with this curriculum, these resources are also on the One in Christ portal, which includes access to links to other Web sites, interactive whiteboard applications, slide presentations, and other resources for the lesson of the day. Tests can be printed out or taken online (with a self-checking feature!). (Unit 8 test answers are: 1-c; 2-d; 3-b; 4-c; 5-a; 6-b; 7-b; 8-d; 9-c; 10-b.) Note that the titles of this unit's lessons are listed in the column at the right to give you an overview of the material covered in this unit.

Unit 8

79. The Emmaus Disciples
80. Doubting Thomas
81. Jesus at the Sea of Tiberias
82. The Ascension
83. Pentecost
84. Peter, John, and the Lame Man
85. Peter and John in Prison
86. Ananias and Sapphira
87. Stephen
88. Philip and the Ethiopian
89. Saul Becomes a Christian

Bulletin Board

This unit's Bulletin Board focuses on Jesus after Holy Week, in His exalted state. Having accomplished all things for our salvation, He was exalted so that all of His power as true God was now revealed. Eventually, using this power, He returned to heaven physically; yet, as true God, He is also with us at all times. We, the people of His Church, are now to be His hands and feet on earth, spreading the Good News, compassion, grace, and mercy of the Lord to all the world. The bulletin board display asks the question, Who will carry on? The disciples must have wondered this as they watched Jesus ascend to heaven, but He promised that He would send the Holy Spirit to empower them in this work. As always, He kept His word, and ten days later, on Pentecost, the Spirit enabled them to carry on the work that He had entrusted to them in the Great Commission (Matthew 28:18–20). As members of His Church, we, too, are part of the answer to that question. Jesus sends the Holy Spirit to teach us through His Word and Sacraments, and He enables us to carry on, spreading the news of salvation.

Jesus Is Exalted on High!

Who Will Carry On?
(Matthew 28:18–20)

Bible Book Overview

The Student Book Appendix has a valuable feature that gives a summary of each book of the Bible. Looking at the summaries of sixty-six books can be overwhelming, so it is suggested that each month/unit, your class look at the summaries of just a few of these books. During Unit 8, introduce what are known as the "Pauline Epistles." These are the letters the apostle Paul wrote to Christians and churches in Rome, Corinth, Galatia, Ephesus, Philippi, Colosse, and Thessalonica. He also wrote letters specifically to Timothy, Titus, and Philemon. There are thirteen of these epistles, which you can briefly learn about using the information in the Student Book Appendix.

Unit 8—The Spread of the Gospel

Lesson 79

The Emmaus Disciples
Luke 24:13–35

Background

Today's Bible story is a beautiful one that takes place on the evening following Jesus' resurrection. Not only is it a story that demonstrates the comforting presence of Jesus, but it is also masterfully written, as it demonstrates several literary techniques. What is so special about the use of literary elements in Bible stories? Each element helps to draw the reader into the story for greater comprehension of its very important message!

One of the most prominent literary elements in this account is that of the "mood" that is conveyed throughout it. The opening verses portray a somber and reflective mood in which two of Jesus' disciples are walking to Emmaus and talking about the day's events. Then, when Jesus first begins talking with them, the mood changes to that of puzzlement. Next, a mood of enlightenment sets in as Jesus interprets the Scriptures for them and shows how God's divine purpose had been revealed already in Old Testament times. When Jesus not only stays but also breaks bread with the disciples and then abruptly disappears, the mood changes to one of sheer amazement. This is followed by a mood of urgency as the two disciples rush to declare that Jesus truly is the promised Messiah called to redeem the world from sin.

This text also is chock-full of irony. The fact that Jesus asks what they are talking about is ironic because with His omniscient nature, He knows they are talking about Him. Also ironic is the disciples' response, insinuating that it was unusual that Jesus didn't know what had happened that weekend. Additionally, when they ask Jesus to stay with them because the day is almost over, it is ironic that they did not yet realize that they needed Jesus to stay with them for spiritual rather than physical reasons; nor did they know that Jesus' time on earth was, indeed, almost over.

Central Truth

After His resurrection, Jesus taught His disciples the purpose of all He had done to prepare them to spread the Gospel.

Objectives
- Confess that we, too, do not always understand all that Jesus has done for us.
- Rejoice that God sends the Holy Spirit, working through Word and Sacrament, to guide us to understanding and truth.
- Diligently share the message of Jesus' love and salvation with others.

Materials
- Hymnals and music CDs
- Web Resource 79a
- Reproducible 79

Bible Prep
Post in advance so students can bookmark references before class time.
- Isaiah 41:13
- Psalm 98
- Luke 24

Devotions

"You see that guy?" Kyle tried to whisper. "He never rips the movie tickets when you enter through his gate—so after I get in, I'll walk to the side of the ropes and hand the ticket back to you so you can get in to the movie for free!"

"But I have money to get in," Daniel said, puzzled.

"Yeah, but if you don't have to buy a ticket, we can spend the money on popcorn!" Kyle's eyes opened wide.

Kyle paid for his ticket at the counter and passed through the gate. His ticket still looked good as new. He walked to the side of the roped section and handed Daniel his ticket to use again. Daniel took it and stood in the line. But Daniel's mind was full of turmoil. He was thinking, "Kyle will call me a wimp if I don't do this, but what if I get caught? But even if I *don't* get caught, it is still wrong." Daniel's thoughts churned.

"May I see your ticket, please?" said the ticket-taker.

Daniel felt the ticket in his pocket, but he could not bring himself to use it because a Bible verse had just popped into his mind: "Finally, be strong in the Lord and in the strength of His might" (Ephesians 6:10). "Um, I'll be right back!" Daniel walked to the ticket counter, paid for one ticket, and then entered the theater—legally and honestly.

Kyle seemed really angry. But Daniel spoke up assuredly: "I just couldn't. In my heart, I knew it was wrong. And I'd rather have a happy heart than a churning stomach."

Do you ever get the feeling that something you are doing just isn't right? Praise God for the gift of the Holy Spirit, who works through God's Word and the Sacraments to keep us faithful. Scripture even says that the Holy Spirit prays for us—interceding for us when we don't know what to say, do, or even think! Sing together "Immortal, Invisible, God Only Wise" (*LSB* 802; recorded as *Hymn of the Month* for grade 6, April). Rejoice together by reading Psalm 98.

337

INTO the Word

On the Road

Begin with the Bible study in the Student Book. Then continue with this discussion. **Today's Bible story contains irony and humor. What part do you consider ironic or humorous?** (The two men assumed that Jesus did not know what had taken place during the last few days when, in fact, it was all about Jesus—His death and resurrection—and He knew every bit of it because He had *lived* it!) **Why do you think Jesus did not let them realize who He was as He was walking with them?** (Jesus probably wanted them to express what was on their minds and wanted them to stay focused on His Word and teachings to prepare them for when He would later reveal Himself as their Redeemer.) **What did it mean that He "opened" the Scriptures to them?** (He explained the Scriptures to them; He made known God's plan as revealed even by Moses of long ago; He showed how He fulfilled the prophecies.) **Jesus not only "opened" Scripture to them, but He also opened their eyes. To what were they opened?** (Their eyes were opened to the fact that it had been Jesus with them all along the road and that He was indeed alive.) **What is the irony in this?** (Only when they realized that Jesus was alive and physically with them did they discover that it was unnecessary for Jesus to be physically/visibly with them—and so He disappeared.) **Scripture says that their hearts burned within them, and they were filled with awe! Explain what that means.** (They were excited as they heard and understood the purpose of all that Jesus had done. They were in awe of Him as true God who did these things for their—and our—salvation.)

Point out: **When Jesus opened their eyes, it was not because they were blind or their eyelids were closed. They could see, but they did not recognize Jesus. When He opened their eyes, they could see with understanding. It is much like when someone explains a puzzle or mystery to you; your response might be, "Oh, I see! I get it now!"** Sing together "Open Our Eyes" (*AGPS* 195; recorded on *JPS*), asking the Lord to give us understanding. You may also wish to use Web Resource 79a, particularly the Easter portion, at this point.

LESSON 79

The Emmaus Disciples

On the Road

It was evening of that first Easter. Two followers of Jesus were walking on the road to Emmaus, a small town about seven miles (nine kilometers) from Jerusalem. As you look at the Bible narrative from Luke 24, notice the changes in mood that take place.

Somber (verses 13–21): Why were the two men so gloomy and sad?
Jesus, who they had hoped was the Messiah, had been crucified.

Puzzled (verses 22–24): What had happened that they found confusing?
People had reported that the tomb was empty and that angels had said Jesus was alive.

Enlightened (verses 25–30): What did Jesus teach them?
Jesus explained why it was necessary for Him to do all this to fulfill the prophecies and to secure salvation for all people.

Amazed (verses 30–32): What amazed them?
They recognized Jesus—and then He disappeared.

Urgent (verses 33–35): What did they immediately do?
They ran back to Jerusalem to tell their friends what they had seen and heard so that they, too, would believe.

Review

Covenant Connection

Jesus was right there with the two travelers from Emmaus when they so desperately needed understanding and hope. Jesus is right here with us too when we need help. The Old Testament prophet Isaiah spoke of this. See Isaiah 41:13.

Stay with Us

Before Jesus made His presence known, the disciples on the road felt sad and dismayed. Have you ever felt alone and wondered what your next move should be? Have you ever been so confused that you don't even know what words to use when you pray? Place a check next to problems you have encountered in your life, and then add two more to the list.

- Parent or sibling died
- Close relative hospitalized
- Experienced a car accident
- Parent lost a job
- Family financial problems
- _____
- Argument with a friend
- Poor grades
- Peer pressures
- Feeling unpopular
- Family has to move
- _____

All of us experience times when we do not understand all that Jesus can do and does for us. In times of weakness and uncertainty, God sends His Holy Spirit to *intercede* (stand up) for us and to *abide* (stay) with us! He also gives us encouragement for the journey through life, on a road that is not always easy, and He equips us to share the Good News of His amazing love!

"The Spirit helps us in our weakness. For we do not know what to pray for as we ought, but the Spirit Himself intercedes for us with groanings too deep for words. And He who searches hearts knows what is the mind of the Spirit, because the Spirit intercedes for the saints according to the will of God" (Romans 8:26–27).

Where specifically on our road through life does Jesus come to us through the power of the Holy Spirit touching our lives?
In the Means of Grace—the Word and Sacraments (Baptism and Holy Communion).

Write a prayer thanking God for the gift of forgiveness for our shortcomings and for the amazing power of the Holy Spirit working within us to keep us faithful! Ask God to abide with you, remaining with you at all times with His help and blessing. Pray also that God will give you the courage to share His message of salvation with all who need to hear it!

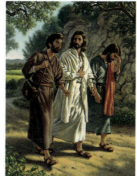

Remember

"If we love one another, God *abides* in us and His love is perfected in us. By this we know that we *abide* in Him and He in us, because He has given us of His Spirit. . . . Whoever confesses that Jesus is the Son of God, God *abides* in him, and he in God." (1 John 4:12–13, 15)

INTO our lives

Stay with Us

This portion of the Student Book connects well with the Covenant Connection, particularly the concept that the Lord is right beside us. We may not see Him visually with our eyes, but He leads us to see Him with our hearts and with understanding and faith. He comes to us directly through the Means of Grace—God's Word and the Sacraments of Holy Baptism and the Lord's Supper. Emphasize these points as you work together through the Student Book activity.

Relate the title of this section to the Bible words to remember. Point out that another term for "stay with us" is the word *abide*. Use Reproducible 79 to expand on this idea. Then look at the words of the hymn "Abide with Me" (*LSB* 878), and discuss how the words relate to the Bible narrative and also to our lives. Then listen to the recording of the song (recorded as *Hymn of the Month for grade 8, March*). If you feel your students are ready to attempt singing a few of the stanzas, close the lesson by doing so, or try singing it with the next lesson.

Lesson Support

Reaching Every Child

The text is set up in such a way that dialogue dominates the presentation of the story. Such writing almost begs to be dramatized by the students in some creative manner, either through student-led skits or through a readers theater. Maximizing student involvement will not only increase the students' self-esteem, but it will also help each student interact with and, therefore, understand the important message shared through the story! Allow students who would appreciate a challenge to use the text and its dialogue to write either a skit or a readers theater. Then have them direct a group of students in planning, presenting, and sharing their performances with other classes. If possible, encourage students to not only tell the story itself but to also lead a short talk after the presentation about the meaning and life application of the story.

Curriculum Connection

If your students are making a drama to retell the Bible story, you'll find plenty of helps and information in section 6.2.2.3, Collaboratively Written and Performed Scenes or One-Act Plays That Define Character, Environment, Action, and Theme. This is located in the sixth-grade Performing Arts volume of the Concordia Curriculum Guide series. Work with students to write the script, find basic costumes and props, and produce the play. Students might enjoy presenting it for chapel or to a class of younger students.

Technology

Three, two, one—action! As students work together to set up and perform today's Bible story as a skit or readers theater, have a few interested students be part of the camera crew. These students could work together to capture the writing, planning, rehearsal, and presentation phases of *Project: Emmaus!* After the initial video has been captured, be sure to have students edit it and make it presentable for viewers to see the entire process in a smooth, logical manner. Encourage the students to also include text for the title of the project, the credits, the acknowledgments, and so forth. After the video has been edited, set up times and places to share the efforts of the entire class, and use the video to tell the story and begin discussions about the Holy Spirit at work in the hearts of His people!

Check it Out

For more information on the work of the Holy Spirit, be sure to read not only the Third Article of the Apostles' Creed and its meaning but also the related questions and answers in *Luther's Small Catechism with Explanation* (Questions 154–168).

Ideas for the Gifted

Emmaus was about seven miles from Jerusalem. Have students who are up for a challenge research the region that was the site of the resurrection and the road to Emmaus. Then have them work in groups of two to four to construct a model of the Jerusalem-Emmaus area. Students who are artistically, mathematically, or engineering oriented will probably enjoy such an activity. Artistic students can help design the landscape and paint or color it accordingly. Students who are "into" math can help to make the model "to scale" as they develop and implement a scale and a key. Engineering-minded students will love the challenge of designing and constructing buildings, roads, bridges, and so forth to make everything as realistic as possible. While certain children will have specific gifts, be sure that *all* children help with different parts of the project—even those outside their comfort zones! When the projects are completed, have each group give a short presentation discussing the model itself and giving the group's reflections on the project as a whole. If possible, display the projects where others can enjoy them!

UNIT 8—THE SPREAD OF THE GOSPEL   LESSON 80

Doubting Thomas
John 20:19–31

Background

Peace—it's a simple little word, but such a loaded one as well! We live in a world that is filled with so much arguing, economic strife, personality clashes, wars, and other hardships to the point that, at times, peace seems far from possible. Although the word has many definitions, most of the ones that fit life as we know it today seem to be focused around the "absence of" certain negative and stressful circumstances. The absence of war equals peace; the absence of loud noise equals peace. Today's Bible story, however, tells about a peace that is quite different from the peace that the world usually knows. It is a peace that passes all understanding—not just human understanding, but that of angels and demons as well! Rather than an *absence* of something, however, it is the *presence* of something far greater! It is a harmony given by God between God and humankind. Such a feeling should be cherished and shared!

St. Paul boldly tells the Colossians, "And let the peace of Christ rule in your hearts, to which indeed you were called in one body. And be thankful" (Colossians 3:15). What a fantastic concept! Peace is supposed to rule in our hearts! It is not just supposed to have a small place in our hearts where we bring it out from time to time; no, it is to "rule" our hearts and our minds and permeate everything we do, say, and feel. Peace is not something that we can create inside ourselves. It is something given by God and intended for our good. Encourage your students to remember that Jesus—a.k.a. "the Prince of Peace"—not only lives in our hearts but also rules in our hearts as well! Remind them that, in spite of their sinfulness, God's forgiveness through Jesus brings a peace that the world does not fully know. Such a peace likewise helps us to believe, even though we do not see!

Central Truth
Jesus comes to us in the truth and assurance of His Word to forgive and reaffirm us in our times of question, doubts, and weakness of faith.

Objectives
- Acknowledge that our sinful nature and the evil in the world around us cause us to sometimes wonder and question what God is doing in our lives.
- Call upon God in prayer, and hear His Word for the strength and certainty of faith that comes only from Him.
- Proclaim the hope and assurance we have in Christ.

Materials
- Hymnals and music CDs
- Web Resource 80a
- Reproducible 80

Bible Prep
Post in advance so students can bookmark references before class time.
- John 20:19–29
- Psalm 98
- Romans 5:1
- John 14:27
- Philippians 4:7
- Luke 24:9–11, 36–48

Devotions

"Joey, look at the pretty sunset!" Alicia tried yet another thing to amuse her little brother.

"Cool! Where's it going?" Joey ran to the window.

"Well, the earth is moving, so the sun will soon be shining below the horizon and then on the other side of the earth—like near China! Then, by tomorrow morning, it will be shining back on our side of the earth where we can see it again." Alicia loved teaching younger children.

"How do you know it shines on the other side of the earth if you can't see it?"

"Well, on television, we can see that they all have sunshine there when it's dark here."

"How do you know the sun will come back to us?" Joey was full of questions.

"We just do."

"Can we go to China so we can see the sun—right now?"

"No, silly boy!" Alicia laughed.

"Hi! I'm home! Will someone please help me carry in the groceries?" Mom called through the garage door.

Joey ran and hugged her. "Mommy, how do we know the sun will come up tomorrow?"

"Because God planned that the sun would do that, and we know we can trust God's plan!"

"Oh. Okay." Joey ran off to play.

Just as Joey trusted his mother's words because he had no reason not to, so we also can trust in the mighty and truthful Word of God, which has never failed us! Just as we can't always see the sun, and yet we know it is there, so also we can, through the power of His Holy Spirit, confidently trust in Jesus, even though we cannot physically see Him. To God be all glory!

Sing together "Immortal, Invisible, God Only Wise" (*LSB* 802; recorded as *Hymn of the Month* for grade 6, April). Say together Psalm 98.

341

INTO the Word

I Told You So!

In times of doubt and confusion, God's Word assures us and leads us to trust in His almighty plan for our lives. Say, **Our devotions today told about little Joey, who wondered how we know the sun still exists on the other side of the earth, even though we cannot see it, and how we know that the sun will rise the next morning. What was the mother's answer to his questions?** (She told him that since God has never failed to have the sun rise, we can trust that it will keep happening for as long as it is part of His plan.) Then say, **Our Bible story today also talks about some people who had doubts about other things. Let's get started by reading John 20:19–29.**

Point out that this story has two parts. Ask, **In the first part of the story, why were only ten of the original twelve disciples there?** (Judas was dead and Thomas was absent.) Point out that the disciples were hiding in a locked room. Recall by way of contrast the reaction of the shepherds when they saw that the Savior was born: "They made known the saying that had been told them concerning this child" (Luke 2:17). They told everyone the happy news. That was not the reaction of Jesus' disciples when they heard the happy news of His resurrection.

Continue with the Student Book discussion, particularly of the word *peace*. Be sure that students understand the meaning of key words, such as *relationship*, *reconciliation*, and *harmony*. If students are unable to explain, ask someone to use a computer dictionary to find an appropriate definition.

Follow this discussion by singing the song "Shalom, My Friends" (*AGPS* 209; recorded on *JPS*). Explain that *shalom* is the Hebrew word for "peace." Sing the song again.

A Bad Reputation

This section of the Student Book is not defending Thomas. It is making the point that he should not be singled out for doing wrong, since all of the disciples had doubts and fears! (Note that on that first Easter morning, the disciples felt that they couldn't trust the word of the women; perhaps Thomas felt the same way about his fellow disciples.)

The discussion questions at the end of this section are very important. The fact that the disciples were hiding out in fear instead of spreading the good news about Jesus' resurrection can remind us again of the great importance of Pentecost. On their own, the disciples would have done nothing. But motivated by the enabling power of the Holy Spirit at Pentecost, the disciples became changed men who courageously spread the Gospel to many people and many places. In fact, that is what most of this unit and the next are about—the growth of the Christian Church.

The other important point for discussion is our own weaknesses and failures. Ask students to think—silently, without responding verbally—about times when they had an opportunity to say something about God's grace and blessings, but remained quiet. Or think about times when they went along with someone's bad idea or imitated their bad behavior because they were afraid to speak out about what was right and what was God's way. Or think about times when they were more concerned about what other kids would say about them than about what Jesus knows and wants. **We can't criticize the disciples, because we have the same weaknesses and sins. But thank God that we also have the same Savior, who forgives us and leads us to be faithful followers.**

A Big Change

The most significant part of Thomas's story is that the power of God changed him so that he was convinced; he was certain that Jesus is true God and true man, risen from the dead as our Savior and Messiah. That is the main thing to take away from his story, because it is also true for us—it is the power of God that works a change in us, bringing us to faith and keeping us in faith. How certain can we be of our salvation through Jesus? Look at the words of the Bible verse to remember—for nothing can separate us from the love of God!

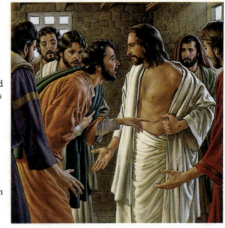

Lesson 80
Doubting Thomas

I Told You So!

It was Easter evening. Jesus had just spent time with two followers from the village of Emmaus. Ten of the disciples were back in Jerusalem in a locked room, frightened that they might be harmed as Jesus had been. Suddenly, Jesus appeared in that room. Read about it and about His second visit several days later in John 20:19–31. Jesus understood their doubt and confusion, and He came to comfort and reassure them. He had often told them that He would die and rise again on the third day (Matthew 16:21), so He easily could have said, "I told you so!" Instead, what were Jesus' first words both times He appeared in that locked room? **"Peace be with you."**

The word *peace* is used in several different ways, some casually, some significantly:

1. *Peace*: "Once there was war and arguing, but now there is no fighting."
2. *Peace*: "Once it was noisy, but now it is quiet and still."
3. *Peace*: "Once there was a broken relationship, but now there is reconciliation and harmony."

What is unique about the peace that Jesus was speaking about in the following passages?

Romans 5:1 — It is peace with God.
John 14:27 — It is not like the peace the world gives.
Philippians 4:7 — It is a peace that is beyond our understanding.

Review

Covenant Connection

Peace explains Christ's purpose. Sin destroyed our relationship with God, but Jesus has reconciled us. By taking away our sin and guilt, Jesus has brought peace and harmony and a new relationship with us as children of God. The Old Testament prophet Isaiah spoke of the Messiah's mission, saying, "His name shall be called Wonderful Counselor, Mighty God, Everlasting Father, Prince of Peace" (Isaiah 9:6, emphasis added). When Jesus was born, the angels sang of "peace on earth." We sing of this peace in Christmas hymns such as "Silent Night" and "Hark! The Herald Angels Sing." Jesus completed that peaceful reconciliation through His death and resurrection! Jesus created peace between heaven and earth!

A Bad Reputation

Two thousand years have passed, and Thomas *still* has a bad reputation. Even the title of this lesson singles him out as "Doubting Thomas." Let's turn to Luke 24:9–11, 36–43, and read additional details about the event. It looks like *all* the disciples were doubters.

What was the disciples' reaction Easter morning when the women told them Jesus is alive (verse 11)? **They didn't believe the women, thinking it was an "idle tale."**

What was their first reaction when they saw Jesus that evening (verse 37)? **They were frightened and thought they saw a ghost.**

How did Jesus reassure them that He was physically there with them (verses 39, 42–43)? **He invited them to touch His hands and feet; He asked them for something to eat, and He ate in front of them.**

Think about this: Why were the disciples in that locked room in the first place? And why were they in that locked room again a week later? Why can we be happy today that Jesus was so patient and forgiving when their faith was weak? **The disciples were afraid for their own safety. We, too, have times of weakness when we have doubts or when we are afraid to speak up about Jesus. Praise God that He patiently forgives us too!**

A Big Change

Think of a time you made an embarrassing mistake. How would you like it if that was the one thing people always remembered about you? Perhaps instead of talking about "Doubting Thomas," we need to recognize that he changed. We need to call him "Convinced Thomas." When Jesus appeared a week after Easter, He didn't come to scold Thomas; Jesus came to strengthen Thomas—and it worked! During the forty days after Easter, Jesus appeared many times, sometimes to one person, and sometimes to as many as 500 people. These appearances proved to many eyewitnesses that Jesus was alive again. But the most important reason for these appearances is that Jesus came to teach His followers, to help them understand about salvation so that they could spread the Gospel to all people, in all places, at all times. Read aloud Luke 24:44–48.

Look again at Thomas's words, which are an affirmation of faith—a creed—as he stated, "My Lord and my God!" (John 20:28). These words are a reflection of similar affirmations from the Old Testament, connecting all of Scripture and pointing to the Savior, Jesus.

Psalm 18:46: "The LORD lives, . . . and exalted be the God of my salvation."
Psalm 31:14: "I trust in You, O LORD; I say, 'You are my God.'"
Psalm 104:1: "O LORD my God, You are very great!"

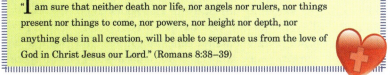

"I am sure that neither death nor life, nor angels nor rulers, nor things present nor things to come, nor powers, nor height nor depth, nor anything else in all creation, will be able to separate us from the love of God in Christ Jesus our Lord." (Romans 8:38–39)

At this time, have students close their eyes and just listen to the hymn "O Sons and Daughters of the King" as recorded on *Hymns of the Season for grade 6, Easter*. Then have them open their eyes and focus on Web Resource 80a. This provides the opportunity to analyze the hymn, placing the stanzas in sequential order. (No peeking at a hymnal!) After the activity is completed, have students open to the text in the hymnal (*LSB* 470), and this time, sing along with the recording, noting how it tells the story of several events of Easter. After this, continue with the next section of the lesson.

INTO our lives

Use Reproducible 80 to make further connections between the Bible narrative from the first century AD and life in the twenty-first century today.

It is important to make students aware that there are many people today who try to contradict and disparage the Word of God. Some are almost like missionaries for unbelief. Make students aware that they will sometimes encounter such people in high school and college classes, in books and magazines, in so-called documentaries on television, and in movies (such as *The Da Vinci Code*); but none of these has the accuracy and documentation that Scripture does.

For your personal study and for any students who are interested in digging deeper, here are authors that speak clearly about the truth of Scripture: Josh McDowell, Lee Strobel, and Ravi Zacharias.

Also encourage students to seek out materials on the CPH Web site. Explain that CPH is the official publishing arm of the Lutheran Church—Missouri Synod, and all the material it publishes is first closely examined to make sure that it tells the truth about God, His Word, and His will for our lives.

Hint: The eight Bible references at the end of Reproducible 80 all have the same words. You may want to assign these verses to different students and have them read simultaneously. Discuss why these words would be repeated so often. (The grace of God and the peace we have through Jesus are vital and essential. But it should also be noted that all of these references are in epistles written by the apostle Paul. An epistle is a letter, and this statement is a special greeting that he included in most of his letters, using a variation of it in others. Consider what statement of your faith you could include to tag along with your signature at the end of all your e-mails.)

Curriculum Connection

Again and again during the forty days after Jesus' resurrection, we see a pattern: doubt . . . Jesus' appearance . . . renewed faith . . . a rush to communicate the news to other people—who nevertheless doubt . . . and so on. Communicating new knowledge so others understand it and believe can be difficult. Make a science connection to this story by using section 6.4.1.10, Communicating the Findings of an Investigation. This is located in the sixth-grade Science volume of the Concordia Curriculum Guide series.

Teacher Tips

Show your students how to make their classroom Bibles into "tabbed Bibles." This can be a great help to students who struggle with finding Bible references, but it is also a big help to students who know how to find their way through the Bible but would like to do so even faster and more efficiently. Provide students with the removable sticky flags available from most office supply stores.

Hint: They could flag each book of the Bible, but that could get cumbersome—and lumpy! Instead, suggest that they choose three or four key books from the Old Testament and in the New Testament that can orient them to the location of other books nearby.

For example, in the Old Testament, don't mark Genesis, because it is the first book and easy to find; mark 1 Samuel, which is the first of the Historical Books about the kings (and thus the pre-king period will also be easy to find); mark the Book of Psalms, because it is so large and is used so often; and then mark the Book of Isaiah, which begins the section of the Prophets, and which also contains some of the most significant messianic prophecies. Also suggest abbreviating the names of the books ("1 Sa," "Ps," "Is"), because there is not much room to write on the flags.

For the New Testament, consider flagging Matthew ("Mt"), because it is the first of the Gospels; next, mark Galatians ("Gal") because it is at the middle of the Pauline Epistles; and then mark James ("Jas"), the beginning of the General Epistles. (Note that there is no single established format for abbreviations; students may find variations on these suggestions.)

Searching Further

Since the fall of Adam and Eve, the world has never been 100 percent peaceful. As a class, look together at a world map and discuss some of the various battles and wars that have occurred since our fall into sin. Hot spots could include the ancient Mesopotamian Valley, Iraq, Iran, Germany, Korea, Japan, Russia, and even the United States. Compare and contrast times of conflict and times of peace, and distinguish between worldly peace and the peace that Jesus gives in spite of any external circumstances!

Critical thinking

Thomas was a typical disciple of Jesus—and yet, the man has been labeled as the infamous "Doubting Thomas," when, in reality, he did what *most* people would have done. Have students think about the following questions and discuss the answers together as a class. **What would you have done if you had been Thomas or one of the other disciples in the room? Would you have been amazed? afraid? confused? elated? bewildered? Would you have experienced some other emotion—or all of the above?** Continue to challenge students' thinking by having them write a journal article from the perspective of one of Jesus' disciples. Their articles should be written from the first-person point of view and should include information, emotions, and reactions during Jesus' appearances. When all entries are finished, display them in a hallway, compile them in a book, or file them in individual work portfolios.

UNIT 8—THE SPREAD OF THE GOSPEL   LESSON 81

Jesus at the Sea of Tiberias
JOHN 21:1–19

Background

"Do you love Me? . . . Do you love Me? . . . Do you love Me?" Jesus asks the question of Simon Peter three times, a dreaded reminder to Simon Peter that he had blatantly denied Jesus three times. Jesus' triple persistence, however, becomes Simon Peter's triple privilege to profess His love for Jesus, each time saying, "Yes, Lord; You know that I love You." The last time, however, Peter indicates profound realization as he says, "Lord, You know everything; You know that I love You." Peter thus admits that there is nothing God does not know; nothing Peter did would ever be hidden. All Peter could do was humbly submit to an omniscient God who loved him enough to give His very life for him. At the Sea of Tiberias, Jesus gave Simon Peter a "do over"; and right here, right now, we are given a "do over" through Christ's saving work on the cross. There is no sin too big that God cannot forgive and forget! He promises in Jeremiah 31:34 that He will remember our sins no more.

Although John calls the location of the great catch of fish "the Sea of Tiberias," it is more commonly known as "the Sea of Galilee," and it is also called "the Lake of Gennesaret." This is the same lake or sea on which a good portion of Jesus' ministry took place. Jesus preached many of His parables and other messages near the Sea of Tiberias, and He healed many people there as well. This sea was known for its large schools of fish, and since nighttime fishing usually yielded good results, the fact that the men had not had a good catch all night was quite unusual. This unfortunate circumstance, however, turns into a wonderful event when Jesus performs a miracle and causes them to catch a large amount (153) of large fish. Praise be to God, who continues to provide for His people through His unique ways and in His perfect timing!

Central Truth

Jesus comes to us, assuring us of His forgiving love and guiding us to live as His disciples.

Objectives

- Acknowledge that we are sinners, but that God's grace is greater than any sin or evil in this world.
- Receive the forgiveness of Jesus, relinquishing feelings of guilt and shame as we are empowered to live boldly for Him.
- Live in discipleship, in faith, serving others, and sharing the hope of eternal life.

Materials

- Hymnals and music CDs
- Web Resource 81a
- Web Resource 81b
- Reproducible 81

Bible Prep

Post in advance so students can bookmark references before class time.
- John 21
- Luke 5
- Matthew 28

Devotions

"Why are you so quiet tonight, Jillian?" said Mom as she sat down beside her.

"I'm not!" Jillian seemed defensive.

"Well, you barely said a whole sentence at dinner this evening," Mom said cautiously.

"Well, I just . . . never mind! It's really no big deal." Jillian's eyes blinked fast now.

"Okay. Just let me know if you want to talk." Mom seemed puzzled. "Or I suppose I could call Lizzie."

"Mom! You wouldn't!" Jillian crossed her arms. "Seriously?"

"Well, I need to find out sooner or later," Mom reasoned.

"Okay—but Lizzie's actually the problem."

"How is Lizzie the problem?" Mom was curious now.

"Well, Lizzie and I were talking with some eighth graders at recess, and they said that they were having a sleepover on Saturday night and they didn't care if they went to church on Sunday or not. Then Lizzie jumped in and said she hates going to church! And that's when I . . . " Jillian paused. "Well, that's when I said I don't want to go to church either! It's like I denied God, just to be cool! I don't really feel that way, though. Honest!"

"I know, Jillian, I know. Try to remember that being with 'cool kids' is never an excuse to lie or to deny God."

"I know," Jillian sniffled.

"Why don't we pray about this?" Mom put her arm around her. "No sin is too big for God. Okay?"

"Okay! You start." Mom and Jillian began praying, and Jillian's smile returned quickly as her load of sin was lifted from her heart.

Sing together "O Sons and Daughters of the King" (*LSB* 470; recorded as *Hymn of the Season for grade 6, Easter*). Rejoice, saying together Psalm 98.

345

INTO the lesson

Explain, **Today we are going to consider the great mercy of God. He loves all people, each one individually, and He cares for us. Let's consider the magnitude of this task.** Use Web Resource 81a to calculate the number of seconds in a year. (Approximately 30 million) Then divide this number up among the approximately 7 billion people in the world. Help students come to this conclusion: **This means that in a year's time, there is less than a half second to spend on each person! Is a half second per year enough for you? How does God accomplish the task of blessing us daily and supplying our needs?** It is important to emphasize that we have access to God *all* the time—not just a half second per year. This is true because **God does not have the limitations that we do. He is God, and with God, nothing is impossible—and all things *are* possible!** See Luke 1:37 and Matthew 19:26. **God is not limited by time because He is eternal and everlasting. Psalm 90:4 says, "For a thousand years in Your sight are but as yesterday when it is past, or as a watch in the night."** Psalm 103:11–12 reminds us that God's merciful kindness is as high as the heavens, and His merciful forgiveness removes our sins as far as the ends of the earth, as it states: **"For as high as the heavens are above the earth, so great is His steadfast love toward those who fear Him; as far as the east is from the west, so far does He remove our transgressions from us."**

LESSON 81
Jesus at the Sea of Tiberias

Mercy[1]

The third time Jesus appeared after Easter to some of the disciples was by the Sea of Tiberias (a.k.a. Sea of Galilee). This Bible narrative can be divided into two parts; in each part, Jesus shows mercy—two different types of mercy. Read John 21:1–14.

Definition

MERCY[1]
Serving those with physical needs
You: Ø ignored.
You: will be helped.

Me Too!

We like to put ourselves into this picture—especially if we are the ones being helped. Solve my problem, give me food, heal my pain, rebuild my house, be my friend. Jesus is truly our helper when we have physical needs, just like in today's Scripture. The disciples needed help catching fish; Jesus provided for them. But Jesus wants more from those who follow Him in faith. More than being the "helped," you are also to be the "helper." How can you help someone:

today? _____ this weekend? _____ at home? _____ far away? _____

Challenge Question

Why, in your opinion, did Jesus repeat the miracle of the catch of fish? He did it when He first met His disciples (Luke 5:1–11), and now, after His death and resurrection, He did it again. **Possibly to open and close His ministry on earth in similar circumstances; but more than that, He probably wanted to show His disciples that He was the same Jesus they had known before—both true man and true God—but now He was in His state of exaltation, using fully His power as the Lord.**

Review

Covenant Connection

"The LORD is merciful and gracious, slow to anger and abounding in steadfast love." This description of God is repeated frequently in the Old Testament. These words—or a variation of them—are given in Exodus 34:6; Nehemiah 9:17; Psalm 86:15; Psalm 103:8; Psalm 145:8; Joel 2:13; and Jonah 4:2. Jesus, true God, continued to show that mercy and steadfast love throughout His time on earth. And He calls His followers to follow His example, as He states in the Beatitudes from the Sermon on the Mount: "Blessed are the merciful, for they shall receive mercy" (Matthew 5:7).

168

INTO the Word

Mercy[1]

The two lesson pages in the Student Book explore the two types of mercy demonstrated in the Bible narrative. Use Web Resource 81b to show the setting of the Bible story. As you work through the page together, emphasize that Jesus showed merciful kindness as He helped the disciples with their physical needs. He continues to show merciful kindness to us also. But the Lord wants us to grow in our faith life, and He wants us to be more than just "receivers." He also desires that we be "suppliers" for the physical needs of others. Mercy is one of the main purposes of our church organization, the LCMS, which stands for "The Lutheran Church—Missouri Synod." Point out that the *M* in LCMS stands for "Missouri," where some of the early work of the Lutheran Church originated in America, and it is where the LCMS has its headquarters. However, it would be good to let that letter *M* also remind you of mercy. To learn more about what the LCMS does to share the mercy and grace of God with others, go to the Web site www.lcms.org and type "mercy works" in the search bar. This will bring up the archives of the free magazine by that name, which has articles about the work of the Church, and pictures

Mercy[2]

Peter had egregiously sinned by denying Jesus three times. Now Jesus singled Peter out to mercifully forgive him, reassuring him three times. Jesus did this by encouraging Peter to continue his work as an apostle with the mission of spreading the Gospel. Read John 21:15–19.

Definition

Mercy[2]
Serving those with spiritual needs
You: Ø punished.
You: are forgiven.

Me Too!

We like to put ourselves into this picture—especially if we are the ones being mercifully forgiven. Jesus calls us to repentance and faith as He, in mercy, forgives us, even though we do not deserve His steadfast love. Jesus took our punishment and gives us His victory. But Jesus wants more from those who follow Him in faith. More than being the "forgiven," you are also to be the "forgiver." He teaches us to pray, "Forgive us our trespasses as we forgive those who trespass against us." What are the limits on when we forgive? What if the person's unkindness is too great? What if the person's unkindness happens too often? What if you just can't stand it anymore?

This can be one of the hardest parts of our Christian life, and that is why it is absolutely necessary to rely on Jesus to make you strong to forgive, because He places no limits on forgiveness. (See Matthew 18:21–22.)

Challenge Question

Jesus could have simply said to Peter, "I forgive you." But He took it a step further, challenging Peter to carry on with the work of "feeding the sheep." In your opinion, why was this so very important at this particular time? **Jesus, the Good Shepherd, knew that it would soon be time for Him to return to His home in heaven. He would turn over the task of feeding His flock (the Church) to His disciples, empowering them through the Holy Spirit at Pentecost.**

Remember

"God ___shows___ His ___love___ for us in that ___while___ we were still ___sinners___, ___Christ___ ___died___ for us." (Romans 5:8)

---

of people around the world who are in need or whose needs are being supplied. Search through several of these online magazines to find an article and pictures that might interest your students, and use your computer to project these on a screen to share with your class.

Before moving on to the next portion of the lesson, sing together "They'll Know We Are Christians by Our Love" (*AGPS* 237; recorded on *JPS*). **This is based on the words of Jesus, who asked His followers to show mercy and kindness to others. He says in John 13:34–35, "A new commandment I give to you, that you love one another: just as I have loved you, you also are to love one another. By this all people will know that you are My disciples, if you have love for one another."**

Mercy[2]

This section focuses on another type of mercy—the forgiveness God supplies for our spiritual needs. We deserve punishment for sin, but God gives mercy instead. And once again, we will see that He asks us to be more than "receivers." We are also called to share forgiveness with others.

As Peter pledged his love to the Lord, join by singing "I Love You, Lord" (*AGPS* 129; recorded on *JPS*). Jesus indicated His total forgiveness of Peter by reinstating him in his role as follower, disciple, and apostle. **God's forgiveness is complete. He doesn't judge the size of our sin; He doesn't make us, as sinners, become "second-class citizens" of heaven. His forgiveness is not based on what we do, but on what Jesus has done for us.** This is also how God wants us to view others—not looking at the wrong they have done to us, but looking toward all the righteousness Jesus has offered for us. Sing together "I Will Sing of the Mercies" (*AGPS* 133; recorded on *JPS*).

Jesus' message to "Feed My sheep" implies feeding His people with the nourishing Word of God and the Sacraments. Read together the Great Commission in Matthew 28:18–20, where Jesus is again leading us to continue His work of spreading the Gospel and sharing His love. Use Reproducible 81 to reflect on how and where we today can share the mercies of the Lord.

Reaching Every Child

As Lutheran schools become centers of mission outreach, you may find yourself teaching immigrant and refugee children whose parents make much less money than most school families do. This means that the incidental costs of schooling—the field trip tickets, the colored T-shirt, the costume for the school play—can be a much greater burden for them than for other families. If you suspect financial problems, talk with a school administrator about it. There may be special funding available, perhaps from an interested donor, to help take care of these needs. Of course you'll want to handle this as quietly and sensitively as possible in order to avoid embarrassment. Also consider whether it's truly necessary to ask all families to purchase those extras—field trip tickets are unavoidable, but the special T-shirt, glue gun, camera, or gardening tool might not be. If a family has no computer or Internet access, can the assignment be handwritten or typed on a typewriter? Is there perhaps an older computer that could be donated instead of discarded? Could research be done at a library or at school instead of online at home? Use your creativity!

Reaching Every Child

Pragmatic Language Disorder. A pragmatic language disorder, which is also referred to as a social communication disorder, limits a child's ability to say the right things at the right times in the right ways. When students are faced with this disorder, they have difficulty with small talk and other social functions of language. Their peers may perceive them as self-centered, rude, or arrogant when, in fact, these students want to be part of the group but display inappropriate mannerisms. They want to be able to answer questions appropriately, but they seem to dominate the conversation, and they do not grasp the concept of taking turns. They are tactless, and they will interpret language literally. It will be difficult for a teacher to incorporate them into their group without making plans ahead of time. Some strategies that can be used with these students include the following:
- Work to improve reading comprehension.
- Provide social skills instruction.
- Provide explanations for academic work.
- Teach students how to draw inferences.
- Create a safe learning environment by eliminating bullying.
- Use precise and literal language.
- Be thoughtful about classroom activities.

Reaching Every Child

Visual Memory. Knowing each student is critical when deciding what modifications and accommodations need to be made when teaching a lesson. If you are aware of your students' strengths and weaknesses, you can look at your curriculum and determine what you want your students to know after the lesson is taught. Once that is decided, the modifications for a student struggling with poor visual memory can include the following:
- Draw a student's attention to the key aspects of the illustrations.
- Have students read and follow one-, two-, and three-step directions.
- Ask students to organize pictures in the correct sequence.
- Use visual cues and auditory information to aid recall.

Reaching Every Child

Writing Disability. Children with this disability may demonstrate illegible writing and/or misspellings, or they may have trouble expressing ideas clearly. Two main kinds of writing disabilities are developmental coordination disorder and disorder of written expression. It has been suggested that 10 percent of students have a writing disability. Students can have a combination of these problems, and most of them dislike the whole writing experience. There are many different strategies one can use with these students:
- Teach prewriting strategies
- Provide class notes for students with writing difficulties.
- Encourage the use of diagrams and other visual tools to organize information.
- Provide opportunities to use a word processor.
- Encourage the use of a dictionary or spelling checker.
- Assign a partner to proofread.
- Provide extra time and reduce lengthy assignments.
- Give two grades for each written assignment, one for content and one for handwriting.
- Allow the students to choose manuscript or cursive writing.
- Be cautious about asking a student to write on the board.

UNIT 8—THE SPREAD OF THE GOSPEL

LESSON 82

The Ascension
ACTS 1:1–14

Background

Lesson 82 moves from the Gospels to the Acts of the Apostles, the history of the Early Christian Church. The inspired author of Acts is the same Luke who wrote the third Gospel. Luke was a physician, historian, and traveling companion of the apostle Paul. A Greek and a Gentile Christian, he is the only known Gentile author in the New Testament. Luke apparently joined Paul and his companions at Troas, as his use of the pronoun *we* indicates in Acts 16:10 through Acts 28. Because Paul and his associates were often subjected to beatings, stoning, and other physical hardships, Luke's skills as a physician must have been in frequent demand.

Luke was a careful historian, concerned with the truth; repeatedly, the details of his descriptions have been proven accurate. The first words in his Gospel indicate his interest in the truth: "Inasmuch as many have undertaken to compile a narrative of the things that have been accomplished among us, just as those who from the beginning were eyewitnesses and ministers of the word have delivered them to us, it seemed good to me also, having followed all things closely for some time past, to write an orderly account for you, most excellent Theophilus, that you may have certainty concerning the things you have been taught" (Luke 1:1–4).

The Book of Acts serves as the connecting link between Christ's life and the life of the Church, between the Gospels and the letters. It was written between AD 63 and 70. Because Acts ends so abruptly, it is thought that Luke may have been planning to write a third book.

Central Truth

When Jesus had accomplished His purpose on earth and prepared His disciples to carry on, He entrusted His disciples and Church with the mission to spread the Gospel message.

Objectives

- Admit that we often fail to see our role and carry on our Christian purpose to share the love and message of the Gospel with others.
- Rejoice in the forgiving and strengthening power of God, who promises the gift of the Holy Spirit to guide us to live as His people.
- Celebrate the victory of our ascended Lord, who, at the same time, never leaves us.

Materials

- Hymnals and music CDs
- Reproducible 82
- Web Resource 82a

Bible Prep

Post in advance so students can bookmark references before class time.
- Acts 1:1–14
- Psalm 98
- 1 John 2:1
- John 14:2–3
- Psalm 110:1
- Ephesians 4:10–12

Devotions

All of the sixth graders were puzzled. Ever since Christmas, when Alan found out his family would be moving to Pittsburgh at the end of the school year, Alan had been complaining about leaving his friends, his school, and his home. As May approached, however, Alan couldn't wait to go. Alan hadn't seen his new house or school. But his father had already gone to Pittsburgh to get everything ready for the family. He would soon return to get his family. Alan wanted to be in his new home with his father, who had prepared a place for him.

On the night before He was crucified, Jesus told His disciples He would be going away. "In My Father's house are many rooms," He said. "If it were not so, would I have told you that I go to prepare a place for you? And if I go and prepare a place for you, I will come again and will take you to Myself, that where I am you may be also" (John 14:2–3). In Jesus' day, when a young man wanted to get married, he and his family would build a new room onto the family's home. When the room was ready, the young man would go to the house where his bride lived. He would bring his bride to the room he had prepared. No one—not even the bride—knew for sure when the young man would come. Sometimes an excited bridegroom would come for his bride in the middle of the night, when no one expected him. But the bride would joyfully go, no matter what the hour, to be with the one who had prepared a place for her.

Jesus ascended into heaven to prepare a place for everyone who believes in Him. He promised He will come again to take us to be with Him in the place He has prepared. We don't know when He will come again, but we look forward to His coming with hope and joy.

Sing "The King of Glory" (*AGPS* 227; recorded on *JPS*) and/or "On Christ's Ascension I Now Build" (*LSB* 492; recorded as *Hymn of the Season for grade 6, Pentecost*). Rejoice as you say together Psalm 98.

349

INTO the lesson

Background: Preparation Time

Jesus' disciples were near the end of three years of intensive preparation for the purpose to which He had called them. They had left their homes and families and followed wherever He went, observing, listening, learning from the Master Teacher. He even sent them out for practical field experience—the equivalent of student teaching or a short-term vicarage (Luke 9:1–6; 10:1–24). Yet they often seemed ill prepared, arguing about who would be the greatest in the kingdom of heaven (Matthew 18:1–4) and not understanding why Jesus would go to Jerusalem, where He would obviously be in danger (Mark 10:32–34).

Remind students that the disciples, like many of the people who heard Jesus teach and saw Him perform miracles, believed that He had come to be an earthly king, one who would restore the glory of the kingdom of David (Acts 1:6). It was only after His death and resurrection, as Jesus opened up Scripture to them, that they began to understand His role as Savior—and they didn't even fully understand until they had received the Holy Spirit on Pentecost. Then as now, the power of the Holy Spirit was necessary for living as God's people and for witnessing to others about what God had done for them—as He has done for us—through Jesus.

Lesson 82

The Ascension

Read Acts 1:1–14 and then fill out this "missing persons report" about Jesus.

MISSING PERSONS REPORT

Name _____
Aliases (a.k.a.) _____
Next of kin _____
Last seen at _____
Witnesses _____

Details of the incident:
_____
_____

Other recent appearances (past 40 days)
_____
_____
_____
_____

Where are the witnesses currently residing?
_____
_____
_____
_____

Review

Covenant Connection

The Last Day, when Jesus will return again, is sometimes called "Judgment Day." That sounds quite frightening, but it shouldn't sound that way to believers. Because of Jesus, we have already been judged and are declared not guilty! Jesus has "now reconciled [us] in His body of flesh by His death, in order to present [us] holy and blameless and above reproach before Him" (Colossians 1:22). As believers, we can look forward to the celebration of Jesus' return, when "the Lord Himself will descend from heaven with a cry of command, with the voice of an archangel, and with the sound of the trumpet of God" (1 Thessalonians 4:16).

170

INTO the Word

Missing Persons Report

Read aloud the account of Jesus' ascension in Acts 1:1–14. Then work together through the "Missing Persons Report" in the Student Book, using the following information.

The name by which Jesus was most often known was "Jesus of Nazareth." His aliases—other names He called Himself or was called by others—would include "Son of Man," "King of the Jews" "I AM," "Light of the World," "Bread of Life," "the Good Shepherd," "the Resurrection and the Life," "the Way, the Truth, and the Life," "Messiah," and "Lamb of God." Ask students to recall as many of these names as possible.

Jesus' next of kin would have included His heavenly Father; His mother, Mary (Joseph apparently was no longer living); and His brothers. But we are also part of His family—as children of God! When He was asked about His family, Jesus replied, "My mother and brothers are those who hear the word of God and do it" (Luke 8:21).

Luke records that the ascension took place near Bethany (Luke 24:50) on the Mount of Olives (also called "Olivet"), "a Sabbath day's journey away" from Jerusalem (Acts 1:12). According to verse 13, those who witnessed the ascension were the eleven remaining disciples: Peter, John, James, Andrew, Philip, Thomas, Bartholomew, Matthew, James the son of Alphaeus, Simon the Zealot, and Judas the son of James. Mary (Jesus' mother), His brothers, and other women may also have witnessed the event (v. 14).

Ask students to write witness statements concerning what people saw (Jesus raised His arms, ascended, and was hidden by a cloud) and what they heard Him say (He promised the Holy Spirit; He commissioned them as witnesses). Another statement could include the angels and their words.

Scripture records many appearances of Jesus in the forty days before the ascension, beginning with the Easter appearances to Mary Magdalene (John 20:10–18) and the other women at the tomb (Matthew 28:8–10), to Peter in Jerusalem (Luke 24:34), to the Emmaus disciples (Mark 16:12–13), to the eleven disciples behind closed doors in Jerusalem (John 20:19–31), to seven disciples while fishing (21:1–14), to eleven disciples on the mountain (Matthew 28:16–20), to a crowd of five hundred (1 Corinthians 15:6), and to Jesus' brother James (v. 7).

Note that after the ascension the disciples returned to Jerusalem to wait for the Holy Spirit.

Why Ascension?

The Bible teaches that 40 days after His resurrection, Jesus, in the presence of His disciples, ascended bodily to the glory of His Father. Before He ascended, He commissioned His disciples to be His witnesses, sharing the Good News about His life, death, and resurrection with others.

Why did Jesus go back to heaven? Why didn't He stay on earth physically and lead this mission in person? Read each of the following statements and Bible passages. Then match the number of each statement to the related Bible verse.

1. Jesus ascended into heaven to prepare a place in heaven for all who believe in Him.	__3__ 1 John 2:1
2. As our Prophet, Jesus sends people to share the Gospel by the power of the Holy Spirit.	__1__ John 14:2–3
3. As our Priest, Jesus pleads and prays for us before His heavenly Father.	__4__ Psalm 110:1
4. As our King, Jesus reigns over the world, ruling and protecting His Church.	__2__ Ephesians 4:10–12

In heaven, Jesus "sits at the right hand of God the Father Almighty." According to Ephesians 1:20–23, God "seated Him at His right hand in the heavenly places, far above all rule and authority and power and dominion, and above every name that is named, not only in this age but also in the one to come. And He put all things under His feet and gave Him as head over all things to the church, which is His body, the fullness of Him who fills all in all."

Jesus is not limited by time or space, and so He promised His disciples He would never leave them alone: "And behold, I am with you always, to the end of the age" (Matthew 28:20). He told them He would return visibly and with great glory on the Last Day to judge the world. Only God knows the day on which Jesus will return. But Christians look forward to that day with hope and joy, knowing they have already been declared righteous through faith in Jesus' death and resurrection.

He's Coming Back! In the Meantime . . .

As Jesus' twenty-first-century disciple, you are also commissioned to spread the Gospel to others "in Jerusalem" (your family, school, and community), "in all Judea and Samaria" (the country in which you live), "and to the end of the earth" (Acts 1:8). But witnessing is hard, isn't it? And surely Jesus meant *adults* should witness, not kids—right?

Wrong! Jesus promised His disciples He would send the Holy Spirit. The Spirit would comfort them, guide them to know His truth, remind them of Jesus' words, give them the right words to say, and fill them with power. The Holy Spirit, whom you received in Baptism, will do the same for you.

Remember

"But you will receive power when the Holy Spirit has come upon you, and you will be My witnesses in Jerusalem and in all Judea and Samaria, and to the end of the earth." (Acts 1:8)

171

Why Ascension?

Share with your students the Second Article of the Apostles' Creed and its explanation in *Luther's Small Catechism with Explanation*, where Questions 146–149 deal with Christ's ascension and second coming, and which form the basis for this section of the lesson.

Jesus ascended so He could send the Holy Spirit to empower the disciples to share the Gospel with others. Explain that Jesus, in His human form, lived and worked in a small area, never traveling more than a hundred miles from the place He was born. But His followers, by the power of the Holy Spirit, would carry the Gospel throughout the world.

Discuss how Jesus can be seated "at the right hand of God, the Father Almighty" and still be with each of His followers here on earth. One of the attributes of God is *omnipresence*, the ability to be present everywhere (Small Catechism, Question 93 F). In Jeremiah 23:24, God asks, "Do I not fill heaven and earth?" Jesus is present in the Church, "For where two or three are gathered in My name, there am I among them" (Matthew 18:20).

He's Coming Back! In the Meantime . . .

Witnessing is indeed for kids—for all who believe the Good News about Jesus, the Savior of the world. We have received the Holy Spirit through Baptism; it is through the power of the Spirit that we live as God's people and share the Gospel with others. Discuss students' previous attempts at witnessing. Assure them that Jesus forgives us for our failure to witness. When we witness, we must rely on God's power through the Holy Spirit, waiting for His timing and instructions. Through the Spirit, He gives us the right words to say at the most effective time.

Provide copies of Reproducible 82, which can be used as a witnessing tool. Teach students how to manipulate it, and then suggest that they share this story with someone in their family, like a younger sibling or a grandparent, or perhaps a neighbor or friend.

Fold the top half of the scene down. Then lift up the top one-fourth section. This will show Jesus standing at the top of the hill with His arms outstretched in blessing as He speaks to His disciples.

Slowly raise the top quarter section so that it looks like Jesus is ascending into heaven.

When the page is fully extended, fold the top quarter section back to indicate that Jesus disappeared from view.

Additional considerations: Suggest that students color the activity—at least the blue sky—to add interest. They can use a scissors to trim off excess paper that is outside of the border.

For an alternative final scene, draw a large white cloud on the back of the top quarter page, and surround it with blue sky. This section can then be folded to the front to indicate that a cloud hid Jesus from view.

Ask students to explain what happened next. (The message of the two angels; disciples returned to Jerusalem to await the coming of the Holy Spirit.)

351

Technology

Use the Internet to find a reproduction of the painting *The Burial of the Count of Orgaz* by the Spanish artist El Greco. The lower part of this famous painting shows the funeral procession of the Count of Orgaz, a prominent nobleman known for his virtue and his faith. Notice the priests and mourners accompanying the body to the grave. The upper part of the painting reveals what most of the mourners cannot see—Jesus, the saints, and the angels waiting to receive the count into heaven. Imagine the scene on the other side of the clouds that hid Jesus from the sight of the disciples at the ascension. Jesus, who had come down from heaven as a human baby, had accomplished everything for which He had been sent. Now He was returning home in triumph. John gives us a hint of what the angel choirs must have sung—"Worthy is the Lamb who was slain, to receive power and wealth and wisdom and might and honor and glory and praise" (Revelation 5:12) and "Hallelujah! For the Lord our God the Almighty reigns" (19:6).

Curriculum Connection

Make a science connection to the story of Jesus' ascension by studying gravity! Look at section 6.3.2.6, Gravity and the Earth's Surface. You'll find it in the sixth-grade Science volume of the Concordia Curriculum Guide series. Discuss with students: **Why do you think God chose to have Jesus leave the earth in this very obvious and physical way rather than simply having Him vanish? What truths does His ascension communicate to us?**

Teacher Tips

Ascension Day has been called "the forgotten festival of the Christian Church." Many congregations who used to have special Ascension Day services have eliminated them due to poor attendance (possibly because it occurs on a Thursday). But Ascension Day is an important observance because it marks God's seal of approval on Jesus' work of redemption. Plan a special Ascension Day celebration for your class. Sing a joyful hymn that celebrates Jesus' triumphant return to heaven, "A Hymn of Glory Let Us Sing" (*LSB* 493). Explore the first four stanzas, which retell the Ascension Day story. While this hymn is not on the One in Christ CDs, the same melody is available with another hymn lyric. You can use the accompaniment version of "From All That Dwell Below the Skies" (*LSB* 816; recorded as *Hymn of the Month for grade 3, May*). This version only has three stanzas; however, you can compensate for this by having students read aloud stanza 1 and then sing stanzas 2–4 along with the recorded accompaniment.

Working in Groups

Divide the class into small groups to assemble packets to be given to people who visit your church by your Board of Evangelism or Friendly Callers group. Discuss what materials might be included to help visitors understand what we believe about Jesus, our Savior, and how they, too, could experience the joy of knowing Jesus as their Savior. Ask your pastor or church secretary for a list of tracts that convey the Gospel message. If possible, include statements from students in your school that tell what Jesus means to them. Be sure to include the name, address, telephone number, and Web site of your congregation and a list of service times and special events.

Hands to Serve

Psychologists remind us that while some people learn most effectively through the written or spoken word, others learn best through music and art. Many composers have written music expressing their view of Jesus seated "at the right hand of God the Father Almighty." Perhaps the most famous of these compositions are found in George Frideric Handel's oratorio *Messiah*. Handel used texts from the Book of Revelation to show Jesus in His ascended glory. Read Revelation 5:11–14; 11:15; and 19:16. Then listen to a recording of the "Hallelujah Chorus" and "Worthy Is the Lamb," the final chorus in Handel's oratorio. As you listen, close your eyes and imagine the heavenly celebration. Draw or paint a picture showing what you have imagined.

UNIT 8—THE SPREAD OF THE GOSPEL

LESSON 83

Pentecost
Acts 2:1–47

Background

In His Maundy Thursday discourse, Jesus told His disciples, "Truly, truly, I say to you, whoever believes in Me will also do the works that I do; and greater works than these will he do, because I am going to the Father. Whatever you ask in My name, this I will do, that the Father may be glorified in the Son" (John 14:12–13). Jesus was not saying that His disciples would do more amazing miracles. They had seen Jesus raise the dead to life, the most amazing miracle of all. But Jesus, in human form, had taught and performed miracles within a limited territory, never traveling a hundred miles from the place He was born (aside from His trip to Egypt as an infant). Now Jesus would return to heaven, and He would send the Holy Spirit to empower His followers. Through the power of the Holy Spirit, the apostles would teach, preach, and perform miracles in Jesus' name throughout the known world. Peter, who had denied Jesus three times in the courtyard of Caiaphas, stood up and boldly preached to the international audience at Pentecost. According to tradition, he was crucified upside down in Rome. Thomas, the disciple who wouldn't believe in the resurrection until he saw Jesus for himself, carried the Gospel to India. Historians believe that John was the only disciple who was not executed for his witness to the Gospel. But even John, the disciple present at Calvary, was exiled to the island of Patmos as part of the persecution that took place under the Emperor Domitian (AD 90–95); he died there of natural causes. The amazing change in the lives of these men was effected by the coming of the Holy Spirit on Pentecost.

Central Truth

Through the Holy Spirit, God empowers His people to boldly proclaim the Gospel to all the world.

Objectives

- Recognize that we often are complacent, keeping what we know about Jesus as Savior to ourselves and our close community.
- Pray that God will send the Holy Spirit to motivate and empower us to boldly, openly, and committedly live for Jesus.
- Worship our redeeming and loving God in all aspects of our lives, welcoming all people in His name.

Materials

- Hymnals and music CDs
- Web Resource 83a
- Reproducible 83

Bible Prep

Post in advance so students can bookmark references before class time.
- Acts 2; 9
- Psalm 98
- Isaiah 11
- John 14; 16
- Romans 5; 8; 15

Devotions

The cheerleaders led the roaring crowd, shouting: "We've got spirit! Yes, we do! We've got spirit! How about *you*?" This type of *spirit* refers to a display of enthusiasm for a school or team, as in "school spirit." Athletes sometimes say the crowd's cheering triggers an excitement that helps them achieve more than they thought possible. In this way, the crowd's spirit acts as a power source for the athlete. Actually, there are many definitions for the word *spirit*. Consider the meaning of the word in the following: "The disembodied spirit floated in the air," refers to a ghostly entity; "a spirited discussion," means an enthusiastic exchange; "the spirit of the law," refers to overall intent rather than a word-for-word recounting; "spirits of ammonia," refers to a substance's gaseous form; "the spirit world," refers to angels and demons; "That's the spirit!" refers to positive attitude or effort; "The thief spirited the valuable diamond away," means that he stole it. When we talk about the Holy Spirit, however, we are talking about much more than a power source or positive attitude. The Holy Spirit is true God, along with the Father and the Son; together, they are one God. The Holy Spirit is much more than just power. The Holy Spirit *has power*, and the Holy Spirit also *gives power* to us. The Holy Spirit guides us, brings us to faith, helps us learn, keeps us in faith, helps us to say and do things in a God-pleasing way, and prays for us when we don't know what to say. The Holy Spirit is a powerful presence who lives and dwells in us and works through the Means of Grace—God's Word and the Sacraments of Holy Baptism and the Lord's Supper. Today we will learn more about the promise Jesus made to send the Holy Spirit at Pentecost and to His people even today. Sing "Breath of the Living God" (*AGPS* 77; recorded on *JPS*) and "Holy Spirit, Light Divine" (*LSB* 496; recorded as *Hymn of the Season* for grade 3, Pentecost).

INTO the lesson

Introduce the lesson with Web Resource 83a to get an overview of the Pentecost story. Then select five volunteers to read the story from Scripture, emphasizing this outline of the narrative.

1. Acts 2:1–4: Amazing changes begin.
2. Acts 2:5–12: An international crowd gathers.
3. Acts 2:22–36: Peter preaches a sermon. (Look at the prophecy later.)
4. Acts 2:37–41: People come to repentance and faith.
5. Acts 2:42–47: The Holy Spirit continues His work.

INTO the Word

The Power of the Spirit

Before Jesus ascended into heaven, He promised His disciples He would send them the Holy Spirit. This Spirit would guide their hearts, empowering them to believe in Jesus as their Lord and Savior, live lives of faith in spite of persecution, and share the Gospel "in Jerusalem and in all Judea and Samaria, and to the end of the earth" (Acts 1:8). From the Mount of Olives, the disciples returned to Jerusalem to wait for the coming of the Holy Spirit.

Then say, **The Holy Spirit brought you to faith through God's Word and when you were baptized in the name of the Father, Son, and Holy Spirit. Since many of us were baptized as infants, we know we didn't come to faith on our own; the power of the Holy Spirit—working through water and the Word of God—planted faith in our hearts and made that faith grow.**

Just as we, as infants, were powerless to come to faith, so we are powerless to live lives of faith on our own. Remind students that the Holy Spirit empowers us for faith-filled living, obeying God because of all that He has done for us. The Spirit gives us the words to say and provides opportunities for us to share our faith with others. When we keep the Good News about Jesus to ourselves, God forgives us and, through the Holy Spirit, empowers us to witness in the future.

Together work through the Student Book section to learn more about the power of the Holy Spirit. *Option:* Devote additional discussion to the miraculous signs at Pentecost, which include the following: John the Baptist had foretold the Holy Spirit's baptizing with fire (Luke 3:16), and fire symbolized God's purifying presence, burning away the undesirable elements in our lives and setting our hearts aflame. The tongues symbolized speech and the communication of the Gospel. The wind may remind students of the Spirit of God hovering over the waters at creation (Genesis 1:2).

The Power of the Spirit in Jerusalem

The story of the outpouring of the Holy Spirit on Pentecost is told from the point of view of Lucas, a fictitious twelve-year-old visitor to Jerusalem. Ask students why they think Lucas was allowed to accompany his father on this trip. Refer them to Jesus' journey to Jerusalem recorded in Luke 2:41–52. Explain that Jewish boys study for and celebrate Bar Mitzvah at about twelve years of age and are considered adults at that time, and so they would make annual pilgrimages to worship in the temple. (Jewish girls today celebrate Bat Mitzvah at the same age.)

Read the story of Pentecost from the Student Book. Explain that Pentecost, the Festival (or Feast) of Weeks, was one of three major Old Testament Jewish festivals, a festival of thanksgiving for the harvested crops (Deuteronomy 16:16). Jews of many nations gathered in Jerusalem to celebrate this festival. Peter's speech was given to an international audience, and it resulted in a worldwide harvest of new believers—the first converts to Christianity.

Peter stood up and addressed the crowd. Ask students to relate as many things as they can about Peter, the impetuous leader of the disciples. While occasionally his words and actions were right on target (such as his

---

LESSON 83

Pentecost
The Power of the Spirit

Why fire and wind at Pentecost? To be exact, Scripture says it was a sound like a great wind, and it looked like tongues of fire on the disciples' heads. In other words, these were not natural phenomena! God the Holy Spirit used them to indicate His supernatural purpose! So why fire and wind? Both elements can be powerful and can bring radical changes; they well represented the Holy Spirit, who is all powerful and makes radical changes in the hearts and lives of people. Yet, why fire and wind to represent the power of the Holy Spirit?

This is not the first time God used fire to indicate His presence and power. Recall the burning bush when God spoke to Moses; recall the tall flame that stayed with the Israelites at night during their wilderness journey. Also, this is not the first time God used wind to represent the working of the Holy Spirit. When Jesus spoke to Nicodemus, He talked about how we cannot see where the wind or the Holy Spirit come from or where they go—but we can recognize the effect of both. What was the effect of the Holy Spirit on Pentecost Day?

The Holy Spirit is the Third Person of the Holy Trinity, true God with the Father and the Son, and not merely the power or energy of God. He dwells in our hearts and prays for us when we don't know what to say. The special work of the Holy Spirit is sanctification—He brings people to faith and empowers them to lead godly lives.

Lives are changed through the power of the Holy Spirit. He empowers Christians to share the Good News about Jesus, their Savior from sin, death, and the power of the devil. When we depend on our own power to witness to others about Jesus, our efforts lead to frustration and failure. Instead, trust the Holy Spirit to give you the words to say at the proper time, just as He gave the right words to Peter on the first Pentecost. It is not your words or someone else's decision that brings another person to faith in Jesus. That is accomplished only by the power of the Holy Spirit working through the Means of Grace.

Review

Covenant Connection

On the Day of Pentecost, the apostle Peter made a direct connection to the words of the Lord in the Old Testament as they were spoken through the prophet Joel (2:28, 32). The Day of Pentecost was the fulfillment of this prophecy. Jesus had done all that was necessary for our salvation. Now it was time for the Christian Church to tell that news to the whole world—and, as Jesus had promised, the Holy Spirit came to the people of the Church, empowering them to speak the Gospel and to live as children of God. We are sanctified through the Holy Spirit, who brings us to faith and keeps us in faith in Christ Jesus, who justified us through His death and resurrection. We can live as God's holy and blameless people because Jesus has taken away our sins and the Holy Spirit enables us to live in faith as God's people!

172

The Power of the Spirit in Jerusalem

My name is Lucas, and my family lives in Rome. Because we are faithful Jews, my father comes to Jerusalem every year for at least one of the religious festivals. This year, he brought me with him to celebrate Pentecost, the Festival of Weeks that comes 50 days after Passover.

Jerusalem is crowded with people from every country to which the Jews have been scattered. You can hear every language imaginable as you walk down the street. But Pentecost Day, I heard a sound that drowned out even the languages of the crowd. It was like a violent wind that seemed to come from heaven and fill a house near where I stood. Through a window of the house, I could see people with what seemed to be tongues of fire on their heads. They began to speak in other languages. People all around me stopped and listened to the men. Each person could understand what they were saying in his own language.

The man they called Peter stood up and spoke to the crowd. He told us we were seeing the fulfillment of the words of the prophet Joel, who said, "In the last days it shall be, God declares, that I will pour out My Spirit on all flesh, and your sons and your daughters shall prophesy, and your young men shall see visions, and your old men shall dream dreams."

Then Peter told about Jesus of Nazareth, whom the people had seen do many miracles. He said this Jesus had been handed over to the people by God's set purpose, and the people—with the help of wicked men—had put Him to death. But God raised Jesus from the dead, God had made this Jesus, whom they had crucified, both Lord and Christ.

You can imagine how upset the people were when they heard Peter's message. They said to Peter and the other apostles, "Brothers, what shall we do?"

Peter told them, "Repent and be baptized every one of you, in the name of Jesus Christ for the forgiveness of your sins, and you will receive the gift of the Holy Spirit." Peter said this promise was for the adults and for their children, even for those who were far away.

Father and I believed what we heard about Jesus. We told God we were sorry for our sins, and we were baptized in the name of Jesus. And we weren't the only ones! Through the power of the Holy Spirit, about 3,000 people were baptized that day.

That day was just the beginning for me. But it was also the beginning of the Christian Church, which grew quickly. In just a short time, the number of Christians had grown to 5,000. Even many of the priests and other church leaders came to faith in Jesus.

"So the church throughout all Judea and Galilee and Samaria had peace and was being built up. And walking in the fear of the Lord and in the comfort of the Holy Spirit, it multiplied" (Acts 9:31).

Remember

"No one can say 'Jesus is Lord' except in the Holy Spirit." (1 Corinthians 12:3)

INTO our lives

The Power of the Spirit in You

Continue with the activity on Reproducible 83, which reminds us that the Holy Spirit comes also to us today. Explore the tasks of the Holy Spirit. Cut out the completed shape, and hang it up as a symbol of the wind, which in a small way reminds us of the Holy Spirit—we cannot see either one, but we can see what they do; we can see that they are powerful and can cause radical changes.

We know that we have been empowered by the Holy Spirit to believe in God, to live lives of faith, and to share the Good News about Jesus. Then why is it so difficult? Why is our faith crowded with doubt? Why is it so hard to give up those favorite sins? And why do we hesitate to share our faith with others when the Holy Spirit gives us the opportunity to do so? Explain to students that although the Holy Spirit empowers us for faithful living and witnessing, the powers of the devil, the world, and our sinful flesh are strong. When we succumb to their influence, the Holy Spirit calls us to repentance, which is turning away from our sinful ways and turning toward Christ. We pray for the Holy Spirit's help, asking Him to strengthen our faith, empower us for faith-filled living, and give us the courage and the words to witness boldly to others.

---

confession of Jesus as Lord recorded in Matthew 16:13–17), he more often was governed by emotion than caution or thoughtfulness; this especially was the case in the courtyard of Caiaphas (John 18:15–27). Notice the difference the power of the Holy Spirit made in Peter, who now boldly addressed the crowd.

Read again Lucas's account of Peter's sermon, and consider this sermon outline:

1. Peter explained that the Holy Spirit had come, just as Joel had prophesied.
2. He reminded the people that they had crucified Jesus, but this was according to God's purpose.
3. He said God had raised Jesus from the dead, as David had foretold in the psalm.
4. He told them God had made Jesus, whom they had crucified, both Lord and Christ.

Peter's listeners were cut to the heart and asked, "Brothers, what shall we do?" Peter told them to repent. **True repentance is not only a turning away from sin, changing the direction of your life from rebellion against God's laws. It is also a turning *toward* Christ, depending on Him for forgiveness and guidance.** Through Baptism, Peter's listeners also received the gift of the Holy Spirit. About three thousand people were baptized that day.

Searching Further

The tongues of fire that accompanied the coming of the Holy Spirit on Pentecost symbolized language and the communication of the Good News about Jesus to all people. The variety of languages spoken in the Middle East often made communication difficult. Remind students how God had confused the language of the builders of the Tower of Babel (Genesis 11:1–9; Unit 1, Lesson 4). The people of Babel built the tower as a monument to their own greatness and not for the glory of God. Their selfish pride was a form of idolatry, as they placed themselves in the place of God. On Pentecost, God undid the confusion of languages that began at Babel. Instead of babbling, the disciples' words were understandable as the Holy Spirit enabled them to speak in other languages. God-fearing Jews from every nation under heaven heard the apostles speaking in their own native languages. As they listened to Peter's sermon, they witnessed the power and presence of the Holy Spirit. This miracle took place so that all could hear the Good News about Jesus, the Savior.

Faith in Action

On Pentecost, God demonstrated that the Good News about Jesus was for all people, no matter where they lived or what language they spoke. Use the map in the Appendix of the Student Book to locate some of the countries people had come from on that Pentecost Day. Learn to sing a song of praise in a foreign language. Foreign language hymns in *LSB* are listed on page 1022 of that hymnal. Also, CD 10 of the *Hymns of the Month* set features recordings by a choir and separate recordings of instrumental accompaniment only for six hymns sung in Spanish.

Technology

On Pentecost, the Holy Spirit brought the mission field to the apostles in Jerusalem, as international visitors to the city heard Peter's sermon, were brought to faith by the power of the Holy Spirit, and carried that faith back with them to their homes in faraway lands. Today, the Holy Spirit has brought a similar mission field to North American Christians as students from all over the world spend time on our college and university campuses. Through International Student Ministry, Inc., our church shares the Gospel with these students. The Holy Spirit works faith in the hearts of some of the students who hear the Gospel, and they are baptized and become Church members. When they return to their homes, they take the Gospel with them and share the Good News about Jesus with their friends and families. Use the Internet to learn more about the work of International Student Ministry, Inc. Report what you learn to your class.

Working in Groups

Divide the class into groups to make posters showing symbols of the Holy Trinity—Father, Son, and Holy Spirit. You will find some of these symbols in *Luther's Small Catechism with Explanation* (copyright © 1986, 1991, 2005 Concordia Publishing House) on pages 275–283. Draw each symbol of the Trinity on poster board. Color the symbols with markers. Beneath each symbol, write an explanation of its meaning. Display your posters in a prominent location in your school or church building.

Critical thinking

Pentecost, or the Feast of Weeks, was one of the three major annual feasts celebrated by Jews. Learn more about these festivals by reading Deuteronomy 16:1–17. The Feast of Passover commemorated the Jews' escape from slavery in Egypt. It was celebrated with a Passover meal of roast lamb, just as the Jews had eaten before leaving Egypt, and a retelling of the Passover story (vv. 1–8). The Feast of Weeks was celebrated seven weeks after the time the farmers began to harvest the grain. This was traditionally fifty days after Passover (vv. 9–12). The Feast of Booths (also called the Feast of Tabernacles) was a seven-day festival celebrated after the produce and wine had all been brought in (vv. 13–17). Three times each year, every male was required to travel to the sanctuary in the city that served as Israel's religious capital, bringing an offering in proportion to what God had given him. *Bonus questions:* **Pentecost took place fifty days after Passover. We celebrate Pentecost fifty days after Easter. What's the connection? How many other words can you think of that begin with *pent* (referring to "five")?**

UNIT 8—THE SPREAD OF THE GOSPEL

LESSON 84

Peter, John, and the Lame Man
Acts 3

Background

The lesson application will refer to the needs of people in Manila, which is located on the island of Luzon, one of 7,107 islands that make up the Republic of the Philippines. What is an island? Did your definition include the fact that an island stands alone, unconnected to any other piece of land? John Donne (1572–1631) was an English poet and a priest in the Church of England. He lived at approximately the same time as William Shakespeare. Donne became dean of St. Paul's Cathedral in London in 1621. In one of his most famous sermons, he wrote these words: "No man is an island, entire of itself; every man is a piece of the continent, a part of the main; if a clod be washed away by the sea, Europe is the less, as well as if a promontory were, as well as if a manor of thy friend's or of thine own were; any man's death diminishes me, because I am involved in mankind, and therefore never send to know for whom the bell tolls; it tolls for thee" (*Meditation XVII*). Those final phrases refer to the old custom of ringing (tolling) the church bell when a member died; neighbors would send someone to the church to find out "for whom the bell tolls." What do Donne's words say about our relationship to those in need around the world? As fellow members of the Body of Christ, what is our responsibility?

Central Truth

God constantly provides us with opportunities to serve others and to proclaim the Gospel of salvation through Christ Jesus.

Objectives

- Acknowledge that we often are silent when we have the chance to speak of God's blessings, grace, and mercy.
- Appreciate the understanding forgiveness of Jesus, who also can transform us into active and bold people of God.
- Live for Jesus, enabled by the Holy Spirit, following His ways and will.

Materials

- Hymnals and music CDs
- Reproducible 84
- Web Resource 84a

Bible Prep

Post in advance so students can bookmark references before class time.
- Acts 3
- Psalm 98
- Luke

Devotion

Many years ago, a bitter war destroyed most of the buildings in a small German village. When the people returned to the village after the war, they found only rubble where their homes had stood. Stores and businesses were closed, their merchandise scattered or stolen. Worst of all, the village church lay in ruins, its steeple broken and stained glass windows smashed. Even the beautiful statue of Christ that had stood above the altar was damaged; shelling had pulverized the statue's hands and feet.

The villagers began the overwhelming task of rebuilding, working on the church during the day and their own homes at night. Debris was swept away, and the church steeple was rebuilt, just the way it had been before the war. Artists created new stained glass to fill the gaping windows. The statue of Christ was cleaned, and new paint covered the places that had been chipped. But no sculptor could be found to carve new hands and feet for the statue.

The people of the village couldn't decide what to do about the statue. Finally, one elderly villager stood up. "The statue of Christ reminds us that Jesus is right here in the village with us all the time, especially when times are hard and people need help. But we must leave the statue just the way it is."

"The way it is?" the others questioned. "Without hands and feet?"

"Precisely," answered the old man. "The statue reminds us that Jesus is here. But *we* are to be His hands and His feet. *We are to reach out to each other in His name, helping the poor, the sick, and the hurting.*"

Sing together "Make Me a Servant" (*AGPS* 174; recorded on *JPS*). Read "Wake Us, O Lord, to Human Need" (*AGPS* 250) as a prayer, perhaps having four volunteers who each read a verse aloud. Or sing "Take My Life and Let It Be" (*LSB* 783; recorded as *Hymn of the Month for grade 6, January*). Say together Psalm 98.

INTO the Word

From Lame to Leaping in Jesus' Name

Help students read the text from Acts 3. Then encourage them to act out the story as presented in the Student Book or use it as a readers theater script. Point out that Peter healed the lame beggar "in the name of Jesus Christ of Nazareth" (v. 6). Ask students, **When do we use the phrase "in Jesus' name"?** (Very often at the end of a prayer) The beggar hoped to receive gold or silver; Peter gave him so much more. According to St. Ambrose, "He gave not money, but he gave health. How much better it is to have health without money, than money without health!" (*The Lutheran Study Bible*, p. 1837, study note on Acts 3:6). *Option:* Look at the song "Silver and Gold" (*AGPS* 212), which is based on today's Bible narrative.

By the power of the Holy Spirit, Peter preached a sermon similar to the one he gave at Pentecost, pointing to Christ as the fulfillment of the Old Testament prophecies. As at Pentecost, the Spirit worked in the hearts of Peter's listeners, and "many of those who had heard the word believed" (Acts 4:4). Point out that through the power of the Holy Spirit, Peter no longer retreated in fear, but used every opportunity when people were gathered to speak of salvation through the Lord Jesus, who through **His death and resurrection provided rescue from sin for all who believe in Him.**

Lesson 84

Peter, John, and the Lame Man
From Lame to Leaping in Jesus' Name

Characters: Peter, John, the lame beggar, crowd of bystanders
Time: The hour of prayer, the ninth hour (about 2:00–3:00 p.m.)

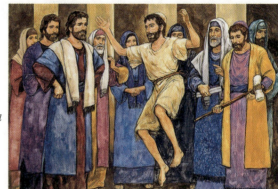

Scene 1—*The gate of the temple that is called "the Beautiful Gate." The lame beggar is carried to his usual spot near the temple gate.*

Beggar: Alms for the poor and lame! In God's name, I beg you to help me! *(He reaches out his hand to receive coins.)*

(Peter and John stop in front of the beggar.)

John: Look at us.

Beggar: *(He focuses his attention on Peter and John.)* A coin, sirs, to help the needy.

Peter: I have no silver or gold, but what I do have, I give to you. In the name of Jesus Christ of Nazareth, rise up and walk! *(Peter takes the beggar by the right hand and raises him up.)*

Beggar: *(He leaps up and begins to walk.)* Praise God! My legs and feet are strong, and I can walk! I can run! I can leap! Praise the God of Israel! *(He enters the temple with Peter and John, continuing to walk, run, and leap for joy.)*

Bystander: Isn't he the one who was begging near the gate? He's been here for years, begging for alms, and now he can walk and run. It's a miracle! Praise the Lord, who has done this wondrous deed!

Review

Covenant Connection
Peter and John did miracles the same way that Elijah and Elisha did in the Old Testament—not by their own power! They all called on God, and He answered their prayers. But it is the power of God that accomplished the miraculous events. (For example, if you prayed for rain, and the next day, it rained, would that make you a rainmaker? No! It is important to recognize that it is the Lord Jesus who answers our prayers and blesses us!) The Lord "heals the brokenhearted and binds up their wounds" (Psalm 147:3). "Bless the LORD, O my soul, and forget not all His benefits, who forgives all your iniquity, who heals all your diseases, who redeems your life from the pit, who crowns you with steadfast love and mercy" (Psalm 103:2–4).

INTO our lives

God's Blessings Today

Emphasize: God does not say He will always heal us, and if He does heal, He may choose a different way and a different time than what we had in mind. We must trust that He knows what is best and when it is best to work for His good purpose in our lives. In the Student Book, look over the possible ways God works in our lives. God can and does still work miracles. But often He blesses us in other ways through other people and other methods. Sometimes God has a reason for *not* changing our circumstances. When it is His will to not remedy the situation, we pray that God will help us cope with our problem—to live with it, adjust to it, accept it in a positive way, and to endure the problems that continue, always trusting in God's will.

Focus now on carrying on God's mission of mercy and compassion through the help that we give to others. Emphasize that your students should never use their youth as an excuse to not help others. Read what the apostle Paul said in 1 Timothy 4:12: "Let no one despise you for your youth, but set the believers an example in speech, in conduct, in love, in faith, in purity." Instead of leaving matters to the adults, encourage your students to look for ways they can serve others. Look for

Scene 2—*Solomon's Portico, on the east side of the Court of the Gentiles. Peter and John enter, with the lame beggar clinging to them. The crowd of bystanders follows.*

Bystander: What a miracle! How could these men do such a wondrous thing?

Peter: Men of Israel, why do you wonder at this, or stare at us as though by our own power we have made him walk? The God of Abraham, Isaac, and Jacob, the God of our fathers, glorified His servant Jesus, whom you delivered over and denied in the presence of Pilate, when he had decided to release Him. You killed the Author of life, whom God raised from the dead—to this we are witnesses. And His name—by faith in His name—has made this man strong, and the faith that is through Jesus has given the man this perfect health. I know that you acted in ignorance, as did your rulers. But what was foretold by the mouth of all the prophets, that His Christ would suffer, He thus fulfilled. Repent, therefore, and turn again, that your sins may be blotted out.

Bystander: Peter is right. This Jesus whom we crucified is really the Son of God. May God forgive us all of our sins and help us to follow the teachings of Jesus, whom He sent to save us.

God's Blessings Today

God continues to help people today through various special ways. Look at each of these and write an example of how someone could be blessed in this way.

1. A direct miracle from God — *Sometimes people are healed or helped and there is no other explanation than that God provided for them in a miraculous manner.*
2. Through other people — *Nurses, firefighters, and other caregivers are blessings from God.*
3. Through tools and other things that assist — *Wheelchairs, hearing aids, glasses, and so forth help people adjust to their problems.*
4. With emotional comfort and coping — *Trust in God and a positive attitude are blessings that help people deal with their difficulties.*
5. The promise of heaven through Jesus — *In heaven, our bodies will be made perfect; there will be no tears or troubles.*

These are all ways God blesses people. The first and the last ones are things that only God Himself can provide. But the examples in between are ways God can use *us* to help other people. God desires that we share the Gospel and the forgiveness we have in Jesus—but we are not to stop there. He also desires that we share kindness, food, care, protection, and other things that people need in their lives today!

As Jesus' twenty-first-century disciples, we, too, are empowered by the Holy Spirit to carry on this ministry.

Remember

"And the King will answer them, 'Truly, I say to you, as you did it to one of the least of these My brothers, you did it to Me.'" (Matthew 25:40)

---

local opportunities; be aware of servant events led by your church community. Use Reproducible 84 and Web Resource 84a to learn about the incredible needs of children in other parts of the world, in this case, the impoverished areas of Manila in the Philippines. The resource will help students to see the squalor in which so many children live and barely survive. Thousands of these children sleep on the streets because they have no parents; they find food only by begging, stealing, or searching through garbage. Emphasize that we can pray to God, thanking Him for the many blessings we have and asking Him to help these children. But the Lord also wants us to put our prayers into action; He wants to use our hands and feet to serve others; He wants us to share our talents and treasures to bless people in need. (*Note:* Tell students to listen for the phrase "the least of these" in today's Bible words to remember and also in the narration of Web Resource 84a.)

As you explore the situation, have students research information, maps, and so forth to learn more about the Philippines and the needs of children there. Encourage students to develop specific plans. For help in determining where to send any funds accumulated, check with your pastor and with organizations such as Lutheran Hour Ministries (www.lhm.org).

Conclude with a moment of meditation and prayer.

More Information about Concordia Children's Services

In response to the growing concern for street children roaming the streets of metropolitan Manila, Concordia Children's Services expanded its ministry, offering three services: street crisis intervention, educational assistance, and family welfare services. More than 70,000 children in Manila between the ages of 5 and 18 live in the streets with or without the care and protection of responsible adults. The majority of these children live with at least one parent, although 25 percent of them live on the streets on their own. Approximately 70 percent of these children are boys, but girls are extremely vulnerable and experience much discrimination. The Street Crisis Intervention Program of Concordia Children's Services has five key components:

1. Alternative education for children not enrolled in public schools
2. Tutoring and other educational assistance to street children already attending formal school
3. Christian education to children and their families
4. Family welfare services
5. Counseling services to children and their families

The goal of Concordia's Street Crisis Intervention Program is to promote a passion for education and provide tools for learning. The ultimate goal is to mainstream street children into a formal school system where they can thrive. Educational assistance is given to families who cannot afford the cost of sending their children to school. This program provides financial assistance for books, uniforms, school supplies, food, and transportation as well as school projects and medical assistance. Volunteer tutors help children who have difficulty with their lessons. Weekly Christian education sessions and Bible studies are conducted with the help of church volunteers. Recreational activities such as sports, games, parties, art, and theater enrich the program. Daily nutritional and medical assistance is provided. A social worker monitors the school performance of the children in the program in coordination with their teachers. The social worker also visits the schools and children's homes to involve the parents in their children's studies.

Celebrating GROWTH

According to the 1995 census, there were 32,894,317 children living in the Philippines, comprising 44.98 percent of the total population. Their age distribution was as follows:

Age Range	Age Proportions	Absolute Numbers
0–4 years	13.85%	10,128,641
5–9 years	12.75%	9,324,202
10–14 years	11.64%	8,512,446
15–17 years	6.74%	4,929,028
0–17 years	**44.98%**	**32,894,317**

Draw a pie chart to show the age distribution of the population of the Philippines. Remember, children comprise 44.98 percent of the population. What will the other portion of your pie represent?

Jesus said, "Let the children come to Me, and do not hinder them, for to such belongs the kingdom of God" (Luke 18:16). What age group did Jesus mean? What about the people represented by the rest of the chart?

Searching Further

The country of the Philippines is made up of 7,107 islands. Only 900 of these islands are inhabited. If you could push all of the islands into one, it would be about the size of Arizona. The islands of the Philippines stretch for 1,100 miles—as far as the distance from New York City to Orlando, Florida. Maps remind us of directions and distances. As we study the map of the Philippines, we ask, "Which way? How far?" What is the greatest distance? According to Psalm 103:11–12, "For as high as the heavens are above the earth, so great is His [God's] steadfast love toward those who fear Him; as far as the east is from the west, so far does He remove our transgressions from us."

Manila enjoys a tropical climate, with warm to hot weather all year. During the "cold" rainy season, the temperature may fall to 62 degrees Fahrenheit at night. In summer, temperatures often climb to over 100 degrees. Some parts of the Philippines experience as many as 20 typhoons a year. ("Typhoon" is the name for a hurricane in the Pacific Ocean.) Discuss the effects of climate and population on the people of Manila. Even in a metropolis of 10 million people, each human being is known and loved by God. Read Matthew 10:29–31. Since God cares so much for each of us, let's care for one another!

Critical thinking

Population density statistics give us the number of people living in the area of a square kilometer. Manila is the most densely populated major city in the world. Put the following population density statistics in order. Then plot the statistics on a bar graph.

Paris	25,934/km²	Moscow	10,275/km²
Tokyo	13,800/km²	Mumbai (Bombay)	29,434/km²
Manila	41,014/km²	Bangkok	4,051/km²
Cairo	36,618/km²	New York	10,292/km²
Chicago	4,923/km²	Detroit	2,647/km²
Grand Rapids	1,710/km²	Buenos Aires	13,680/km²

Measure an area of 1 km² (about one half mile × one half mile). Imagine 41,014 people living in this area. How does overcrowding in the city of Manila contribute to the problems of the street children and their families?

Read Matthew 9:35–38. "When He [Jesus] saw the crowds, He had compassion for them, because they were harassed and helpless, like sheep without a shepherd" (v. 36). Pray for the staff and supporters of Concordia Children's Services who share Jesus' compassion with the crowds of Manila.

Faith in Action

The Republic of the Philippines is the largest Christian country in Asia. The second most popular religion in the Philippines is Islam. Followers of the religion of Islam are called Muslims. Islam was brought to the Philippines from Brunei in the 15th century. More than 2 million Filipinos are Muslims, who believe that God is called "Allah." Muslims must stop what they are doing and pray to Allah five times each day. Muslims do not believe in Jesus as their Savior. They do not believe Jesus is God. They do not believe the Bible is God's Word. In the past decade, Muslim extremists have kidnapped Christian missionaries in the Philippines and made other threats against Christian churches. Pray for our missionaries and their families in the Philippines. Ask God to give them courage to do His work in the face of these threats and to keep them safe in times of danger.

UNIT 8—THE SPREAD OF THE GOSPEL

Lesson 85

Peter and John in Prison
Acts 4

Background

There are all sorts of things that seem unstoppable. As they overcome the opposing team, football players move the ball toward their goal. Bulldozers move earth and debris, pushing dirt, rocks, and trees out of the way. More dangerously, powerful tornadoes and hurricanes rip across the landscape, leaving a wide wake of destruction as they pass. Ocean waves shape the shoreline with sudden tsunamis as well as the steady movement of the tides. In today's Bible story, the enemies of the Gospel try to stop the saving message of Jesus from going out into the world. But the Word of God—the Gospel of Jesus Christ—moves forward and cannot be stopped. The apostles are arrested, imprisoned, and told to stop preaching about Jesus. But even so, people still come to faith, and the number of believers continues to increase. Again the apostles are ordered to stop teaching about Jesus, but they keep on teaching the Good News, even when they are on trial in front of the Jewish council. A crippled man is healed by the power of Jesus' name, and the enemies of the Gospel have no answer for that. They have to release the apostles. The people listen and believe and want to hear more. The apostles join with the other believers in prayer, rejoicing in the unstoppable message of salvation in Jesus' name. In prayer, they rejoice as they review earlier attempts to stop the Good News. King Herod, the Roman governor Pilate, Gentiles, and Jews line up together to oppose God's promised Messiah. But unknown to them, even their attempts to stop Jesus are all part of God's unstoppable plan! The Holy Spirit fills the disciples with boldness. The Good News of salvation would continue to "speed ahead and be honored" (2 Thessalonians 3:1).

Central Truth

Though people may try to stop the spread of the Gospel, Jesus, His Word, and His salvation endure forever.

Objectives

- Recognize that in today's world there are people, organizations, and even governments that oppose Christianity.
- Pray for forgiveness and boldness to speak and live for Jesus, especially when we feel overwhelmed or powerless to make a difference.
- Glorify God in all we do and say, letting our new life in Christ be a witness to others.

Materials

- Hymnals and music CDs
- Reproducible 85
- Web Resource 85a

Bible Prep

Post in advance so students can bookmark references before class time.
- Acts 4

Devotions

Ask your students to suggest things that seem unstoppable. Possible examples include natural disasters such as wildfires, tornadoes, hurricanes, tsunamis, and man-made machines like tanks and bulldozers. Discuss the power and force of the things that are suggested. **How can some of these forces be stopped?** (Fires can be put out; machines can be destroyed or turned aside from their destructive paths.) **What kinds of things cannot be stopped?** (Natural forces such as tsunamis and storms cannot be stopped. Weather forecasters can only warn people that they are coming.) **What do people do who live in the path of some of these natural forces?** (Some people try to protect their property. Others leave their homes until the danger is past.) **Why are some things unstoppable?** (Some things have too much strength and force to be stopped by human efforts.)

In today's Bible lesson, it is not a storm or fire that cannot be stopped; it is the plan of God. The Good News of life and forgiveness in Jesus' name is unstoppable! When Jesus lived on earth, many forces tried to stop Him from completing His work. King Herod wanted to kill Him when He was just a baby. The devil tempted Him. The religious leaders wanted to arrest Him. Finally, it seemed that Jesus' enemies were successful in stopping Him. Jesus was captured, put on trial, and crucified. But that was all part of God's plan to save us. How did Jesus show that He could not be stopped? (He rose from the dead!) **Even today, people might try to prevent the story of Jesus from being told. But as we will see in today's story, no matter what people do, the Good News of Jesus Christ cannot be stopped! "The word of the Lord remains forever!"** (1 Peter 1:25)

Sing "Go into the World" (*AGPS* 101; recorded on *JPS*) or "Immortal, Invisible, God Only Wise" (*LSB* 802; recorded as *Hymn of the Month* for grade 6, April). Listen to Web Resource 85a, which is the chanted version of Psalm 98. (Listen to this recording each day during devotions until you feel your students are ready to join in chanting.)

INTO the Word

Roadblocks

Many things seem unstoppable, but as we discussed in the devotion, people do try to stop some of them. For example, **how do police try to stop a car driven by a criminal?** (They set up roadblocks, put out spike strips, or follow the car with a helicopter.) **How does one football team try to stop another from scoring a touchdown?** (Team members try to block opposing players or intercept a pass.) **How do doctors try to stop the spread of disease?** (They use antibiotics or vaccines.)

All through history, enemies of the Christian Church have tried to stop the spread of the Gospel message. Even the apostle Paul himself, before he believed in Christ, arrested and imprisoned Christians. For several centuries, the Roman emperors and other authorities persecuted Christians and murdered many of the apostles, including Peter and Paul. Today there are countries all over the world whose governments persecute Christians or place restrictions on Christian teaching and worship. Christians today can be imprisoned and killed in some of the countries of the Middle East, Asia, and Africa. In our country, we have the freedom to worship as we choose, but there are still many people who ridicule the Christian faith. There are false teachers who try to lead people away from the truth of Christ. We know, however, that even **death could not stop Jesus. His death was part of God's plan to save us, and on the third day, Jesus rose from the dead. Nothing can stop the spread of the Good News about Him!** In today's lesson, the enemies of the Gospel try to put roadblocks up to stop the apostles from preaching the Good News, but the Holy Spirit makes the spread of the Gospel unstoppable!

Work through the entire first page of the lesson in the Student Book, which is a Bible study outline of today's narrative.

Lesson 85
Peter and John in Prison

Roadblocks

The priests and Sadducees and the scribes and Pharisees thought they were done with Jesus. They had crucified Him. But now His disciples were everywhere, talking about Jesus and His resurrection. Jesus' enemies thought, "Something must be done to stop those disciples!" So what did they do?

- Acts 4:1–3   *They arrested several disciples.*
- Acts 4:17–18   *The disciples were forbidden to teach about Jesus.*
- Acts 4:21   *The leaders threatened the disciples.*

Unstoppable

The plan didn't work. The followers of Jesus were so certain of their faith in Him that nothing could stop them now. They felt they must speak about what they had seen and heard. They would not quit! They openly testified:

- Acts 4:8–10   *The crippled man was healed in Jesus' name.*
- Acts 4:12   *Salvation is found only in Jesus' name.*
- Acts 5:29   *They would obey God rather than the leaders.*

The disciples were supported in their efforts to spread the Good News of the Gospel by:

- Acts 4:23–24, 29   *prayers to God to give them courage.*
- Acts 4:31   *the Holy Spirit, who filled them with boldness.*

Results

- Acts 6:7   *The number of believers in Jesus multiplied.*
- Acts 5:34–39   *A leader, Gamaliel, warned other council members to wait and see what would happen. If the disciples were wrong, their efforts would fail. But if this was from God, no one could overthrow the message of Christ Jesus.*

Review

Covenant Connection

From the very beginning when sin entered the world, God faithfully gave His covenant promises to send the Messiah. Now that these promises had been fulfilled in Jesus Christ, the Lord continued to be with His people so that the Good News of the Gospel would be spread to all the world. Luke 24:47 says, "Repentance and forgiveness of sins should be proclaimed in His [Jesus'] name to all nations."

INTO our lives

Your Roadblocks

Point out: **Today, our most damaging roadblocks are from our own thinking and willfulness, and from things that are close to us, like our friends and possessions. Those are the things that stop us from speaking up for Jesus and His ways; those are the things that stop us from living as disciples of Jesus.** Discuss the attitudes in this activity on the Student Book page.

1. Often our own worries about the opinions of others lead us to retreat from living as people of God. When we are afraid of what other people will say or think, we are putting their will above the will of the Lord.

2. Sometimes the roadblock is that we want to live according to the ways of the world, even if it is contrary to God's ways. If being cool means doing things that are wrong, and if doing what is right is considered the "uncool" way to go, then you need to consider your priorities: What is guiding your life, and who is determining your values?

Your Roadblocks

Today, you don't have to worry about being arrested by priests and Sadducees or by scribes and Pharisees. But there are definitely roadblocks today that stop people from speaking up about Jesus and living as His disciples. Find these roadblocks by unscrambling and rewriting these sentences.

1. afraid others I'm what of think of will me **I'm afraid of what others will think of me.**

2. don't uncool I "holy" want to or seem too **I don't want to seem uncool or too "holy."**

3. can't I important talk like a with words pastor **I can't talk with important words like a pastor.**

4. already know I Everybody Christian is a **Everybody I know is already a Christian.**

5. have time TV I don't because I'm video games using Internet texting busy and **I don't have time because I'm busy using video games, TV, Internet, and texting.**

6. my business what's speak up for to It's none of right **It's none of my business to speak up for what's right.**

Unstoppable Support

We all need help! Here are ways to be strengthened. Each is a blessing from God!

- Pray for courage to stand up for Jesus.
- Trust that the Holy Spirit will empower you.
- Use God's Word and the Sacraments.
- Be encouraged by other faithful Christians.

Remember

"In your hearts honor Christ the Lord as holy, always being prepared to make a defense to anyone who asks you for a reason for the hope that is in you; yet do it with gentleness and respect." (1 Peter 3:15)

177

---

3. Speaking up for Jesus does not have to sound like a sermon. Often a simple and spontaneous witness is very effective. Just a short "Yes, God is good to us" or "No, that's not the Christian thing to do" can give an important message.

4. God wants us to share His message of love and forgiveness with everyone, and that includes people who are already believers. We do this to comfort them, encourage them, and support them in their faith in Jesus.

5. If screen time is all you have time for, then electronics have taken over your life (and your heart and soul). If that is what is number one in your life, that has become your god.

6. It's every Christian's business to speak up for Jesus. God calls on us to be concerned about the welfare of other people, and that includes their spiritual and eternal welfare.

Unstoppable Support

Emphasize the blessings of God that support us in living our lives as people of God. Then continue with Reproducible 85, pointing out that sometimes we need "tools" that are reminders for—or signs of—living in faith as our priority. Have students cut apart the four activities and discuss each one.

First, we have a reminder of the biggest roadblock in our faith life: putting ourselves first. Perhaps our thinking goes something like this: "I want this and I want to do that, and so forth." When all we can think of is "what I want" rather than what *God* wants, then "I" becomes the priority and replaces God and His will in our lives. What change is needed? Have students cut out the shape and fold the sections on the dotted lines, overlapping the horizontal sections and creating the shape of a cross. **This is what we need to keep before our "I's" and before our eyes!** Suggest that if someone ever asks them about their faith, they can use this little tool to explain the concept of Jesus as the priority in life as a Christian.

Second, explain that we are going to look at another major roadblock in living faithfully for the Lord. Ask students to explain what a "thumbs up" sign means, as well as a "thumbs down" sign. Then direct their attention to the picture, noting that it shows "thumbs across." Point out that this is a reminder of activities that often take over a person's life—using their thumbs for texting, playing video games, working on the computer, and so forth. Electronics are not necessarily a bad thing unless they become the priority in our lives, affecting our choices, and working against the will of God. If you are playing video games when you are supposed to be helping your mom or dad, using electronics has supplanted God's will. If you are texting messages that ridicule or slander someone else, or if you keep silent when you receive such messages instead of speaking up for what is right, your thumbs are leading you into sin. If your thumbs (and fingers) are using a computer keyboard to find pornographic Web sites, you have succumbed to the easy access that leads to easy sinning. How can this be changed to a "thumbs up"? Discuss positive ways to use electronics and when they should be set aside in order to focus on other things.

Third, speaking up for Jesus does not need to be complicated. Perhaps use or design a simple symbol like the one pictured. Add this design in a variety of places and see if anyone asks you about it. Their question opens up the opportunity to talk about Jesus. You can explain that the sign tells about two of the important parts of our Christian life. The top part is a *W* for "worshiping" God, and the bottom is an *M* for the "mercy" that we share with others in kindness.

Fourth, use these simple examples to encourage students to explore a way they can incorporate a Christian symbol into their own name. Look at the examples, but you may have to point out that this will not necessarily work with all letters and names. **If you can't think of one today, just be open to possibilities that may inspire you in the future. When you have designed a signature that incorporates a Christian symbol, you can share a simple message each time you sign your name.**

Lesson Support

Curriculum Connection

Peter and John found themselves under pressure from the authorities to deny Jesus and stop speaking and serving in His name. Your students, too, will come under pressure to give up their Christian witness. Help them find ways to handle it using section 6.3.1.5, Behaving in a Safe and Healthy Manner When Confronted with Negative Peer Pressure. You'll find it in the sixth-grade Physical Education volume of the Concordia Curriculum Guide series.

Working in Groups

In Acts 4:12, Peter says, "And there is salvation in no one else, for there is no other name under heaven given among men by which we must be saved." The name *Jesus* means "God saves" or "God is salvation." We also refer to the Son of God in many other ways and by other names. Jesus is called "Lord" and "Christ." He is "the Bread of Life," "the Good Shepherd," and "the True Vine." Jesus also called Himself "the way, the truth, and the life" (John 14:6) and "the resurrection and the life" (11:25). Have students work in groups to research the names of Jesus. They can report back to the class and design posters that illustrate the name *Jesus* or other favorite names by which our Savior is known.

Searching Further

Annas and Caiaphas are among the rulers who tried to stop Peter and John from preaching about Jesus. This was not the first time that these two priests tried to put up roadblocks to the Gospel. They were present when Jesus was arrested and brought to trial in front of the Jewish ruling council. In John 18:13, it is Caiaphas who is called the high priest, and Annas is described as his father-in-law. In v. 22, Annas is also described as "the high priest," although it appears that Caiaphas was the ruling high priest at the time. (Perhaps they served at different times, but retained the title, just as a former U.S. President retains that title, even though out of office.) It was Caiaphas who earlier prophesied that Jesus should die for the people of Israel (John 11:49–52). Even though he did not believe in Jesus, Israel's high priest unknowingly spoke God's truth. Jesus died for Israel and for *all* people and rose from the dead. No priestly roadblocks could stop Him!

Critical thinking

When Peter and John were arrested, they were forbidden to teach the Gospel. They answered, "Whether it is right in the sight of God to listen to you rather than to God, you must judge, for we cannot but speak of what we have seen and heard" (Acts 4:19–20). Later, the apostles were again arrested and forbidden to speak about Jesus, and again they answered, "We must obey God rather than men" (5:29). As Christians, we are told to obey the government and others in authority over us (Romans 13:1–7), yet the apostles could not obey the rulers' commands. Discuss the apostles' disobedience with your students. **If God tells us to obey the government authorities, when is it acceptable in the sight of God to disobey our leaders?**

Teacher Tips

In Acts 4:11, Peter describes Jesus as "the stone that was rejected." But that rejected stone is now the Cornerstone, the Foundation stone of the Church. Peter is talking about a prophecy found in Psalm 118:22–23: "The stone that the builders rejected has become the cornerstone. This is the Lord's doing; it is marvelous in our eyes." Psalm 118 was used each year by the Jews as part of the Passover celebration. The rulers in the Jewish council were no doubt familiar with the prophecy of that psalm, and now Peter tells them that the stone is Jesus Christ. Jesus was rejected and crucified, but God raised Him from the dead and made Him the foundation stone: "For no one can lay a foundation other than that which is laid, which is Jesus Christ" (1 Corinthians 3:11). Scripture also calls Jesus a "stone of stumbling" because unbelievers reject Him and stumble over Him, but "whoever believes in Him will not be put to shame" (Romans 9:33).

Check it Out

Perhaps your students have experienced the frustration of talking to someone about Jesus, only to have that person reject the Good News or ridicule the message. Remind the students that it is our job to be witnesses about what we know about Jesus. It is the work of the Holy Spirit to call the person to faith in Christ. We are witnesses—and the Spirit convinces!

Unit 8—The Spread of the Gospel

Lesson 86

Ananias and Sapphira
Acts 4:32—5:11

Central Truth
God looks at the heart for faith and trust rather than at an outward show or pretense of faithfulness.

Objectives
- Confess times when we are Christian in name and word only.
- Celebrate the forgiveness of Jesus, and rely on His power to strengthen us with boldness and certainty in our hearts and lives.
- Live faithfully for Jesus in all we say and do.

Materials
- Hymnals and music CDs
- Web Resource 86a
- Web Resource 86b
- Reproducible 86

Bible Prep
Post in advance so students can bookmark references before class time.
- Acts 4–5
- Hebrews 10:22
- Ephesians 4

Background

Lessons about synonyms and antonyms usually take place during a grammar lesson, but we can use them in religion too. We compare faith and works, and rightly so. Our good works cannot save us—we are saved only through faith in Christ; but the two go hand in hand. Outward works reveal the inward faith of the heart. Outwardly, it appears that all of the early Christians in today's story shared the same faith. To all outward appearances, the believers were "of one heart and soul" (Acts 4:32). Visible works of the believers' hands testified to the unseen faith of their hearts. But the story suddenly shifts from synonyms to antonyms. Ananias and Sapphira hid a lack of faith behind a false front of pretended good works. They, too, sold property and brought money to the apostles. But the Holy Spirit revealed the truth, and Peter confronted them. Ananias and Sapphira lied to the apostles and to God, keeping some of the money for themselves. (The sin was not in the amount of money they gave, but rather in the lies they told.) They were given the opportunity to repent, but they did not. Swift and terrible judgment followed. Their outward show of good hid unrepentant hearts. God calls us to repent of our sin when our works do not testify to our faith. Confident in the forgiveness we have in Christ, we live in love and service toward others. The works of our hands reflect the faith of our hearts!

Devotions

Things are not always what they appear to be. For example, have you ever cut open a shiny red apple only to find a worm and brown fruit inside? Have you ever seen an advertisement for a diamond ring on sale for ten dollars? What a bargain—until you notice the initials *CZ*, which stand for "cubic zirconia," an imitation, man-made stone that only *looks* like a diamond. Why are we fooled by these things? (We are deceived by outward appearances. It may seem valuable, but a closer look reveals the truth.) Ask your students to suggest other examples of things with an outward appearance that may fool us, such as clothing that looks like a big name brand, **"You can't judge a book by its cover." What does that saying mean?** (We can't tell if a book will be exciting or boring just by looking at its cover.) Discuss the ways in which we judge people by their outward appearance.

Little children pretend to be soldiers, firefighters, and superheroes. They pretend to be the people they want to be when they grow up. **When you were younger, what did you want to be when you grew up? What did you pretend to be?** Sometimes older children and even adults pretend to be someone they are not. **Why do they do that? Why, for example, might people who have very little money pretend to have a lot of money, buying things they cannot afford?** (They want to impress people and be popular.) **There are times when all of us pretend to be someone we are not. When might you pretend to be like someone else? When might you act one way outwardly but think differently inwardly?** We can often fool people by hiding what we feel or think. We can fool them with our outward words and actions. We might even be able to fool our parents or close friends. **But who can never be fooled by our outward actions and words?** (God)

God cannot be fooled. The Bible says He sees the heart; He does not see as people see. When the prophet Samuel looked at the outward appearance of men to find a king for Israel, God told Samuel not to judge by appearance or height. God said, "For the LORD sees not as man sees: man looks on the outward appearance, but the LORD looks on the heart" (1 Samuel 16:7). As Christians, we want our outward words and actions to match the faith and love in our hearts. Let's pray: Lord Jesus, forgive us for our sinful thoughts, words, and actions. Help us to show our faith by our outward words and actions. Amen.

Sing "Christ Be My Leader" (*LSB* 861; recorded as *Hymn of the Month for grade 7, September*). Speak or chant Psalm 98 (Web Resource 85a).

Lesson 86

Ananias and Sapphira

Action—Reaction

Read Acts 5:1–11. What do you think? Why was God's reaction so harsh? __God saw the lie in their hearts; it was not a matter of money but of motivation.__

What do you think? Why did Ananias and Sapphira do this in the first place? Read Acts 4:32–37. __They probably wanted to impress other people; envy probably led them to want to appear to be as good as Barnabas.__

Deception

When Barnabas sold his field and gave all the money to the Church, he was not required to do that—it was his choice. Ananias and Sapphira could have chosen to give just a portion of their money—but they chose to lie. They lied not just to other people, but also to God (Acts 5:4). Scripture says in 2 Corinthians 9:7, "Each one must give as he has decided in his heart, not reluctantly or under compulsion, for God loves a cheerful giver"—not a dishonest one! The amount of the offering was not the concern either; recall how Jesus praised the widow who gave two tiny copper coins, saying that she gave more in her offering at the temple than all the rest of the people (Luke 21:1–4).

Ananias and Sapphira were not simply pretending to be more righteous than they were. It was not simply a fake gift. Consider these synonyms for the word *fake*: dishonest, deceptive, fraud, bogus, imposter, misrepresentation. This was a serious matter, and God dealt with it in a serious way. Ananias and Sapphira did not recognize that God is omniscient and omnipotent. They were only concerned with external appearances. But God went right to the *heart* of the matter!

What's wrong with the half-hearted thoughts above? Read God's response to the half-hearted church in Revelation 3:15. What does God want from us? See Hebrews 10:22. __A true heart__

Review

Covenant Connection

"Out of sight, out of mind." This type of thinking may have prompted Ananias and Sapphira's fraudulent behavior. Jesus had ascended to heaven. He was no longer physically present. However, He did not leave us on our own to do whatever we want. Today's Bible narrative reminded the people of the Early Church—just as it reminds people of the Church today—that Jesus is still with us, as He promised: "Behold, I am with you always, to the end of the age" (Matthew 28:20).

INTO the lesson

Introduce the lesson by looking at Web Resource 86a, which shows several optical illusions. Explain that an optical illusion is based on appearances. What may look like one thing may actually be something else. Discuss the illusions, and connect them to today's Bible narrative, which is also about appearances that proved to be deceptive.

INTO the Word

Action—Reaction

In this section, students will speculate about the actions in the story. Some students may think the punishment was harsh—you lie, you die. But the problem was much bigger than that. Ananias and Sapphira were lying to God, which showed disrespect and dishonor to the Lord. By doing this, they seemed to minimize God's involvement in their lives. God was not angry about the amount of money they gave, but about their motivation of self-interest. If they had given even much less but had done it out of compassion for others and out of thankfulness to God, the Lord would have been happy with their gift. But their motivation appears to have been to impress other people and to not be "outdone in giving" by Barnabas. These were selfish and self-centered motives. God saw what was in their hearts; the main thing lacking was faith in Him.

Point out another factor to consider, which is the timing of the event. God was making a strong statement about the Christian Church—that this was not a church abandoned by God's divine power. Jesus returned physically to heaven, but that does not mean He is no longer with us. Jesus is true God, and He is not limited by time or space. Jesus is Lord—and He is still in charge!

Imitation

Ananias and Sapphira were imitation Christians. They gave the appearance of being Christian, but it was only an external illusion. They were concerned mostly about the opinions and evaluations of the people around them. This is contrary to the way Jesus lived. Even His enemies recognized that when they said, "Teacher, we know that You are true and teach the way of God truthfully, and You do not care about anyone's opinion, for You are not swayed by appearances" (Matthew 22:16).

God does not want us to just be imitation (fake, faux) Christians. However, He does want us to imitate: He desires that we imitate Jesus, following His example of truth and compassion.

Write what Scripture tells us about this in Ephesians 4:32–5:2. _____

"Be kind to one another, tenderhearted, forgiving one another, as God in Christ forgave you. Therefore be imitators of God, as beloved children. And walk in love, as Christ loved us and gave Himself up for us, a fragrant offering and sacrifice to God."

Reflection

ACTION BUT NO HEART   HEART BUT NO ACTION

The first circle represents what was happening in today's Bible narrative (and in many lives today). The actions (good works) were there, but their hearts were empty. Good works do not save us! "By grace you have been saved through faith" (Ephesians 2:8). Draw a large *X* over the first circle to indicate that it is not acceptable—God looks at the heart for faith in Christ Jesus as our Savior.

The second circle is also not acceptable, so draw large *X* over it too. Saying we have faith in Jesus but never living in faith is an empty faith or no faith at all. Again, good works do not save us—however, good works *are* a reflection of the faith that is in a person's heart. James 2:17–18, 22 says: "Faith by itself, if it does not have works, is dead. But someone will say, 'You have faith and I have works.' Show me your faith apart from your works, and I will show you my faith by my works. . . . You see that faith was active along with his works, and faith was completed by his works." Faith is necessary, but it is not separate or isolated from good works. First we are justified by faith in Christ Jesus, and that is immediately followed by the sanctification work of the Holy Spirit in our lives and actions. Praise God that He brings us to faith and then keeps us in faith, as He sanctifies our hearts and lives.

Remember

(See Ephesians 4:32–5:2, which you wrote on the lines above.)

179

Deception

This section of the Student Book expands on the seriousness of the situation. We could very likely become casual with regard to our own truthfulness and faithfulness because we do not see people struck down every time someone tells a lie. (If that did happen, none of us would be standing.) God has warned us through the example of Ananias and Sapphira; but He is also full of grace and mercy, and He has an amazing amount of patience. Still, we should never become complacent about sin—God sees and God knows. As stated in 1 Samuel 16:7, "The Lord sees not as man sees: man looks on the outward appearance, but the Lord looks on the heart."

Discuss and analyze the cartoon. This is not a "funny" cartoon; it is very serious. Encourage your students to analyze their own hearts and to pray that God would lead them to fully commit themselves to faith in Jesus and to their faith life.

The Covenant Connection speaks to the concept of "cheap grace," in which people focus on "Forgive, forgive, forgive." Jesus is ready and willing to forgive—but "I sin, He forgives" is not the one and only dimension of being a Christian. **God calls us to repentance and faith, which results in change. We cannot ignore sanctification and the work of the Holy Spirit; this follows the actions of Christ for our justification, but they cannot be separated. They go together. Jesus justifies us; the Holy Spirit transforms us. We now look at God's Law not as a "have to" but as a "can do" because of God working in us.** Jesus said He came not to get rid of the Law but to fulfill it. Furthermore, He leads believers in faith to not only obey the Law as new people in Christ, but even to exceed it, to go beyond the Law. (This is the theme of the Sermon on the Mount.) Read Matthew 5:17–20.

Imitation

Point out that there are several definitions of the word *imitation*. Ananias and Sapphira were *imitation* Christians—they were fake; they were not real believers.

However, there is another meaning of *imitation* that God *does* ask of believers. This type of imitation copies the example of another: we are to imitate the kind, compassionate, forgiving actions of Jesus. Sing together "Make Me Like You," which specifically calls on God to empower us to follow Jesus' example. We can't do it on our own, but Jesus promises to guide and bless us through the enabling power of the Holy Spirit. Web Resource 86b contains the lyrics and accompaniment of the song.

Reflection

This section of the Student Book focuses on the relationship between faith (in our hearts) and good works (in actions and speech). Good works do not save us; but if you have saving faith, good works will accompany it. Some people are uncomfortable with the Book of James, thinking it emphasizes good works too much. However, the Book of James is trying to put things into perspective. Good works are a reflection of the faith that is already in the person's heart. If there is no faith, there will be no reflection (good works). But the reverse is also true: if there are no good works, that indicates a blank heart with nothing to be reflected.

This is like the old adage about putting the cart before the horse. You won't get anywhere if you put good works first (the cart before the horse). Likewise, if horse and cart are disconnected, you will get nowhere (faith disconnected from works is dead faith, as James says). But if the horse is first and the cart follows, the will of the driver will be accomplished; this is like having faith followed by good works, which is the will of God.

The love and compassion we show to others is a reflection of the love and compassion Jesus gives to us, and this is also a reflection of the faith He has placed in our hearts. Sing about this in "They'll Know We Are Christians by Our Love" (*AGPS* 237; also recorded on *JPS*).

Celebrating GROWTH

The story of Ananias and Sapphira offers an opportunity to talk about sin and forgiveness. The couple refused to repent and accept the forgiveness available to them in Christ. The terrible judgment brought against them shows us that God takes sin very seriously. But we see an even greater lesson about the seriousness of sin when we look to the cross of our Lord. Jesus carried our sins in His body to the cross (1 Peter 2:24). Because He suffered the penalty of death for us, our sins are forgiven. The first Christians knew the love of Christ and demonstrated that love by sharing their material blessings with fellow believers. Certain of God's love and forgiveness for us, we in turn can share that love and forgiveness with others.

Teacher Tips

Jesus said, "By this My Father is glorified, that you bear much fruit and so prove to be My disciples" (John 15:8). The first Christians bore fruit in good works as they shared their possessions with those in need. We know that we are not saved by good works. The apostle Paul wrote, "We know that a person is not justified by works of the law but through faith in Jesus Christ" (Galatians 2:16). Along with those early Christians, we are saved only by God's grace through faith in Jesus Christ. Yet we also know that we are "created in Christ Jesus for good works, which God prepared beforehand, that we should walk in them" (Ephesians 2:10). We testify to our faith in Christ as we follow the path of love and good works to which God directs us in His Word. By those loving works, we show the world that we really are Jesus' disciples.

Curriculum Connection

Lying is widespread in our world, particularly in advertising, politics, and on unregulated sites on the Internet. The false information spread there can have very bad effects on your students' lives. Help them learn to tell the difference between reliable and unreliable sources using section 6.7.1, Reliability of Information, located in the sixth-grade Health volume of the Concordia Curriculum Guide series.

HANDS TO SERVE

The first Christians were "of one heart and soul" (Acts 4:32). They demonstrated their unity by the way they lived. Believers with many possessions shared with those in need. Your students can demonstrate their faith by sharing their blessings with others in your church and community. They can donate clothing, personal care items, or food for a mission or food pantry. Students can also show that they are "of one heart and soul" by the way they treat others at school and at home. Another student may be "in need," simply needing a kind word. Students can listen to a friend who is experiencing difficult times at home, or they might help others who want to bring their grades up in a certain class. There are many ways each day in which we can demonstrate the power of Jesus' resurrection in our lives and the "great grace" that has been poured out on us in His name!

Check it Out

The early believers were "of one heart and soul" (Acts 4:32) and put their faith into action through works of love. What was their source of strength and power for such unselfish acts? Verse 33 tells us: "And with great power the apostles were giving their testimony to the resurrection of the Lord Jesus, and great grace was upon them all." Jesus died on the cross and conquered death when He rose from the dead. Because of His death and resurrection, those first Christians enjoyed the forgiveness of sins and the promise of eternal life. Jesus gave His life for them, and they gave their lives in joyful service to others. The hope found in the resurrection of Jesus empowers us to share with those in need.

Faith in Action

The generosity of the first Christians is a lesson in good stewardship. A *steward* was a servant who managed the money and property of his master. We are to be stewards of God's gifts to us. Use Reproducible 86 to see what Scripture says about this. Ask your pastor to talk to the class about stewardship and the sharing of time, talents, and treasures. Ask him to explain the way that the funds collected through Sunday offerings are used for the work of the Church. Students can also volunteer to assist with church projects, helping with clean-up days or serving at a potluck or fund-raiser. Older students can volunteer to help with Vacation Bible School. Some of your students might be interested in being pastors, teachers, deaconesses, or missionaries. Talk to them about future careers in church work. Invite the pastor and other staff members, to talk to the students about full-time work in the Church.

Unit 8—The Spread of the Gospel

Lesson 87

Stephen
Acts 6:7–8:3

Background

Stephen was one of the seven deacons chosen by the Early Church to oversee the distribution of food to needy widows (Acts 6:1–6). His name indicates that he was probably a Hellenized Jew—that is, one who had come under the influence of Greek culture and language. Hellenized Jews were often in conflict with more traditional Jews, but the Early Church defused this conflict by appointing several to leadership positions, where they could ensure fairness.

Although Stephen's primary job involved meeting physical needs, he soon became known as a powerful speaker and also a miracle worker (vv. 8–10). This brought him into conflict with the Jewish religious leaders of Jerusalem, where the young Church was located. Stephen's last sermon made it clear that he would not compromise the truth; he told his hearers flat out that they had "betrayed and murdered" the Messiah, whom Stephen called "the Righteous One" (7:52).

Predictably, his hearers were enraged. They threw him out of the city and stoned him, which was an illegal execution (John 18:31). But before he died, he uttered this prayer to Jesus: "Lord Jesus, receive my spirit" (Acts 7:59).

Stephen's murder touched off a wave of persecution that scattered the Christians throughout Palestine. But this actually had a positive impact, as Christians began sharing the Good News of Jesus far more widely, and many new churches sprang up.

Central Truth

Being a Christian is not an easy path, but God promises to be near with His strength and blessing and the ultimate certainty of heaven.

Objectives

- Recognize that many people in the world are persecuted physically and emotionally for following Jesus.
- Pray for those who suffer in the name of Jesus, and ask for strength to stand firm in our faith.
- Dedicate our life to Jesus, who gave His life for us.

Materials

- Hymnals and music CDs
- Reproducible 87
- Web Resource 87a

Bible Prep

Post in advance so students can bookmark references before class time.
- Acts 6–8; 22

Devotions

John logged off the computer, looking sick to his stomach. His dad glanced up and said, "Are you done already? John, what's wrong?"

John sank down on the sofa and said, "I was reading the news . . . there was a church in the Middle East . . . they were having worship, and some people came and burned it down! With the people inside it!"

His dad came over and put an arm around him. "I'm sorry, son," he said. "That is terrible news. I heard about it this morning on the way to work."

John dashed away the tears from his eyes and said angrily, "How can people do that? How can God allow that?"

"It isn't what God wants," his dad said gently. "But Jesus did warn us that people would hate us because of Him, and that there would be suffering."

"Suffering?" asked John. "You mean it could happen *here*?"

"I hope not," said his father, shutting his eyes for a moment. "We're very blessed to live in a country where it's illegal to persecute people on account of their faith. But you may still meet people who ridicule Christianity, and you may have to deal with people who treat you harshly because you belong to Jesus. Being a Christian is not an easy path."

"What do you mean?" John asked.

"Well, compared to what our brothers and sisters are going through around the world, it's nothing. But you may get teased or left out by some friends. Some people will give you a hard time if they see you praying, or if you tell them you won't do something because it is against God's way. When you get older, you may miss out on jobs or special opportunities because the people offering them want you to do something unethical or unchristian."

John looked thoughtful. "I suppose it's all worth it?" he asked.

His dad hugged him. "Yes, it certainly is. Having Jesus is worth everything, and it's everlasting."

Let's pray: Dear Lord, watch over the Christians who suffer for Your sake. Keep them close to You and protect them from evil. In Jesus' name we pray. Amen.

Sing together "Immortal, Invisible, God Only Wise" (*LSB* 802; recorded as *Hymn of the Month* for grade 6, April). Speak or chant Psalm 98 (Web Resource 85a).

INTO the lesson

Say, **Today, we will hear about Stephen, the first martyr who died for his faith in Jesus. Let's look at this short skit that introduces the Bible story, and then we will study it more thoroughly and discover what a first-century story can teach twenty-first-century people like you and me!** Distribute Reproducible 87 and discuss the readers theater script.

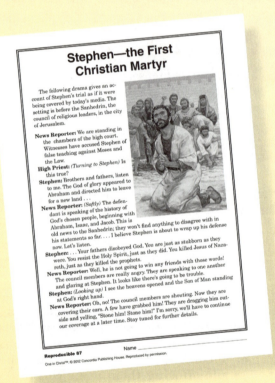

Lesson 87

Stephen

Reach Out

After Pentecost, the Christian Church grew by the thousands. There was so much work to be done by the twelve apostles. Their main task was preaching and teaching the Good News of salvation through Jesus. But they didn't want to neglect other matters, such as helping the poor. So seven helpers (deacons) were chosen to assist in the work of the Church.

What qualifications did they need to have? See Acts 6:3. **A good reputation; they were to be filled with the Holy Spirit and wisdom.**

Give the names of the seven who were chosen. See Acts 6:5. **Stephen, Philip, Prochorus, Nicanor, Timon, Parmenas, Nicolaus**

Stand Up

Stephen spoke up boldly about salvation through Christ Jesus. What happened next paralleled what happened to Jesus. This was no coincidence. Stephen learned from and followed Jesus' example. As you read Stephen's story in the Book of Acts, write what was similar in Jesus' story.

Acts 6:8–10 **Jesus had enemies who disagreed with Him.**
Acts 6:12 **Jesus was brought before the Sanhedrin council.**
Acts 6:13 **False witnesses accused Him.**
Acts 7:54 **The leaders were angry, even though Jesus spoke the truth.**
Acts 7:59 **As He was dying, He committed His spirit to the Lord.**
Acts 7:60a **He forgave His enemies.**
Acts 7:60b **He died.**

Both stories end in victory! Three days later, Jesus was resurrected from the dead. Stephen awaits the resurrection on the Last Day. We can be certain of this because of the promises of Jesus, our living Lord and Savior.

Covenant Connection

God kept all of His covenant promises about the Messiah—Christ Jesus. This gives us the assurance and certainty that He will continue to keep all the promises He has made—promises yet to be fulfilled. We can be certain that we and all believers will join Stephen and many others on the Last Day, when we will be resurrected to live a new life in heaven eternally! The victory is ours!

180

INTO the Word

Reach Out

As you look at this portion of the Student Book, remind your students: **The work of the Church is not just the job of the pastors. They have a very specific role in preaching God's Word and administering the Sacraments. But they cannot do everything that is needed; furthermore, they should not *have* to do everything. God desires that we all become active in the Church, dividing up the tasks among us, and using our individual skills to take on specific responsibilities.**

Belonging to a church does not mean that you are the audience to be entertained or helped when needed. Belonging to a church means participation, taking your part actively in worshiping God and in helping others.

Also point out that active church membership is not just for adults. Discuss things your students can do now to take an active part in worship and in serving others.

Stand Up

Point out that Stephen was murdered—the Sanhedrin had no power to carry out a sentence of death. Their actions were illegal. But more than this, Stephen was martyred—he was killed

Powerful Words

Why did the people in the council murder Stephen? It was because of the powerful words he spoke as he was guided by the Holy Spirit. Look at portions of Stephen's speech, and rate how the Sanhedrin council must have felt about what he said.

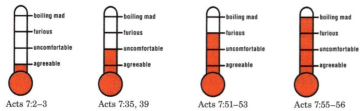

Acts 7:2–3   Acts 7:35, 39   Acts 7:51–53   Acts 7:55–56

Loud Silence

A response of silence can be very powerful because it implies acceptance and even approval. During the stoning of Stephen, Saul stood silently by, indicating that he approved. See Acts 7:58 and 22:20.

Silence is not neutral. It is acceptance. You must speak up in order to stand up for Jesus and to defend another person. How could you respond to these statements?

1. "Don't invite Jennifer to your party. She is so uncool. She never has any nice clothes to wear."
   I'm going to invite her. She needs a friend. I don't even notice her clothes because she is always so much fun to be with.

2. "Look, Jackson dropped the ball again. That is so stupid!"
   He didn't do it on purpose. Maybe we should practice together so we all improve. I'm sure glad Jesus accepts us the way we are!

3. "Let's put this up on the Internet. It's just a joke. And Jacob will never know that we are the ones who did it." *You know Jacob won't be laughing. I'm sure it will hurt his feelings. No matter what, God will know. If I have to choose between your bad joke and God's good way, I know what I will do.*

4. "Those people talk weird! I don't want those foreigners coming to our church."
   Hey, you are talking about my family! They are your brothers and sisters too because Jesus has made all believers part of God's family.

Pray for the right words to say and the courage to say them when you run into similar situations. It takes courage to stand up for what is right. Stephen boldly spoke words that he knew would get him into trouble. Where did he get the courage to do this? See Acts 6:5, 8, 10.
From the power of the Holy Spirit working in Him

Remember

"Lord, . . . grant to Your servants to continue to speak Your word with all boldness." (Acts 4:29)

181

INTO our lives

Loud Silence

This title is an *oxymoron*—a phrase that seems to contradict itself. Ask students to interpret what it means. (Silence often speaks as loudly as words. Silence has a strong impact. Silence about something that is wrong implies that you not only accept the wrong, you approve of it!) Look first at the silence of Saul in Acts 7:58. Later, in his own words, Saul (also called Paul) admitted that his silence gave approval (22:20). Continue to look at Saul's actions as you read 8:1–3. Saul's silent approval of Stephen's death exploded into a terrorizing persecution of Christians.

Continue then with the Student Book activity, which explores issues in today's world where a response of silence is often very negative. We cannot excuse silence as neutrality, because it isn't! Allow students time to work on their responses. After that, incorporate Web Resource 87a into your discussion as volunteers share what they wrote.

because he stood up unrelentingly for his belief in Jesus as Savior. This was just the beginning of a period of persecution for the Christian Church. All of the disciples except the apostle John would eventually be martyred for standing firm in their faith. Persecutions of the early Christian Church would continue for about three hundred years, until the time of the Roman Emperor Constantine.

Have students turn to "By All Your Saints in Warfare" (*LSB* 517), which speaks of the faith of many martyrs. Read aloud stanzas 1, 4, and 7, and then go back to 3, which is the concluding stanza. The Church Year calendar includes the commemoration of some of the saints of old. Look at page xi in the front of *LSB* to see a list of some of these dates. Jesus had told His followers that persecutions would come, but He also offered promises of support. Read about this in Matthew 10:16–20.

Note: Often there is a morbid interest in how the martyrs died. Focus instead on how they lived—in faith—and the fact that they will continue to live eternally in heaven because of Jesus.

Powerful Words

This section provides an opportunity to explore some of the powerful things Stephen said at his trial before the Sanhedrin. **He spoke openly about Jesus' death and resurrection, which accomplished forgiveness, life, and salvation for us.** The Student Book activity shows that as Stephen's words became more convicting, the heat of the anger in the room also increased until, as Scripture states, the council was enraged, grinding their teeth, shouting, and covering their ears so that they could hear no more of Stephen's words.

How was Stephen able to withstand all this? It was not his own doing. He was not alone; he was not without support. He had the example of Jesus before him, and he had the Holy Spirit working in him!

371

Searching Further

Persecution is not strictly a Christian problem—other religious, ethnic, and political groups suffer persecution as well. Ponder these questions: **What leads people to persecute others? How can it be stopped? What can we do?** Emphasize that the most important thing students can do for persecuted Christians is pray for them. Some may see this as too indirect and too easy. Make it clear that this is not so. Christians who suffer ask specifically for our prayers again and again, because they know from experience that God listens. It is a high privilege to take a situation before the throne of God and ask for help. God has given this privilege to your students also.

Critical thinking

Discuss with students: **How are the smaller problems Christians experience in our own country (teasing, prejudice) related to the much more serious problems our brothers and sisters face elsewhere in the world? How are they the same, and how are they different? How should we deal with these problems when they happen to us?**

Curriculum Connection

In connection with Stephen's speech and its result, consider using section 6.4.1.4, Characteristics of Effective Presentations, found in the sixth-grade Language Arts volume of the Concordia Curriculum Guide series. Discuss with students: **In what sense could we say that Stephen's presentation was effective? In what sense was it not effective? What elements do you see in his speech that are clearly geared to his audience of Jewish religious leaders? Why do you think he included the biblical stories and examples that he did?**

Celebrating GROWTH

It takes courage to stay faithful to the Lord in hard times. Your students, too, are growing in courage—whether that means trying new things, standing up to people who tease them, or making hard choices to do what is right. Think of the students in your class, and identify several you have seen showing courage in ways big or small. Then write them encouraging notes to be given to them privately.

Technology

Persecution of Christians continues today, especially in parts of Asia and Africa. If students want to learn more about persecuted Christians, it would be wise for you to check out their sources before turning them loose on the Internet. Web sites are full of graphic material that is inappropriate for sixth graders. If students are interested in service projects for Christians under persecution, consider checking the LCMS World Mission Web site. There may be prayer suggestions, missionaries' personal newsletters or blogs, or special fund-raising projects for various areas around the world. Be aware that you will *not* be given all the details or contact information you might wish for; much work must be carried out quietly and without publicity in order to avoid drawing the attention of persecutors. For example, you will probably not be able to develop an e-mail pal project. But you *will* make a difference!

UNIT 8—THE SPREAD OF THE GOSPEL

Lesson 88

Philip and the Ethiopian
Acts 8:26–40

Background

The story of Philip and the Ethiopian is remarkable because it shows just how much trouble God will go to in order to save a single person. (Philip was one of the seven deacons chosen to help with the food distribution to the poor, as recounted in Acts 6:5; at this point, all the apostles still remained in Jerusalem.) An angel told Philip just where to go in order to meet up with this traveler. Once Philip had evangelized and baptized him, the Holy Spirit took Philip away, leaving the Ethiopian to continue on his way home—now a Christian himself, and a witness to his own people for Jesus Christ. Indeed, the Ethiopian Christian Church traces its beginning to this man's witness.

Philip overheard the Ethiopian man reading a passage from Isaiah 53, a messianic portion that Christ fulfilled through His death on the cross. People normally read aloud in those days, so asking about the reading made it easy for Philip to start a conversation. To emphasize his high standing in the court of the queen, the Ethiopian man is identified as a eunuch in charge of his government's treasury. Although he was a Jewish proselyte, he would have been considered a "second-class believer"—but that all changed when Jesus Christ threw open the gates of God's kingdom to everyone who believes. Although he is not mentioned directly, there was apparently a servant driving the chariot, freeing his master to read. This servant would have heard Philip's explanation about Jesus and been a witness to his master's Baptism (Acts 8:36–38). We have no idea what his own response was to the Gospel, but we can hope that he, too, eventually came to faith in Jesus.

Central Truth

God desires that people of all nations, races, and statuses come to know Jesus as Savior.

Objectives

- Recognize that God's Church is wherever two or three people are gathered together in His name.
- Ask God to open our hearts to openly share the love of Jesus with anyone and everyone.
- See our role sometimes as student, sometimes as teacher, but always as disciple of Jesus.

Materials

- Hymnals and music CDs
- Web Resource 88a
- Reproducible 88

Bible Prep

Post in advance so students can bookmark references before class time.
- Acts 8
- Isaiah 41; 43; 53; 60
- 1 Timothy 2
- 1 Corinthians 3

Devotions

Susan complained, "It seems like a lot of trouble to go to for just a few kids. They're mostly Muslim anyway. Why don't we run a VBS program for the kids in our church?"

"The kids at church already know Jesus," said Lisa patiently. "They have plenty of chances to learn more about God: at home, at school, and at church. But the kids in this neighborhood don't even know who Jesus is."

"Yeah, but they're immigrants," argued Susan. "They're poor, and they don't speak much English."

Lisa smiled. "I'm an immigrant too, you know," she said quietly.

"What?" asked Susan, sitting up abruptly.

"Sure," Lisa answered. "My parents came here from Vietnam when I was only three. I wasn't born here."

"Well, okay," Susan said. "But you're a Christian now, and you go to our church and school!"

"Yes, I do *now*," said Lisa. "But my family originally worshiped our ancestors. We had a shrine in our house, and we used to offer fruit and incense on it. When my grandma died, the Buddhist priest came to our house, and we had to do all these rituals."

Susan was fascinated. "But how did you end up in our church then?" she asked.

"Well," said Lisa, "someone invited me. You know Megan? Our families became friends and they invited us to VBS one year. We were all baptized when I was eight years old. Now I want to share the blessings of Jesus with other people. That's why it is so important for me to help with this Vacation Bible School."

Susan jumped up. "Well then, let's get going. We have a VBS program that needs these kids because they need Jesus!"

Have a special reading of Isaiah 53:3–10. This is the text that the man from Ethiopia was reading in today's Bible narrative. It is also the portion that Philip explained as a messianic prophecy fulfilled in Christ Jesus. And it is through this Scripture that the Holy Spirit worked faith in the Ethiopian's heart. Sing together "Immortal, Invisible, God Only Wise" (*LSB* 802; recorded as *Hymn of the Month for grade 6, April*).

INTO the lesson

Begin the lesson with Web Resource 88a, which visually tells today's Bible story. Then read it directly from the Bible (Acts 8:26–40) to learn more details of the account

INTO our lives

What Is Important to the Lord?

This is one of the important lessons we can take away from today's Bible narrative: Jesus did not come just for one nation—He came for all people. That was shown by the Spirit's amazing efforts to bring the man from Africa to faith. This is also significant for you and me, because for the most part, the people in your classroom are probably Gentiles (not Jewish people).

It might even be surprising to your students that this is significant, because they may be accustomed to thinking of this as a Christian nation; and they may even think that Jesus came for people in the United States. However, if Jesus had come for only one nation, it would have been the Jewish people, who were direct descendants of Abraham. If that had happened, we would all be on the outside, unable to receive the blessings of faith and forgiveness!

Thank God that He loves and cares for all people. In Scripture, over and over again, God assures us that Jesus came to save all people who believe in Him. Consider one of the most famous Bible verses—John 3:16. It says, "God so loved the world that . . . ." (Have students complete the verse.) Another reassuring verse says that anyone who believes in the true God and the fulfillment of His promises is a true descendant of Abraham by faith. We actually *are* descendants of Abraham—by faith, not by birth—because we have been made members of God's family through Christ Jesus!

Lesson 88

Philip and the Ethiopian

What Is Important to the Lord?

Is it numbers? The Book of Acts lists big numbers of people who came to faith in Jesus. On one day (Pentecost), 3,000 people became believers. A short time later, the number was up to 5,000. And the numbers continued. However, God cares about each individual too. In Acts 8, we see that God sent Philip on an amazing journey to talk to one man in the desert. You can be certain that God knows and cares about you too. He knows you so well that He calls you by name. See Isaiah 43:1.

What is important to the Lord? Is it race or nationality? Those two men discussing Scripture in a chariot were different in many ways. One was a Greek and one was an Ethiopian; one was white and one was black; one was from Judea and one was from Africa. But God called both of them to faith in Jesus, who was prophesied in the words of Isaiah 53, which they were reading.

What is important to the Lord? Is it wealth or social standing? The Ethiopian was an important government official. As treasurer for the queen, he had power and influence. Philip, however, was on the run, escaping from angry leaders in Jerusalem. Yet God loved them both and kept them in His care. Read about God's personal care for you in Isaiah 41:13.

What is important to God? See 1 Timothy 2:4. **God wants all people to be saved and to come to the knowledge of the truth.**

How Easy Was That?

Look at how God worked through the power of the Holy Spirit to guide Philip in his task.
1. God set it up so Philip and the man would be in the same place at the same time.
2. The man was already reading the Bible, so he was clearly interested.
3. He was reading out loud, so Philip could hear and start a conversation about it.
4. He asked Philip to explain the reading, so Philip was actually *invited* to speak about Jesus.
5. Later, the African man himself asked to be baptized.

Trust God to help you witness your faith and tell what you know.
Trust God to handle the rest. That's the Holy Spirit's job, not yours!

Covenant Connection

When God gave His covenant promises to Abraham, God said that through this, "all the families of the earth shall be blessed." That includes people who are Greek, Ethiopian, American, Canadian, Mexican . . . we could go on and on. God desires all people to be saved! Isaiah 60:1, 3 speaks this messianic promise: "Arise, shine, for your light has come, and the glory of the LORD has risen upon you. . . . And nations shall come to your light, and kings to the brightness of your rising."

182

How Easy Was That?

Being a witness—telling what we know—for Jesus is not exactly easy, but it is also not as difficult as many people think. The Holy Spirit makes the difference, helping us, guiding us, blessing us. What is important is to be natural and sincere about talking about your faith, not using flowery language or giving long speeches. You don't have to preach a sermon or even tell a Bible story; you can simply say why Jesus is an important part of your life or talk about how He has blessed you. God wants us to "plant the seed"; that's the small part, just a beginning. He will water and nourish this message through the Word and Sacraments so that it grows into faith. At the same time, out of concern and love for others, we will want to do all we can to continue to encourage such people as they grow in faith.

Help your students to see that God also prepares the way for us to share our faith with people we care about. In many cases, God has been preparing those opportunities for years—through experiences, questions, curiosity, and encounters with other Christians before us. We are not on our own when we seek to tell someone about Jesus; the Holy Spirit goes ahead of us and follows up after us. And He uses many other people's contributions to ultimately bring a person to faith.

The Holy Spirit in Word

Jesus promised to send us the Holy Spirit to be our Counselor and Helper. The Holy Spirit comes to us through the Means of Grace. (This is an important reason for us to stay connected to God's Word and His Sacraments!)

The Spirit helps us in ways we cannot help ourselves. He helps us by giving us saving faith; He helps us understand God's will; He helps us live God-pleasing lives; He helps us remain firm in faith; and He helps us as we tell others about salvation through Jesus.

We can be certain of the Spirit's help as He works through God's Word because we have His promise that "My word . . . shall not return to Me empty, but it shall accomplish that which I purpose, and shall succeed in the thing for which I sent it" (Isaiah 55:11).

The Holy Spirit in Baptism

The Ethiopian man asked to be baptized in the name of the Father, Son, and Holy Spirit. For many of you, your parents and sponsors asked that you be baptized, and at your confirmation, you will have another opportunity to reaffirm your faith in Jesus. For others of you, the opportunity to ask to be baptized is yours; you have come to faith as the Holy Spirit worked through God's Word, and you can look forward to your own Baptism day.

Why be baptized? It is one of the ways God gives us His special blessings. Look in the Appendix of this book for the Small Catechism, and write here the answer to the question "What benefits does Baptism give?" __"It works forgiveness of sins, rescues from death and the devil, and gives eternal salvation to all who believe this, as the words and promises of God declare."__

The Holy Spirit in You

At one time, sin made us enemies of God. But Jesus has removed that sin by His death and resurrection, making us holy and blameless by His grace through faith. God now mercifully and graciously is willing to make our hearts His home. We are His temple; the Holy Spirit lives in us! What is the Spirit doing in our hearts? He is guiding us to grow in faith and leading us to live in faith as people of God. He is with us, doing what we cannot do on our own! The Holy Spirit empowers us and enables us. What does that mean? __He gives us power to become people of God in faith, and He makes us able to live in faith.__

How do we know this to be true? Once again, we find the truth in God's Holy Word. Read about it in 1 Corinthians 3:16 and 6:19.

Remember

"Such is the confidence that we have through Christ toward God. Not that we are sufficient in ourselves to claim anything as coming from us, but our sufficiency is from God." (2 Corinthians 3:4–5)

INTO the Word

The Holy Spirit in Word, in Baptism, in You

The essential part of this Bible narrative is the work of the Holy Spirit. Use these three portions of the Student Book to explore how the Holy Spirit works through God's Word, blesses us in the gift of Baptism, and humbly dwells within us as He continues to work in us.

Distribute Reproducible 88 at this time. Explain that in a moment, at your signal, each student will go around the room to each desk (in an orderly pattern determined by you) and write his or her name in one heart on each paper. If you need more than thirty hearts because your class is larger, assign certain students to draw a heart each time and then add their names. If you have too many hearts, students may later add the names of other Christians to those hearts. These might include the pastor, teacher, family members, and friends who are believers in Jesus.

When that part of the activity is finished, have everyone take their seats. Tell them to write this title in the blank box at the top: "The Holy Spirit Dwells in . . . ." Then have students draw a line from that box to every name on the page. What is the message of this page? God is always with us. The Holy Spirit lives in us—we are His temple. Thank God for such amazing blessings!

Curriculum Connection

Christianity spread widely as a result of the persecution that began with Stephen's death. Christians went everywhere, preaching the Gospel. Learn more about this diaspora using section 6.2.1.36, Jewish Migration and the Spread of Christianity in the Roman Empire. You'll find it in the sixth-grade Social Studies volume of the Concordia Curriculum Guide series.

Bringing it home

Challenge students to "bring it home" by asking the Lord to place them in a situation this week where they can tell someone else about Jesus. Ask Him to make it clear when and how they can talk about Him, and to help them not to be nervous or shy. This activity should be voluntary; making it a class assignment could be a big problem for timid children or for those who are not yet believers or are just beginning in faith. After a week, invite children to report on their experiences if they wish to do so.

Reaching Every Child

Visual Problems. Creating an environment that reaches all learners is critical for teachers today. There is so much information that needs to be relayed, but the way students interpret that information affects their final output/understanding of the concepts. Students who have visual challenges need to have material presented in a multitude of ways. Visual problems include fluctuating eyesight, slowly or rapidly deteriorating vision, or eye problems that are subject to improvement over the course of the year. It has been proven that visually impaired students learn more by listening than their sighted counterparts do. It will be very important that these visually impaired students have accommodations in place such as preferential seating, bright lighting, and print size that they can see. Some modifications teachers can make that will help these students succeed include the following:

- Face the visually impaired student when speaking.
- Say aloud everything that is written on the board.
- Ensure that handouts are clear, dark, and legible.
- Assign a buddy to provide additional assistance.
- Allow the student to record information being taught to listen to again later.
- Give detailed descriptions so that the visually impaired student can picture the lesson in his or her mind.

Reaching Every Child

Hearing Loss. Some students have difficulty hearing the information the teacher is giving to the class due to a sustained hearing loss. This loss, depending on its cause, can be permanent or temporary. It has been found that children with a hearing loss can experience substantial setbacks in learning unless some type of assistive device is provided. To ensure that these students get the most from the lessons, there are many modifications and accommodations that can be made:

- Provide preferential seating.
- Use visual cues (overheads, maps, drawings, demonstrations).
- Face student directly when speaking.
- Emphasize key points.
- Repeat or rephrase what other students say.
- Highlight texts or study guides.
- Use preprinted outlines of materials.
- Minimize background noise.
- Use alternative testing methods.
- Preteach the vocabulary.
- Use peer tutoring.
- Use captioned films or videos.
- Provide note-taking assistance during lessons to allow the hearing-impaired student to concentrate on the teacher.

Technology

Just for fun, do a little research on ancient chariots. How were they constructed, and how were they driven? How many people fit in a chariot? How easy would it have been to read the Bible in one of them? And what were the roads like?

UNIT 8—THE SPREAD OF THE GOSPEL

LESSON 89

Saul Becomes a Christian
ACTS 9:1–31

Background

Saul's zeal is evident in both parts of this story. In the beginning, he is eager to persecute the Christian Church. By the end, not only has he received Baptism, he is actively preaching Christ to his enemies. Saul, who persecuted Christians, now treats suffering for Christ as a joy and honor (Romans 5:3; 8:18; 2 Corinthians 11:23–33; Ephesians 3:13). Saul's escape in a basket was necessary because many ancient cities were surrounded by thick walls, and the city gates were the only normal way of entering or leaving. However, homes might be built into the city walls, and a window or other opening in one might have been how the Christians were able to smuggle Saul out. Ananias seems to be a minor character in the story of Saul's conversion; the Lord sends him to heal Saul and baptize him, and then Ananias fades out of history. Yet there is much to learn from him. He appears to be nobody in particular, simply "a disciple at Damascus" (Acts 9:10)—not a church leader, as far as we know, or an especially notable person. Ananias's name means "The Lord is gracious," and this is very appropriate for the man God uses to bring Saul to know Jesus and His forgiveness. Ananias is also faithful; he is frightened and questions Jesus' command, but he carries it out nonetheless. He even addresses the persecutor Saul as "brother" when he lays hands on him (v. 17). What a wonderful example of Christ's forgiving love this ordinary Christian was!

Central Truth

Expect that God can make amazing changes in the hearts and lives of people, including ours.

Objectives

- Recognize that God chooses us and comes to us with His call for repentance and His gifts of faith and salvation.
- Rely on the power of the Holy Spirit to use us as His tools/instruments for sharing God's love and message.
- Give thanks for the blessing of Christian friends who support us in our Christian lives.

Materials

- Hymnals and music CDs
- Reproducible 89

Bible Prep

Post in advance so students can bookmark references before class time.

- Acts 9
- Luke 9
- 2 Corinthians 11
- Romans 8

Devotions

Aidan slammed into the house. "Mom!" he shouted. "Mark and Lucas say that Uncle Bill is a murderer!"

His mother looked up and sighed. "Come here, sweetheart," she said. "I need to talk to you."

Aidan's face went white. "What?" he said. "Why do we need to talk? They are liars, aren't they?"

His mom led him to the couch and sat with him. "When Bill was a teenager, he got involved with a bad group," she said. "They were doing drugs, and some were even selling them to make money. Your uncle didn't do that, but his best friends did—and one day, they asked him to go with them to pick up a new supply.

"Nobody knows exactly what happened next—Bill says there was an argument, and someone pulled out a gun. Bill had a gun too—he used to carry one because he thought it was cool—and he pulled his gun out, and, well . . ."

Aidan looked sick. "Somebody died?"

His mother nodded. "Bill said he didn't intend to kill anybody, but it did happen. And he went to jail for a long, long time."

"But—" said Aidan. "But- but- Uncle Bill's a Christian! He's not a bad guy! He's even studying to be a pastor now! How could that story be true?"

"I know it's hard to believe," his mother said, "but it's true. When he was in jail, someone told him about Jesus and gave him a Bible to read. And the Holy Spirit turned his life around. Over the years, I've watched him grow and change from the man I remember. And now he wants to tell other people about Jesus by becoming a pastor."

"But what should I say to Mark and Lucas?" asked Aidan.

"Tell them the truth," his mother advised. "Tell them that Jesus changed Uncle Bill's heart, and He can do that for anybody. Only Jesus could make such a dramatic change. God promises to forgive and forget, and we should too. He says in Jeremiah 31:34, 'I will forgive their iniquity, and I will remember their sin no more.'"

The grace of God is amazing, and He blesses each of our lives with His grace and forgiveness. Let's sing about that now. Sing "Amazing Grace" (*LSB* 744; recorded as *Hymn of the Month* for grade 5, December).

INTO the lesson

Explain: **Today we are going to talk about a conversion. To *convert* means to make a significant change. For example, if people convert an empty basement into a family room, what changes might they make?** (New paint, flooring, furniture, and so forth) **A conversion van is a van that has been changed considerably since it was built in a factory. What changes might have occurred?** (Perhaps decorative detailing on the outside paint, high-powered CD and DVD players, and so forth) **What is different about the kind of car that is called a convertible?** (It can change from having its top up or down.) **People can change too. As we will see in today's Bible narrative, the Holy Spirit can change people from hopeless, unbelieving sinners into forgiven people of God.**

LESSON 89

Saul Becomes a Christian

Converted

Read about the great change (conversion) in Saul (a.k.a. Paul) in Acts 9:1–31. Then tell what each of these had to do with Saul's experience.

1. A bright light — The supernatural light came from heaven and signaled the presence of God.
2. The voice from heaven — Jesus Himself spoke to Saul, demanding that he stop persecutions, and giving him instructions about what would happen next.
3. Saul's blindness — Though it related to Saul's spiritual blindness, his physical blindness forced Saul to be dependent on God's timing, power, and plans.
4. Ananias — Chosen by God, he was instructed to commission Saul in the work he should do—taking the Gospel to the Gentiles—and to baptize Saul in the Christian faith.
5. Barnabas — When others still feared Saul, he spoke well of Saul and the changes that had occurred in his heart and in his life. He was a defender and encourager.

Instrument

The task God gave His new instrument, Saul/Paul, was to spread the Gospel to the Gentiles. He was well suited to this task because he had grown up in a Greek-speaking city (Tarsus), he had been raised in the Jewish faith (as a Pharisee), he was a Roman citizen, and now he was a follower of "the Way." All of these factors combined to give him direct access to many different groups of people.

Saul/Paul used two key methods in his work of spreading the Gospel. He went on missionary trips, using various means of transportation to reach many parts of the Roman Empire (the then-known world). After establishing Christian churches in an area, he would move on, but he would continue to contact these growing churches through letters, which are also called "epistles." Most of these epistles are in the Bible, in the New Testament.

Covenant Connection

Saul knew many facts about Jesus. He knew Jesus with his head; but he didn't know Jesus with his heart. It was Jesus who came and gave Saul a change of heart. The grace of God turned Saul's life around and sent him in another direction. In Ezekiel 36:26 God says, "I will give you a new heart, and a new spirit I will put within you." When the Spirit of the Lord comes on you, 1 Samuel 10:6 says, you are changed into a different person. And the apostle Paul himself, now chosen and changed by the Lord, says in 2 Corinthians 5:17, "If anyone is in Christ, he is a new creation. The old has passed away; behold, the new has come." Paul also described this in 1 Timothy 1:14, saying, "The grace of our Lord overflowed for me with the faith and love that are in Christ Jesus."

184

INTO our lives

Converted

Read the Bible narrative and then use the Student Book activity to explore it further. Point out that Saul/Paul knew he was blessed because after his encounter with the risen Lord Jesus, **he recognized that he had been the worst of sinners, fighting against the Lord Himself. But by God's grace, he was forgiven in the name of Jesus.** Have students use a red pen or marker and print this phrase on the picture of Saul: "New and Improved." It was the power of the Holy Spirit who made Saul a new person.

Point out that when Ananias spoke to Saul, he called Saul his "brother." This is very significant because it is an indication of forgiveness for the past misdeeds, and it is a welcoming invitation into the fellowship of Christians. (Make sure your students understand that this Ananias is *not* the deceptive liar of the same name who was married to Sapphira [Lesson 86].)

Note: The name *Saul/Paul* is listed in the Student Book along with the abbreviation *a.k.a.*, which stands for "also known as." These are given because Saul was known by both names. Some people think that Saul changed his name after his conversion.

378

Suffering

What a privilege it was for Saul/Paul to be called in Acts 9:15 as an instrument of the Lord! But wait! Put on the brakes! Things change very quickly in verse 16, where the Lord says, "I will show him how much he must suffer for the sake of My name."

Whoa! Some might say, "Shouldn't life as a Christian be a bed of roses because Jesus is there to take care of all our troubles?" Jesus never said that! In fact, what did He say in Luke 9:23?

"If anyone would come after Me, let him deny himself and take up his cross daily and follow Me."

Read Paul's list of the troubles that he encountered as he spread the Gospel of Jesus in his missionary travels. Read 2 Corinthians 11:24–27.

As long as we are in this sinful world, we will have troubles. There will be times that people tempt, intimidate, laugh at, or reject us for standing up for Jesus. But He promises to be with us and to bless us even in the midst of our difficulties. What comfort and encouragement do we have in Romans 8:28, 38–39? *God will work good, even from a bad situation, and nothing can separate us from His love.*

Paradoxes

A *paradox* is a situation or saying that seems to contradict itself, in which the before and after are opposites. There were many paradoxes in the life of Saul/Paul. Complete the chart to indicate the reversals in his life.

Planned to hurt the apostles	Planned to help the apostles
Enemy of Christians	Became a Christian—and their friend
Unbeliever	Faithful follower of Jesus
Proud, self-righteous	Humbly described himself as the worst sinner
Full of anger and turmoil	Full of peace
Wanted to stop the Gospel	Wanted to spread the Gospel

"Chief of sinners though I be,
Jesus shed His blood for me."

Remember

"You are a chosen race, a royal priesthood, a holy nation, a people for His own possession, that you may proclaim the excellencies of Him who called you out of darkness into His marvelous light." (1 Peter 2:9)

185

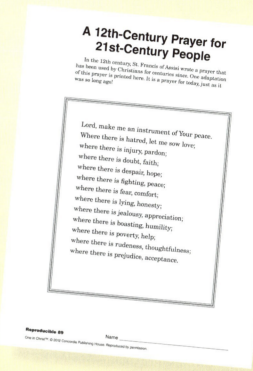

A 12th-Century Prayer for 21st-Century People

In the 12th century, St. Francis of Assisi wrote a prayer that has been used by Christians for centuries since. One adaptation of this prayer is printed here. It is a prayer for today, just as it was so long ago!

Lord, make me an instrument of Your peace.
Where there is hatred, let me sow love;
where there is injury, pardon;
where there is doubt, faith;
where there is despair, hope;
where there is fighting, peace;
where there is fear, comfort;
where there is lying, honesty;
where there is jealousy, appreciation;
where there is boasting, humility;
where there is poverty, help;
where there is rudeness, thoughtfulness;
where there is prejudice, acceptance.

Reproducible 89   Name _____
One in Christ™. © 2012 Concordia Publishing House. Reproduced by permission.

Actually, *Saul* was his Jewish name and *Paul* was the Greek version. He did not change it because both names already existed. However, once he began his ministry, working mostly among the Gentiles in Greek-speaking areas, he was usually referred to by his Greek name, *Paul*.

We, too, are sinners who have been mightily blessed with the grace of God. Sing together "Chief of Sinners" (*LSB* 611; recorded as *Hymn of the Month* for grade 3, February).

Instrument

Point out that in Acts 9:2, Saul was wanting to arrest people who followed "the Way." **What is "the Way," and where does it lead?** ("The Way" was an early term for Christianity. We know where the Way leads—to forgiveness and eternal life. In John 14:6, Jesus Himself says, "I am the way, and the truth, and the life." Saul/Paul, through the call of Jesus, became a follower of the Way!)

God's purpose for Paul was to use him as a tool and instrument for spreading the Gospel. A tool has no power of its own; it is dependent on the person and the person's power source. Paul, as a tool, was dependent on the Holy Spirit in all that he did in spreading the Gospel. The same is true of all that we do for and in the name of Jesus. Let's sing now about passing God's love and forgiveness and message of salvation to others. Sing "Pass It On" (*AGPS* 196; recorded on *JPS*).

Suffering

Point out that some people today have the mistaken notion that God will give us everything we want and life will be easy. Then, when troubles come along, these people question God and even blame Him! But God did not promise to remove all problems and pain *until* we are in heaven. We can be certain that when we are taken from this sin-filled world full of the consequences of sin, we will live forever with Jesus. (See Revelation 21:3–4.)

Paradoxes

After working through the Student Book activity, distribute Reproducible 89. Say, **This is an ancient prayer from medieval times that is still relevant to today's lesson and to our lives today. The prayer begins by asking God to use us as His instruments. The prayer continues with paradoxes that indicate the changes that take place in our lives as the Lord lives and works in our hearts and lives.** Explore the prayer, perhaps underlining words that are opposites. Then pray the prayer together.

Lesson Support

Reaching Every Child

Learning Disabilities: Research estimates that approximately 5–10 percent of the population has some type of learning disability. A learning disability is defined as a neurobiological disorder that affects one's ability to process information. These students usually have above-average intelligence, but their academic achievement falls below expectations. These disabilities can be evident in written and/or spoken language, listening, and reasoning. There are many teaching strategies and modifications that you can incorporate into a lesson you are teaching. Some helpful ideas include—but are not limited to—the following:

• Relate your lesson to a personal experience.
• Limit expectations to two or three per unit.
• Evaluate projects instead of doing traditional testing.
• Concentrate on students' strengths, and incorporate them into the lesson.
• Model assignment expectations; show an example of the product.
• Create small group activities.

Curriculum Connection

As you study one of the greatest missionaries of the Christian Church, consider using section 6.2.1.34, Origins and Rise of Christianity, found in the sixth-grade Social Studies volume of the Concordia Curriculum Guide series. Together with students, trace the ways Christianity spread—first in Palestine, then abroad among the Jews, then to the Gentiles, and to the farthest reaches of the Roman Empire. How did Roman rule make the task of spreading the Gospel easier?

Searching Further

Find out as much as you can about the city of Damascus of Saul's time. Also find out how far Damascus was from Jerusalem, and how long it would take to get there—and to return with walking prisoners! What does this say about Saul's attitude toward Christianity? Why do you think Saul chose this distant city as his base for persecuting more Christians? (When persecutions began in Jerusalem, many Christians fled to Damascus for safety among other Christians already living there.)

Critical thinking

Jesus said to Ananias, "I will show him how much he must suffer for the sake of My name" (Acts 9:16). This is an ominous, even frightening thing to say, yet Saul seems joyful about his sufferings! (See Romans 5:3–5; Colossians 1:24–26.) **Why do you think Saul is able to rejoice in his sufferings? Are you ever able to do that?**

Faith in Action

Ananias did what the Lord told him and went to help and heal a man who was his enemy. Encourage your students to identify one person in their lives with whom they don't get along very well—even an enemy—and share a secret kindness with that person.

Ananias went to visit Saul to heal him as Jesus commanded. Later, the Christians of Damascus helped their old-enemy-turned-friend escape the city by lowering him from the wall in a basket. These were both very practical ways of showing love to a person in need. During the coming week, can your students come up with a practical way of showing love to someone in need? Do some brainstorming together.

Unit 9—The Christian Church Grows

Theme

This unit continues to look at the Early Christian Church after Jesus ascended into heaven and sent the gift of the Holy Spirit at Pentecost. This unit will focus on individual Christians and significant incidents in their lives, so another theme for this unit could be "Heroes of Faith." While acknowledging that Jesus is the ultimate hero of the entire Scriptures, it is also of value to see how Jesus worked in the hearts and lives of His people as they came to faith, lived by faith, and shared that faith with others. This is a most appropriate time to bring in the Heroes of Faith book series, available from Concordia Publishing House. Written for fifth and sixth graders, these paperback books share the stories of Christians from the sixteenth century to more recent times. While celebrities and sports figures tend to be the heroes of many children, it is important for young people to see the examples of people courageously and generously living their lives for Jesus. Through all of these Bible stories, we want to connect to contemporary students, encouraging them to live their lives for Jesus in these times that are often not friendly toward a Christian way of life. Also, living for Jesus today requires the faithfulness and determination that come only from the blessings of the Holy Spirit as He works in our hearts to guide us in faith and in our faith walk through life!

Worship

Appropriate to this unit's theme, the hymn "Thine Forever, God of Love" (*LSB* 687; recorded as *Hymn of the Month for grade 6, May*) is a hymn of dedication that will be featured this month. The psalm of the month is Psalm 95:1–7, a psalm of praise and rejoicing. We will also be learning to sing this psalm from the Matins Liturgy (*LSB*, p. 220). Since this is the concluding unit of this level of the One in Christ series, it would be appropriate to review some of the hymns learned this year that are found on the *Hymns of the Month* and *Hymns of the Season* CDs. Also consider reviewing hymns from *All God's People Sing!* (*AGPS*), particularly those recorded on the *Jesus' People Sing!* (*JPS*) CD. Another possibility for review is CD 10 from the *Hymns of the Month* set, which has hymns with lyrics sung in Spanish.

Resources

Though the *Teacher Resource Book* provides many extra materials to use with this curriculum, these resources are also available on the One in Christ Portal, which includes access to links to other Web sites, interactive whiteboard applications, slide presentations, and other resources for the lesson of the day. Tests can be printed out or taken online (with a self-checking feature!). Unit 9 test answers: (1) a; (2) c; (3) b; (4) d; (5) c; (6) b; (7) e; (8) a; (9) c; (10) b. Note that the titles of this unit's lessons are listed in the column at the right to give you an overview of the material covered in this unit.

Unit 9

90. Cornelius
91. Rhoda
92. Tabitha
93. A Mission Trip
94. Lydia
95. The Jailer at Philippi
96. Paul at Mars Hill
97. Paul's Nephew to the Rescue
98. Paul on Trial
99. Shipwrecked
100. Paul and Timothy

Bulletin Board

As we study the Early Christian Church, it is important to remember that the Church continues throughout time with the blessings, grace, and power given by the Holy Spirit. Cut apart and display the sections of this bulletin board starting with the cross, because Jesus is the center of everything in the Church. Add the first section as a reminder of the many early believers we learn about in the Book of Acts. Add the second section, which illustrates faithful Christians throughout various centuries. (Their stories are available in the Heroes of Faith paperback series, available from Concordia Publishing House.) Add the third section to indicate that your students are the continuation of the Church today. Ask students to bring a photograph of themselves and pin the photos onto this section of the display. The last section reminds us that the Christian Church consists of people of all ages, genders, races, and nationalities. Ask students to find a variety of people pictured in magazines or newspapers and add their photos to the final section. Pray that God's Word will spread to people all over the world!

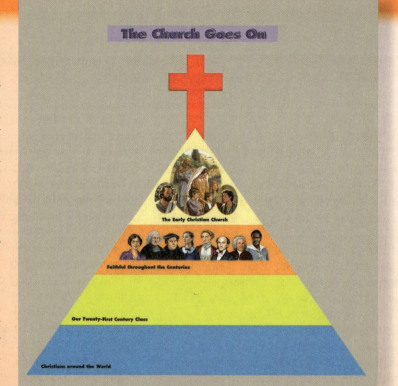

Bible Book Overview

The Student Book Appendix has a valuable feature that gives a summary of each book of the Bible. Looking at the summaries of sixty-six books can be overwhelming, so it is suggested that each month/unit, your class look at the summaries of just a few of these books. During unit 9, introduce the last nine books of the New Testament. Eight of these books are known as the "General Epistles," written by several authors (as compared to the previous Pauline Epistles), but all inspired by the Holy Spirit. The last book is unique in that it is written by John, who also wrote a Gospel book and three epistles. It tells of the vision of heaven that God revealed to him, so it is a fitting conclusion to the Holy Scriptures. Point out to students that the book is symbolic, not literal, because John's look into heaven could not be described in earthly terms. So he uses figurative and symbolic language as the only tools for understanding something so incomprehensible. Read together and discuss the summaries of these nine books in the Student Book Appendix when you have available time. (Note that a copy of the Student Book Appendix is included in the back of this Teacher Guide.)

Unit 9—The Christian Church Grows

Lesson 90

Cornelius
Acts 10:1—11:18

Background

We have all heard stories about people who do the right things for the wrong reasons. In Luke's account of Peter and Cornelius, we see the opposite side of the coin. Peter is doing the wrong thing for what he perceives to be the right reason. As a practicing Jew, Peter had been taught never to associate with Gentiles, not to visit them in their homes, and especially not to eat with them. But God used a startling vision, repeated three times, to show Peter that salvation through Christ was for *all* people, Jew and Gentile alike. The old paradigm Peter knew was based on Scripture—the Law given to Moses. The new paradigm came by grace through Jesus Christ.

Paul, too, was doing what he believed was right when he persecuted the Christians. Then Christ's appearance to him on the Damascus Road changed his mind forever. How often do we, as Christians and as a Church, do the wrong things for the right reasons? Are our attitudes toward people who are "not like us"—foreigners, followers of other religions, punk rockers in Goth apparel, and others with alternate lifestyles—based on what we believe the Bible teaches us? Are we missing the point of Jesus' message of love, forgiveness, and acceptance for all people? They, too, need to hear the truth of God's grace and mercy. Do we share this in action as well as in what we say?

Jesus criticized the Pharisees for following the letter of the Mosaic Law while completely missing its spirit: "You tithe mint and dill and cumin, and have neglected . . . justice and mercy and faithfulness. . . . You clean the outside of the cup and the plate, but inside they are full of greed and self-indulgence" (Matthew 23:23, 25). Let's reexamine our own attitudes, asking for guidance in showing compassion.

Central Truth
God wants all people from every nation, both Jews and Gentiles, to believe in Jesus Christ and be saved.

Objectives
- Acknowledge that we find it hard to love people who are different from us in language, culture, class, or ethnicity.
- Rejoice that God has chosen us Himself to be among His loved and redeemed people.
- Share the Good News of Jesus, through words and actions, with those around us, regardless of whether they are like us or not.

Materials
- Hymnals and music CDs
- Reproducible 90

Bible Prep
Post in advance so students can bookmark references before class time.
- Psalm 95
- Acts 10

Devotions

In some communities, adults and children who are deaf, like other people with handicaps, are regarded as different from you and me. Hearing-impaired children may be excluded or isolated from activities that other children enjoy. Adults may have trouble finding jobs or understanding directions given to them orally. Sometimes deaf people are regarded as unintelligent if they do not respond when someone speaks to them. Often they are ignored or excluded when others feel it is too hard to communicate with them.

Hearing-impaired residents at the Florida State School for the Blind and Deaf in St. Augustine have found a place where they are welcomed and accepted at St. Mark Lutheran Church, located across the street from the school. Each week, deaf residents fill the front rows at St. Mark for Sunday worship services. An American Sign Language interpreter faces the residents and signs the words of the hymns, prayers, Scripture readings, liturgy, and sermon. When the Lord's Supper is celebrated, the pastor himself signs the Words of Institution—"Our Lord Jesus Christ, on the night when He was betrayed, took bread . . ."—and the deaf worshipers receive the body and blood of Jesus. With their fingers, hands, and voices, the deaf worshipers praise God for the gift of salvation.

St. Mark the Evangelist, after whom that church is named, recorded the account of Jesus healing a man who was hearing impaired (Mark 7:31–37). Jesus put His fingers into the man's ears and touched the man's tongue. Then He looked to heaven, sighed, and said, "'Ephphatha,' that is, 'Be opened'" (v. 34). Immediately, the man could hear and speak plainly. The people who had witnessed the miracle were astounded. Remembering the prophecies of Isaiah, they declared, "He has done all things well. He even makes the deaf hear and the mute speak" (v. 37).

While our first reaction to someone who is different from us might be to stare, to whisper about them, or perhaps even to laugh or walk away, Jesus calls us to reach out with kindness, overlooking any differences, and seeing in that person a potential brother or sister in Christ.

Sing "Brothers and Sisters in Christ" (*AGPS* 78; recorded on *JPS*). Speak together Psalm 95:1–7.

INTO the Word

Two Dreams and a Sermon

Call it a culture clash, a collision of two opposing worlds, resulting in a paradigm shift for Peter and the Early Christian Church. **God used an inspired dream to teach Peter that His grace through Jesus Christ was not only for the Jews, but for all people, regardless of language, culture, class, or ethnicity.** God called Peter to step out of his comfort zone and bring the Good News about Jesus to Cornelius and his household; He poured out the Holy Spirit on these Gentiles, and they were baptized into the family of faith.

Read about Cornelius's dream with your students from the Student Book and then in Acts 10:1–8. Explain that a Roman legion consisted of six thousand soldiers, divided into ten cohorts of six hundred soldiers. Cornelius was a centurion, commanding a hundred soldiers in the Italian Cohort. Cornelius and his household (family and servants) knew the God of the Jews, prayed to Him as the Jews did, and gave generously to help the poor. Cornelius did not yet know Jesus as his Savior, although he must have known that the prophets had promised a Messiah. The angel who appeared to Cornelius in his dream called him by name, terrifying Cornelius. Through this inspired dream, God prepared Cornelius to hear and receive the Good News about Jesus, his Savior. Following the angel's words, Cornelius immediately sent two servants and a trusted soldier to Joppa to find Peter.

Then read about Peter's dream, which came around noon, when he was up on Simon's roof, praying. You can almost imagine his stomach growling as his mind wanders to thoughts of food. But the food presented to Peter in the sheet that descended from heaven was unlike anything Peter had ever eaten. Peter, as a pious Jew, had always obeyed the Jewish dietary laws. **Among other restrictions, he had never eaten pork or other mammals that didn't have a split hoof and chewed their cud, no sea creatures other than fish with scales, no birds of prey, nor birds that feed on the carcasses of dead animals.** These animals had been listed as unclean in Leviticus 11. But now a voice from heaven told Peter, "Kill and eat" (Acts 10:13). Peter protested that he had never eaten anything that was unclean. But the voice told him, "What God has made clean, do not call common" (v. 15). This was repeated two more times, and the sheet full of animals was taken back to heaven. The emissaries from Cornelius arrived, and the Holy Spirit told Peter to go with them immediately. These visions were not random incidents; God's exact timing was in effect.

Read about Peter's sermon. Remind students that Peter's audience on Pentecost consisted of Jews from all parts of the world; the listeners at Cornelius's home were all Gentiles. God gave His blessing on Peter's sermon by pouring out the Holy Spirit on Cornelius and his household. This served as a witness to Peter and the other Jewish Christians who had accompanied him that God truly wanted all people to be saved. **Peter's paradigm shift led to an encounter with the Christian leadership in Jerusalem. When Peter related the story of his experience with Cornelius and the outpouring of the Spirit on the Gentiles, the Church glorified God: "Then to the Gentiles also God has granted repentance that leads to life"** (Acts 11:18).

LESSON 90

Cornelius

Two Dreams and a Sermon

Cornelius's Dream:
As a Roman centurion stationed in Palestine, I have become familiar with the religion of the Jews. I believe their God will send a Messiah through whom I will be declared righteous before God. I give generously to help the poor, and I pray to God as the Jews do, even though I know the Jewish people do not accept me because I am a Gentile.

Yesterday afternoon, as I was praying, I dreamed I saw an angel who called me by name. I was terrified and asked, "What is it, Lord?" The angel told me God had heard my prayers and saw my heart. The angel told me to send men to Joppa to find Simon Peter, who was staying with Simon the tanner in a house by the sea. When the angel had departed, I told two of my servants and a trusted soldier everything that had happened, and I sent them to Joppa to find the man called Peter.

Peter's Dream:
As I was praying on the roof of Simon's house, I became very hungry, since it was about noon. I must have fallen into a trance, because I dreamed I saw the heavens open, and something like a great sheet holding all kinds of animals, reptiles, and birds. A voice called, "Rise, Peter, and eat." Well, I was very hungry, but I have never in my life eaten anything the Jewish law declares to be common or unclean, and I said so. The voice came again and told me, "What God has made clean, do not call common." This happened three times.

As I was puzzling about what the vision meant, three men came looking for me. The Holy Spirit told me, "Rise and go down and accompany them without hesitation, for I have sent them." So I went down and told the men I was the one they were looking for. The next day, I went with them to meet Cornelius.

Peter's Sermon:
Cornelius greeted me, and he told me about his vision. He had invited many of his friends and relatives to hear about Jesus. Now I understood what my strange vision meant. I told Cornelius, "You yourselves know it is unlawful for a Jew to associate with or visit anyone of another nation, but God has shown me that I should not call any person common or unclean. . . . Truly I understand that God shows no partiality, but in any nation, anyone who fears Him and does what is right is acceptable to Him.

"As for the word He sent to Israel, preaching Good News of peace through Jesus Christ—He is Lord of all. Everyone who believes in Him receives forgiveness of sins through His name."

While I was speaking, the Holy Spirit fell on all who heard the Word, even on the Gentiles. I called for water and baptized them in the name of Jesus Christ.

Review

Covenant Connection
Peter and some of the other Jewish Christians were still hanging on to some of the practices of the Old Covenant of the Old Testament, requiring that new converts adhere to old Jewish rituals. The Lord dramatically reminded Peter that Jesus gives us the New Covenant in the New Testament, which is for all who believe in Him as their Savior. Jesus has removed obstacles and boundaries, offering His grace and forgiveness to all. There are no restrictions of nationality or ethnicity. As Christians, we are one family by faith in Jesus.

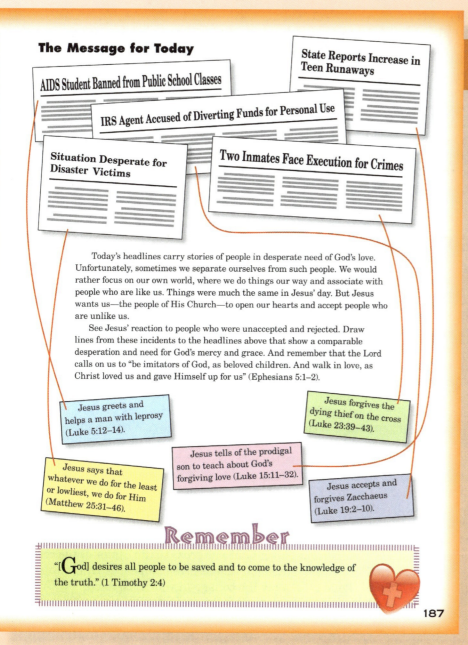

INTO our lives

The Message for Today

Your students are growing up in a global village, surrounded by diversity in language, culture, class, and ethnicity. Yet the membership of your congregation and the enrollment of your school probably represent a more homogeneous group. Are your students comfortable to remain with people who are "just like me"? Or do they reach out with the Good News about Jesus to all people, regardless of language, culture, class, or ethnicity?

Read and discuss the five headlines as displayed in the Student Book. Consider that the student with AIDS was banned from school because parents of the other students feared he would expose their children to the illness. Teen runaways usually have a history of family problems, perhaps involving truancy, run-ins with the police, and drug or alcohol use. Criminals facing execution usually have a long record of serious criminal activity. Embezzlement or misuse of public funds costs taxpayers money and destroys trust in government. The hungry, homeless, and those struck by tragedy present problems for governments and social service agencies; their presence on the streets of our cities bothers residents and visitors alike. Are these the kinds of people you would want to avoid—you know, people who are "not like me"?

First-century Palestine was a global village too. Roman soldiers walked the streets, and officials sent by Rome kept order throughout the region. Roman roads brought traders and visitors from all over the Mediterranean region. Faithful Jews were taught not to associate with people who were not Jewish like themselves. So what did Jesus do? What do His words and actions tell us about the way He wants us to treat people who are different from us?

In Luke 5:12–14, Jesus heals a man with leprosy. People with leprosy were required to leave their families, jobs, and synagogues because of the fear of contagion, much like AIDS patients today. Jesus reached out and touched the sick man. According to Jewish law, touching the man with leprosy would defile Jesus; on the contrary, Jesus' touch made the leper clean. Jesus' example teaches us to reach out to the suffering in spite of the social stigma involved.

In Luke 15:11–32, Jesus tells the story of the prodigal son, who demanded his share of his father's wealth and ran away from home and lived a sin-filled life. When he returned in poverty, his father forgave him, just as our heavenly Father welcomes sinners who return to Him in repentance.

In Luke 23:39–43, Jesus forgives the dying thief on the cross. His example shows us that no sin is too great to be forgiven. The second stanza of the hymn "Today Your Mercy Calls Us" (*LSB* 915) exemplifies this, saying, "The past shall be forgotten, A present joy be giv'n, A future grace be promised."

In Luke 19:2–10, Zacchaeus the tax collector had diverted public funds for his own use, just like the IRS agent in the headline. Although the people of Jericho shunned him, Jesus called him, forgave him, and went to visit him in his home. Through Jesus' acceptance and forgiveness, Zacchaeus's life was changed forever. Following Jesus' example, we forgive those who are guilty of public wrongdoing.

In Matthew 25:31–46, Jesus tells Christians that whatever they have done for others in need, they have really done for Him. God wants us to back up our words about people in need with action.

Now ask your students to dig a little deeper, look at their daily lives, and examine attitudes that are not the "headline makers" we have just observed, but are still serious. Very often the things that separate us from other people are simple differences. With such types of prejudices, we are setting ourselves up as the standard, avoiding or even harming those who have divergent qualities. Instead, God desires that we learn about them, appreciate these differences, and welcome them into a friendship that includes welcoming them into the family of God. Use Reproducible 90 to discuss some of these issues.

Lesson Support

Curriculum Connection

God used an odd but powerful dramatic scene and dialogue to help Peter understand that he should not shun the Gentiles but instead tell them about Jesus. As a result, people from all the nations of the world will be included among God's people at the Last Day, praising our Savior. Your students can imitate God's wisdom here by writing scripts that support similar social messages; have them use section 6.2.5.3, Script That Supports Political or Societal Issues or Goals. You can find this in the sixth-grade Performing Arts volume of the Concordia Curriculum Guide series.

Hands to Serve

Invite a guest who knows American Sign Language to visit your classroom. Ask him or her to teach the students one of their favorite hymns in sign language. When students are comfortable singing the hymn with the hand signs, encourage them to teach the song with its hand signs to a class of younger children. They may also want to teach the younger children a few simple phrases in sign language—"Jesus loves you," "I love Jesus," "Jesus died for you and me," and other such phrases would be appropriate. The two classes could then sing and sign their song together for a school chapel service. Sixth-grade students may also enjoy reading a simple biography of Helen Keller, who, though deaf and blind, become an inspiration to many.

Searching Further

What would it be like to have a handicap? Ask each student to pretend he or she has a handicap. Students may choose blindness, deafness, developmental disability, autism, cerebral palsy, paralysis of the legs or arms, or any other disability with which they are familiar. Then take your students on a tour of your church and school buildings, considering from this viewpoint what obstacles can be observed. How would the disability they imagined affect their participation in the activities that take place in your church or school? What changes to the buildings would be necessary to enable them to participate more fully? What changes to the activities themselves would make participation more possible or enjoyable? Ask students to compile their ideas in a letter to your church council.

God showed Peter that the Good News about Jesus was meant for all people, regardless of language, culture, class, or ethnicity. His message to us today is exactly the same. Work together as a class to make a collage of pictures of people from magazines and newspapers and arrange and glue them on a large piece of poster board. Overlap the pictures until the entire poster board is covered. Then cut a cross from black construction paper. Glue the cross to the center of the collage as a reminder that Jesus loves, died for, and forgives all people. At the top of the collage, write "Just Like Me." Display the collage in your classroom.

Teacher Tips

A wise teacher once observed that the attitudes we want to see in our children are caught, not taught. Think about your own attitudes regarding people who are "not like me." Do your students see you treat all adults and children with respect, regardless of language, culture, class, or ethnicity? Are you open to new ideas and new ways of doing things in your classroom? Do you show as much enthusiasm with the slow learner as you do with your more gifted students? Do you adapt your teaching methods to the learning styles of children from other classes or cultures? As you answer these questions privately, ask God to forgive you for the times you have failed to reach out to students and parents who are different from you or the majority of members of your congregation. Ask the Holy Spirit's guidance as you continue to teach all of God's children, whatever their language, culture, class, or ethnicity.

UNIT 9—THE CHRISTIAN CHURCH GROWS

LESSON 91

Rhoda

ACTS 12:1–24

Background

Prayer is a vital part of our Christian life, a precious gift God has given us in promising to hear and answer us when we pray. Jesus said, "Ask, and it will be given to you" (Matthew 7:7). Paul commanded the Thessalonian Christians to "Pray without ceasing" (1 Thessalonians 5:17). Yet prayer is not an additional Means of Grace, nor is it a work by which we please God. We come to God in prayer as He has commanded, often speaking His own inspired words back to Him, as when we pray the Psalms or repeat His scriptural promises. He does not come to us through prayer, however, but through His Holy Word. "Long ago, at many times and in many ways, God spoke to our fathers by the prophets, but in these last days He has spoken to us by His Son, whom He appointed the heir of all things, through whom also He created the world" (Hebrews 1:1–2). God answers prayers in His own way and in His own time, according to His own will. Jesus encouraged His disciples to always pray and not lose heart, illustrating this point with the parable of the persistent widow (Luke 18:1–8). Following this command of Jesus, some of today's charismatic religious groups have made a work of prayer, endeavoring to please God by their constant elaborate petitions and thinking that an unanswered prayer means the person has not prayed enough or has not prayed properly. But this is not what God has told us. We are to trust that He will answer because of His grace and mercy, not because of our actions. And He will answer at the time and in the way that is best for us. Plus, what comfort it gives to Christians to know that "the Spirit helps us in our weakness. For we do not know what to pray for as we ought, but the Spirit Himself intercedes for us with groanings too deep for words" (Romans 8:26).

Central Truth

God hears and answers us when we pray.

Objectives

- Repent of the many times we fail to pray or pray only halfheartedly because of our weak trust in God.
- Recognize the wonderful, gracious gift God has given us in promising to hear our prayers.
- Begin to pray more regularly in every need, asking for help and giving thanks and praise.

Materials

- Hymnals and music CDs
- Reproducible 91
- Web Resource 91a

Bible Prep

Post in advance so students can bookmark references before class time.

- Psalm 95:1–7
- Acts 12:1–24
- Acts 7:59–60
- Acts 2:38
- Acts: 4:24
- Acts 12:5
- Romans 1:8
- Ephesians 1:3
- Ephesians 1:16
- 1 John 1:9

Devotions

The summer drought was entering its third month. On farms, the cornstalks stood stunted and drooping. Tractors raised clouds of dust as they crossed the hard, cracked earth of the fields. Gardens produced only a few small tomatoes and peppers. City lawns lay dead and brown, since residents had been asked to conserve water by not watering their grass. Everyone was desperate for rain. The president of the church council came to talk to the pastor. "We've tried everything else, Pastor," he said. "It's time to pray." So the pastor scheduled a special prayer service to pray for rain.

The little church was filled on the afternoon of the prayer service. The congregation sang; the choir offered special anthems. The pastor, the president of the church council, and all of the people prayed for rain. As the pastor raised his hands to bless the congregation at the end of the service, a deafening clap of thunder shook the building, and rain began to fall. The people in the church looked at one another in amazement. They had not trusted that God would answer or answer so quickly. No one had brought an umbrella!

We are often like the people in that little church. We fail to pray, or we pray as a last resort when everything else has failed. We pray halfheartedly, not really trusting God to hear and answer our prayers. When we don't get the answer we want—the answer that is according to our will, not God's will—we are disappointed and think our prayers have not been answered. But God does hear and answer our prayers—in accord with His will, which is always best for our eternal good.

Sing together "Thine Forever, God of Love" (*LSB* 687; recorded as *Hymn of the Month for grade 6, May*). Speak together Psalm 95:1–7. Pray, **Forgive us, Lord, for failing to pray or for praying halfheartedly. Help us to trust You to hear and answer our prayers in accord with Your good and perfect will. We pray in Jesus' name. Amen.**

INTO the Word

A Servant Girl's Story

Rhoda's excitement at hearing Peter's voice . . . the disbelief of the people praying for Peter's release when they heard the servant's report . . . Peter—a wanted man—left standing in the dark . . . it's no wonder students love this story! But in addition to all of these details Luke records for us, this story is about prayer—God's power to answer prayer, and our need to trust Him to hear and answer our prayers according to His will.

Refer back to the story of the first martyr, Stephen. After he was stoned, the rapid increase in the number of believers in the Early Church clearly alarmed the religious leaders in Jerusalem, and persecution faced the followers of the Way. In an effort to put down the new religious movement, King Herod executed James, who was the brother of John and a son of Zebedee. Students should recall that this James, along with Peter and John, formed the inner circle of Jesus' disciples, present with Him at the transfiguration and in the Garden of Gethsemane. This King Herod was probably Herod Agrippa (who ruled AD 37–44), tetrarch of Galilee, Judah, and Samaria.

When Herod saw that James's death pleased the Jewish religious leaders, he arrested Peter. He planned to keep Peter in prison under heavy security until the Passover crowds had left Jerusalem, at which time Peter would be tried and executed. The Early Christian Church responded to his imprisonment with earnest prayers on Peter's behalf.

The thrilling account of Peter's rescue from prison follows. God works through the means of both angels and apostles. Throughout the Book of Acts, angels serve primarily as messengers of salvation and freedom from persecution, often emphasizing that they are real, rather than mere visions. In this case, the reality of the angelic escort is seen as the angel pushes Peter, who was sleeping calmly, and then opens the iron gate.

The angel leaves Peter before he reaches Mary's house. Remind students that this Mary is the sister of Barnabas and the mother of John Mark, not the mother of Jesus. Mary probably hosted one of the house churches in Jerusalem, and the believers had gathered in her home to pray for Peter. When Rhoda reported that Peter was at the gate, the people refused to believe it. When they finally saw Peter in person, they were amazed. Ask students to compare this reaction to that of the disciples on Easter evening. Peter tells the gathered believers all that has happened and asks them to "Tell these things to James and to the brothers" (Acts 12:17). Explain to students that this is a different James—the brother of Jesus, and the acknowledged leader of the Jerusalem Church.

Postscript: King Herod was furious that Peter had escaped. After he had searched for Peter without finding him, he questioned the sentries and ordered that they be put to death. Then Herod left for Caesarea. At Caesarea, Herod put on his royal robes, sat on his throne, and gave a speech. The people shouted that Herod was a god, not a man. Immediately, an angel of the Lord struck Herod dead, because he did not give God the glory.

Use the riddles in the "Who Said This" section and also Reproducible 91 to review the events of the Bible narrative.

Lesson 91

Rhoda

A Servant Girl's Story

My name is Rhoda, and I am a servant girl in the household of Mary, the mother of John Mark. Mary and many of her friends are followers of the Way, people who believe in Jesus, who was crucified and arose from the dead three days later. I, too, believe in Jesus as my Savior, the way to heaven.

Being a follower of Jesus has become very dangerous. Recently, King Herod had James, the brother of John, killed. When Herod saw that this pleased the Jewish people, he arrested Peter and planned to kill him too. On the night before Herod planned to execute him, Peter was bound with chains, sleeping between two soldiers, with sentries guarding the doors of the prison. Suddenly an angel stood next to Peter, and a light shone in his cell. The angel woke Peter and said, "Get up quickly." The chains fell off Peter's hands. Then the angel told Peter, "Dress yourself; put on your sandals. Wrap your cloak around yourself, and follow me." Peter followed the angel past the first and second guards. When they reached the iron gate, it swung open, and they went out into the city. Peter realized the Lord had rescued him from the hand of Herod and from certain death.

While Peter was in prison, the believers had gathered here at Mary's house to pray for him. Peter came to the house and knocked on the gate. I, of course, went to answer. When I recognized Peter's voice, I was so excited that I ran to tell the others that Peter was here, leaving Peter standing out at the gate. The people who were praying told me I was out of my mind. I insisted that it was Peter, but they said it was only his angel. Poor Peter! He knocked and knocked, until someone finally opened the gate. Peter told the amazed believers how the Lord had brought him out of prison. He asked us to tell James, the brother of Jesus, and the other church leaders all that had happened. Then Peter left and went to another place where he would be safe.

Who Said This?

1. Peter's in prison! Proclaim the news!
   Maybe this will please the Jews.
   Herod

2. Four at a time, four shifts each night,
   We kept Peter right in our sight.
   Soldiers

3. Chained between two guards I lay
   While all the Christians met to pray.
   Peter

4. Get up, put sandals on your feet.
   Then follow me into the street.
   Angel

5. When I heard Peter at the gate,
   I left him there! He had to wait!
   Rhoda

6. We prayed for Peter, and we see
   God heard our prayers and set him free.
   Christian friends

Review

Covenant Connection

The prophet Isaiah said the Lord has come to "proclaim liberty to the captives, and the opening of the prison to those who are bound" (Isaiah 61:1). Jesus announced that He was the fulfillment of that prophecy. These words were true for Peter in a very physical sense. But they are true for all believers in an even greater sense: we were held captive by sin, death, and the power of the devil, but Jesus has set us free and opened heaven to all who believe!

188

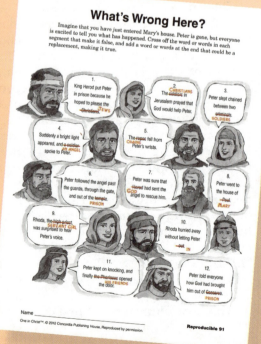

Prayer in ACTS/ACTS of Prayer

In the Book of Acts, Luke records the history of the Early Christian Church. After the outpouring of the Holy Spirit on Pentecost, Luke writes, "They [the Christians] devoted themselves to the apostles' teaching and the fellowship, to the breaking of bread and the prayers" (Acts 2:42). These Jewish Christians continued to use liturgical-style prayers they had memorized and always recited, much as Christians today use the Lord's Prayer. Their prayer life also included gathering together in homes to ask God's help in time of need.

Prayer is speaking to God in words and thoughts. God invites and commands all who believe in Jesus Christ to pray. But what should we include in our prayers? The word *ACTS* gives us a pattern for our prayers. (Your teacher will guide you through this activity.)

A Adoration	Acts 4:24	Ephesians 1:3
C Confession	1 John 1:9	Acts 2:38
T Thanksgiving	Romans 1:8	Ephesians 1:16
S Supplication	Acts 7:59–60	Acts 12:5

The Book of Acts and the writings of the apostle Paul give us examples of all four kinds of prayers used in the Early Church. Read the following passages from your Bible. Then write each verse in the category above in which it belongs: Romans 1:8; Acts 12:5; 1 John 1:9; Ephesians 1:16; Acts 7:59–60; Acts 4:24; Ephesians 1:3; Acts 2:38.

We sometimes pray halfheartedly or even fail to pray when our trust in God is weak. We ask Him to forgive us for our lack of trust and to strengthen our faith as we come to Him often in prayer. Pray with confidence. God answers, saying, "Yes," "Wait," or "I have a better idea," according to His good and holy will. We accept His answers in faith, knowing that He loves us and will always do what is for our eternal good.

Remember

"Do not be anxious about anything, but in everything by prayer and supplication with thanksgiving let your requests be made known to God." (Philippians 4:6)

189

INTO the lesson

ACTS of Prayer

Introduce students to the *ACTS* acronym, talking about the kind of prayer each letter stands for (Adoration, Confession, Thanksgiving, Supplication). Use Web Resource 91a to display a definition and a keyword for each part of this acronym. Students are to write the keyword in the first blank after each letter in the acronym in the Student Book. Continue together with the activity, asking volunteers to read the selected Bible references aloud; decide as a group which type of prayer is being mentioned, and write the references in the two other blank lines behind each letter.

INTO our lives

Continuing with the same Student Book activity, have students review the "ACTS of Prayer" again. This time, they are to write a simple prayer statement on the longer line next to each acronym letter. Their statements should represent the type of prayer indicated. Use these statements in a group prayer. Begin with "Adoration," and ask any volunteers to lead by standing and reading their prayer statements. Point to each reader; after reading, the student may be seated. Follow this procedure with "Confession," "Thanksgiving," and "Supplication."

Then take another look at Web Resource 91a. Say, **Using the acronym *ACTS* to describe prayer is appropriate for this lesson from the Book of the Acts of the Apostles, in which they prayed for and received God's blessing. However, there is another way we can arrange these letters to again give a significant guideline for prayer.**

Have a student switch the first two lines on the screen. **Now we are beginning with "Confession." It is always appropriate to first come to God in prayer, admitting our sinfulness and receiving His grace and mercy. From these blessings will flow "Adoration"—the praise and honor we give to God for all He has given to us in Jesus.**

Have another student switch the last two lines. Say, **We must admit that the large part of our prayer is often devoted to "Supplication"—asking God for things we want and need. He welcomes that, but He also welcomes our "Thanksgiving," which follows our requests, showing our trust that God will answer, and thanking Him that He will answer in the right time and right way that is best for us.**

Point out that the acronym has now changed from *ACTS* to the word *CAST*. This is another significant connection to prayer in light of the apostle's words in 1 Peter 5:7—"[Cast] all your anxieties on Him, because He cares for you." Also point out that this Bible verse relates to today's Bible words to remember. **God does not want you to worry or be anxious about what you want or need. He calls on you to give those cares to Him in prayer, trusting in His grace and mercy.**

Curriculum Connection

Although the events of Peter's rescue from prison are hard to believe for those who are not Christians, the individual reactions of the people involved are obviously realistic. Peter thinks he is dreaming, Rhoda is so happy she forgets to open the door, and the people praying refuse to believe that God has actually said yes to their prayer. Help your students learn more about plot lines and characters by using section 6.2.3.3, Contrived or Realistic Characters and Plot, found in the sixth-grade Language Arts volume of the Concordia Curriculum Guide series.

Searching Further

Understand that God answers according to *His* will, not ours. Write God's three answers to prayer on the whiteboard: "Yes, because I love you"; "Wait, because I love you"; "I have a better idea for you, because I love you." Ask your students to suggest situations in which God may give each of these answers. You might use the following situations for discussion starters:

1. A sixth-grade boy prays that God will help him learn to pray more frequently and with greater trust. (Yes, because this is God's will for us.) 2. A sixth-grade girl asks God to make her grandmother well. (Could be any of the three, depending on God's will.) 3. A sixth-grade student prays for his own motorcycle. (Wait, because it would not be good for him at this age.) 4. Two brothers ask God to forgive them for fighting. (Yes, this would be according to God's will.) Remind students that we can always trust God to love us and to answer our prayers in the way that is best.

Bringing it home

In addition to translating the Bible into German and writing the Small and Large Catechisms, Martin Luther wrote many hymns and prayers for use in church worship services and in the home. Section 2 of Luther's Small Catechism is entitled "Daily Prayers: How the Head of the Family Should Teach His Household to Pray Morning and Evening." In this section, Luther included his Morning Prayer and Evening Prayer, and they are as appropriate today as when he wrote them nearly five hundred years ago. Encourage parents to teach these prayers to their children and use them together as a family every morning and evening. Luther also included in this section his suggestions for prayers to pray before and after every meal.

Critical thinking

Write and use prayers for missionaries and other Christians who are facing persecution in our country and in other countries around the world. Using the ACTS formula, praise God for the Good News of salvation being shared by these missionaries. Confess that we have not always been bold in our own witness and in our support of Christians facing persecution. Thank God for faithful witnesses, by whose words and actions many have come to know Jesus. Thank Him for a government that allows us the freedom to worship God without physical persecution. Then ask His protecting care over all who suffer for their faith. Choose a missionary serving in a foreign mission field. Write a letter telling the missionary you are praying for God's blessings on his or her work and for protection for the missionary and his or her family.

Reaching Every Child

Peter, miraculously released from prison, appeared first to Rhoda, a simple servant girl. It was up to Rhoda to spread the good news of Peter's release to the believers engaged in prayer for Peter. Think how often God appeared to and used ordinary people to tell the Good News about Jesus—the women at the Easter tomb, the former fishermen empowered by the Holy Spirit, the shepherds at Bethlehem. A modern theologian said it was a good thing the Christmas angels appeared to shepherds and not the theologians of the day. The Pharisees would have questioned the orthodoxy of the angels' message, while the Sadducees would have denied the existence of angels. The shepherds simply ran to Bethlehem to "see this thing that has happened. . . . And when they saw it, they made known the saying that had been told them concerning this child" (Luke 2:15, 17). Never underestimate God's power and plan to use each child in your classroom for His purposes—the slow learner as well as the gifted.

UNIT 9—THE CHRISTIAN CHURCH GROWS

LESSON 92

Tabitha
ACTS 9:36–43

Background

"Now there was in Joppa a disciple named Tabitha" (Acts 9:36). The Greek word used here for "disciple" is *mathetria*, "female disciple," and this is the only time the word is used in Scripture. Luke, who records more of Jesus' interactions with women than any of the other Gospel writers, tells us that in His earthly ministry, Jesus was accompanied by the twelve disciples (all male) "and also some women who had been healed of evil spirits and infirmities: Mary, called Magdalene, from whom seven demons had gone out, and Joanna, the wife of Chuza, Herod's household manager, and Susanna, and many others, who provided for them out of their means" (Luke 8:2–3). This was a break with Jewish rabbinic tradition, since women did not usually follow Jewish rabbis. Mary, from the village of Magdala, was present at Jesus' crucifixion, witnessed His burial, and helped anoint His body. Joanna, whose husband served in the household of Herod Antipas, was of a higher social class; she accompanied Mary to anoint Jesus' body. Susanna is not mentioned again in Scripture. These women disciples made important contributions to Jesus' ministry and God's plan of salvation for all people. In the same way, the Church today calls *all* of its members to various forms of service. The Lord has provided appropriate opportunities for service for every member of His kingdom, regardless of gender, ethnicity, or social standing. For a chart detailing the roles of women disciples in the ministry of Jesus, see *TLSB*, page 1726.

Central Truth
The Holy Spirit causes Christians to love and care for one another in Jesus Christ, their Lord.

Objectives
- Admit that too often, our love for others never gets translated into action.
- Celebrate the awesome love that God has shown to each of us in His Son, Jesus Christ.
- Find practical ways to love fellow Christians around us.

Materials
- Hymnals and music CDs
- 8-inch squares of white paper, enough for the class
- 9-inch squares of black paper, enough for the class
- Tape or glue
- Web Resource 92a
- Reproducible 92

Bible Prep
Post in advance so students can bookmark references before class time.
- Acts 9:36–43
- Exodus 22:16–23:9

Devotions

Matt, Alex, and Justin couldn't remember a better afternoon. They had come to the ballpark early with Matt's dad, in time to see batting practice and the pitchers warming up. The ball game itself had been exciting, and the home team won with a walk-off home run in the bottom of the ninth inning. Then, as a special attraction after the ball game, a group of contemporary Christian musicians put on an inspirational concert for the audience at the ballpark. The three boys were spellbound by the music, moving with the beat and listening to every word.

"Wow!" exclaimed Matt. "You can really hear them sing about their faith in Jesus in their music."

"Yes," agreed Alex. "Their music made me feel even more sure of my own faith in Jesus."

"Me too," said Justin. "It's great to be with so many people who believe in Jesus like we do."

"Let's go, guys," said Matt's dad. "We'll stop at the concession stand on the way out of the park, and you can spend the rest of your money on snacks for the ride home."

As the boys walked along with the crowd, Matt almost tripped over a small boy who had fallen a few feet ahead of him. Pushing past the crying child, Matt grumbled, "Stupid kid should have watched where he was going."

A little girl looked anxiously from one person to the next. "Mommy," she cried. "Mommy, where are you?" Alex ignored her, hoping somebody else would do something about the noise the child was making.

As the group reached the concession stand, Justin almost stepped in an ice-cream cone a little boy had dropped. "Don't worry, kiddo," Justin said, reaching into his pocket for his own snack money. "We'll get you another ice-cream cone right away."

According to James 2:17, "Faith by itself, if it does not have works, is dead." Which of the boys put his faith into action, sharing the love Jesus gave him with others?

Sing "They'll Know We Are Christians by Our Love" (*AGPS* 237; recorded on *JPS*).

INTO the lesson

A Quilt of Many Colors

In many congregations, you will find members who, like Tabitha, have a special heart for those in need. Often these people are organized into groups with names like "the Dorcas Circle" or "the Tabitha Society." These dedicated Christians live out their faith in service to the poor and needy, often by sewing quilts, clothing, or other articles for those in need. If your congregation has such an organization, arrange a visit for your students to observe them at their work. Be sure to ask them about the motivation for their charitable actions. As an alternate activity, arrange a quilt display in your classroom.

The Tabitha Society referred to in the Student Book made quilts for distribution through the Lutheran World Relief program. Quilt distribution is just one of many vital activities carried on by this relief agency. Discuss the many ways people use the quilts they receive through these acts of mercy. **Why is it important for people in need to know that Christians in a far country care about them? How does this help them to understand Jesus' love?**

Christians have a special reason to love and serve others. On the night before His death, Jesus gave His disciples a new commandment—that they love others *as He had loved them* (John 13:34). **Jesus' love was sacrificial, offering His own life on the cross for the sins of the world.** Our love for others is to spring from our faith in Him, loving and serving as He loved and served. He demonstrated this love and service in washing the feet of His disciples, telling them, "If I then, your Lord and Teacher, have washed your feet, you also ought to wash one another's feet. For I have given you an example, that you also should do just as I have done to you" (vv. 14–15). Also remind students that Jesus told His disciples that when He returns on the Last Day, He will say to the believers, "I was hungry and you gave Me food, I was thirsty and you gave Me drink, I was a stranger and you welcomed Me, I was naked and you clothed Me, I was sick and you visited Me, I was in prison and you came to Me. . . . 'As you did it to one of the least of these My brothers, you did it to Me'" (Matthew 25:35–36, 40). Jesus calls us to give evidence of our Christian love in Christian actions.

LESSON 92

Tabitha

A Quilt of Many Colors

The students in Mrs. Wilson's sixth-grade class were on a very short field trip—one that involved traveling to their church's basement meeting room on Monday morning. That's where the Tabitha Society met each week to make quilts. In the basement, they found six women sitting around a wooden frame on which a colorful piece of fabric was stretched. The women pulled lengths of heavy thread through the fabric and tied the thread in knots.

One of the women stood to greet the students. "Welcome to our Tabitha Society," Mrs. Carter said. "We get together every Monday morning to make quilts. Our organization is named after a hero of faith in the New Testament who believed in Jesus and shared His loving kindness with others."

"This quilt is beautiful!" exclaimed Sarah. "I bet you could sell your quilts for lots of money."

"Perhaps we could," answered Mrs. Carter. "But that's not why we're making them. These quilts will be sent to poor families here and in other countries through the church's mercy and world relief agency. We make these quilts to share the love that God has shown to us through Jesus."

"I can just see someone using this quilt to stay warm on a cold night," commented Jake.

"The quilts are important for warmth," explained Mrs. Carter, "but they serve other purposes as well. Quilts are used as baby carriers, tied around the mother's back. A quilt may serve as a bag to transport goods to market, or for a place to display fruits and vegetables for sale on the ground. A quilt may be a shade from the hot sun or a shawl on a cool day. Most of all, a quilt is a reminder that someone cares a lot."

The Tabitha Society served out of love for Jesus and love for other people. They remembered that Jesus said: "Just as I have loved you, you also are to love one another. By this all people will know that you are My disciples, if you have love for one another" (John 13:34–35). Our love and compassion for others are the results of our faith in Jesus, who loved us enough to die for us to bring us forgiveness, life, and salvation.

Review

Covenant Connection
We could not keep our part of the covenant in obedience to God, so Jesus fulfilled all things for us. We no longer live under the Law. We live by faith, and a result of that faith is showing loving kindness to others. We do not help others so that we will be saved; we help others *because we are saved!*

190

INTO the Word

A Surprising Funeral

Acts 9:36–43, the account of the death and raising of Tabitha, can be read directly from the Bible by most sixth graders. After reading Luke's account, read this section of Lesson 92 in the Student Book. Explain to your students that an *obituary* is the newspaper article announcing someone's death. **What information is generally included in an obituary?** Notice that Tabitha's obituary includes the important facts of her life: she was a follower of Jesus; she lived her faith in acts of charity and good works.

Tabitha's funeral was probably a large one. Those she had helped by sewing clothes gathered to mourn her passing, showing the tunics and other garments she had made for them. Peter was nearby, at Lydda, and so two men were sent to invite him to attend the funeral. When Peter arrived, he sent the mourners out of the room. Then he knelt and prayed. Turning to the body, he said, "Tabitha, arise."

Compare these events with the account of Jesus raising Jairus's daughter (Luke 8:40–42, 49–56). Remind students that when Jesus sent His disciples out in ministry, He gave them authority to "heal the sick, raise the dead, cleanse lepers, [and] cast out demons" (Matthew 10:8) in His name. Through the power of the Holy Spirit, the Christian Church continues to do works of mercy.

392

A Surprising Funeral

AN OBITUARY

Tabitha, also known by her Greek name, Dorcas, died in the city of Joppa following a short illness. Tabitha was a follower of the Way, followers of Jesus, who was crucified and arose at Easter. Tabitha was well known in the community for her good works and acts of charity. She is survived by many widows and orphans for whom she made tunics and other garments. Funeral arrangements will be announced later, following notification of the rest of the believers.

As is the custom, her friends washed her lifeless body and laid it in an upper room. The poor of Joppa stood around her, weeping, showing the pieces of clothing she had made for them. A message has been sent to Peter, an apostle, who is visiting in a nearby town.

A MIRACLE

The disciples in Joppa knew Peter would want to come for Tabitha's funeral. When Peter arrived, he sent the tearful mourners out of the room. Then he knelt down and prayed to the Lord God. Turning to the body, Peter said, "Tabitha, arise." Tabitha opened her eyes and sat up. Peter called to the mourners to come in, and he presented Tabitha to them alive, in the name of Jesus. News of the miracle traveled, and many believed in the risen Lord and Savior.

Tabitha knew that Jewish law required her to show charity to the poor and needy. But she had an even better reason: her faith in Jesus moved her to show mercy to others, just as Jesus had shown mercy to her.

A Quilt of Faith

The women of the Tabitha Society stitched together quilts for the poor and needy because of their faith in Jesus as their Savior. As a class, make a paper quilt expressing your faith. Each class member is to take an 8-inch-square piece of white paper. On your square, you are to write a favorite Bible verse, tell what your faith in Jesus means to you, draw a picture from one of your favorite Bible stories, or decorate it with Christian symbols. Glue your square to a 9-inch square of black paper. Take all the squares in the class and overlap the black edges, taping them together to make a paper quilt. Display your "Quilt of Faith" in the hall outside your classroom as a message of God's love to all who pass by.

Remember

"For we are His workmanship, created in Christ Jesus for good works, which God prepared beforehand, that we should walk in them." (Ephesians 2:10)

copies, reading assigned chapters and discussing them in a large or several smaller discussion groups.

This unit of the One in Christ curriculum is the best time to make use of the Heroes of Faith series because unit 9 focuses on heroes of faith in the Early Christian Church. Reproducible 92 provides a format that students can use to make their own "Heroes of Faith" booklet based on the Bible characters they are studying right now. Follow these steps to make a booklet that does not require tape or staples to hold it together:

1. Use a scissors to cut the page in half along the solid dark line; then cut the half pages only on the solid dark lines.
2. Fold the half pages along the dotted lines so that each half page folds like a card.
3. Working with the half page that has the dotted lines in the center of the fold, gently roll the top and bottom edges inward to make something resembling a cone.
4. Insert this rolled shape through the center slit of the other half page.
5. Gently pull the rolled shape through the slit until the center folds in each half page line up; then unroll the top and bottom edges of the first half page and smooth them out. You will have an eight-page booklet. (Some smoothing and refolding may be needed.)

Students could print "Heroes of Faith" on the cover page and then devote individual pages to some of the people—Tabitha, Rhoda, Peter, and so on—they are currently studying. Students might write the person's name at the top of the page, give a summary of their story, and perhaps add an illustration or design. Make extra copies of the reproducible available in case students want to make more booklets. For example, they could make a booklet of heroes of faith they know personally, such as grandparents, mom and dad, the pastor, and so forth.

INTO our lives

A Quilt of Faith

After working on the project mentioned in the Student Book, which is a witness to others of your faith, explore further the concept of "Heroes of Faith." There is no denying that Jesus is the ultimate hero of Scripture. But there is also no denying that the Lord blesses people with strength and courage in faith through the Holy Spirit to enable His followers to be strong as they live their firm faith in Christ Jesus. Web Resource 92a presents illustrations of Christians through the centuries who, by God's grace, have lived out their faith in action, motivated by the love of Jesus and enabled by the Spirit. The eight illustrations presented are from the covers of the Concordia Publishing House series titled Heroes of Faith. These are chapter books intended to be of interest to fifth- and sixth-grade students. Web Resource 92a is an introduction to these people and to the book series. The books can be used in your classroom in a variety of ways: the teacher could read the stories to the class; the books could be made available in the classroom library; or with classroom sets, students could read individual

393

Curriculum Connection

Tabitha (Dorcas) was well-known for the clothing she made to help people in need. Ancient clothing was different from what your students wear, both in the way it was made and in its value (which was much greater in an age of hand-sewing and weaving). Students can explore ancient clothing more fully using section 6.3.4.2, Aspects of Culture, in the sixth-grade Social Studies volume of the Concordia Curriculum Guide series.

Bringing it home

Plan a Day of Caring for the families of your school or congregation. Contact three or more social service agencies in your community, and offer volunteer workers for a Saturday project of the agency's choice. Agencies might include Habitat for Humanity, the local food bank, a soup kitchen, a senior citizens' center, or Goodwill Industries. Then invite families to sign up to work for that agency as a family on that day. Begin the Day of Caring with a brief worship service, thanking God for caring for all of us and giving us the ability to care for others, and asking Him to bless our work to His glory and our neighbors' good. Hold a contest to design a logo for your Day of Caring; use the logo on posters and other promotional materials. To identify your workers, find a sponsor who will provide T-shirts printed with your Day of Caring logo and the date of the event. On the Day of Caring, provide water bottles and nametags for all of your volunteer workers.

Teacher Tips

Many of the activities in Lesson 92 involve donations of money or materials. Learning to offer our financial resources and physical goods is an important element of Christian education. After all, "God loves a cheerful giver" (2 Corinthians 9:7). But take a careful look at your students. You may have children whose families are experiencing the same kind of financial needs as the people you are trying to help. These families may be overwhelmed by your frequent requests for donations of one kind or another. Their children may be embarrassed when they are unable to contribute to every project. Yet these children and their parents need to experience the joy of giving too. Look for ways in which students and parents can make contributions that are not of a financial nature. For example, a parent might help keep the shelves of the congregation's food pantry organized. A student might be in charge of posting promotional materials around the church and school. A family might deliver food baskets from the church to a needy neighbor.

Working in Groups

Divide into groups to organize and carry out a project in which members of your congregation and school families provide Personal Care Kits to be distributed to homeless people in your community. One group will plan and organize, while another group will create promotional posters and announcements to advertise the project. A third group will assemble the kits, while a fourth group will raise money for needed materials, supplies, and shipping costs. Each Personal Care Kit could contain the following items:

1 light- to medium-weight bath towel
2 bath-size bars of soap in original wrapper
1 adult-size toothbrush in original wrapper
1 sturdy comb
1 metal nail clippers
Toothpaste
Shampoo
Wrap all of the items in the towel; tie with ribbon or yarn.

Reaching Every Child

Just as God has given each believer spiritual gifts to be used for the building of His kingdom, so He has also given us a variety of abilities to use in service to Him and to one another. Divide your students into groups of three or four. Ask each student to list one or more skills he or she has observed in each of the other students in his or her group. When students have finished, ask them to share their lists with the rest of the class. Then discuss how these various God-given abilities can be used to serve God and to help others, especially people in need.

UNIT 9—THE CHRISTIAN CHURCH GROWS

LESSON 93

A Mission Trip
ACTS 13–14

Background

We honor many people—and rightly so—for their service to the nation or to the community: soldiers, firefighters, and police. Others are honored for their talent, their leadership, or simply because of their status in society: politicians, athletes, and celebrities. The composer J. S. Bach added the initials "S. D. G." to many of his musical manuscripts. The initials stood for the Latin words *Soli Deo Gloria*, "To God Alone Be Glory." The brilliant musician assigned the glory to the One to whom it truly belonged.

If anyone on earth should have received honor, it was Jesus. He was God in human flesh. Yet, during His earthly ministry, Jesus laid aside His heavenly glory. The apostle Paul writes in Philippians 2:6, "[He] did not count equality with God a thing to be grasped." Instead, Jesus Christ humbled Himself and took the form of a servant. He was falsely accused and condemned, suffering a degrading and humiliating death on the cross. But that cross of humiliation has become a sign of triumph and glory, a symbol of victory greater than any earthly trophy or medal. When Jesus had suffered for our sins, God the Father raised Him from the dead and exalted Him to the highest place of honor. Jesus is the one to whom saints and angels shout their praise: "Worthy is the Lamb who was slain, to receive power and wealth and wisdom and might and honor and glory and blessing!" (Revelation 5:12). *Soli Deo Gloria!* To God alone be glory!

Central Truth
Glory belongs to God alone, who saves us.

Objectives
- Acknowledge that God alone deserves all glory and honor for every good gift He gives us.
- Rejoice that He honors us by working through us to serve others in Jesus' name.
- Dedicate our gifts, talents, and blessings to the Holy Spirit's use for God's glory.

Materials
- Trophies, ribbons, award certificates
- Hymnals and music CDs
- Web Resource 93a
- Reproducible 93
- Pair of gloves

Bible Prep
Post in advance so students can bookmark references before class time.
- Psalm 95
- Acts 13–14
- Galatians 2–6

Devotions

Bring items such as trophies, ribbons, or school award certificates to display, and discuss the awards with your class. **Why do people receive such awards? What do actors and athletes do to receive awards? Why are medals given to soldiers, firefighters, or police officers? What do you think about people who receive these honors? Do they all deserve equal honor and attention?**

Discuss awards that your students might have received. **How did you feel when you received the award? Have you ever felt a little jealous when someone received an honor and you did not?** Discuss with your students the ultimate source of our talents and abilities. **We learn certain skills in music, sports, or academic areas, and we practice to perfect them, but it is God who created us and gave us our bodies and minds to use for His glory.**

In part of today's lesson, we will hear about people who wanted to give glory to the wrong persons. The crowds of Lystra wanted to honor the messengers, Paul and Barnabas, rather than the message. Paul and Barnabas tried to direct the people to the one person who should have received honors and awards, and that was Jesus.

During His earthly ministry, Jesus was rejected by many people. He was welcomed as a King and Savior when He entered Jerusalem, but by the end of that same week, people shouted for His death. He was crowned not with gold, but with thorns. Jesus died on the cross for our sins. He was raised from the dead and exalted to God's right hand, the place of power and authority. Everyone who trusts in Him has eternal life in His name! The Bible says that God "has qualified you to share in the inheritance of the saints in light" (Colossians 1:12). Jesus did the work, and we receive the prize!

Sing "Glory Be to God the Father" (*LSB* 506; recorded as *Hymn of the Season for grade 5, Christian Education month [September]*). Praise and honor God by reading together Psalm 95:1–7.

INTO the lesson

Travelogue

Throughout this lesson, refer frequently to the illustration in the Student Book, which shows Paul and Barnabas in Lystra in Galatia, and also to the map of Paul's journeys in the Student Book Appendix.

The "Travelogue" section gives a general overview of Paul's journeys. This background information will help students understand this lesson and the lessons that follow. The focus in the rest of this unit and in the rest of the Book of Acts is on taking the message of salvation through Jesus Christ to the rest of the world, to Jews and Gentiles alike.

As you explore the "Covenant Connection," assign the Bible verses to individual students to read aloud. (Since all of these are in Galatians, it should be easy for everyone else to follow along in their Bibles.) While these are being read, display the opening illustration of Web Resource 93a, which shows some of the writing tools of that day. Also point out the Greek language on a scroll. After finishing the Galatians verses, scan the rest of the resource, pointing out that Paul wrote to Christians in several other cities and to some individuals, and that we have many of these epistles (letters) in our Bible today. (Note: Do not read all of the Bible verses listed on the Web resource at this time. Instead, return to this resource on other days, hearing the Bible verses during your devotions time as volunteers read them. Also note that these are taken from the NIV.)

LESSON 93
A Mission Trip

Travelogue

We see now, beginning in Acts 13, a new outlook for the Christian Church that focuses on mission outreach to all parts of the world known at that time.

God had chosen the apostle Paul especially for this task (see Acts 9:15). The Church in Antioch (Syria) now sent Paul on a missionary journey, one of several that tended to follow this pattern:

1. Paul usually traveled with a fellow missionary or an assistant. On this first trip, he traveled with Barnabas, the man who spoke up for Paul when he first became a Christian, defending him to people who did not trust the motives of this former persecutor of Christians.
2. On entering a city, Paul would go directly to the synagogue to preach Jesus Christ to the Jews first, knowing there would be people there who were eager to learn that the promised Messiah had come. Many of the Jews would rejoice and believe in Jesus; others would refuse to believe and would become violent in their protests against Paul. Then Paul would also preach to the Gentiles. Again, there were many Gentiles who would rejoice and believe in Jesus; and others would refuse to believe and would protest. This up-and-down pattern followed Paul wherever he went.
3. This first missionary journey may seem like a short one (see map in Appendix). However, Paul often spent weeks in a single location, equipping the believers, training leaders, and strengthening the growing Christian Church through the Gospel. This was the first of three missionary trips, plus a trip when he traveled as a prisoner (and continued to spread the Gospel message).
4. Paul continued to keep in contact with new Christian churches through his letters (epistles), many of which are in the Bible. During his first trip, Paul visited cities in an area known as "Galatia" (also known as "Asia Minor" and "Turkey"). Paul later wrote the Epistle to the Galatians, which was passed from one congregation to others nearby, spreading the Good News in that way and eventually to us today.

Review

Covenant Connection

Paul's message to the Galatians emphasized that Jesus fulfilled the Law for us, so we no longer live by the Law but by faith in Jesus. (The Law threatens; Jesus saves.) By faith in Jesus, we are all heirs of Abraham and are children of God, receiving the covenant promise. There no longer is a separation between Jews and Gentiles, because in faith, in Christ, we are one! See Galatians: 2:16 and 20; 3:11-14 and 26-29; 4:4-5; 5:1 and 22-23; and 6:10.

INTO the Word

Itinerary

Use the Student Book to follow the location of events on this missionary trip and the unique circumstances the missionaries encountered. Use Reproducible 93 to review.

Then place a pair of gloves on a desk or table, and ask the students to "command" the gloves to pick up a pencil or piece of paper. Put on the gloves, or ask a student to do so, and perform the task while wearing the gloves. Ask the students, **Who is really doing the work—the gloves alone, or the person whose hands fill the gloves? We know, of course, that the hands receive the credit for the work that is done. The gloves cannot work by themselves.**

In all of the work that we do, at home or at school or anywhere else, we are like gloves on the hands of God. We remember that it is God who has given us our bodies, our minds, and our talents and skills. When we help someone or show kindness and forgiveness—even if those things are unnoticed by other people—God is at work in us.

In today's lesson, Paul and Barnabas received honor and glory that they did not want, for something they did not do! They knew that the glory belonged to God alone. They were only like gloves on the hands of God.

In the city of Lystra, God worked through Paul and Barnabas to heal a man who had been crippled from birth. Crowds were watching, and they began to honor and worship Paul and Barnabas. How did Paul and Barnabas react? (The apostles tore their clothes and told the people to stop.) Tearing their clothes was a sign of grief or sadness. The apostles told the people that they were not gods; they were ordinary men. They came to bring Good News from the true God. They wanted the crowds to stop worshiping the false gods and worship instead the living God. God alone deserved the glory!

Itinerary

Antioch of Syria: The leaders of the Christian Church in Antioch (in Syria), led by the Holy Spirit, sent Paul and Barnabas on their first missionary journey, into parts of Asia. John Mark went along for a while as a helper. This trip is recorded in Acts 13–14.

Cyprus: On Cyprus, an island in the Mediterranean Sea, the Roman proconsul, Sergius Paulus, summoned Paul and Barnabas because he wanted to hear the Word of God. A magician and false prophet named Elymas tried to turn Sergius Paulus against the Christian faith. But Paul bravely spoke up, calling Elymas a son of the devil and much more. The Lord struck Elymas with blindness. Seeing all of this, the proconsul believed in the Word of God (Acts 13:4–12).

Antioch of Pisidia: Paul and Barnabas spoke to the Jews about how Jesus had fulfilled the Old Testament prophecies. Read especially Acts 13:38–39. The Jews were interested in hearing more; in fact, "almost the whole city gathered to hear the word of the Lord" (verse 44). But the Jews were so angered to see so many Gentiles coming to faith in God that they turned against Paul and Barnabas and sent them away.

Iconium: This city was divided—some Jews and Gentiles believed in Jesus, some Jews and Gentiles did not. When troubles arose, Paul and Barnabas "remained for a long time, speaking boldly for the Lord" (Acts 14:3). They faced their troubles, not wanting to give up.

Lystra: In the crowd at Lystra was a man crippled from birth. He listened to the message of the Gospel and believed. Seeing his faith, Paul told the man to stand up. When the crippled man began to walk, the crowds of people shouted out that Paul and Barnabas were gods. They called Barnabas "Zeus" (the head of the Greek gods), and they called Paul "Hermes" (the messenger of the gods). The people brought garlands and sacrifices to honor them. But Paul and Barnabas tore their clothes in grief. They tried to direct the people to the true God, but the people hardly listened. In the meantime, enemies from Antioch of Pisidia and Iconium came into town and turned the crowd against Paul and Barnabas. One minute the people of Lystra were honoring them as if they were gods, and the next minute, they were stoning them as if they were criminals. The people dragged Paul outside of the city, supposing that he was dead. Amazingly, with God's blessing, Paul survived! He got up and went back into the city! The next day, he continued with Barnabas on their mission trip to another town.

Return Trip: For their return trip, the two missionaries backtracked over the same route they had come. They returned to the new Christian churches they had started earlier. Read Acts 14:22 to see the purpose of this part of their trip. Eventually, they returned to Antioch in Syria, where they had begun their journey. They reported on their experiences, and "they declared all that God had done with them, and how He had opened a door of faith to the Gentiles" (verse 27).

Remember

"To the only God, our Savior, through Jesus Christ our Lord, be glory, majesty, dominion, and authority, before all time and now and forever. Amen." (Jude 25)

INTO our lives

Like the apostles, you can be like gloves on God's hands. When you tell others about Jesus, the Holy Spirit works through the message of the Gospel to bring people to faith. This is not an easy task. Like the apostles, you will have ups and downs, but don't get discouraged. It is God who is at work in you and through you. He will bless you and the life you live as a follower of Jesus Christ.

Discuss with your students the ways in which God can work through them. Talk about different talents and skills that God has given to them. Sometimes, people notice only certain abilities, such as talents in sports or music. Those skills are gifts of God and should be used and developed to glorify God. Discuss other gifts and abilities with your students, gifts that may not be so noticeable. Some people are talented in certain academic subjects, such as math or history. Ask your students to suggest ways that those gifts can be used to help others. Others may be especially friendly or kind to others. They may be good listeners and able to help friends in difficult times. These, too, are gifts from God to use for His glory. If some students feel that they have no special skills, help them to realize that they can always show kindness and care for others. Listening and encouraging are important gifts of God too, although they are not always noticed. **Emphasize that any good we do is in response to the greater good we receive through Jesus and the salvation He offers us.**

The scene changes very much as the story continues, and the people turn against the missionaries. The cruel treatment he received does not discourage Paul. He is still acting as gloves on the hands of God. How do we know that God was still at work through him? (Paul and Barnabas went to another city, Derbe, and preached the Gospel. Many people there believed in Jesus.)

Who Was at Work Here?

Directions: Unscramble the mixed-up capital letters and rewrite the words onto the answer blanks of the puzzle at the bottom of the page. Solve the puzzle to answer the question in the title.

The Christians in (1) ATICHNO sent Paul and Barnabas on a missionary journey. (2) OHJN KARM went along as an assistant. The three men sailed to the (3) LSNIDA of Cyprus. There, Paul confronted a magician and false prophet named (4) SMELYA; however, the Roman proconsul (5) SSREGIU AUULSP came to faith in Jesus. This was typical of the high and lows, ups and downs that the missionaries faced on their journeys. Sometimes they were welcomed, and sometimes they were (6) SEPERCUTED, by Jews and Gentiles alike. They traveled on to places in Galatia such as (7) CIINOMU and Lystra. There, Paul saw a crippled man who had faith in the Lord. Paul called on him to stand up, through the power of God. The crowds who saw this gave Paul and Barnabas the glory, calling them by the names of Greek gods. They called Barnabas "Zeus" and Paul (8) MERHES. Once again, enemies turned the people against Paul and Barnabas. Paul was stoned and dragged outside the city, where he was left to (9) EID. However, God's grace and mercy were with Paul, and the next day, the missionaries continued on their travels to spread the Gospel. They revisited the places where they had established churches so that they could encourage the Christians there in their faith. Then they returned to (10) TICNAOH in Syria, where they had begun their trip.

1. A N T I O C H
2. J O H N M A R K
3. I S L A N D
4. E L Y M A S
5. S E R G I U S P A U L U S
6. P E R S E C U T E D
7. I C O N I U M
8. H E R M E S
9. D I E
10. A N T I O C H

Name _____

One in Christ™ © 2012 Concordia Publishing House. Reproduced by permission. Reproducible 93

Lesson Support

Curriculum Connection

The man God healed through Paul had never been able to walk in his life. Something was wrong with his muscles, nerves, bones, or some combination. Yet God healed his body and set those systems right. Learn more about body systems, using section 6.2.3.1, Skeletal and Muscular Systems, and section 6.2.3.2, Digestive, Circulatory, Respiratory, Excretory, and Nervous Systems. Both can be found in the sixth-grade Science volume of the Concordia Curriculum Guide series.

Searching Further

In today's story, the apostle Paul was stoned by the people of Lystra, dragged out of the city, and left for dead. He recovered, by God's grace and power, and continued his ministry. When the risen Christ appeared to Paul (then referred to as "Saul") on the road to Damascus, the Lord showed him "how much he must suffer for the sake of [His] name" (Acts 9:16). Defending his apostolic ministry in 2 Corinthians 11:23–28, Paul describes the suffering he experienced in service to Christ: imprisonments, beatings, stoning, shipwrecks, adrift at sea, dangers while traveling, sleepless nights, hunger, thirst, cold, and his worry for the churches. Paul responded to all of these hardships and dangers with trust in Christ, knowing that God's power was "made perfect in weakness." Paul wrote, "For the sake of Christ, then, I am content with weaknesses, insults, hardships, persecutions, and calamities. For when I am weak, then I am strong" (2 Corinthians 12:10).

Check it Out

Becoming a Christian does not mean becoming free of trouble. Jesus told His disciples, "In the world you will have tribulation. But take heart; I have overcome the world" (John 16:33). Paul and Barnabas were persecuted for their faith in Christ. The Bible tells us about the martyrdoms of St. Stephen (Acts 7:54–60) and St. James (12:2). Peter and the other apostles were often imprisoned, put on trial, and threatened (4:1–22; 12:3–5). Paul, like many of the apostles, was very likely martyred. Although we may not suffer persecution, earthly troubles can still shake our faith. But no earthly trouble, not even death, can separate us from the love of Christ. With confidence in Christ, St. Paul was inspired to write, "For I am sure that neither death nor life, nor angels nor rulers, nor things present nor things to come, nor powers, nor height nor depth, nor anything else in all creation, will be able to separate us from the love of God in Christ Jesus our Lord" (Romans 8:38–39).

Reaching Every Child

Some students may feel that they have no particular talent or gift to use in service to Christ. Help them to realize that as they grow in faith and in experience, they may develop special interests and talents. Encourage the students with the knowledge that they can serve God by helping others in the many small things they do each day. They can treat others with kindness and respect. They can listen to a friend who is hurting or invite a new student to join them at the lunch table. They can volunteer to help with a cleanup project around the school or church. The "gloves" on God's hands are not necessarily made out of velvet and covered in shining, eye-catching jewels. Hardworking gloves may be made out of ordinary and useful materials! As Paul reminded the young pastor Timothy—who may have compared himself with older, more experienced Christian workers—what matters is being "useful to the master of the house, ready for every good work" (2 Timothy 2:21).

Ideas for the Gifted

Some students might wish to research the myths of the Greek gods. Have them find out more information about the chief god, Zeus, and the winged messenger of the gods, Hermes. When the Romans conquered the Mediterranean world, they adopted the worship of the gods of Greece, giving them new names. Zeus is sometimes better known by his Roman name, Jupiter, and Hermes by his other name, Mercury. Students can do some research in astronomy and find out why the planets are named for the Roman gods. Ask them to report their findings to the class. In their report, they can give special attention to the gods mentioned in today's story, Zeus and Hermes.

UNIT 9—THE CHRISTIAN CHURCH GROWS

LESSON 94

Lydia
Acts 16:11–15, 40

Background

There are many people in the Bible whom we do not know much about. Farmers, priests, or soldiers may be mentioned in passing as characters in a narrative, but their names are never written down for us. We know the names of other individuals and even know a little bit of information about them. At the end of his Letter to the Romans, for instance, Paul greets a man named Persis. We don't know exactly what Persis did, but Paul writes that he "worked hard in the Lord" (Romans 16:12). Sometimes we learn a little bit more about the characters in a story, even some important information, such as the things we learn about the woman named Lydia in today's lesson. Lydia was a seller of purple goods in Philippi (in Europe) and was originally from the city of Thyatira (in Asia). She worshiped the God of Israel, and she heard Paul preach in Philippi. But certainly the most important thing we know about Lydia isn't really about *her* at all. The most important piece of information is what the Lord did in and through Lydia.

We learn that the Lord opened Lydia's heart to pay attention to Paul's teaching. She believed in Christ and was baptized. The Holy Spirit led this newborn Christian to put her faith into action immediately. Lydia welcomed Paul and his companions into her home, giving them a place to stay as they went about their ministry. It was a place of welcome to which they returned after their imprisonment. As He did with Lydia, the Spirit opens our hearts to hear the Word of God. He draws us to faith in Christ and keeps us in the true faith, daily forgiving our sins. And as He did with Lydia, the Spirit leads us then to put our faith into action in works of humble service.

Central Truth

God opens our hearts to believe in Jesus through His Word.

Objectives

- Understand that the Holy Spirit works faith in our hearts through God's Word and Sacraments.
- Appreciate the wonderful gifts of forgiveness and life the Lord gives us freely.
- Respond to this great love by serving others.

Materials

- Hymnals and music CDs
- Web Resource 94a
- Reproducible 94

Bible Prep

Post in advance so students can bookmark references before class time.

- Psalm 95:1–7
- Acts 16:6–15, 40
- Ephesians 2:8–10
- Philippians 4:4–13

Devotions

Ask your students to think of the names of famous people, such as actors or athletes or other celebrities. We know quite a bit about many of these people because of TV programs and magazines. Then name your pastor or another member of your school or church staff. What do the students know about that person? They probably know something about the individual's personality and family. Next, name a member of your congregation that your students may not know, perhaps someone who has been active in serving the church for a long time. Ask students to describe that person if they know any information. Finally, name some students in your class. Are those students famous? Your students may know many things about one another, but they are probably not famous—at least, not yet!

You may not be well-known to many people, but you are known to God. Remember that God the Holy Spirit called you to faith in Jesus Christ. You were baptized, and the Holy Spirit created faith in your heart. Each day, the Spirit forgives your sins and keeps you in the true faith. Today you continue to grow in faith and in your knowledge of God's Word. Perhaps none of us will be well-known or famous. But what is important is that we are well-known to God. His Spirit leads us through the Word to grow in grace each day and then leads us to serve others.

Today we will hear about a woman we know very little about, except for the most important thing: she believed in Jesus as her Savior. You and I share that same important thing in our lives. Being well-known by God is all we really need! Let's pray: Heavenly Father, we are glad to be known by You. Lead us by Your Spirit to grow in grace. Amen.

Sing "I Want to Walk as a Child of the Light" (*LSB* 411; recorded as *Hymn of the Season for grade 7, Epiphany*). Rejoice together in the words of Psalm 95:1–7.

INTO the lesson

On the Road Again

The events of Paul's many missionary trips seem to run together, so it helps to identify what is unique about each of the various journeys. His second trip is unique because he traveled with different companions. Also, Paul had wanted to revisit the churches in Asia, but the Holy Spirit led him to go instead to new places in Europe.

The main portion of this journey was spent traveling among large seaports around the Aegean Sea. These were centers of commerce and trade, and they attracted many visitors from all around the world. Students may be interested in learning more about this area; today, it is a beautiful region where people often take vacations on cruise ships. The area is also home to interesting ruins of Greek and Roman buildings that Paul would have seen when they were in their prime. Use Web Resource 94a to encourage an interest in this.

LESSON 94 — Lydia

On the Road Again

"After some days Paul said to Barnabas, 'Let us return and visit the brothers [fellow Christians] in every city where we proclaimed the word of the Lord, and see how they are'" (Acts 15:36). The second missionary journey was about to begin, but big changes would occur. First of all, Barnabas did not go with Paul because they had an argument. Barnabas wanted to take John Mark along again and give him a second chance. But Paul refused to take John Mark because he had quit and gone home early on their first trip. Without criticizing Paul, we can see that Barnabas was a very forgiving person, helping to "rescue" and build up John Mark in his faith and in his skills. John Mark traveled with Barnabas to Cyprus on a mission trip; later, he became an assistant to the apostle Peter; and eventually, he was the author of the second book of the New Testament (writing down the life of Jesus as told to him in part by Peter, and always through the inspiration of the Holy Spirit). Paul chose to travel instead with Silas, a faithful Christian, and he also took along young Timothy as a helper and student.

Paul intended to go again to Asia, but the Holy Spirit had other plans, and He directed the team of missionaries to Europe. Their most significant stops were at large seaport cities along the Aegean Sea. This was a longer trip that took many months, possibly even years. They preached the Word of God in Philippi, Thessalonica, Athens, Corinth, and Ephesus. Once again, Paul kept in contact with the new churches in these areas, writing letters to the Christian congregations there. Many of these epistles are in the New Testament of the Bible. Do you recognize which epistles would have been sent to which cities?

Review

Covenant Connection

Look at Ephesians 2:8–10, one of the most important Scripture readings of the New Testament. Paul was showing the people of Ephesus their connection with the grace and mercy they have in Christ Jesus. Thankfully, we, too, can read those words showing us our connection to our Lord and Savior. Paul learned to be an encourager too. Read Philippians 4:4–13. May the Holy Spirit bless and encourage you, too, through these words!

INTO the Word

An Open Heart

The woman in the Bible story is Lydia, and the most important thing we know about her really isn't about *her* at all. The most important thing about Lydia is what the Lord did in her life. He opened her heart to pay attention to Paul's teachings about Jesus Christ. Lydia believed the Good News and was baptized. The Holy Spirit led this brand-new Christian to put her faith into action right away. Lydia invited Paul and his companions into her home, giving them a place to stay for as long as the apostle stayed and taught in the city. Believers in the city also may have gathered in Lydia's home for prayer or worship. After Paul and Silas were imprisoned and then released by a miracle of God, they returned to Lydia's home to visit and encourage the believers before they left the city to continue their work elsewhere.

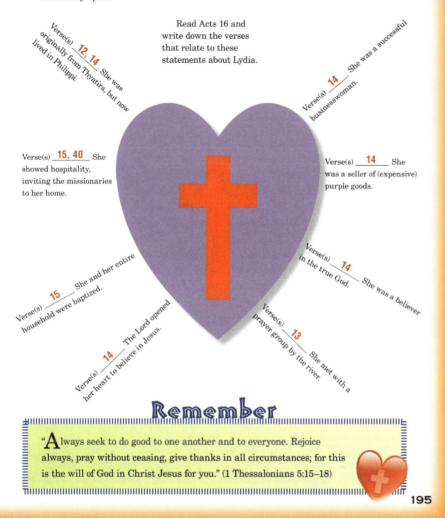

An Open Heart

There are just a few verses in Scripture about Lydia, so we don't know much about her. Yet we know what was most significant in her life: she believed in Jesus as her Savior, and she actively lived out her faith for God's glory and to serve others! We don't need to know any more than that to call her a hero of faith, through the enabling power of the Holy Spirit.

Read Acts 16 and write down the verses that relate to these statements about Lydia.

Verse(s) **12, 14** She was originally from Thyatira, but now lived in Philippi.

Verse(s) **14** She was a successful businesswoman.

Verse(s) **15, 40** She showed hospitality, inviting the missionaries to her home.

Verse(s) **14** She was a seller of (expensive) purple goods.

Verse(s) **15** She and her entire household were baptized.

Verse(s) **14** She was a believer in the true God.

Verse(s) **14** The Lord opened her heart to believe in Jesus.

Verse(s) **13** She met with a prayer group by the river.

Remember

"Always seek to do good to one another and to everyone. Rejoice always, pray without ceasing, give thanks in all circumstances; for this is the will of God in Christ Jesus for you." (1 Thessalonians 5:15–18)

Just as the Spirit opened Lydia's heart to listen to Paul, **the Spirit opens our hearts to hear God's Word. The Holy Spirit is at work in the preaching and teaching of the Word. The Spirit calls us to faith and keeps us in faith, daily forgiving our sins for the sake of Jesus Christ. Then the Spirit leads us to put our faith into action as we help and serve others.**

INTO our lives

The Holy Spirit led Lydia to put her faith into action. She invited Paul and his friends to stay in her home while they taught in the city of Philippi. The Spirit also leads us to put our faith into action. Lydia did what she could to support the Lord's servants when they came to Philippi. On Reproducible 94, have students write a note of thanks and a prayer asking the Lord to bless your pastor or another staff member at your church or school. Include a special Bible verse, if you wish. Give the notes to the staff members and thank them in person for their work of service to the Lord.

Curriculum Connection

Lydia was a dealer in purple dyed material. This color was very expensive because the dye was derived from a shellfish that only produced a tiny amount of the necessary substance at one time. Explore color, using section 6.2.1.3, Drawing Using Varying Tints, Shades, and Intensities. You'll find it in the sixth-grade Visual Arts volume of the Concordia Curriculum Guide series.

Searching Further

Paul and his companions made plans to travel through the regions of Phrygia, Galatia, and Bithynia and preach the Gospel. But we are told that in the case of the first two regions, the missionaries "were forbidden by the Holy Spirit" (Acts 16:6), and that when they wanted to go to Bithynia, "the Spirit of Jesus did not allow them" (v. 7). God's Word does not tell us why the Lord forbade them to do mission work in those regions at that time. We learn that the Lord sent them to take the Gospel into Macedonia instead. Talk to your students about prayer. God always hears and answers our prayers, although He may not answer those prayers in the way we think He should. But Scripture is clear: "My thoughts are not your thoughts, neither are your ways My ways, declares the Lord" (Isaiah 55:8). The Lord Jesus taught us to pray, "Thy will be done." In Gethsemane on the night He was betrayed, Jesus Himself prayed for His Father's will—not His own—to be done. In the Small Catechism, Martin Luther reminds us that God's will is done without our prayer, but that with these words, we pray that His will "may be done among us also." We can trust our wise God to answer our prayers for our good and to His glory.

Bringing it home

Send a letter to the parents of your students in which you explain the importance of worshiping together as a family. Parents usually want their children to develop good habits as they grow older—taking care of personal property, being polite to others, showing respect to people in authority, and much more. Ask parents to help your students develop the good habit of going to church each week. In doing so, they are following the example of our Lord. The Bible tells us that Jesus was in the habit of attending worship each week: "And as was [Jesus'] custom, He went to the synagogue on the Sabbath day, and He stood up to read" (Luke 4:16). Parents can help their children grow strong in faith as they worship together, nurtured by God's gifts of Word and Sacrament. Pray that the Lord will open the families' hearts to listen to the saving message of the Gospel.

Faith in Action

Lydia believed and was baptized. The Lord opened her heart to hear the Word, and Lydia opened her home to the apostles. Her hospitality gave Paul and his companions a place to stay and gather with other believers. Help your students learn about the gift of hospitality. Host a classroom open house for parents or for another class of students in the school, perhaps younger "buddies." Students can create and send invitations to the event. They can plan a menu and help prepare refreshments. Students may wish to plan a program for the open house, perhaps reading stories to younger students or presenting a skit to parents. They may wish to act out some of Paul's missionary adventures and use the open house as an opportunity to present the Gospel.

Check it Out

In his Gospel, as Luke explains, he "dealt with all that Jesus began to do and teach, until the day when He was taken up" (Acts 1:1–2). Now, in his second volume of the story of Jesus, Luke begins with Jesus' ascension into heaven (vv. 6–11) and takes up the story of the apostles as they carry the message of the risen Lord to the end of the earth. In the earlier chapters of Acts, Luke describes the activities of the apostles in third person (e.g., "They were on their journey" [10:9]). But within the verses from today's lesson, a change takes place. In 16:8, Luke writes that "*they* went down to Troas"; then, in verse 10, Luke begins to use the word *we* as he describes the journey: "Immediately *we* sought to go on into Macedonia" (emphasis added). In the city of Troas, Luke joins the apostle Paul, and then travels with him to Philippi. Luke is apparently with Paul at times and serves as an eyewitness to some of the events he describes. He is with Paul when the apostle arrives in Rome for trial at the close of the Book of Acts (28:16).

UNIT 9—THE CHRISTIAN CHURCH GROWS

LESSON 95

The Jailer at Philippi
Acts 16:16–40

Background

Paul was annoyed—"greatly annoyed," the text tells us (Acts 16:18)—with the slave girl who followed him through Philippi. It may seem that Paul is using the power of Christ to serve his own ends by removing an annoyance in his ministry. But by commanding the demon to depart, Paul is serving Christ, not himself. The slave girl is healed, and people who saw the healing witnessed the power of Christ. We might expect the healing to be received with thanksgiving. That is what happened in Lystra when the crippled man was healed. But Paul did not receive any thanks for helping the slave girl. In fact, he and Silas were seized and imprisoned.

Not too much later, in the city of Thessalonica, the apostles were described as men who "turned the world upside down" (Acts 17:6). Paul and Silas do behave in an upside-down way. They are beaten and imprisoned, but instead of cursing, they sing hymns. Set free by an earthquake, they do not run for safety, but stay and preach some more. They are not filled with hate for their jailer—they baptize him. Paul and Silas proclaim the Good News of Jesus Christ, who, by His death and resurrection, came to turn people right side up again, placing them in fellowship with God and others as they were created to be. Jesus Himself put our needs ahead of His own, and our Christian life is also one of opposites: humility instead of pride; service instead of demands; life instead of death. Like our Savior and His apostles, we are called to turn the world upside down, because Christ has turned our lives right side up!

Central Truth

The Holy Spirit turns our priorities upside down, causing us to love God and our neighbor before ourselves.

Objectives

- Contrast the behavior of Paul and Silas with that which would be expected of people concerned first for their own welfare.
- Appreciate the wonderful way Christ's love shines through His people, including us.
- Pray that the Lord would help us to become ever-clearer witnesses to His love and mercy in Jesus.

Materials

- Hymnals and music CDs
- Web Resource 95a
- Reproducible 95

Bible Prep

Post in advance so students can bookmark references before class time.

- Acts 16:16–40
- Matthew 5:44
- Matthew 6:25
- Romans 12:17
- Philippians 2:4
- Hebrews 13:5
- Mark 16:16

Devotions

Before class, prepare a sentence to display in class. Write the words backward, out of order, even upside down. Ask volunteers to try to read the sentence. **Why can't you read the sentence?** (All of the words are in the wrong place; the sentence is backward and upside down.) Next, ask your students to turn around in their chairs so they are facing the back of the room. Then write something (in regular writing) on the board in the front of the room, and ask a student to read what you wrote (without turning around). **Why is it hard to read that way?** (They are facing the wrong way; they have to turn around if they want to see something.)

When God created the world, everything was just right, the way God designed things to be. But when Adam and Eve disobeyed God, sin entered God's perfect creation. Their relationships with God and with each other were ruined. Life was turned "upside down," and the penalty for the ruin of sin was death. But God did not want the ruin to go on forever. He sent His Son, Jesus Christ, to suffer the punishment for sin. When we are baptized, we become a new creation, put back into a right relationship with God. We are turned "right side up" again, but we live in a world that is still "upside down" in its relationship to God. The people of the world look at life from a different point of view and often think that Christians are the ones behaving in strange ways. When Jesus' apostles went out to proclaim the Gospel, some people described them as "these men who have turned the world upside down." Because we belong to Jesus, we also live that "upside-down" life, knowing that we are really "right side up" with God!

Sing "Thine Forever, God of Love" (*LSB* 687; recorded as *Hymn of the Month* for grade 6, May).

INTO the lesson

Unexpected

Use Web Resource 95a to tell today's Bible story; review it by reading aloud the Scripture from which it is taken (Acts 16:16–40). Then explore the story, looking in the Student Book at the unexpected things that happened. As stated in the "Covenant Connection," God's thoughts are not like our thoughts, and His ways are different from ours and what we would expect.

Say, **We live right side up with God in a world that is turned upside down by sin. People who do not believe in Jesus think that the way Christians act is what is really "upside down." Of course, we know that we are not really turning the world upside down; instead, we want to turn the world right side up to believe in Christ and to follow God's will. As we see in today's lesson, Christians do often act in unexpected ways. In this, we are imitating God's way of doing things. He often acts in unexpected ways too!**

When God acted to save us, He did not act in expected ways, at least not as the *world* might have expected Him to act. Jesus did not come as a mighty king and warrior. How did the Son of God come to earth? (He was born as a baby in Bethlehem.) **Jesus did not save us by fighting the Roman soldiers and sending fire from heaven to destroy evil people. How did Jesus save us?** (He died on the cross for us.) **Jesus was condemned and crucified, the kind of death usually suffered by criminals and slaves in the Roman world. Jesus was taken down from the cross and buried in a borrowed tomb. But on the third day, the most unexpected thing happened! Jesus rose from dead! In Jesus, God was setting the upside-down, sinful world right with Himself. Everyone who trusts in Jesus receives forgiveness of sins and eternal life. Each believer is put right with God.**

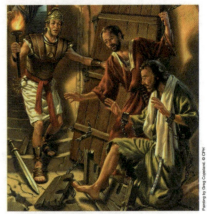

Lesson 95
The Jailer at Philippi

Unexpected

Unexpected: When Paul healed a slave girl in the name of Jesus, her owners became angry. (They had been making a lot of money off of her telling fortunes through the evil spirit in her.)

Unexpected: Paul and Silas were beaten and thrown into prison for doing something good (healing the slave girl).

Unexpected: Even though it was midnight and they were in jail, Paul and Silas sang hymns of praise to God, as other prisoners listened. (They were joyful in all circumstances.)

Unexpected: An earthquake opened the doors of the prison, and the chains of all the prisoners fell off, yet no one tried to escape.

Unexpected: Paul prevented his jailer from committing suicide, saying, "Do not harm yourself, for we are all here" (Acts 16:28).

Unexpected: This Roman soldier got down on his knees and asked what he must do to be saved.

Unexpected: Paul gave the surprisingly simple answer: just believe in Jesus.

Unexpected: The jailer took Paul and Silas to his home, cleaned their wounds, and fed them. This was a dangerous thing for a Roman soldier to do; it was punishable by death.

Unexpected: The jailer and his entire household came to faith in Jesus as their Savior and were baptized.

Unexpected: The next day, the city magistrates said Paul and Silas could go free, but Paul said no! (Paul announced that he and Silas were Roman citizens who had been mistreated by being flogged and thrown unjustly into prison.)

Unexpected: The city magistrates were afraid that now they would get into trouble for harming Roman citizens, so they went to the jail themselves and apologized to Paul and Silas. The missionaries were now cleared of all false charges; they returned to the home of Lydia, where they met with fellow Christians; and then they resumed their journey.

Review

Covenant Connection

God often works in unexpected ways. The greatest examples of this are seen in His plan for fulfilling His covenant promises through Jesus. No one expected the Messiah to be born as a baby in a stable, with a manger for a bed. No one expected the Messiah to die on a cross to take the punishment for our sins. No one expected the Messiah to arise from the dead at Easter. But, as the Lord says, "My thoughts are not your thoughts, neither are your ways My ways" (Isaiah 55:8).

196

INTO the Word

Expect the Unexpected

Living as a Christian can be difficult if you expect that life to be easy. Actually, as a Christian, you will be going against the main currents of thought in the world. **You've all heard the expression "everybody does it." That is a justification for doing something only if you intend to follow the ways of the world. Jesus sets us on a different path, where our guide is what *He* does in loving mercy and grace, and our goal is to do as "every Christian does it."**

Think about all the things you do each day, the places you go, and the people you meet. How can you live today as a witness for Jesus Christ? How will your words and actions show that you follow Jesus? Plan some unexpected ways to act and speak today. Say a prayer with your class, asking God to help them witness to Christ by the way they speak and act.

Continue these thoughts with Reproducible 95. Read aloud the incorrect version of the Beatitudes, noting how this represents the attitude of the

Expect the Unexpected

Living as a Christian is very different from living in the ways of the world. We could say that being a Christian is often countercultural, especially when we put God first, forgive others, and follow Jesus' example (because He turned the world upside down). Read each Bible verse, and write down what it says about the unexpected ways in which Christians act, as they are enabled by the Holy Spirit.

Matthew 5:44: **Love your enemies and pray for those who hurt you.**

Matthew 6:25: **Don't worry or be anxious about what you need; God will take care of you.**

Romans 12:17: **Don't try to get revenge. Despite the evil someone may do, you should always do what is good and honorable.**

Philippians 2:4: **Don't put yourself first; take care of other people and what they need.**

Hebrews 13:5: **Don't love getting more money and possessions; be satisfied with what you have.**

Baptized in the Name of the Lord

Read Mark 16:16. Who is saved? Who is not saved? What does that tell us about Baptism? Mark tells us that whoever believes and is baptized is saved, but he also tells us that whoever does not believe is condemned. Scripture does not say that believers who have not yet been baptized are condemned. Only those who do not believe are condemned.

In today's Bible narrative, Paul tells the jailer that he will be saved if he believes in Jesus. Once the jailer believes, he wants to be baptized. One of the great blessings of God is that He comes to us in several ways to bring us, keep us, and strengthen us in faith. He does this through the Means of Grace, and each means contains the essential Word of God!

What are the three Means of Grace? **God's Word, Holy Baptism, the Lord's Supper**

Remember

"Do nothing from rivalry or conceit, but in humility count others more significant than yourselves. Let each of you look not only to his own interests, but also to the interests of others. Have this mind among yourselves, which is yours in Christ Jesus." (Philippians 2:3–5)

The Beatitudes

Jesus spoke of the upside-down and right-side-up behaviors of people of God in the Sermon on the Mount. He said we are not to just live by the Law, but live by love, as we are led by the love of God for us. Jesus wants us to exceed the Law, going beyond what the Law expects in order to show kindness and the love of Jesus. Time and again, especially in the Beatitudes, He speaks of this topsy-turvy life of a Christian, which, in humility, does not put ourselves first (as the world does), but first serves the glory of God and then serves the needs of others.

Look at this version of the Beatitudes (Matthew 5:3–10). This incorrect version demonstrates the way of the world—every man for himself, everyone trying to be number one, everyone wanting the most money and possessions. In each verse, cross off the words that are wrong, and on the answer line, write the words that make the statement correct.

Matthew 5

Verse 3: Blessed are the ~~proud~~ in spirit, for theirs is the kingdom of heaven. **poor**

Verse 4: Blessed are those who ~~have no problems~~, for they shall be comforted. **mourn**

Verse 5: Blessed are the ~~brave and courageous~~, for they shall inherit the earth. **meek**

Verse 6: Blessed are those who hunger and thirst for ~~money~~, for they shall be satisfied. **righteousness**

Verse 7: Blessed are those who are ~~tough and bossy~~, for they shall receive mercy. **merciful**

Verse 8: Blessed are the ~~famous celebrities~~, for they shall see God. **pure in heart**

Verse 9: Blessed are the ~~powerful~~, for they shall be called sons of God. **peacemakers**

Verse 10: Blessed are those who are ~~rewarded~~ for righteousness' sake, for theirs is the kingdom of heaven. **persecuted**

---

world around us. After working on the activity, have everyone read aloud the corrected Beatitudes together.

Baptized in the Name of the Lord

Review Baptism and its benefits by reading aloud the Small Catechism section on Baptism, found in the Appendix of the Student Book. Point out that when Lydia's household and the jailer's household were baptized, there were likely people of all different ages—young and old—being baptized. Survey the class to see how many of your students do not remember their Baptism, how many do remember it, and how many are still looking forward to their Baptism. Relate this discussion to the rite of confirmation, which many in your class will experience in the next few years. Point out that confirmation provides an opportunity to stand up before everyone and state what you believe in faith about Christ Jesus, your Savior.

Curriculum Connection

Paul and Silas turned down a chance to escape after a great earthquake shook the foundation of the jail. Learn more about earthquakes, using section 6.3.2.3, Plate Tectonics. This can be found in the sixth-grade Science volume of the Concordia Curriculum Guide series.

Critical thinking

Paul and other early Christians were described as people who "turned the world upside down" (Acts 17:6). Certainly, riots and trouble seemed to follow Paul wherever he proclaimed the Gospel; but as we have seen in this story, the Christians often lived in an upside-down sort of way, when compared with the way unbelievers acted. When they were hated and ridiculed, they responded in love. They prayed for their enemies, as the Lord Jesus had taught them. Talk to your students about ways in which Christians are the same as unbelievers and ways in which they are different. **Christians work, dress, and act in just about the same way as everyone else, so what is it about Christians that is different?** Being "different" in any way is especially difficult for teens and preteens. Talk to your students about times when they may need to act or speak differently than others. How might other people react to them? How can your students use that different approach to life as a witness to Jesus Christ?

Tell your students' parents about Paul and Silas and the other Christians in the Book of Acts who turned the world "upside down" for Christ. Ask them to encourage their children, by word and by example, to live "right side up" as God's redeemed people. They can pray together as a family and bring their children to church and Sunday School. Students may not listen to a lecture, but they learn quite a bit by watching and listening. Parents teach their children how to live "right side up" by the ways in which they react to the circumstances of daily life.

Check it Out

After Paul and Silas's prison bonds were shattered by the earthquake, the city authorities decided to set them free, telling them to "go in peace" (Acts 16:36). Paul, however, was not about to go in peace. Taking full advantage of his rights as a Roman citizen, Paul replied, "They have beaten us publicly, uncondemned, men who are Roman citizens, and have thrown us into prison; and do they now throw us out secretly? No! Let them come themselves and take us out" (v. 37). The authorities apologized and asked Paul and Silas to leave the city. This was not the only time that Paul used his rights as a Roman citizen. In 22:25–29, a Roman tribune quickly abandoned his plan to scourge Paul when he learned that the apostle was a Roman citizen by birth. In 25:11, Paul appealed to Caesar, asking that his case be tried in front of the emperor in Rome. With that appeal, Paul was sent to Rome—as a prisoner. God worked through Paul's citizenship to protect His apostle and bring the Gospel of Jesus Christ into the judgment hall of the emperor himself!

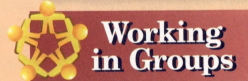

Have the students work in groups to design posters about "turning the world upside down" for Christ and the unexpected ways of the Lord. They might illustrate with scenes from the life of Christ. The mighty Savior of the world was born as an infant in a Bethlehem stable. The King of kings died on a cross, crowned with thorns instead of gold. Use scenes from the life of Paul: two prisoners sat in jail, singing hymns; and then, when set free by an earthquake, they remained in the jail and eventually baptized their jailer! How can your students encourage others to live as God's people and turn the world upside down?

Faith in Action

The demon-possessed slave girl in Philippi was a source of income for her owners. Using her satanic powers to tell fortunes, she brought her owners "much gain" (Acts 16:16). When the demon left the slave at Paul's command and in Christ's name, the source of income for her owners left with it. Many people today are influenced by the satanic arts, although we do not always recognize the practices as demonic. People turn to fortune-tellers, tarot cards, or astrological charts in an effort to learn what the future holds. Talk to your students about the Second Commandment. We are not to use God's name to swear or deceive others. We must not become involved in fortune-telling. When we are worried about what the future holds for us, we must turn to our heavenly Father in prayer, calling on His name "in every trouble."

UNIT 9—THE CHRISTIAN CHURCH GROWS

LESSON 96

Paul at Mars Hill
ACTS 17:16–34

Background

Today's story reveals another stop on a long journey taken by Paul. It doesn't take long for Paul to see that Athens, too, needs attention as far as spreading the truth and beauty of God's plan is concerned. Pagan statues and idols are prominently displayed throughout the city, and it is clear that the people don't dare miss out on sacrificing to every god imaginable, as the inscription on one of the city's main altars reads, "To the Unknown God."

Many of the city's people spent much of their day studying and philosophizing about many misconceptions and beliefs. The Epicurean philosophers believed in seeking a life of pleasure (right-brained thinking), while the Stoic philosophers believed in the rational order of nature (left-brained thinking) combined with the acceptance of their natural fate. Not grasping the full message, some of these philosophers thought Paul was preaching about a foreign deity. Others were simply fascinated to learn yet another "theory" upon which to ponder away their days. Life and faith for them were all based on learning, pondering, thinking, debating, and rationalizing rather than on the solid truth of God's Holy Word!

As you guide students through the pages of the Student Book, supplement their base of knowledge with some of the ideas and practices of the time so that they can appreciate how Paul had to use his God-given intelligence to effectively communicate with groups of people who desperately needed to hear the truth of God's salvation plan. Emphasize that just as God gave Paul the capacity for using his intelligence, so also God has given us gifts of body and soul and enables us to reach out to those in need. Everything we have and are is from God; pray together that our gifts are used for His glory!

Central Truth
God uses His gifts to us of intelligence and education in order to strengthen our faith in Jesus.

Objectives
- Recognize that all our gifts of body and soul, including intelligence, are from God and not of our own doing.
- Affirm that God is the God of all truth, not merely "religious" truth.
- Honor and love the Lord with all our mind (Matthew 22:37).

Materials
- Hymnals and music CDs
- Web Resource 96a
- Reproducible 96

Bible Prep
Post in advance so students can bookmark references before class time.
- Psalm 96
- John 8:32
- Colossians 3:17
- Acts 17–18
- James 1:17
- 1 Corinthians 12:4–6; 14:12
- Romans 12:3–11
- 1 Peter 4:10–11
- 2 Timothy 1:6–7

Devotions

"I stink at math! I wish I could at least just get one B or C on a test this year!" Devon said as he swished a rimless free throw.

"Yeah, I don't like math either. Actually, *all* of the subjects are stupid!" Matt grabbed the ball from his front yard and unsuccessfully tried to copy the shot.

"Matt, please come here and help me for a minute," called his mother. Matt passed the ball to Devon and carried some groceries into the kitchen.

"Okay—what's going on, Matt?" his mom asked.

"What do you mean?"

"You *love* math! And you don't think school's stupid!" Mom looked him right in the eye. "Something tells me you are avoiding telling Devon the truth for a reason."

"I don't want Devon to feel bad that schoolwork comes easy for me, while it's so hard for him. Besides, some guys think it's not cool to be smart!"

"Matt, you are blessed! God didn't give you the wonderful brain you have for you to not use it. I'm not saying you should ever brag about it, but you should certainly use God's gift of intelligence!"

"But what do I do about Devon?" Matt put a pile of grocery bags in the recycling bin.

"Why don't you find a way to put both of your gifts to good use?"

Matt thought for a minute and then went outside.

"Hey, Devon, I actually think I understand the math unit we're on right now. How about I help you with math, and you show me some tips on your jump shots?"

"Works for me! Let's do the math thing first, though, because our test is tomorrow!" Devon said.

"You know," Matt said, "if you do well on tomorrow's test, you might like school more. I'm kind of liking it myself lately!"

Read together John 8:32 and Colossians 3:17. Then sing "Go into the World" (*AGPS* 101; recorded on *JPS*). Use Web Resource 96a to learn to chant Psalm 95 as it is presented in the Matins liturgy in *LSB*, page 220.

INTO the lesson

Do a brief overview of the opening verses of Acts 17 to give students some background for today's lesson. Say, **After leaving Philippi, Paul and his fellow travelers went to Thessalonica. How long were they there? See verse 2.** (The answer is not three days. It says "three Sabbath days," which would be three Saturdays, which would indicate two or three weeks.) **What success did they have? See verse 4.** (There were new believers among the Jews and the Greeks.) **But then jealous enemies stirred up a mob. What is so dangerous about mob behavior?** (Too often, people get caught up in the emotion and do not think about what they are doing, or they let someone else do the thinking for them. Mob behavior seems to lower the intelligence of the group, and stupid and even dangerous things happen. Good things are unlikely to result from mob behavior.) **What accusation was brought against Paul and his friends? See verse 6.** (They have "turned the world upside down.")

In verse 10, who are the "brothers" who sent Paul and Silas away by night to Berea? (Fellow Christians) **What were the Bereans like? See verse 11.** (They listened eagerly to God's Word and studied the Scriptures daily.) Unfortunately, those enemies from Thessalonica followed Paul to Berea and caused more trouble. So Paul left town by sea, with Silas and Timothy planning to follow him as soon as possible. This leads us to today's story; now Paul is in the city of Athens, waiting for his friends.

INTO the Word

Follow the Flow

Point out that this Bible story follows a classic pattern of written narratives, showing exposition, rising action, climax, conclusion, and falling action. This pattern can be found in many well-written stories. Use the Student Book to explore the Bible story using this outline. Then return to the five main elements of the story and have students find and read the verses in the Bible that correspond to them. (Exposition, Acts 17:16–17; rising action, 17:18–21; climax, 17:22–31; conclusion, 17:32–34; falling action, 18:1–5).

Use Your Head!

Say, **God gave each healthy human a brain that has two sides, or *hemispheres*. Each side does different types of jobs to help our bodies do what they need to do. God has made us each unique, however, so the ways and amounts in which we use the parts of our brain varies from person to person. Some of us might be more right-brained, while others of us might be more left-brained. Depending on the situation, we might use one side over the other. God is the one who gave us the gift of intelligence, and it is He who enables us to use that intelligence to help strengthen our faith and share the truth of His Word with others!** Study the chart, noting that the left side of our brain is more attuned to reasoning and logic, while the right side is more into artistic thought and emotional feelings. Then explore how the apostle used his brain (left and right sides) to connect with the people of Athens. Because he was speaking to philosophers, he tended to focus more on intellectual eloquence. Paul knew the importance of knowing your audience—their interests, their background, their abilities—and using that information to lead them to **the truth about the Lord Jesus, our Savior, who offers forgiveness, life, and salvation.**

Use Your Head!

In the midst of a very philosophical society, Paul did not just rattle off biblical statements and hope to convert people; first, he considered the background and beliefs of his audience. Through the power of the Holy Spirit, he chose his words carefully; in order to reach the people, he had to know them! Like Paul, God has blessed each of us with a brain too! Study the chart that describes the two hemispheres (halves) of the human brain and the functions each side controls.

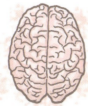

LEFT BRAIN HEMISPHERE | RIGHT BRAIN HEMISPHERE

a. Language usage	Face recognition
b. Logical thinking	Shape and color recognition
c. Analytical time-sequence processing	Expressive emotions/speech
d. Numbers/computation	Intuitive/thoughtful thinking
e. Objective thinking	Subjective thinking (based on feeling/opinion)
f. Skilled movement	Musical intelligence
g. Reasoning	Creative thinking

Paul used both sides of his brain as he bore witness to God's plan of salvation for all believers. But primarily, he spoke with logic and reasoning, knowing that was the type of thinking that interested Greek philosophers. Match these teachings of Paul with the left-brain function that they match.

- **a** Paul used language skills to speak logically to the people.
- **g** Paul reasoned with them to compliment and also counter their philosophical worldview.
- **c** Paul used sequential thinking as he included pre-creation, creation, and events through the final Judgment Day.
- **c** Paul mentioned time factors when he pointed out that God created humans with determined allotted periods.
- **b** Paul used logic when he asserted that God's offspring would not likely be created of stone.

Paul also used some right-brain thinking as he quoted well-known Greek poets and used his God-given intuition to connect with the needs and concerns of his listeners. Also, he spoke expressively as well as emotionally because he had a heart for the people.

Remember

"This is good, and it is pleasing in the sight of God our Savior, who desires all people to be saved and to come to the knowledge of the truth." (1 Timothy 2:3–4)

199

INTO our lives

Know Your Audience!

Say, **Paul was given a brain and intelligence to reason with the people in Athens. What a blessing! But what does that mean for us today, in the twenty-first century?** Give students time to answer, and lead them to see that they, too, have been equipped with intelligence, education, and other gifts to help share the Good News. Then say, **Many of us have already had the chance to share the Good News with other people. Raise your hand if you have been blessed to do so.** Give students the chance to share any of their witnessing experiences, if desired. **As I said, some of you have had the privilege of witnessing to others already, and some of you may have had chances that you never even realized were chances! Could you witness to people at the grocery store? Could you witness to someone at a restaurant? How about at a public school? How about at church? How about in your house, to your family? Yes, we can witness to many people from all walks of life, using the talents and gifts God gives us!** Look at Reproducible 96, and ask students to consider how to witness and what to say to these different people, based on what you know about them. Perhaps discuss this in small groups.

Continue then by reminding students that everything they have comes from God. Ask a student, **Where did you get those nice clothes?** Encourage an "Ultimately, from God" response. Ask someone else, **How did you get such a good grade in some of your homework last week?** Again, encourage an "Ultimately, from God" response. Ask another student, **How have you gotten so good at some sports?** Encourage again an "Ultimately, from God" response. Have students find passages in the Bible that talk about different gifts and about all gifts coming from God, such as 1 Corinthians 12:4–6; 1 Corinthians 14:12; Romans 12:3–11; 1 Peter 4:10–11; 2 Timothy 1:6–7; James 1:17.

Say, **In today's devotion, Matt tried to hide the truth that he actually likes school and is good at schoolwork. How do the Bible passages we just studied apply to Matt and his gifts?** (His gifts came from God, and he should not be ashamed to use and share them.) **You, too, have been blessed in many ways—some of you more with the left side of your brain, some of you more with the right side of your brain, and some of you with the ability to balance between both. Whatever your abilities and skills, pray that God will guide you to use them for His glory and for the good of other people!**

Lesson Support

Curriculum Connection

Challenge your students to use their God-given intelligence with section 6.2.5, Information Needed to Solve Problems, which is found in the sixth-grade Math volume of the Concordia Curriculum Guide series. The God of all truth will help them discern which information is needed and which is merely a distraction. Remind them to ask for God's help as they study!

Reaching Every Child

Differentiated Instruction: You have certainly noticed the unique differences your students bring to your classroom. God has blessed each of your students with various talents, strengths, and preferred learning styles. Children may come to your classroom with diverse personal interests, cultural backgrounds, and readiness for learning. You may ask yourself, how can I ensure that I am reaching all of my students with the saving message of the Gospel when they bring such diverse learning styles to my classroom? In differentiated classrooms, teachers do whatever they can to ensure that *all* students experience the opportunity for spiritual growth every day of the school year. Differentiated instruction starts with teachers who assess the needs of their students, understand the differences that each child brings to the classroom, and respond to the needs of each student. Take a good look at each of your students. How do they learn best? Through visual, auditory, tactile, or kinesthetic modes? What are their interests? What faith-building events have they already experienced? Getting to know your students well is the first step in learning how to help them grow in their faith. Be ready to connect your students with the essential truths of the Gospel message by using various learning modalities and activities that appeal to students with different backgrounds, and by adjusting the rate and complexity of learning to individual student needs. Teachers who differentiate their instruction know that students learn differently and may need to take different paths to reach the same understanding of the lesson's essential truths. Ask yourself, what adjustments or changes can I make in teaching the lesson to meet the diverse learning needs of my students?

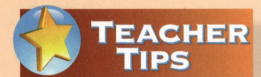

Most people are fascinated by how the human brain works. In teaching today's lesson, do not get caught up in the psychology of the human brain to the point that it detracts from the biblical truths of the lesson itself. Always drive home the theme of the lesson: God uses His gift of intelligence in us to strengthen our faith! Remember that Paul used his brain to basically tell the people of Athens that they were using *their* brains too much as they rationalized their days away. He had to use his brain to communicate effectively with the people. Our brains are only as good and as sharp as they are because our loving God created them! They are to be used for His glory!

Reaching Every Child

Memorization Difficulties: Memorizing always seems to be a difficult task for students with disabilities. Giving these students meaningful strategies to use during the lesson will help them to gain the most from the material that is taught.
- Write a visual pyramid using key words from the lesson.
- Chunk meaningful words together.
- Use imagery to form a visual picture of each phase.
- Set a verse, passage, or series of items to a tune that students know well.
- Write the important material on an index card, and have students place the card where they will see it daily.
- Practice the information in pairs.
- Encourage students to say it aloud to themselves or to another student daily.
- Play a game or create an activity that relates to the lesson.

UNIT 9—THE CHRISTIAN CHURCH GROWS

LESSON 97

Paul's Nephew to the Rescue
ACTS 18–23

Background

Paul was no stranger to prison! In fact, a good amount of his witnessing took place in prison, where he was able to take advantage of a captive audience to tell the Good News of salvation through Christ Jesus! In today's narrative, in the midst of danger, God offers protection through the actions of someone quite unexpected—Paul's young nephew, who was probably in his preteen or early teen years. Regardless of his age, his role in the story is significant because it is yet another example of how God is in control in the midst of trouble and chaos! Paul also saw himself as an unexpected instrument of God because he was still troubled by his earlier actions of ordering Christians to be put to death. Even though Paul firmly believed in the forgiveness of his sins and all sins won by Jesus on the cross, he often reminded himself and others of how sinful he had been. He did this to show that God even uses sinners like him to further and strengthen His kingdom, which is another example of God using the unexpected! Help students to see that even though they, too, are sinful, God can use each of them in wonderful, unexpected ways. Encourage them to keep the idea of service in the Church in the forefront of their minds as they interact with the themes of today's lesson. Remind them of Paul's humble words: "To me, though I am the very least of all the saints, this grace was given, to preach to the Gentiles the unsearchable riches of Christ" (Ephesians 3:8).

Central Truth

God is always in control of our lives, even in the middle of chaos and danger.

Objectives

- Admit that there are times in our lives when we are afraid and are unable to help ourselves.
- Depend on the Lord to guide and protect us when we are afraid.
- Give thanks for the ways God brings us help, even from unexpected sources.

Materials

- Hymnals and music CDs
- Web Resource 96a
- Web Resource 97a
- Reproducible 97

Bible Prep

Post in advance so students can bookmark references before class time.

- 1 Corinthians 1:26–29
- Ephesians 3:8
- Acts 18–23
- Philippians 4:11–13
- John 14:27
- Matthew 18:20
- Isaiah 43:1

Devotions

"Not now, Timmy! I can't find my tape measure, and Mom said we need to leave in three minutes. If I don't have one for science class today, I'll lose points for my science project!" Trevor's ankles and feet were sticking out from under the bed as he slithered from side to side, trying to find it.

"But Trevor, I—"

"Not *now*, Timmy!" snapped Trevor. "I know it's under here, and I've got to find it!"

"Okay, but Trevor I think you need—"

"You don't know *what* I need because you are only a second grader! Let me look for it in peace!"

Timmy's eyes filled with tears. "Here. I just thought this might help you find it." Timmy dropped his most special flashlight next to Trevor's feet and ran out to the car, where he and Mom sat and waited for Trevor.

A few minutes later, Trevor rushed out to the car and took his place in the backseat next to Timmy. The silence was long and awkward, but eventually Trevor looked at his little brother and said, "Sorry for yelling at you, Timmy. Your flashlight helped me find my tape measure. Thanks!"

"Sure!" Timmy smiled from ear to ear.

"Boys, do you have your lunches?" Mom broke in.

"Yes!" answered the boys.

"Hey, did you put my flashlight back in my room?" Timmy asked Trevor.

"No, I thought I'd keep it safe under my bed." Trevor smiled. "Just kidding!"

Both boys laughed. Deep inside, Trevor was refreshingly surprised that God could use someone smaller and unexpected to bring him help at just the right time! In today's Bible story, we will see someone else who was refreshingly surprised that God could use someone smaller and unexpected to bring him help at just the right time!

Read together 1 Corinthians 1:26–29 and Ephesians 3:8. Then sing together "Thine Forever, God of Love" (*LSB* 687; recorded as *Hymn of the Month for grade 6, May*). Speak or chant the first portion of Psalm 95. (See *LSB,* p. 220, and Web Resource 96a.)

411

INTO the lesson

Good Grief!

Today's story is one of complexity and suspense! During the lesson, try to re-create the feeling of suspense that is present throughout most of the story, and emphasize that God often uses the unexpected to help us in times of trouble.

Choose students to read the various paragraphs in the Student Book that present this complex story, which actually covers most of Acts 18–23. But the heart of the story is in 23:12–35. Have students also read aloud this Scripture section.

Continue to review the Bible narrative by using Web Resource 97a. **This story will be explored as if it were a big pizza puzzle, and it's up to us to put the wedges and the edges in the right places to piece the story together!** (Note: Some of the statements may require students to search the Scriptures for names and references that were not previously mentioned.)

LESSON 97

Paul's Nephew to the Rescue
Good Grief!

The apostle Paul went on a third missionary journey, to revisit the churches established on earlier trips. This trip, as usual, had high and low points, but all was done to spread the Gospel of salvation through Jesus Christ. Finally, it was time to return to Jerusalem, where . . .

Good Grief! Paul encountered some of the same troubles he had survived in Europe and Asia. The Roman tribune and his soldiers arrived to stop the mob uprising, but the only thing they could do was to get Paul back to their barracks and then figure out what to do. Acts 21:35 says, "When he came to the steps, he was actually carried by the soldiers because of the violence of the crowd." Then . . .

Good Grief! The crowd quieted down as they heard Paul speak to them in Hebrew. He said he was a Jewish man, as they were. He talked about the days when he had persecuted Christians. He talked about when Jesus came to him and he came to faith and began to preach the Gospel. Then the crowd turned on him again, saying, "He should not be allowed to live" (Acts 22:22). So then . . .

Good Grief! The Roman tribune ordered that Paul be taken into the barracks and flogged. He thought he could beat the truth out of Paul. But Paul spoke up about his dual citizenship—he was Jewish, but he was also a Roman citizen, and it was illegal to beat a Roman citizen who had not been condemned. Read Acts 22:25–29 to see the reaction of the Roman soldiers. They needed to dump this problem on someone else. So . . .

Good Grief! Paul was sent back to the Jews—this time, to the Sanhedrin council. Paul wisely knew that the Pharisees believed in a resurrection but the Sadducees did not. So as Paul defended himself, he mentioned that he was a Pharisee who looked to the hope of the resurrection. This started an argument among the members of the council themselves. They were so mad at one another that they seemed to ignore Paul. Some of them even said, "We find nothing wrong in this man" (Acts 23:9). There was such an uproar that the Roman tribune had no choice but to take Paul back to the barracks. In the meantime . . .

Review

Covenant Connection
In all of this chaos, Paul could rely on the promises of Christ Jesus, who said in John 14:27: "Peace I leave with you; My peace I give to you. Not as the world gives do I give to you. Let not your hearts be troubled, neither let them be afraid."

INTO the Word

From Chaos to Comfort to Contentment

Throughout all this chaos, Paul never seems to lose his calm. That's because he is living in the peace of the Lord. As a class, look through this section and read aloud the Scripture references. After filling in the Bible verses for the "Review" and "Remember" sections, read those verses aloud as a group. Say, **Paul was given many opportunities to practice his "trusting" skills. In the midst of danger, Paul continually remembered that God was in control and that He would always be with** Paul. Paul could have just given up witnessing to avoid the danger, but instead, God enabled Paul to trust in Him for protection, comfort, and, of course, love!

Have students look up and highlight Matthew 18:20. Then read it aloud together as a class: **Jesus says, "For where two or three are gathered in My name, there am I among them."** Then pair students up to form prayer partners, and have each pair pray about things that are chaotic in their own lives, asking for God's blessings of peace and contentment.

Good Grief! Forty men met secretly with a plot to ambush and kill Paul the next day. They knew the route by which he would be taken from the Roman barracks to the Jewish Sanhedrin, and along the way, they would jump him and kill him. The conspiracy was well planned, except . . .

Good Grief! The plan was overheard by a young boy—Paul's own nephew! What could a young boy do? He talked to his uncle about what he had heard, and his uncle Paul called for the centurions to take the boy to the head officer—the Roman tribune. We don't know how old the nephew was, perhaps 10–14 years old, and he was now in great danger too. But the Roman tribune treated him kindly, taking him by the hand to reassure him, and stepping aside where they could talk privately. When the tribune heard about the plot, he was determined to not let a small band of Jewish men attack his Roman soldiers. He made plans to rescue Paul, taking him by night, and . . .

Good Grief! He formed an entourage of 470 men, all charged with protecting Paul (see Acts 23:23). The Roman tribune was determined to get rid of this problem—and he got rid of it by giving it to someone else! He sent Paul and the Roman soldiers to the city of Caesarea with a letter explaining matters and turning Paul over to the Roman governor, Felix. Felix's first thought probably was . . .

Good Grief!

From Chaos to Comfort to Contentment

Chaos: Paul endured much and gave up lots to share God's Word with those who needed to hear it! His life often was chaos. List a few of the chaotic things that happened to Paul. _____
Answers will vary.

Comfort: Paul indeed had comfort, but it was definitely not physical comfort. It was the comfort and peace that only Christ can give. One night in a vision, God spoke directly to Paul these words of comfort: "Do not be afraid, but go on speaking and do not be silent, for I am with you" (Acts 18:9).

Contentment: Paul learned to be content with whatever happened to him, as long as he was able to continue to preach the Gospel. (See Acts 20:24.) Paul's journeys continued, but for the rest of his life he traveled as a prisoner rather than a missionary. Yet he was able to share his joy and contentment with others. At the bottom of this page, write his message to fellow believers from Philippians 4:11–13.

Remember

"I have learned in whatever situation I am to be content. I know how to be brought low, and I know how to abound. In any and every circumstance, I have learned the secret of facing plenty and hunger, abundance and need. I can do all things through Him who strengthens me." (Philippians 4:11–13)

INTO our lives

Whose Am I?

Continue working with partners on Reproducible 97. Then highlight and read together Isaiah 43:1. Say, **Think of the most loving father in the world. Know that your heavenly Father is infinitely greater than the best father this side of heaven! From the beginning of time, God has called us by name. We are indeed His children.** He loves us so much that He sent His only Son, Jesus, to die on the cross so that our sins would be washed away and so that we will live eternally in heaven someday! **God is in** *control.* **In the midst of** *chaos,* **we are** *comforted.* **Jesus gives us the assurance of life eternal, which brings us** *contentment!*

Say, **As He did with Paul, God uses our times of trouble to strengthen our faith and our walk with the Lord. Sometimes, He even uses unexpected people to help us through our problems as well. Perhaps God is planning to use** *you* **as that young person who comes to the rescue of someone else! Perhaps God is planning to use** *your words* **to share the contentment and peace that are found in God's Word!**

Lesson Support

Curriculum Connection

On several occasions, Paul used his Roman citizenship as a "Get Out of Trouble Free" card. Your students can learn more about Roman citizenship by using the ideas and information in section 6.4.1.6, Types of Ancient Government. This is located in the sixth-grade Social Studies volume of the Concordia Curriculum Guide series. Discuss with students: **What is similar between Roman citizenship and citizenship in our own country? What is different?**

Searching Further

Paul traveled mile upon mile on land and sea to spread the Word of God. Help students look at several maps, such as the one in the Student Book Appendix, that show Paul's journeys, and have them pay attention to the various markings that indicate how, where, and when he traveled. **Did he walk? Did he take a boat? When did each of the different journeys take place?** Encourage students to search further by answering some or all of the following questions: **With whom did Paul travel on each of his journeys? What notable and/or dangerous events happened on each journey? What was accomplished through each journey physically and, especially, spiritually? What specific messages can we learn from each journey?**

Have students work together in groups of four to either make their own individual presentations or to divide the work based on certain journeys. When all information is compiled, students should work together within their groups to develop an oral/visual presentation to share their findings with the class and possibly even other grades.

Hands to Serve

Plan to have a secret-service search over the course of one week. Ask the students to each secretly search for opportunities to help others in unexpected ways in a variety of locations. Give each student ten index cards to record the activity and place of the service being provided (e.g., "Shop-a-Lot Foods, bagging groceries for Mom"; "Immanuel Lutheran School, helping Miss Hente carry boxes to her car"; "1802 Chesterton Rd., helping rake Mrs. Miller's leaves"; "Trinity Lutheran Church, sharpening pencils to put in the pew racks"). On each card, also include a section for an appropriate person to "sign off" on the service, verifying that the service was performed willingly and satisfactorily. If desired, reward the class with a small party if the entire class successfully completes "Secret Service Week."

Faith in Action

In keeping with the theme of God's children being helpful in times of need, plan a service auction that is "stocked" with services to be performed by the students themselves! Brainstorm several ways in which they can be helpful, and then have them offer their services to someone willing to buy them at the auction. This auction could be a separate event in which other grades in the school participate, or it could include only the members of your class and be held in conjunction with a PTA meeting. Note that parental supervision will be needed in most cases.

The services auctioned should be reasonably priced and aimed directly at meeting the needs of the people in your school, church, or community. Some examples could include babysitting during a church function, a meeting, or a parents' night out; raking leaves at someone's house or at church or school; scrubbing walls or mopping floors at church or school; organizing papers for the pastor, teacher, or secretary; helping a teacher put up a bulletin board; helping a single parent or the pastor's wife with her children by sitting with them in church; helping to paint a classroom; and so forth.

To connect this service project with your language arts curriculum, have students type up their own descriptions of the services they are offering, and display descriptions on the service auction table. After the service has been purchased, have students each give their "client" a thank-you they have written, thanking the person for their purchase and giving them any necessary contact information to set up the date and time the service is to be completed. Then, following completion of the service, have each student write a follow-up report on how the job went, explaining the jobs performed, for whom, when, and how. Additionally, have students write about any challenges and joys they encountered while completing their service projects.

UNIT 9—THE CHRISTIAN CHURCH GROWS

LESSON 98

Paul on Trial
ACTS 24–26

Background

Our story takes place when Paul is under house arrest. Because neither Roman Governor Felix nor his successor, Governor Festus, dared to upset the Jews by pronouncing him innocent, Paul was forced to appeal to Caesar for fair judgment. When King Agrippa heard Paul's case, however, he privately implied to Festus that Paul should have been declared innocent long before he had to appeal to Caesar. What's the point of all this? Paul was held captive for nothing! Or *was* it for nothing?

As with many situations in life, we need to ask ourselves "What if?" What if Paul hadn't been arrested and remained in captivity for so long? Looking at today's texts, it is easy to see that God was able to use Paul right where he was! "And we know that for those who love God all things work together for good, for those who are called according to His purpose" (Romans 8:28). Through the power of the Holy Spirit, God used Paul, who eagerly witnessed to Agrippa and many others—and He also uses His people today to share the news of His saving love!

When reading today's text with your students, take note of the number of times the phrase "the way" (or "the Way") is used (e.g., "according to the Way . . . I worship the God of my Fathers" [Acts 24:14]; they plotted to kill him on "the way" [25:3]). Point out that "the Way" with a capital *W* refers to the teachings embraced by early Christians, who were sometimes called "followers of the Way." Note also that "the way" is used here and in several other places in Acts to refer in general to "the way of salvation," which is Jesus Christ, who is "the way, and the truth, and the life" (John 14:6). Rejoice with your students that our God is such a wonderful God and that Jesus is the way to eternal life in heaven with Him!

Central Truth
God gives us opportunities and the Holy Spirit's help to share the Gospel of Jesus with the people around us.

Objectives
- Recognize the great need for a Savior that every human being has.
- Rejoice that God has given us His own dear Son to be our Redeemer and Lord.
- Respond to the needs of those around us by lovingly sharing the Good News with them also.

Materials
- Hymnals and music CDs
- Reproducible 98

Bible Prep
Post in advance so students can bookmark references before class time.
- Romans 1:16; 8:28
- Matthew 28:18–20
- John 14:1–7
- Acts 24–26

Devotions

"Mom, have you ever been friends with someone who isn't a Christian?" Kelly waited intently for her mother's reply.

"Sure I have. Why do you ask?" Mom wondered.

"Well, did you ever try to talk about Jesus to that friend?"

"Actually, I did. Why all these questions?" Mom was curious.

"Well, I just found out that the new girl, Aimee, is not a Christian. It was really creepy, hearing her actually say the words 'I don't believe in Jesus.'"

"I'll bet it was," agreed Mom.

"In fact, it caught me so off guard that all I could say was, 'Well, I do. Jesus died on the cross and forgave my sins.' And then I got really nervous and just stopped talking about it. She looked at me like I was some space alien or something!"

"Those were actually really *good* words to say, Kelly! You never need to be nervous or ashamed to talk about your faith in Jesus, but if you are, remember that God is the one doing the work. We are just His instruments."

"I suppose you're right."

"Maybe if you get nervous with her again, try to say a quick prayer asking the Holy Spirit to give you the confidence and the words to say. In fact, I'm sure it was the Holy Spirit who helped you today too!"

"So those weren't stupid words?"

"Not at all! And never feel like you're too young! God works through all kinds of people—big and small—to carry out His plan of salvation."

"So whatever happened to your friend who wasn't a Christian?"

"Well, after lots of talking, the Holy Spirit had His way in that situation too—because now that friend of mine is your dad!"

Read together Romans 1:16 and Matthew 28:18–20. Pray together that God will lead you to see opportunities to witness to others about salvation through Christ Jesus. Then sing together "Go into the World" (*AGPS* 101; recorded on *JPS*). Speak or sing the first portion of Psalm 95.

INTO the lesson

Knock! Knock!

Today's lesson is a beautiful one telling of Paul's persistence as he witnessed to others, even in times of frustration and danger. Throughout the lesson, remind students that as they witness, the Holy Spirit will help them in times of uncertainty. Begin the lesson by asking, **In our devotion today, what was Kelly's problem?** (She found out her friend Aimee wasn't a Christian, and she wasn't sure what to say.) **How was her problem solved?** (Her mom told her that the Holy Spirit is with her and will give her the words to say as she shares the love of Jesus.)

Do any of you have friends who are not Christian? Allow students to answer. If some do have non-Christian friends, ask, **Have any of you talked to your non-Christian friends about Jesus?** Again, allow students time to respond. **What have you said to them?** Based on their responses, guide students to the realization that God gives them the words to say as they stand up for the truth of God's Word and share the message of salvation. Say, **I hope that you will not be afraid to share the truth about Jesus with those who need to hear His message. When you have the opportunity to witness, know that God is with you always. Remember, the Holy Spirit will help you know what to say. You do not have to be afraid; He will give you the right words to say when the time comes.**

Choose three students and have each read one of the "Opportunity knocked!" statements. To check for understanding, ask, **In today's Bible story, to whom did Paul end up witnessing?** (Paul ended up witnessing to King Herod Agrippa and also to Felix and Festus—even though none of them seemed to come to faith.) Follow up by asking, **What is unique about Paul witnessing to these people?** Paul was a lowly prisoner witnessing to a king and two Roman governors! But he didn't care about status; he knew that sharing the message of salvation was more important. He seized the opportunity to witness, even in the midst of captivity. Say, **Remember, Paul used to be higher up in status when he was "Saul," who was not a Christian. However, God stopped Saul on the "way" in his sin and changed his heart to believe in "the way, and the truth, and the life"!** The Paul we hear about today definitely follows in "the Way"! As a class, read together John 14:1–7. Explain the irony of the words *way* and *Way* as they are seen in today's story and surrounding text. (See more information on this connection in the *Background* section.) Then read Romans 8:28 together as a class. Ask, **How does this verse fit the story today?** (Because Paul was in captivity, things didn't look good for him. God, however, worked all things for good because, during this time, He helped Paul witness to many people.)

Say, **Paul was extremely diligent about seizing any opportunity he could to share the Gospel message. Wouldn't it be wonderful if we could be as bold as Paul and share the message of salvation as much as he did? Well, each and every one of you can share God's Word with others! Just as God was with Paul, He is also with you and with me as we share the news of God's love!**

Note: You may want to use Reproducible 98 to help students understand more about the many different Herods mentioned in the New Testament.

Lesson 98
Paul on Trial

Knock! Knock!

Opportunity knocked! Governor Felix was in charge when Paul was brought to trial. Paul's accusers began by flattering Felix, saying he was most excellent and had brought peace and reforms to the nation (Acts 24:2), and then they presented false charges against Paul. When the governor motioned for Paul to speak, Paul used the opportunity to speak the truth about God (verses 14–15). Felix had the opportunity to learn about Jesus; he met often with Paul when it was "convenient," but he did nothing about the truth concerning Paul or the Lord Jesus. Felix was hoping Paul would pay him a bribe. But he did show some leniency, allowing friends to visit Paul in prison. Paul had been imprisoned for two years when Felix was replaced and recalled to Rome for being inept (verses 24–27).

Opportunity knocked! Festus was the new governor, replacing Felix, who had not been well liked. Festus saw an opportunity to please the people of his new jurisdiction by suggesting that Paul be taken to Jerusalem and placed on trial there, which would provide Paul's enemies with another opportunity to harm him (Acts 25:1–3, 9). Paul recognized that Festus was only interested in politics and was not going to give him a fair trial either, so once again, he brought up his dual citizenship. As a Roman citizen, he appealed to be tried before Caesar (the emperor Nero). Festus replied, "To Caesar you have appealed; to Caesar you shall go" (verse 12). This would give Paul many more opportunities to spread the Gospel, even as far away as Rome!

Opportunity knocked! The Judean king, Herod Agrippa, arrived in Caesarea for a visit, and Festus asked for his help. He explained the situation with Paul's appeal to Caesar, but he didn't know what to write down about charges that were to be brought against him. He hoped the Jewish king would have a better understanding of the matter. Agrippa said, "I would like to hear the man myself." (See Acts 25:22–27.) Paul recognized another opportunity, and he spoke at great length about his conversion to Christianity. Read the reaction to Paul's witness in Acts 26:24–32.

What was Festus's startling response to Paul's sermon?  He said Paul was out of his mind.

What was Agrippa's sad response to Paul? "Do you think you could lead me to become a Christian so quickly?" What a missed opportunity for Agrippa to receive salvation!

Paul would now set sail for Rome as a prisoner. But this was all part of God's plan as He said to Paul "Take courage, for as you have testified to the facts about Me in Jerusalem, so you must testify also in Rome" (Acts 23:11). God was in control!

Review

Covenant Connection

Throughout his trials, Paul could rely on the promises of Jesus Christ, who told His disciples in Luke 21:12–13, 15, "You will be brought before kings and governors for My name's sake. This will be your *opportunity* to bear witness. . . . I will give you a mouth and wisdom, which none of your adversaries will be able to withstand or contradict" (emphasis added).

Who's There?

Paul, indeed, had many opportunities to reach different people with the message of the Gospel! Consider the people in today's Bible story, and use the clues below to figure out who is behind each door. Then, write the name of the character on the center crossbeam of each numbered door.

1. I am someone to whom Paul preached; I am not a Jew.
2. I heard Paul's case and determined he could have been released.
3. When I made no declaration of Paul's innocence, he appealed to go before Caesar.
4. We made charges against Paul through our lawyer, Tertullus.
5. I died for the sins of the world.
6. I am King Herod Agrippa's wife.
7. I am the Roman emperor.
8. We are people who are very self-righteous.
9. For two years, I talked often to Paul, but I did not help him.
10. We are citizens of one of the most influential cities of Paul's time.

Look at the highlighted letters in the clues. Throughout the entire story, during every opportunity to share the Gospel, who was there, working in and through Paul to reach the people? __Holy Spirit__

In your own life, know that God is the one who is there, always with you. Pray that God will strengthen and equip you to seize opportunities to tell others about His love!

"Be strong and courageous. Do not fear or be in dread of them, for it is the LORD your God who goes with you. He will not leave you or forsake you." (Deuteronomy 31:6)

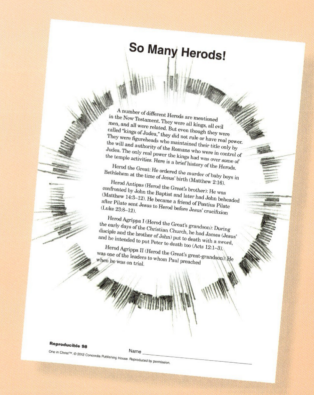

INTO the Word

Who's There?

Read each clue aloud and pause to give students time to write the correct name on the corresponding door (e.g., the answer to clue 1 should be written on door 1, and so forth). Continue until all clues have been read and all the students have finished writing their answers. Then discuss the answers.

Emphasize, **The message Paul always shared was of the forgiveness and salvation offered through Jesus.**

Say, **Notice that the heading for this section is "Who's There?" Why do you think that these words were chosen?** (Because the clues tell us about the people who were there in today's story.) Say, **You're correct, but let's continue to think about who *else* was in today's story as we answer the next question in the Student Book.** Lead students to answer that the Holy Spirit was also present, helping Paul witness about Jesus' love.

Read together the Bible words to remember (Deuteronomy 31:6), then ask, **How does this verse apply to your life?** Guide students to realize and rejoice that God will never leave them or forsake them. Say, **What joy it gives us to know that the Holy Spirit helps us as we share Jesus' love with others! God will indeed never leave us or forsake us.**

Lesson Support

Reaching Every Child

Language Disorders: Students with language disorders have challenges in many academic areas. They have trouble understanding and remembering one-step instructions. At times, adults assume that the child is not paying attention or is behaving inappropriately. It has been proven that between 3 and 5 percent of primary school students experience some type of language disorder, although it seems that half of these students will outgrow these disorders during adolescence. Many of these students exhibit difficulty in understanding words with multiple meanings and have limited reading comprehension. Here are some strategies to use in the classroom with these students:

- Repeat and clarify instructions as needed.
- Deliver information in more than one way.
- Simplify daily language use.
- Help students to compare and contrast objects and ideas.
- Be specific when giving instructions.
- Provide written directions.
- Provide a preview of the class or lesson.
- Show a sample of the finished product you are assigning.
- Preteach the vocabulary.
- Allow for flexibility in the coursework.

Reaching Every Child

Disruptive Behavior Disorders: Teaching to a diverse group of students is always a challenge for teachers. It is difficult when the group includes a student with a Disruptive Behavior Disorder. It has been proven that 10 percent of children and adolescents have these types of disorders. Half of these young people have Attention Deficit Hyperactivity Disorder, and there are a substantial number with mood disorders. It is sometimes difficult to identify these disorders because all children are upset at times. It is natural for children to test the limits of their parents and teachers. As teachers, we need to focus on how to address these disorders and still maintain a healthy learning environment for our other students. Here are some simple strategies and interventions to help these students:

- Clearly establish rules and behavior expectations in the classroom.
- Provide positive reinforcement.
- Teach anger-management and conflict-resolution skills.
- Facilitate kind acts.
- Use a behavior contract to address misbehavior.
- Establish provisions for students to cool off.
- Use a timer to encourage positive behavior.
- Teach children to self-monitor their behavior.
- Provide a warm and encouraging environment.

Reaching Every Child

Stuttering: Children who stutter repeat sounds or words, have broken speech, or hesitate. According to psychologist and author Myles Cooley, Ph.D., about 1 percent of young people experience stuttering issues. Most will grow out of this problem during early adolescence. The academic difficulties these children experience are related to participation in class. These students don't want to read aloud, nor do they want to recite their memory work, because they don't want their peers to hear them and tease them. Many of these children become severely isolated socially because of the fear of speaking with their classmates. Here are some ways to help the student become more willing to participate:

- Show patience when the student is speaking.
- Reduce your rate of speech while speaking to the student.
- Maintain eye contact with the student while he is stuttering.
- Ask questions that the student can answer simply.
- Minimize students' oral reading requirements and oral reports.
- Create a special time outside class when the student can speak with you.
- Take immediate action if any student mimics, laughs at, or teases a child who stutters.
- Provide social skills instruction for the entire class.

Curriculum Connection

Paul was just as eager to tell King Agrippa about Jesus as he was to tell any merchant, philosopher, or slave he met in a foreign city. Social status meant nothing to him when he had the opportunity to share the Gospel. Discuss social status with your students and how it impacts our lives. Section 6.3.3.6, Social Status, will help. It's located in the sixth-grade Social Studies volume of the Concordia Curriculum Guide series.

UNIT 9—THE CHRISTIAN CHURCH GROWS

LESSON 99

Shipwrecked

ACTS 27 (SHIPWRECKED); 28:1–11 (MAROONED)

Background

It is probable that the evangelist Luke traveled with Paul on the way to Rome, because Luke, the writer of Acts, often refers to "we" in the narrative and gives an eyewitness description of the events. Initially, they traveled on a "coaster," a ship that hugged the coastline, stopping frequently at ports along the way. Probably hoping to speed up the trip to Rome, the centurion moved his soldiers and prisoners to a ship from Alexandria, probably carrying grain from Egypt to Rome, which sailed on a more direct route out to sea (and also out to danger, because the stormy season was approaching). The first time they ignored Paul's warnings, they sailed into trouble. The second time Paul advised them, they listened (they had no alternative because they were about to sink). Through all of these dangers, God kept Paul informed and safe. God had a significant purpose for getting Paul safely to Malta and then safely to Rome: Paul was to spread the news of salvation through Christ Jesus to more and more people.

Central Truth

God is strong to save us, even in the worst situations.

Objectives

- Realize that there are times when fear and trouble overwhelm us.
- Believe God's promise to be with us and keep us in His mercy, no matter what.
- Entrust ourselves to Him wholeheartedly whenever we are in need.

Materials

- Hymnals and music CDs
- Reproducible 99
- Web Resource 99a
- Web Resource 99b

Bible Prep

Post in advance so students can bookmark the reference before class time.
- Acts 27:1–28:11

Devotions

Carmen's first mistake that day was getting into the kayak when she knew it was too windy. Her second mistake was not telling her family where she was going. Another mistake was not listening to her dad earlier when he had told her to practice her kayaking skills with her brothers. It would be a morning of mistakes. When the strong winds and waves pushed her downstream, away from camp, and she was not able to control the kayak, she knew she was in trouble and wouldn't be able to right herself if she tipped over.

Now here she was, heading farther away from their cabin, being pushed along against her will. *I should have told someone I was going out on the water,* Carmen thought with regret. With all her strength, she dug the paddle into the muddy river bottom. She slowed for a second, but then she spun around backward. Suddenly, the kayak flipped—and she was underwater.

God, please help me! Carmen prayed. *I'm in trouble!* Her mind raced as she tried to remember what she had heard her dad tell her brothers. There was some sort of trick to flipping upright, but she couldn't think of what it was. A surge of panic welled up in her chest, and again she prayed frantically for help, knowing she wouldn't be able to hold her breath much longer. *Lord, please give me the strength to get out of this mess!* she prayed.

In what felt like an eternity—but was really just a matter of seconds—she pulled her body out of the kayak while still underwater. She found her footing in the murky water and pushed herself to the surface, hitting her shoulder on the kayak on the way up. Struggling against the strong wind and current, she reached for the boat before it could float away.

Thank you, Lord! I am so sorry for trying to do this by myself. Please forgive me for not listening to my dad! Now Carmen prayed with a sense of relief. With an ache in her shoulder, she pulled the kayak closer and gave it a flip. Here, the water was shallow enough for her to walk in the water and push the kayak back to shore.

Her relief was cut short when she reached the shoreline. Soaking wet, she pulled her ruined cell phone out of her pocket. Though mad at herself over ruining her phone, she said another silent prayer of thanks that God had kept her safe. She knew she would make a lot of mistakes in life, yet she was grateful that God would always be near.

Sing "O God, Our Help in Ages Past" (*LSB* 733; recorded as *Hymn of the Month for grade 3, November*). Chant or speak Psalm 95:1–7 to praise the Lord.

419

INTO the lesson

Say, **Today we are going to talk about disasters.** Some disasters are smaller, such as forgetting to bring your homework to school the day of your big report. Some disasters are enormous, such as the earthquakes, tsunamis, tornadoes, and hurricanes we hear about in the news. In today's world, there are many ways to call for help when a disaster strikes. Use Reproducible 99 to explore some of these, and then emphasize that the most important call for help is at the bottom of the page. **God will always hear our cries for help. That doesn't mean we always will be rescued in the way and at the time we want. We must trust that God knows what is best. And we also can be certain that He has saved us from the greatest disasters of all—sin, death, and the devil—by sending Jesus to be our Savior.**

After looking through the reproducible activity, point out that the Bible story today is about Paul and stormy seas and a shipwreck. Point out that the song on Web Resource 99a was originally written for the Bible narrative about Jesus in a ship with His disciples on the Sea of Galilee. But the song is just as appropriate for today's lesson, because God was also with Paul in the ship on the Mediterranean Sea. And it also applies to us, because Jesus is with us in any kind of trouble or danger. Sing the song together.

Lesson 99

Shipwrecked

Sailing for Rome

Paul was now the prisoner of a Roman centurion named Julius, of the Augustan Cohort. As they set sail for Rome, winter was approaching, which is a dangerous time for storms on the Mediterranean Sea. What follows is best read step-by-step from Scripture in Acts 27:9–44.

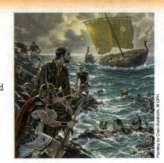

Message in a Bottle

Communication was often difficult in Bible times. There were no phones, radios, telegraph, or e-mail to send a message from a ship. Sometimes, people would put a message to their family into a bottle, cork it, and toss it into the sea, hoping that somehow—perhaps after months or even years—it would be found and taken to their family. The message often shared faith, encouragement, and hope. If you were tossing a message in a bottle into the sea, what message of faith and hope about Jesus would you share with friends and family? Write it here.

Review

Covenant Connection

In all of Paul's troubles, trials, and shipwrecks (he was in four), God was with him, setting his focus always on the Gospel. As was promised of old, and to the Early Christian Church, and to us today, God is near, with His shelter and salvation. Psalm 91:1–2 says, "He who dwells in the shelter of the Most High will abide in the shadow of the Almighty. I will say to the LORD, 'My refuge and my fortress, my God, in whom I trust.'"

204

INTO the Word

Sailing for Rome

The best way to look at this Bible story is to read it directly from Scripture. The author, Luke, gives a detailed, step-by-step look at all the events, almost as if he were writing a ship's log. Go around the classroom and have each student read one verse (to capture the single moment). Invite students to stop at any time to ask a question or add a comment about what is happening. Read Acts 27:9–44. Here are additional questions you might ask:

1. **When the gentle south wind began to blow, how do you think the crew felt?** (In v. 13, it says they "supposed that they had obtained their purpose"; in other words, they thought their strategy had been successful.)

2. **This is an example of "the calm before the storm." Think about a time in your own life in which you experienced calm before trouble started. Was prayer a part of that experience?**

3. **What is symbolic about the crew throwing all the cargo overboard during the storm?** (This was a cargo ship; sometimes we need to give up everything and rely only on God.)

4. **Why did Paul wait until the crew was starving and had given up all hope before he offered them words of encouragement?** (Just the night before, he had a dream in which an angel told him that God would spare him and all the lives that sailed with him. Paul wanted to offer hope in a time of great despair. Weathering storms can make our faith stronger, knowing that we must rely on God.)

5. **Why did Paul pray before eating in front of the crew?** (He wanted to set a good example and continue to offer encouragement and hope.)

6. **Why did God spare the entire crew?** Our God is a loving God, and He wished for the crew to come to know Him. He used Paul to further His kingdom, even during Paul's imprisonment.

420

Survival!
Acts 28:1–10

Narrator: As the ship began to break apart and sink, Paul and the rest of the crew swam or floated to an unknown island, where they were greeted by friendly islanders.

Islander 1: Welcome to Malta, our little island. You must be wet and cold.

Islander 2: Come and sit. We will build you a fire.

Paul: Let me help gather some firewood. Whoa, a snake has attacked my arm!

Islander 1: It's a poisonous viper!

Islander 2: *(To other islanders)* He must be a criminal because even though he escaped from the sea, justice has not allowed him to live!

Luke: Quick, shake the viper off, into the fire!

Narrator: Paul suffered no ill effects, and after waiting a long time, he did not swell up and die like the people thought he would. Then they changed their minds and said he was a god.

Paul: No! No! It is God who has saved me! He has saved me in many ways. Let me tell you about my God and Savior.

Publius: As chief official of the island, I welcome you to my home. We will need to be quiet, though, because my father is sick in bed with a bad fever.

Paul: I will visit him if you would like, and pray for God to bless him.

Narrator: So Paul went in to see him. After praying, Paul placed his hands on him, and the man was healed in the name of the Lord.

Father of Publius: *(Seated)* Wow, I feel so much better! Thanks be to God! *(Stands and shakes Paul's hand and gives Luke a high five)*

Narrator: After this had happened, the rest of the sick came to see Paul, and many people heard the Gospel message of salvation in Jesus. After three months, the stormy winter was over, and it was time to continue on their journey.

Paul: Thank you for all your kindness.

Islander 1: *(Giving Paul a pat on the back)* No, let us thank *you* for sharing the message of the one true God with us!

Islander 2: *(Giving Paul a high five)* If you must leave, here—have some supplies for your journey to Rome. Wherever you travel, know that distance does not separate us, for we are one in Christ.

Narrator: They honored Paul and the crew, and when they were ready to sail, the islanders gave them what they needed. God blessed Paul and his crew in spite of the shipwreck so that others could see the work of God and hear His saving Word.

Remember
"So take heart . . . for I have faith in God that it will be exactly as I have been told." (Acts 27:25)

Message in a Bottle

Continue with this activity in the Student Book, which provides for an opportunity for a faith witness.

Survival!

Paul's troubles were not over. He was bitten by a poisonous viper, he was called a criminal, and he was called a god, all while wet and shivering in the cold on the beach of an unknown island. But God used this incident to capture the island people's attention and make them receptive to Paul's important Gospel message. Read Acts 28:1–10 and the readers theater in the Student Book.

They spent three months (the winter) on the island before traveling on to Rome and Paul's trial before Caesar. An interesting side note is that Paul stayed in Rome under "minimum security" house arrest. He was allowed to stay by himself with just one soldier guarding him, and he could have visitors (Acts 28:16–17). This, too, was part of God's plan to allow Paul's ministry to continue.

Say, **Through all of this, Paul "kept his eyes on the prize." He focused on the Gospel message of the salvation we have in Jesus. In Philippians 3:14, he wrote, "I press on toward the goal for the prize of the upward call of God in Christ Jesus." That "prize" is not something Paul earned—it was won by Jesus when He died on the cross and arose at Easter. That prize is eternal life, and we can rejoice, along with the apostle Paul, that Jesus gives that prize to us too. "Thanks be to God, who gives us the victory through our Lord Jesus Christ" (1 Corinthians 15:57).** Sing together about pressing on to receive the prize of eternal life from Jesus Christ, who gives us the victory He has won for us! Use Web Resource 99b to sing "Don't Look Back."

Then explore the Bible words to remember. While Paul was speaking to a specific situation, we can apply this observation to all of God's Word. We can be certain of God's truth. We can be certain of all of God's promises!

Lesson Support

Curriculum Connection

While Paul was on Malta, he was bitten by a poisonous snake, and the islanders expected him to die (Acts 28:3–6). Make a health connection to Paul's story by learning first aid. Use section 6.3.6, Health and Safety Practices, found in the sixth-grade Health volume of the Concordia Curriculum Guide series. If applicable to your area, see to it that students also learn what to do in case of snakebite.

Ideas for the Gifted

Let several students work together to simulate what would have occurred if Paul could have had a GPS mapping system. Students may trace the journey on a map and record these directions to indicate the journey's path.

GPS directions:
1. Begin voyage by leaving Caesarea and sailing north along the coast of Asia.
2. Arrive at Sidon on the right.
3. Pass the lee of Cyprus on the left.
4. Sail across the open sea off the coast of Cilicia and Pamphylia on the right.
5. Arrive at Myra in Lycia on the right.
6. Recalculating; cannot arrive at Cnidus.
7. Sail to the lee of Crete opposite Salmone.
8. Continue along the coast to Fair Havens, near the town of Lasea on the right.
9. Continue to sail along the shore of Crete.
10. Recalculating; pass the island Cauda.
11. Recalculating; unable to arrive at destination; swim to the island of Malta.

Check it Out

Would sailors in ancient times have had glass bottles to throw into the sea with their message? Yes; the Romans were good at glassmaking. Archaeologists today find many pieces of glass in ancient Roman digs. Often these are just broken bits that had been tossed onto a refuse pile, but these shards of discarded glass have become valuable today. Roman glass often has a greenish-blue color, much like the color of a gem or of the sea. It has become popular for higher-end jewelry makers to use these two-thousand-year-old pieces of glass to make mosaics for decorating silver jewelry. Imagine being able to wear a piece of jewelry that contains Roman glass from biblical times!

Critical thinking

Prepare a large T-chart on the board with the column headings "A Dangerous Voyage" and "A Venomous Snakebite." With the whole group, compare and contrast the two incidents and the events involved. Challenge the students to provide ideas that show what we know about God and life itself. Some possible answers may include the following:

A Dangerous Voyage
God spared the crew.
The trip was dangerous to many.
Crew members doubted.
God allowed the storms to come.
Paul gave glory to God.

A Venomous Snakebite
God spared Paul.
The snake was dangerous to one person.
Islanders were certain Paul would die.
God allowed Paul to be bitten.
Paul gave glory to God.

Technology

Divide the class into teams, and challenge the students to create a list of nautical terms used in Acts 27. Have them compete to see which team can create the longest list. Set a time limit, such as two minutes. The list below can be used to check the lists and declare a winning team. Have teams visit a variety of Web sites that will create free word puzzles with the terms they enter. Allow students to print their word puzzles and distribute them to the other teams to try and solve.

Terms: *aground, anchor, bay, beach, bow, cargo, coast, foresail, gear, harbor, island, jettison, lee, northeaster, open sea, overboard, pilot, planks, port, reef, ropes, rudders, sailed, sailors, sandbar, ship, shore, soundings, stern, surf, tackle, tempest, vessel, voyage.* (Note: These terms are found in the ESV; your lists may vary if you use another version of the Bible.)

UNIT 9—THE CHRISTIAN CHURCH GROWS LESSON **100**

Paul and Timothy
1 AND 2 TIMOTHY

Background

As true God in the flesh, being a mentor was part of who Jesus was here on earth. He was a mentor to His twelve disciples, to individuals such as Nicodemus, and to crowds of thousands. The Church would increase in numbers due to the mentoring of these and other Christians. Our job as Christian educators is to mentor those around us, be they children, colleagues, congregations, or family members. If we have children of our own, they, too, carry the blessing of the mentoring business on their young shoulders. Is it a burden? It's a tall order, but the Lord's yoke is easy, and His burden is light.

During Paul's ministry, his letters became part of his mentoring program. His pastoral letters offered instructions to Timothy in caring for the Church. Today we can use technology to mentor others. We can reach far more people and have impact in ways never before possible, whether it be a note of encouragement or simply an e-mail with a Bible verse attached. God will guide us to mentor others as we grow in faith and share the love of Jesus.

It's important to remind our students to respect the advice and wisdom of people who are older and have more experience. While students do need to find things out for themselves, the hard way is still the hard way. Share with them the knowledge of others in your classroom. Have personal daily devotions in order to receive God's wisdom yourself.

C. S. Lewis once said, "The Christian does not think God will love us because we are good, but that God will make us good [sanctification] because He loves us." Part of what made the apostle Paul a strong mentor was his willingness to accept his own shortcomings. In 1 Timothy 1:15, Paul writes, "The saying is trustworthy and deserving of full acceptance, that Christ Jesus came into the world to save sinners, of whom I am the foremost." God will use us to further His kingdom in ways that He sees fit.

Central Truth
God gives us older Christians to teach us, mentor us, and help us grow up in faith and service to Christ.

Objectives
- Acknowledge our need for teaching, wisdom, and counsel as we grow in Christ.
- Appreciate the older Christians God has placed in our lives to provide this loving guidance for us.
- Honor, thank, and listen to these parents, pastors, teachers, and mentors.

Materials
- Hymnals and music CDs
- Web Resource 100a
- Reproducible 100

Bible Prep
Post in advance so students can bookmark references before class time.
- Acts 16:1–5
- Philippians 2:19–24
- Philippians 2:3
- 1 and 2 Timothy

Devotions

Julia loved her grandmother's new cell phone. She opened and closed the cover again and again, looking at the cool keypad. She was jealous. She didn't even *have* a cell phone, but her grandma would need a cell phone now that Grandpa was gone. He passed away right before Christmas, and Grandma was now living alone. Her family thought that she needed to learn how to use a cell phone, just in case there was an emergency. But Julia continued to play with the phone. Just then, her big sister Kayla walked into the room, and Julia was startled. She dropped the phone and it crashed to the floor, landing on the tiles with a crunching sound. Both girls watched in horror as the phone bounced under the table. "It was an accident! I didn't mean to drop it! Besides, you scared me when you came in!" Julia tried to make excuses, but she knew she shouldn't have been playing with it—and her sister reminded her of this fact. Kayla retrieved the phone and shook her head. Sure enough, it was broken. Julia felt sick to her stomach. "*Now* what do I do?" Julia asked, as tears stung her eyes. "You have to admit it, of course," Kayla replied. "Besides, that's what Grandpa would tell you to do." Julia thought for a moment, remembering how kind and caring her grandfather had been. Grandpa would always ask the girls if they had learned a lesson from their mistakes. Julia knew he would have told her to talk to Mom and Grandma and ask for forgiveness. But before Julia could say anything, Kayla spoke again. "Let's go talk to Grandma first. Otherwise, she won't know what happened to it, and she will think *she* broke it herself." Julia was grateful to have such caring parents and grandparents and an older sister who would remind her to do the right thing. Julia knew her mom and grandmother would forgive her. They were truly blessings from God. Sing "Thine Forever, God of Love" (*LSB* 687; recorded as *Hymn of the Month* for grade 6, May).

INTO the lesson

Plenty of Good Advice

Tell students that a *mentor* is a person who gives good advice to someone. Look over the first page of the lesson as you think about mentors. Ben Franklin gave advice that has been passed on through generations of people. Your students are mentored by parents, grandparents, coaches, and teachers. (It is a good process for students to consider the advice various people have given them.) Emphasize, though, that the best mentoring we have for our lives is found in Scripture.

Point out that today we will look at the relationship of Paul as mentor to a young person named Timothy. Project from your computer onto a screen so that your class can look at an online thesaurus to find other words that are similar to *mentor*. It is likely that you will find words such as *adviser, counselor,* and *guide,* among others.

Ask the students if they have a mentor or if they feel as though they may *be* a mentor to someone else. Ask them to think about the best possible mentor that ever lived. Pray together that God would lead them to listen and apply good advice, to discern advice that is not appropriate, and to be good mentors to others they may serve.

At some point in the lesson, you can explore Web Resource 100a, which is a review of the Bible words to remember in this unit. It is also an exploration of the best advice we have—advice from the Lord. **This advice focuses on life: our justified lives, as we are made holy and saints as Jesus takes away our sins with His perfect sacrifice, and our sanctified lives, as the Holy Spirit empowers us, bringing us and keeping us in faith, and enabling us to live that faith as people of God.**

INTO the Word

Mentoring a Young Disciple

As you look at the illustrations and read aloud the Scripture verses about Timothy, encourage your students to take a similar look at their own lives. They, too, are young like Timothy, and they, too, have the blessings of the Lord to guide their lives, now and in the future through the enabling power of the Holy Spirit.

Look at more advice on Reproducible 100. Then, as you look at the final memory verse, think of how appropriate this is as a conclusion to this level of the One in Christ series. (If you are not at the end of the school year, consider that extra time as an opportunity to explore more information in the Appendix and in other related biblical materials.)

Mentoring a Young Disciple

Paul was a teacher and mentor to young Timothy. Eventually they became co-workers, as Paul trained Timothy to become a pastor and missionary for the Gospel message of Christ Jesus.

1. Read about Timothy's background in Acts 16:1–2; and 2 Timothy 1:1–5 and 3:14–15. Write about your own background. _____
_____
_____
_____ .

2. Read about Timothy's life as a young person in 1 Timothy 4:12. Write about your life as a Christian. _____
_____
_____
_____ .

3. Read about Timothy as a faithful helper in Philippians 2:19–22. Write about what you can do to help others as you share the love and kindness of our Lord Jesus. _____
_____
_____
_____ .

Together share these words of encouragement by the epistle writer to Christians long ago and to us today. (See the Bible words to remember.)

Remember

"May the God of endurance and encouragement grant you to live in such harmony with one another, in accord with Christ Jesus, that together you may with one voice glorify the God and Father of our Lord Jesus Christ." (Romans 15:5–6)

Fight the Good Fight

The apostle Paul often traveled with Timothy, who was his helper on his missionary journeys. Sometimes, Paul had Timothy stay at a congregation to teach the new Christians while he moved on to another city.

Timothy visited Paul when he was in prison. Paul wrote at least two letters (epistles) to Timothy, especially to encourage him to grow up in faith in Jesus and faithfulness to the Scriptures.

Here is a piece of advice from Paul's Second Letter to Timothy: "God gave us a spirit not of fear but of power and love and self-control" (2 Timothy 1:7). What does this mean? What does this mean to you? What does this mean for your life as a Christian?

_____
_____
_____

Here is more of Paul's advice: "Fight the good fight of the faith. Take hold of the eternal life to which you were called" (1 Timothy 6:12). What does this mean for you and your life today?

_____
_____

First and foremost, Paul looked to the grace and mercy of God in Christ Jesus, giving Him all thanks and praise: "The grace of our Lord overflowed for me with the faith and love that are in Christ Jesus. The saying is trustworthy and deserving of full acceptance, that Christ Jesus came into the world to save sinners. . . . To the King of ages, immortal, invisible, the only God, be honor and glory forever and ever. Amen" (1 Timothy 1:14–15, 17).

Reproducible 100   Name _____
One in Christ™ © 2012 Concordia Publishing House. Reproduced by permission. Scripture: ESV®.

Curriculum Connection

Paul knew Timothy very well, and when he wrote to him, he was able to write appropriately, with a warm, personal style that paid attention to issues Timothy was likely to be concerned about. Make a connection to this story by helping your students learn to focus on a known audience in their own writing. Section 6.3.3.7, Format, Style, and Tone Appropriate for the Audience and Purpose, will help. You'll find it in the sixth-grade Language Arts volume of the Concordia Curriculum Guide series.

Searching Further

Create a PowerPoint presentation of encouragement for other Christians. Use Scripture from this lesson and other favorite verses to encourage others to be of service to one another. Focus on Paul's use of the phrase "The saying is trustworthy" (Timothy 1:15). Add the music of Christian hymns as a background for your presentation.

Working in Groups

Use 1 Timothy 4:12 to create an attractive poster to display on the bulletin board. Have students use the computer to create their own printouts of this verse to take home to display. Encourage them to be creative and use artwork and appealing font sizes. Mount the finished printouts on construction paper for a finished look.

Critical thinking

Newspapers and magazines often have an advice column in which an editor responds to the questions and concerns of people who write to him or her, seeking advice. Read aloud the following letters and have students work in groups to craft responses for their own "advice column."

Dear Mentor,
My parents have been divorced for a little over a year now, and my dad keeps telling me to "get over it" whenever I tell him that I am still sad that they aren't together. I have a hard time trying to keep my schoolwork caught up because I live in two households, and I keep forgetting my assignments and books at one house or the other. It's depressing to get such bad grades! How can I get over it and try to be happy?

Dear Mentor,
My older brother has started hanging out with some troublemakers. He seems very moody lately and has even come home late at night, smelling like smoke. Whenever I ask him what's going on, he tells me to mind my own business. My parents are clueless and don't think there's a problem. Am I too young to give advice? What can I do to get through to my big brother?

Dear Mentor,
My best friend moved away, and now it seems as though I am all alone. We used to do everything together, and now I don't have anyone to talk to. What can I do to try to make new friends so I am not so lonely?

APPENDIX

Table of Contents

Bible Overview	209
Bible Concordance	218
Bible Timelines	233
Bible Atlas	236
Bible Dictionary	242
Small Catechism	249

BIBLE OVERVIEW

Books of the Bible
(Sixty-Six Books)

Old Testament
(Thirty-Nine Books)

Genesis: This is a book of beginnings—the beginning of the world, the beginning of sin, and the beginning of God's promise to Adam and Eve to send a Savior to rescue humankind from sin and death. Because of the extent of sin, God makes a new beginning by sending the great flood and starting anew with Noah and his family. But sin remains, and God chooses a family to build into a nation that will carry the promise of the Messiah—the only salvation from sin. God gives this promise to Abraham, who passes it on to his family through Isaac, Jacob, Judah, and so on. As in the story of Joseph, we see that even when all around us seems to go wrong, God has a plan to give us hope and blessing.

Exodus: The story of God's chosen people—known then as the Hebrews or Israelites—continues in the Book of Exodus, which means to go out. The people go out of slavery in Egypt, led by the Lord and His appointed leader, Moses. This is a story of God's faithfulness, patience, and blessing to a people who, like us, are undeserving and continue to fall into sin. God's grace and forgiveness are constant as He leads them to the Promised Land.

Leviticus: Leviticus is the third of the five books known as the Pentateuch (which are also known as the Books of Moses and the Books of the Law). Leviticus focuses on God's people as a special people set apart to worship Him and to live through obedience, rededicating their lives to God's service. The sacrifices, feasts, and offerings foreshadow, or point to, the Messiah, Jesus, the perfect sacrifice to come; so, though this is called a Book of the Law, it also contains a Gospel message of hope through the promised Savior.

Numbers: The name of this book refers to the counting of people and property, but it is largely about the Israelites wandering in the desert wilderness. Time and again, we see God faithfully providing for His people. The mercy and grace of Jesus is foreshadowed through the account of the bronze snake (lifted up for God's promise of deliverance), the rock that brings saving water, and the daily manna. These are a preview of Jesus as the eternal living water and the bread of life eternal.

Deuteronomy: Deuteronomy is the retelling of God's law. This is a review of what God has done and of God's will for a new generation of people, preparing them for their life in the Promised Land. God calls His people to rededicate their lives to Him, reminding Israel again of the promise God has made to them and the promise they have made to Him in the covenant that He will be their God and they will be His people. We have this promise, too, in the new covenant, or New Testament, which we have through the work of Christ Jesus.

Joshua: This begins the Books of History, which continue through the Book of Esther. Joshua, meaning "the Lord is salvation," becomes the new leader, taking the people into the Promised Land (Canaan) after the death of Moses. Joshua calls on the people to remain faithful to God, who has always been faithful to them. Joshua foreshadows Jesus, who leads us to the promised land of heaven through His death and resurrection.

Judges: This Book of History tells of the ongoing cycle of people "doing what was right in their own eyes," turning away from God, falling under the power of evil enemies and tribulation, God's call to repentance, and God's deliverance through His chosen leaders (such as Gideon, Deborah, and Samson). This is a cycle that continues even today as God continues to call us to repentance from our sinfulness and as He offers deliverance from the evils of sin, death, and Satan through the salvation we have in Jesus. God's faithful love is constant.

Ruth: The story of Ruth is about a woman who was not an Israelite but came to faith in God and became one of the ancestors of Jesus, reminding us that God's Kingdom is for all people who have faith in Him. The Book of Ruth examines the concept of redemption, or "buying back," which foreshadows Jesus as our Redeemer who bought us back from the power of the devil; the price was His own body and blood on the cross. The story of Ruth again shows the faithfulness of God in the midst of difficult circumstances in a changing world.

1 and 2 Samuel: The story of Samuel as prophet, priest, and judge foreshadows Jesus, the greatest Prophet, Priest, and King! Up until the time of Samuel, leaders were chosen by God to carry out His will because God Himself was the true ruler of the people. In time, however, the people wanted a king like other nations around them. The first two kings, Saul and David, were anointed by God's prophet Samuel. Both of these kings were sinners, as are all people; but Saul turned away from God while David turned to God in repentance and received forgiveness. God made a wonderful promise to David that the Messiah, the King of kings, would come from his family. This promise is completed through Jesus (often called the Son of David), who rules forever as our Savior and who will someday take all believers to His kingdom in heaven.

1 and 2 Kings: These books are a continuation of the history found in 1 and 2 Samuel, from the time of the united kingdom (when David and Solomon ruled as kings) through the times of the divided kingdom (with Israel in the north and Judah in the south). The Northern Kingdom never had a king who was faithful to God; eventually, God allowed the Assyrians to capture and exile that nation. The Southern Kingdom of Judah was largely unfaithful, though occasionally, there were God-fearing kings who tried to lead the people back to the Lord. But eventually, Judah, too, was taken into captivity, in exile in Babylon. Throughout these years of turmoil, God continued the royal line of David in Judah and maintained the promise of the Messiah to come. God continued to send His words of Law and Gospel through the prophets, whose writings are found in the latter portion of the Old Testament.

1 and 2 Chronicles: These books focus on the reigns of King David and his son Solomon (who built the temple), continuing on through their royal family line in the Southern Kingdom. This family line also carried the promise of the Messiah, who came centuries later in the fullness of time in Christ Jesus. The author of Chronicles reminds the people that God has cared for them in the past and His care will continue throughout the ages. Leaders and governments change, but God remains unchanging in His call to repentance, grace, and mercy.

Ezra: The books of Ezra, Nehemiah, and Esther continue the story of God's people who had been in captivity in Babylon for seventy years and who finally began to see their need for reliance and hope in the true God. Ezra was part of a group who returned to Jerusalem to complete the rebuilding of the temple, assuring the people that God continued to be present with them. Ezra, a priest, taught the people God's Word and prayed for their forgiveness and renewed faithfulness. God kept alive the promise of the Savior, who was to be born in the land of Judah.

Nehemiah: God worked through Ezra to rebuild His people spiritually; God worked through Nehemiah to rebuild His people physically. Without the protection of city walls, the people who had returned to Jerusalem from captivity were in constant danger. God answered Nehemiah's prayers, choosing him to guide the people to rebuild the walls in just fifty-two days, using armed guards working side by side with the construction workers to protect the project. At the dedication of the wall, the people gave all glory to God!

Esther: This is the story of Jewish people who stayed in Persia instead of returning to Judah. Again, we see how God can work through ordinary people, such as Esther, to accomplish His will. Through God's plan, Esther, though Jewish, became a queen in Persia and bravely spoke up for her people, even at the risk of her own life. We see again that God is with His people blessing them and working through them to make a difference. This ends the historical section of the Old Testament.

Job: This begins the section of five books called Wisdom and Poetry. These were originally written in Hebrew and do not rhyme as many poems in English do. (Hebrew poetry repeats ideas rather than repeating sounds.) This is the story of a man who loses everything and suffers much. Through his story, we learn that the devil, not God, is actually responsible for sufferings, but God is in control and limits how much Satan may do. We cannot always understand God's wisdom and loving plans, but He is always with us, working to accomplish His good purpose. Job's life is a witness to others that even troubles can provide opportunities to praise God. God heard Job's pleas in his time of trouble and restored Job to health and gave him many new blessings. One of the clearest Old Testament passages on resurrection is in chapter 19, where Job says, "I know that my Redeemer lives."

Psalms: The Book of Psalms is sometimes called the hymnal of the Old Testament—a book of prayer and praise. Psalms gives us examples of how God's people deal with both joys and sorrows. The psalms express the personal relationship that believers have with their God. David (as shepherd, warrior, and king) wrote about half of the psalms. This book repeats the theme that God is the good and faithful King of all creation and to His people. There are also frequent references to the coming Messiah.

Proverbs: This is a collection of wise sayings that tell us how to live a godly life. There is practical advice on many subjects, such as making friends, handling money, and caring for the poor. But real wisdom is based on honoring and faithfully following God. Proverbs appears to be very law oriented, telling you what to do and not do. However, a repentant sinner, justified through Christ Jesus, can look at these verses as guidelines for living a sanctified life through the enabling power of the Holy Spirit.

Ecclesiastes: The author of this book directs us to the real purpose of life and encourages us to stay away from things that are meaningless. Some things in life are empty, but life with God brings true joy and direction. Fame, possessions, power, and wealth cannot bring the eternal blessings of forgiveness, life, and salvation, which we receive only through Christ Jesus.

Song of Solomon: Also known as Song of Songs, this book tells of the relationship between a husband and wife and, in turn, illustrates the love God has for us. God's love is perfect, faithful, and He wants us with Him always. This is a love that is willing to give up everything for the loved one, which is what Jesus did when He gave up His life for our salvation.

Isaiah: The remainder of the Old Testament contains the books of the prophets: the first five are considered the Major Prophets, and the next twelve are the Minor Prophets. The prophets spoke messages from God, mostly during the time of the divided kingdom, but with words that are still significant in today's world. They spoke warnings about sin, pleaded for repentance, and continued to give more information about the coming of the Messiah. Although Isaiah lived centuries before Christ, he told how Jesus would be born, suffer, die, and rise again to take away our sins. God's promises of the Messiah comforted His people, even when Judah was in misery because of sin. The prophets Amos, Hosea, and Micah were also living at this time.

Jeremiah: Jeremiah loved his Lord; He also loved his nation enough to speak out the truth about its sin and the coming consequences. Jeremiah dramatically called the people to repent and spoke compassionately of God's forgiveness, mercy, and the promise of the Savior—the Lord, "our Righteousness"—who was yet to come. His harsh warnings often made him unpopular with his countrymen, who ridiculed and even hated him. Although many people did not consider Jeremiah to be successful in changing the hearts of the people, he was truly successful in that he faithfully and boldly proclaimed God's Word.

Lamentations: Lamentations is a poetic book of weeping. The author, thought to be Jeremiah, is crying over the destruction of Jerusalem—the consequence of sin, as prophesied. However, even in the middle of terrible sadness, with God there is hope. God's compassion never fails. God did later restore His people, and through them, He kept His promise of the Messiah.

Ezekiel: The prophet Ezekiel lived in the time when Jerusalem had been conquered and the temple burned. In the middle of these difficult times, God chose Ezekiel to call the people to repentance and to restore and renew them spiritually. Ezekiel used picture language and even acted out some of his prophecies to explain the visions he had received from the Lord, telling of God's grace and mercy.

Daniel: The Book of Daniel is partly narrative story and partly visionary prophecy. Though Daniel and his friends are in exile in a foreign country, God blesses their faithfulness and bold witness in amazing ways. The book emphasizes that God is the ruler over all kingdoms and His reign is forever. The latter half of the book records amazing visions Daniel received from God about the future, and particularly about the coming Messiah. God is in charge of all history, and He directs all things for the purpose of saving His people through Christ Jesus.

Hosea: This is the first book of the Minor Prophets. It tells of the prophet Hosea's relationship to his unfaithful wife Gomer. Hosea's life becomes a picture or symbol of God's constant, continual love for His people. Even when they are unfaithful to Him, God continues to call His people to repentance. Unlike most prophets, who were from Judah, Hosea was from the Northern Kingdom of Israel.

Joel: This prophet speaks of the destruction in Judah recently caused by a swarm of locusts that destroyed the crops as God's punishment for sin. Joel warns that if the people do not repent, there will be even greater destruction, caused by the swarm of an enemy's army. He says that the Day of the Lord will come to punish sin, but those who trust in God will be saved. God still promises salvation to all who trust Him, in Jesus.

Amos: Amos was a shepherd who became God's prophet to warn the people at a time of great wealth and idolatry. He warned the people not to trust in money or images, but to trust in the true God. Though the message is of condemnation, the book ends with a word of hope in the continued promise of the Savior for all who believe.

Obadiah: Obadiah is the shortest book in the Old Testament. This prophet speaks against the people of Edom, who were glad to see Judah suffering when taken captive by Babylon and rejoiced and benefited from Judah's despair. The prophet repeats God's promises to one day restore His people to their land.

Jonah: Jonah was an unwilling prophet who tried to run from God's command. He did not want God's message of repentance and forgiveness to be shared with the people of Nineveh, Israel's Assyrian enemy. God clearly wants all people to hear His Word and to come to faith—a message for us today to share with all people. Centuries later, Jesus compared sorrow over the sin of the people, but His burial in the tomb and resurrection that sadness turns to joy as the prophet on the third day to Jonah's three days in speaks of God's deliverance and salvation. the belly of the great fish.

Micah: The Book of Micah explains that God hates sin but loves the sinner. Though the people would be punished for their refusal to repent of sin, the prophet also speaks a message of hope in the coming Messiah. Micah points to Bethlehem as the birthplace of the Savior, who would care for His sheep and lead them like a shepherd. Though the people would still have to wait centuries for the fullness of time, God kept these promises in Christ Jesus, who, as Micah prophesied, came with strength, majesty, greatness, and peace.

Nahum: About 150 years after the time of Jonah, the people of Nineveh in Assyria had returned to their wicked and idolatrous ways. Nahum pronounced God's judgment on this nation that had taken Israel captive. Nahum said that God is slow to anger, but He brings justice on those who are guilty and is a refuge in times of trouble for those who trust in Him.

Habakkuk: This is a conversation, as the prophet asks God many questions and God answers, revealing His plan. God assures us that we can hope in Him even when surrounded by troubles because He is still in control and His will will be done. The prophet concludes by saying, "I will take joy in the God of my salvation" (3:18).

Zephaniah: This book begins with sorrow over the sin of the people, but that sadness turns to joy as the prophet speaks of God's deliverance and salvation. God will lead the people to repentance so that He may then rejoice over them and gather them to Himself. The prophet says that when the people return to the Lord, He will bless them and through them the whole earth will be blessed. That blessing is the promised Messiah by making strong connections to the Old Testament. Matthew shows time and again how Jesus fulfilled the prophecies of old, specifically and completely: The book begins with a genealogy showing that Jesus came from the royal line of David, but then goes on to show Jesus as King of kings who brings salvation to all people.

Haggai: The prophet Haggai encouraged the people returning from captivity to Jerusalem in order to rebuild their temple, and he called them to action. While this temple would not be as beautiful as Solomon's, it would have greater glory in that the Savior would one day come to this new temple.

Zechariah: As Zechariah encourages the rebuilding of the temple, he gives even greater encouragement through specific prophecies about the promised Savior, foretelling Jesus' triumphant entry into Jerusalem on Palm Sunday, His being betrayed for thirty pieces of silver, and His cleansing away of sin by His blood.

Malachi: The last Old Testament prophet, Malachi, foretold of the messenger (John the Baptist) who would come and get people ready for the coming of the Messiah (Jesus). Malachi is a bridge between the Old and New Testaments, a time span of four hundred years.

New Testament
(Twenty-Seven books)

Matthew: The four Gospels tell the stories of Jesus' life, death, and resurrected life, each with a unique perspective. Matthew, writing to a largely Jewish audience, emphasized that Jesus indeed is the promised Messiah by making strong connections to the Old Testament. Matthew shows time and again how Jesus fulfilled the prophecies of old, specifically and completely: The book begins with a genealogy showing that Jesus came from the royal line of David, but then goes on to show Jesus as King of kings who brings salvation to all people.

Mark: The style of the Gospel of Mark is full of action about what Jesus did (rather than what He fulfilled). The primary audience was Roman Christians, who would appreciate this active style of writing, which is brief and to the point. Mark was an assistant to the disciple Peter (Mark's mentor and primary source of information).

Luke: The author of this book, Luke, was a doctor who followed a second career as a missionary and also as a writer. Luke emphasizes Jesus' compassion for people as he tells of Jesus' teachings (especially in parables) and also of the miracles in Jesus' healing ministry. Jesus' compassion for people includes the poor, humble, the unpopular, and even the outcasts. Luke's primary sources appear to be Mary (Jesus' mother) and also the apostle Paul, with whom he traveled on many missionary journeys. Luke wrote this Gospel—as well as the Book of Acts—to Theophilus, a Gentile.

John: John's viewpoint tends to be more philosophical than the other Gospels, focusing more on the teachings of Jesus. This would relate especially well to John's Greek audience. His constant theme is the love of Jesus for all people. John states the purpose of this book when he says, "that you may believe that Jesus is the Christ, the Son of God, and that by believing you may have life in His name" (20:31). John emphasizes that Jesus is God's Word in the flesh; we know God by knowing Jesus, who Himself is true God.

Acts: Luke wrote this book of history called the Acts of the Apostles (which could actually be called the Acts of the Holy Spirit). It tells of the early growth of the Christian Church from the time of Christ's ascension into heaven through the giving of the Holy Spirit at Pentecost and then to the spread of the Gospel throughout the world. Acts also tells how the Holy Spirit works in the lives of individual believers such as Stephen, Peter, Paul, Philip, Lydia, and Dorcas.

Romans: Romans through Philemon are the Pauline Epistles, letters written by the apostle Paul to Christian churches (nine letters) and individual believers (four letters). The Book of Romans was written to the Christian church in Rome around the time of the emperor Nero. This epistle gives an eloquent account of the basic details of our Christian faith as it emphasizes the grace and mercy that is a gift from God through Christ Jesus. The focus is on eternal salvation for all who believe that we are justified through Christ's death and resurrection for our forgiveness.

1 and 2 Corinthians: These epistles were written to people in the seaport city of Corinth, a city known for its many idols to false gods. Paul heard that the church in Corinth had many problems. He wrote these letters to encourage them to remove their divisions and to be united in teachings about salvation through Jesus. He wanted them to restore order as they celebrated the Lord's Supper and to show loving care to others, especially those in need. The message of these letters is clear, strong, and very direct to the people then as well as people today.

Galatians: Paul's Letter to the Galatians reminds the Christians there that they need to clearly separate Law and Gospel. Some of the people were demanding that new Christians follow old Jewish law. Paul emphasizes that faith in Jesus alone is all that is necessary for salvation, not rules or works. This letter was probably passed around to several churches in Galatia, which is part of modern-day Turkey.

Ephesians: Ephesus was a very large commercial city. In this letter, Paul emphasizes clearly the message of salvation by grace alone in Christ. Paul wants the church in Ephesus to understand that there is nothing they can do to earn salvation; it is a gift of God through faith created by the Holy Spirit. As Paul describes and directs the church in Ephesus, he is speaking to us today, too, that the church is not a building but believers in Christ Jesus who want to serve Him.

Philippians: Philippi was a wealthy Roman colony in Macedonia. This letter to the Philippian church was a thank-you note from Paul for the gift they had sent him. It is a letter full of joy and expresses the love that Paul had for them, encouraging them to be faithful and to be united as troubles come to them. Paul encouraged them to face hard times with joy, knowing that in Christ they could do all things.

Colossians: Paul wrote to the church in the city of Colossae that they should be careful of the false teachings that were challenging them. He wants them to know that human ideas are nothing compared to the greatness of God. Knowledge combined with other philosophies and religions does not bring saving truth. Paul encouraged people in this church to let their faith be shown in good works. Since Colossae was on an important trade route, information could easily be passed on from this church location to other churches.

1 and 2 Thessalonians: Thessalonica was a busy seaport that served as an important trade center. These epistles were written to Christians there who were under attack and physically persecuted. Paul encouraged the believers in Thessalonica to continue in their faith and look forward to the hope that is theirs in Christ Jesus. Paul also replied to their questions concerning the second coming of Christ, assuring them that this will not be a fearful time for believers, but rather a time of comfort and joy.

1 and 2 Timothy: Having been raised in a godly home, Timothy was led to Christ and trained by Paul as Timothy accompanied Paul on several mission trips. Paul wrote these two letters to Timothy to explain how church workers should teach and live. Paul also gives Timothy information on recognizing and dealing with false teachers. Paul is handing over his ministry to the church to a new generation as he challenges Timothy to put his hope and trust in the message of Christ Jesus.

Titus: This letter is to Titus, a Greek, who is a church worker on the island of Crete and had traveled with Paul on some of his missionary journeys. Paul gives Titus instructions about organizing the church and about the daily life of a Christian living in faith, emphasizing that godly living is always motivated by God's love for us in Christ Jesus.

Philemon: Paul writes this personal letter to Philemon, who is a slave owner. Paul intercedes for the runaway slave Onesimus, offering to pay off his debts and pleading that Philemon welcome him back. This is a picture of us as sinners who are slaves to sin. Jesus has paid the debt for our guilt and intercedes on our behalf before God the Father, who now welcomes us back to His family.

Hebrews: The remaining epistles are known as the General Epistles. The writer (unknown) to the Hebrews writes to Jewish communities, sharing information on the priesthood, with which they would be very familiar, to teach about the person and work of Jesus. It shows that Jesus is the fulfillment of the Old Testament laws and that He is greater than the prophets. Not only is He the great High Priest, He is also the perfect and complete sacrifice.

James: James is a practical book of Christian living. He wants people to understand that works are an important indication of faith and that "faith without works" is dead. Good works do not create saving faith, but when saving faith in Jesus exists, it is always followed with Christian living. (Justification is followed by sanctification.)

1 and 2 Peter: Peter writes these letters to people who are being persecuted for their faith. He reminds them that Jesus understands, for He suffered too. Jesus gives them an example of how to suffer and offers grace and hope in their time of trial. Peter reminds them that the troubles they face as Christians will make their faith strong. Peter warns about false teachers and encourages the people to be faithful until Christ comes again.

1, 2, and 3 John: John was an old man when he wrote these letters and often refers to the readers as his "dear children." He summarizes the love and mercy we have in Christ Jesus, which is our motivation to show love and mercy to others. John emphasizes that Jesus is both Son of God and Son of Man.

Jude: Jude (probably a half brother of Jesus) was written to Christians who have problems with false teachers. He reminds Christians that they are kept in their faith by Jesus. Jude challenges Christians of all times and all ages to stand up for what they believe in Christ and clearly protect the true faith.

Revelation: This book of prophecy is different from the other Bible books because it contains messages about the end of the world written in picture language. Revelation is a message from the apostle John, revealing, or showing, that Jesus will return triumphantly at His second coming. As Genesis starts with the beginning of time, Revelation speaks of the end of time, when we will see Jesus Christ's complete victory over sin, death, and the power of the devil. Christians are challenged to be strong and alive in their proclamation of faith and to remain faithful to the Last Day.

BIBLE CONCORDANCE

Based on the ESV
(English Standard Version)

ABUNDANT

Genesis 41:49 And Joseph stored up grain in great **abundance**, like the sand of the sea, until he ceased to measure it, for it could not be measured.

Numbers 20:11 Moses lifted up his hand and struck the rock with his staff twice, and water came out **abundantly**, and the congregation drank.

Psalm 51:1 Have mercy on me, O God, according to Your steadfast love; according to Your **abundant** mercy blot out my transgressions.

Psalm 147:5 Great is our Lord, and **abundant** in power; His understanding is beyond measure.

John 10:10 I came that they may have life and have it **abundantly**.

Ephesians 3:20–21 Now to Him who is able to do far more **abundantly** than all that we ask or think, according to the power at work within us, to Him be glory in the church and in Christ Jesus throughout all generations, forever and ever. Amen.

BAPTIZE

Matthew 28:19 Go therefore and make disciples of all nations, **baptizing** them in the name of the Father and of the Son and of the Holy Spirit.

Acts 2:38 And Peter said to them, "Repent and be **baptized** every one of you in the name of Jesus Christ for the forgiveness of your sins, and you will receive the gift of the Holy Spirit."

Galatians 3:27 For as many of you as were **baptized** into Christ have put on Christ.

BELIEVE

John 6:40 For this is the will of My Father, that everyone who looks on the Son and **believes** in Him should have eternal life, and I will raise him up on the last day.

John 11:25 Jesus said to her, "I am the resurrection and the life. Whoever **believes** in Me, though he die, yet shall he live."

John 20:31 These are written so that you may **believe** that Jesus is the Christ, the Son of God, and that by **believing** you may have life in His name.

Acts 16:31 And they said, "**Believe** in the Lord Jesus, and you will be saved."

BENEFITS

Psalm 103:2 Bless the LORD, O my soul, and forget not all His **benefits**.

Psalm 116:12 What shall I render to the LORD for all His **benefits** to me?

CLEAN

Psalm 51:2 Wash me thoroughly from my iniquity, and **cleanse** me from my sin!

Psalm 51:10 Create in me a **clean** heart, O God, and renew a right spirit within me.

1 John 1:9 If we confess our sins, He is faithful and just to forgive us our sins and to **cleanse** us from all unrighteousness.

COMFORT

Psalm 23:4 Even though I walk through the valley of the shadow of death, I will fear no evil, for You are with me; Your rod and Your staff, they **comfort** me.

Psalm 119:50 This is my **comfort** in my affliction, that Your promise gives me life.

2 Corinthians 1:3 Blessed be the God and Father of our Lord Jesus Christ, the Father of mercies and God of all **comfort**.

2 Thessalonians 2:16–17 Now may our Lord Jesus Christ Himself, and God our Father, who loved us and gave us eternal **comfort** and good hope through grace, **comfort** your hearts and establish them in every good work and word.

COMPASSION

Isaiah 49:13 Sing for joy, O heavens, and exult, O earth; break forth, O mountains, into singing! For the LORD has comforted his people and will have **compassion** on his afflicted.

Colossians 3:12 Put on then, as God's chosen ones, holy and beloved, **compassionate** hearts, kindness, humility, meekness, and patience.

CONFESS

Psalm 32:5 I acknowledged my sin to You, and I did not cover my iniquity; I said, "I will **confess** my transgressions to the LORD," and You forgave the iniquity of my sin.

Psalm 38:18 I **confess** my iniquity; I am sorry for my sin.

Romans 10:9 Because, if you **confess** with your mouth that Jesus is Lord and believe in your heart that God raised Him from the dead, you will be saved.

Philippians 2:11 And every tongue **confess** that Jesus Christ is Lord, to the glory of God the Father.

1 John 4:15 Whoever **confess**es that Jesus is the Son of God, God abides in him, and he in God.

CONTINUE

Acts 4:31 And when they had prayed, the place in which they were gathered together was shaken, and they were all filled with the Holy Spirit and **continued** to speak the word of God with boldness.

Acts 13:43 And after the meeting of the synagogue broke up, many Jews and devout converts to Judaism followed Paul and Barnabas, who, as they spoke with them, urged them to **continue** in the grace of God.

Colossians 1:23 Continue in the faith, stable and steadfast, not shifting from the hope of the gospel that you heard, which has been proclaimed in all creation under heaven.

Colossians 4:2 Continue steadfastly in prayer, being watchful in it with thanksgiving.

2 Timothy 3:14 But as for you, **continue** in what you have learned and have firmly believed.

Hebrews 13:1 Let brotherly love **continue**.

COURAGE

Deuteronomy 31:6 Be strong and **courageous**. Do not fear or be in dread of them, for it is the LORD your God who goes with you. He will not leave you or forsake you.

Joshua 1:9 Be strong and **courageous**. Do not be frightened, and do not be dismayed, for the LORD your God is with you wherever you go.

Psalm 27:14 Wait for the Lord; be strong, and let your heart take **courage**; wait for the LORD!

CREATE

Psalm 51:10 Create in me a clean heart, O God, and renew a right spirit within me.

Isaiah 42:5 Thus says God, the LORD, who **created** the heavens and stretched them out, who spread out the earth and what comes from it, who gives breath to the people on it and spirit to those who walk in it.

Ephesians 2:10 For we are His workmanship, **created** in Christ Jesus for good works, which God prepared beforehand, that we should walk in them.

Ephesians 4:24 And to put on the new self, **created** after the likeness of God in true righteousness and holiness.

Colossians 1:16 For by Him all things were **created**, in heaven and on earth, visible and invisible, whether thrones or dominions or rulers or authorities—all things were **created** through Him and for Him.

Hebrews 1:2 But in these last days He has spoken to us by His Son, whom He appointed the heir of all things, through whom also He **created** the world.

Revelation 4:11 Worthy are You, our Lord and God, to receive glory and honor and power, for You **created** all things, and by Your will they existed and were **created**.

CREATION

Mark 16:15 And He said to them, "Go into all the world and proclaim the gospel to the whole **creation**."

2 Corinthians 5:17 Therefore, if anyone is in Christ, he is a new **creation**. The old has passed away; behold, the new has come.

ENCOURAGE

Romans 15:4 For whatever was written in former days was written for our instruction, that through endurance and through the **encouragement** of the Scriptures we might have hope.

Romans 15:5 May the God of endurance and **encouragement** grant you to live in such harmony with one another, in accord with Christ Jesus.

1 Thessalonians 5:11 Therefore **encourage** one another and build one another up, just as you are doing.

ENDURE

Psalm 100:5 For the LORD is good; His steadfast love **endures** forever, and His faithfulness to all generations.

Psalm 104:31 May the glory of the LORD **endure** forever; may the LORD rejoice in His works.

Psalm 117:2 For great is His steadfast love toward us, and the faithfulness of the LORD **endures** forever. Praise the LORD!

Psalm 135:13 Your name, O LORD, **endures** forever, Your renown, O LORD, throughout all ages.

Psalm 136:1 Give thanks to the LORD, for He is good, for his steadfast love **endures** forever.

Lamentations 5:19 But You, O LORD, reign forever; Your throne **endures** to all generations.

Hebrews 12:2 Looking to Jesus, the founder and perfecter of our faith, who for the joy that was set before Him **endured** the cross, despising the shame, and is seated at the right hand of the throne of God.

ETERNAL

John 3:16 For God so loved the world, that He gave His only Son, that whoever believes in Him should not perish but have **eternal** life.

John 6:40 For this is the will of My Father, that everyone who looks on the Son and believes in Him should have **eternal** life, and I will raise him up on the last day.

Titus 3:7 So that being justified by His grace we might become heirs according to the hope of **eternal** life.

FAITH

Galatians 3:11 Now it is evident that no one is justified before God by the law, for "The righteous shall live by **faith**."

Ephesians 2:8 For by grace you have been saved through **faith**. And this is not your own doing; it is the gift of God.

1 Timothy 1:14 And the grace of our Lord overflowed for me with the **faith** and love that are in Christ Jesus.

1 Timothy 4:12 Let no one despise you for your youth, but set the believers an example in speech, in conduct, in love, in **faith**, in purity.

FAITHFUL

Psalm 86:15 But You, O Lord, are a God merciful and gracious, slow to anger and abounding in steadfast love and **faithfulness**.

1 John 1:9 If we confess our sins, He is **faithful** and just to forgive us our sins and to cleanse us from all unrighteousness.

Revelation 2:10 Be **faithful** unto death, and I will give you the crown of life.

FORGIVE

Ephesians 1:7 In Him we have redemption through His blood, the **forgiveness** of our trespasses, according to the riches of His grace.

Colossians 3:13 Bearing with one another and, if one has a complaint against another, forgiving each other; as the Lord has **forgiven** you, so you also must **forgive**.

GRACE

Romans 1:7 To all those in Rome who are loved by God and called to be saints: **Grace** to you and peace from God our Father and the Lord Jesus Christ.

Romans 3:24 And are justified by His **grace** as a gift, through the redemption that is in Christ Jesus.

2 Corinthians 9:8 And God is able to make all **grace** abound to you, so that having all sufficiency in all things at all times, you may abound in every good work.

Ephesians 2:8 For by **grace** you have been saved through faith. And this is not your own doing; it is the gift of God.

2 Peter 3:18 But grow in the **grace** and knowledge of our Lord and Savior Jesus Christ. To Him be the glory both now and to the day of eternity. Amen.

HELP

Psalm 18:6 In my distress I called upon the LORD; to my God I cried for **help**. From His temple He heard my voice, and my cry to Him reached His ears.

Psalm 28:7 The LORD is my strength and my shield; in Him my heart trusts, and I am **helped**; my heart exults, and with my song I give thanks to Him.

Psalm 40:13 Be pleased, O LORD, to deliver me! O LORD, make haste to **help** me!

Psalm 79:9 Help us, O God of our salvation, for the glory of Your name; deliver us, and atone for our sins, for Your name's sake!

Psalm 124:8 Our **help** is in the name of the LORD, who made heaven and earth.

John 14:26 But the **Helper**, the Holy Spirit, whom the Father will send in My name, He will teach you all things and bring to your remembrance all that I have said to you.

Acts 26:22 To this day I have had the **help** that comes from God.

Romans 8:26 Likewise the Spirit **helps** us in our weakness. For we do not know what to pray for as we ought, but the Spirit Himself intercedes for us with groanings too deep for words.

Hebrews 4:16 Let us then with confidence draw near to the throne of grace, that we may receive mercy and find grace to **help** in time of need.

Hebrews 13:6 So we can confidently say, "The Lord is my **helper**; I will not fear; what can man do to me?"

HOLY

Psalm 97:12 Rejoice in the LORD, O you righteous, and give thanks to His **holy** name!

Psalm 103:1 Bless the LORD, O my soul, and all that is within me, bless His **holy** name!

Isaiah 6:3 And one called to another and said: "**Holy, holy, holy** is the LORD of hosts; the whole earth is full of His glory!"

Acts 2:38 And Peter said to them, "Repent and be baptized every one of you in the name of Jesus Christ for the forgiveness of your sins, and you will receive the gift of the **Holy** Spirit."

Romans 15:13 May the God of hope fill you with all joy and peace in believing, so that by the power of the **Holy** Spirit you may abound in hope.

HOPE

Psalm 33:22 Let Your steadfast love, O LORD, be upon us, even as we **hope** in You.

Psalm 42:11 Why are you cast down, O my soul, and why are you in turmoil within me? **Hope** in God; for I shall again praise Him, my salvation and my God.

Psalm 71:5 For You, O Lord, are my **hope**, my trust, O LORD, from my youth.

Psalm 119:114 You are my hiding place and my shield; I **hope** in Your word.

Psalm 147:11 But the LORD takes pleasure in those who fear Him, in those who **hope** in His steadfast love.

Hebrews 10:23 Let us hold fast the confession of our **hope** without wavering, for He who promised is faithful.

Hebrews 11:1 Now faith is the assurance of things **hoped** for, the conviction of things not seen.

1 Peter 1:3 Blessed be the God and Father of our Lord Jesus Christ! According to His great mercy, He has caused us to be born again to a living **hope** through the resurrection of Jesus Christ from the dead.

1 Peter 3:15 But in your hearts honor Christ the Lord as holy, always being prepared to make a defense to anyone who asks you for a reason for the **hope** that is in you; yet do it with gentleness and respect.

Colossians 1:23 Continue in the faith, stable and steadfast, not shifting from the **hope** of the gospel that you heard, which has been proclaimed in all creation under heaven.

Titus 3:7 So that being justified by His grace we might become heirs according to the **hope** of eternal life.

JUSTIFY

Romans 3:24 And [we] are **justified** by His grace as a gift, through the redemption that is in Christ Jesus.

Romans 5:1 Therefore, since we have been **justified** by faith, we have peace with God through our Lord Jesus Christ.

Galatians 3:11 Now it is evident that no one is **justified** before God by the law, for "The righteous shall live by faith."

LAMB

John 1:29 The next day he saw Jesus coming toward him, and said, "Behold, the **Lamb** of God, who takes away the sin of the world!"

Revelation 5:12 Saying with a loud voice, "Worthy is the **Lamb** who was slain, to receive power and wealth and wisdom and might and honor and glory and blessing!"

Light

Psalm 27:1 The LORD is my **light** and my salvation; whom shall I fear? The LORD is the stronghold of my life; of whom shall I be afraid?

Psalm 119:105 Your word is a lamp to my feet and a **light** to my path.

John 8:12 Again Jesus spoke to them, saying, "I am the **light** of the world. Whoever follows Me will not walk in darkness, but will have the **light** of life."

1 John 1:7 But if we walk in the **light**, as He is in the **light**, we have fellowship with one another, and the blood of Jesus His Son cleanses us from all sin.

Mercy

Psalm 23:6 Surely goodness and **mercy** shall follow me all the days of my life, and I shall dwell in the house of the LORD forever.

Psalm 145:9 The LORD is good to all, and His **mercy** is over all that He has made.

Hebrews 4:16 Let us then with confidence draw near to the throne of grace, that we may receive **mercy** and find grace to help in time of need.

Peace

Isaiah 9:6 For to us a child is born, to us a son is given; and the government shall be upon His shoulder, and His name shall be called Wonderful Counselor, Mighty God, Everlasting Father, Prince of **Peace**.

Luke 2:14 Glory to God in the highest, and on earth **peace**.

John 14:27 Peace I leave with you; My **peace** I give to you. Not as the world gives do I give to you. Let not your hearts be troubled, neither let them be afraid.

Romans 5:1 Therefore, since we have been justified by faith, we have **peace** with God through our Lord Jesus Christ.

Philippians 4:7 And the **peace** of God, which surpasses all understanding, will guard your hearts and your minds in Christ Jesus.

Persecution

Matthew 5:10 Blessed are those who are **persecuted** for righteousness' sake, for theirs is the kingdom of heaven.

Matthew 5:11 Blessed are you when others revile you and **persecute** you and utter all kinds of evil against you falsely on My account.

Matthew 5:44 But I say to you, Love your enemies and pray for those who **persecute** you.

1 Corinthians 4:12 And we labor, working with our own hands. When reviled, we bless; when **persecuted**, we endure.

Redeem/Redemption

Job 19:25 For I know that my **Redeemer** lives, and at the last he will stand upon the earth.

Isaiah 43:1 But now thus says the LORD, He who created you, ... "Fear not, for I have **redeemed** you; I have called you by name, you are Mine."

Ephesians 1:7 In Him we have **redemption** through His blood, the forgiveness of our trespasses, according to the riches of His grace.

Renew

Psalm 51:10 Create in me a clean heart, O God, and **renew** a right spirit within me.

Isaiah 40:31 But they who wait for the LORD shall **renew** their strength; they shall mount up with wings like eagles; they shall run and not be weary; they shall walk and not faint.

Romans 12:2 Do not be conformed to this world, but be transformed by the **renewal** of your mind, that by testing you may discern what is the will of God, what is good and acceptable and perfect.

Titus 3:5 He saved us, not because of works done by us in righteousness, but according to His own mercy, by the washing of regeneration and **renewal** of the Holy Spirit.

Resurrection

John 11:25 Jesus said to her, "I am the **resurrection** and the life. Whoever believes in Me, though he die, yet shall he live."

Romans 6:5 For if we have been united with Him in a death like His, we shall certainly be united with Him in a **resurrection** like His.

1 Peter 1:3 Blessed be the God and Father of our Lord Jesus Christ! According to His great mercy, He has caused us to be born again to a living hope through the **resurrection** of Jesus Christ from the dead.

Save

Acts 4:12 And there is salvation in no one else, for there is no other name under heaven given among men by which we must be **saved**.

1 Timothy 1:15 The saying is trustworthy and deserving of full acceptance, that Christ Jesus came into the world to **save** sinners, of whom I am the foremost.

Separate

Romans 8:35 Who shall **separate** us from the love of Christ? Shall tribulation, or distress, or persecution, or famine, or nakedness, or danger, or sword?

Romans 8:38–39 I am sure that neither death nor life, nor angels nor rulers, nor things present nor things to come, nor powers, nor height nor depth, nor anything else in all creation, will be able to **separate** us from the love of God in Christ Jesus our Lord.

Serve

Psalm 100:2 Serve the Lord with gladness! Come into His presence with singing!

Mark 10:45 For even the Son of Man came not to be **served** but to **serve**, and to give His life as a ransom for many.

Sheep

Psalm 95:7 For He is our God, and we are the people of His pasture, and the **sheep** of His hand.

Psalm 100:3 Know that the Lord, He is God! It is He who made us, and we are His; we are His people, and the **sheep** of His pasture.

Isaiah 53:6 All we like **sheep** have gone astray; we have turned—every one—to his own way; and the Lord has laid on him the iniquity of us all.

Ezekiel 34:15 I Myself will be the shepherd of my **sheep**, and I Myself will make them lie down, declares the Lord God.

John 10:11 I am the good shepherd. The good shepherd lays down His life for the **sheep**.

John 10:27 My **sheep** hear My voice, and I know them, and they follow Me.

Shepherd

Psalm 23:1 The Lord is my **shepherd**; I shall not want.

Isaiah 40:11 He will tend His flock like a **shepherd**; He will gather the lambs in His arms; He will carry them in His bosom, and gently lead those that are with young.

John 10:11 I am the good **shepherd**. The good **shepherd** lays down His life for the sheep.

John 10:14 I am the good **shepherd**. I know My own and My own know Me.

Sin

Psalm 32:5 I acknowledged my **sin** to you, and I did not cover my iniquity; I said, "I will confess my transgressions to the Lord," and You forgave the iniquity of my **sin**.

Psalm 38:18 I confess my iniquity; I am sorry for my **sin**.

Psalm 41:4 As for me, I said, "O Lord, be gracious to me; heal me, for I have **sinned** against You!"

Psalm 51:2 Wash me thoroughly from my iniquity, and cleanse me from my **sin**.

Romans 3:23 For all have **sinned** and fall short of the glory of God.

Romans 5:8 But God shows His love for us in that while we were still **sinners**, Christ died for us.

Romans 6:23 For the wages of **sin** is death, but the free gift of God is eternal life in Christ Jesus our Lord.

1 Corinthians 15:3 For I delivered to you as of first importance what I also received: that Christ died for our **sins** in accordance with the Scriptures.

2 Corinthians 5:21 For our sake He made Him to be **sin** who knew no **sin**, so that in Him we might become the righteousness of God.

Sing

Psalm 30:4 **Sing** praises to the LORD, O you His saints, and give thanks to His holy name.

Psalm 57:9 I will give thanks to You, O Lord, among the peoples; I will **sing** praises to You among the nations.

Psalm 89:1 I will **sing** of the steadfast love of the LORD, forever; with my mouth I will make known Your faithfulness to all generations.

Psalm 95:1 Oh come, let us **sing** to the LORD; let us make a joyful noise to the rock of our salvation!

Psalm 96:1 Oh **sing** to the LORD a new song; **sing** to the LORD, all the earth!

Psalm 96:2 **Sing** to the LORD, bless His name; tell of His salvation from day to day.

Psalm 146:2 I will praise the LORD as long as I live; I will **sing** praises to my God while I have my being.

Strength

Psalm 28:7 The LORD is my **strength** and my shield; in Him my heart trusts, and I am helped; my heart exults, and with my song I give thanks to Him.

Psalm 29:11 May the LORD give **strength** to His people! May the LORD bless His people with peace!

Psalm 73:26 My flesh and my heart may fail, but God is the **strength** of my heart and my portion forever.

Psalm 96:7 Ascribe to the LORD, O families of the peoples, ascribe to the LORD glory and **strength**!

Psalm 118:14 The LORD is my **strength** and my song; He has become my salvation.

Ephesians 6:10 Finally, be strong in the Lord and in the **strength** of His might.

Philippians 4:13 I can do all things through Him who **strength**ens me.

Temple

2 Chronicles 7:1 As soon as Solomon finished his prayer, fire came down from heaven and consumed the burnt offering and the sacrifices, and the glory of the LORD filled the **temple**.

2 Chronicles 7:3 When all the people of Israel saw the fire come down and the glory of the LORD on the **temple**, they bowed down with their faces to the ground on the pavement and worshiped and gave thanks to the LORD, saying, "For He is good, for His steadfast love endures forever."

Habakkuk 2:20 But the LORD is in His holy **temple**; let all the earth keep silence before Him.

Luke 2:46 After three days they found Him in the **temple**, sitting among the teachers, listening to them and asking them questions.

John 2:19 Jesus answered them, "Destroy this **temple**, and in three days I will raise it up."

John 2:21 But He was speaking about the **temple** of His body.

Acts 5:42 And every day, in the **temple** and from house to house, they did not cease teaching and preaching Jesus as the Christ.

Acts 17:24 The God who made the world and everything in it, being Lord of heaven and earth, does not live in **temples** made by man.

1 Corinthians 3:16 Do you not know that you are God's **temple** and that God's Spirit dwells in you?

1 Corinthians 6:19 Or do you not know that your body is a **temple** of the Holy Spirit within you, whom you have from God? You are not your own.

Worship

Psalm 29:2 Ascribe to the LORD the glory due His name; **worship** the LORD in the splendor of holiness.

Psalm 86:9 All the nations you have made shall come and **worship** before you, O Lord, and shall glorify Your name.

Psalm 95:6 Oh come, let us **worship** and bow down; let us kneel before the LORD, our Maker!

Luke 4:8 And Jesus answered him, "It is written, 'You shall **worship** the Lord your God, and Him only shall you serve.'"

BIBLE TIMELINES

Old Testament
CHRONOLOGY

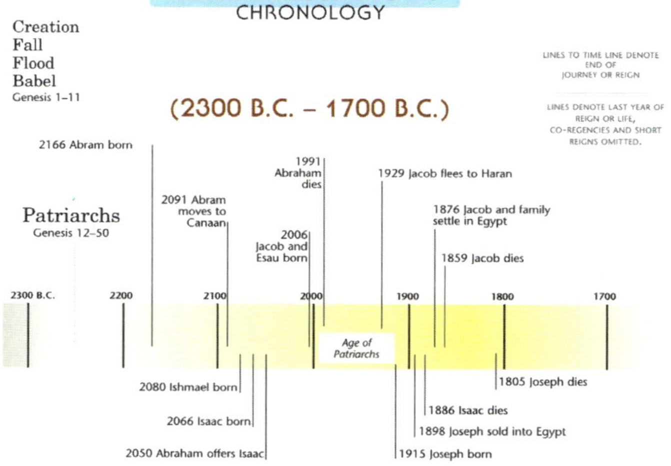

LINES TO TIME LINE DENOTE END OF JOURNEY OR REIGN

LINES DENOTE LAST YEAR OF REIGN OR USE. CO-REGENCIES AND SHORT REIGNS OMITTED.

(2300 B.C. – 1700 B.C.)

Creation
Fall
Flood
Babel
Genesis 1–11

2166 Abram born

Patriarchs
Genesis 12–50

- 2091 Abram moves to Canaan
- 2080 Ishmael born
- 2066 Isaac born
- 2050 Abraham offers Isaac
- 1991 Abraham dies
- 2006 Jacob and Esau born
- 1929 Jacob flees to Haran
- 1876 Jacob and family settle in Egypt
- 1859 Jacob dies
- 1886 Isaac dies
- 1898 Joseph sold into Egypt
- 1915 Joseph born
- 1805 Joseph dies

Age of Patriarchs

2300 B.C. — 2200 — 2100 — 2000 — 1900 — 1800 — 1700

(1600 B.C. – 900 B.C.)

Exodus and Conquest
Exodus 1:1–Joshua 24:29

- *Sojourn in Egypt*
- 1526 Moses born
- 1446 The exodus, Red Sea crossed
- 1406 Moses dies; Joshua appointed leader; Israelites enter Canaan
- 1375 Joshua dies

Exodus & Conquest

Judges
Judges 1:1–1 Samuel 9
1375–1050

- 1367–1327 Othniel
- 1309–1229 Ehud
- 1209–1169 Deborah
- 1162–1122 Gideon
- 1105 Samuel born
- 1075–1055 Samson

Period of Judges

United Kingdom
1 Samuel 10–1 Kings 11

- 1050–1010 Saul
- 1010–970 David
- 970–930 Solomon
- 930–913 Rehoboam

HISTORICALLY VERIFIABLE DATES

1600 — 1500 — 1400 — 1300 — 1200 — 1100 — 1000

BIBLE CONCORDANCE

John 4:24 God is spirit, and those who **worship** Him must **worship** in spirit and truth.

Romans 12:1 I appeal to you therefore, brothers, by the mercies of God, to present your bodies as a living sacrifice, holy and acceptable to God, which is your spiritual **worship**.

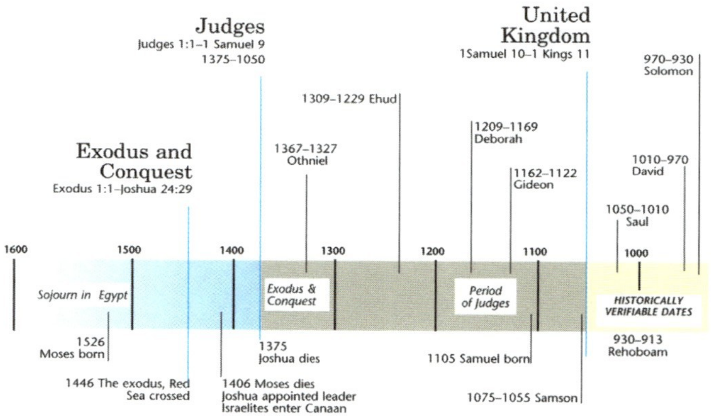

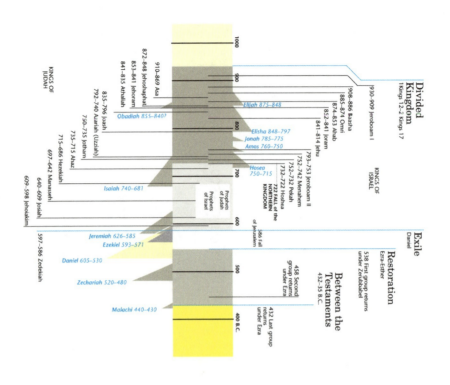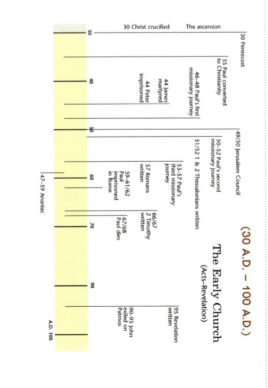

BIBLE ATLAS

TO THE PROMISED LAND

A view of the Great Sphinx with the Great Pyramid of Khufu in the background in Giza, Egypt.

Mount Sinai, where God gave the Ten Commandments to His people.

The Sinai Desert. The children of Israel traveled through this land on their way to Canaan.

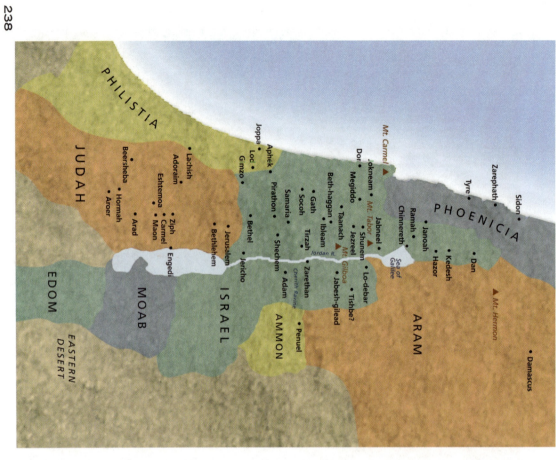

The Divided Kingdom 900 BC

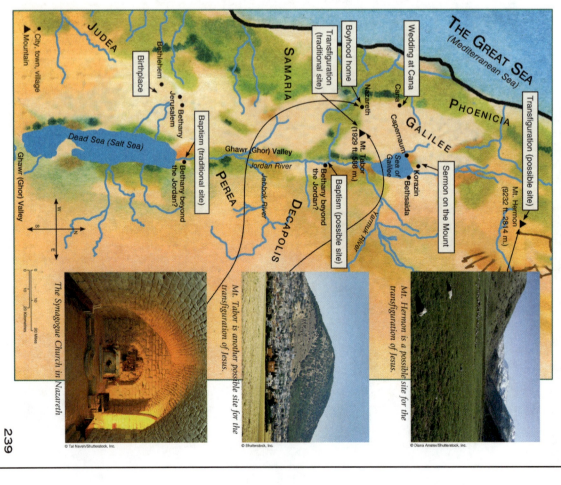

The Land Of Jesus

Paul's Missionary Journeys

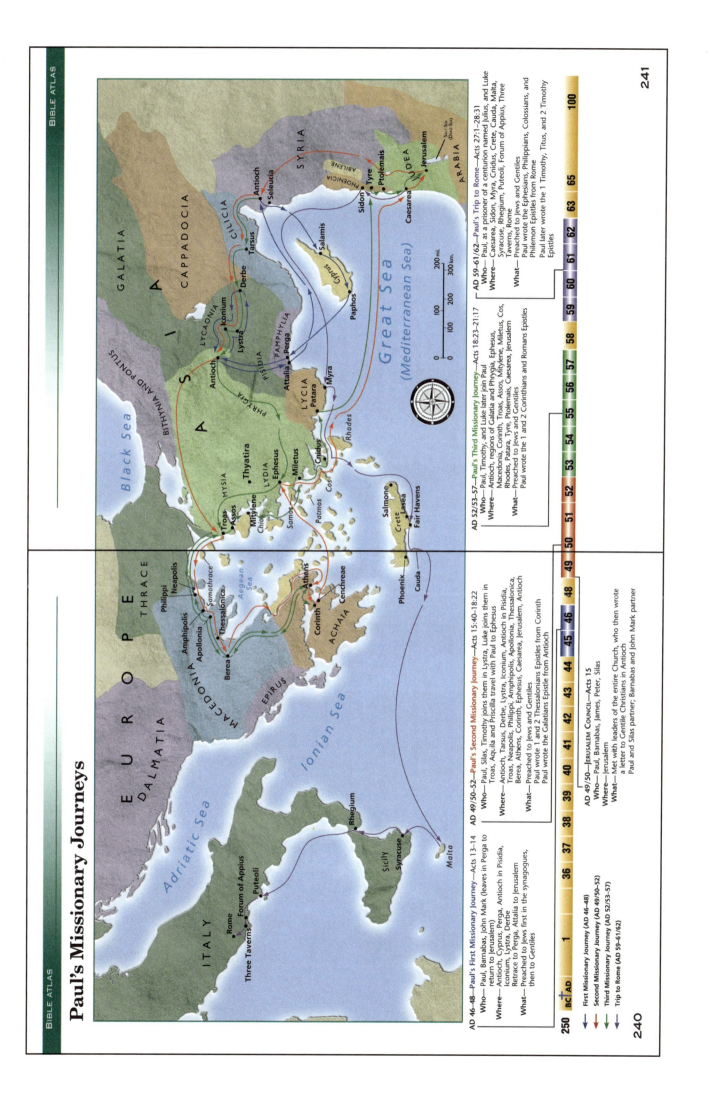

AD 46–48—Paul's First Missionary Journey—Acts 13–14
Who— Paul, Barnabas, John Mark (leaves in Perga to return to Jerusalem)
Where— Antioch, Cyprus, Perga, Antioch in Pisidia, Iconium, Lystra, Derbe
What— Preached to Jews first in the synagogues, then to Gentiles

AD 49/50–52—Paul's Second Missionary Journey—Acts 15:40–18:22
Who— Paul, Silas, Timothy joins them in Lystra, Luke joins them in Troas, Aquila and Priscilla travel with Paul to Ephesus
Where— Antioch, Tarsus, Derbe, Lystra, Iconium, Antioch in Pisidia, Troas, Neapolis, Philippi, Amphipolis, Apollonia, Thessalonica, Berea, Athens, Corinth, Ephesus, Caesarea, Jerusalem, Antioch
What— Preached to Jews and Gentiles
Paul wrote 1 and 2 Thessalonians Epistles from Corinth
Paul wrote the Galatians Epistle from Antioch

AD 49/50—Jerusalem Council—Acts 15
Who— Paul, Barnabas, James, Peter, Silas
Where— Jerusalem
What— Met with leaders of the entire Church, who then wrote a letter to Gentile Christians in Antioch
Paul and Silas partner; Barnabas and John Mark partner

AD 52/53–57—Paul's Third Missionary Journey—Acts 18:23–21:17
Who— Paul, Timothy, and Luke later join Paul
Where— Antioch, regions of Galatia and Phrygia, Ephesus, Macedonia, Corinth, Troas, Assos, Mitylene, Miletus, Cos, Rhodes, Patara, Tyre, Ptolemais, Caesarea, Jerusalem
What— Preached to Jews and Gentiles
Paul wrote the 1 and 2 Corinthians and Romans Epistles

AD 59–61/62—Paul's Trip to Rome—Acts 27:1–28:31
Who— Paul, as a prisoner of a centurion named Julius, and Luke
Where— Caesarea, Sidon, Myra, Cnidus, Crete, Cauda, Malta, Syracuse, Rhegium, Puteoli, Forum of Appius, Three Taverns, Rome
What— Preached to Jews and Gentiles
Paul wrote the Ephesians, Philippians, Colossians, and Philemon Epistles from Rome
Paul later wrote the 1 Timothy, Titus, and 2 Timothy Epistles

First Missionary Journey (AD 46–48)
Second Missionary Journey (AD 49/50–52)
Third Missionary Journey (AD 52/53–57)
Trip to Rome (AD 59–61/62)

BIBLE DICTIONARY

Glossary

abortion Taking the life of an unborn person.

absolution An announcement or declaration of forgiveness.

abundance More than enough; more than we need.

advent Something or someone is coming.

almighty This adjective means having all power, unlimited might. *Body builders may be strong. Earthly rulers may be powerful. Only God is almighty.*

angel A spirit being, created by God, having a mind and will, but no physical body (though, at times, for God's purposes, angels have taken on a human form). There are good angels and those that turned evil.

atlas A collection of maps.

atonement The payment that pays the penalty to correct the relationship between God and humans, which was broken through sin.

attitude How you look at the world; perspective; viewpoint; point of view; mind-set; outlook; how you observe, understand, and perceive things. *Attitudes can be positive or negative. If you look for good, you will find it. If you expect problems, they will probably happen.*

authority Having power to make decisions and to establish and enforce commands and rules.

avoid To keep away from.

baptismal font Receptacle for water used in Baptism.

benediction Proclamation of a blessing, especially the short blessing with which public worship is concluded.

betray To tell someone's secrets; to act disloyally.

bless (1) To give joy or gifts. (2) To pray for someone's welfare. (3) To give God glory and praise.

blessing God blesses us with His good gifts; we bless Him with our thanks and praise.

calling A strong inner desire toward a particular course of action. *Often a person's calling is fulfilled in their chosen profession or vocation.*

catechism A book of instruction giving a summary of basic principles in a question-and-answer format. Martin Luther's Small Catechism is based on the Six Chief Parts of Christian Doctrine, which are based on God's Word.

chant To sing with repetitive tones.

charity (1) Kindness shown, especially to those in need. (2) Love. *In older translations of 1 Corinthians 13, the word love has been translated as charity.*

chaste Morally and sexually clean and pure.

cherubim Angels of a specific rank or grouping; in Hebrew, the word implies nearness, perhaps indicating the cherubim's nearness to God. These angels are sometimes described as having four wings.

Christ Greek for "Messiah."

Christian discipleship The actions of being a disciple—listening, supporting, and living in faith, following the ways and will of our Lord Jesus.

cling To hold on tightly, firmly, tenaciously.

collaborate To work jointly with others, especially in an intellectual endeavor.

commit (1) To put in charge or entrust. (2) To carry into action deliberately.

communicant Someone who is eligible to receive Holy Communion.

compassion Feeling the joy or the sadness of someone else, leading to a positive response.

condemnation Being judged and found guilty for your actions.

confession (1) Stating accurately what we believe is true. (2) Admitting sins and recognizing what God says about our wrongdoing.

consecrate To set someone or something apart for a special, holy purpose.

consequence The result of an action.

contrition Sincere regret or sorrow for one's sins; remorse.

conversion A change, turn around, transformation; new life in Christ.

cooperation Acting together toward a common purpose.

coordination Harmonious adjustments and interactions.

covenant A promise or pledge; a formal agreement. An agreement of faithfulness. "I will walk among you and will be your God, and you shall be My people" (Leviticus 26:12).

culture The socially shared behavior patterns, arts, beliefs, institutions that characterize an ethnic, religious, or social group (including shared attitudes, values, goals, and practices that characterize that particular group).

curse (1) To speak evil of God or mock Him. (2) To call God's anger down on someone or something.

decent Meeting accepted standards of moral behavior.

demons Evil angels; a name for the angels who joined Satan when he rebelled against God.

denomination A religious organization uniting congregations in a single administrative body.

despise Neglect, ignore.

devil Another name for Satan; this name means "slanderer" or "accuser." Because of Jesus' death on the cross, our heavenly Father does not listen to Satan's accusations.

devote To set apart for a special person or for a special reason; to set apart for God's use.

disciple One who listens, understands, and follows the teachings and beliefs of another. See also *Christian discipleship*.

empower When an outside source gives you the power or ability to do or be something.

emulate Strive for accomplishments similar to someone else.

enable When an outside source helps you to be able to do something or makes it possible to be something.

enchiridion Refers to the brief portion of questions and answers written by Luther, which is often memorized by people who study Christian doctrine, which is based on God's Word. In the book *Luther's Small Catechism with Explanation*, the enchiridion is the first small section of the book (approximately 10 percent), followed by a deeper exploration of the enchiridion itself.

endure To last a long time; continue.

environment Surroundings, conditions, influences, external factors affecting us and our lives.

envy To want for oneself something that belongs to another person.

epistle A letter; often meaning the letters in the Bible written by an apostle.

esteem To think highly of someone or something; to respect.

euthanasia Ending the life of someone too infirm or helpless to care for themselves.

faithful Loyal, trustworthy, constant, devoted, dutiful, reliable, genuine, dependable, honest, upright, honorable, unswerving, unwavering, enduring, unchanging, steady, dedicated, steadfast, sincere, conscientious. *God is faithful; He enables believers to become faithful.*

fame To be well known or popular.

fear (1) To be afraid. (2) To honor and respect.

follow (1) Walk behind. (2) Try to imitate or emulate.

forgiveness Through Christ, our wrongdoings are taken away and forgotten. We forgive others in thanksgiving for God's forgiveness.

fortune Money, wealth, accumulation of material possessions.

fruit (1) The sweet part of a seed-bearing plant. (2) The edible part of a plant. (3) Results that have been produced.

genealogy The record of ancestry and descendents of a family.

God's will What God wants and desires for humankind, which includes living in obedience to God's commands, and above all, it is God's will that all people come to faith in Jesus and be saved.

Gospel (1) One of the first four books of the New Testament. (2) The story of Jesus' birth, life, death, and resurrection. (3) The promise of God in both the Old and New Testaments to forgive our sins and offer eternal salvation through the Messiah—Jesus Christ.

gossip Telling someone's personal or private matters.

grace Receiving kindness you *do not* deserve.

greatness (1) Worldly definition—having the most or best of what is valued. (2) God's definition—serving others in humility and for the glory of God.

greed Selfish desire for more money or possessions than one needs.

hallowed Respected as holy and sacred.

holy Set apart for a sacred purpose; pure, without sin.

holy matrimony A man and woman's pledge of faithfulness before God to fulfill their marriage vows.

honor To show respect to; to give credit to.

hope The hope we have in Christ is the certainty (not just a wish) that our faith is based on. "Now faith is the assurance of things hoped for, the conviction of things not seen" (Hebrews 11:1).

humble (1) Not proud. (2) Submissive.

hymn A song of praise to God.

hypocrite A person who pretends to be something they are not; false appearance.

identity The characteristics by which something is specifically recognized or known.

image God's likeness placed in humans, gifting them with reasoning ability and many other attributes, so they can relate to God and live as caretakers of His world.

imitate Copy the actions or behaviors of someone else.

Immanuel Hebrew for "God with us."

incarnate In the flesh, in human form.

inerrant Never wrong.

inexpressible Beyond description.

influence The act or power of producing an effect on a manner of thinking, decision, course of action, or resulting events.

inherit To receive a gift from the estate of someone who has died. One can inherit money, property, jewelry, or something intangible.

inspired Guided directly by a message from God.

invaluable Priceless.

invocation A prayer asking for help and support at the beginning of a service of worship.

jealousy (1) Fear of losing someone's love or affection. (2) Anger, envy, unhappiness because of what someone else has that you want.

Jesus Greek form of Joshua or Jeshua; "the Lord saves."

Judgment Day Also known as the Last Day, the second coming, Christ's return.

justification What God does *for us* through Jesus. We are rescued by Jesus' death and resurrection.

justified To be declared guiltless or innocent; to be absolved of guilt.

kingdom An area or group of people headed by a king; God's kingdom, or the kingdom of heaven, is made up of all believers.

law Commandment, statute, rule, command, instruction, decree, ordinance, requirement, regulation, mandate, precept, order, direction, summons, obligation.

liturgical arts Various skills, methods, and media used to give glory to God in the construction of a church sanctuary for the purpose of proclaiming a message of God's grace through Christ Jesus.

liturgy The order Christians follow in public worship. Liturgy may be highly formal or more flexible, but it always has some structure that allows worshipers to participate together. A liturgy usually includes hymns, Confession and Absolution, a creed, Bible readings, a sermon, prayers, the Lord's Prayer, Holy Communion, and a benediction.

manifest Apparent, noticeable, straightforward, visible, revealed, easy to see, clear, obvious, unmistakable, proclaimed, shown.

materialism (1) An intense focus on physical things, comforts, or possessions. (2) A false trust that looks to possessions to make one happy or secure.

Means of Grace The tools by which the Holy Spirit gives to individuals the forgiveness Jesus won for all on the cross. The Means of Grace are the Word of the Gospel (both written and spoken) and the Sacraments (Baptism and the Lord's Supper). These means are the only ways God has promised to create and strengthen faith in people's hearts.

medieval A period of many centuries of domination by royalty and clergy in European history.

merciful Characterized by compassion, pity, concern; the willingness to help someone in need, especially an enemy.

mercy *Not* receiving punishment you *do* deserve.

Messiah Hebrew for "anointed."

modest Humble in appearance.

morality Good character/behavior that follows a value system of right and wrong.

Office of the Keys The authority Jesus gave to His Church here on earth to forgive the sins of those who repent and to refuse absolution to the impenitent; congregations call pastors to use the Office of the Keys publically on the congregation's behalf.

opportunity Favorable occasion, a fortunate possibility, or a convenient time.

organization People or groups working together for a united purpose.

Pentecost (1) Old Testament times—a harvest thanksgiving festival held fifty days after Passover. (2) New Testament times—a celebration of the pouring of the Holy Spirit on the Christian Church fifty days after Easter.

perish (1) To die physically (Matthew 8:25). (2) To die spiritually and eternally (John 3:16).

persecution Mistreatment, including verbal and physical assault, of a person or a group because of their beliefs.

petition Request; ask for something.

plainsong A rhythmically free liturgical chant.

pledge A heartfelt, sincere promise or agreement.

preserve Protect; safeguard.

primary source Spoken or written information from a person who actually witnessed or participated in an event.

prophet One who speaks a message from God (can be a prediction or warning or an encouragement).

prophesy To tell what or who is coming.

propitiation The act of gaining or regaining favor or goodwill. Something that gains or regains the favor or goodwill, specifically, an atoning sacrifice.

protestant (1) Broadly—a Christian church denomination not of the Catholic Church or Eastern Orthodox Church. (2) Specifically—a member of any of several church denominations denying the universal authority of the pope and affirming the Reformation principles of justification by faith alone, the priesthood of all believers, and the primacy of the Bible as the only source of revealed truth.

pure Innocent, without guilt, free from impurities.

redeem To buy back or to pay a debt owed by someone else. Jesus came to redeem all people from slavery to sin and death.

He paid the price to set us free not with money but with His own blood.

redeemer Person who buys back.

reflect To mirror the likeness, image, or characteristics of someone else.

Reformation A point in history where God blessed the Church with reformers who bravely proclaimed a return to the pure truth of God's Word, especially in the Gospel of salvation through Christ Jesus.

regeneration Spiritual rebirth, becoming new again.

relationships Your connection to, interactions with, and associations with other people.

rely (1) To be dependent on. (2) To have confidence based on experience.

remember Celebrate, observe a ceremony.

Renaissance An era of great changes in culture and academics led by greater individual independence of thought.

renewal To begin again, restored to a condition that had been lost or damaged.

repentance The change of heart and the renewed trust for God that leads to changed behaviors.

reputation The respect and value in which someone's character is regarded.

restored As Jesus forgives us, we live new lives in repentance and faith.

revere To feel deep respect, honor, and awe.

rival One who attempts to compete to equal or surpass another or pursues the same object or goal.

Sabbath Rest and relief from cares and troubles.

Sacrament A sacred act instituted by God, in which He has joined His Word of promise to a visible element and in which He offers the forgiveness of sins earned by Christ's death and resurrection. The two Sacraments are Holy Baptism and the Lord's Supper.

sacred Honored as holy and dedicated to God.

sacrifice To give up something you value very much.

saints Christian believers; people whom God has made holy through the forgiveness of Christ Jesus. A saint can be either a Christian who is alive on earth or one who is already in heaven.

sanctification What God does *in us* through the Holy Spirit. We are set free by the empowering gifts of the Spirit. The ongoing work of the Holy Spirit to keep us in faith, strengthen that faith, and live a life of faith; the Holy Spirit sanctifies us as He works through the Means of Grace, which are God's Word and the Sacraments of Holy Baptism and the Lord's Supper.

sanctuary (1) A consecrated place of safety, peace, and meditation. (2) A place set aside where we worship God—God's house.

Satan The chief of the fallen angels; created holy by God, Satan later rebelled against Him. The name "Satan" means "adversary." He is the enemy of God and God's people.

seraphim Angels of a specific rank or grouping; in Hebrew, the word means "the burning ones," perhaps because the seraphim burn with love for God and zeal to serve Him. These are sometimes described as having six wings.

slander To spread malicious or false rumors.

BIBLE DICTIONARY

soul The breath of life from God that gives the rational immortal spirit by which humans are distinguished from animals.

spontaneous Automatic, free, impromptu, improvised, natural, uncontrived, unplanned, unpremeditated, voluntary.

state of:
(1) **humiliation** Christ did not always or fully use His divine powers (Philippians 2:5–8).
(2) **exaltation** Christ now fully and always uses His divine powers (Philippians 2:9–11).

stewardship Being responsible for what someone has entrusted to your care; managing someone else's property or possessions wisely and well.

suicide Taking one's own life.

swear To call on God's name to witness to the truth of what you say, asking Him to punish you if you break your promise.

synagogue The house of worship and instruction for a Jewish congregation.

testament A declaration; a covenant.

treasurer Someone in charge of the receipt, care, and disbursement of something valuable; trustee; steward.

Trinity The one true God in three persons: Father, Son, and Holy Spirit; Three in One; also called the triune God.

trust (1) To have confidence in. (2) To be certain.

vocation A person's career, occupation, role, or calling.

vow A solemn promise, made before God and witnesses; to make a personal commitment regarding actions in the future.

walk (1) Take steps. (2) Behave or live in a certain way.

will Desire; what is wanted. Seeking God's will means looking to do what God wants to be done.

witness Telling others what you know is true.

worthy Deserving, honorable, upright, of value.

LUTHER'S SMALL CATECHISM

SECTION 1

THE TEN COMMANDMENTS

The First Commandment:
You shall have no other gods

What does this mean? We should fear, love, and trust in God above all things.

The Second Commandment:
You shall not misuse the name of the Lord your God.

What does this mean? We should fear and love God so that we do not curse, swear, use satanic arts, lie, or deceive by His name, but call upon it in every trouble, pray, praise, and give thanks.

The Third Commandment:
Remember the Sabbath day by keeping it holy.

What does this mean? We should fear and love God so that we do not despise preaching and His Word, but hold it sacred and gladly hear and learn it.

The Fourth Commandment:
Honor your father and your mother.

What does this mean? We should fear and love God so that we do not despise or anger our parents and other authorities, but honor them, serve and obey them, love and cherish them.

The Fifth Commandment:
You shall not murder.

What does this mean? We should fear and love God so that we do not hurt or harm our neighbor in his body, but help and support him in every physical need.

The Sixth Commandment:
You shall not commit adultery.

What does this mean? We should fear and love God so that we lead a sexually pure and decent life in what we say and do, and husband and wife love and honor each other.

The Seventh Commandment:
You shall not steal.

What does this mean? We should fear and love God so that we do not take our neighbor's money or possessions, or get them in any dishonest way, but help him to improve and protect his possessions and income.

The Eighth Commandment:
You shall not give false testimony against your neighbor.

What does this mean? We should fear and love God so that we do not tell lies about our neighbor, betray him, slander him, or hurt his reputation, but defend him, speak well of him, and explain everything in the kindest way.

The Ninth Commandment:
You shall not covet your neighbor's house.

What does this mean? We should fear and love God so that we do not scheme to get our neighbor's inheritance or house, or get it in a way which only appears right, but help and be of service to him in keeping it.

The Tenth Commandment:
You shall not covet your neighbor's wife, or his manservant or maidservant, his ox or donkey, or anything that belongs to your neighbor.

What does this mean? We should fear and love God so that we do not entice or force away our neighbor's wife, workers, or animals, or turn them against him, but urge them to stay and do their duty.

The Close of the Commandments:

What does does God say about all these commandments? He says, "I, the Lord your God, am a jealous God, punishing the children for the sin of the fathers to the third and fourth generation of those who hate Me, but showing love to a thousand generations of those who love Me and keep My commandments." (Exodus 20:5–6)

What does this mean? God threatens to punish all who break these commandments. Therefore, we should fear His wrath and not do anything against them. But He promises grace and every blessing to all who keep these commandments. Therefore, we should also love and trust in Him and gladly do what He commands.

THE CREED

The First Article *(Creation)*

I believe in God, the Father Almighty, Maker of heaven and earth.

What does this mean? I believe that God has made me and all creatures; that He has given me my body and soul, eyes, ears, and all my members, my reason and all my senses, and still takes care of them.

He also gives me clothing and shoes, food and drink, house and home, wife and children, land, animals, and all I have. He richly and daily provides me with all that I need to support this body and life.

He defends me against all danger and guards and protects me from all evil.

All this He does only out of fatherly, divine goodness and mercy, without any merit or worthiness in me. For all this it is my duty to thank and praise, serve and obey Him.

This is most certainly true.

The Second Article *(Redemption)*

And in Jesus Christ, His only Son, our Lord, who was conceived by the Holy Spirit, born of the Virgin Mary, suffered under Pontius Pilate, was crucified, died and was buried. He descended into hell. The third day He rose again from the dead. He ascended into heaven and sits at the right hand of God, the Father Almighty. From thence He will come to judge the living and the dead.

What does this mean? I believe that Jesus Christ, true God, begotten of the Father from eternity, and also true man, born of the Virgin Mary, is my Lord, who has redeemed me, a lost and condemned person, purchased and won me from all sins, from death, and from the power of the devil; not with gold or silver, but with His holy, precious blood and with His innocent suffering and death, that I may be His own and live under Him in His kingdom and serve Him in everlasting righteousness, innocence, and blessedness, just as He is risen from the dead, lives and reigns to all eternity.

This is most certainly true.

The Third Article *(Sanctification)*

I believe in the Holy Spirit, the holy Christian church, the communion of saints, the forgiveness of sins, the resurrection of the body, and the life everlasting. Amen.

What does this mean? I believe that I cannot by my own reason or strength believe in Jesus Christ, my Lord, or come to Him; but the Holy Spirit has called me by the Gospel, enlightened me with His gifts, sanctified and kept me in the true faith.

In the same way He calls, gathers, enlightens, and sanctifies the whole Christian church on earth, and keeps it with Jesus Christ in the one true faith.

In this Christian church He daily and richly forgives all my sins and the sins of all believers.

On the Last Day He will raise me and all the dead, and give eternal life to me and all believers in Christ.

This is most certainly true.

THE LORD'S PRAYER

The Introduction: Our Father who art in heaven.

What does this mean? With these words God tenderly invites us to believe that He is our true Father and that we are His true children, so that with all boldness and confidence we may ask Him as dear children ask their dear father.

The First Petition: Hallowed be Thy name.

What does this mean? God's name is certainly holy in itself, but we pray in this petition that it may be kept holy among us also.

How is God's name kept holy? God's name is kept holy when the Word of God is taught in its truth and purity, and we, as the children of God, also lead holy lives according to it. Help us to do this, dear Father in heaven! But anyone who teaches or lives contrary to God's Word profanes the name of God among us. Protect us from this, heavenly Father!

The Second Petition: Thy kingdom come.

What does this mean? The kingdom of God certainly comes by itself without our prayer, but we pray in this petition that it may come to us also.

How does God's kingdom come? God's kingdom comes when our heavenly Father gives us His Holy Spirit, so that by His grace we believe His holy Word and lead godly lives here in time and there in eternity.

The Third Petition: Thy will be done on earth as it is in heaven.

What does this mean? The good and gracious will of God is done even without our prayer, but we pray in this petition that it may be done among us also.

How is God's will done? God's will is done when He breaks and hinders every evil plan and purpose of the devil, the world, and our sinful nature, which do not want us to hallow God's name or let His kingdom come; and when He strengthens and keeps us firm in His Word and faith until we die. This is His good and gracious will.

The Fourth Petition: Give us this day our daily bread.

What does this mean? God certainly gives daily bread to everyone without our prayers, even to all evil people, but we pray in this petition that God would lead us to realize this and to receive our daily bread with thanksgiving.

What is meant by daily bread? Daily bread includes everything that has to do with the support and needs of the body, such as food, drink, clothing, shoes, house, home, land, animals, money, goods, a devout husband or wife, devout children, devout workers, devout and faithful rulers, good government, good weather, peace, health, self-control, good reputation, good friends, faithful neighbors, and the like.

The Fifth Petition: And forgive us our trespasses as we forgive those who trespass against us.

What does this mean? We pray in this petition that our Father in heaven would not look at our sins, or deny our prayer because of them. We are neither worthy of the things for which we pray, nor have we deserved them, but we ask that He would give them all to us by grace, for we daily sin much and surely deserve nothing but punishment. So we too will sincerely forgive and gladly do good to those who sin against us.

The Sixth Petition: And lead us not into temptation.

What does this mean? God tempts no one. We pray in this petition that God would guard and keep us so that the devil, the world, and our sinful nature may not deceive us or mislead us into false belief, despair, and other great shame and vice. Although we are attacked by these things, we pray that we may finally overcome them and win the victory.

The Seventh Petition: But deliver us from evil.

What does this mean? We pray in this petition, in summary, that our Father in heaven would rescue us from every evil of body and soul, possessions and reputation, and finally, when our last hour comes, give us a blessed end, and graciously take us from this valley of sorrow to Himself in heaven.

The Conclusion: For Thine is the kingdom and the power and the glory forever and ever. Amen.

What does this mean? This means that I should be certain that these petitions are pleasing to our Father in heaven, and are heard by Him; for He Himself has commanded us to pray in this way and has promised to hear us. Amen, amen means "yes, yes, it shall be so."

THE SACRAMENT OF HOLY BAPTISM

FIRST

What is Baptism? Baptism is not just plain water, but it is the water included in God's command and combined with God's word.

Which is that word of God? Christ our Lord says in the last chapter of Matthew: "Therefore go and make disciples of all nations, baptizing them in the name of the Father and of the Son and of the Holy Spirit." (Matthew 28:19)

SECOND

What benefits does Baptism give? It works forgiveness of sins, rescues from death and the devil, and gives eternal salvation to all who believe this, as the words and promises of God declare.

Which are these words and promises of God? Christ our Lord says in the last chapter of Mark: "Whoever believes and is baptized will be saved, but whoever does not believe will be condemned." (Mark 16:16)

THIRD

How can water do such great things? Certainly not just water, but the word of God in and with the water does these things, along with the faith which trusts this word of God in the water. For without God's word the water is plain water and no Baptism. But with the word of God it is a Baptism, that is, a life-giving water, rich in grace, and a washing of the new birth in the Holy Spirit, as St. Paul says in Titus, chapter three: "He saved us through the washing of rebirth and renewal by the Holy Spirit, whom He poured out on us generously through Jesus Christ our Savior, so that, having been justified by His grace, we might become heirs having the hope of eternal life. This is a trustworthy saying." (Titus 3:5–8)

FOURTH

What does such baptizing with water indicate? It indicates that the Old Adam in us should by daily contrition and repentance be drowned and die with all sins and evil desires, and that a new man should daily emerge and arise to live before God in righteousness and purity forever.

Where is this written? St. Paul writes in Romans chapter six: "We were therefore buried with Him through baptism into death in order that, just as Christ was raised from the dead through the glory of the Father, we too may live a new life." (Romans 6:4)

CONFESSION

What is Confession? Confession has two parts. First, that we confess our sins, and second, that we receive absolution, that is, forgiveness, from the pastor as from God Himself, not doubting, but firmly believing that by it our sins are forgiven before God in heaven.

What sins should we confess? Before God we should plead guilty of all sins, even those we are not aware of, as we do in the Lord's Prayer; but before the pastor we should confess only those sins which we know and feel in our hearts.

Which are these? Consider your place in life according to the Ten Commandments: Are you a father, mother, son, daughter, husband, wife, or worker? Have you been disobedient, unfaithful, or lazy? Have you been hot-tempered, rude, or quarrelsome? Have you hurt someone by your words or deeds? Have you stolen, been negligent, wasted anything, or done any harm?

What is the Office of the Keys? The Office of the Keys is that special authority which Christ has given to His church on earth to forgive the sins of repentant sinners, but to withhold forgiveness from the unrepentant as long as they do not repent.

Where is this written? This is what St. John the Evangelist writes in chapter twenty: The Lord Jesus breathed on His disciples and said, "Receive the Holy Spirit. If you forgive anyone his sins, they are forgiven; if you do not forgive them, they are not forgiven." (John 20:22–23)

What do you believe according to these words? I believe that when the called ministers of Christ deal with us by His divine command, in particular when they exclude openly unrepentant sinners from the Christian congregation and absolve those who repent of their sins and want to do better, this is just as valid and certain, even in heaven, as if Christ our dear Lord dealt with us Himself.

THE SACRAMENT OF THE ALTAR

What is the Sacrament of the Altar? It is the true body and blood of our Lord Jesus Christ under the bread and wine, instituted by Christ Himself for us Christians to eat and to drink.

Where is this written? The holy Evangelists Matthew, Mark, Luke, and St. Paul write: Our Lord Jesus Christ, on the night when He was betrayed, took bread, and when He had given thanks, He broke it and gave it to the disciples and said: "Take, eat; this is My body, which is given for you. This do in remembrance of Me." In the same way also He took the cup after supper, and when He had given thanks, He gave it to them, saying, "Drink of it, all of you; this cup is the new testament in My blood, which is shed for you for the forgiveness of sins. This do, as often as you drink it, in remembrance of Me."

What is the benefit of this eating and drinking? These words, "Given and shed for you for the forgiveness of sins," show us that in the Sacrament forgiveness of sins, life, and salvation are given us through these words. For where there is forgiveness of sins, there is also life and salvation.

How can bodily eating and drinking do such great things? Certainly not just eating and drinking do these things, but the words written here: "Given and shed for you for the forgiveness of sins." These words, along with the bodily eating and drinking, are the main thing in the Sacrament. Whoever believes these words has exactly what they say: "forgiveness of sins."

Who receives this sacrament worthily? Fasting and bodily preparation are certainly fine outward training. But that person is truly worthy and well prepared who has faith in these words: "Given and shed for you for the forgiveness of sins." But anyone who does not believe these words or doubts them is unworthy and unprepared, for the words "for you" require all hearts to believe.

SECTION 2

DAILY PRAYERS

MORNING PRAYER

In the morning when you get up, make the sign of the holy cross and say:
In the name of the Father and of the Son and of the Holy Spirit. Amen.

I thank You, my heavenly Father, through Jesus Christ, Your dear Son, that You have kept me this night from all harm and danger; and I pray that You would keep me this day also from sin and every evil, that all my doings and life may please You. For into Your hands I commend myself, my body and soul, and all things. Let Your holy angel be with me, that the evil foe may have no power over me. Amen.

EVENING PRAYER

In the evening when you go to bed, make the sign of the holy cross and say:
In the name of the Father and of the Son and of the Holy Spirit. Amen.

I thank You, my heavenly Father, through Jesus Christ, Your dear Son, that You have graciously kept me this day; and I pray that You would forgive me all my sins where I have done wrong, and graciously keep me this night. For into Your hands I commend myself, my body and soul, and all things. Let Your holy angel be with me, that the evil foe may have no power over me. Amen.

Asking a Blessing

The eyes of all look to You, [O Lord,] and You give them their food at the proper time. You open Your hand and satisfy the desires of every living thing. (Psalm 145:15–16)

Returning Thanks

Give thanks to the Lord, for He is good. His love endures forever. [He] gives food to every creature. He provides food for the cattle and for the young ravens when they call. His pleasure is not in the strength of the horse, nor His delight in the legs of a man; the Lord delights in those who fear Him, who put their hope in His unfailing love. (Psalm 136:1, 25; 147:9–11)

We thank You, Lord God, heavenly Father, for all Your benefits, through Jesus Christ, our Lord, who lives and reigns with You and the Holy Spirit forever and ever. Amen.

SECTION 3

TABLE OF DUTIES

Certain passages of Scripture for various holy orders and positions, admonishing them about their duties and responsibilities

To Bishops, Pastors, and Preachers

The overseer must be above reproach, the husband of but one wife, temperate, self-controlled, respectable, hospitable, able to teach, not given to drunkenness, not violent but gentle, not quarrelsome, not a lover of money. He must manage his own family well and see that his children obey him with proper respect. (1 Timothy 3:2–4)

He must not be a recent convert, or he may become conceited and fall under the same judgment as the devil. (1 Timothy 3:6)

He must hold firmly to the trustworthy message as it has been taught, so that he can encourage others by sound doctrine and refute those who oppose it. (Titus 1:9)

What the Hearers Owe Their Pastors

The Lord has commanded that those who preach the gospel should receive their living from the gospel. (1 Corinthians 9:14)

Anyone who receives instruction in the word must share all good things with his instructor. Do not be deceived: God cannot be mocked. A man reaps what he sows. (Galatians 6:6–7)

The elders who direct the affairs of the church well are worthy of double honor, especially those whose work is preaching and teaching. For the Scripture says, "Do not muzzle the ox while it is treading out the grain," and "The worker deserves his wages." (1 Timothy 5:17–18)

We ask you, brothers, to respect those who work hard among you, who are over you in the Lord and who admonish you. Hold them in the highest regard in love because of their work. Live in peace with each other. (1 Thessalonians 5:12–13)

Obey your leaders and submit to their authority. They keep watch over you as men who must give an account. Obey them so that their work will be a joy, not a burden, for that would be of no advantage to you. (Hebrews 13:17)

Of Civil Government

Everyone must submit himself to the governing authorities, for there is no authority except that which God has established. The authorities that exist have been established by God. Consequently, he who rebels against the authority is rebelling against what God has instituted, and those who do so will bring judgment on themselves. For rulers hold no terror for those who do right, but for those who do wrong. Do you want to be free from fear of the one in authority? Then do what is right and he will commend you. For he is God's servant to do you good. But if you do wrong, be afraid, for he does not bear the sword for nothing. He is God's servant, an agent of wrath to bring punishment on the wrongdoer. (Romans 13:1–4)

Of Citizens

Give to Caesar what is Caesar's, and to God what is God's. (Matthew 22:21)

It is necessary to submit to the authorities, not only because of possible punishment but also because of conscience. This is also why you pay taxes, for the authorities are God's servants, who give their full time to governing. Give everyone what you owe him: If you owe taxes, pay taxes; if revenue, then revenue; if respect, then respect; if honor, then honor. (Romans 13:5–7)

I urge, then, first of all, that requests, prayers, intercession and thanksgiving be made for everyone—for kings and all those in authority, that we may live peaceful and quiet lives in all godliness and holiness. This is good, and pleases God our Savior. (1 Timothy 2:1–3)

Remind the people to be subject to rulers and authorities, to be obedient, to be ready to do whatever is good. (Titus 3:1)

Submit yourselves for the Lord's sake to every authority instituted among men: whether to the king, as the supreme authority, or to governors, who are sent by him to punish those who do wrong and to commend those who do right. (1 Peter 2:13–14)

To Husbands

Husbands, in the same way be considerate as you live with your wives, and treat them with respect as the weaker partner and as heirs with you of the gracious gift of life, so that nothing will hinder your prayers. (1 Peter 3:7)

Husbands, love your wives and do not be harsh with them. (Colossians 3:19)

To Wives

Wives, submit to your husbands as to the Lord. (Ephesians 5:22) They were submissive to their own husbands, like Sarah, who obeyed Abraham and called him her master. You are her daughters if you do what is right and do not give way to fear. (1 Peter 3:5–6)

To Parents

Fathers, do not exasperate your children; instead, bring them up in the training and instruction of the Lord. (Ephesians 6:4)

To Children

Children, obey your parents in the Lord, for this is right. "Honor your father and your mother"—which is the first commandment with a promise—"that it may go well with you and that you may enjoy long life on the earth." (Ephesians 6:1–3)

To Workers of All Kinds

Slaves, obey your earthly masters with respect and fear, and with sincerity of heart, just as you would obey Christ. Obey them not only to win their favor when their eye is on you, but like slaves of Christ, doing the will of God from your heart. Serve wholeheartedly, as if you were serving the Lord, not men, because you know that the Lord will reward everyone for whatever good he does, whether he is slave or free. (Ephesians 6:5–8)

To Employers and Supervisors

Masters, treat your slaves in the same way. Do not threaten them, since you know that He who is both their Master and yours is in heaven, and there is no favoritism with Him. (Ephesians 6:9)

To Youth

Young men, in the same way be submissive to those who are older. All of you, clothe yourselves with humility toward one another, because, "God opposes the proud but gives grace to the humble." Humble yourselves, therefore, under God's mighty hand, that He may lift you up in due time. (1 Peter 5:5–6)

To Widows

The widow who is really in need and left all alone puts her hope in God and continues night and day to pray and to ask God for help. But the widow who lives for pleasure is dead even while she lives. (1 Timothy 5:5–6)

To Everyone

The commandments . . . are summed up in this one rule: "Love your neighbor as yourself." (Romans 13:9)

I urge . . . that requests, prayers, intercession and thanksgiving be made for everyone. (1 Timothy 2:1)

SECTION 4

CHRISTIAN QUESTIONS WITH THEIR ANSWERS

Prepared by Dr. Martin Luther for those who intend to go to the Sacrament. After confession and instruction in the Ten Commandments, the Creed, the Lord's Prayer, and the Sacraments of Baptism and the Lord's Supper, the pastor may ask, or Christians may ask themselves these questions:

1. **Do you believe that you are a sinner?**
   Yes, I believe it. I am a sinner.

2. **How do you know this?**
   From the Ten Commandments, which I have not kept.

3. **Are you sorry for your sins?**
   Yes, I am sorry that I have sinned against God.

4. **What have you deserved from God because of your sins?**
   His wrath and displeasure, temporal death, and eternal damnation. See Romans 6:21, 23.

5. **Do you hope to be saved?**
   Yes, that is my hope.

6. **In whom then do you trust?**
   In my dear Lord Jesus Christ.

7. **Who is Christ?**
   The Son of God, true God and man.

8. **How many Gods are there?**
   Only one, but there are three persons: Father, Son, and Holy Spirit.

9. **What has Christ done for you that you trust in Him?**
   He died for me and shed His blood for me on the cross for the forgiveness of sins.

10. **Did the Father also die for you?**
    He did not. The Father is God only, as is the Holy Spirit; but the Son is both true God and true man. He died for me and shed His blood for me.

11. **How do you know this?**
    From the Holy Gospel, from the words instituting the Sacrament, and by His body and blood given me as a pledge in the Sacrament.

12. **What are the Words of Institution?**
    Our Lord Jesus Christ, on the night when He was betrayed, took bread, and when He had given thanks, He broke it and gave it to the disciples and said: "Take, eat; this is My body, which is given for you. This do in remembrance of Me." In the same way also He took the cup after supper, and when He had given thanks, He gave it to them, saying: "Drink of it, all of you; this cup is the new testament in My blood, which is shed for you for the forgiveness of sins. This do, as often as you drink it, in remembrance of Me."

13. Do you believe, then, that the true body and blood of Christ are in the Sacrament?

    Yes, I believe it.

14. What convinces you to believe this?

    The word of Christ: Take, eat, this is My body; drink of it, all of you, this is My blood.

15. What should we do when we eat His body and drink His blood, and in this way receive His pledge?

    We should remember and proclaim His death and the shedding of His blood, as He taught us: This do, as often as you drink it, in remembrance of Me.

16. Why should we remember and proclaim His death?

    First, so that we may learn to believe that no creature could make satisfaction for our sins. Only Christ, true God and man, could do that. Second, so we may learn to be horrified by our sins, and to regard them as very serious. Third, so we may find joy and comfort in Christ alone, and through faith in Him be saved.

17. What motivated Christ to die and make full payment for your sins?

    His great love for His Father and for me and other sinners, as it is written in John 14; Romans 5; Galatians 2; and Ephesians 5.

18. Finally, why do you wish to go to the Sacrament?

    That I may learn to believe that Christ, out of great love, died for my sin, and also learn from Him to love God and my neighbor.

19. What should admonish and encourage a Christian to receive the Sacrament frequently?

    First, both the command and the promise of Christ the Lord. Second, his own pressing need, because of which the command, encouragement, and promise are given.

20. But what should you do if you are not aware of this need and have no hunger and thirst for the Sacrament?

    To such a person no better advice can be given than this: first, he should touch his body to see if he still has flesh and blood. Then he should believe what the Scriptures say of it in Galatians 5 and Romans 7. Second, he should look around to see whether he is still in the world, and remember that there will be no lack of sin and trouble, as the Scriptures say in John 15–16 and in 1 John 2 and 5. Third, he will certainly have the devil also around him, who with his lying and murdering day and night will let him have no peace, within or without, as the Scriptures picture him in John 8 and 16; 1 Peter 5; Ephesians 6; and 2 Timothy 2.